## DATE DUE

| DUE - 4 79 | | | |
|---|---|---|---|
| | | | |
| | | | |
| | | | |
| | | | |
| | | | |
| | | | |
| | | | |
| | | | |
| | | | |
| | | | |
| | | | |
| | | | |
| | | | |
| | | | |
| | | | |
| | | | |
| | | | |

DEMCO 38-296

# A NEW HISTORY OF
# EARLY ENGLISH DRAMA

# A NEW HISTORY OF EARLY ENGLISH DRAMA

*Edited by John D. Cox*
*and David Scott Kastan*

Foreword by Stephen J. Greenblatt

COLUMBIA UNIVERSITY PRESS

*New York*

Columbia University Press
Publishers Since 1893
New York   Chichester, West Sussex
Copyright © 1997 Columbia University Press

a

ın D. Cox and David

‑231-10243-7 (pbk.:

1. English drama—Middle English, 1100–1500—History and
criticism. 2. English language—Early modern and Elizabethan,
1500–1600—History and criticism. 3. English drama—17th century—
History and criticism. 4. Civilization, Medieval, in literature.
5. Renaissance—England. I. Cox, John D., 1945–      . II. Kastan,
David Scott.
PR641.N49      1997
822'.009dc21

96-29670

Case bound editions of Columbia University Press books are printed on permanent
and durable acid-free paper.
Printed in the United States of America
c 10 9 8 7 6 5 4 3 2
p 10 9 8 7 6 5 4 3 2 1

*For David M. Bevington*

# CONTENTS

# ACKNOWLEDGMENTS

IT IS FITTING that this book about early drama began in ritual, even if the ritual was attenuated and commercial—a Halloween party, to be exact. Members of the editorial board first met at John Cox's house for a bonfire on the evening of October 31, 1992. An intensive work session followed on All Saints' Day, during which the principal divisions of the book gradually took shape. The editors are grateful to Provost Jacob E. Nyenhuis and President John Jacobson of Hope College for underwriting the costs of the editorial board meeting. We are also grateful to members of the editorial board, who gave a weekend of their time to travel to Hope College for an extraordinarily productive and stimulating discussion. From it everything else has sprung.

Peter Saccio and Charles Forker read the bulky manuscript for Columbia University Press and offered many incisive and helpful suggestions. Jennifer Crewe represented the press with firmness, patience, and unfailing encouragement. Jesse Lander provided invaluable help and wisdom throughout the production process. Myra Kohsel assisted with unstinting cheerfulness and efficiency at every stage of the project and prepared the manuscript in the face of deadlines that no one else could possibly have met.

Our principal debt, however, is acknowledged in the dedication. Members of the editorial board have in common that they were David Bevington's doctoral students at the University of Chicago over the course of the last thirty years. His learning, graciousness, and intellectual energy continue to affect all of us, and no doubt it was the example of his and Peggy's unfailing hospitality that inspired us to begin the book with a party. Many of those who contributed to this *New History* mentioned how pleased they were to be acknowledging David's own remarkable contribution to the study of early English drama, and those who had never met him characteristically remarked how important both David's scholarship and his support for their own work had been in their careers. Among all the admiring comments about David's scholarly achievements, *generous* was the word people most frequently used; and we concur, for his life, like his work, has been marked by a wonderful generosity of both mind and spirit, and those of us who planned this book and saw it through to completion are deeply aware of his generosity to us. Though such bounty can never be repaid in full, this book is intended at least to acknowledge our debt and hint at our gratitude.

# FOREWORD

*Stephen J. Greenblatt*

LIKE MOST of the best literary scholarship of the past few decades, A *New History of Early English Drama* does not tell a simple story. It does not invite the reader to imagine that the theatrical activities of several centuries were an elaborate preparation or rehearsal for the career of William Shakespeare, nor does it offer a straightforward, unitary definition of the objects — the textual and material traces of the past — that it analyzes. It forgoes the satisfaction of linear narrative and literary triumphalism in order to present a more capacious, confusing, and complex picture of early drama.

There are simple pleasures in life, but the theater is not one of them. To be sure, at its core there seems to be a set of familiar, virtually timeless games, variations on the childhood theme of "Let's pretend." Indeed, we could liken the scene that emerges from this book to Pieter Brueghel's famous *Children's Games* (1560), a painting that contains many of the basic motifs of early English drama and of Western drama in general: from the little boy who is riding a hobby horse to the little girl wearing a tinsel crown, from mock fights to sweet embraces, from comic processions to solitary self-absorption to what looks like a make-believe crucifixion. But the scene Brueghel paints is amazingly complex. So many and various are the figures, so fragmentary and multifaceted the represented actions, that it would be virtually impossible to give a single, coherent account of what is happening. The swirling confusion of distinct groups and diverse motives seems to defy a unitary order, a resolution of the scene into a narrative or a set of stable, interlocking propositions. It is tempting to say, as a first principle, that the space of Brueghel's painting, in all its mad variety, excludes the serious world and hence decisively demarcates play from earnest. But no sooner does one congratulate oneself on finding at least this small patch of stable ground on which to stand than one notices in a corner of the painting, at the far end of a street leading off the main square, a crowd of men and women engaged in some action. On closer inspection, the action becomes clear: they are burning someone at the stake.

This glimpse of one of the vicious games that adults play is no more the truth of the painting than any one of the frenzied games of the children. The artist seems to invite us to imagine a space, to attend to the peripheries as well as the center, to understand the complexity of the activities that go on within its confines, and to think about the institutions—church, inns, market stalls, and so forth—that frame these activities. Above all, he invites us, as do the authors of this volume, to savor the astonishing energies that at once compel and radiate out from the human beings passionately absorbed in their forms of play.

INTRODUCTION

# Demanding History

*John D. Cox and David Scott Kastan*

THIS *New History of Early English Drama* is at once very much like and unlike other reference books. It is recognizably a "history" of its subject, but to its readers it should equally be recognizably "new." Its primary aim is to provide the most comprehensive account yet available of early English drama. Twenty-six essays by twenty-eight scholars attempt to delimit and define the field, to summarize the state of knowledge, and to suggest new lines of inquiry and research. In this regard, the volume is much like any such reference work. It builds its subject out of single blocks, and readers can consult individual essays on specific topics in the confidence that what they are reading is reliable and authoritative.

What makes this book unique, however, is that it regards and presents the field from an unfamiliar perspective, one that has been made not only possible but in fact necessary by the theoretical shifts of the last twenty-five years. Whatever else these theoretical initiatives have accomplished, they have successfully challenged the largely unexamined and naturalized categories that have dominated literary analysis. Literary texts are now understood not merely as exclusive sources but as contested sites of meaning, their authors as something less simple and more constrained than the solitary producers and sole proprietors of the meanings that circulate through them. If the author is not actually "dead," as theorists have provocatively claimed, authorial intention has been recognized as only one of the multiple and often contradictory intentions involved in the production of texts; if texts do not allow totally free play of meaning, meaning is nonetheless inescapably plural — "meanings" that emerge in the contest over the text's representations; if there is a world of agents and agency "outside of the text," it is a world largely structured and apprehended in language; and if literature itself is not an indiscriminate field of signification, it has been importantly discovered as a historically constructed and historically specific field of interests and value that has changed and will continue to change over time.

Theory has thus exposed the mystifications that have dominated our categories of literary analysis, though *theory* itself is construed here not as monolithic but as a productive set of concerns about the possibilities of meaning and value. Nevertheless, theory has now brought us to the place where we must respond to its challenges by producing not more theory but more facts, however value-laden they may be, that will illuminate the historical conditions in which early drama was written, performed, read, published, and interpreted. Theory has convincingly demonstrated that all these activities are inevitably mediated, taking place only and always in context and action; nonetheless, the specific contexts and actions that produce meaning cannot merely be gestured at but must be recovered and analyzed.

One major goal of this history is just such specification, recovery, and analysis. Accordingly, no essays about individual authors will be found here. To some, no doubt, this will seem a major drawback of the volume; to others—to most, we hope—it will be the volume's principal strength. Of all the literary forms, drama is the least respectful of its author's intentions. Plays inevitably register multiple intentions, often conflicting intentions, as actors, annotators, revisers, collaborators, scribes, printers, and proofreaders, in addition to the playwright, all have a hand in shaping the text. Drama is always radically collaborative, both on stage and in print, and this volume seeks to restore the collaborative sense of early English dramatic activity by focusing on the conditions and constraints of playmaking, the networks of dependency, both discursive and institutional, that motivated and sustained it. Individual playwrights and plays are, of course, not absent from the volume, but they are distributed throughout the various essays, relocated in the cooperative economies in which drama is always produced. Shakespeare figures prominently in these pages, but he is treated as a working playwright functioning within the enabling (and inhibiting) circumstances of the playhouse and printing shop, rather than as the implicit goal toward which drama before him is seen to move.

In other respects, too, this history self-consciously attempts to avoid tendentious teleology and chronology. The word we use to identify the drama discussed herein, *early*, is a descriptive adjective that seeks to remove—or perhaps more accurately, to evade—many of the difficulties raised by traditional period markers such as *Elizabethan, Jacobean, Medieval, Renaissance,* or the increasingly common *early modern*. No doubt we have not been entirely successful. Customary period designations occasionally appear in these pages because we are editors, not ideological law enforcers, and *early* itself carries freight that cannot be easily abandoned—but less freight, we think, than any of the alternatives. We intend *early* in much the same sense as it has been used by the *Records of Early English Drama,* which covers the beginnings of dramatic performance in England to 1642, when Parliament ordered the theaters closed.

This descriptive usage of *early* achieves a number of desirable purposes. First, it avoids the obvious problem of regnal designations, with their implication that dramatic conditions or sensibilities somehow conveniently changed with the passing of the monarch. *Early* also works to erase the sharp distinction between *Medieval* and *Renaissance* that has traditionally been used to mark a period boundary. "Renaissance" scholars have too often posited the "Middle Ages" as a unique cultural phenomenon, thereby reenacting the humanist bias against the prehistory of the Renaissance itself, as humanism claimed to invent itself in its rediscovery of classical culture. The culture called the "Renaissance" was more continuous than this self-interested narrative allows. With regard to drama, for example, the Corpus Christi plays, apparently that most quintessentially "medieval" dramatic form, were performed in Kendall well into the seventeenth century. And if *early* does obviously commit us to some notion of temporal development (though not thereby to a Whiggish notion of inevitable progress), it manages to escape the troublesome implication of *early modern*: that the essence of "the period" is to be found primarily in its relation to a modernity of which of course it could know nothing. Our discomfort with periodization, however, should be taken as a recognition of cultural and historical change, not a denial of it, and we have structured this volume precisely to register the distinctive qualities of *early English drama*. The volume organizes its individual essays into three categories, a taxonomy that is innovative but, more important, is intended to be comprehensive and productive. The three sections work to clarify the specific circumstances and conditions in which drama was produced and by means of which its achievement can be assessed: (1) "Early English Drama and Physical Space"; (2) "Early English Drama and Social Space"; (3) "Early English Drama and Conditions of Performance and Publication." The organization thus aims not only to remap the field but also to redirect study of it in response to the remarkable shift in emphasis in recent years away from formal analysis to material and cultural concerns.

The essays in part I, "Early English Drama and Physical Space," go beyond the description of traditional "playing areas" to consider the social and material ramifications of theatrical performance in the various locations that the drama occupied. Part II, "Early English Drama and Social Space," turns from consideration of the physical space for dramatic performance to questions about its social locations as they affected dramatic composition and performance and the formation of a dramatic canon. Finally, the essays in part III, "Early English Drama and Conditions of Performance and Publication," take up questions about the material conditions under which plays were produced and disseminated, both in performance and in the form of scripts and playbooks. In each of these sections we no doubt might have covered additional topics as well as treated some of those here in greater breadth and depth. Virtually all readers will no doubt find something missing that they will regard as indispensable. Still, we hope that the principle of organizing the essays in the way we have is both clear and clarifying.

Our historical focus is designed to release the drama both from the mystifications of idealist criticism and from the no less mystifying moves of poststructuralist theory, where playmaking also disappears — not into the putative unity and self-sufficiency of symbol and form but into the assumed priority of the linguistic order itself. It may be objected that the turn to history takes us away from the drama itself, focusing attention on its background instead of on the rich and various play texts that are the essence of dramatic activity. But the singular focus on texts is precisely what this volume contests, as it seeks to reconceptualize the achievement of early English drama, shifting the emphasis from drama as the timeless achievement of sovereign authorship to drama as collective activity that ties the play to history. Playwrights are of course essential to playmaking, but they write always and only within specific conditions of possibility, both institutional and imaginative, connecting the individual talent to preexisting modes of thought, linguistic constructions, literary conventions, social codes, legal restraints, material practices, and commercial conditions of production. We intend to restore drama to the rich field of its social origins, insisting that its embeddedness in history (or, rather, histor*ies*) does not contaminate it but is the very condition of its existence.

In other words, these essays focus on what Ben Jonson might have called the *body* of dramatic history, as opposed to its *soul*. Jonson used these terms to distinguish his own contribution to court masques (namely, the text and the commentaries he wrote on the text) from Inigo Jones's contribution, which consisted of stage design, machinery, props, lighting, and costumes. For Jonson, the terms of distinction were loaded, and he borrowed them from Christian tradition precisely to insist on the priority of his own achievement: the soul was more important than the body, because the soul was immortal, whereas the body existed only as the soul's conveyance, perhaps making a good show but enduring only briefly.

But Jonson's understanding of the soul and body has a strong Platonic bent, and its bias misrepresents the theater. What Jonson called the soul could as easily be dismissed as the residue of theater, hardly more substantial — and certainly no more representative — than a quark, which can be perceived only by its effect, though its effect can hardly be thought of as the thing itself. Drama is indeed a temporal art, ineluctably tied, like a quark, to the event of its performance, for performance changes from one afternoon (or night) to the next in a particular run, and even more from one run to another, which might occur decades or even centuries apart, in what are, in effect, different cultures. To maintain that the text of a play (or *a* text, for texts, too, change over time) is real and performance merely ephemeral is to mistake the effect of a quark for the thing itself.

So it is in the history of drama. We have become accustomed to regarding playwrights and play texts as the substance of dramatic history, organizing our narratives around a chronology of successive playwrights and their plays. Such histories are not, of course, irrelevant, because the most persuasive evidence of performance is found in the texts that remain to us. But if texts and commentary on texts are the soul of drama, the sine qua non of performance, as Jonson maintained, they are not a substitute for performance or for the negotiated collaboration (of which the author or authors are only a part) that makes performance possible.

Hence the decision of this history to dislodge authors and scripts from the center of dramatic history. Both are pointedly relocated here within the social and material circumstances in which early English drama was enabled and inhibited. Authors and plays are recognized within the determining contexts in which plays were written, produced, performed, sold, published, patronized, read, censored, exploited by the powerful, and watched and listened to by a socially diverse population that changed remarkably over the course of the roughly 150 years under consideration. Restoring to the collaborative economies in which plays were produced is not to denigrate or neglect them, however. We have chosen to attend to what might be thought of as the body of dramatic history here because the traditional focus primarily on the soul has resulted in a misleading teleology that privileges the later over the earlier, the literary over the performative, elite terms of cultural value over the popular, the putatively complex over the apparently simple. If the result of our focus is to enable a new vision and appreciation of the "soul" of early English drama, we will have achieved half of our purpose; the other half, and our first task, is to restore the "body" to its proper place and dignity in a narrative in which it has too long suffered neglect. Or, perhaps better, it is to suggest that to separate the play text from the specific circumstances in which it was required, produced, witnessed, and read is radically to misunderstand the very nature of the drama's engagement with the world in which and to which it is alive.

CHAPTER 1

# World Pictures, Modern Periods, and the Early Stage

*Margreta de Grazia*

> The fact that the world becomes picture at all is what distinguishes the essence of the modern age.
> — HEIDEGGER, "The Age of the World Picture"

PERIOD HISTORIES tend to begin, paradoxically, with a disavowal of historical periods. C. S. Lewis, for example, divides his *English Literature in the Sixteenth Century* into three picturesque periods: the silver age, the drab age, the golden age. All the same, he urges that period concepts be avoided as "mischievous conceptions" (64). Like puckish elves, goblins, and hobbits, they play tricks on us, lead us astray, make us see things that are not really there. Figments of our imagination, they possess little more "reality than the pictures we see in the fire" (63).

In the middle of the century, Lewis's reference to "pictures . . . in the fire" would have seemed less whimsical than it does now at the century's end. In a discussion of Renaissance periodization, it would have targeted E. M. W. Tillyard's vastly popular *Elizabethan World Picture*. In Tillyard's account, Elizabethans pictured the world as a divinely ordered cosmos whose various realms (divine, human, animal, vegetable) were held together hierarchically by links, correspondences, and sympathies. In Elizabeth's time, this "fixed system" (5) was "so much taken for granted, so much part of the collective mind of the people, that it [was] hardly mentioned" (9). Inherited from the Middle Ages, the picture "inspirited the minds and imaginations . . . of all men of the Renaissance." By the Enlightenment, however, it was no longer in view. The encroaching modern age—with its new and destabilizing forms of statecraft, astronomy, and commerce—had effectively effaced it. Through Tillyard's account of the ruling ideas and metaphors of the time, however, the picture has been restored for modern-day viewing.

The notion of an Elizabethan world picture, it must be said, now seems quite odd. (Could an upstanding Elizabethan produce one, like a passport, upon demand: stand and unfold yourself? And what form would it take? sketch in commonplace book? snapshot in wallet? portrait above mantel?). Our postmodernist mistrust of hegemonies, discontinuities, and totalities has little use for such categories as "the ordinary educated Elizabethan" with a "habit of mind" and "ruling ideas." Needless to say, the notion would have seemed odder still to Elizabethans. For world pictures postdated them, like photography, by more than two hundred years. World pictures (*Weltbild*) or worldviews (*Weltanschauung*) were devised in the eighteenth century to provide a philosophical basis for the diverse systems by which different cultures represented the world to themselves.[1] The concept enabled both ethnographers and historians to accept as equally valid highly disparate structures of thought and experience.

In the first half of this century, *world picture* was used interchangeably with an array of psychologizing terms to designate the distinctive feature of an era—*spirit, character, mind-set, temperament, mentalité*. Heated and learned debates centered around such issues as whether the world picture of the Renaissance should be considered medieval or modern, or some transitional composite of the two.[2] In recent years, such controversies have died down. Radical alternatives to traditional period concepts have been proposed: Braudel's variant durations, Foucault's Nietzchean genealogies, Benjamin's blasted continuum, Althusser's differential temporality, and Derrida's disjunctive time line. The days of uniform, coherent, and comprehensive historical pictures seem to be over.

Unless, perhaps, they now survive in less idealized and aestheticized forms than Tillyard imagined. Suppose instead of world pictures we called them "reflections on the forms of social life," "systems of representations," "imaginary transpositions," "cognitive mappings," or "fantasy-construction[s]."[3] Is it possible, in other words, that ideology might have slipped into the place of world pictures as a way of thinking about cultures of the past? Certainly some of the same questions apply to both terms. Where do they reside—in consciousness, in the unconscious, in practice, in discourse? What is their effect—mystification, distortion, palliation? Whose interest do they serve—that of the dominant power, of the social formation, of a particular class? For our purposes, it is important only to remark that ideologies, like world pictures, are generally thought to work as screens or representations that mediate between perception and the world, between the imaginary and the real. Historical pictures, then, may be more relevant than the misty projections that Lewis had us seeing—or imagining we were seeing—in fires, clouds, or inkblots.

When framed by termini (for example, 1500–1600, 1558–1603, 1576–1660), time is bracketed off from the rest of the temporal continuum in order to be set squarely in view. If this is the case, a world picture or period concept or ideology may be less a methodological convenience than an epistemological necessity. Without such an act of enframing, the past would appear either as massive monolith or as myriad details. In addition, it would blur into the present. Once bounds are drawn, however, a historical object can emerge. Putting a frame around a temporal span is what enables us to see something inside it.[4] It is the very condition of visibility or intelligibility—or so it seems to have been since the end of the eighteenth century.

## Epochal Frames: Centuries, Early Modern, Medieval/Renaissance

The division of the past into one-hundred-year units seems as self-evident as arithmetic itself. Yet even this system of periodizing presupposes a surprisingly long series of developments. To begin, a point from which to start counting the years needs to be determined. This means, in effect, agreeing upon the most important event in history. For Muslims it was Mohammed's flight from Mecca to Medina; for Jews it was God's creation of the world; for Romans it was the founding of the Eternal City. Christendom agreed upon the nativity of Christ, but only after other events in the life of Christ had been considered—for example, the annunciation, the circumcision, the crucifixion; in Spain up until the fourteenth century, time was counted from the resurrection (Poole, 37–38). The nativity was not familiar as a starting point for counting forward (A.D.) until more than eight centuries after Christ's birth (Wilcox, 142–44); it was not standard for counting backward (B.C.) until another ten centuries after that (Wilcox, 8, 208). Discrepancies in the Gospels raised doubts about the starting point of the Christian Era: Christ's birth date was reckoned to lie anywhere between 12 B.C. and 4 A.D., depending on the dating of Herod's death, Quirinius's governorship, Roman censuses and enrollments, and even Halley's comet. For many—indeed, for most of the world—the miraculous birth never took place at all, and sensitivity to that point has recently led to the substitution of B.C.E. (Before the Common Era) for B.C. and C.E. (Common Era) for A.D.

Lacking a fixed starting point, ancient and medieval historians and chroniclers employed numerous units for computing past time, among them olympiads, indictions, generations, and consulships. Often several time frames are used to locate a single event. Thucydides dates the beginning of the Peloponnesian War in relation to a truce, a battle, three different terms of office (of a priestess in Argos, an ephor in Sparta, and an archon in Athens), the seasonal cycle, and the watch of night (*History of the Peloponnesian War*, 2.2). Augustine dates Christ's birth in relation to Herod's reign, the change to republican government in Rome, and Augustus Caesar's bringing peace to the world (*City of God*, 18.46). The thirteenth-century chronicler Robert of Clari dates the Fourth Crusade with reference to the papacy and the reigns of two kings, in addition to the incarnation of Christ (Wilcox, 144). As Donald Wilcox has demonstrated, a single chronological time line starting from the fixed point of Christ's nativity was a long time in coming (16–39). It was not until Newton that the various systems of relative time were replaced by a single, uniform absolute time, which, according to Newton, "flows equably without regard to anything external" (Wilcox, 16).

The term *century* secured its present temporal signification around the time Newton published his chronologies (1726, 1728). In the sixteenth and seventeenth centuries, a century was a generic unit, not a temporal one, referring to a group of any hundred items. In one notable instance, centuries referred to time: the Lutheran ecclesiastical history known as the *Magdeburg Centuries* (1559). But centuries referred to groupings of numerous kinds: Watson's *Hecatompathia or Centurie of Love* consists of one hundred sonnets, Erasmus's *Adages* is divided into units of ten (decades), hundreds (centuries), and thousands (chiliades), A *Centurie of Meditations* comprises Traherne's spiritual poems. Only after the seventeenth century was the centurial unit applied primarily to years (Wilcox, 9). At the same time, the French *siècle* and the Italian *secolo* took on new specificity. Once referring, like *saeculum*, to an age of indefinite duration, sometimes as brief as a generation (the approximately thirty-year interval between parents and their offspring) or an indiction (the fifteen-year interval between Roman tax collections), these two terms came to refer to hundred-year spans. In Germany, the new concept was met with a new word altogether, *Jahrhunderte* (Koselleck, 246).[5]

The tripartite division of history into ancient/medieval/modern also has a long and complex history. For Petrarch, history consisted of only two divisions, the past, *aetas antiqua*, and the present, *aetas nova*. Separating the two was the calamitous fall of Rome in 410. The barbarian invasions cast civilization into the blackout that Petrarch termed the "Dark Ages" and that he saw as extending up through his own tenebrous times (Mommsen, 118, 122). The fifteenth-century humanists, however, felt they had emerged from this thousand-year era of *tenebrae*. Petrarch's *aetas nova* was then pushed back to become the *medium aevum* separating the present from antiquity. While breaking with their proximate past, the humanists were interested less in defining themselves as *new* than in establishing continuity with the remote *old* of antiquity. Repeatedly they refer to the project of rebirth, recovery, renewal, revival, reawakening, and restoration of the ancient world (Ullman, 116–17). So too the Reformation assigned itself a similarly recuperative relation to history, identifying itself not as a rupture with the past but as a reinstating of an older, purer past—that of the apostolic church prior to papist corruption (Huizinga, 277).

Hegel's *Philosophy of History* also establishes continuity through historical time, not by returning to the past, however, but by tracking the progress of Spirit through the course of World History. Spirit (or Reason) courses through all historical time, from the most ancient civilizations of the Orient, through the Greek and Roman epochs, and up to Hegel's contemporary Germanic or modern era. Yet its movement along the historical trajectory is hardly even—it moves strenuously, by gradations, each dialectical step moving closer to the final end: the absolute consciousness of freedom. Hegelian history thus allows for both diachronic continuity (Spirit progresses on its temporal trajectory) as well synchronic coherence (discrete epochs form along the way).

And yet, in Hegel's World History a decisive break occurs just at the point where the humanist and Reformation writers insisted upon continuity: the fifteenth century separates the modern era from earlier history. The Reformation is the decisive event precisely because it marks the onset of the new or modern, "that blush of dawn . . . at the termination of the mediæval period" (*Philosophy*, 412). Luther is the key figure, "a simple *Monk*" who knows that the Deity is to be found not "in an earthly sepulchre of stone" (414) but rather in "infinite subjectivity" (415). It is this movement inward—"the meditative introversion of the soul upon itself" (421)— that is so critical to Hegel's history of the emancipation of consciousness. Luther's break from Catholic authority marks the abrogation of "the external in a coarse material form" (412), that is, in the form of the rituals, vestments, and icons that Hegel consigns to the realm of the medieval and Catholic "supersensuous."

It is impossible to overstate the importance of Hegel's history to the subsequent understanding of that stretch of the past that precedes the modern. For once it is put at the beginning of the modern trajectory (once it is named *early* modern), it is committed to anticipating the modern. It serves to inaugurate whatever features are seen to characterize the present moment of the modern. Since the modern is, after Hegel, identified with consciousness, subjectivity, Cartesianism, individuality, then the early modern is constrained to display the early stages of their emergence. The very term *early modern* upholds the teleology of modern consciousness, what Foucault has called "the history of the sovereignty of consciousness" (*Archaeology*, 12), that relentless ideational history toward emancipation that is our Hegelian legacy.

It is a legacy of which Karl Marx was acutely aware, for his history of capitalism is basically an economic materialist recasting of Hegel's philosophic idealist history of consciousness (302). Both histories unfold dialectically on a teleological continuum toward a prescribed emancipatory end: in one case, the freedom of consciousness; in the other, a classless society. And both histories assign the same inaugural importance to the sixteenth century. For Marx, it is in sixteenth-century England that the "rosy dawn of the era of capitalist production" (435) can be observed in "classic form" (434). The enclosure acts and the dispersal of feudal retainers provided a population of wage-laborers; New World gold and silver and African slavery supplied the necessary capital. While Marx is bitterly critical of these historical transformations, or "idyllic proceedings" (436), they do all the same constitute an advance from feudalism in the movement toward overthrowing capitalist society. And while Marx repeatedly criticized Hegel for his inverted priorities, for having put the spiritual over the material (301–2), his history, like Hegel's, is teleological, progressing out of necessity and toward freedom, though consciousness is no Hegelian given for Marx but rather the final product of transformed social relations and material conditions.

Jacob Burckhardt, an exact contemporary of Marx (both were born in 1818), was also a reader of Hegel, though as the very structure of his work into self-contained chapters indicates, he resisted Hegel's narrative of progress. The span of time covered in Burckhardt's *The Civilization of the Renaissance in Italy* (1860) is sealed off from any historical continuum: it neither issues from the past nor extends into the future. And yet for Burckhardt, too, the modern age begins with the stirring of consciousness in Italy, around the same time it does for Hegel in Germany and Marx in England.

Burckhardt's Renaissance emerges from Italy's singular and temporary political situation. Poised between the feudalism of the Middle Ages and the mid-sixteenth century absolutism of the French and Spanish monarchies, Italy for a century and a half was divided into independent city-states. Free from civic and religious strictures, these city-states (whether republics or despotisms) gave rise to Renaissance genius, both political and artistic (1:143). The absence of repressive laws and mores encouraged calculated and unscrupulous aggression, putting despots and artists in rapacious but productive rivalries that brought about the flourishing of the arts and the "state-as-art." For Burckhardt, medieval man failed to attain "full consciousness of himself" not because he failed to discover antiquity, but because he remained locked into secular and religious communities: "Man was [in the Middle Ages] conscious of himself only as a member of a race, people, party, family, or corporation—only through some general category" (1:143).

As is often noted, Burckhardt's history, along with Jules Michelet's *La Renaissance* (1855), introduced the term *Renaissance* as a period designation. Yet he himself minimized the importance of antiquity, maintaining that the Renaissance would have occurred even if antiquity had *not* been recovered (1:443, 2:175). In the German edition, he often distanced himself from the term by putting it in quotation marks, and he chose to use "beginning of the modern age" at least thirty times as an alternative to *Renaissance* (Gilbert, 61). Properly speaking, for Burckhardt there had been no *re*-birth, only a birth, the "birth of man," a nativity that, not unlike Christ's, provided a crucial historical marker, a point from which to start reckoning time—*modern* time, "the beginning of the modern age." His despots, condottieri, diplomats, courtiers, and artists exemplified the full flowering of the individualism he associated with the modern age, and to crown their new internal condition, "a new sort of outward distinction" was introduced—"the modern form of glory" (1:151).

What the preceding sketches suggest is that the period designations *fifteenth/sixteenth century*, *early modern*, and *medieval/Renaissance* were not in general use before 1800, a good two or three centuries after the time in history that they were devised to designate. What it also suggests is the degree to which the nineteenth-century formative accounts concur in their identification of the emergent period with heightened consciousness—whether it be Hegel's "introversion of the soul upon itself," Marx's worker released from feudal manors and guilds, or Burckhardt's self-determining and self-regarding individual. Even the century designation seems sympathetic to this historical focus on consciousness. After Hegel, hundred-year spans start to look like superannuated life spans; centuries start to develop anthropomorphic traits, not only character and feeling but also consciousness, especially consciousness of being at the end of the century, so that fin de siècle malaise seems as symptomatic of the senescent century as of the enervated culture experiencing its run-down (de Grazia, "Fin-de-Siècle Renaissance," 48).

As Marx quizzically put it, Hegel's history of consciousness turned history into "a person ranking with other persons" (172). It also could be said to have done the reverse: turned persons into history. Historical subjects become identified with historical periods, an honor formerly reserved for monarchs like Charles V, Elizabeth I, or Philip II. Thus we have the Age of Luther, Age of Gutenberg, Age of Columbus, Age of Bacon, Age of Machiavelli, Age of Alberti, Age of Copernicus, and Age of Descartes. The subjects in this list do more than epitomize their times. Each is seen to have initiated the break with the Middle Ages and the rush into the modern: Luther by posting reformational theses, Gutenberg by inventing the printing press, Columbus by discovering the New World, Bacon by fathering empirical science, Machiavelli by defending practical statecraft, Alberti by devising the laws of perspective, Copernicus by demonstrating the earth's rotation around the sun, Descartes by formulating the cogito.

## The Theater

If there is any event in the history of the early English stage comparable to the epochal ones listed above, it would have to be the building of the first public theater in London in 1576. The event is invariably singled out in the annals of English stagecraft as the beginning of commercial theater. The name of that edifice, the Theatre, recalled the theaters of ancient Greece (*theatron*, a place for viewing), but in sixteenth-century London a fixed building for dramatic performance was a decided novelty. That novelty rapidly became an institution as the number of theaters in London multiplied.

The Theatre emerged from new dispensations of both time and space. Performance in 1576 was no longer bound to a religious and official calendar: by royal patent, it was permitted on work days as well as calendar holidays. So, too, it no longer depended on securing church and civic quarters, and since it did not have to move from one site to another, it could now take place in a fixed structure of its own. Once occasional, performance time was now regular; once makeshift and borrowed, performance space was now stationary and owned. In 1576, it might be said, the theater became free to occupy its own time and space.

Cast in such emancipatory terms, the building of the Theatre would seem perfectly in keeping with the Hegelian histories that push arduously but purposefully toward the telos of freedom. Indeed, it could support either of the two most influential accounts of the beginning of the modern. It could illustrate Burckhardt's cultural history, in which the Renaissance broke away from the constraining laws and mores of church and state. It could also be drawn into Marx's economic analysis of the transition from feudalism to capitalism: from the constraints of dependency to the opportunities of capital, investment, and profit.

Is it because 1576 is an insular phenomenon, limited to London and its environs, that it is not accorded epochal status? The example of a slightly later event from this same theatrical provenance suggests otherwise: the emergence of not a historical figure but a dramatic character—Shakespeare's *Hamlet*, first played, as history would have it, by the son of the Burbage who built the Theatre. To an extraordinary degree, *Hamlet* has served to mark not only Shakespeare's transition from early to mature work (from comedies and histories to tragedies and romances), but more momentously, Western history's transition from medieval to modern. It is not only Shakespearean editors and critics who conventionally highlight Hamlet's epochal status. In Freud's *Interpretation of Dreams*, for example, Oedipus and Hamlet represent "two widely separated epochs of civilization" (264), the Age of Realization and the Age of Repression, to be followed by Freud's own Age of Psychoanalysis. So, too, in Derrida's recent *Specters of Marx*, Hamlet and his Ghost loom large in a work that ends with the suggestion that an "*epochal* history of haunting" be brought to bear upon Hegel's "*epochal* history of Being" (193)—that deconstructive ages of the specter be set against ontological ages of the spirit. And while the specters that Derrida discusses are primarily those feared and generated by Marx, it is Hamlet who "comes back in advance from the past" to set the course for times to come (10).

So what has Hamlet got that the Theatre lacks?

As the account above on the nineteenth-century construction of the span of time between approximately 1400 and 1600 should suggest—he has consciousness. Since the end of the eighteenth century, Hamlet has been identified with introspective thought, thought turned inward away from world and others; his soliloquies have been seen to stage Cartesian solipsism—thought thinking itself, Hamlet meditating upon a skull. From the nineteenth century on, Hamlet's inwardness becomes synonymous with emergent consciousness, the Hegelian motor of modern history. The epochal events listed above represent the pull away from the alleged dark ignorance of the Middle Ages and toward the Hegelian "blush of dawn" at the emergence of early modern consciousness. Indeed, it is precisely that troop of epochal figures who are the subjects of Foucault's "history of the sovereignty of consciousness."

The novelty of a fixed theatrical space has proven incidental if not irrelevant to such a history. This is not to propose that 1576 be added to the already ample list of epochal moments. It is instead to ask if there might not be a bias against it in our temporal schema. Is 1576 of limited consequentiality because spatial transformations cannot be run into a narrative of consciousness? Indeed, the old Cartesian mind/body dualism may be behind the exclusion. What distinguishes mind from body is precisely that only the latter is extended and possesses magnitude, figure, and number. Space is then the domain of bodies and matter, not of mind and consciousness. Consciousness possesses its own metaphoric spaces, the vast interior recesses that convince Hamlet he could count himself king of infinite space though bounded in a nutshell. What this essay suggests is that the modern may be predicated on a profound antipathy between consciousness and space—an antipathy that may explain why modern temporal schema tend to subordinate or bar spatial transformations.

## Time and Space Coordinates

The spatial was not always excluded from temporal schema. Up through the sixteenth century the two most common schemas for organizing historical time were spatiotemporal units. Histories were generally divided either into six eras on the model of the six days of creation in Genesis or into four eras on the model of the four empires in Daniel. In Genesis, each of the six days of creation corresponded with an expansion of the cosmos; the filling of the spatial void coincided with measurements of diurnal time. In Daniel 2:36–45, the prophet interprets Nebuchadnezzar's dream to mean that future time will be divided into four kingdoms (of gold, brass, iron, and clay), which will be shattered at the end of time and replaced by the eternal kingdom of God. Augustine's monumental *City of God* collapses Daniel's four kingdoms into two, a worldly kingdom and a heavenly kingdom running concurrently through secular time, with only the latter surviving the apocalyptic end of both world and time. Temporal duration and spatial extension were the properties of empire, according to the principle of *translatio imperii*, transferred from kingdom to kingdom throughout world history from Assyria, Persia, Macedonia, and Rome, and then after the fall of Rome to Byzantium, France, and finally Germany.

Eras and empires generally occurred in cyclical patterns, on the model of the movements of the stars and planets (Trompf, 201–7). The very concept of a cycle involved both categories, for temporal cycles were patterned on astrological ones. Many of the terms used for describing the division of history have their origin in astral movements. In astronomy, an *epoch* refers to a star's transit through its zenith (Blumenberg, 459). A *revolution* is the orbital movement of one planet around another (Koselleck, 42). Both terms suggest chronic recurrence rather than irreversible change. The very word *time* derives from astronomical phenomena, the cyclical rise and fall of the sea determined by the gravitational pull of the sun and moon, the sea's advance and retreat on land serving as the spatial coordinate of the passage of time.

A range of terms bears semantic witness to the interdependence of the two elements in which things exist and happen. Spatial concepts are invariably invoked to mark changes on the temporal continuum. The beginning and end of temporal duration are marked with spatially derived termini (*a quo* and *ad quem*), boundaries, thresholds, and horizons. So, too, the intervals between them are imagined as spatial areas: stretches, spans, terms, periods. These terms demonstrate the coordination of time and space, as does their conjunction in astrological and navigational charts, on legal documents, in indexical markers specifying the place (*where?* here, there) and the time (*when?* now, then) of being, in Newtonian physics, which located matter in absolute time and absolute space (Wilcox, 20–22). Something has happened, therefore, when space drops away from time—when time is considered alone. The alteration is encapsulated in a crucial modification of the standard word for *historical period* in German. In the Hegelian nineteenth century, *Zeitraum* (time-space) is modified to *Zeitgeist* (time-spirit) (Koselleck, xx, 258). Spirit supplants space as time's coordinate.

This displacement may have its rationale in Hegel. In his *Philosophy of History* he formulates the modern notion of epoch—as both synchronic and diachronic, a static cultural system (spanning across time) and a dynamic teleological thrust (driving through time). His *Zeitgeist*, or Spirit of the Time, becomes the animating force of a history that courses through time toward the end of full self-consciousness. His four divisions of world history—into Oriental, Greek, Roman, and Germanic epochs—track the developments of increasing consciousness: "The East knew and to the present day knows only that *One* is Free; the Greek and Roman world, that *some* are free; the German World knows that *All* are free" (104). The last stage of the Germanic gives rise to Modern Time, precipitated when Luther extricates Spirit from the sensuous and external embodiments of Catholicism and invests it instead with "infinite subjectivity . . . in no way present and actual in outward form." It is this "abrogation of externality" (415) that frees Spirit to consciousness: "Time, since that epoch, has had no other work to do than the formal imbuing of the world with this [Free Spirit]" (416).

Time and consciousness prove in modern history to be mutually sustaining and reinforcing. This is among Foucault's great insights into modern history: consciousness and periods make up "the two sides of the same system of thought" (12). The "subject of consciousness" needs Hegelian periods in order to secure its primacy by extending its sway backward over the historical continuum. These modern epochs, according to Foucault, protect the sovereignty of consciousness from the discourses that disturb the subject's privileged centrality: discourses like psychoanalysis, Marxist economics, ethnography. With consciousness thus threatened, continuous and coherent epochs provide the accommodation that consciousness needs in order to retain its sovereignty.

In such a temporal schema, space proves subordinate to, rather than coordinate with, time. It does not, however, disappear altogether. In Hegel's philosophical history, consciousness progressing in time encounters space in the form of opposition. Like Nature and Necessity, space is an obstacle to be overcome dialectically on Spirit's progression toward freedom. Space and time constitute two separate realms: the one of Nature and the other of History. "History in general is therefore the development of Spirit in *Time*, as Nature is the development of the Idea in *Space*" (72). Nature develops in space without struggle, smoothly and directly; History progresses in time through conflict, dialectically: "Development, which in nature is a quiet unfolding, is in Spirit a hard, infinite struggle against itself" (*Reason*, 69). And yet in order for consciousness to be fully realized, it must assimilate or subjectify what is other. On its progress to freedom, consciousness must encounter alienated and estranged Nature and through dialectic struggle convert it into itself in order to continue onward.

The shift from *Zeitraum* to *Zeitgeist* reflects Hegel's rearrangement of the two coordinates we have been tracing. At one time conjoined with time, space becomes its subordinate, replaced by Spirit or consciousness. Insofar as space still figures on the historical trajectory, it is as an adversary to be overcome, an antithesis to be synthesized.

## 1576

What happens to the history of a place—the theater, the stage—in a temporal schema biased against space? Space in early English stage history is clearly the critical category. Its transformations can be tracked throughout time: from transient to fixed locales, from outdoor to indoor settings, from city to suburbs to provinces, from public to private theaters, from auditorium to stage to attiring room, in relation to the position of actors and of props.

In no study of the subject are such transformations more in evidence than in Glynne Wickham's magisterial three-volume *Early English Stages: 1300–1660*. It is also a study that highlights 1576: "I have chosen the building of The Theatre in 1576 as my point of demarcation . . . though arbitrary and approximate . . . it does nevertheless represent a climacteric within the subject" (1:xxix). Deeming 1576 "the watershed in the affairs of the theatre" (3:xix), Wickham organizes each of his three volumes in relation to it by titling the volumes, in order, as *1300–1576*, *1576–1660*, and *Plays and Their Makers to 1576*.

The materials are arranged around the 1576 dateline by genre rather than by chronology in order to avoid what Wickham repeatedly denounces as Victorian narratives of progress. All the same, his history does tell a story of development: 1576 is "a point toward which everything seems inexorably to move and after which those same things are never quite the same again" (1:xxix). After a thousand years of stability, of uniform religion and government over all of Europe, the Reformation strikes England, disrupting a long heritage of shared values. The drama, once so closely affiliated with Catholic belief and ritual, is perforce shaken by the schism. No sooner does authority pass from Church to Crown than the drama is subjected to the constraints of censorship. It suffers from foreign as well as native influence in the form of the humanist, neoclassicist, and secularizing values of the Italian Renaissance. Despite these pressures—religious and secular, internal and external—the drama stands up "to assaults of religious, political, and social changes" well into the sixteenth century (2:x), heroically enduring, with enough vigor to inspire and support Shakespeare, but gradually losing ground, declining from an amateur "public service theatre" of devotion and recreation to a professional "commercial theatre" of investment and profit (2:xii), "drained of vitality," so that eventually nothing remains of its original verve and dedication.

The building of the Theatre in 1576 hardly provides protection for the embattled medieval drama. Unexpectedly, it spells its demise rather than its preservation. It is, indeed, for this reason that Wickham selects it as his watershed point. The date, he reasons, is critical for three reasons: (1) because performances were then regular rather than occasional, (2) because Crown censorship regulated production, and (3) because a new style of play came into being (3:xix). But for Wickham, each of these events signals decline: regular performances reflect interest in profit ("pleasures that can be bought" [3:xix]) over traditional cultural value; censorship enforces conformity and silences spontaneity; and the emergence of a different style points to the switch from an emblematic tradition of shared ideals and values to an imagistic one catering to the coterie fashion for perspectival verisimilitude.

In short, Wickham identifies the building of the first theater with the beginning of the end of traditional English drama. After a millennium of "homogeneity," the drama "finally crumbled in the period 1576–1642" (3:xxi). His account tells of how a vital, native drama, once established in a place of its own, gradually submitted to the temptations of lucre, the force of power, and the whims of effete taste. In effect, it is a teleological narrative in reverse, like the nineteenth-century accounts of degeneration that were the counterpart to narratives of progress. It is also Marxism in reverse. For rather than progressing from a feudal to a capitalist to a classless society, the theater regresses from a popular form, to bourgeois enterprise, to elitist indulgence.

As Wickham allows, his history is driven by the desire to understand "how a drama of religious inspiration, universally appreciated, came to be transformed by 1670 to a drama of rationalist philosophy and secular entertainment for fragmentary coteries." His climacteric event of 1576 is the key to that explanation. As long as the drama was itinerant, it remained attached to its *"fons et origo"*; once situated in a theater of increasing spatial definition, it paradoxically became rootless so that it "has drifted ever since whither the winds of commerce have cared to blow it" (2:xix). Thus the building of the 1576 Theatre marks an irreversible turn that "sealed the fate of the open stage of visual suggestion" (2:xxvii) well before the closing of the theaters in 1642, preparing the way for the triumph of the proscenium-arched stage in 1660, the endpoint of Wickham's history.

## 1660

Wickham's endpoint is a date more momentous than his "point of demarcation." Unlike 1576, 1660 *can* be extended beyond the history of stagecraft into the history of the modern. And this is not for the obvious reason that it coincides with the end of the Commonwealth and the Restoration of monarchy. It is because when the theaters reopened, a new kind of stage was on view. The proscenium stage had replaced the platform stage; a perspectival space set off from the audience had supplanted an open stage continuous with the audience. For Wickham, this spatial innovation is so radical that no continuity with the medieval stage remains. The

1660 stage is, for him, "revolutionary," in the modern sense that it marks a definitive cutting off from the past, a break as radical in the history of the stage, he maintains, as the printing press was in the history of literature.

What makes 1660 an epochal marker is that its significance can be extended to nondramatic phenomena that have come to signal the onset of the modern (R. Williams, *Writing*, 31–74; Belsey, *Subject*, 23–26). In a difficult and brilliant essay, "The Age of the World Picture," Heidegger discusses *representation* as the distinctive feature of the modern period. While he makes no mention of the theater, the proscenium stage seems, like the framed picture, a striking materialization of what he terms "enframing": a setting up of the world in such a way that it can be perceived and known. This mode of knowing is credited to Descartes (undoubtedly the most vaunted epochal figure of them all), whose cogito established new grounds for knowability in man's positing of himself as its foundation. In the ancient period, knowledge made itself known through presence; in the medieval, revelation was the basis of certainty; in the modern, certainty is obtained through what Heidegger describes as *a setting out before* and *a setting forth in relation to oneself* (132)—through the representation of "the world conceived and grasped as picture" (129).

Cartesian or modern knowledge requires, for Heidegger, the enframing or enclosing of what is to be known—a cordoning off of the object from the subject, which both constructs the object as something knowable and defines the subject as the one, apart and against the object, who not only does the knowing but is itself the grounds of knowability. Enframing thus mutually constitutes subject and object; it relates the two by setting them apart and against one another in such a way as to define and differentiate each. Objects receive "the seal of Being" by being represented before and in relation to a subject. But at the same time, this representation or "picture character of the world" calls man into being as subject. Yet the relation is, as we might expect, not equal and symmetrical. The subject's secure self-determination of itself upholds, once again, its sovereignty: "Man becomes the relational center of that which is as such" (128); his perception of the world as picture is predicated upon his having brought himself "into precedence over other centers of relationship" (134).

The proscenium stage, like the framed painting, seems a perfect materialization of this modern condition of visibility and knowability. It is self-contained, isolated from the space of the audience by its enclosing walls, just as the painting is separated from viewers by its frame. Not only is the space blocked off from that of the audience; it is artificially defined by its own perspectival and geometrical axes. It is precisely because this enframed space is voided of properties of its own that it lends itself to artificial scenic transformation. *Scene* is a key word here, for once the proscenium stage has been installed, *scene* blurs into the homonymic *seen*. What was once a place in which action occurs becomes a *representation* or *picture* of a place in which action occurs. *Scenery* or *scenary*, even as late as Johnson's 1765 dictionary, refers to the order of a play's scenes. (Pope in editing Shakespeare complains of the drudgery of having to rectify the *scenary* [OED].) After the Restoration, however, *scenery* takes on a new sense of pictured landscape. *Scene* as locale turns into *scene* as backdrop. At the same time that the enframed space becomes more defined by abstract geometric design, it becomes less significant in terms of what is enacted before it. It is decorative, suggestive, atmospheric but in no sense a necessary precondition for what occurs there—for what takes place.

By enframing dramatic action over and against the viewer, the proscenium stage achieves the representation that is Heidegger's condition of modern intelligibility. Its framing of illusion can be compared with the example that Heidegger does discuss: the framing of nature on which the scientific research experiment is predicated. As Heidegger explains, the experiment stipulates its limits in advance; so, too, it might be said, the proscenium stage displays from the moment the curtain is raised the enabling terms of its own illusionistic projection. And this framing, whether dramatic or scientific, by circumscribing the object secures the autonomy of the subject, as well as the subject's control over the "enframing" as the grounds of its own certainty.

Heidegger's argument offers still more for stage history. For the essay discusses two types of modern enframing or representation: the framing of nature by experiment and the framing of history by epoch. Thus epochal representations or "world pictures" are themselves a modern innovation. An epoch itself turns out to be one of those Cartesian forms of representation by which we make the world knowable to ourselves, by enframing the past as a discrete and coherent unit continuous with times past and times future. The concept of the epoch is no more (or less) than an epochal feature of the modern: the modern age was the first and only age that understood itself as an epoch and, in so doing, simultaneously created the other epochs (Heidegger, 130; Blumenberg, 468; Koselleck, 234).

If Heidegger is right, it is only logical that the proscenium stage should qualify for epochal status, for in enframing dramatic enactment, it packages or parcels performance in the very form that the modern requires for understanding. In focusing on that epochal development, we remain ourselves locked in the epoch of epochality, seeing not only the picture of world pictures but ourselves as part of the pictorial system we have set up.

Yet what is to be made of that earlier spatial transformation of 1576? What does it mean that a cultural activity once dependent on makeshift location comes to have a place of its own? And what of the vast array of spatial negotiations surrounding that date—of inside and outside, public and private, city and suburb, the here and there, actors and props? Our notion of the epochal, biased against space as it is, tends to undervalue such transformations. To pursue them beyond their documentary value in the annals of stagecraft is to begin to break out of the limitations of modern epochality and the subjectivity it upholds. It is, perhaps, to follow what Jameson has called the "spatial turn" of the postmodern, an attempt to offset the modern privileging of time over space in order to make sense of contemporary phenomena that have pushed beyond its pale: multinational capitalism, electronic information networks, virtual realities—all of the simulacral transactions that cannot be sited, pinpointed, or grounded, real as they may be.

NOTES

1.  For an account of how "world pictures" emerged in the eighteenth century as a solution to the conflicting claims to universal validity in different historical and cultural systems, see Dilthey, 133–54.
2.  For example, all of the 1943 volume of *Journal of the History of Ideas* (vol. 4) is devoted to this debate; for an account of the simultaneous debate over *Romanticism*, see Parker, *Theatrical Issues in Literary History*, 227–47.
3.  The first quotation is from Marx, the second and third are from Althusser, the fourth is from Geertz, all in Eagleton, 21, 88, 102, 279; the fifth is from Zizek, 45.
4.  I would like to thank Rayna Kalas for sharpening my sense of how critically *frames* and *framing* have figured in modern perceptions of the past.
5.  If the century is a relatively recent historiographic device, so too may be the millennium. Some historians have argued that it is an eighteenth-century invention (Milo, 63–100). Patristic exegesis could be offered in support of this view; Augustine mocked "Chiliasts" and "Millenarians" for their attempts to correlate worldly time with the thousand years mentioned in Revelation 20:1–6 (*City of God*, 906–8). "Relax your fingers," he urged them as they tried to calculate the time of the Second Coming, reminding them of Christ's response when asked when the last things would happen: "It is not for you to know the times or the seasons, which the Father has put in his own power" (838; citing Acts 1:6).

# PART I

*Early English Drama and Physical Space*

## CHAPTER 2

# The English Church as Theatrical Space

*John M. Wasson*

THOSE SITES most neglected by twentieth-century scholars for performance of early English religious drama have been the churches themselves, despite the fact that every village in England had a parish church large enough to hold all the inhabitants and almost none had any more suitable acting space. Even as late as 1983, a scholar as well informed as A. C. Cawley, while admitting that liturgical plays (those based on expansions of the liturgy and written in Latin) doubtless stayed inside the church, argued that all vernacular plays were moved outdoors for the laity, to be performed in marketplaces, theaters-in-the-round, on pageant wagons, or elsewhere (12). This has been the standard view at least since E. K. Chambers's *The Medieval Stage* in 1903. More recent discussions of where vernacular plays were acted seem to ignore churches as even possible venues, but especially given the evidence established by the Records of Early English Drama (REED) project, it is arguable that far more than half of all vernacular plays of the English Middle Ages and Renaissance were in fact performed in churches.[1]

Judging only by currently printed sources and other records waiting to be printed, we already know of 143 parish churches and other religious houses that performed plays in the church, plus twenty-three other performances that moved no farther than the churchyard. With regard to the Devon records, it is likely that less than 10 percent of the relevant records survive. If that percentage is accurate across England, and it almost surely is (far less than 10 percent survived in Suffolk, Norfolk, Derbyshire, and the West Riding of Yorkshire), a very great number of churches must have had their plays. In those 143 churches, records remain of 211 different plays that were performed, some of them many times. If the 10 percent

survival-of-records estimate is close to correct, more than 2,000 plays were performed in churches before 1642.

Given the constant objections by bishops over five centuries to plays' being performed in churches, even in sees where no extant performance records of such survive, that number is doubtless a low one. In 1213–1214, Archbishop Stephen
Langton of Canterbury prohibited "inhonesti" plays in churches and churchyards
(I. Lancashire, *Dramatic*, 105). In 1217–1219, Bishop Richard Poore of Salisbury prohibited such "inhonesti ludi" (I. Lancashire, *Dramatic*, 261). At least as early as
1225, plays in churches and churchyards were forbidden in Scotland. By 1236,
Bishop Grosseteste of Lincoln had joined in this objection; four years later, the
bishops of Norwich and Worcester also objected. In a few more years, the bishops
of Chichester and Durham did the same. And about that time, the bishops of
Coventry and Bath voiced similar complaints.

One might assume, with all of these prohibitions, that "inhonesti ludi" would
have ceased in churches, but throughout the centuries bishops and deans all over
England continued to issue prohibitions of plays in churches and churchyards, at
least as late as 1638. That these prohibitions did not seem to stop "lewd" or "inhon-
est" plays in parish churches might be illustrated from Devon. Between 1287 and
1641, there are some sixteen extant prohibitions of plays in Devon, yet for those 355
years the plays seem to have continued. Old habits apparently are hard to break,
despite the orders of bishops and quarter sessions. As late as 1641–1642, in a sermon
at Exeter, Thomas Trescot praised the most recent ban on church ales and revels,
encouraging the congregation "to give over Ben, and Shakespeare, and fall upon
Moses and the Prophets" Wasson, *Records: Devon*, 206–7). Not only were there
parish plays, but the earliest notice of professional actors' playing in a churchyard
also comes from Devon. In 1339, Bishop John de Grandisson ordered that a stage
erected in the churchyard of St. Martin's, Exeter, by one Robert Lucy be torn
down. Not only did the stage obstruct church processions, but it was frequented by
"a gathering of rogues, actors, whores, and other vile persons" (Wasson, *Records:
Devon*, 320).

The fact that ten times as many plays were acted inside the church as were acted
in the churchyard may seem surprising. Doubtless most of them were intended to
be performed before the local parishioners, who of course could fit into the nave.
Accommodating the local audience in the nave also seems to have been the rule
when the actors took their play to nearby villages, as there are numerous references
by churchwardens to such visiting players. In Scotland, on the other hand, the
practice seems to have been to stage the plays either at the west front or in the
churchyard and to advertise them at other villages. At least most of the prohibitions
after 1225 refer to these two sites. The effect of the Scots' advertising seems to be
reflected by the Reverend George Wishart of Haddington, East Lothian, who complained in 1545–1546 that although scarcely one hundred people would come to

church for a sermon, two or three thousand would show up for "ane vane Clerk play" (I. Lancashire, *Dramatic*, 320).

London, as one would expect from its population, had the most parishes putting on plays at their churches. In addition to Westminster Abbey, published accounts list no fewer than eleven such churches between 1451 and 1565, a figure that no doubt will vastly expand as the collection of the London records progresses. Laurels for the most plays in one church over the longest period of time, however, currently must go to Lincoln Cathedral. Between 1317–1318 and 1543–1544, records survive for no fewer than seventeen different plays performed there. The apparent favorite was *The Coronation of the Blessed Virgin*, presented over some ninety-five years, from 1399–1400 to 1543–1544. The second most popular was *The Assumption*, performed nineteen times from 1461–1462 to 1519. Considering that accounts are missing for 66 of the 227 years 1318 to 1544 inclusive, the total number of performances would doubtless be higher had the other records survived. We nevertheless have contemporary notes of 146 performances in the 160 years of extant records, most of the years when no performance was recorded coming before 1440. While no extant text of any of the seventeen different plays survives, the huge space before the choir screen in Lincoln Cathedral would have accommodated almost any play's acting needs. We are clearly told, for instance, that in 1483 *The Assumption* and *The Coronation of Mary* were both performed in the nave just west of the choir. On the other hand, it is probable that the nine performances of the Corpus Christi play between 1473 and 1481 were presented in the great space between the west front and the castle wall, as at least in 1479 and 1481 the canons watched the play from the chamber of John Sharp in the cathedral close.

The parish church that seems from the available records to have had the most different groups of players, both amateur and professional, was Long Sutton in Lincolnshire. In addition to fourteen plays by what were apparently local parishioners from 1543 through 1574, the churchwardens made payments to the professional companies of the Duchess of Suffolk (1550–1551 and 1565–1566), Lord Robert Dudley (1565–1566), Sir John Gaskins (1566–1567), and Master Samples (1573–1574). The churchwardens also rewarded amateur actors from Frampton (1542–1543), Walsoken (1555–1556), Bolingbroke (1560–1561, 1564–1565, 1566–1567), four boys being strangers (1563–1564), Spalding (1554–1555, 1573–1574), Ipswich (1564–1565), Wisbech (1565–1566), Gosberton (1566–1567), Moulton (1566–1567), Nottingham (1556–1557), Kesteven (1570–1571), and Lincoln (1572–1573). Why so many different groups of players came to Long Sutton is not clear. Perhaps the parishioners had a reputation as supporters of drama, for in addition to all these visiting players, banns criers from Freston, Donington, Leake, Boston, and Kirton also came to town to advertise their plays (Kahrl, *Records*, 70–74).

Despite all our knowledge of the names of the plays and the parishes, abbeys, and cathedrals where they were acted, we have precious few extant texts of those plays. Morality plays, on the other hand, tended to be written for court or by schoolmasters for their students to perform and so were more likely to be preserved, though there were not nearly as many of them. And since Corpus Christi cycles were of course performed by larger towns with sufficient guilds and managed by the city council, the council would understandably have insisted on having, and keeping, copies of the various plays involved; hence these too had a fair chance of survival.

Parishes, however, seem to have had no reason to preserve their plays, at least not after they were no longer being performed. Like the Saint George and Robin Hood plays, it is possible that many of the other parish plays were never written down at all but simply more or less remembered and passed on from one year to the next. Even so, it can be argued that the few extant church plays do give a fairly clear notion of how and where they were presented. In considering those plays and their staging, it is important to remember that most churches did not begin to incorporate pews or stalls until the late sixteenth century; before then, the nave was a large open space, with no more furniture than a lectern and perhaps benches along the south wall for the disabled and aged.

The earliest known but not typical English church play is the Winchester *Visitatio Sepulchri*—or *Quem Quaeritis*, as it is more commonly known—dating from the second half of the tenth century. The text exists in two versions, one to be acted by Benedictine monks throughout England, the other apparently to be acted at Winchester Cathedral. While the versions are virtually identical in their brief speeches, there are some interesting differences. The Winchester text has the angel and the three Marys, as was common in its Continental counterparts. The stage directions, however, are minimal at best: no movements or properties are listed, presumably because these were well known and thus not needful of written explication at Winchester.

The Benedictine play, while just as short, has extensive stage directions. The brother who is to be the angel enters wearing an alb and goes to the Easter sepulchre. Then three other brothers, not dressed as women but simply wearing copes, enter with thuribles and incense rather than with the usual spices of the Marys. When told that Christ has risen, they turn to the choir and sing the Alleluia. The angel consequently takes them to the sepulchre and shows them that while the burial shroud is there, the cross representing Christ is gone. The three brothers pick up the shroud and spread it before the monks, showing them and singing that Christ has risen. Both of these plays, of course, were clearly to be performed before the clergy, not the laity, and apparently in the choir, not the nave.[2]

The assumed presence of the Easter sepulchre, however, may be indicative of a more widespread use of some such playlet for (or by) the laity. Easter sepulchres were common in churches all over Britain throughout the Middle Ages. On Good Friday, the cross (or a consecrated host) would be placed in the sepulchre and "buried"; on Easter morning, the sepulchre would be opened and the cross would be gone. Unfortunately, not a single description of what took place on these two occasions seems to survive, except for the Winchester clerical play. Clearly, two playlets would have been possible, a burial and a resurrection. One can assume neither that nothing dramatic took place nor that the little dramas were so common that no one bothered to describe them. All one can say is that given the two examples from Winchester, it is clear that the possibilities for dramatic impersonation certainly existed. We do know that little plays were taking place on Easter morning all over England, certainly, at least, in Benedictine monasteries. The existence of such plays in parish churches across the Continent would suggest that they were commonplace in England as well, and not merely at monasteries.

The twelfth-century play of *Adam* is hardly typical of a parish play, requiring as it does some seventeen or eighteen actors, very elaborate properties, and some clearly expensive costumes—all of that just in the part of it that is extant. It must have been designed for performance at a cathedral or a large and wealthy monastery. It was performed not in the church but at the west front, for stage directions indicate that whenever God exits he goes into the church. The directions call for a paradise surrounded by silk hangings with sweet-smelling flowers, shrubs, and fruit trees. When Adam and Eve are expelled from Eden, there must be a place for them to rake and spade and plant their wheat and for the devil to come and plant thorns and thistles in it. There must be a smoking hell mouth, large enough to contain (or provide a rear exit for) at least four devils, Adam, Eve, Cain, Abel, Abraham, Moses, and presumably the rest of the prophets. There are two "great stones," Abel's stone to God's right, Cain's to his left. A bench must be provided for Abraham, Daniel, and Habakkuk to sit on, and an ass for Balaam to ride on. Finally, there should be something representing a synagogue from which the Jew comes to Isaiah. The script breaks off at Nebuchadnezzar's complaining about Shadrach, Meshach, and Abednego walking unburnt in the fiery furnace. There is no telling where the play went from there, but the surviving text at least illustrates the fact that twelfth-century drama was hardly crude or minimal. One can certainly see why it was performed outside the church. Parishioners who wanted to do their own play could have derived some ideas from *Adam*, even if not hoping by any means to imitate it.

While the twelfth-century play of *Daniel* was written to be acted in the Anglo-Norman cathedral of Beauvais in northern France, the only extant copy of it is among the Egerton manuscripts at the British Library (MS 2615). Whether it was ever acted in England is not known, but it clearly seems to be a church play. In this play and in *The Conversion of Paul*, the drama, while still biblical, is no longer a mere expansion of the liturgy. As the play is in Latin with only a few French phrases (e.g., "benvois al roi"), and as Beauvais was a monastic cathedral, the play likely was written for and probably acted by the boys of the choir school; the intended audience seems clearly to have been the residents of the monastery and likely some local nobility. As the choirboys were quite used to processions but apparently not very familiar with drama, *Daniel* contains more spectacle than interactive drama. There is almost no characterization and very little action and reaction. But we get the processional entrance of King Belshazzar at the beginning, the procession of the satraps with the holy vessels, the processional of the queen, the processional of Daniel, the recessional of the satraps with the vessels, the recessional of the queen, the processional of King Darius, and a second processional of Daniel's coming to Darius.

While the playing place is not indicated, the logical place would be at the east end of the nave, before the choir screen. This would allow the satraps to bring the holy vessels from the high altar down through the choir. The processionals of Belshazzar, the queen, Daniel, and Darius could be from the Galilee porch at the west end, down through the audience. At the screen there would need to be a throne for the two kings and a place beside them for Daniel to sit. The "house" where Daniel is caught praying could be either the north or the south aisle beside the choir screen, and Habakkuk's place the other aisle. The real problem is the lion's den. We need to see Daniel and the angel in it, but not necessarily the lions. In fact we cannot very well see the lions devouring the satraps later. As the unseen can be more moving than the seen, a few choirboys roaring out of sight could simulate the lions. I would suggest that the entrance to the crypt at the north edge of the south transept would have made a fitting den. Daniel and the angel could stand a step or two down and still be seen. When the satraps are thrown in, they could simply scream and disappear into the crypt. The angel who appears on high at the end could be in the rood loft above the choir screen. Thus not much in the way of stage setting is really needed for this play, in contrast to *Adam*, which clearly had to be moved outside. How the right hand appears and writes "Mene, Tekel, Peres" on the wall, however, is not explained: possibly someone reached around from behind the choir screen.

Costuming is rather complicated. There are two kings, who need to be dressed regally, and the satraps in their purple robes (probably the choirboys wore the canons' robes). There are also three angels, who would need something, at least white albs, to indicate their rank, and Belshazzar's queen would have to be elegantly dressed in her golden apparel. Presumably a wealthy cathedral could provide such costumes. There are numerous songs in the play, and in fact the opening lines are a song. The satraps sing another when they bring in the sacred vessels. At the queen's recession there is another song, not written in the text but presumably familiar, since the audience is invited to join in. Daniel's second processional seems also to be accompanied by a song, while at the end the play apparently slips into the beginning of Lauds with the Te Deum Laudamus. There are also calls for various musical instruments and dances. At the entrance of the sacred vessels, a harp is played and hands are clapped. At the queen's entrance there are both "joyful applause" and "sonorous strings." When Darius enters, zither players accompany the song. Then the drummers, zither players, and other instrumentalists play for the dance, in which the audience is invited to participate.

Thus, while bishops all over Western Europe were forbidding use of the church for "the bringing in of May" and other "ludos ineptos et noxios," the choirboys of Beauvais managed to come up with a Christmastide play with singing, dancing, and instrument playing in the cathedral. A play about Daniel is not especially appropriate for Christmas, except that Daniel, having been saved by God, represents a precursor of the coming of Christ to save humankind. But one suspects that the music, singing, and dancing, none of which is integral to the story of Daniel, were what the choirboys had in mind when they conceived this play. How the rest of the monastics felt about joining in the singing and dancing is not made clear. The idea for the nonbiblical music and dancing would almost surely have come from the folk plays and celebrations in the parish churches in which the choirboys were raised and in which the bishops' efforts were failing to put a stop to such events.

Since the only place name mentioned in the late fifteenth-century Croxton *Play of the Sacrament* is Babwell Mill, near Bury St. Edmunds, it is possible that it was written by a monk at the abbey there, but no extant records suggest that this play was ever acted at Bury. In any case, the banns make clear that it was to be performed at Croxton, twenty miles north of Bury. This deduction is supported by the fact that in 1506–1507 the monks of the Cluniac priory at Thetford, about a mile from Croxton, donated twenty pence "in regard to the gylde of Crokeston." In 1524–1525 they made a similar donation of twelve pence to the guild (Wasson and Galloway, 106, 111).

As it happens, Croxton has an ideal playing space for the performance of this particular play. On the one main road, just across from the west front of the church, is a rather high embankment, running parallel to the street. If the audience were in the street below and most of the play were performed on this embankment, there would be good sight lines and plenty of room on the embankment for Aristorius's stage, the Jew Jonathas's stage, the post, the cauldron, and the oven. When the oven collapses, Christ can simply rise from the other side of the embankment. When the presbyter returns to the church, he need only cross the road to the parish church. Similarly, Aristorius can cross the road with the church key, open the door to the west front, go in, and return with the host.

At the end of the play, fittingly, the bishop, the Jews, and the audience enter the church, where the bishop returns the host to the altar, preaches his sermon, and ends with the Te Deum Laudamus, inside the church, as appropriate. If the seven "miracles" had taken place up on the embankment, it would have been much easier to make their appearance convincing. The audience below would have seen an impressive show and would have felt that they were part of the action as they entered the church for the grand finale. There is no way to prove that this is how the play was staged, but since most of the action has to take place within sight of the church, the guild most likely would not have ignored the advantages of using that embankment across the road. It is almost as if the play were written with this site in mind.

The play *Wisdom*, dating from the second half of the fifteenth century, was almost surely performed by the choirboys of the abbey at Bury St. Edmunds in Suffolk. Although no performance record survives, one must note that only six Bury accounts, between 1422 and 1506, are extant. They include one entertainment entry, a 1494–1495 payment to the boy bishop, but for the sake of argument, one can assume an entertainment traffic pattern in Bury similar to those of religious institutions whose records have survived. This play is aptly suited to performance in a large church like the former abbey at Bury. It requires at least thirty-two actors, as well as trumpeters, a bagpiper, and a hornpiper—clearly not a small parish play.

No stage properties are required for the production, but considerable open space is called for, and the logical playing place would again be the west front of the choir screen. This location would allow entries for the numerous actors and musicians from the north and south transepts, the choir entry, and the north and south choir aisles. The siting also would allow ample room for the devil's dance, Madam Regent's dance, the jurors' dance, and the six women's dance. As one would expect from a choirboys' play, at least five songs are indicated in the stage directions, and more were probably sung without being so specified, as in the numerous Latin quotations from the Vulgate in the text—likely songs that the choirboys knew beforehand and therefore did not need a cued stage direction for. Although requiring no stage properties, unlike the *Daniel* choirboys' play, *Wisdom* is a very lively and spectacular play, with a devil, the seven deadly sins, and prostitutes, all clad in flagrant clothing, with dancing, piping, and singing of the sort in which the boys of Bury St. Edmunds Abbey could normally only dream of being engaged. The play does end, of course, with the return of Mind, Will, and Understanding to proper behavior and repentance and with the saving of Anima's soul. For the choirboys, however, *Wisdom* must have been something of a holiday from normal monastic life.

The Brome *Abraham and Isaac* presents a different setting for a church play. The parish church at Brome, Suffolk, is very small and has no areas that would be suitable for the performance of this play; consequently, one can speculate that the actors moved it to (or perhaps it was written for) the motte-and-bailey castle site right next door to the church. Now overgrown with weeds and thistles, in medieval England it would have been an exemplary place for performance of *Abraham and Isaac*. The audience would be on the inner slopes of the ramparts, leaving the platea, or "this green," as the angel calls it, open for playing space. Heaven, or God's station, would be atop the rampart to the east. The motte to the south would be the hill where the angel leads Abraham to sacrifice his son. Given the size of the castle site, the audience would have no difficulty hearing the actors when they were on the motte, an outdoor performance consideration that often is neglected in isolated textual analyses.

Unlike Wisdom, this play is appropriate to a small parish like Brome. While it needs the available acting space of the motte-and-bailey castle site, the play requires only five actors: God, the angel, Abraham, Isaac, and the doctor at the end (even Sarah, Isaac's mother, about whom he talks so much, does not appear). Aside from the rampart for God and the motte for the sacrifice, very few stage properties are required—only the fire and the wood for the burnt offering, Abraham's sword, and of course the ram tied in the briars up on the motte. Given the need for the hill and the killing and burning of the ram, the play could not possibly have been performed in the church itself, but with the castle site virtually abutting the church, there would have been no need to go inside.

The Digby Killing of the Children was performed somewhere in the East Anglia area on Saint Anne's Day (July 26) 1512, a Monday.[3] No stage properties are needed except a burning taper at the purification of Mary; consequently, the play could have been acted in any open space, but since Poeta, in her role as prologue and epilogue, stresses that the audience has come here "in the worshippe of Oure Lady and hir moder Seynt Anne," the logical performance place would have been in a parish church dedicated to Saint Anne. Killing of the Children clearly is a parish play, with a cast of ten men and eleven women. The requisite hand properties are only five swords for four knights and Watkyn; five babies for four mothers at the slaughter of the innocents and for Mary's baby, Jesus; five tapers for virgins at the purification; two doves for the purification; and four distaffs for the mothers to beat Watkyn with after the death of their children. Herod dies onstage in the middle of the play, but his four knights and Watkyn are there to carry him off, despite the lack of a stage direction to that effect. While the virgins sing the Nunc Dimittis and dance three dances accompanied by the minstrels, these actions hardly would have been difficult to perform in the open area at the east end of a church nave. With Simeon's procession "about the tempille" with Jesus in his arms and the seeress Anna present (see Luke 2:36–39), the nave of the church seems the most likely acting area for this play. Given the wild dances and songs of the play of Wisdom, these serene virgins' performances would hardly seem inappropriate to a performance in the church, and any other space would in fact seem somewhat inappropriate.

William Rastell wrote The Pardoner and the Friar and published it in 1533, for intended performance in a church. The pardoner and the friar do not mention this locale in their long argument, although the friar apparently goes to the lectern to try to preach a sermon. When the parson and constable Prat come in to break up the fight, however, the parson three times blames them for polluting "my church" and for wrangling in it. There is not a lot of action in the play except for the two fights at the end, but there must have been many laughs at the attempts of the pardoner and the friar to outshout one another, and of course to get the audience to donate money to them.

No stage properties at all are needed for this play, unless the friar indeed goes to the pulpit to attempt his sermon, nor are hand properties needed except the pardoner's many ridiculous "holy relics" and his pope's pardon. In short, it would be an easy play to put on in the nave of the church, with no stage required and very few properties. It also would have been a source of great enjoyment for the audience of that time—and perhaps would have cured any pre-Reformation notions, which was clearly Rastell's purpose in writing the play. Any setting except the nave of the church would have been entirely inappropriate for this particular play.

The *Processus Satanae* of c. 1570–1580 was apparently from the village of Limebrook, Herefordshire, where the church would have been the only building of a size for this play (Greg, "*Processus Satanae,*" 239–50). Although we have from this fragment only God's speeches and his cues, it is clearly a village play, with far too many actors for a professional company at that time period. The plot of the play is clear enough: Satan complains to God that because Christ has died to save men's souls he can no longer take everyone off to hell. As a one-hour break is noted between God's first speeches and his last, clearly God was not at the trial or hearing that decided in his favor.

All that would be needed in the way of stage properties would be a throne for God and a table for the judges at the trial. Even with most of the play's text missing, it is clear that numerous actors are needed: God, Christ, Satan, an angel, the four daughters of God (Truth, Justice, Peace, and Mercy), Isaac, Joseph, Samson, Solomon, Moses, Isaiah, David, John the Baptist, and the thief on the cross—at least seventeen actors. With so few properties required, the play would be ideal for performance in the church. With probably only two skilled actors needed, those who play God and Satan, it would have been suitable for a parish of amateurs.

Except for these few extant plays, most of the remaining records do not make clear what the many church plays were about, not even including their titles. If a record of a Robin Hood play or a Saint George play survives, one has a fair notion of its content, but a play listed as acted on Corpus Christi Day or Christmas may not be so revealing. At Ashburton in 1517, for instance, the play on Corpus Christi requires expenses for rattle bags, visors, and five heads of hair. In 1538, Herod is the only one mentioned as being in the Corpus Christi play. The Christmas play of 1542 calls for devils' heads and rattle bags, but these expenses tell us very little about the plays (Wasson, *Records: Devon,* 332–36).

A list of players for a performance at Donington, c. 1563–1565, is equally puzzling (Kahrl, *Records,* 6–7). One would expect this play to have been based on the Apocryphal Gospel of Judith, so popular in the Middle Ages. Unfortunately, only the cast list survives, and it names only "rex," who should be King Nebuchadnezzar; "holofernes," his commander-in-chief; four messengers; a steward; the herald; a duke; and several knights. If the "iij yong men" included Judith and the maid who went with her to behead "holofernes" and save the Israelites from the Assyrian invasion, we would have a regular Saint Judith play, but it does seem odd that neither Nebuchadnezzar nor Saint Judith is mentioned by name in the cast list. What else the play could have been about, however, is hardly clear. Certainly the cast list would fit a Saint Judith play, and hardly implies an early version of Shakespeare's *Love's Labour's Lost*, with Holofernes as a stuffy schoolmaster.

Only one other cast list gives some idea of what the play was about. Saint Oswald's, the parish church of Methley in the West Riding of Yorkshire, was an impressive and wealthy church, but in the 1590s a large and complex collection of stalls was erected in the church, making it an impossible place for any large dramatic performance. Consequently, when a parish play was put on in 1614, it was acted in a large barn next to the vicar's house, presumably the tithe barn. A local gentleman, Richard Shann, wrote in his commonplace book the names of the seventeen actors who played the twenty roles, probably because at least six of them were relatives. Oddly for a parish play, however, this was not a religious play but apparently a knightly romance. Shann does not give us the plot, only the title and the names of the actors (fols. 71–71v). *Canimore and Lionley* was the title: these two characters were a prince (son of a King Padamon) and a princess (daughter of a King Graniorn). The other characters included a duke, earls, knights, two knight adventurers, a vice figure, and a ghost. Clearly the play must have been a romance, whether or not Canimore and Lionley lived happily ever after. The cast list, including not a single religious figure, could hardly have been that of a standard church play, but again we have no plot to go with the list.

Something more should be said here about professional actors' performing in churches. The standard view, still accepted by most scholars after nearly a century, is that expressed by E. K. Chambers in 1903: "The drama which had already migrated from the church to the market-place, was to migrate still further, to the banqueting-hall. And having passed from the hands of the clergy to those of the folk, it was now to pass, after an interval of a thousand years, not immediately but ultimately, into those of a professional class of actors" (*Medieval*, 2:180–81).

Contrary to Chambers's position, it is now apparent that drama did not necessarily pass from the church to the marketplace and elsewhere; that it did not develop in any chronological order from clergy to folk to professional actors; and that clerical, folk, and professional actors existed together throughout the time period under consideration. The last professional performance in a church seems to have been in 1625–1626, the earliest in 1339; the last nonprofessional church play recorded in our time period was in 1642, the earliest in 1348; and, of course, liturgical drama extended at least until the middle of the sixteenth century. The stubborn assumption that professional companies never performed in churches is particularly exasperating, given the extant evidence to the contrary.

Even with only the relatively limited documentation as yet available, there are explicit records of sixty-five performances by professional players in sixteen different churches, not counting the numerous payments to "players in the church" who are not identified. Thus far, the Records of Early English Drama project has identified sixteen different professional companies who performed in churches, some of them many times and in several places. Most of their patrons are named, but one or two are not, such as those who broke the church windows at Kilmington in 1625–1626.

The most frequently named are the players of King Henry VII and King Henry VIII, who came to Exeter Cathedral almost every year from 1490 to 1541. Queen Elizabeth's players appear seven times at four different churches between 1561 and 1596. The Earl of Leicester's Men seem from the records to have traveled the farthest, from Devonshire to the West Riding of Yorkshire in the 1570s. In 1574 Leicester's Men were paid twenty shillings "for playing in the Churche" at Doncaster; on July 18 of that year, Lord Monteagle's Men also received ten shillings "for playing in the Churche."[4]

Since traveling professionals were more likely to play in the churches of villages too small to have a town hall or a guild hall, and since those small towns are the least likely to have preserved their expense accounts, these statistics must be seen as a very small percentage of the whole. One hopes that the forthcoming portions of the Records of Early English Drama project will expand our knowledge of traveling professional companies, but the early idea that drama went from churches to elsewhere, and from priests to professional actors, is clearly demolished by the gathering evidence. Obviously, churches were centers of dramatic activity from the beginning of the Middle Ages to the end of the Renaissance. While we do not have descriptions or texts of more than a tiny minority of the hundreds of known church performances, we do know that these plays were being acted all over England, from the twelfth century to the seventeenth century.

NOTES

1.  E. K. Chambers and those generations that followed him were largely dependent on dramatic records accessible at the British Library and the Public Record Office or available through printed antiquarian accounts. The Records of Early English Drama (REED) project, with its editors' mandate "to locate, transcribe and publish systematically all surviving external evidence of dramatic, ceremonial and minstrel activity in Great Britain before 1642," has significantly altered the scholarly landscape since the publication of the first REED volumes in 1979. Electronic and international data communication has further altered collaborative scholarship in ways unimaginable to Chambers and his peers. Many of these efforts to amplify and reassess the materials of early English entertainment

have been supported by financial help from the National Endowment for the Humanities, which here is gratefully acknowledged.

2. The most convenient access to the Winchester *Visitatio Sepulchri* and to the following three plays, *Adam, Daniel,* and the Croxton *Play of the Sacrament,* is found in Bevington, *Medieval Drama.*

3. The original text is in Bodleian Library Digby MS 133, to which the most convenient access is Coldewey, *Early English Drama.*

4. The entertainment records of the West Riding, Yorkshire, edited by Barbara Palmer, will be published for the first time in the *Records of Early English Drama.* The payments to Leicester's and Monteagle's players are found in the Doncaster Mayor's Account Book, Doncaster Record Office, AB.2/1/1, fol. 80.

# CHAPTER 3

# "A Commonty a Christmas gambold or a tumbling trick": Household Theater

*Suzanne Westfall*

IN THE INDUCTION scene of *The Taming of the Shrew*, Christopher Sly, under the delusion that he is lord of the manor, is about to be entertained by his household players, but he hasn't the least idea what this entertainment will be—a play, a dance, or a vaudeville act. The variant *The Taming of A Shrew* records a fascinating slip of the tongue or pen, when one of the servants calls the performance a "comoditie" (A. Thompson, 58 n). Household drama was certainly a commodity and did indeed wear many generic hats, so until postmodern criticism expanded our definitions of theater, most scholars were disinclined to examine these diverse and generally unscripted constructs in great detail.

Traditional histories of early modern theater have also slighted household theater as a genre because it was almost always occasional, deliberately ephemeral, multimedial, and frequently nontextual or metatextual; all these qualities indicate events that are notoriously difficult to document without visual representation, musical scores, or some early equivalent of the glyphic Laban notation to record movement and dance. In addition, household drama appears, at first glance, to be a very poor relation indeed to the textual drama of the church, schools, and public stage. Since its effects depended on production values that were at best tangential to our highly rhetorical concept of drama, tournaments, masques, and jests were relegated to the disciplines of social and music history, until the great artist Inigo Jones and the great dramatist Ben Jonson gave us reason to pay attention.

It is hardly surprising, therefore, that most of our theater historians have collected, to the best of their abilities, records and descriptions of household revels and entertainers, storing the references in appendixes and footnotes but omitting analysis. Consequently, besides expanding the parameters of the word *theater* (performance), and differentiating it from the word *drama* (text), we must employ unusual sources and deconstructive readings to recover these performances. Eyewitness accounts—except at the royal court, where gossip or political intrigue provide the motive—are virtually nonexistent. Even today, who but a diarist or letter writer would record the activities at her weekend dinner party? If such sources ever did exist, they have not survived or have only recently been collected and edited. Financial accounts, long our mainstay, are preserved for the royal court, but aristocratic courts lower in the hierarchy were frequently less fastidious in their record keeping.

With these difficulties in mind, I will attempt to outline the borders of this recently rediscovered country, depending on my colleagues in other chapters to fill in the geography on more specific issues, and update the map as we go along. For any discussion of great household entertainments naturally engenders a profusion of contiguous considerations, from the influence of patronage on major playwrights (including political ideology, religion, touring patterns) to the aesthetics of royal court performances (jousts, disguisings, and masques, as well as the ubiquitous plays) to cookery, music, art, heraldry, ceremony, and architectonics (great halls, chapels, outdoor, domestic versus public spaces).

To explore households properly as theater venues, we must shift our paradigms of theater history a bit, to consider such theater from novel angles, to read the available evidence from different perspectives. So, in my commentary on the revels, I will discuss traditional components of theater, perhaps with a slightly unconventional attitude toward elements such as: (1) the household as "stage," including diverse spaces, from fishponds to bedchambers; (2) the resident household personnel as performers and technicians; (3) the producers—both the aristocratic patrons and the artists they employed; (4) the audiences, including the circumstances and opportunities for performance; and (5) the performances themselves, concentrating on the production values, the forms and aesthetics that distinguish household theater from church, school, and public theater.

Household performance is indeed affected by geographical space, as the title of this section of *The New History* suggests. The household is also, however, a social space and a condition of performance, which will be the foci of subsequent sections. To make matters more difficult, a household is often not a material space at all, but a sphere of influence dominated by an aristocrat.

So household theater will not allow us to foreground the traditional aspects of drama—playwrights or actors or texts; nor does it fit neatly into any niche in what I call the "big bang" theories that perceive an almost linear evolution from trope to tragedy, implying if not stating outright that earlier and variant forms (indeed *variant* itself implies a "norm") are simplistic and monovalent. Most of us agree that the very notion of "development" is suspect, a concept made more clear, ironically, through the study of great household revels.

An aristocratic household is itself a paradoxical establishment, embodying binary oppositions; it is a static/active, private/public, and domestic/commercial institution. The patron, an epicenter of family, bureaucrats, officers, and servants, moved from property to property—from manor to castle to London town house—to manage the financial affairs and sociopolitical networks that ensured the preservation of power. Family "seats" were rather public homes to the resident household, which could number as many as 250 persons. And, of course, a household was an economic unit, a corporation of managers and workers who happened to live (occasionally) under the same roof. Consequently, entertainments in the noble households tended to represent a curious admixture of the public and the private, an opportunity for the formal pretensions of largesse and flattery, as well as for the casual celebration of personal leisure.

A great household was not a specific architectural structure; it was not a place per se. Rather, a great household was a collection of people assembled to serve a master in the maintenance of person and property. These masters were not limited to members of the aristocracy (I include, of course, the fountainhead of aristocracy: the royal households) or even to males (although the majority of heads of households tended to be men, for which reason I frequently use the masculine pronoun here). Household structures could envelop powerful ecclesiastics and sometimes the officers of schools and inns of court, which required the services of administrative and artistic personnel in order to function efficiently.

A household could also comprise concentric circles of smaller households; the king's household would incorporate households of the queen, princes, and princesses, each of whom retained a personal staff of bureaucrats, functionaries, servitors, and artists. These, in turn, especially when they themselves were members of the upper aristocracy or clergy (like Henry VIII's chancellor Cardinal Wolsey or Elizabeth's secretary Lord Burleigh), also retained their own households.

The size of a great household varied both from time to time and from patron to patron. Henry Algernon Percy, fifth earl of Northumberland (1478–1527) retained 166 domestic servants at a cost of one thousand pounds per annum, one quarter of his yearly income. This number included Percy's chief household officials, such as the chamberlain, treasurer, and steward, as well as henchmen (noble youths sent by their parents to be educated at Percy's court), scores of gentlemen, yeomen, grooms, clerks, chaplains, chapel children, minstrels, players, and various domestic servants from tailors to cooks, requiring seventeen carriages to transport personnel and "movable stuff"—furniture, beds, carpets, and cooking and eating utensils (Grose, 12, 55–56, 179, 289; Van Brun Jones). Traveling noblemen often brought along their artists—particularly their heraldic minstrels, trumpeters, and drummers, who musically "announced" their patron's movements.

At the time of his arrest in 1546, Thomas Howard, third duke of Norfolk, maintained 147 in his household (N. Williams, 15); Edward Stafford, third duke of Buckingham (1478–1521), kept a staff of 225, including the 86 in the household of his duchess, Eleanor Percy (Rawcliffe, 88). Henry VII was so disturbed by the potentially threatening size of his subjects' household retinues that he frequently resorted to fining them, euphemistically for ostentation, thus acknowledging the theatrical power of extravagant displays; financial penalties effectively restricted the nobility, while simultaneously adding to royal coffers (Brenan, 1:141, 168–69; I. Lancashire, "Auspices," 101).

Just as the size and geographical locus of the household were fluid, so were the spaces for performance. Although few architectural structures from the early modern period survive intact, we do have a good idea from blueprints, descriptions, and remodeled properties of what manor houses and castles looked like during the fifteenth to seventeenth centuries. Household theater took advantage of a variety of spaces, not limited to the great hall that Richard Southern discusses thoroughly in his *The Staging of Plays Before Shakespeare,* a discussion that John Orrell continues later in this volume.

In actuality, any space, from bedchamber to a field in Calais, could and did become a stage, a fact that challenges twentieth-century notions of appropriate theater space, suggesting once again that early modern aristocrats conducted their lives with a complex understanding of "public privacy." Household revels commingle communal and personal space, public and private experience, as the participants, both performers and spectators, progress through the geographical space inhabited by the household.

Henry VIII once surprised his first wife, Queen Katharine, by bursting into her bedchamber in a disguising (an early form of masque), and the Spanish ambassador reported that the bedridden Queen Anne Boleyn listened to her favorite minstrel, Mark Smeton, while her ladies danced (Giustinian, 2:75). The fact that Smeton was tried and executed for adultery with the queen is evidence that retained minstrels could be quite intimate with their patrons, at least in the popular imagination and in the political agenda of Henry VIII.

Churches and cathedrals had long provided playing spaces in England, and private chapels did the same. The earl of Northumberland's Household Ordinances (c. 1510) specifically direct his chapel gentlemen and children to perform the "Play of the Nativity uppon Cristynmes-Day in the morning," as well as the "Play of Ressurection upon Estur-Day in the Mornynge," presumably in conjunction with divine services for the holidays in the chapel of Percy's main seat of Wressel, for which blueprints survive (Westfall, 19–21).

The earl's chapel singers also performed in the great hall, where we generally expect theater to occur. The "Play before his Lordship uppon shrofteusday at night yerely" took place in the context of a banquet, in a tripartite revels consisting of the chapel's play, a disguising, and a morris dance by the earl's henchmen (I. Lancashire, "Orders," 39–43). Since household revels frequently centered on banquets (thus prompting some scholars to interpret the Latinate term *interlude* as "entertainments *between* courses"), the great halls, and even the galleries, kitchens, and passages that gave access to them, were naturally very active performance spaces.

At such major celebrations as Christmas, New Year's Day, and weddings, virtually the entire property became theatrical space, as noblemen and their guests
processed throughout the house from chapel, to antechamber, to great hall, to bed-
chamber, and outdoors for hunting and dancing. In good weather, great household
entertainments could take place almost entirely outdoors. Although allegorical
tournaments were usually staged by sovereigns who could afford the financial and
ideological expense of a mock military muster, Henry Herbert, second earl of
Pembroke, and his friend Sir Philip Sidney did produce tilts at the earl's seat at
Wilton; Pembroke's son William staged an elaborate and emblematic tournament
to celebrate his wedding to Mary Talbot in 1604 (Brennan, 108). These athletic
events contained all the conventional elements of drama—dialogue, conflict, plot,
costume, character, set—and were framed by banquets, musical entertainments
with costumed minstrels, and disguisings.

A household might have temporary structures (such as tents) or permanent
structures constructed specifically for banquets and entertaining under the changeable weather conditions that are a permanent feature in England and France.
Henry VIII watched and participated in many such revels at permanent banqueting halls constructed at Greenwich and at temporary ones, such as at the 1520 Field
of the Cloth of Gold in Calais, where he entertained Francis I with banquets, disguisings, and allegorical tournaments (Russell, 169–74). Inigo Jones's Whitehall
Banqueting House still survives.

Outdoor spaces, including city walls, streets, and squares, were constantly used
by civic producers when welcoming visiting dignitaries. These "environmental
theaters" employed icons from popular culture, courtly romance, biblical history,
and classical literature—the same combination of tropes that frequently occurs in
great household entertainment, which was created for a more specific but still culturally and economically diverse audience. Like the civic pageantry, household
pageantry exploited the physical estate of the aristocrat to produce a performance
environment.

As an example of the many environmental productions for Queen Elizabeth,
one outdoor performance, "The Princely Pleasures of Kennilworth," certainly
stands out. Produced by Robert Dudley, earl of Leicester, a great patron of the
drama who was frequently in charge of performances at the Inns of Court and the
royal court, "Pleasures" (named, significantly, for the household rather than the
producer or writer) honored Queen Elizabeth on her summer progress of 1575.

Beginning at the entrance to the "set," Dudley stopped his castle clock at the
queen's approach and throughout her visit. Actors entered from gardens and
woods—figures from high and popular folk culture: Greek gods, and a wildman or
greenman (played by George Gascoigne, the author of the verses). Dudley's technicians had designed and created an artificial crescent-shaped lake, complete with
islands, to stage a disguising that featured the Lady of the Lake; this figure of courtly
romance incidentally reflected the Arthurian tropes that marked one of the earli-

est performances of the Tudor dynasty, Henry VII's marriage celebrations for Elizabeth's late uncle Prince Arthur and her stepmother Queen Katharine, three-quarters of a century before. Jousts, dancing, hunting, fireworks, a historical battle reenactment, and lavish banquets completed the revels. (Sanders et al., 2:34, 3:10–11; Withington, 1:207–9).

Performances of this scope, form, and structure were clearly not possible on the public stage, which could little afford the expense or the specificity. Church authorities could afford to put on the shows but would have little interest in these themes or aesthetics. Civic celebrations used the same forms and mounted similarly extravagant pageants, but would rarely alter city landscape to suit the occasion; in addition, the multiple producers of civic pageantry had various agendas and expected individual appreciation and attention, whereas the single producer—Dudley—had no competitors. Allusions to these sorts of household performances appear in the geography of the imagination, in, for example, the masque of *The Tempest* and as inspiration for such scenes as Oberon's "love-in-idleness" speech in *A Midsummer Night's Dream*.

While the geographical space of the household is fluid, the duties and privileges of the people who inhabited that space are, ironically, quite specific. As I have demonstrated elsewhere, most aristocratic households retained many different types of entertainers as permanent residents in the court. Prescriptive accounts, household books of ordinances and regulations, such as *The Black Book* of Edward IV and *The Second Northumberland Household Book*, delineate the privileges and duties of various household members, including theatrical performers.

Chapel gentlemen and children were literate musicians, preachers, and singers who were responsible primarily for religious service but also performed as a theatrical company. These choristers, like the professional children at whom Hamlet rails, were accustomed to performing in classical satires and interludes, sometimes in Latin or Greek. Many quite naturally became professional actors as they outgrew their household roles. Chapel gentlemen were frequently playwrights and designers for household theatrics, like William Cornish Sr. and Jr., extraordinary producers of disguisings for Henry VII (Anglo, "William Cornish"), or William Peres, Northumberland's almoner and "maker of interludes," who revised the Beverley mystery plays (Grose, 61, 92, 97, 199). Other playwrights, such as John Redford, John Heywood, Nicholas Udall, and William Hunnis, worked with chapel performers.

Musicians of various sorts also resided permanently in the household. The most vital, those who invariably traveled with their patrons, were the heraldic minstrels—pipes, trumpets, and drums—who served as watchmen, waits, and military signalmen. We also find these musicians serving as costumed performers in household entertainments, blowing and beating ceremonial tattoos at banquets, jousts, and processions, constantly signaling the movements and actions of the nobility, just as sound tracks direct audience response in theater and film today.

For more subdued and private (but hardly less professional) music, households employed mixed consorts, soloists, and secular singers. These were expected to provide music for singing and dancing, the assumed skills of any courtier. Traditional musicians, such as harpers, functioned like the Celtic bards, composing and performing lyrics exceedingly specific to the household: elegies, family histories, battle victory songs, and records of household achievements. More subversively, and certainly proving the intimacy of these particular soloists, the duke of Norfolk used his harpers as messengers and spies. This intimacy was also double-edged, however, for Henry VIII's solo organist Dionisius Memo was also reputed to be a spy for the Spanish court (Westfall, 76–77).

In addition to retained actors, who have always been the dominant players in theater history, household theater frequently foregrounded the arts of various entertainers that have never been considered in the mainstream of theater history, entertainers marginalized by their class, technique, or gender. Like today's stand-up comedians, fools, both "natural" (mentally and/or physically abnormal) and "artificial" (professional wits and jesters), were audience-specific in their jibes and frequently subject to household whims. These figures, perhaps more than any other household entertainers, became resonant icons on the popular stage, yet their antics have never been analyzed as theater.

Animal managers tended menageries, which sometimes included dancing bears. Traveling acrobats, jugglers, mimes, or anyone with an unusual artifact to display could visit a noble household and expect a reward. As early as 1306, Edward I received 119 prestigious retained minstrels for a Whitsun feast. At the same time, the king was also entertained by more coarse acts, such as "John de Coton, a Lombard, making his minstrelsy with snakes" and "Bernard, The fool, and 54 of his companions coming naked before the King, with dancing revelry." Royal accounts for 1331 record a land grant to Roland le Fartere for "making a leap, a whistle and a fart" (Bullock-Davis, *Menestrellorum*, 66–67; Bullock-Davis, *Register*, 108–9).

By neglecting these marginalized performers, long regarded as too trivial or unsophisticated for scholarly consideration, we risk distorting and misinterpreting early modern theater. Let us consider, for example, performers marginalized by their gender. While the early modern professional, civic, school, and religious theater was an exclusively male domain, in records of private household theater we find as early as 1297 an entertainment for King Edward I by Matilda Makejoy, a female acrobat and dancer (Bullock-Davis, *Register*, 108–9, 174).

We know that while female actors were proscribed from most stages, they found freedom to perform in disguisings and masques at the royal court, beginning during the reign of Henry VIII and culminating in the Stuart court masques of Jones/Jonson and Samuel Daniel (see Parry, chapter 11, this volume), which included such performers as the queen herself, Susan Vere, Countess of Montgomery, Lady Anne Herbert, and Lady Mary Wroth (Brennan, 109–10). Even after the official closing of the theaters in 1642, the women of the Cavendish family produced their domestic theatrical *The Concealed Fancies* (Braunmuller and Hattaway, 156).

Some entertainers were resident, while other retained performers were expected to travel, to export household entertainment in the livery and under the protection of their households, at least until James I created a royal monopoly on patronage. Edward IV's *Black Book* stipulates that of the king's thirteen retained minstrels, some "are strengmen, coming to this court at v festes of the yere, and than to make theyre wages of household after iiij^d ob. a day if they be present in court; and than they to auoyde the next day after the festes be don" (Myers, 131–32). They were also cautioned not to be too aggressive in demanding rewards from the king's friends. By 1515, Henry VIII had divided his players into two troupes, one resident and one traveling.

Entertainers who did not travel could hold other occupations in the household, such as teaching music and repairing instruments. In 1311, Richard Pilke and his wife, Elena, served sometimes as royal minstrels and sometimes as waferers, or pastry chefs, for banquets (Bullock-Davis, *Register*, 51). The *Manuscripts of the Duke of Rutland* show that one Anthony Hall was provided with board for four weeks because he was "lernyng a play to pley in Christemes." Later, he was paid for "scowrying away the yerthe and stones in the tennys playe" (4:322). Many have pointed out Richard Gibson's occupational metamorphosis from player to Yeoman of the Wardrobe. Henry VII's interluder John English was also a tailor; Henry VIII's George Mallor was a glazier, and John Young was a mercer (Chambers, *Elizabethan*, 2:78 n, 80 n).

Today, popular "fakelore" insinuates that early drama was improvisational and rather haphazardly organized and produced, a fallacy we still find expressed in our popular culture via film, "medieval" banquets, Renaissance "fairres," and Society for Creative Anachronism fetes. But period accounts show clearly that household theater was meticulously planned and stage-managed with precision. Here again we must look to unusual sources, to household ordinances, for evidence of staging details.

These texts indicate that, from very early on, theater was integral to the court, especially if we accept a wider, less text-based definition of theater that includes aristocratic ceremonialia, in which the nobility were self-consciously creating and performing their roles, a concept that Stephen Greenblatt makes quite clear. Multimedial displays were as common to public life as they were to private theater; "Henry's [VIII] taste for lavish dress, ceremonial banquets, pageantry, and festivity astonished his contemporaries and profoundly affected their conception of power" (Greenblatt, *Renaissance*, 28). Henry's children, particularly his daughter Elizabeth, also became as expert as their father and grandfather in the manipulation of signs. Sir Thomas More's comparison of court life to "Kynges games, as it were stage plays, and for the more part plaied vpon scofoldes" not only articulates a complex theory of performance and performance reception (More, *History*, 80) but reiterates the almost commonplace early modern metaphor of life as a theater and political arenas as stages.

Peter Brook's *The Empty Space* taught us long ago that the essence of theater is a person performing a role and another observing it, a definition that embraces the self-conscious exhibition of which Greenblatt speaks and certainly includes many of the alleged "proto-dramatic" revels I have assumed in my definition. But household ceremonies contain many elements more traditionally linked to drama: theme, subtext, set, costume, blocking, character, and gesture.

Ordinances dictate the administrative details that accompany the theatrical events, such as the organization of the household for the occasion, the sequence of events, and the placement of the physical "set" and properties in the performance space. As an example of how these documents may be used, let me examine one ordinance, in combination with lists of Percy's household "stuff," as a theatrical rather than exclusively social or historical document, so that it functions like a twentieth-century stage manager's annotated script, the "bible" of theatrical production.

The twelfth order of the *Second Northumberland Household Book*, which concerns the marriage of an earl's daughter, delineates what would in theater be called set construction and blocking. The earl took the opportunity to display his wealth as set decoration for the theater that was to come. Thus the earl "produces," in the Marxist sense explored by Lefebvre, a theatrical space from a social space, marking his territory by transmogrifying the church (which many might consider an egalitarian and public space where all the assembled company could be equal in the sight of God) into a locus, a chamber within his home, foregrounding his possessions as properties and set dressing.

The first four of the six articles within the order stipulate that the high altar, the choir (including the desks, stalls, and walls), the body of the chapel, and the two altars at the chapel door were to be covered with "the best stuf that they have," hung with "arras or counterfeat arras" (fol. 22), and that carpets cover the floor of the choir and the body of the chapel. Percy's church plate, including "a crosse vppon a stage," "ymages" of saints, silver and gilt candlesticks, basins, ewers, cruets, and chalices, was displayed on the high and doorway altars (fol. 22). From these details we can form quite a vivid mental image of the stage.

Later in the manuscript, the tenth order describes the blocking—the bride's progress to the service, which falls to the technical and production crew, the chamberlain and the gentlemen ushers, who were responsible for ensuring that each signifier in the cultural code of social order was properly placed. Concerned primarily with matters of hierarchy and protocol, the order has three functions: to ensure that each "character" is properly placed according to rank; to facilitate the precise timing of the procession; and to prescribe the attendance and costume of the bride, manipulating semiotics to indicate her marital history—whether she was a maiden, a widow, or a previously betrothed woman.

The first function of the order is the blocking, dictated by precedence. After the bride has "made redy in the Chamber of my lady her moder," the stage manager gives the cue: "my lordes chamberlayn when she is comyn Down into the saide chamber" commands "a gentleman ussher to fetche the two gentlemen whiche shall lede hir to the chirche as be bachelors yf she go for a made" (fol. 23). Then the chorcography of the bridal party is prescribed: "Item the iiijth article is That all thois Gentilwomen as schalbe Attending vppon hir that Day shall go behind hir to the churche And from the churche in Degree next hir as two and two togeder as they be of birth ande the best to go next hir" (fol. 23v).

The document specifies an intermission ("Item the xxvjth article is That when the bride haeth restid her a spac in hir chaumbre where sche commeth too aftir dynnar"), outlines the movement of the principal players ("Than a gentillman vscher to com to hir and schew hir that the mynstrallis be redy"), and stipulates gestures ("and yf sche be a countesse Doughter and hir moder present Than sche to yef hir moder hir right hand when sche goith to the chambre to Daunc") and even the casting of characters: "Than a gentillman to com and make his obeisaunc to hir and Daunc *with* hir and if sche have breder at Age or Vncles the auncientest of theim to Daunc with hir Or ellis the most auncientest gentillman their that vsith to Daunc" (fol. 29v).

The document also supplies the chamberlain/stage manager with options if the actors are recalcitrant: "And if my Laidy hir moder be not Disposide to go furth with hir to the Dansing Than sche to go alloon and all the gentilwomen to follow hir and my Lord and my Laidy to com into hir When they ar in Daunsing if it be their plea*ser* so to Doo" (fol. 29v). And finally, the "bible" frustrates theater historians by providing the cue only, not the content, for what we may consider the main attraction: "And When they have souped that then they be brought into the great chambre again to se suche passe tymes as is their ordirid for theim As Disguisinges enterludes or playes" (fol. 30), concluding with the curtain calls, exits, and set strike.

Since the orders were designed to be guidelines for the household's servants, to be followed when the occasion arose, they were general in nature, omitting specific details of any particular occasion in order to be generally useful, preserving the form and structure but not the content of household revels. Perhaps precisely for this last reason, these ordinances were long neglected by critics of early modern drama, who were interested in text, not in the logistical problems and procedures that concern stage managers and producers.

While household retainers were responsible for the mundane details of production, other producers, like many Broadway "angels" today, lurked not so quietly in the wings: the patrons. In the last twenty years, patronage has become an important focus for theater studies, and it is obviously integral to the analysis of household theater. Many have written in a tangential fashion about patronage: E. K. Chambers and Glynne Wickham have included references to aristocratic performances in their histories, and the Malone Society and the Records of Early English Drama project have gathered evidence of noble patronage in their shire and city accounts. Albert Feuillerat and other royal revels accounts have preserved information that relates specifically to the entertainments of the royal patrons. Some, like Mary Blackstone, Sally-Beth MacLean, and Michael Brennan, are focusing more specifically on individual patrons. Paul White has written about patronage and religious ideology, while Stephen Orgel's and Stephen Greenblatt's more general studies have revolutionized our views by approaching patronage and early modern ideologies from the perspective of the new historicist. In *Patrons and Performance* and in this essay, I approach patronage as an integral component of the genre of household drama.

The patron exercised ownership over his revels, in that he ordered them and paid for them. At the same time, however, he was also the object of the revels, which were designed to glorify him by representing his ideas, his wealth, and his artistic tastes. The patron's dual role as producer and spectator formed an elaborate fugue, unarticulated in the dramatic theory of the period but omnipresent and subtextual. The earliest explication of this complex contrapuntal role is suggested not by theatrical or even musical theory but by Serlio's theory of perspective in *Architettura* (1545), a work that influenced Inigo Jones and consequently virtually all Stuart masque. Serlio's scenery was designed to be in perfect perspective when viewed from one and only one point: the seat of the patron. In the Stuart courts of Jonson and Jones, therefore, the quintessential but invisible role of the patron is concretized.

Patrons of great households were responsible for providing clothes (usually in the form of livery), food, and shelter for servants while they were resident in the household. Patrons were also expected to keep this small army under control, to keep them loyal to their lord and to his household, and thus, theoretically, to the sovereign. This structure was crucial, of course, while the feudal system was economically and ideologically organized in pyramidical fashion, with warrior pledged to knight pledged to overlord pledged to king. By the beginnings of what Lawrence Stone calls "bastard feudalism," noble courts seem to have been more symbolically considered to be microcosms of the kingdom as a whole.

The patron was also expected to protect those in his service and to facilitate their dealings with outside organizations. As Richard Dutton has pointed out, royal censors might be more lenient with potentially seditious materials if they were to be performed in household auspices (*Mastering*, 41–45). As early as 1285, the Statute of Winchester attempted to control masterless wanderers, an effort that was repeated by statutes and royal proclamations throughout the Tudor period (*Statutes of the Realm*, 1:97, 3:328; Hughes and Larkin, 1:172; Chambers, *Elizabethan*, 5:269–71 and app. D, 260; P. W. White, 56–61, 123–24). Players and minstrels who could produce proof of noble patronage were exempt from vagrancy laws and frequently received permission to play, while unpatronized entertainers would not.

As Mary Blackstone has suggested, noble patronage might also inspire higher wages and rewards on tour ("Patrons," 121–22). In 1540–1541, for example, the duke of Suffolk's players received six shillings eight pence in Dover, a city within his sphere of influence, while other communities tended to reward them twelve pence (Dawson, *Records*, 39, 69). Household regulations for the fifth earl of Northumberland specify that entertainers patronized by a "speciall Lorde Frende or Kynsman" would receive higher rewards (Grose, 253). The complexities of touring are discussed by Peter Greenfield later in this volume.

On the opposite end of the performance spectrum, patronage once again allowed women a theatrical voice. Many women acted as producers, as patrons to drama, like Lady Honor Lisle, who purchased a text of an interlude called *Rex Diabole* for her household in 1538 (Brewer et al., vol. 1, pt. 2, 1362). Most queens and princesses royal retained their own troupes of players and minstrels. Scores of noblewomen patronized poets and playwrights who may have contributed to performances in their households, and many also wrote literature themselves, including, to name but a few: King Henry VII's mother, Margaret Beaufort, dowager countess of Richmond and Derby; Sir Philip Sidney's sister Mary, the countess of Pembroke; Mildred Cooke, wife of William Cecil, Lord Burleigh; Anne Seymour, duchess of Somerset; Lucy Russell, countess of Bedford; Christiana Cavendish, countess of Devonshire; Lady Elizabeth Carey; and Lady Mary Wroth (Brennan, 8–9; Pollet, 7–9; Stone, *Crisis*, 208). So, while the public stage may indeed have been exclusively male-gendered (with occasional queenly forays through patronage), household revels certainly felt the influence and occasionally reflected the interests of women.

Within these households, the elaborate web of allegiance and service was woven primarily through wages, but patrons also inspired loyalty through largesse, by rewarding attentive servants with gifts, properties, privileges, money, feasts, and—our chief interest here—entertainment. Since all of these benefactions required an outlay of cash, it is hardly surprising that we have a paper trail of theatrical evidence in the household and civic account books. These accounts are now being systematically examined and printed by the Malone Society and the Records of Early English Drama project, endeavors that are revolutionizing our understanding of early drama and rewriting its history.

The records tell us not only who was employed by aristocratic households but also precisely what each artist could expect to receive in wages and livery. Also preserved in accounts, particularly the revels accounts in the royal household of the later Tudor and Stuart periods, are outlays for set and costume expenses that allow us sometimes to connect texts with specific performances and frequently to reconstruct, at least in part, what a performance might have looked and sounded like.

Many scholars have been working to attribute anonymous early Tudor play texts to patrons and great household auspices. In particular, Sydney Anglo's *Spectacle, Pageantry, and Early Tudor Policy* and David Bevington's *Tudor Drama and Politics* examine entertainments in the period, proving, if we had any doubt, that theater was central to court life as early as the turn of the fifteenth century. Anglo demonstrates clearly that royal court entertainments were influenced by the Burgundian style that Henry VII had observed while in exile and that they therefore adopted specific allegories designed to reinforce and compliment the new Tudor dynasty. Bevington argues that drama was polemical and that patrons either chose or commissioned works that would communicate their own ideologies, an idea that has proved a bountiful fountainhead for patronage studies.

Tracing source materials and stressing ideological affinities, Ian Lancashire has attributed *The World and the Child* to the household of the earl of Kent about 1508, *The Interlude of Youth* to the household of the fifth earl of Northumberland about 1513, and *Hick Scorner* to the duke of Suffolk's court about 1514 (I. Lancashire, "Auspices" and *Two Tudor Interludes*). T. W. Craik has also investigated this angle in *The Tudor Interlude* and suggests that *Wealth and Health* was written for Queen Mary Tudor's interluders at the beginning of her reign (Craik, "The Political Interpretation," 98–108). Milton Gatch, and more recently Milla Riggio, have discussed *Wisdom who is Christ* as a household play, perhaps for the bishop of Ely. Recent research and publications are continually demonstrating that many extant texts, particularly in the early sixteenth century, can be traced to household sponsorship, either in composition or in performance.

While tracking specific auspices and patrons for anonymous texts is a comparatively recent movement, theater historians have long been engaged in connecting known playwrights firmly with specific aristocratic patrons. As we focus increasingly on anonymous playwrights, "minor" (read: uncanonized) writers, and unprivileged forms, we discover that, in fact, most dramatists before the Elizabethan age of the public theater either were in the service of a noble household or were closely connected with a noble patron. Henry MacCracken edited John Lydgate's *The Minor Poems* in 1934, but no one seemed particularly interested in Lydgate's mummings for Henry V and VI; certainly few took them very seriously, either as poetry or as theater. We have almost as thoroughly ignored such artists as Gascoigne and the Cornishes, mentioned above. Even canonized writers like Ben Jonson are acclaimed more for their plays than for their household revels.

John Heywood, author of *Four PP, Johan Johan, The Play of Love, The Play of the Weather, The Pardoner and the Friar*, and *Witty and Witless*, was a retained minstrel for Henry VIII. David Bergeron has examined patronage as it affects Thomas Heywood. Nicholas Udall, author of *Rafe Roister Doister* and *Respublica*, wrote verses for the coronation pageants of Queen Anne Boleyn and produced plays and Christmas entertainments for Queen Mary Tudor (Withington, 1:181–87; Chambers, *Medieval*, 451–52; Bevington, *Tudor*, 121). Henry Medwall, author of *Nature* and *Fulgens and Lucrece*, was employed by Cardinal Morton; Alan Nelson also connects Medwall with Sir Thomas More and the Rastells, who printed his plays (Moeslein, 1–19; Nelson, *Medwall*, 3, 17). John Skelton was connected both to the Percy family, earls of Northumberland, and to Henry VII's mother, Margaret Beaufort (Carpenter, 138).

Other examples abound. Paul White, here and elsewhere, has written extensively on Protestant patronage, including that of William Cecil, Lord Burghley, Elizabeth's secretary of state; Thomas Cranmer, archbishop of Canterbury; and Robert Dudley, earl of Leicester, among others. He persuasively connects John Bale with John de Vere, earl of Oxford, and with Thomas Cromwell, Secretary of State and Lord Privy Seal to Henry VIII.

I cannot here enter into a thorough discussion of patronage to 1642, a topic that certainly deserves more attention than it has been granted and that is explored in this volume later by Kathleen McLuskie and Felicity Dunsworth, Peter Greenfield, Paul Whitfield White, Graham Parry, and W. R. Streitberger. Anyone who even glances at the records cannot fail to notice that, while the names of players and the plays they performed are conspicuously missing, page after page and year after year of civic and household account books record the names of hundreds of patrons.

And if playwrights were writing for aristocratic patrons, it is not so far a stretch to assume that the patrons and their households also performed, viewed, and even read the plays, an issue that Heidi Brayman Hackel addresses later in this volume. Certainly poets in hope of social and financial attention were in the habit of broadcasting dedications to many noble patrons who did not, perhaps, request the honor. But the writers I have mentioned above have been shown to have close geographical, personal, and ideological connections to their patrons, and presumably, to their households.

My point here is that household entertainments were not necessarily limited to the nontextual disguisings or offerings of visiting or retained troupes of minstrels and the occasional traveling acrobat. Households could and did see plays written expressly for them, plays that mingled the structures of the mysteries, miracles, and moralities that John Wasson has examined above, with the classical structures of the university plays that Alan Nelson and John Elliott speak of next.

Spectators at household revels, like those at schools and unlike those at church dramas, civic pageants, and public theaters, were a very specific audience. Besides living and working together, they shared particular cultural paradigms, they gathered in a private space for specific reasons, and they understood personal, topical, and local allusions. Consequently, a performance could assume a particular audience reception and predict a response, could tailor its content to a social or religious occasion, like the progress of the monarch or a local saint's day, and could refer specifically to those present.

Performances at the royal court, such as entertainments for visiting dignitaries, exploited this specificity. Sydney Anglo has examined early Tudor revels and demonstrated very thoroughly that entertainments reflected not only the occasion and auspices but also the particular audience. For example, Henry VII's elaborate entertainments at the wedding of his son Prince Arthur to Princess Katharine of

Spain demonstrate that Henry was consciously promulgating specific Tudor policies and ideologies by using the emblems of England and Spain and impersonat-
ing the guests of honor, thus manipulating signs to consolidate his dynasty and to
ensure that he and his descendants were firmly established as permanent features
on the international stage.

Household entertainments, especially those of Elizabeth's courtiers, made topical use of local history, current events, or persons in attendance as systems of reference devised to entertain, to deliver subtle and not-so-subtle suggestions, and to
include household members in a hermeneutic circle. This circle could be so
closed that at times the line between spectators and performers becomes blurred;
early modern theater is full of what modern readers would consider breaches of
fourth wall in the form of prologues and epilogues, verses designed to contact the
audience directly with recommendation for their behavior, pleas for applause and
reward, and straightforward flattery.

In an era when all aristocratic display was theatrical, and when the reactions of
the viewers were as riveting as the actions of the performers, the audience was at
the very least bifocal. The Stuart masque is perhaps the best example of this split
focus, as aristocratic masquers mingle with professionals; Henry VIII seems to have
started the tradition of disguisers' breaking the barrier of the dance-fiction to
choose partners from the audience. The generalized performance space of the
great hall or tiltyard could easily lead to mistaken identities, a fact that Medwall
capitalizes on in *Fulgens and Lucrece*:

A. For I thought verely by your apparell
   That ye had bene a player.
B. Nay, never a dell.
A. Than I cry you mercy:
   I was to blame. Lo, therfor, I say
   Ther is so myche nyce aray
   Amonges these galandis now aday
   That a man shall not lightly
   Know a player from a nother man. (43–56)

Neither costume nor physical position distinguishes spectator from the spectacle.

Martin Butler has explored this prohibition of willing suspension of disbelief, citing many examples, such as Thomas Nashe's *Summer's Last Will and Testament*
(performed for Archbishop Whitgift at Croyden), in which Will Summers, as narrator, interrupted and interacted with the performance, thus functioning as interlocu-
tor for the spectators (Braunmuller and Hattaway, *Companion*, 136). Elizabeth and
James always sat where they could be seen, sometimes in places where they themselves could not see or hear very well. And several performances actually reached out
and touched them, such as Peele's *The Arraignment of Paris*, in which Elizabeth is
offered Paris's prize golden apple (Braunmuller and Hattaway, 128–35).

Other performances were satisfied with letting the content touch the spectators. Shakespeare's "The Mousetrap" within *Hamlet* is perhaps the most famous fictional example of the effects of this phenomenon, although Elizabeth's reactions to various performances that purported to give her personal or political advice are equally notorious.

From all of these references, we can see that one of the signifying characteristics of household theater was the nature of its audience. Certainly their socioeconomic standing and, in certain cases, their sophisticated literary taste made elevated language and sentiments appropriate. But scores of financial records indicate that so-called lowbrow entertainments were also rewarded, particularly as ancillary diversions. Audiences participated both explicitly and implicitly, as the aristocrats took to the stage themselves or as they assumed that the assembled household was closely marking their behavior and response.

Many features of household drama discussed thus far are similar to theater in other venues. I would like now to discuss in more detail some of the forms and structures that make household drama distinct. Obviously, my attempt here is not to be exclusive, for private drama indeed shares many features with public, academic, and church drama. But great household audiences, aesthetics, and production values do differentiate the private theater of the aristocracy from other types. Some interludes, and the disguisings in particular, require a variety of performers, multimedial production values, and an extravagance in set and costume that not only preclude touring but seem to necessitate the stable and abundant space, time, and finances of aristocratic or ecclesiastical household auspices. This I believe to be a key to understanding the aesthetics of household entertainment.

Household performances tended to be far more expensive and multimedial than those of the public stage, for the simple reason that a variety of entertainers was conveniently available and because of the aristocratic doctrine of excess: MORE is more. Since patrons retained within their households a variety of artists (including singers, jesters, players of instruments, painters, poets, dancers, actors, educators, and rhetoricians) of various ages (from chapel children to adult entertainers), genders, and even species (let us not forget the menageries), the designers of household revels could conceivably call upon a great variety of talented professionals to create and perform for the occasion.

I use the term *designers* quite specifically, since most household performances seem constructed by a design team rather than an individual, with no particular artist in tyrannical control but rather with many artists participating, with varying degrees of cooperation. Poets, musicians, painters, tailors, and laborers collaborated to design, write, build, sing, play, and dance one unified performance piece. And since these occasional performances had to adapt to a number of different political, social, and religious agendas, the makers had to be prepared to be subtle and complex.

As the noble and royal revels accounts clearly demonstrate, the households were prepared to allocate their resources for these occasional and multimedial extravaganzas. Entertainments required the capital of the sponsor to supply raw materials, carpenters, craftsmen, and laborers. Households also provided time, space, and money to design, construct, and perform, as well as a storehouse of costume and set materials in the possessions of the household chapels and wardrobes. While many household artists did travel for a variety of reasons, during performances in their homes, in the great households that retained them, they could produce different sorts of theater than they did when performing on the road or on the public stage.

Although a household performance might contain a tourable text (like Percy's tripartite Twelfth Night revels, which contained a play, a disguising, and a morris dance), generally the full presentation did not wear or travel well; far too occasional and cumbersome in set and costume, it could barely move, let alone return a financial profit. Complex staging, properties, music, dance, participation by performers of various ages, specific references to occasion, topical references, focus on audience—all these, particularly in combination, indicate household performance. Allegorical jousts, masques, and disguisings are, from all the available evidence, strictly private occasional forms.

Many plays also show evidence of household production values. For example, I have argued elsewhere that the Wakefield Master's *Secunda Pastorum* shows the influence of chapel production and seems designed for indoor staging. At the opposite extreme of complexity, we have the elaborate *Wisdome Who is Christ*, a performance that requires actors, seven mute boys, dancers, and at least three minstrels. With doubling, the thirty-eight characters can be played by six speakers and seven children, coincidentally the average number of performers in great household chapels (Westfall, 50–54).

In some cases, plays designed for household performance are identifiable through their production values and requirements. John Rastell's *Four Elements* clearly demonstrates the difference between a text designed for household performance and one suited to touring. The full version of the play incorporates a disguising, which requires dancers, minstrels, and elaborate costuming, but Rastell edits his own text to allow for simpler dances and *a cappella* song. Ben Jonson's *Bartholomew Fair* also edited itself, including different prologues and epilogues depending on whether the play was to be performed at court or in the public playhouse.

The aesthetics of household theater were as diverse as the households that produced it, but a few common features by which we may recognize the genre do emerge. The close personal relationships among performers, patrons, and audiences; the specific and occasional nature of the revels; the expenses in time, sets, costumes, space, and consequently the money required; and the multimediality engendered by the cooperation of various artists all characterize household revels. But we cannot neglect to account for taste, for most patrons made their ideological and personal preferences quite public.

As early as Richard the Lionhearted, we have evidence (at least in folklore) of the intimacy of retained minstrels, for Richard's minstrel is credited with finding the king's prison at Trifels Castle by singing the king's favorite lays, to which Richard responded. The pious Henry VI supposedly rushed from the room when a bare-breasted woman danced. Henry VII, as Sydney Anglo has shown, imported Continental style that he had observed while he gathered his invasion force in Burgundy, but the king never actively participated. His son, in contrast, always took center stage, and he also frequently mixed elite with retained entertainers. Henry's children, using theater in their ideological warfare, increased national interest in plays while following their own tastes and agendas: while Edward viewed childish shows of jesters in mock battles, his Protestant courtiers paid for polemical plays; frugal Elizabeth presumed she was the star without performing and preferred to be flattered with entertainments paid for by others. The Stuart clan once again took over the stage, footed the bills, and used the masque as their own personal fantasyland.

Some might allege that these movements are evolutionary: royal spectators of simple emblematic "shows" become royal spectacles themselves, thereafter reverting to a seemingly more passive audience for sophisticated (read: Shakespeare) texts, and finally shifting to royal performers in professional extravaganzas that were elitist and expensive. Postmodern critics, however, tend to see a shift in context, rather than a progression. These shifts are changes rather than developments, and they articulate more about the personalities of the sovereigns than about theatrical evolution or technological advancement. For while Inigo Jones's state-of-the-art pageants and Ben Jonson's refined verses were astonishing the royal court, noble households outside London were still celebrating simple family affairs.

The influence of these family entertainments on the public stage (along with the influence of civic pageantry and school drama) has been relegated to brief footnotes, perhaps because the multimedial aesthetics and socioeconomic conditions of performance were difficult to reproduce on the public stage and seem to have evolved into variant genres of theater such as ballet and opera, genres that have until recently received far less attention than the privileged literary texts. The closest living relative to household theater may perhaps be found in the avant-garde forms of happenings and performance art, which also blur generic borders, leave little evidence in script, and seem to many to be exclusive in audience reception and response.

By the turn of the seventeenth century, Shakespeare was repeatedly referring to household drama and patronized players in plays for the public stage. Household drama is not important *because* Shakespeare refers to it; Shakespeare refers to it because it was *already* important. Indeed, plays for the public theater attest to the influence of private theater and provide some imaginative examples of great household performance, though these must of course be read with caution.

Thomas Middleton and William Rowley's *The Changeling* mentions a disguising of madmen at the three-day revels surrounding the marriage of Beatrice-Joanna. I have already mentioned "The Mousetrap" of *Hamlet*; all of *The Taming of the Shrew* is a performance by the unnamed lord's players before Christopher Sly; *The Tempest* includes a banquet and masque; *A Midsummer Night's Dream* not only includes a wedding play but also describes the process by which it is introduced to the household. Volpone is entertained by his fool, dwarf, and castrato in Jonson's play.

Household accounts record payments to various traveling entertainers, some wearing the livery of noble households, some under civic patronage, some probably slipping through loopholes in the laws against vagrancy. Vivid descriptive accounts, again particularly of royal household revels, survive in chronicles and letters. Edward Halle's *Vnion of the Two Noble and Illustre Famelies of Lancastre and York* preserves eyewitness accounts of scores of entertainments in the early Tudor period. But Halle is frequently so subjective in his concerns that he omits details about the performance in favor of details about the spectators. Nevertheless, Halle's chronicle presents a court almost constantly in performance mode. Similarly, letters and papers of foreign diplomats and the sovereigns themselves are often concerned more with politics than with art, but they still provide visual and auditory details that financial accounts and ordinances lack, especially when the entertainment reflected some social or political point.

Rude vaudeville acts, liturgical plays by singing boys, an opulent tournament in France, the onset of "The Mousetrap" in *Hamlet*, and political ballets at the royal court do appear at first glance to have very little in common. The entertainments I have mentioned above range over four hundred years, span the reigns of many sovereigns, occur in various spaces on two continents, and comprise many types of entertainments, mostly nontextual and exceedingly ephemeral. What they do have in common is that all constitute household theater, a topic (like most of the topics in this volume) that is elusive, complex, and impossible to discuss thoroughly in a few pages.

Household revels did affect English theatrical traditions; indeed, performances in the royal court set fashions in theater that were imitated throughout the kingdom. And, since postmodern theory has begun decentering text and authority as primary focus for scholarship, we are finally beginning to understand that the source of theater is not limited to its immediate creators in the persons of writers, musicians, and performers. Rather, social conditions and specific locations can and do create vectors of influence that affect not only the form of theater but also the audience reception and response.

For years scholars have dismissed household entertainments as fleeting and somewhat embarrassing because of their allegedly unsophisticated texts—and sometimes, quite frankly, there has been good reason for such dismissal. Yet a reconsideration of this art form, with text and writer no longer exclusively foregrounded, offers many implications for this *New History*. By enlarging our definition of theater, we begin to entertain more complex notions of its function, including the nature of the audiences and the contexts within which they viewed performances. Interdisciplinary methodologies in research are continually yielding new insights, and the impact of new historicism and cultural materialism has revolutionized our understanding of the place of theater in early modern life. By paying more attention to the stage than to the page, and to the private as well as the public theaters, we are finally including uncanonized performances and marginalized performers in our representations and acknowledging the places of ideology, patronage, and power in the creation and performance of theater.

CHAPTER 4

# The Universities

## Early Staging in Cambridge

Alan H. Nelson

ENGLISH RENAISSANCE academic theaters of the kind that flourished at Cambridge, Oxford, and the Inns of Court had a character of their own and should be studied and appreciated in their own right.[1] Reconstructions of such professional theaters as the Rose and the Globe, whether on paper or in timber, should not draw on evidence from the academic theaters, at least not in the first instance; nor should academic theaters be reconstructed in the image of the Rose and the Globe.[2]

Queens' College theater at Cambridge, first constructed over the years 1546–1547 to 1548–1549, some thirty years before the Theatre in Shoreditch, was erected annually in the college hall and survived for well over ninety years (Nelson, *Early*, ch. 2). This theater (fig. 4.1) consisted of strong timber scaffolding, which was normally kept in storage. At least once a year the college hall was cleared of its dining tables, and the theater scaffolding was erected and covered with floorboards. After two or three weeks of rehearsals and perhaps a single performance, the whole structure was then dismantled and put away until the following year.

The Queens' College stage, made up of some five hundred pieces of timber, was inventoried in 1638, at a time when it looked as if some years might pass before it would be set up again. The inventory served not only as a record of the pieces of timber but as a set of instructions for assembly, perhaps with the thought in mind that at least a generation of carpenters might pass before the stage was put to use once more (Nelson, *Records*, 688–93; Nelson, *Early*, app. 3).

The principal parts of this theater included a stage platform, which ran from one side of the hall to the other, near the upper end; stage houses, which flanked the stage platform and backed against the side walls; scaffold seating for college and university dignitaries and noble visitors above the stage, at the upper end of the hall; and scaffold seating and floor space for students and for visitors from the town below the stage, toward the lower end of the hall.

Each of the two stage houses was in effect a multistory structure with a railed platform on top (Nelson, *Early*, 25). The first platform above the hall floor stood at the same height as the stage. The four posts and studs facing the stage platform were probably so disposed as to create three structural openings, which under dif-

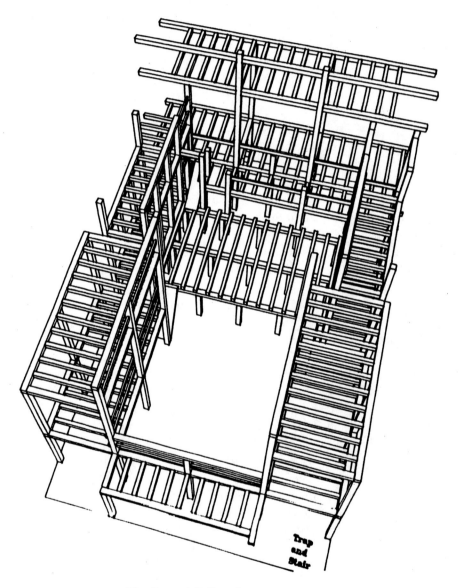

FIGURE 4.1. The Queens' College theater.

ferent circumstances might provide one, two, or three doorways. The top platform by contrast might represent a balcony or a city wall, but most commonly, as we shall see, it provided the possibility of upper-story windows.

A similar, though much larger, stage was built in the great hall of Trinity College, Cambridge, from about the time construction was completed on that hall in 1608 (Nelson, *Early*, ch. 3). This stage (fig. 4.2) was used annually by the college until 1642: it was the site of plays produced for the royal (or noble) visits of 1613, 1615, 1623, 1628, 1629, 1632, 1636, and 1642 (Nelson, *Records*). Accordingly, it seems

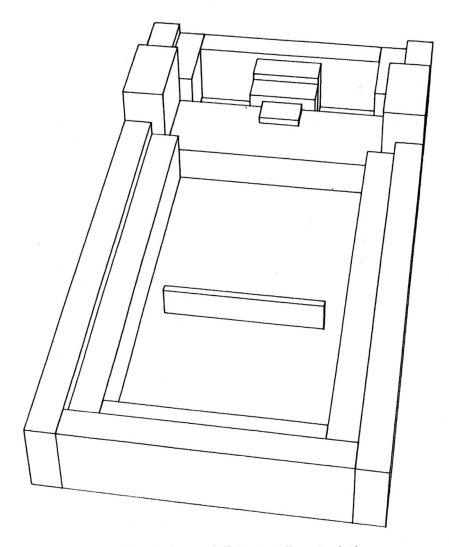

FIGURE 4.2. Stage in the great hall, Trinity College, Cambridge.

to have been supplied with a dais or throne platform to be used whenever the king or a prince of the blood was in attendance (Nelson, *Early*, 45–52).

These two reconstructions of Cambridge college theaters are based almost exclusively on college and university archival records. But surviving playtexts can be correlated with these reconstructions to discover how the stages were used for actual productions. Some 60 plays written specifically for Cambridge college theaters survive today, along with twenty-five cast lists (Nelson, *Records*, apps. 6–7): this record compares favorably with some 474 plays and fifteen cast lists for professional theaters in London during the same period.[3]

Three Cambridge plays warrant special scrutiny: *Leander* and *Labyrinthus* by Walter Hawkesworth, dated c. 1599–1600 and 1603 respectively; and the anonymous *Cancer* (in English, *The Crab*), c. 1613.[4] These plays were all performed at Trinity College, all come down to us with complete cast lists, and all are richly supplied with stage directions. *Leander* and *Labyrinthus* were written for and performed in the old college hall, a medieval structure inherited from Michaelhouse at the time Trinity was first established in 1546–1547, while *Cancer* was written for the college's magnificent new hall, which survives virtually unchanged from the time of its completion in 1608 and which should be regarded as an authentic Jacobean theater, yet older and more representative than Inigo Jones's Banqueting House in Whitehall (Nelson, *Early*, 39–40).

*Leander*, *Labyrinthus*, and *Cancer* constitute a test case. If the Cambridge college staging conventions survived unchanged through such a massive alteration of venue as the replacement of a decaying, cramped medieval college hall with a spanking-new Jacobean showpiece for royal visitors, with three times the floor space of its predecessor and with a built-in tiring house for college actors—an important characteristic of the new hall (Nelson, *Records*, 43–52)—then we can say that Cambridge had a tradition that changed very little for almost a century, and we can assume, at least provisionally, that the same tradition governed the staging of other Cambridge plays as well.

The three Cambridge plays we are examining have much in common. The characters are all organized by households, as shown by the dramatis personae from *Labyrinthus* (Nelson, *Records*, 904–5). Two of the *Labyrinthus* manuscripts improve on this organization by identifying the households further as *Domus decani superioris*, *Domus bacaulariorum in medicinae*, and *Domus decani inferioris*—that is, "House of the senior dean," "House of the bachelors in medicine," and "House of the junior dean." George Charles Moore Smith, who first called attention to this phenomenon, thought that the notations might refer to "structures or partitions already existing in the hall" (27);[5] a more likely explanation, now that we have reconstructed the college theater, is that the first house was situated near where the senior dean sat to watch the play, the second near the bachelors in medicine, and the third near the junior dean. The senior dean and the bachelors in medicine probably sat above the stage, the junior dean below the stage, near the undergraduates whom he supervised. Next to the name of the braggart Spaniard Don Piedro Pacheo D'Alcantara occurs the notation *semper è Foro*, "always from the forum" (marketplace). Since the Spaniard did not have a house of his own, he was compelled to enter from the "wings."

We are now ready to work out a stage plan. *Cancer* is a good example, since it may well contain more original stage directions than any other play from the entire English Renaissance. *Cancer* requires four houses: those of Ursilia, Sempronius, Rodericus, and Granchio. Offstage exits are to the forum of the bachelors of medicine and to the forum of the senior dean (perhaps stage left and stage right). The action also requires exits and entrances through an *angiportus*—a kind of narrow alley, which can be conjecturally placed, somewhat arbitrarily, between the houses of Ursilia and Sempronius (fig. 4.3).

Another important feature of the academic stage is the upper-level window. Cambridge plays with window scenes include but are not limited to *Hymenaeus* (1579?), *Victoria* (1582?), *Hispanus* (1597?), *Machiavellus* (1597), *Leander* (1599?), *Labyrinthus* (1603), *Zelotypus* (1606?), *Albumazar* (1615), *Ignoramus* (1615), *Susenbrotus* (1616), *Adelphe* (1612, 1613), *Cancer* (1613?), *Fraus Honesta* (1619), *Alphonsus* (date unknown), *Loiola* (1623), *Pseudomagia* (1627?), *Paria* (1628), and

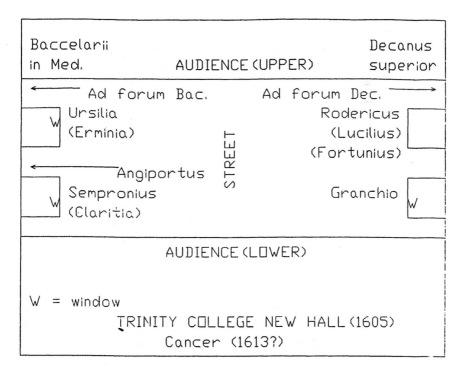

FIGURE 4.3. Alley between the houses of Ursilia and Sempronius in the play *Cancer.*

*Rival Friends* (1632). Often the heroine speaks from the window, which represents her bedroom, or at least an upper-story room, while her suitor and others speak to her from the street. Letters may be handed up to or down from the window; occasionally the window is entered from below by means of ropes or scaling ladders, or the heroine may take flight by climbing down from her window to the street. Three of the four houses in *Cancer* require functional windows, represented in figure 4.3 by the letter W.

The window openings seem to have been supplied with functional shutters, the doorways with hinged wooden doors or with curtains. Subsidiary structures were sometimes provided, including trees, posts, doghouses, and in one instance a functional tomb, with doors and with places for concealment within.

Perhaps the single most distinctive characteristic of the academic theater lay in the fixity of its locales. For the kind of comedy that is the norm for Cambridge — that is, for at least half of the surviving plays — the stage platform is always and only the main street of a named city or town, for example, Florence or Bordeaux. A house once assigned to a given mater- or paterfamilias retains its identity unchanged to the end of the play. A particular exit is understood as leading to a particular forum or port, and nowhere else. For convenience, let us call this characteristic "fixed locale" staging, in contrast to the "dynamic locale" staging we are used to in Shakespeare, in which the stage platform may be a throne room, a field of battle, a garden, the interior of a house, or a street, or even nowhere in particular, and whose identity usually changes from one scene to the next.

Fixed-locale staging restricts action in certain ways. It is virtually impossible, for example, to play an interior scene, except perhaps by having actors hang their heads out an upper-story window. All conversations, including the most private, must occur outdoors. It is impossible for the action to alternate between one city and another or to shift from the city to the country. Characters must often be given reasons, however lame, why they should appear on the city street.

Cambridge also had a tradition of pastoral plays, including one identified as a "piscatory" (Phineas Fletcher's *Sicilides, a Piscatory* [Nelson, *Records*, 923–24]), but these plays were set in the country, and their settings did not alternate with locations in the city. In such plays, the superfluous stage houses may have been concealed behind a painted "pastorall clothe" of the kind recorded in 1613 (Nelson, *Records*, 500).

In the anonymous *Return from Parnassus*, first performed at St. John's College, Cambridge, c. 1602, and printed in 1606, the character Will Kemp observes of an academic play he had witnessed at Cambridge: "tis good sporte in a part, to see them neuer speake in their walke, but at the end of the stage, iust as though in walking with a fellow we should neuer speake but at a stile, a gate, or a ditch, where a man can go no further" (Leishman, act 4, scene 3; details noted in Nelson, *Records*, app. 6.1). Presumably "at the end of the stage" means "at the fore-edge of the stage." On this evidence, a fair inference is that the action of the play was projected out toward the main part of the audience, even though the actors would have had their backs to dignitaries, including the monarch, seated behind the stage platform.

A similar point is made by reports concerning the theater built by Simon Basil and Inigo Jones in 1605 at Christ Church hall, Oxford, which incorporated the first perspective set in England (Orrell, *Human*, ch. 8). King James objected so vehemently to being placed in the center of the audience where the theatrical illusion would be most nearly perfect that the designers were forced to alter the placement of his throne. He complained that spectators would see "his cheek only"—that is, they would see him from the back or side rather than head-on (Orrell, *Human*, ch. 8). James, who was not much enamored of plays in any case, cared nothing for perspective. His main purpose in attending a play was not to see but to be seen.

The principal document for the traditional Oxford college theaters is John Bereblock's Latin account of the stage erected in Christ Church hall for Elizabeth's royal visit of 1566. Glynne Wickham's reconstruction (Wickham, *Early*, app. H, 355–59) reflects close attention to documentary detail, but he may have been misled by taking the word *theatrum* to signify the scaffolding for spectators rather than the stage platform and its appurtenances: with this false start, he placed the stage platform at the lower or eastern end of the hall and the primary seating scaffolds at the western or upper end. If, as seems more likely, the *theatrum* was the site of the dramatic action, then the stage platform was situated at the upper end of the hall, as at Cambridge. The validity of this reconstruction is confirmed, I believe, by the further description: "Ex utroque scenae latere comoedis ac personatis magnifica palatia aedesque apparatissimae extruuntur" [And on both sides of the stage, magnificent palaces and splendid houses were set up]. These houses must have been like the substantial flanking houses in Cambridge theaters, rather than the minuscule boxes of Wickham's reconstruction. Finally, the queen sat above the stage, beneath a baldachino. In short, the Christ Church stage of 1566 must have looked much like the reconstructions proposed here of the Queens' College and Trinity College stages at Cambridge.

Fewer playtexts survive from Oxford than from Cambridge, with a tendency toward the tragic rather than the comic, so to some extent we are comparing apples and oranges. With the major exception of *Gorboduc*, Inns of Court plays tended to follow the Cambridge comic tradition: George Gascoigne's *Supposes*, set on a single street in Florence and featuring fixed houses, is a perfect example of academic staging (Fraser and Rabkin).

With some idea what an academic comedy looked like onstage, we may turn now around and ask whether any of the presumed professional plays from the English Renaissance belonged rather to the academic staging tradition. Although many plays lack a strong sense of location and may thus be imagined as transpiring at a single fixed site, at least one scene will usually be found that is set elsewhere than on a given city street—in another city, indoors rather than outdoors, on a ship, or in a pasture or a wood.

One play that adheres in strictest possible measure to the rules for academic comedy is Shakespeare's *The Comedy of Errors*. The action is set in Ephesus, on a city street, flanked by one house, called the Phoenix; at least one inn, called the Centaur (perhaps the Tiger and the Porcupine as well); and finally an abbey. One exit leads to other streets of Ephesus, a second to the port. A functional door and a functional window at the Phoenix (the house of Antipholus of Ephesus) are of considerable importance to the action. The setting never changes. As we know from contemporary references, *The Comedy of Errors* was written for Gray's Inn, 1594, evidently on commission. We know of no productions on a professional stage, and the play was not printed until the 1623 First Folio (Shakespeare, *Works*, ed. Bevington, 2).

Bevington comments on two staging possibilities for *The Comedy of Errors*:

> Some editors argue that the play was staged according to classical practice with three visible doors backstage representing three "houses"—that of Antipholus of Ephesus (in the center), that of the Courtesan, and that of the Priory—with the stage itself representing a marketplace or open area. More probably, the stage may have been open and unlocalized. The [opening] scene may be at the Duke's court. (5 n. 1.1)

But surely there is a third possibility: the localized setting of an academic theater, in which the stage platform represents a street in the city of Ephesus, with the stage houses (not necessarily limited to three) ranged on either side. Admittedly, when and if *The Comedy of Errors* was translated to a London professional theater, the setting may have lost its localization.

*Love's Labor's Lost* may also belong to the academic tradition, not only because of its scholars and pedants but by virtue of its fixed pastoral setting. *The Taming of the Shrew* has many characteristics of the academic theater as well, set on a street in Padua, but with the major exception of a scene at Petruchio's country house.[6]

By contrast with their academic counterparts, the Rose and the Globe were theaters in the dynamic tradition: the stage platform might change its identity at any time, and locations were not fixed. Actors strolled about the stage, speaking as they walked, rather than standing stock-still at the fore-edge like Cambridge academic players or modern opera singers. We learn from the character Will Kemp, in a continuation of the passage already cited, that facial expressions at Cambridge inclined to the grotesque: "I was once at a Comedie in Cambridge, and there I saw a parasite make faces and mouths of all sorts on this fashion" (he demonstrates). Clearly, facial expressions as well as stage movements were more naturalistic on the public stage.

Despite these differences, London commercial theaters were in some ways similar to academic theaters. As at the academic theaters, members of the audience at the Rose and the Globe might well sit above the stage, in the "lords' room," content to observe the action from behind (Hotson, *Shakespeare's*, 152–54; Nelson, *Early*, 176–77 n. 24). We know from the academic theaters that English carpenters were expert at devising timber structures that could be set up and taken down quickly and repeatedly, so thrones, beds, funeral monuments, and tombs might be set on the stage for special effects, then cleared away as quickly again.

The disposition of the theater at Blackfriars remains a great unknown. Most reconstructions of this important venue simply squeeze down and square off arena theaters like the Rose and the Globe, with little concern for antecedent traditions of hall staging.[7] Is it not possible, however, that private and court theaters conformed rather to the tradition of the academic theaters, with audiences above and below the stage platforms, and stage houses on either side (Nelson, *Early*, 125–26)? Though we have no proof that they were so organized, this possibility must be maintained as one of several equally tentative hypotheses until further proof is forthcoming one way or the other.

NOTES

1. This essay was first presented at the annual meeting of the Shakespeare Society of America, Chicago, March 25, 1995. Figures 1 and 2 are reproduced from Nelson, *Early*, 31, 42, by permission of Cambridge University Press.

2. Court, college, and Inns of Court theaters constitute a major part of Hotson's preliminary analysis in *Shakespeare's Wooden O* (ch. 6), while Southern (*Staging*) treats hall stages as the venue for virtually all plays prior to the construction of the Theatre in 1576. Gurr (*Playgoing*, 240, no. 161) includes an order for a 1632 performance at Trinity College, Cambridge, among documents meant to illustrate playgoing in London.

3. King, *Casting*, ch. 3. I am grateful to Leslie Thomson for information concerning London playtexts.

4. Publication details are in Nelson, *Records*, app. 6.1. For facsimile reprints, see *Cancer* and *Hawkesworth*.

5. For precise manuscript information, see Nelson, *Records*, 169 n. 25.

6. Although he is not thought to have had a university education, and so far as we know was not a member of Gray's Inn, Shakespeare in his early plays adhered much more closely than any of his professional colleagues to the English academic staging tradition. Perhaps he learned of the academic performance tradition at the grammar school in Stratford.

7. I. Smith; Orrell, *Theatres*, ch. 12. I am more inclined to agree with the argument in Berry, "Stage and Boxes," 163–86.

# Early Staging in Oxford

*John R. Elliott, Jr.*

BEGINNING IN THE 1540s and largely copying the model pro-
vided by Cambridge, drama in Oxford played an extensive role both in college life
and in the public life of the university.[1] This role was often recreational or ceremonial, but it was also sometimes quasi-curricular. We know of at least two occasions, for instance, in which students in the Faculty of Arts were required to write
a play in order to supplicate for their B.A., one of whom described the practice as
"bringing a trifle to receive a hood" (Oxford Archives, Register G 143; Llewellyn,
80).[2] Less trifling were the annual expenditures by Christ Church between 1554
and 1604 for productions by its students of a pair of comedies and a pair of tragedies,
one of each pair to be spoken in Latin and the other in Greek. Similar support of
student plays was given at St. John's College and at Magdalen College throughout
the period before the Civil War.

These formal endorsements of dramatic activities reflected the value that drama was deemed to have in the training of young men for public life. For Oxford
as for Cambridge humanists, drama was a branch of rhetoric whose educational
function was to hone the skills of the future preacher and statesman. As the
Christ Church don and playwright William Gager put it, acting in plays enabled
students to

> practise their style either in prose or verse, to be well acquainted with Seneca or
> Plautus, to try their voices and confirm their memories, and to frame their speech and
> conform it to convenient action, whereby never any one amongst us, that I know, was
> made the worse, and many have been much the better. (Corpus Christi Archives,
> MS 352, 41–65)

So widely shared was this opinion among the Oxford authorities that the number of play productions in the colleges in the early seventeenth century actually increased, at a time when plays were becoming fewer at Cambridge.

Student plays at Oxford, as at Cambridge, were most usually performed in the college halls, and only rarely outdoors in the college gardens, as a present-day visitor to Oxford in the summer might assume. In addition to the Greek and Latin classics, some plays were written by undergraduates, whose names were seldom recorded, and others by senior members of the university, who generally kept an amateur profile by not seeking to publish their works, William Gager being a notable exception. No plays written for the commercial London stage were ever performed by Oxford students; no plays written by Oxford academics were ever performed by professional actors; and no professional companies ever performed within university precincts. By carefully maintaining the distinction between educational drama and the work of "common players," Oxford managed to preserve its humanist theatrical tradition down to the eve of the Civil War.

Oxford plays staged primarily for entertainment mainly served the purpose of keeping the students occupied during the long Christmas vacation, when they were required to remain in residence (Salter 149).[3] The fullest record of such entertainments is preserved in a manuscript anthology of playtexts with linking narratives, now generally referred to as *The Christmas Prince*, chronicling the performance of eight different plays over the Christmas vacation of 1607–8 at St. John's College (Boas, *Christmas*; for a manuscript facsimile, see Richards). As at the Christmas revels of the Inns of Court, on which they were modeled, the individual plays in this collection marked the stages of a larger festive occasion: the election, coronation, and reign of a mock prince or Lord of Misrule.

The eight plays began as early as November 30 and continued until Shrovetide in early February. The performance of a ninth play, whose text was lost before it could be copied, is mentioned, as well as three more plays partially written but prevented from performance "by the shortness of time and want of money" (Boas, *Christmas*, 287). A point was made of giving every member of the college a part in the festivities, since "it was thought fit that in so publick a business everyone should do something" (135). The plays, which were variously called comedies, tragedies, interludes, "devices," "shows," "mock plays," and "wassails," were performed in the hall and opened to the "public," meaning members of other colleges (152). The student audience was frequently unruly, and to control them, sword-bearing ushers called "whifflers" were appointed, who locked the rowdiest of them in the porter's lodge and carried out others who had fainted or been trampled in the crowded hall. Despite the presence of the whifflers, there were at least two stabbings of actors and spectators during the festivities, and many broken windows in the hall.

Such behavior seems today to be more in keeping with a football crowd than with a theater audience, yet at Oxford in the early seventeenth century it was taken for granted as part of a holiday ritual. Only one young man was brought before the college officials for discipline, the rest of the miscreants being dealt with by the "prince's" court itself, which devised various imaginative but largely symbolic punishments. The stage dramas were thus overshadowed by the metadramatic "misrule" of the college by the student prince, whose judgments were little more indulgent than those of the college authorities themselves. When the president of the college, on the day before the Lent term was to begin, found the hall "still pestered with the stage and scaffolds" and filled with snow because of the broken windows, he simply prorogued the term by a week so that more plays could be performed (Boas, *Christmas*, 152).

The tradition of Christmas revels at Oxford was considerably older than the tradition of humanist educational drama, reaching back into the pre-Reformation past. Such revels were first recorded in the Merton College register for 1486, and later records reveal that they remained a popular feature of college life until the Civil War (Salter, 94). The diary of Peter Heylyn, chaplain to Charles I, for example, tells us that the custom of electing a Christmas Prince was still flourishing at Magdalen in the 1620s and 1630s (Heylyn, x–xxiv), while the St. John's account books continue to show payments for plays during the Christmas vacation until 1641.

The most ambitious dramatic entertainments at Oxford, however, came on the occasion of official royal visits, of which there were four between 1566 and 1636. At such times the university as a corporate body acted as the producer of the plays, with the vice-chancellor and his deputies overseeing their texts, venues, financing, and mode of production, in close consultation with court officials. With one exception, these plays were all put on in Christ Church hall, both because Christ Church as a royal foundation traditionally acted as host to the sovereign and because its hall was the largest in Oxford (larger, too, than any in Cambridge).[4] Actors in these plays were usually drawn from all the colleges combined, although occasionally individual colleges might assume responsibility for the casting of an entire play, as with Magdalen's version of Sophocles' *Ajax* for James I in 1605, or the St. John's production of George Wilde's *Love's Hospital* for Charles I in 1636. The latter was the only occasion when the royal party ventured out of Christ Church to see a play; it was staged at St. John's to celebrate the opening of Archbishop Laud's new Canterbury Quadrangle, a gift of the former president to his old college.[5] Oxford records give us abundant information not only about the stages built for these plays but about the style and quality of the acting as well.

Our principal information about the plays staged for Queen Elizabeth in August 1566 comes from two eyewitness accounts. One is by a spectator, John Bereblock, a Christ Church don, who wrote in Latin; the other is from an actor in one of the plays, Miles Windsor, an undergraduate at Corpus Christi College, who wrote in English. Bereblock says little about the content of the plays, none of whose texts survive, but gives a vivid description of how Christ Church hall was fitted out for the occasion. The walls and ceiling were lined with gold paneling to simulate the opulence of an ancient Roman palace (*"veteris Romani Palatii"*).[6] Scaffolds for the audience were placed at one end of the hall and along each of the side walls. Boxes or booths for the more important spectators were built at the top of the scaffolds, while the less privileged (*"populus"*) stood on the floor around the stage, which, as at Cambridge, was probably placed at the western, or high-table, end of the hall. At the back of the stage a throne, or "state," was placed for Elizabeth, who sat facing the audience. The scenery consisted of classical stage houses, resembling "splendid palaces," which also served as the actors' dressing rooms. Bereblock seems to have considered the playtexts themselves the least important part of the occasion, since he fails to mention either their titles or their authors.

Miles Windsor's account of the occasion, on the other hand, as one might expect from a member of the cast, concentrates on the texts and the actors (Corpus Christi Archives, MS 257, 104–23; see also Elliott, "Queen"). He lists the three plays and their authors as follows:

1. *Marcus Geminus*, a Roman history play in Latin by Toby Mathew of Christ Church
2. *Palamon and Arcyte*, a two-part play in English, based on Chaucer's "The Knight's Tale," by Richard Edwards, formerly of Corpus Christi College and now Master of the Children of the Chapel
3. *Progne*, a tragedy in Latin by James Calfhill of Christ Church.

Although Windsor, who played the part of Perithous in Edwards's play, appears not to have seen the other two performances, he nevertheless gives a list of actors who took part in all three plays. The characters they played are not given, but the list includes the name of Toby Mathew, the future archbishop of York, who presumably acted in his own play, *Marcus Geminus*, possibly in the title role.[7] It also includes the name of a nonstudent, a boy actor named Peter Carew, the fourteen-year-old son of George Carew, a former dean of Christ Church. Peter was evidently something of a child prodigy, since in addition to playing one of the leading female roles in the plays, he also regaled the queen with an oration in Latin and Greek earlier in her visit (Wood, 2:158).

Windsor's most detailed information is naturally about the play in which he himself performed, Edwards's *Palamon and Arcyte*, a play based on the same story later dramatized by Shakespeare in *The Two Noble Kinsmen*. The main interest of his account lies in the fact that while he was onstage he was close enough to the throne to hear the queen's reactions to the student players. Elizabeth behaved much as the courtiers do during the performance of "Pyramus and Thisbe" in *A Midsummer Night's Dream*, interrupting the actors and speaking back to them as well as to the audience. Occasionally she was even cruel, the chief victim of her wit being an unfortunate young man named John Dalaper, who played a character called Trevatio. This character does not appear in Chaucer's tale, but he was probably the Vice, since the name would appear to come from the Italian *traviare*, "to lead astray or corrupt." Dalaper became so nervous in the presence of the queen that he went dry and, after exclaiming, "by the Mass and God's blood I am out!," decided in desperation to whistle a hornpipe instead. At this the queen exploded, "Go thy way" and, turning to her secretary, Lord Burghley, said, "God's pity what a knave it is." Taking his cue from the queen, Burghley banished the unhappy Dalaper from the stage with the words, "Go thy ways! Thou art clear out! Thou mayst be allowed to play the knave in any ground in England!" (Corpus Christi Archives, MS 257, 118).[8] (We may wonder whether Shakespeare was not giving his Theseus and Hippolyta, in 1593, when Elizabeth was again in the audience, a chance to get even with the queen for her behavior at an earlier play about them!)

While this misfortune undoubtedly put an end to the stage career of poor Dalaper, other student actors in *Palamon and Arcyte* fared better at the queen's hands. At the end of the second night of the play the queen spoke appreciative words to the two men who played the title roles and gave rewards of eight angels each to the two female impersonators: John Rainolds, the future president of Corpus Christi College and translator of the King James Bible, then seventeen, who played Hippolyta; and the talented Peter Carew, who played Lady Emilia and gained the queen's praise for "gathering her flowers prettily in the garden and singing sweetly in the prime of May."[9]

The queen also intervened in another incident during the play, which involved one of the costumes she had lent the students from the royal wardrobe. These were mainly old cloaks and gowns that had belonged to King Edward VI and Queen Mary, a fact that was apparently well known to the audience. At the moment in the play when Theseus, Emilia, and Perithous all threw mementos onto Arcyte's funeral pyre, one of the spectators standing near the stage grew alarmed and, grabbing Miles Windsor's arm, exclaimed, "God's wounds, will ye burn the King Edward cloak in the fire?" At this, Edwards the author (who must have been nearby with the playbook), Windsor, and the queen (who must have been given a plot synopsis beforehand, like the King of Spain at the performance of "Soliman and Perseda" in *The Spanish Tragedy*) all berated the interrupter, the queen shouting, "What aileth ye? Let the gentleman alone, he playeth his part!"

Whether this spectator was unusually credulous or just a Cambridge provocateur is not known. It is difficult to believe that the royal cloak, out of fashion or not, would actually have been burned in the performance, but we do know that at least one expensive garment was never returned to the Office of the Wardrobe (Arnold, 33), and that similarly realistic effects were aimed at in other parts of the play. Theseus's hunting scene, for example, took place outside in the Christ Church quadrangle with live hounds, the sounds of the horns and dogs reaching the queen through the windows and prompting her to observe that "those boys [student spectators?] are ready to leap out at window to follow the hounds" (Corpus Christi Archives, MS 257).

The queen's next official visit to Oxford in 1592 is not as well documented, since the only surviving eyewitness account of the entertainments is that of a Cambridge "spy," Philip Stringer, who made notes at the time but did not write them up until shortly before his death in 1603. By that time he had forgotten, or found indecipherable, everything except the titles of the two plays acted before the queen, and his judgment that they were "but meanly performed" (Stringer, 6v).[10] Anthony Wood, researching the event many years later for the first published history of the university, could discover even less: "but what they were or how applauded, I know not" (2:248–49).

From other evidence, however, we know that one of the plays was Leonard Hutten's Latin comedy, *Bellum Grammaticale*, originally performed in Christ Church as long before as 1581 (McConica, 719), now fitted out with two new prologues and an epilogue by William Gager. The other was Gager's own play, *Rivales*, another Latin comedy, now lost but first performed at Christ Church in 1583 and revived at Shrovetide 1592, a few months before the queen's visit.[11] The trotting out of two old plays for the occasion suggests that the arrangements for the visit must have been made at short notice, and the fact that Christ Church expended only a meager thirty-one pounds "for the stage and towards the plays" suggests that they were indeed more "meanly" set forth than in 1566.[12] Beyond the fact that the costumes were borrowed from the Revels Office, we know nothing else about the staging of the plays or about the queen's reaction to them.

Much more is known about the visit of the newly crowned King James to Oxford thirteen years later. In August 1605 four plays were presented in Christ Church hall for the royal party, three in Latin aimed at the erudite king and one in English for Queen Anne and the young Prince Henry. Another play was given in Magdalen College hall for Prince Henry alone, while a sixth entertainment, a short "device" called *Tres Sibyllae* (The Three Sibyls), in which the prophecies of the witches to Macbeth were spoken to the king by three little boys outside the gates of St. John's, may have planted the seed of the most famous English play of the following year.

The Christ Church plays of 1605 were a combined showcase for Oxford's classical learning and Inigo Jones's revolutionary neoclassical stage designs, which now supplanted the traditional college-hall staging examined above in Cambridge. As John Orrell has shown, the three Latin plays chosen for the king were intended to demonstrate the three "kinds" of classical drama as labeled by the Roman architect Vitruvius, whose work Jones was busy introducing into England (30).[13] *Alba*, one of whose authors was Robert Burton (Nochimson, 325–31), was a satyr play featuring shepherdesses, hermits, various gods and goddesses, and a magician. Though its text is now lost, a costume list survives indicating its classical pastoral characters, and a member of the audience noted that it made use of a live flock of wild doves (Boas, "James," 251–59; Wake, 48). The tragedy was Sophocles' *Ajax Flagellifer*, an obvious choice for Jones, since his Italian edition of Vitruvius gave specific instructions for the staging of this play in a Roman-style amphitheater (Orrell, *Theatres*, 33). The comedy was supplied by Matthew Gwinne of St. John's in the form of an allegory of the four seasons called *Vertumnus* (The Year About).

The choice of these works was designed to show off the new perspective scenery that Jones, who had designed his first Whitehall masque only a few months before, was using for plays for the first time in England. The stage, we are told, held five "stately pillars which would turn about"—that is, copies of ancient Greek *periaktoi*—in order to change the scene, erected against a permanent backdrop.[14] In *Ajax* a different scene was painted on each face of the "pillars," which were rotated by winches located under the stage. The machinery remained in place throughout the four days of performance, furnishing new scenes for *Alba, Vertumnus*, and the last play, Samuel Daniel's *Arcadia Reformed* (later renamed *The Queen's Arcadia*). Since the stage was steeply raked, the king could not sit on it. Unlike Elizabeth, James and his throne were placed on an "isle" in the center of the auditorium, with his courtiers seated on benches in front, as well as in boxes fastened to the side walls. From here the king and his officials had the best sight lines, though some courtiers complained that they could not now be seen by the rest of the audience as well as they could before, and the king complained that he could not hear. The needs of the new technology prevailed, however, and the king stayed where he was put.

Inigo Jones's scenic innovations were to transform English theater, but in 1605 they had a mixed effect on their first audiences. A Cambridge observer, perhaps predictably, claimed that neither *Alba* nor *Ajax* came up to the standard of comparable plays at his university, and that the king found both of them "tedious."[15] He found *Vertumnus* better "penned and acted" than the others but says that during this play the king "fell asleep, and when he awaked, he would have been gone, saying, 'I marvel what they think me to be.'" Even Jones's "rare devices" he dismissed as having accomplished "very little to that which was expected." Oxford officials, of course, gave a more favorable verdict, one of them claiming that the king pronounced himself as "much delighted" with *Vertumnus* "as with any sight of the like nature at any time heretofore presented unto him" (Nixon, E1v). We may doubt that this is really what the king thought, however, since for the rest of his reign he preferred the more traditional offerings of Cambridge, partly because of that university's proximity to the races at Newmarket.

Thirty-one years were to elapse before the next royal visit to Oxford, by Charles I in 1636, the last such occasion before the king settled permanently into Christ Church for the duration of the Civil War. By that time Inigo Jones had become Surveyor of the King's Works, and the splendor of his court entertainments had grown far beyond his earlier experiments for King James. In Christ Church in August 1636 he abandoned his antique *periaktoi* and instead used the new Italian style of creating visual perspective by means of wing-flats, hinged shutters, sculpted reliefs, and painted backdrops (Orrell, *Theatres*, 37). The plays too were in the now fashionable genre of tragicomedy or romance, rather than decorous adaptations of the classics. The two plays performed in Christ Church were William Strode's *The Floating Island* and William Cartwright's *The Royal Slave*, both of which used exotic plots as political allegories to extol the benefits of monarchy. Both, too, were in English, as was the third play, performed at St. John's, George Wilde's romantic comedy, *Love's Hospital*. The abandonment of any pretense of "academic" drama was noticeable and was epigrammatically justified by Cartwright in a couplet in the epilogue to *The Royal Slave*:

> There's difference 'twixt a College and a Court:
> The one expecteth Science, the other Sport. (Cartwright, 252)

Not surprisingly, eyewitness accounts of this occasion say nothing about texts or "pen men" but concentrate upon Jones's scenic wonders. Brian Twyne of Corpus Christi College, Oxford's first archivist, left a long description of the two productions that took place on the "goodly stage made at Christ Church," extolling the splendors of what to him was "the new fashion." Perhaps only an Oxford archivist could have compared Jones's wing-flats to "partitions much resembling the desks in a library," but the rest of his description indicates that his imagination quickly left behind any academic preoccupations to marvel at "the great variety and admiration" of the scenes.[16]

Although the texts of the royal plays of 1636 were written by Oxford men, the performances themselves were, in every other respect, the product of the king's usual purveyors of court entertainment. The scenery and costumes were provided by the Office of the Works and the Office of the Revels; the music was written by William and Henry Lawes, for performance by the King's Musick and the Children of the Chapel; the actors were coached by Joseph Taylor, the leader of the King's Men at the Globe; and even a set of candelabra was dismantled in Whitehall Palace and reassembled to light the Christ Church stage (Elliott and Buttrey). Cartwright's *Royal Slave* so closely resembled the court plays favored by the queen that she commanded it to be transferred to Hampton Court and performed by her own company. What she saw both there and at Oxford was not a representative of Oxford culture but an imitation of the prevailing Stuart court taste. Oxford, with its unerring eye for lost causes, had ceased to instruct and now bent to flatter the monarch.

NOTES

1. The subject of Oxford plays and players is also treated at greater length in Elliott, "College." It is a pleasure to acknowledge the support of my research by the Fulbright Commission for the International Exchange of Scholars, Washington, D.C.

2. Since the first of these "degree plays" was written in 1512 and the second in 1640, we may assume there were others in between. For a list of the surviving manuscript texts that look as though they may have been written for this purpose, see Elliott, "Degree."

3. For similar requirements at the Inns of Court, see Prest, 15–16.

4. Originally founded by Cardinal Wolsey in 1529 as Cardinal College, Christ Church was refounded by Henry VIII after Wolsey's fall and called King Henry VIII College during the rest of his reign. In 1548 it was again refounded as Christ Church by Edward VI, in the dual role of college and see of the diocese of Oxford.

5. The production was also paid for entirely by Laud. The expense sheets survive in the Public Record Office, SP 16/348, no. 85.

6. Bodleian Library MS. Add. A. 63, fols. 1–22. This manuscript was copied no later than 1571 and seems the most authoritative of the three surviving scribal copies of Bereblock's narrative of the royal visit. The others are Bodleian MS. Rawlinson D. 1071, fols. 1–25; and Folger Shakespeare Library MS. V.a.109, fols. 1–24.

7. If so, he set a precedent repeated in 1619 when Thomas Goffe both wrote and starred in *The Courageous Turk* in Christ Church (Carnegie, "Identification").

8. The sense of the remark is: "You could get the role of a knave in any playing-place in the country," i.e., "you would be a knave wherever you were." See *OED*, ground 10.a, 14.a.

9. In his narrative, Windsor says that the actor who played Palamon was named Lynhame, but this name does not appear in his list of actors, nor does it occur in any other list of Oxford or Christ Church students. The actor who played Arcyte was Brian Baynes, an undergraduate at Christ Church. More than thirty years later John Rainolds acknowledged in print his youthful cross-dressing role but failed to mention his reward by the queen (Rainolds, 45).

10. Stringer was a fellow of St. John's College, Cambridge. The purpose of his mission to Oxford was to help his own university prepare for its next visit from the queen. It is not known how many such "spies" were sent to Oxford in 1592 besides Stringer and his companion, Henry Mowtloe, fellow of King's College, to whom he gave his manuscript account. In 1605, however, there were forty of them, whose job was "to view in secret and note the whole event," then to record their observations in shorthand in a "table-book" (i.e., a tablet or notebook) (Fennor, E1v).

11. *Bellum Grammaticale* was not published until 1635. The prologues and epilogue added to it by Gager for the queen's visit, however, were printed in Gager's *Meleager* (1593). See also Boas, *University*, 181–83.

12. The Christ Church Disbursement Book for 1592–1593 indicates that the committee to "oversee and provide for the plays" was not appointed until August 17, with the queen due to arrive on September 22 (Christ Church Archives, xxii.b.35 97).

13. That the choice of the three "kinds" of plays was made by the Court, at Jones's instigation, and not solely by Oxford playwrights is shown by a document in the University Archives, containing an order by the delegates responsible for the entertainments for "three plays to be made in Latin, viz., two comedies and a tragedy." The colleges were left the "choice of actors and pen men to help to pen them" (Oxford Archives, W.P. gamma/ 19/ 1 2v).

14. Wake, 46; translated in Orrell, *Theatres*, 31. Orrell has reproduced the original plan for the auditorium constructed in Christ Church hall by the office of the King's Works for this occasion in "Theatre" and *Human*, plate 28, 121.

15. Cambridge University Library, MS. 34, fols. 28–45v. The account is anonymous, but the author may have been Henry Mowtloe, who once possessed the manuscript (see n. 10).

16. Bodleian Library MS. Twyne 17 201. The complete description, as copied by Wood, 2:408–9, is reproduced in Bentley, *Jacobean*, 5:1191.

# CHAPTER 5

# Streets and Markets

*Anne Higgins*

IN 1486, WHEN Henry VII entered York, he was met at the bridge outside the city first by the two sheriffs, then by the mayor and aldermen in their long gowns of scarlet. Closer in, the ecclesiastical authorities of the city greeted him, and last, "the generall procession of al the parisshe Chirches of the saide Citie with merveolous great nombr of men women And Childern on foote whiche in ReIoysing of his commyng criden king henry king henry" (Johnston and Rogerson, 1:147).

At the gate of the city the king was met by a tableau vivant, from which stepped the figure of a crowned king, the legendary founder of York, Ebrauk. Calling himself "a primatyve of yovre progenye," Ebrauk saluted King Henry and gave him the key of the city. This royal entry, like others, crossed the River Ouse and turned left onto Coney Street. The 1486 procession stopped at several places, among them the Common Hall, where the show carried on with a speech by a figure of King David, who gave Henry a sword. The procession then turned right along Stonegate, and finally into York minster, where the king dined and lodged (fig. 5.1).

In another neighborhood of York in 1486 there had long been a stone statue of a man, affixed to a house. This much venerated image was popularly believed to be that of York's eponymous founder, Ebrauk. In 1501 the statue was removed from the corner of Colliergate and St. Saviourgate, on the boundary of one of the religious liberties, to the Common Hall, center of York's civic government. But no gesture in a town was simple or innocent. While slavishly greeting its monarch, the city also asserted its own authority. By giving him its key, the city, not the king, permitted entry. The translation of Ebrauk's statue to the Common Hall, like the pause of the royal entry there before it moved on to the minster, is emblematic of the endless jockeying of civic and ecclesiastical groups for dominance in town life, and of the ascendancy and confidence in 1501 of the civic authorities.

In York, as in other English cities, much of the competition for influence was
played out in ceremonies in the city's streets and markets. Royal entries were but
one kind of the traditional processions that year after year served to mark the
claims of different official groups to territory, prestige, and power in late medieval
English towns. Ancient processions did more than beat the bounds of influence.
They depicted visually the unity and hierarchy of those who lived in the town.
What Phythian-Adams wrote about Coventry is true in general: there was "a conspicuous correspondence between social structure and its ceremonialization in
time and space" ("Ceremony," in Holt and Rosser, 262). Furthermore, processions extended that correspondence by investing the city's streets, buildings, and
markets themselves with meanings. What processions created was a dramatic
and sophisticated demotic of space and movement, one that expressed the
common identity of citizens within the bounds, as well as the hierarchies that
ordered them.

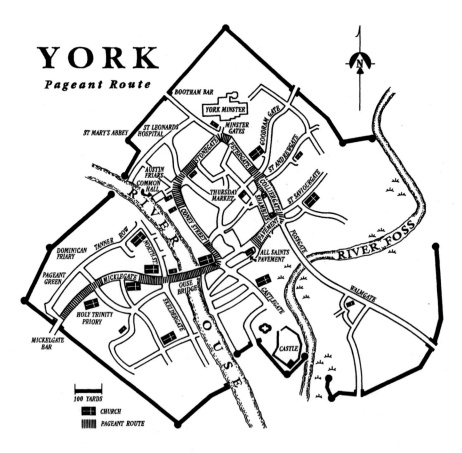

FIGURE 5.1. York pageant route.

The greatest of all such processional displays of influence and efforts at self-definition were the Corpus Christi plays. Each town's play had a unique style and emphasis, though they are generically closely related in structure and in many aspects of staging. After years of research and debate, a general view of the great English civic plays has emerged. Meg Twycross, one of the chief investigators of this drama, offers this view of their common features:

> All the surviving pageant wagon-cycles have a basic structure in common. The great story that composed the Corpus Christi play (the whole cycle was called a *play*, while the individual portions were *pageants* . . . ), a history of the universe from just before its Creation to its ending at the Day of Judgement, was parcelled up into episodes. Each episode was delegated to a separate group, a trade or religious guild, which was totally responsible for its production. Each group had or shared a mobile stage also called a *pageant*, which when their turn came they pulled through the city along a traditional route, stopping at prearranged *stations* (the word means "stopping places") to perform their episode. ("THEATRICALITY," 39)

In their processional movements through the streets of their towns, Corpus Christi plays used and extended the ancient system of beating the bounds, a ritual practice employed variously, in the mayor's perambulation of the common lands, in the Rogationtide processions that marked the limits of parishes, and even in some sense in royal entries and in the Corpus Christi procession, which was maintained even in towns that did not develop cycles of plays and to which elsewhere Corpus Christi plays were long attached.

To understand the sense of early dramatic performances in the streets and markets of older English towns, it is essential first to understand in general how a topography of status, wealth, occupation, and self-consciousness was mapped onto urban space. My examination of this question will depend on the evidence of one town, York, for a number of reasons. First, York has preserved detailed civic, guild, and private records likely to illuminate such a study; second, York is one of only four towns in which an entire Corpus Christi play is extant; third, York as it was in the fifteenth century is well preserved (Swanson, "Artisans," 1; Twycross, "'Places,'" 38). Furthermore, as Martin Stevens has argued, York more than any other city dramatized itself in its play (17–87).[1]

But what is true of York's use of its own streets and markets in dramatic representations is true in general for other English cities: the Corpus Christi procession and play told the story of many bodies, from the body of Christ in life and in the Eucharist to the extended body of Christ in the corporate body of all believers (James). When townspeople saw their own work and bodies dramatized in the history that the tableaux and plays represented (Higgins, "Work"), they often also saw their towns so used. The conclusion we may draw from York's well-documented experience with drama in the streets may be useful broadly as another way to think about other towns' Corpus Christi plays, because of similar official concerns with boundaries of all kinds and because of "their shared grand design" (M. Stevens, 327).

## Franchise, Freedom, Liberty

Towns were not single political entities, even within their own walls. In the contest for influence and control, different official bodies had authority over different areas. Movement and work within the town, like stopping places in a procession, were significant, and closely regulated. Such spatial signification can be read, however, only within a social and political organization that may seem alien, one in which terms like *franchise, freedom,* and *liberty* meant very different things from their modern senses.

To be a freeman meant that a merchant or artisan could practice his craft and sell his goods, that he had obligations and rights in the precinct, or liberty, to which he belonged, and that he was free from the payment of tolls within his liberty. A man could become free "by patrimony, as the son of a freeman; by apprenticeship; by redemption, that is by purchasing the freedom" (Swanson, *Medieval*, 108). (Women were seldom admitted to the franchise except as widows or daughters of freemen [Dobson, 13–14; Phythian-Adams, "Ceremony," in Holt and Rosser, 240; Swanson, *Medieval*, 107].) Initially in York the franchise was granted primarily to merchants, but in the fourteenth century it was extended not only to artisans, who were skilled workers in a craft, but also further downward socially to independent masters in service trades, such as barbers and cooks (Dobson; Swanson, *Medieval*, 109).

It seems likely that the post-plague broadening of the franchise was mostly achieved by a rise in the proportion of men made free by redemption, a revenue-raising strategy for the town government. But it is important to realize that admission to the freedom (except by patrimony) was always controlled by the merchant class and "extended the obligations more than the opportunities of artisans" (Swanson, *Medieval*, 109). It is not at all evident that the privileges conferred by freedom outweighed its duties. What is clear is that no resident who was not free could "use byying or sellynge in ony craft or occupacon as Maister" (York freemen's oath, MS Register, fo. Ir; quoted in Dobson, 15). And it is equally clear that most residents of a liberty were not free.

The rights of freemen obtained only in their own franchise, that is, only in the area that received them to its freedom. A city like York "was honeycombed with other franchises, some of them older than the franchise of the city" (Tillot, 38). From as early as the eleventh century the liberty of St. Peter (the minster), and later those of St. Mary's Abbey and St. Leonard's Hospital, built up their rights and authority in their precincts of the city. St. Peter's liberty at various times maintained the right of the dean to hold a court at minster gate for all transgressions in the lands of his church both within and without the city; and of the archbishop to take all "customs" (including husgable [a hearth tax]) from his property in the city, all the tolls within his liberty, and a third of the tolls, husgable, and profits of the pleas in the Walmgate and Fishergate areas of the city (Tillot, 38). The archbishop furthermore had a mint, one-third of the tolls from the Foss bridge, and a "yearly fair, during which his bailiffs took over, from those of the city, the keeping of the peace, the collection of tolls, and doing justice upon thieves" (Tillot, 38). St. Mary's Abbey and St. Leonard's Hospital secured rights in their liberties similar to those of the minster.

York was divided, then, into a complicated map of areas of intertwined privileges, obligations, and influence, shoulder to shoulder in the narrow streets. The ecclesiastical liberties were exempt not only from the city's authority but also, in certain matters, from the king's. The rules were confining and confusing, as Tillot explains:

> The tenants of these exempt churches were excluded from the jurisdiction of the city courts; nor did they attend the sessions of the king's justices for the pleas of the city: special sessions were held at the doors of the minster, St. Leonard's, and St. Mary's to deal with matters arising within their respective liberties. Finally, the administrative powers exercised by the city officials were exercised by the officers of the privileged churches in places where they had property and tenants in the city and also, in the case of the minster and St. Mary's, in complete districts of the city. (38–39)

Such complex jurisdiction gave birth to endless disputes. At different times during the thirteenth century both king and pope intervened, the king censuring the churches for their claim to be exempt from such common burdens as murage (a tax to maintain the city walls), the pope placing the city under interdict for such offenses as efforts to make St. Mary's men pay toll in York; the arrest, trial, and hanging of a tenant of the chapter; and riots in which some of the abbey's men were killed. A settlement imposed by the king in 1275 reconfirmed the ecclesiastical liberties and their rights but failed to "draw lines of demarcation between the competing jurisdictions" clearly, creating what Tillot called "the context of future discords" (40). When in 1493 the weavers and cordwainers of York asked the abbot of Saint Mary's to mediate their dispute with the city, the mayor defied the abbot and the king himself, anxiously acknowledging their claims but defending the city's rights in a firm reply:

> whervnto My lord the Maier answerd and said how that the kynges noble progenitours of theyr especiall gracez of auncien tyme hath grant vnder theyr lettrez patentes vnto the Maier Shireffes aldermen & other of the comon Counseill of this Citie fful power to make ordinancez & other establischmentes for the publike well of this Citie & cociticinz of the same and ferthermore to here & determyn that al maner causez quarels contraversiez debatez & demaundez emargyng & surdaunt emong the any personz beyng cociticinz within this said Citie or elles before the Iusticez of assisez & by suche mene other al whiche grauntez libertiez & priviligiez oure soueraigne lord the kyng that nowe is of his most tendre grace hath confirmed & Ratified ffor whiche consideracion my said lord Maiour his brether Shireffes and al other of the comon counseill of this Citie wold not in any wise consent That the said abbot & Richard Chomley or any other foreyn shuld by coloure or virtue of any wryttyng from the kynges grace or from any other entermett theym of any cause Matier or accion Surdaunt or meved betwix any of the Citicinz of this Citie whiche in any wise shuld

Sound into the breche of the fraunchesiez and libertiez of the same. (Johnston and
Rogerson, 1:170)

This was the frantic legalistic response of a mayor who had to prevent a terrible
precedent: the intervention of royal and ecclesiastical authority, however cautious,
in a matter that was strictly the city's affair. The term *foreyn* is especially noteworthy
(in "the said abbot & Richard Chomley or any other foreyn"). A *foreyn* might be
someone from another town or country, or a non–guild member from the same
franchise of the town, or, as we see here, someone from another liberty, regardless
of his rank or wealth. One could be only *fre* or *foreyn*; *foreyn* workers who were not
masters might well live in the same district as their *fre* employers. Foreignness
might be one's civic status, then, as unfree in the district of one's birth; all strangers
and freemen from other liberties were evidently foreign.

R. B. Dobson has argued that the hostility of York civic authorities to the immunities enjoyed by the other liberties might have prevented strong artisanal development in them (13). Still, residents of the ecclesiastical liberties escaped civic regulation in their practice of crafts and their trading. York's council was irritated by master
cappers who put out piecework to men and women living in the liberties, "wher we
have no power to correk tham," and it forbade the practice in 1482 (*York Memoran-
dum Book* ii, 285, quoted in Dobson, 13; Swanson, *Medieval*, 51). The advantage of
employing unfree workers in one's own liberty was that their work could be regulated.
A 1483 ordinance forbade giving work to anyone within other franchises, where the
city's searchers had no jurisdiction, because they could not examine goods outside
the liberty to ensure quality and control prices (Swanson, *Medieval*, 59). Stevens is
surely right to insist that resentment against the religious houses and the residents of
their liberties "was, in general, not based on anticlericalism, but on the unfair economic competition that the system of liberties fostered" (82). What Parliament and
the king could not or would not do, the contestants tried to do for themselves, and
the proliferation and tenacity of ceremonies to beat the bounds of jurisdiction within
York mark how crucial their concrete and visible efforts to assert authority were.

### Beating the Bounds

A number of prominent ceremonies marked boundaries in fifteenth-century York,
and their unchanging routes were defended by claims of antiquity. Henry VII's royal
entry in 1486 shows how the king moved from his own jurisdiction into that of the
city, and finally to that of the minster, at each stage making some gesture acknowledging the authority of the franchise he entered. The whole population of the city
was represented in a carefully ordered sequence of greeters. Order always matters in
visual demonstrations like this one; the privilege of the mayor and aldermen to be
first to welcome the king is balanced by the archbishop's honor of hosting him.
Some city spaces, inevitably, had to be used by all the franchises of a city. Micklegate,
a great street that then had York's only bridge across the Ouse, seems to have been a
less strictly defined space in various processional routes, a place of mutual royal,

civic, and ecclesiastical influence, or at least of mutual tolerance in the name of practicality. Progress along Coney Street to the Common Hall was movement permitted through, and by, the city's mercantile and artisanal liberty, while Stonegate, the boundary between liberties, seems to have been territory equally claimed by the city and the minster as they regarded each other across that street. All jealously guarded their jurisdictions and were alert to slights against their authority.

In ancient ceremonies medieval cities explicitly marked the bounds of the liberties and of their common lands. Parishes marked their boundaries annually at Rogationtide, the three days before Ascension. With crosses, banners, and bells, all parishioners joined together to beat the bounds of their parish and religious community. This ritual was about more than demarcation, however. It was also a ceremony of purification, in which demons were exorcised from the parish and its animals and fields cleansed and blessed. The Rogationtide procession was a powerful assertion of parish identity and unity. "Processions from neighbouring parishes which happened to converge might come to blows, in part because they believed that the rival procession was driving its demons over the boundary into their parish" (Duffy, 136).

The mayor's perambulation of the city's common lands was a regular event, notionally an annual one, that took place in October or early November. The riding of the boundaries of the city's common lands was a two-day affair, and floods or expense often obliged its cancellation. Since freemen had the right to use common lands to keep cattle for milk and meat, it is clear that both council and residents were eager to ensure that the city's rights of pasturage outside the boundaries of the city's liberty should be asserted and maintained. When the mayor's perambulation could not be ridden, ward officers were alerted to prevent encroachments (Tillot, 315–17). Soon after this beating of the bounds came another, this time inside the city's bounds, called the sheriffs' riding, in which they "rode through the main streets, making an ancient proclamation about law and order" (Palliser, 85). There was even a summer custom called Fishing Day, in which the city caused the Ouse to be ceremonially fished from civic barges, thereby asserting its rights in the river (Palliser, 84).

As all these ceremonies demonstrate, an ancient, invincible literalism and explicit public action governed the syntax of the late medieval demotic of space; the concrete town itself—streets, buildings, churches, markets—provided the content. The bounds had to be beaten in plain sight of everyone, before the eyes of this community and of the communities of its brothers and rivals. Whatever townspeople intended to have and use forever they had to walk around with their own feet, fish with their own hands, and purify with their bells and prayers.

## York's Corpus Christi Procession and Play

The demotic of physical space informs in deep ways the meanings of York's other rituals of movement and demarcation in the streets and markets. The procession with the host in honor of the feast of Corpus Christi followed a route that was considered traditional in 1399, the year of the first surviving reference to it (Johnston and Rogerson, 1:12). In his investigation of Corpus Christi processions in Germany, Charles Zika argues that it was not the body of Christ but the processional form itself that acted as an instrument for working out social identity and political structure (44). This would seem to be true as well of English Corpus Christi processions and pageant routes. The processional form celebrating this feast of bodies expressed the organic unity and interdependence of the town's body religious, while its linearity stretched out and differentiated constituent parts, like clothes on a line. But no procession was really a mirror of the city (M. Rubin, 266). It was an idealized representation of unity and hierarchy, a "spectacular advertisement of specific status" (Phythian-Adams, "Ceremony," in Holt and Rosser, 244). Its representation of space was equally idealized. As in England, German procession routes "symbolically linked parish and collegiate churches to the mother church, the cathedral to the marketplace or town square, the quarters of the city to each other and to both bishop and town council" (Zika, 39). With the host, greatest of relics, as focus, the Corpus Christi procession and its tableaux vivants mapped out not just the city's space but its ideal social and political hierarchies, and they did so (as in Germany) "at a point in historical time when territorial consolidation, the integration of jurisdictions within geographical space, was becoming the expression and path of political power" (Zika, 44).[2]

It matters that York's procession with the host for Corpus Christi shared its first movements with, and then diverged significantly from, the route followed by the city's Corpus Christi play. With only three surviving records regarding the processional route and seventeen for the play route, it is clear as well that the routes were both distinct and unvarying for generations, starting, it would seem, well before 1399 and not ending until the late sixteenth century (J. F. Hoy, 167). How are we to interpret the shared beginning and the very different conclusions of these processions?

The procession began at the gates of Holy Trinity Priory, traveled along Micklegate, crossed the Ouse, moved to York minster, and concluded at St. Leonard's Hospital. Surviving records do not specify the route from the junction of Coney Street and Castlegate, nor from the minster to St. Leonard's. But since the procession's beginning echoes the movement of that other notable procession with tableaux vivants, the royal entry, one might well surmise that the Corpus Christi procession turned left on Coney Street and then right on Stonegate, direct to the minster gates. That is, since the royal entry took this route to the minster, clockwise (as it were) through the city streets, it is likely that the demotic of movement required the procession with the host to do the same, in order clearly to assert its own demarcation of community, authority, and welcome. (Crouch calls this route, as far as the minster gates, the "traditional route for all civic processions" [66].)

The pageant wagons associated with the Corpus Christi play followed this clockwise route as well, proceeding after the minster right on Petergate and Colliergate, and right again to wind up on the Pavement. Had the procession gone counter-clockwise through the city (straight through the Pavement, then left along Colliergate and Petergate), then in the era when York performed its Corpus Christi procession and pageants together on the feast itself, the procession would have had to move against the flow of the guilds' pageant wagons (that is, probably, in the years before 1426 [Hoy, 167 n. 6; see below and n. 3]). It seems that royal entries, Corpus Christi processions, and Corpus Christi plays in York all started off the same way, moving clockwise around the city center.

The streets of the traditional routes form a sort of diamond shape, set on a north-south axis. Processions came into York from the west, on an eastward route along Micklegate, and crossed the River Ouse. They turned left onto Coney Street (the diamond's southern tip), then right on Stonegate (the western tip of the diamond) until they reached the minster (the northern tip). Royal entries terminated at the minster; the king stopped there to dine and lodge. Other ceremonies took different routes away from the minster. The ecclesiastical procession turned from the minster to streets to the north and west, outside the processional diamond, to go on to St. Leonard's Hospital. But the guild pageants of the Corpus Christi play paused before the minster and then continued clockwise around the central artisanal precinct (the center of the diamond) along Petergate/Colliergate (to the eastern point of the diamond), and from there to their final station, the Pavement. They nearly completed the full shape of the diamond in this route (ending just northeast of the southern tip). Nelson argued that the pageant wagons simply were not able to enter the minster and therefore could not have completed the route of the church's traditional Corpus Christi procession. That the guild pageant wagons did not go in, but instead carried on along a route that circled their own liberty, may have been construed as an insult. For this and other reasons, Nelson thought conflict between the ecclesiastical and civic franchises must have been inevitable (*Medieval*, 44).

The initial recapitulation by each ceremony of a route used in other ceremonies may seem a little surprising, but it does indeed seem to have been the best way to make clear to the entire polity how the different occasions and sponsors used their particular processions to redefine the city in their own terms. They entered York by the same route and moved through the same territory in order to redefine them and to assert their authority among rival official groups; each then moved into different territory as a way of beating the bounds of its particular influence and power. The religious procession ended up demarcating the religious liberties of York by visiting the three chief religious foundations. It claimed authority in the whole city by recapitulating the royal and civic routes up to the minster gates. On the other hand, the guild pageant route redefined the route of ancient royal and religious processions and then swung farther along in the clockwise arc to the Pavement, to mark out boldly all the territory that was part of the mercantile and artisanal franchise.

The meaning of these curiously overlapping and distinct routes may be clearer if we consider the single great change in medieval York's Corpus Christi celebrations, the 1426 separation of procession and play. In that year Brother William Melton, a minorite friar, objected to the traditional practice of mounting both procession and play on Corpus Christi Day. He regarded the play as "good in itself and most laudable" but said too many townspeople attended not only to the play but also to "feastings, drunkenness, clamours, gossipings, and other wantonness" and especially that they failed to observe the liturgical offices or to attend Mass at the end of the procession (Johnston and Rogerson, 1:42–44, 2:728–30). Melton persuaded the city that the procession and play should be performed on different days. It would be a mistake to see in this affair simple hostility to the civic drama. Melton's comments show that the friars supported the plays but resisted any interference with the religious rituals for the feast (Clopper, "Lay," 115). The commons agreed that the play should go first, on the eve of Corpus Christi (that is, the preceding Wednesday), and the religious procession always stay on the feast itself. It was an intelligent effort to avoid conflict. At the same time, the full and formal separation of play and procession served to make even more evident that each did, in fact, beat the bounds of its own power in the city of York. So the feast of corporate unity, like the processional form itself, served as well to differentiate the competing groups in York, all of which constituted their city in different ways.

After 1468, for reasons that are not clear in the surviving records, the procession was moved to the day after Corpus Christi, and the play, apparently, to Corpus Christi itself.[3] The two shifts, in 1426 and 1468, are revealing. The first change avoided competition for the attention of the citizens of York's franchises, and, it would seem, allowed the religious procession to recover a bit from the loss of audience and worshipers to the play, while retaining the honor of owning the feast day itself. Brother Melton's proposal tacitly admits as much. But the 1468 change, in which the guilds took over Corpus Christi Day for their dramatic performances, probably marks an ascendancy of the guilds over the ecclesiastical foundations. The contestation between these official bodies for precedence in this matter was a long struggle—one, I think we must conclude, that the guilds won.

Yet another issue concerned with the physical space of the plays needs attention here, and that is the matter of the stations, or playing places, for the play. Year by year individuals or syndicates leased the right to erect scaffolds at specific playing places, and they charged spectators who wished to sit there to see the play. The usual number of stations for lease each year was twelve, though the actual number paid for varied over the years from eight to sixteen (Johnston, "York," 362). Twycross, White, and Crouch have all studied the names of stationholders throughout the play's history in an effort to determine exactly where the episodes were played. Crouch documents a shift in the status of stationholders, with the mercers in decline and locally trading artisans rising in the fifteenth century (93–96). This fact would seem congenial with my argument that as the century wore on the play's organizers had new corporate confidence (or a different sort of confidence) and negotiated better playing arrangements, ending in their taking over the feast of Corpus Christi itself.

Some of the most intriguing facts that Twycross uncovered, and White and Crouch modified and generally confirmed, led to what they refer to as the "left-hand-side theory." Twycross's early study identified stationholders, all of whom lived on the left-hand side of the pageant route (" 'Places,' " 18–20). Eileen White showed that some in the sixteenth century clearly lived on the right-hand side of their streets. But she also demonstrated that those exceptions may all have been at road junctions, where pageant wagons could be positioned so that stationholders of corner sites could view the play from either side of the road (56–57).

What is at issue in this discussion is the practical necessity that a single wagon be able to play always to the same side of the street (or, as White argued, be carefully placed for a corner site). But in terms of the demotic of physical space in York, the "left-hand-side theory" makes good sense in a route that is essentially clockwise, circumscribing the guild territory. If the wagons faced left, their episodes were presented not *inward*, toward the heart of the artisanal city, but *outward*, toward the rival franchises. It would seem crucial in a play that defined a community that it be directed to the others, the foreigns, to instruct them who the freemen of York were and how their freedom constituted itself. The York play's perambulation of the artisanal city, its efforts to make the past meaningful as a way to understand who contemporary residents of that franchise were and what they believed, were themselves artisanal products exported to their neighbors and competitors. Important as it was to the working people of the corporation, the play was the production of those people on the inside of what they knew as the city looking outward, toward the foreigns. The movement of pageant wagons through the streets asserted the city liberty's ordered unity; out of that unity this freedom performed scenes to tell the others who it was.

If Martin Stevens is right that civic hostility to the religious liberties was not anticlericalism but an objection to unfair economic competition, then perhaps one could look at the guilds' efforts to make the Corpus Christi play the central celebration of the feast as a response in kind to the religious foundations. It might make sense to view York's detailed control and tenacious maintenance of the Corpus Christi play as an effort to show the religious franchises what unfair competition felt like. In this instance, the guilds arrogated for themselves the church's role of teaching about the meaning of the feast, by depicting in their own way the central moments in the sacred history. From early on, the play interfered with religious observance for Corpus Christi Day; eventually the civic play usurped the great feast day itself. If the ecclesiastical liberties practiced unfair economic competition, perhaps it might also be true that the guilds practiced unfair religious competition by so energetically pushing forward their pageants and by taking over as the chief celebrant on Corpus Christi Day. Historians such as Zika have insisted that religious rituals are in fact very much about social relations and political identities (26). It would hardly be surprising if civic rituals were also about religious convictions. As the evidence from the honeycombed liberties of York shows, religious behavior cannot be separated from other forms of social and cultural practice, including competition.

### Other Streets, Other Markets

"The most intriguing question is why civic governments put on cycles of religious plays in the streets" (Clopper, "Lay," 128). The experience of York leads us to consider to what degree the Corpus Christi drama arose as an act of piety that also served to preserve the city's role in teaching its own people and others and to assert the city's right to have its own ceremony for beating the bounds of its authority during the great feast of community. It is hard to imagine that York's play would have developed as it did without the invigorating strain, the felt necessity, of competition with the other liberties of the city. "The development of these plays during a period of economic stress occurred as a consequence of the city's coming to supremacy in the local power arena," wrote Lawrence Clopper, who went on to argue that as a consequence of its dominance the city assumed responsibility for its citizens' moral and religious welfare as well.

Competition itself seems to have been the driving force for outdoor civic drama. When there was no rivalry with other liberties for authority in the city, a great play was hardly needed. When competition faded, so did civic, or at least artisanal, desire to maintain the play. What is revealing is the way Corpus Christi drama developed (or failed to develop) in other English towns. Despite the hazards of generalization, it seems true that the church nowhere controlled or directly participated in the civic cycle plays. "Their composition and development," wrote Clopper, "often reflect the power structure of the corporation" ("Lay," 118). Like York, Coventry had a strong civic government early on, and early on it developed its cycle. Chester's civic government was not strong enough to dominate until the early sixteenth century, and by 1531 or 1532 it moved its cycle from Corpus Christi Day to Whitsun, after which the play quickly expanded. Chester's Whitsun play was announced by a riding of the banns, a procession through the main streets that stopped at two prisons to give alms; this riding was clearly a kind of beating of the city bounds. And Chester's play was performed in four principal streets of the city rather than at St. John's cathedral, outside the walls (Clopper, *Records*, 106). So space and boundaries mattered in Chester as well. Like Chester, Norwich developed its cycle only after the city government achieved substantial authority. Lincoln provides the negative example. In Lincoln, there was little competition between civic and ecclesiastical liberties, since the cathedral was dominant. The cathedral had a play of the Coronation of the Virgin, for instance, but held it separate from the city's Corpus Christi and Pater Noster plays, producing it only in years that the civic plays skipped.

Clopper articulated what seems to have been the rule: "Cycles of religious dramas appeared in northern England in those cities that established strong govern-

ments centered in the trade guilds." Conversely, where church foundations dominated, or religious guilds rather than trade guilds, cycle plays do not seem to have
developed (Clopper, "Lay," 112). One might suggest that the civic authorities had
little reason to defend their great plays after the reformed English church abolished
all processions in 1547 and the Corpus Christi feast itself in 1548 (Duffy, 451). Guild
dramas and their annual displays of social order, wealth, religious conviction, and
political authority slowly disappeared. There were no outdoor processionals left to
compete with to define the city.

### The Pavement

The York Corpus Christi cycle always ended its performance in the Pavement,
even in years when the station there had not been leased. Clearly this great market
square, "the earliest paved open space in the city" (Raine, 177), was considered for
some reason vital to the play. York had two markets, the Pavement and Thursday
Market. The three weekly markets in the Pavement were for the sale of grain and
other food; Thursday Market twice a week opened for the sale of cloth and merchandise. The markets were for foreigns; citizens were obliged to sell their goods in
their shops and leave these markets to outsiders. The clockwise circumscription of
York's city center by the pageants missed Thursday Market, but that is not surprising if the pageant route was indeed a kind of perambulation of guild turf: Thursday
Market is well within the guild area.

The Pavement, however, was an ancient broad space, the center of the city's commerce. From time out of mind it had been where traitors were executed, drunks pilloried, rogues whipped, kings and queens proclaimed, bulls baited. Despite the difficulty of moving the great play through the streets of York in daylight, it is clear this
market was well suited to play a crucial role in the last performance of the Last
Judgment episode. Where better to proclaim judgment and to exact punishment
after separating the saved from the damned? But there's more to the investing of this
medieval space with cosmological meaning. Audiences all along the route were
constantly brought into the play's action, as nosy neighbors, as crowds screaming for
Barabbas, as the saved and the damned. Similarly, guilds were cast appropriately for
their episodes, using their own tools and products in the action of the play (Higgins,
"Work"). So too the streets, houses, churches, and markets were employed in a specific, sophisticated, and concrete anachronism in order to bring home to the spectators the figural sense of the play's representation of history. Martin Stevens shows
how the principles of spatial self-reference and meaningful anachronism inform
and deepen the sense of the Entry to Jerusalem episode (57–62). While apparently
all episodes were performed at each station, it seems clear that the last Last
Judgment, the final performance of an exhausting day, was particularly significant.
The full burden of its meaning depended on the Pavement being understood as the
world at its end, with heaven and hell beckoning simultaneously, and at the same
time the Pavement remained the familiar market of old York.

Scholars have long wondered why York maintained the Pavement as a station for the play's performance, since it was often difficult to rent at all. Its spaciousness was surely one reason. The streets of fifteenth-century York were very narrow; the great street of Micklegate alone was as wide as thirty-five feet, and the overhang of buildings would have narrowed the streets even more (Crouch, 99). (The streets on the map in figure 5.1 are not drawn to scale; the Shambles, for example, is very narrow.) The research of Eileen White shows that the other stations could permit only a fairly small audience to see an episode, whether seated or standing (56–57). Crouch makes the intriguing suggestion that the Pavement was the only space large enough for a big crowd. He surmises, in fact, that potential stationholders might not have wished to rent that station, since in such a crowd they would have had to rub shoulders with the poor (Crouch, 100).

Appealing as Crouch's suggestion is, the Pavement is a more complicated space socially. Here the mayor's wife and her friends watched the play (the mayor himself watched from the Common Hall, with the council). The great merchants of York largely kept their houses on the Pavement (Twycross, " 'Places,' " 21). In the Pavement's two churches, All Saints Pavement and St. Crux, sixty-eight of York's mayors were buried (Raine, 177–80). This was the place where farm people from all around the countryside, as well as other foreigners, came to sell their produce to freemen and to each other. The bullring, too, was here, and the street of the slaughterhouses, the Shambles, opened onto the Pavement, its stinking gutter running downhill into a grate where the streets met. If the wealthy and powerful of the mercantile city lived on the Pavement, their artisanal brethren, the butchers, lived and worked just beside it in the Shambles. The butchers' trade was traditionally regarded as the lowest occupation in what LeGoff has called the guilds' "hierarchy of contempt" (59–62), whatever the wealth of individual butchers. The market on the Pavement was the place of business of the victualing trades, traditionally viewed as scarcely better than that of the butchers. These were also the trades most practiced by women (Swanson, *Medieval*, 47–48). Like Doomsday itself, the Pavement embraced all people, both the mayor's wife and foreign regrators. Here York's merchants and artisans made their final statement to themselves and to outsiders about what kind of freedom theirs was.

The actual space of the Pavement mattered in the staging of the last Last Judgment. First, Corpus Christi plays traditionally used the ground level before the pageant wagons, or *platea*, as a nonlocalized, nontemporalized playing area. The Pavement offered the largest area of this kind of staging. Platea staging would seem to have been especially vital for the representation of the Last Judgment, in which sinners and the saved of all time are despatched to their fates.

Second, the wide space and actual streets and buildings of the Pavement afforded the civic drama an opportunity to make use of a long-established tradition of positional symbolism. The spatial orientation of churches was carefully attended to in western Europe, and this practice permitted a consistent use of positional symbolism in their construction and liturgies. The church door faced roughly west; its altar was in the east end of the building. The right (or north) side of the altar was favored. Every movement within the carefully oriented space of the church gained symbolic sense: "The movement of the gospel from left to right for the reading was interpreted as symbolic that Christ first preached to the Jews and then, when rejected by them, was accepted by the Gentiles. Its return at the end of the service foreshadows the conversion of the Jews" (Hardison, 50). The many churches in York show that efforts were made to preserve as much as possible the traditional east-west orientation of the nave, reasonably constrained by York's geometry. The minster, remarkably, is exactly aligned on the east-west axis, in defiance of the actual alignment of the streets, which are some degrees off square (see fig. 5.1.). The liturgical correctness of the alignment of York's churches, even the minster's extreme precision, defiant of the city's geometry, were doubtless apparent to, and had some meaning for, most of York's people.

It therefore seems reasonable to propose that the staging of the last Last Judgment scene on the Pavement employed that durable and persistent tradition of positional symbolism. Such a staging would have made sense of the actual space: hell to stage left, toward the stinking Shambles, and paradise to the right, near the church of all the saints, the burial place of the mayors. The fact that the episode's action calls for the crowd itself to be searched and divided into souls damned and saved may help, too, to explain why stations on the Pavement were not always rented, scaffolds not always built. Where, in good conscience, would one elect to sit?

Native popular drama in late medieval and sixteenth-century England was widespread and so long-lived that we must attend to it if we are to make sense of the native popular drama that succeeded it, in the era of the public playhouses. Many strategies devised for the medieval demotic of physical space that informed Corpus Christi plays lost little of their power for a long time. But the dramatic space itself changed. The open public areas of English towns, the spaces where freemen and foreigners lived and worked, no longer echoed with outdoor performances of plays that told townspeople in crucial ways who they were and marked out their liberty. With the rise of performance in privately owned, not public, spaces, the rough equality of citizens in the streets of their own city, watching a play produced and largely performed by their neighbors, was lost forever. No longer would they see guildsmen whom they knew performing in plays using the tools and products of their daily work; no longer would they see their neighborhood changed for the nonce into Jerusalem, or heaven and hell. There was a time when townspeople owned their play, and they also owned the playing places. The audience suffered the play to go on. The drama itself was situated within the bounds of their home, the *erev*, their freedom. In the sixteenth century, however, "ceremony and religion together withdrew indoors from the vulgar gaze" (Phythian-Adams, "Ceremony," in Holt and Rosser, 263). Not surprisingly, so did drama. Entrepreneurs came to own the playing place as well as the play, and they suffered the play-goer to surrender his penny to enter and watch (cf. Kahrl, "Medieval," 232). It took a long time for spectators to learn passively to watch someone else's play, silent in someone else's theater, ignored by the play itself, but eventually, we did.

NOTES

Several people greatly helped my work for this essay. Christopher Holmes was the ideal research assistant, energetic, discerning, and imaginative. As always, Janet Fox was the sounding board for all my notions, and shared with me insights about the theatrical space used by Corpus Christi plays. Susan Brown, Jonathan Curtin, C. J. Neville, Lee Oliver, and Catherine Stephenson aided me at crucial moments. I'm grateful to them all.

1. This essay is greatly indebted to Martin Stevens's insights about the York play and its strategies for bringing the city and civic life itself into the play's meaning.

2. Zika notes that before the sixteenth century there seem to have been no plays in German Corpus Christi processions, but there are some examples of tableaux vivants presented by guilds or confraternities. What may interest students of English drama is the fact that these *figurae* portrayed the *Heilsgeschichte*, with scenes from both Old and New Testaments, and ended with the Last Judgment (Zika, 49).

3. I am persuaded by Martin Stevens that the procession and play probably were indeed moved to separate days in 1426, and that after 1468 their order was changed, the procession to the day after Corpus Christi, and the play to the feast itself. In this view he has disagreed with Alexandra Johnston, who has argued that the procession and play were not separated until 1468 ("Procession," 55–62; M. Stevens, 48 n. 38). Both shifts would seem to be evidence of the ascendancy not just of the play but of the corporation over the religious liberties.

CHAPTER 6

# The Theaters

*John Orrell*

## Court Theaters

Court theaters were built as a branch of court policy. Their construction was undertaken by the King's Works, a department of government based in Whitehall, and the design was a matter for the King's Surveyor, often working under instruction from members of the Privy Council. As a result, they tended to be more cosmopolitan than might otherwise have been the case, both in conception and in detail.

In his aptly titled *Spectacle, Pageantry, and Early Tudor Policy*, Sydney Anglo traced the connection between politics and regal show, and particularly noted the events of 1520, when Henry VIII met the king of France in the Field of the Cloth of Gold at Guisnes, and subsequently the emperor Charles V at Calais (158–69). For the latter occasion the King's Works set up a great polygonal timber theater intended to house the major banquets of the encounter. Richard Turpyn describes the elaborate decor of this theater in detail, much of it intended as balanced political protocol, but in the event it all came to nothing. A great wind blew away the canvas roof, and a rainstorm quenched the lights. What remained was a useless timber frame, boarded on the outside, its walls covered with canvas painted to represent ashlar, or hewn stone. Without its delicate imagery, the empty building had little political value, the meeting was removed elsewhere, and the Works carpenters set about dismantling the remains and transporting the timbers back to London.

Variously characterized by contemporaries as a theater or an amphitheater, the building evoked the glories of an antique past: it was intended as a Roman setting for a stately modern encounter. A few weeks earlier a similar disaster had occurred at Ardres, where Francis I had built another round "Roman" theater:

It was covered with canvas . . . and it was made in a form like that which the Romans, in past ages, used for their theatre: all in a round, constructed of wood, with loges, rooms and galleries. [It had] three storeys, one above another, and all the foundations were made of stone. (DE LA MARCK 69; my translation)

Here too the canvas roof had blown away. The writer, the seigneur de Fleurange, checks off the characteristics of the Roman theater as understood early in the sixteenth century: round shape, wooden construction, stories of galleries.

The round houses of 1520 seem to have been a passing fashion, though many later festive halls — usually rectangular in plan — used their structural techniques and elaborate decor. The Greenwich "Disguising Theatre" in 1527 was the most spectacular, with a ceiling probably by Holbein and even an early version of a proscenium arch. In 1581–1582 Queen Elizabeth entertained the duc d'Alençon in a specially built rectangular hall made of masts and enclosed with boards and canvas painted to look like ashlar, in the Calais fashion (BL Harleian MS. 293: 217; PRO E351/3216). This building, though intended at first as a temporary affair, stood until it was replaced by the first Jacobean Banqueting House in 1606; in that time it was gradually converted into a court theater of a type that was becoming well known in Italy and abroad, especially through the prints in Serlio's *Architettura*.

Serlio's first two books (the second containing the theater scheme) appeared in Paris in 1545, with an English translation in 1611 (Dinsmoor, 72–77). They are among the first printed books to be so extensively illustrated and were often used as pattern books by English sixteenth-century builders. The theater scheme forms part of a developing argument about the geometry of perspective, and the plan and section of an exemplary theater (Serlio, 2:24v and 23v) convey some of Serlio's principles, the first of which is to follow the ancient example, even within modern formal constraints (Serlio, *Architettura*, 2:24r). Features of the ancient Roman theater are pressed into the space provided by a courtyard or hall, including a semicircular orchestra, surrounded by concentric stepped degrees forming a *cavea*, cut off to either side by the flanking limits of the space.

Serlio's favored source is Vitruvius, the Roman commentator on architectural design, whose theater scheme observes that the width of the orchestra is the normative measure from which all else is derived. Inigo Jones was aware of the scheme: "noat," he wrote in his copy of Vitruvius, "that $y^e$ Diamiter of the orchestra ruiles $y^e$ measurey of all"; and, a few pages earlier, "The sceane is duble $y^e$ diamter of $y^e$ orchestra," "or pedistal of $y^e$ sceane ye 12 part of $y^e$ dimiter of $y^e$ Orcestra," "the collombs $y^e$ fourth part of the diamter the orchistra" (Barbaro, 255, 252). For Vitruvius the whole *cavea* is just twice as wide as the orchestra, but Serlio's narrow space forces him to another expedient: his orchestra is related to the whole width as $1:\sqrt{2}$, one of the preferred proportional ratios with which he begins his discourse (Serlio, *Architettura*, 1:12r). Thus the width of the orchestra, though it differs from Vitruvian precept, is still "$y^e$ measurey of all." In addition, the depth of each of the seating degrees — a dimension for obvious reasons suited to the human body—provides the module by which the whole scheme is measured: the orchestra is twelve such units in diameter and the squared-up actors' stage thirty-four units wide by five units deep. The same unit also enters the mathematics of the stage perspective. In sum, Serlio's theater scheme adapts Vitruvian theory to contemporary conditions, emphasizes the geometric primacy of the orchestra, and offers a literally human basis for its dimensioning.

After the 1580s the court theaters of Westminster and elsewhere began to show signs of Serlian (and, at some remove, Vitruvian) influence. At the Whitehall Banqueting House the first developments were structural: the canvas walls were strengthened and filled in with more substantial stuff. But in 1583–1584 a strongly built proscenium arch or border was introduced, decorated with two "Personadges"; the following year the painters made a new sky cloth to replace the old wickerwork and evergreens, and at the northern end "iij Rounde Skaffoldes" (probably semicircular) appear to have given the theater a U-shaped auditorium (PRO E351/3218–19). In this state, with an elevated stage to the south bordered by a prototype proscenium arch, and a galleried U-shaped auditorium flanked by stepped degrees, the theater outlived Queen Elizabeth, in whose name it had been built. *Othello* was staged there in 1604, but for Jonson's *Masque of Blackness* a few weeks later much of the seating appears to have been rearranged and a great mobile stage introduced at the northern end (PRO E351/3240): what had begun as a traditional banqueting house and had been developed into a Renaissance theater was now transformed once more into a *salle des spectacles*.

Evidence for the Banqueting House is fragmentary, but in 1605 Inigo Jones designed scenes for a series of plays put on in the hall at Christ Church, Oxford, for a court audience. The royal Works, headed on this occasion by Simon Basil, designed and built the theater structure. A plan and section of the auditorium survive (Foakes, *Illustrations*, item 27; BL Add. MS. 15505: 21r) and show it to have been resolutely Serlian in inspiration. The Italian's orchestra now housed the royal halpace, or viewing platform. Behind it were stepped concentric degrees—polygonal rather than curved—reaching to the back of the hall: it was, as contemporaries observed, a Roman theater in a narrow room. In fact, the Christ Church scheme was a thoroughly proportionate design following the principles rather than the accidents of Serlio's method.

The Whitehall Banqueting House, "old rotten, sleight builded" (Stowe, 891), was dismantled in 1606 and replaced by something more substantial, whose interior decor gives a useful example of current practice among the artificers of the Works (Colvin and Summerson, 322–24, plate 21). It provided a space that could be fitted up as a regular court theater, sometimes for plays but more regularly for Inigo Jones's spectacular masques, with libretti by Jonson. Scenic stages were still a rarity, most plays performed at court being housed in time-honored fashion in the hall or great chamber with little in the way of special provision beyond the usual seating degrees. But at Somerset House from 1616 onward a tradition of scenic drama was established, at first by Ann of Denmark and then by Queen Henrietta Maria. For the latter, Jones designed some highly accomplished scenes, usually employing fixed wings (either flats or book-wings) leading to changeable backshutters with a backscene beyond to close the vista. His imagery was often derived from Serlio, but the theater architecture—especially in the border or frontispiece that framed the scene—was more eclectic, drawing from prints by Bartolomeo Neroni, G. B. Aleotti, or the Parigi (Peacock, 210—11). The actors, who sometimes included royal participants, entered through the wings but generally made directly for a level acting space in front of the proscenium border, sometimes indeed on the floor of the room, reached by steps down from the stage. The scenes were, therefore, great pictures, only partly changeable, set behind the dramatic action and only dimly lit by candles and lamps located between the flats. The chief action, and most of the artificial light, was effectively in the auditorium.

For two such theaters, one set up in the Paved Court at Somerset House (1633; Foakes, *Illustrations*, item 32) and the other in the great hall at Whitehall (1635; Foakes, *Illustrations*, item 33), we have complete sets of drawings, showing the scenery as well as the theater fittings (Orrell, *Theatres*, 113–48). Both sets show that the old tradition of the central dancing floor flanked by raised degrees of seating still persisted, enabling the royal halpace to be positioned where no members of the audience would have their backs to it.

There is little evidence that scenic theaters were built outside the circle of the court: they were extremely expensive and tinged with alien culture. Plays continued to be performed in the halls and great chambers at Whitehall, Greenwich, and elsewhere, usually with the minimum of special preparation. In the reign of James I the old Tudor cockpit at Whitehall, often in use for its original purpose, was sometimes commandeered for plays, and in 1629 Inigo Jones converted the building into a permanent court playhouse (Foakes, *Illustrations*, item 30). He evidently had two important models in mind: the commercial playhouses of contemporary London, because the new house would be used by the professional players, and Palladio's well-known treatment of the ancient theater theme at the Teatro Olimpico in Vicenza, which Jones had visited. Within the central, top-lit octagon of the building he placed a level platform stage, its front extending almost to the diameter, doubtless in recognition of Vitruvius's recommendation that it should do so (Orrell, *Theatres*, 90–112). There was a broad, shallow acting stage, 34 feet wide by 5 feet deep. Behind that stood a segmentally planned *frons*, but where, in Vicenza, there was a blank second story and an attic filled with statuary, at Whitehall Jones provided a central window or framed opening over the main one below, in the manner of the public playhouses. The auditorium, which can be reconstructed from Webb's plan of 1660 together with the Works accounts, appears to have been a polygonal *cavea*. In the pit (the site of the original cockfight table) broad degrees rose to the height of the original low gallery. Beyond this the degrees were much steeper, no more than narrow perches for leaning on. Overhead, to encourage the neo-Roman feel of the house, a sky cloth or velarium was stretched on wires, retractable on copper rings to let an ingenious descent machine work through it (PRO E351/3265). Together with the *frons* and a plaster ceiling over the stage, these fittings effectively closed off the fabric of the original structure from view, so that the audiences found themselves in a space whose limits were entirely "Romanized." Yet the Cockpit-in-Court was no chaste academic reinterpretation of classical theater architecture like the Olimpico: it was a working playhouse, designed for and enjoying constant use by commercial players. Nevertheless, the greatly emphasized central bay of the *frons*, with its *porta regia* and articulated window above, the central gangway through the auditorium, and the elevated state opposite the stage gave the house a firm axial emphasis quite unlike anything in the public theaters. The shallow actors' stage lay on the transverse axis, with almost all of the audience housed in front of it.

A balanced design such as Jones's *frons* tends to be lifeless if there is no variation in the symmetry. He tricked it out with statuary, nicely varying his theme to give the architecture direction. Plaster statues of Melpomene and Thalia (the Muses of Tragedy and Comedy) stood on plinths flanking the central stage opening, the first stage right and the second stage left.[1] Above, in niches to either side of the central opening, were places for two more pairs of statues. The inscriptions show that they also followed the left/right polarity, but in two parts, as it were. The labels are not as readable as they might be beneath Webb's cross-hatching, but they appear to show that within each pair the figure associated with tragedy was to stage right and the one representing comedy, stage left. Beside the central opening were labeled brackets with brass busts, Thespis to stage right and Epicharmus to stage left (the former the reputed founder of tragedy and the latter, of comedy).

In 1619 the Whitehall Banqueting House burned down. Jones designed the new one, which still stands, as a great double cube, roughly the same size as its predecessor but made of stone and finely proportioned. The aisled basilica character of the older building was retained, even though the columns that had limited its usefulness were done away with: the new building contained an uninterrupted space for court ceremonies, receptions, and especially for conversion to spectacular theater. The superimposed orders were now set back against the walls as attached Ionic half-columns below and Composite pilasters above, forming seven bays where the earlier building had ten. Between the orders a cantilevered gallery, too shallow to be of much practical use, recalled the previous galleried form. To the south a coffered niche gave the room focus, and together with the compartments in the ceiling defined the width of the central nave. Where the burned building had been encrusted with ornament, much of it figurative, Jones's great shell was chastely restrained, only a subfrieze of swags in the upper order breaking the austere mood. The result, even before the removal of the niche in 1625, was an interior of what Sir John Summerson called "a formidable and even forbidding immobility" (53).

This is, however, to misrepresent the character of the room as a *salle des spectacles*. When a stage was prepared at the northern end, ranges of stepped degrees down either aisle, and a vast frontispiece or border in front of the scenes, its quality radically changed. For *Albion's Triumph* in 1632, for example, the frontispiece was scaled to fit exactly between the opposite gallery fronts of the Banqueting House. Its entablature contained enormous swags on which sleeping *putti* reclined. The entablature was supported by lofty Doric pilasters, wreathed in crimson velvet, with figures of Theorica and Practica standing on pedestals (Orgel and Strong, 2:458–59). The pilasters measured 31 feet tall, including their pedestals, and made a giant order in a room that was itself designed to avoid such flashy monumentality.

The acoustic quality of the masonry hall may not have suited the voice and music of the masque, and in any case when Rubens's specially commissioned paintings were installed in the compartments of the ceiling, candle smoke became a liability. In 1638, therefore, a similar-sized Masquing House was built alongside, out of wood: critics called it a Dancing Barn. This was the last court theater to be built before the Restoration.

### Private Theaters

Court theaters were usually interiors, where plays and masques were performed by candlelight. Most commercial drama before the last quarter of the sixteenth century seems to have taken place indoors too, in town halls and the halls of great houses and city inns, between which the companies of strolling players customarily traveled. When permanent playhouses came to be established in London after 1567, they were of two main types, one indoors and lit by candles, the other exterior and lit by daylight. The latter seems to have been the greater innovation. Indoor playhouses were more expensive to run than outdoor ones, if only because of the need to provide the candles and torches; and the cost of building (or adapting) and lighting the enclosed auditorium limited their size and audience capacities, with the result that entrance prices were higher. Throughout the Elizabethan and early Stuart period the so-called private houses—the enclosed theaters— enjoyed a higher social status than the open public playhouses, where the audience included people of every rank except the highest and the lowest.

The first private theater opened in 1576 in a converted room at the old Blackfriars priory, long since dissolved, between St. Paul's Cathedral and the river. It was constructed by Richard Farrant, deputy master of the Children of the Chapel Royal, for use by his boy actors, in an upstairs room about 26 feet by 46 feet, 6 inches (I. Smith, *Shakespeare's Blackfriars*, 134–37, 143). Almost nothing more is known about its design, and in this it is joined by several of the other private houses: unlike the court theaters, their conversions were not registered in Works accounts, nor did they produce the substantial building contracts of some of the public theaters. Paul's playhouse, located somewhere in St. Paul's Cathedral precinct, flour-

ished from 1599 but may have been fitted up as early as 1575. It was certainly small,
though its actual dimensions are unknown. One speculation is that its stage and
auditorium formed an irregular hexagon about 25 feet in diameter between the but-
tresses of the cathedral's chapter house and the cloisters flanking its nave (Gair,
66–69). The Whitefriars playhouse, built c. 1608 in the refectory of the old Carmel-
ite priory a little to the east of Blackfriars, was larger, about 35 feet by 85 feet (Gurr,
*Shakespearean*, 160); the conversion of Porter's Hall into a theater was begun in
another part of Blackfriars in 1615 by Philip Rosseter, but its size is unknown; in
1629 at Salisbury Court, close to the Whitefriars, Richard Gunnell and William
Blagrave made a theater out of an old barn, possibly 40 feet wide and of unknown
length (Bentley, *Jacobean*, 6:77–117); and finally a temporary theater—31 feet by 40
feet, boarded and covered with pantiles—was built in the grounds of a riding
school in Drury Lane for a season of French plays in 1635–1636, on the site of the
later Theater Royal (E/BER, Drury Lane, survey, 1635).

Internal evidence from plays written for the private theaters suggests that their
auditoriums were galleried and that their platform stages were provided with doors
of entrance, some sort of discovery space, a quantity of hangings, and usually a
small acting area "Above." They were also raised sufficiently to permit trapwork
beneath, and some of the theaters contained descent machines (T. J. King,
"Staging"; D. Stevens). All relied on candles for lighting, requiring act intervals
while the wicks were trimmed. References to their audiences in prologues and epilogues suggest that several of them had rounded, U-shaped auditoriums in the
manner of the Christ Church fit-up of 1605 (Orrell, "Private," 83–88).

Two of the private houses achieved much greater prominence than the rest: the
Second Blackfriars as the home of the King's Men after 1609, and the Cockpit in
Drury Lane, its closest rival, built in 1616. The Second Blackfriars was built by
James Burbage for the Lord Chamberlain's Men in 1597, though in the event the
objections of influential neighbors barred them from using it. It was leased to a
boys' company until the adult players—now the King's Men—were at last able to
take it over in 1609 to house plays like *Cymbeline* and *The Tempest*.

The first Blackfriars theater had closed in 1584; the second was built in the upper
frater of the monastery, a chamber some 46 feet by 66 feet internally (I. Smith,
*Shakespeare's Blackfriars*, 164–71; Hosley, 197–216). It was therefore the largest of
those private theaters whose dimensions are known. The stage was probably at the
south, opposite the stairs, and ran east and west across the room. Leonard Digges,
in verses prefacing the 1640 edition of Shakespeare's *Poems*, refers to "The Cockpit
Galleries, Boxes" at the Blackfriars: evidently there was a pit, with surrounding galleries, some of them partitioned as boxes. An account of a quarrel at the theater in
1632 tells how a dandy standing on the stage obscured the view of spectators seated
in a box, one of whom reached out a hand and "putt him a little by," provoking a
sword thrust in reply (PRO C115/M35/8391). Evidently the box was within arm's
reach of the stage and much on a level with it. The auditorium appears to have

been galleried and U-shaped, framed as part of a polygon. Jonson's Blackfriars play *The Magnetic Lady* has a snobbish stage spectator refer to people "that sit in the oblique caves and wedges of your house" (A3r-v), an allusion to the *cavea* and *cunei* of the Roman theater; and Davenant in *The Wits* described the audience as "this our Hemispheare" (A4r).

To the south the stage with its flanking boxes had three entrance doors: "Enter Maister Touch-stone," says a stage direction in the boys' play *Eastward Ho* (1605), "and Quick-silver at several [i.e., separate] dores . . . At the middle dore, Enter Golding discouering a Gold-smiths shoppe" (A2r). Because the central door could be used for small scenic "discoveries" it was probably larger than the other two. As in most of the theaters of the period, Blackfriars play texts require a small acting space (and sometimes music) above, a single trap (sparingly used), and a descent machine enabling vertical drops close to the stage balcony (T. J. King, *Shakespearean*, passim).

Digges's use of the word *cockpit* for part of a theater's interior is a sharp reminder that in one case the term was literally true: at the Phoenix or Cockpit in Drury Lane the theatrical pit was established precisely where the old cockfight table had stood. In 1616 this playhouse was converted out of a round brick cockpit of traditional design (*Middlesex*, 2:125–26; 3:310). Cockpits were commonly circular structures some 30 or 40 feet in diameter, with a central table 12 feet across and concentric rings of degrees forming a miniature amphitheater around it (Orrell, "Inigo Jones," 163–65). The whole was too small for professional theatrical use and required some radical transformation if it were to become a playhouse.

An undated set of drawings by Inigo Jones may show the scheme for the theater, though whether in its first state of 1616 or as refurbished in 1639 one cannot be quite sure (Foakes, *Illustrations*, item 29). In any case, the drawings show all the characteristics of the private playhouse as we have come to know them through other types of evidence: the U-shaped galleried auditorium, the raised stage with its three doors of entrance, the stage balcony with its central "window" or music room, the boxes within arm's reach of the stage, the seated pit located in the round part of the house. The drawings are detailed and worked up to a high presentation standard. Because they include all the known main features of the Stuart private playhouses, they enable us to approach the details of their design with some assurance.

Like the court theater plans, the present drawings are developed by means of a repeated module. For the exterior shell, which probably derived from a round cockpit structure 40 feet in diameter, this is 5 feet. But the interior proportioning is more interesting, for here the module is precisely the depth of a seating degree, or 18 inches. As in Serlio's theater scheme in *Architettura*, the dimension of the seat gives the commensurate unit (U) from which the design is developed. The stage is 10 U deep (15 feet); the centerpiece of the *frons* is 4 U wide (6 feet); the gallery floor is 10 U above the pit; the pit entry door is 2 U wide by 4 U tall (3 feet by 6 feet); and so on. If this were a court theater we should expect to find the orchestra to be half the whole width of the house, or in this case 20 feet. But in fact it is rather wider than that, about 21 feet, 3 inches, a measure that derives from the stage depth of 15 feet (10 U) by means of an *ad quadratum* construction: $15 \times \sqrt{2} = 21.21$. Adequate space for pit seating required the greater width, and the stage was wider still, at 24 feet (16 U), yielding an aspect ratio of 5:8.

With a main cell 40 feet by 55 feet, the Jones theater was probably about the same size as most of the private houses, though rather smaller than the second Blackfriars. Its flat rectangular stage was 4 feet high, and railed at the front. The two main doors of entrance were only 5 feet, 6 inches high in the clear, but the central arched opening was wide enough to be used as a small discovery space. The stage balcony was fitted with degrees for spectators, though its central bay, framed with a nicely proportioned and pedimented aedicule, formed an area 6 feet wide by 10 feet deep that was cleared of seating. The balcony degrees doubtless extended into the corners of the building, where they met those of the upper gallery, with the result that the audience at this level entirely surrounded the action below (except in the hiatus of the music room).

Entrance into the theater, wherever one's chosen seat, involved passage through some very restricted spaces. The main door was large enough, but the way to the pit involved ducking through the narrow arch, and the stairs to the galleries were tight winders with small headroom. Once inside, a modern theatergoer would be appalled by the accommodation: the bench seating allowed the standard eighteen inches fore and aft. The rake of the galleries was more than forty degrees, a vertiginous slope hardly countered by the tiny two-foot barrier at the bottom (blank parapet below, balustrade above). To reach the front benches one clambered down the steep degrees from the rear gangway, there being no other passage.

The *frons* was more intensely decorated than the rest of the house. Its lower story was made of brick, the front surface plastered and therefore probably painted or grooved as ashlar. The composition was closed at either end by a flat pilaster into which the stage box rails were let. Above the two doors of entrance, with their simple doorcases, were plaster swags in relief, while beside them stood four-foot-high sculptured figures in niches. The central opening was treated in the manner of a miniature triumphal arch, with a scrolled cartouche in its entablature. At this level, then, the design was restrained, even monumental; at the upper level everything flowed more freely. The tiny balustrade that circled the auditorium continued here across the *frons*, linking the stage balcony visually with the rest of the upper gallery and boxes. The central aedicule with its broken pediment supported a life-size bust that seemed to preside over the whole, while on plinths set against its piers stood bound Terms holding urns. Beneath the entablature to either side was a swagged subfrieze, a tender Palladian detail that Jones was to repeat in the Whitehall Banqueting House.

Because the idiom of the drawings is so Jonesian, they probably give only a distant idea of the decor of other private theaters, from Blackfriars to Salisbury Court, which will have been much less refined. But they provide full information about other matters that are certainly more typical: the provisions for audience accommodation, for example, and for stage boxes, doors of entrance, the stage balcony. Above all, they give a clear idea of how space was organized in such a theater, especially with regard to its social function. The U shape of the auditorium left many audience members facing one another rather than the play, as did the limited seating in the stage balcony. Those who sat on stools on the stage itself, diminishing its narrow twenty-four-foot width even further, were also thoroughly on view. But some people, seated at the back of the stage boxes, enjoyed a measure of privacy, protected as they were by a partition between the galleries and the boxes. Modern performers generally dislike a central axial gangway through the auditorium because it creates a blank at the middle of their focus. Jones included a central door at pit level with an axial gangway through the pit seating; there are no similar doors in the galleries in the section of the auditorium, but they were necessary and one is present in the plan. The effect of these central accents would have been to reinforce the bifurcation of the house, which was already encouraged by the opposed lateral seating. The auditorium as social meeting place competes with its strictly theatrical function.

Two of the private theaters survived until the Restoration, when for a year or two they resumed their productive life. Salisbury Court, though damaged more than once by Parliamentary troops, was thoroughly refitted, apparently in the old way, but the Cockpit in Drury Lane, after similar injury, was made capable of housing the scenes and machines that were soon to characterize the revived Caroline theater. The theater shown in the Jones drawings, though not a scenic house as it stands, was capable of such transformation: even as early as 1639 Jones had designed a scene exactly proportioned to its stage, endorsed "for yᵉ cokpitt" (Orgel and Strong, 1:26). Later scenic performances at the Drury Lane playhouse included some quite elaborate operas by a visiting French company, whose published libretti possibly exaggerate their visual effects but show that the theater anticipated the new scenic developments that were to shape Davenant's Bridges Street playhouse and the theaters of the eighteenth century (Visser; Orrell, "Scenes"). It appears that the private theaters of the late sixteenth and early seventeenth centuries, as known to us through the medium of Jones's drawings, stood directly in the mainstream of English theater history.

## Public Playhouses

The first substantial London playhouse of which notice survives is the Red Lion in Whitechapel, built in 1567. Like all the earliest theaters it was a speculative venture, put up by a businessman with an eye to profit. There is no reason to believe that it lasted very long, but its pattern appears to have anticipated that of the more famous and longer-lasting Theatre and Curtain, erected in Shoreditch almost a decade later.

Surviving documents allude to two separate building contracts for the Red Lion, one for the spectator seating or galleries and the other for the stage, with a "turret" mounted on it (Chambers, *Elizabethan*, 2:379–80; Loengard). The stage was large— 40 feet by 30 feet, and 5 feet high—and apparently rectangular, with a void space in it possibly for a trap. The turret was mounted on or beside the stage, 30 feet high, with a floor 7 feet below the top. All this was framed in the normal Elizabethan way, in the builder's yard or framing-place, then brought to the site and erected as a kit of pre- fabricated parts. The owner, John Brayne, a London grocer, was determined to exer- cise close control over the building process: he complained about every part of it, both the "skaffoldes" (or galleries) and the stage and turret. The stage area was slightly greater than that of the later Fortune playhouse, for which we have a contractual description, and probably larger than that of the Globe. If some yard space sur- rounded it, in front of the galleries, the whole structure must have been almost as large as the Fortune (80 feet square). At a minimum there were presumably two lev- els of spectator space, one a raised gallery story perhaps over standing room or degrees below. If some yard-level space was left around the stage there must have been at least 160 running feet of gallery work "about the . . . courte" (PRO KB27/1229 m. 30). If each had room even for only four rows of seating space the galleries will have held more than 850 people in addition to any standing in the yard. In short, the Red Lion was a substantial and complex theater, of whose subsequent life we know nothing.

Where did Brayne, who evidently knew what he wanted, conceive his idea of the theater? It is often said that the animal-baiting arenas on Bankside formed the model for the earliest playhouses, but by 1567 nothing substantial enough had been built in that line to offer Brayne a precedent. The Victorian notion that inn yards were the source of the Elizabethan public playhouses has not been supported by recent scholarship: when actors performed at inns they usually occupied a large room rather than a yard and performed by candlelight. And the arrangements made for playing in Tudor halls, guildhalls, and the like can hardly have suggested the 40-foot-wide stage with its 30-foot turret.

Nine years later, Brayne set up in business with a London joiner-turned-actor, James Burbage, to build another playhouse, which they tellingly called the Theatre. The use of the antique name suggests that their imaginative source was the Roman theater as currently understood, for surviving evidence of the building indicates that it was like the round house built by French carpenters at Ardres, more than fifty years earlier. The Theatre's foundations were doubtless of brick, and its frame was polygonal rather than truly round (as was Henry VIII's similar the- ater at Calais); otherwise, the Theatre in Shoreditch answers the description belonging to the timber frame at Ardres. The Theatre is shown in an engraved view of London as seen from the north, where it is a polygonal structure, conventionally attenuated and therefore much too tall for its width as drawn, but evidently of three stories (Foakes, *Illustrations*, item 5). Documents tell us that it had galleries and ways of "going vppe" to them; it had a yard and a tiring house, and there were "vpper romes" for spectators (Berry, "Aspects," 30, 36). No masons or thatchers seem to have worked on the building, which probably had a tiled roof. The engraving shows what appear to be stair turrets attached to either side of the frame, providing access to the galleries and upper rooms; it also shows what may be the top of a turret rising higher than the main gallery frame within the yard.

It is unlikely that there was any direct connection between Brayne and Burbage's idea for the Theatre and that which informed the French and English round houses of 1520. It is, rather, that they all stem from the same root: all are modern versions of the Roman theaters of antiquity. There is, too, a substantial social and political difference. The theaters of 1520 were like chalices containing sacred truths: their galleries and stages were the mere framework for what was far more telling in the way of emblematic political decor, the most persuasive part of which was their elaborately painted canvas roofs. There is no sign in the Theatre in Shoreditch of any such programmatic scheme, nor did it have a canvas roof to be decorated. It contained paying spectators rather than hieratic imagery; what Brayne and Burbage provided was a physical plant designed to please the visitors with a painted luxury they couldn't find at home. In the following years, as more such buildings appeared, especially along Bankside, visitors repeatedly saw the Roman connection. A schoolmaster, preaching at St. Paul's, condemned the Theatre for being "after the maner of the olde heathnish Theatre at Rome" (Stockwood, 134–35). In 1600 a tourist wrote in his diary after seeing a play: "The theatre was constructed in the style of the ancient Romans, out of wood." Johannes de Witt, describing the Swan in 1596, observed that "its form seems to approach that of a Roman structure" and called its building type that of the "amphiteatra" (Chambers, *Elizabethan*, 2:366, 362).

English building at the end of the sixteenth century gives many examples of designs that were governed—with various degrees of rigor—by intellectual programs. Sir Thomas Tresham built a triangular lodge in the grounds at Rushton to illustrate the theme *tres testimonium dant* ("there are three that bear witness"—the theme also plays on Tresham's name) (Jencks, 26–30; Mowl, 188–91). Or the semiotic theme might be more literary and could emerge piecemeal during construction, as when Sir Edward Pytts developed Kyre Park (Baldwyn-Childe, 204). From many other examples, some of them instances of garden rather than house design, one sees that the relation between an initial design impulse and the final product was complex, but where a program was used the primacy of the owner was normally undisputed. Workmen did as they were told, interpreting their instructions according to the traditions of their craft.

The Theatre in Shoreditch was all of a piece, more Triangular Lodge than Kyre Park. Some sort of geometric program must have been invoked if the great three-storied polygon was to be carried through, and there could be little room for changing one's mind during the process of construction. Preparing the timbers for so complex a structure was no easy matter. It would have been undertaken remote from the Shoreditch site, involving extremely delicate jointing of green oak cut or

split into balks of large dimensions. There is some reason to believe that the
Theatre was a twenty-sided polygon 99 feet in diameter, each gallery being 12 feet,
6 inches deep measured face-to-face at ground level. The carpenters needed essentially to know the geometry of the plan, both at ground level and at that of the wall
plates, if the stories of the galleries were to be jettied. They would proceed by cutting the sills, beams, and posts of one of the radial cross-frames, then assembling
the frame horizontally, set up on chocks on the ground. While these timbers were
in position they would cut and joint the horizontal beams (bressumers) that were
to connect this cross-frame to the next, marking each timber so that it could eventually be reassembled in its proper place. In order to cut the joints accurately, they
needed precisely made jigs or templates, which they prepared using the compasses
and dividers, probably on a plaster tracery floor, into which they scored their constructions with the points of the instruments. Their command of geometric procedures was the essential precondition of their work.

In 1576 no Elizabethan carpenter can have had much experience in constructing such elaborations of polygonal geometry as the Theatre and the Curtain.
Burbage and Brayne had to be possessed of an idea powerful enough to make the
peculiarity of the work worthwhile: imagination had to lead geometry. And it seems
that the idea of the ancient Roman theater was what led their imaginations to the
task. Yet one of the most powerful graphic motives was apparently denied them.
The Roman theater was commonly covered, according to Alberti, by a *vela*, supported by ropes and strewn with stars. The canvas roofs at Ardres and Calais
recalled the ancient example, and so did others in the court theaters.

But there is no evidence for such a thing at the Red Lion or the Theatre in
Shoreditch, where most of the audience might be sheltered in the galleries and
daylight was needed to illuminate the performances. In these theaters a stage turret rose within the compass of the surrounding galleries, but there was no separate
cover over the stage (Wickham, "Heavens," 1–13). The earliest evidence for a stage
roof comes in 1595, at the Rose on Bankside, when a carpenter was paid for
"mackinge the throne In the heuenes" (Henslowe, *Diary*, ed. Foakes and Rickert
[unless otherwise noted], 7). Doubtless this was a reference to a descent machine,
but it takes the presence of the Heavens for granted. We now know that the Rose's
stage and tiring house were demolished and substantially rebuilt in 1592, with posts
at the front of the stage evidently intended to support a covering roof. There is no
firm archaeological evidence of such a roof in the original build of 1587.

At the Swan, recorded by de Witt, c. 1596, a stage turret of the Red Lion kind
was supplemented with a lean-to stage roof covering only part of the platform
below and supported at the front by great Corinthian pillars (Foakes, *Illustrations*,
item 26). This arrangement was surely unsatisfactory, as it left the most useful part
of the stage open to the weather and inevitable decay. By 1613, when the Bear-
gardens was rebuilt as a dual-purpose baiting-arena-cum-playhouse called the
Hope, the builder's contract called for a "Heavens all over the saide stage" (I.

Smith, *Shakespeare's Globe*, 220); and at the second Globe, built in the following year, there was a great twin-ridged stage roof tied into the main polygonal frame and extending forward to the diameter of the house. The simple turret of the Red Lion had by then been replaced by something much larger and more fully integrated with the rest of the structure.

John Norden's 1600 bird's-eye view of the city shows the Rose and the Globe as polygonal structures (though of only six or eight sides) with integral stage roofs tied into the frame and presenting a gable toward the front (Foakes, *Illustrations*, item 6). This is the same essential pattern that Hollar was later to record at the second Globe (Foakes, *Illustrations*, item 16). It therefore seems likely that both the Rose and the first Globe had roofs generally of the pattern Norden recorded. In those theaters the old turret form had been superseded, though doubtless the change was not a matter of smooth sequential development, the Swan's turret and improvised stage roof probably dating some three years after the Rose's Heavens.

From the first, then, an upper element was a necessary part of an Elizabethan public stage, but the earliest playhouses had no decorated Heavens that might govern their imaginative program. In this they differed from the court banqueting and disguising theaters. Nevertheless, contemporary allusions show that they were gorgeously painted places, recalling the splendors of ancient Rome. When, during the 1590s, the stage turrets were sometimes superseded by large roofs covering the whole of the stage, the Roman connection was maintained. Thomas Heywood, describing a Roman amphitheater, wrote of "the couering of the stage, which wee call the heauens" (D2v), and Cotgrave followed with his 1611 definition: "a place ouer a stage which we call the Heauen" (sig. Mmmiij$^r$). Although it had been no part of the original public theater design, the Heavens confirmed the Romanness of the scheme.

When the lease on the site of the Theatre in Shoreditch ran out and the landlord failed to renew it, the Lord Chamberlain's Men hired the carpenter Peter Street to dismantle the old Theatre and transport its useful timbers—doubtless those of the main polygonal frame—across the river to Bankside, there to re-erect them as the Globe. This translation was effected after Christmas 1598, and the Globe went up during the following year. If Norden's View is to be trusted, the Globe was now equipped with an integral stage roof of the kind already established over the road at the Rose, and vested with a cosmic potential that could on occasion be realized by the poets.

In 1989 both the Rose and the Globe sites were dug by archaeologists, who provided us for the first time with direct physical evidence from the playhouses. Enough of the Rose was revealed to show that its original plan, established in 1587, was a regular fourteen-sided polygon, with the tiring house evidently occupying somewhere between three and five of the bays in the northern quarter. Each bay was 12 feet 6 inches deep, face-to-face at ground level, and just over 11 feet wide at the front (and 16 feet wide at the rear). The stage, some 36 feet, 9 inches across at the widest point, tapered toward the front to about 26 feet, 10 inches. The yard was covered in mortar and raked upward from the foot of the stage at about 14 degrees for a few yards before leveling off to the south (Bowsher and Blatherwick, 63–67). There was no sign of any stage posts that might have supported a Heavens in the original build, nor were any remains found of attached stair turrets for access to the galleries. The diameter overall was about 72 feet, and that of the yard 49 feet, 6 inches (or 3 rods). It seems likely that the plan was developed using the medieval *ad quadratum* method: the diameter to the joints of the exterior sills being equal to that of the yard (also measured to the shoulders of the joints) multiplied by $\sqrt{2}$ (Orrell, "Beyond," 102, fig. 3B). In a fourteen-sided polygon the length of one of the faces is almost exactly 2/9 of the diameter, a condition that would have proved useful to the carpenter when he set out the geometry of his joints on the tracery table (Orrell, "Beyond," 104–7).

In 1592 the owner, Philip Henslowe, paid for a good deal of construction work at the Rose, and the dig revealed that the improvements entailed dismantling the whole of the northern half of the building and reconstructing it several feet further north in a new D-shaped plan. At the same time the stage was removed northward with the rest, thus extending the north-south dimension (and capacity) of the yard, while leaving the size and shape of the platform much the same as before. The tiring house, which appears to have been located within the bays of the main frame, was similarly removed. The original yard was now filled with a black ashlike substance probably derived from a nearby soap yard, for although it had set rock hard, crushed hazelnut shells, a by-product of the soapmaker's oil press, were liberally distributed throughout its depth. The surface of the yard was raised somewhat, so that its original rake was filled in, and the ashes covered what remained of the footings of the original stage. The second stage's foundations were established about a foot higher than those of the first and were provided with footings for stage pillars located close to the front corners, about 21 feet apart on centers (Bowsher and Blatherwick, 67–72).

Over the road only a small part of the Globe could be investigated, hardly as much indeed as a single bay of the galleries. Enough was found, however, to make possible deductions about the size and shape of the whole. The one bay was, like most at the Rose, 12 feet, 6 inches deep face-to-face. Geometric analysis of the whole dig, which included the footings of a lobby, or possibly a stair turret attached to the outer wall, revealed that the section discovered was approximately consistent with a polygon of twenty sides, 99 feet in diameter, and with a yard almost 74 feet across. In the yard there was some evidence of ashes like those found at the Rose (Orrell, "Beyond," 98, fig. 2).

### The Globe and the Fortune

The Globe was evidently much bigger than the Rose, which could just have squeezed into its yard. Its dimensions may be interpreted with the help of the builder's contract for the Fortune, built by Peter Street in 1600 and generally taking the Globe as its model (Henslowe, *Diary*, 307–10). The Fortune was, however, to be square in plan, 80 feet each way externally, with galleries 12 feet, 6 inches deep at ground level, leaving a 55-foot-square yard within. The gallery depth matched that of the Globe (and the Rose), but the identity of the two plans was closer still: the area of the Fortune's galleries at ground level was 3,375 square feet, while that of the Globe's was 3,376.8 square feet. The difference, 1.8 square feet, was less than the space accorded to one paying customer and probably failed to enter Street's estimates (fig. 6.1). The Fortune was simply the Globe squared: all the important gallery space, where most of the owner's revenue was generated, was preserved, while the area of the less-profitable yard was significantly diminished to provide a more intimate auditorium (Orrell, "Architecture," 18–20).

At the Fortune the galleries were jettied forward in the Elizabethan way, 10 inches at each story so that the top ones were 14 feet, 2 inches deep. Analysis of Hollar's sketch of the second Globe shows that its galleries at the top level (the only place where their depth can be estimated) were about 14 feet, 6 inches deep, measured radially, so it too almost certainly had jettied fronts. Eleven-inch jetties in each story would bring the proportions of the top gallery at the Globe precisely to

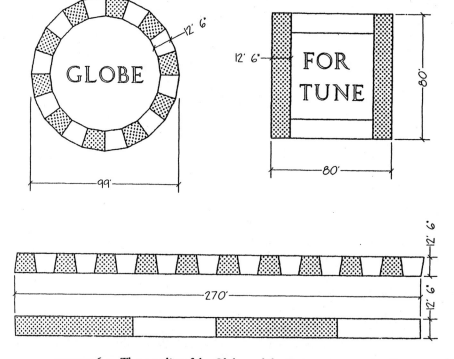

FIGURE 6.1. The equality of the Globe and the Fortune: a computer diagram.

those of an *ad quadratum* construction. (The gallery would measure 14 feet, 4 inches face-to-face, or 14 feet, 6 inches radially, for a yard diameter of 70 feet; 70 × $\sqrt{2}$ = 99 feet.) On this evidence one cannot prove that the carpenters cut the Globe's wall plates (and the Theatre's) using an *ad quadratum* construction on the tracery floor, but their need to invoke some geometric method or other makes it a good bet that they did, measuring their work in this case from the presentation surfaces rather than the shoulders of the joints.

At the Fortune the stage was 43 feet wide and extended forward to the center of the yard. The parity of gallery area with the Globe suggests that this stage may also have equaled that of the model, and a stage 43 feet wide set in the twenty-sided, 73-foot, 8-inch diameter yard of the Globe neatly chords four of its bays. But the model of the Rose suggests that the stage would have been placed so that it fronted an odd number of bays, leaving a clear space at the center to permit uncluttered stage entry through a central door. As at the Rose, therefore, the Globe's stage probably fronted five bays in all, its flanks returning to mid-bay at either side. Again the Fortune provides a useful check: the contract doesn't specify the bay widths, but they were likely 11 feet, 2 inches, yielding the yard width of 55 feet if five bays were constructed in each side, for a total—as at the Globe—of twenty bays in all. The 43-foot stage will have fronted all five bays in the tiring house range of the Fortune, though it will have extended only across rather less than half of those at either end.

One further characteristic of the Fortune's dimensions suggests that Edward Alleyn, the famous actor whose wealth funded the building, was seeking to advance on the Globe/Theatre's rather old-fashioned polygonal geometry. The best gallery at the Fortune must have been the middle one, on a level with the lords' rooms over the stage and decently removed from the sweaty fray in the yard. This *piano nobile* was proportioned according to those simple ratios that we have found favored in the court theaters: the galleries here were 13 feet, 4 inches deep, so that the yard at this level was 53 feet, 4 inches wide. The yard width was therefore proportioned to the total width of 80 feet as 2:3 (Orrell, "Architecture," 20–22).

### Decor

Street's contract required him to shape all the main front posts of the galleries and stage as pilasters, with carved satyrs attached to the top of each (Henslowe, *Diary*, 308). They were, that is, classical Terms. At the end of the sixteenth century such devices were much explored in lavish pattern books published all over Europe, each illustrating the theme of a chaotic, wild energy (represented by the satyrs) literally disarmed, bound, and put to architectural service (Hersey, 132–47). On the back of the Fortune contract a series of acquittance accounts reveals that in January Street went down into the country with a gang of workmen to acquire, prepare, and frame the green timbers of the theater; he then sent the wood down the Thames by barge to arrive in London during April and May. Work on the foundations had to be postponed until the danger of frost had passed, but on May 8, with the aid of a number of carpenters specially brought in from Windsor, the frame could be erected (Orrell, "Building," 130–41). Exactly when the Terms were carved the accounts do not say, but they are likely to have been prepared separately from the pilaster posts themselves (green wood not being good for carving) and attached, as the contract implies, later on.

The posts at the Globe differed from the Fortune's Terms, but their form is unknown. At the Hope there were turned columns, and de Witt recorded something similar at the Swan. He also remarked on the trompe l'oeil nature of the marbling, a painted finish so expertly done as to fox the most alert eye. There are many general allusions to the painting of the stages and their allied parts, but very little detail. Contemporary documents of the Royal Works, however, give a good idea of what such painting entailed: wood was frequently painted stone color, plaster was troweled to resemble ashlar, columns and balusters were marbled, architectural friezes were commonly painted "bice" or gray-blue, and enrichments such as rosettes, pendants, and finials were gilt (or painted yellow). Above all, whatever was of such lowly material as wood and plaster was converted by illusionistic means to something richer and more monumental (Mercer, 154–55). This imaginative transformation, so common elsewhere, was surely at the heart of theater decor too.

Analysis of stage directions and other textual references shows that the stages at the Globe, the Fortune, and most other public playhouses had two main doors of entrance separated by a larger opening capable of effecting small visual "discoveries": it is essentially the pattern of the Inigo Jones "Cockpit" drawings. As in those drawings, there was a stage balcony above, intended mostly for paying spectators but capable also of housing a small acting area (the "Above"). Poetic allusions to the details of the tiring house front, in which these features were built, are obviously unreliable evidence. It has been argued that the lowest story must have been squat, because of the occasional need of actors to climb up to or down from the Above, or even (as Arthur does in *King John*) to jump down. But such incidents are so rare (and scattered among texts written for a variety of theaters at different dates) that it seems unlikely that they encode a principle of theater design: much more often the *frons* is called upon to stand in for the front of a noble house (as, for example, at the first Globe for Brabantio's house, or Gloucester's, or Macbeth's castle entrance). These moments merely reinforce what ought to be obvious enough: the *frons* was the most impressive part of the public theater's architecture and was designed accordingly. The wide central opening required a certain height if it were not to appear cramped, and because the *frons*'s floor level was some 5 feet above that of the yard, its story heights could hardly coincide with those of the galleries. Contracts from the Red Lion on insist that the tiring house and galleries were framed as two separate structures, reflecting the visual distinction.

There is little direct evidence that the *frons* was designed in the manner of a Tudor hall screen. It was once believed that the players, accustomed to performing in front of such screens during their provincial tours, re-created familiar acting conditions when they began to organize themselves in permanent theaters. But recent scholarship gives no explicit support to this theory (Somerset, " 'How chances it,' " 54–60). It is more likely that the *frons* was a piece of deliberately showy architecture, of the sort refined by Jones in the two Cockpit schemes. A more reliable clue to the appearance of the *frons* at the first Globe and the Fortune may be the elaborate funerary sculpture of the Southwark School, a strongly architectural style, realized in rich stone, precisely of the kind that late Elizabethan painted decor strove to emulate (Esdaile, 117–24; Mowl, 31–36).

If the comparative refinement of the *frons* details suggests indoor architecture, an equally prominent feature of the public theaters toward the end of the century—the great columns that supported the Heavens—suited the outdoors. Those shown in the Swan drawing are columns of a giant Corinthian order, rising through two or three stories, and must have seemed a stunning innovation. Such an order was as yet a purely exterior device, as it still was in 1634 when Inigo Jones added a portico of giant columns to the west face of old St. Paul's (Summerson, 104–6).

There were other external characteristics too: at the Rose (and probably at the first Globe) the yard was surfaced with a soap-ash mortar sometimes used for paving streets. And at the Fortune, as always the imitator of the Globe, there were metal "pikes" atop the lowest gallery balustrade, doubtless meant to dissuade the groundlings from clambering into the more expensive seats. We have no illustration of such theatrical spikes from the Elizabethan period, but they were found in most English playhouses from the Restoration to the early nineteenth century, and appear in many theatrical prints (Thomas and Hare, 178, 363). Deterrent spikes are part of any city's exterior streetscape, and the more murderous they look the more effectively they do their job. The visual style of the turn-of-the-century public playhouses seems therefore to have combined indoor with outdoor characteristics in a manner well suited to the flexibility (but not anonymity) required by the play texts.

Expenditures listed in one of Alleyn's notes show that considerable changes must have been made to the Fortune over the years, just as they had been at its predecessor, the Rose (Greg, *Henslowe Papers*, 110). But with the Globe and the Fortune the form of the public theater seems to have reached a kind of zenith: subsequent playhouses built before the Restoration did not develop the type much further. The Red Bull was constructed in a square inn yard in 1605, and—to judge by the plays written for it—seems to have been equipped in the normal way (Reynolds, *Staging*). The Hope, built for both theatrical and animal-baiting uses in 1613, had a portable stage and tiring house, but otherwise was generally modeled on the Swan (Foakes, *Illustrations*, item 16). One piece of evidence, however, does suggest that the design of such playhouses was returning to the imaginative patronage and architectural taste of the court, whence in its origins it had flowed. When the Fortune burned down in 1622, Alleyn replaced it with a round brick theater. While the workmen were busy on the site, the old actor went off to visit the most aristocratic of his friends, the earl of Arundel, patron of Inigo Jones. On June 12 he

entered in his diary: "I went to ye Lord off Arundle showed ye fortune plott . . ."
(Young, 2:238). The Second Fortune drawings were exposed to the criticism of the
foremost aesthetic arbiter of the age: did they pass muster, one wonders, as "architecture"?

NOTE

1. Webb's drawings, as reproduced in Orrell, *Theatres*, 98–99 (plates 16 and 17) are unfortunately reversed.

CHAPTER 7

# "Rowme" of Its Own:
# Printed Drama in Early Libraries

*Heidi Brayman Hackel*

WHEN SIR Thomas Bodley selected books for the new public
library at Oxford at the beginning of the seventeenth century, he excluded most
English drama as unsuitable "riffe raffe" that could bring only discredit to the institution.[1] Ever conscious of the public's perception of the library, Bodley feared that
his critics would charge him with inflating the size of the holdings if he were to
accept "Almanackes, plaies, & proclamacions" (Wheeler, *James*, 219). Although
perhaps one English play in forty may be "worthy the keeping," Bodley maintained
that it was not worth the risk:

> Were it so againe, that some litle profit might be reaped (which God knowes is very
> litle) out of some of our playbookes, the benefit therof will nothing neere conteruaile,
> the harme that the scandal will bring vnto the Librarie, when it shalbe giuen out, that
> we stuffe it full of baggage bookes. (222)

Distinguished from Continental drama, which was "compiled, by men of great
fame, for wisedome & learning," and dismissed instead with ephemeral almanacs
and proclamations, English drama had no place at the Bodleian (222, 219). Bodley's
objections, in fact, focus on the physical space that these playbooks would occupy:

> the more I thinke vpon it, the more it doth distast me, that suche kinde of bookes,
> should be *vouchesafed a rowme*, in so noble a Librarie. (222, emphasis mine)[2]

And yet many men and women did make "rowme" for English playbooks—in their
closets, on their shelves, and in their bedchambers. Denied by Bodley, granted by
many of his contemporaries, this "rowme" for drama is the subject of this essay.

Usually thought of in terms of performative space, early English drama quite literally took up space in households and, eventually, in universities. This essay,

accordingly, will consider the drama not as an event but as an object that was collected, bound, and placed within the structure of a library. Such a consideration raises several interrelated questions: who owned playbooks? what was the status of playbooks in private and institutional libraries? what was the relationship between the playbook and the play, the study and the stage?

Attention to the study, as well as to the stage, is necessary to the understanding of early English drama, for it helps situate the drama in the larger contested category of literature, and it illuminates the relationships between drama and privacy, class, and gender. Even a masque, when performed for an aristocratic household, remains an insistently public occasion. What happens to the drama, then, in the privacy and silence of the book closet? And why was early English drama excluded from the Bodleian, the period's most ambitious public library, which had unique access after 1610 to every playbook printed in England?

### Reading Spaces

Between 1500 and 1650 in England, libraries and book ownership underwent a "period of revolution" (Jayne, 29) that included the introduction of vernacular drama into many sizable collections. Ecclesiastical institutions were the chief bookowners in England at the beginning of the period, but Henry VIII's dissolution of the monasteries in 1538–1539 shifted much of that ownership to private and university libraries (Jayne, 39–43). As ecclesiastical collections became less prominent, new institutional libraries took their place: the Bodleian opened in 1602, and the first independent town library was founded in Norwich in 1608.[3] The four fixed fields of medieval collections—theology, law, medicine, philosophy—gave way in many libraries to more dynamic subject categories, and libraries with only a few costly manuscripts yielded to collections dominated by printed books of various sizes and prices (Jayne, 29).

As library holdings increased in size and became more varied in content, the physical spaces that they occupied also changed. When Bodley undertook the project of restoring the University Library at Oxford, he found only the shell of Duke Humfrey's library, "which then in every part lay ruined and wast" (Bodley, 15). Not only the books but also all the furniture of the fifteenth-century library had been dispersed by the 1550s.[4] Much of Bodley's correspondence with Thomas James, the first keeper and librarian of the Bodleian, concerns the outfitting of this space. Desks, bookcases, cupboards, locks, chains—all these "mechanicall workes" consumed Bodley's attention. And when aristocratic families began to devote whole rooms to their book collections, they imitated institutional libraries like the Bodleian in furnishing them.[5]

By the 1630s, as large private libraries were becoming increasingly common, a new level of materiality shows up in the representations of book collections on the English stage. Bookish characters fret upon the stage, surrounded by the tools and fruits of their preoccupation, denounced by their fellows as "booke-wormes." In Beaumont and Fletcher's *The Elder Brother* (1637), Thomas Nabbes's *Tottenham*

*Court* (1638), and Henry Glapthorne's *Wit in a Constable* (1640), young men have given themselves over not only to the mental world of books but to all its paraphernalia as well: book receipts, bookcases, and bookworms. *Wit in a Constable*, for instance, opens with a discussion of the organization and shipment of Jeremy Hold-fast's increasingly unwieldy library, which is beginning to show signs of decay. Unlike Marlowe's Faustus and Shakespeare's Prospero, who mystify books, Hold-fast brings with him onto the stage the thud of books. Title pages, too, dramatize the presence of books on the stage and the physical realities of bookowning. George Ruggle's *Ignoramus* (1630) and Edward Forsett's *Pedantius* (1631), for instance, were each printed with a frontispiece engraving of the title character backed by a shelf of papers and books, the titles of which can be discerned on the fore-edges of the volumes.[6]

Like the producers of plays and playbooks, critics of the theater also focused increasingly on the materiality and physical bulk of playbooks. In the letter "To the Christian Reader" of *Histrio-mastix*, the virulent antitheatrical tract for which the author got his ears cropped, William Prynne laments that more luxurious materials are used in the production of playbooks than of Scripture:

> Some Play-books since I first undertooke this subject, are growne from *Quarto* into *Folio*; which yet beare so good a price and sale, that I cannot but with griefe relate it, they are now (e) new-printed in farre better paper than most Octavo or Quarto *Bibles*, which hardly finde such vent as they.

Prynne annotates this passage with a reference to Shakespeare's Second Folio in a marginal complaint about paper stock: "(e) Shackspeers Plaies are printed in the best Crowne paper, far better than most Bibles." Particularly in a polemic subtitled "the players scourge," such attention to the book as an object suggests the importance of the playbook itself in the antitheatrical debates. The materiality that Prynne seizes upon—format and paper stock—signifies for him the lure of playbooks in the marketplace where they find such successful "vent."

Even as Sir Thomas Bodley excludes from his library "an infinit number [of unworthy books], that are daily printed," he envisions the proliferation in gossip of any English playbooks that are admitted:

> And though they should be but a fewe . . . yet the hauing of those fewe (suche is the nature of malicious reporters) would be mightily multiplied by suche as purpose to speake in disgrace of the Librarie. (WHEELER, *James*, 221–22)

Despite the universally small formats of playbooks before 1616 and the near absence of any vernacular drama in the Bodleian in 1612, when this letter was written, Bodley again reveals his attention to the physical bulk of "baggage books" when he imagines critics exaggerating not the content but the number of playbooks. With slightly more basis in reality, this vision of "mightily multiplying" playbooks reappears in William Prynne's polemic two decades later. Sharing Bodley's astuteness to the growing numbers of playbooks, Prynne excuses the tremendous bulk of his thousand-page *Histrio-mastix* by citing the profusion of playbooks:

And can then one *Quarto* Tractate against Stage-playes be thought too large, when as it must assault such ample Play-house *Volumes*? Besides, our *Quarto*-Play-bookes since the first sheetes of this my Treatise came unto the Presse, have come forth in such * abundance, and found so many customers, that they almost exceed all number, one studie being scarce able to holde them, and two yeares time too little to peruse them all: And this made this Treatise swell the greater, because these Play-bookes are so multiplied. ("TO THE CHRISTIAN READER")

While most of *Histrio-mastix* focuses on the perils of the playhouse, Prynne isolates the playbook here, stressing the threat that it poses. In a printed marginal note, he claims that more than 40,000 playbooks have been printed and sold in the past two years. For Prynne, playbooks are dangerous precisely because they take up too much time and too much room—at bookstalls and in studies where they may crowd out worthier books.

Prynne's calculations are telling, for his figure of 40,000 must refer to individual books rather than editions. If an average edition ran roughly 1,000 copies in the early seventeenth century, Prynne's figure of 40,000 playbooks would translate to forty editions for these two years, a number identical to W. W. Greg's tally of new and reprinted professional plays in 1631 and 1632.[7] The distinction between playbook and play text is important because it reveals both the obsession and the exaggeration in Prynne's polemic: no one would "peruse" or collect into "one studie" all *copies* of all plays printed in 1631 and 1632. Forty or so individual plays, on the other hand, would take up less than two feet of shelf space in a study, even if they were individually bound, and a reader would make much faster work of them than two years' time.[8] To dramatize the threat of the proliferating press, however, Prynne piles up all the printed volumes against which his *"one* Quarto Tractate" must vie. (Had he reminded the Christian Reader that 999 other copies of the hefty *Histrio-mastix* might join in the "assault," the reader might not have worried so.)

Prynne's and Bodley's insistent, exaggerated emphases on the physical space that playbooks occupy may well reflect contemporary anxieties about the space of the playhouse and even the changing space of London. The constellation of words that Bodley uses in association with playbooks—"riffe raffe," "baggage," "idle," "rowme," "multitude"—revolves around twin concerns about the lower classes and crowded spaces. These concerns meet in the word *vulgar*: the quality of a mob (from the Latin *vulgus*), which is both debased and populous. Throughout his letters to his librarian, Bodley appeals to notions of worth and nobility, alerting James to books that are "not worthy the buieng," "not worth the taking," "hardly worth the hauing," "not worth the custody" for so noble a library.[9] The language that Bodley uses for these books locates his distaste within a discourse of class: the nobility of his library stands in opposition to "riffe raffe bookes," "baggage bookes," and "idle bookes" (35, 171, 219, 222). Bodley had referred with similar disdain to the workmen at the Library as "all that idle rabble" (Wheeler, *James*, 1). In its primary contemporary meaning, *riffe raffe* refers to people of the lowest social class: "persons of disreputable character or belonging to the lowest class of community" and "refuse or scum of a community . . . the rabble" (*OED*). Similarly, meanings of *baggage* include "a worthless or vile fellow" (1594) and "a strumpet" (1596). The application of these words to books exposes Bodley's appeal to taste and inherent worth as an anxiety about access and social hierarchy.

Bodley's insistent anthropomorphizing of playbooks with these words resonates with much of the antitheatrical literature in early modern England and with the social and material conditions of the London public playhouses. "Riffe raffe," "baggage," and the "idle" were precisely the people figured in the antitheatrical tracts as playgoers. In an early account, *A Third Blast of Retrait from Plaies and Theaters* (1580), a "worshipful and zealous Gentleman" imagines the scene at a playhouse:

> Whosoeuer shal visit the chappel of Satan, I meane the Theater, shal finde there no want of yong ruffins, nor lacke of harlots, vtterlie past al shame . . . yea, they seeme there to be like brothels of the stews. (89)

By 1615, in *A Refutation of the Apology for Actors*, J.G. can "particularize" his list of the "vulgar sort" who "runne madding vnto playes": prophane gallants, city dames, country clowns, bawds, whores, courtesans, cutpurses, pickpockets, knaves, and youths (I1–I1ᵛ).[10]

The public playhouses, like playbooks, were linked not merely to the "riffe raffe" but to large numbers of them. The *Third Blast* bemoans "with what multitudes those idle places are replenished" (65); J.G. recounts an accident that befell "a great multitude" at the theater (F3); and Thomas Platter recalls the "great swarms" of prostitutes at the playhouses (175). During the two decades following the opening of commercial theaters in 1576, the population of London doubled. And throughout the century, the number of vagrants and "masterless men" was growing—a social crisis countered by a series of royal acts, culminating in the Elizabethan Poor Laws in the 1590s.[11] A disproportionate number of these "baggage" and "idle riffe raffe" occupied the spaces surrounding the playhouses. The theaters shared Southwark with brothels; these suburbs, which were the poorest neighborhoods in London, were home to the "refuse or scum of the community"—prostitutes, lepers, exiles, vagrants, criminals.[12] Therefore, when Bodley repeatedly dismisses playbooks as "idle," "riffe raffe," "baggage" books, he invokes a set of social anxieties and transfers contemporary concerns about playhouses onto playbooks.

Many of Bodley's contemporaries, particularly critics of the theater, similarly viewed playbooks and performances as points on a continuum: playbooks, albeit less subversive than the performances themselves, nevertheless were tainted by their association with the stage. For Prynne, the reading of playbooks is one of the activities that consume the "Play-haunter" (***2ᵛ, 307, 309). Most telling, perhaps, are Prynne's references throughout *Histrio-mastix* to playbooks as "play*house* books," a phrase that links the printed texts not to a notion of the author or printer but to the arena of performance itself. The expression further suggests Prynne's inability to separate the playbook from the playhouse. Indeed, the printed texts support this association: of the 500 or so extant plays published during the reign of Charles I, 150 name the playhouse in which they were performed on the title page (Gurr, *Playgoing*, 76).

While the reading of plays was associated with attendance at the theater, the two sites—the study and the stage—were often opposed to one another. Young men at the Inns of Court, for instance, are satirized for making the playhouse "their Studie."[13] To read a play in a study was often figured as a paradox, for it gave the activity of reading a play a degree of seriousness—literally, of studiousness—not usually accorded it. In a poem in Abraham Cowley's *Poeticall Blossomes* (1636), a young schoolboy curses a "Semy-gentleman of th'Innes of Court" who has offended him: "may hee / Bee by his Father in his study tooke / At *Shakespeares* Playes, instead of my L. *Cooke*" ("A Poeticall Revenge" E5$^v$-E6).

Where then were plays read? In a prefatory address to *The Roaring Girle* (1611), Thomas Middleton presents his "book" as "fit for many of your companies . . . and [the book] may be allowed both gallery-room at the playhouse, and chamber-room at your lodging" ("To the comic Play-readers"). Middleton's presentation of the "gallery-room" and "chamber-room" as alternative spaces for his play suggests a continuity between the watching and reading of plays. One seventeenth-century gentlewoman documents this fluidity between the two activities. Deprived of the opportunity to attend the theater in London, Ann Merricke turns to her books instead:

> I cu'd wish my selfe with you, to ease you of this trouble, and with-all to see the Alchymist, which I heare this tearme is revis'd, and the newe playe a freind of mine sent to Mr. John Sucklyn, and Tom: Carew (the best witts of the time) to correct, but for want of these gentile recreationes, I must content my selfe here, with the studie of Shackspeare, and the historie of woemen, All my countrie librarie.[14]

Writing to her friend Mistress Lydall, Merricke presents the reading of Shakespeare as a substitute for playgoing, something with which she may "content" herself. For Merricke, the relation between a performance and a playbook seems based upon a dichotomy between city and countryside: in London, she has the playhouse; in the country, her library.

As Middleton's preface suggests, early modern scenes of reading occur in many sites—galleries, bedchambers, gardens, parlors, coffeehouses—yet it is in the library, the book closet, or the still more modest "chestful of books" that these scenes originate. During the period 1500–1650, the spaces in which early modern readers made "rowme" for their books were evolving. Among aristocratic families, records of books stored in chests and trunks give way to inventories of entire closets and studies stocked with books.[15] Certainly, books were taking up more space as private collections grew in size; they were also, however, occupying a space that was becoming increasingly private and specialized. In his discussion of the rise in "personal privacy" in the seventeenth century, Lawrence Stone demonstrates the emergence of a sense of "architectural privacy": interior, separate, specialized rooms—like the study—provided previously unavailable opportunities for seclusion. While such architectural developments bear most directly on lives of the aristocracy, the houses of yeomen and tradesmen also "became more varied, more subdivided and more specialized in function" during this period (L. Stone, *Family*, 254–55). The book closet, or indeed any closet, may be distinguished from a chamber on the basis not of size but of accessibility and the potential for privacy: a chamber has two or more doors while a closet has one.[16]

Often seen as the exclusive domain of male householders,[17] book closets served also as rooms for women. Even at the beginning of the period, household inventories document the presence of paired closets, one for the lord and one for the lady. Often it is this physical separation of men's and women's books that leaves a trace in the historical record: when a woman's books take up a discrete and gendered space like a wife's book closet, a listing of her collection may survive in household records. The household accounts of the fifth earl of Northumberland refer in 1512 to "my Lord's Library" and "my Lady's Library"; Sir William More records in 1556 the contents "In my *wyfes* closet," as well as those "In myne owne closette." An inventory in 1586 lists thirty "bookes and reliques" in the studies of siblings George, Elizabeth, and Briget Brome.[18] By the seventeenth century, mentions of women's book closets are common among the gentry. Lady Anne Clifford writes of spending a winter day in 1617 with a book in her closet while her lord read in his closet (Clifford, 47). And in 1679, an advertisement in *The Domestick Intelligence* records a list of books "Stollen from the Lady Mohun, out of her Closet on Tuesday night."[19]

While no book closet survives in its original state from the sixteenth century (Girouard, 166), contemporary architectural designs and household inventories preserve a glimpse of what such rooms contained and how they may have functioned. Along with books, these closets held a range of other objects: scientific equipment, sea compasses, "watch-clocks," glass bottles, spice boxes, footstools, taffeta curtains, even petticoats.[20] Many contained a good deal of furniture—cabinets, cupboards, shelves, stools, desks, chairs—and Elizabeth Freke's was self-sufficient enough to have its own fireplace.[21] Certainly by the seventeenth century, people were reading in their closets. I turn now to an assessment of what early modern men and women may have been reading in the changing spaces of public and private libraries.

## Holdings of the Bodleian and Private Libraries

The catalogs of the Bodleian, compiled by Thomas James and printed in 1605, 1620, and 1635, provide a useful counterpart to Bodley's letters because they suggest the control his policies exercised over the library's acquisitions. Three years after it opened, the Bodleian recorded in its first catalog a collection of more than five thousand titles, only three of which were classified as English literature and none of which was vernacular drama (Philip, *Bodleian*, 32–33). Yet, after Bodley's death, a few "Almanackes, plaies, & proclamacions" had found their way into the collection by 1620, as its benefactor had feared.[22] But, in general, Bodley's disdain for playbooks and his favoring of Latin and Continental over English literature appear to have been successful. For example, one of the few English playwrights in the 1620 catalog, Thomas Dekker, is represented by his one work with a Latin title, *Troia Nova Triumphans*, a pageant celebrating the mayor's entry into London.

A 1610 agreement with the Stationers' Company entitled the library to "one perfect Booke" of every work newly printed by members of the company. This agreement should have introduced far more vernacular drama into the collection than is recorded in the 1620 catalog. While this agreement faltered and nearly collapsed after 1640, it nevertheless became the library's "main, though imperfect, source of English books."[23] The 1620 catalog, however, does not record a single one of the plays by Beaumont and Fletcher, Jonson, Marlowe, or Shakespeare that the library might have obtained through this arrangement. Similarly, the catalog lists Webster's elegy for Prince Henry but not his play *The White Divel* (1612), even though the two quartos were printed within a year of each other.[24] Though members of the Stationers' Company were dilatory about depositing new books, the staff of the Bodleian failed, at the very least, to insist upon its rights to these books of vernacular drama.[25] And it is likely, too, that many playbooks were rejected by the library after their deposit by the Stationers' Company.

In 1640, the Bodleian greatly increased its store of English drama when Robert Burton bequeathed to the library all of his books that the Bodleian "hath not" (Kiessling, vii–ix). By the terms of the will, John Rous, the Bodleian's second librarian, sorted through more than 1,700 books, ultimately augmenting the university library by 872 volumes (vii–viii). At the end of his record of the books taken from Burton's collection, Rous characterizes the bequest and explains his basis for selection: "Among these [I chose] especially comedies, tragedies, poetry, and comic works mainly in the vernacular, collections which because of their multitude we have not added."[26] Although Rous in his choices effectively reverses Bodley's exclusion of "riffe raffe" books, he nevertheless, like Bodley, casts their earlier absence from the collection in terms of space: their "multitude" has made them impractical to collect.

From Burton's library, Rous plucked 417 books that he characterized as "English books" in quarto or octavo and 66 books that he described as "Maskes, Comedies, & Tragedies" (viii). The strengths of Burton's collection complemented the Bodleian's: 70 percent of the literature in Burton's library interested Rous, while only 20 percent of its philosophy added to the Bodleian's already rich holdings (ix). Among the "riffe raffe" books the Bodleian acquired from Burton are ten plays and entertainments by Heywood, nine by Beaumont and Fletcher, eight by Shirley, six by Chapman, six by Middleton, four by Jonson, and three by Webster. Rous's choices reveal at once the range of Burton's collection of popular literature and the narrowness of the Bodleian's. Burton, for example, owned nearly half of all the Shirley plays printed before his death in 1640, while not one seems to have found its way into the Bodleian, even though all might have been obtained through the Bodleian's agreement with the Stationers' Company.

Although Rous had the good sense to snap up the "baggage books" that Bodley had scorned, he recorded them in categories much as Bodley might have, separating the English books from the Latin ones and cataloging drama in a field of its own. Further, only the Latin titles were copied from Rous's list and entered into the Benefactors' Register (viii), a book that Bodley had taken great care to establish as an incentive to potential donors. Absent from this register, the bulk of the bequest, therefore, quite literally went unrecognized. Many of Burton's playbooks were also not entered by hand into the Bodleian's copy of the 1620 catalog, the interleaved copy that ordinarily was updated with new titles and made available to readers. In fact, seven of the nine plays by Beaumont and Fletcher were not listed until the publication of the 1843 catalog (Philip, *Bodleian*, 33). Therefore, although the Bodleian had yielded some "rowme" to drama by 1640, it neither acknowledged the acquisitions fully nor made them accessible to readers.

Was Bodley's scorn for drama typical of a group of book collectors, or was he trying to set a standard that few of his contemporaries observed in their private collections? Bodley's correspondence itself suggests that his opinions were not universally held and that the gaps in his collection were exceptional in the period. Although their disagreement is muted, Bodley's standards for the library's acquisitions seem to have been a point of contention with his librarian, James. Even after years of working with James, Bodley corrects him for admitting unsuitable books:

> Sir, I would yow had foreborne, to catalogue our London bookes, till I had bin priuie to *your* purpose. There are many idle bookes, & riffe raffes among them, which shall neuer com into the Librarie, & I feare me that litle, which yow haue done alreadie, will raise a scandal vpon it.[27]

Bodley differentiates here between his purpose and James's; had he been "priuie" to James's intentions sooner, he clearly would have intervened. And, in a letter written two weeks later, Bodley seems to respond to a challenge to his judgment:

> I can see no good reason to alter my opinion, for excluding suche bookes . . . as, me thinkes, both the keeper & vnderkeeper should disdaine to seeke out, to deliuer vnto any man. (221–22)

Thus, within the institution itself, there seems to have been debate about the admission of books. Even among the contributions from James's own library, Bodley singles out several copies for inspection:

> Of your lesser bookes . . . [and] some fewe other litle ones, because I knowe them not, and and [*sic*] make doubt of their goodnesse, I leaue to your owne discretion, to keepe, or reiect.[28]

James's apparently greater tolerance for vernacular "lesser bookes" shows up as well in his role in establishing the Bodleian as a deposit library for the Stationers'

Company. After securing the grant of deposit copies from the company, Bodley recognizes James's foresight: "I thinke I had hardly thought vpon it, if yow had not moued the mater at first" (Wheeler, *James*, 206).

James, not Bodley, seems to have been more representative of contemporary attitudes toward book acquisition. For James and Bodley were not lurking about the stalls of St. Paul's or approaching chapbook peddlers and trying to buy "riffe raffe bookes": they were, for the most part, sorting through the donations of aristocrats whom Bodley had courted and buying books from a select group of Oxford and London booksellers. The "London bookes" that provoked disagreement between Bodley and James, for instance, do not include deposits from the Stationers' Company, for the same letter notes that the master of the company "hath not taken any order" yet (Wheeler, *James*, 219). Among the earliest donors to the library were Lords Essex and Hunsdon and Sir Robert Sidney (Wheeler, *Oxford*, 7–8). Yet it is in these collections that Bodley finds cause for alarm.

Bodley's suspicions about the contents of donors' collections were justified: "riffe raffe bookes" *do* appear in his contemporaries' libraries and catalogs. Sir John Harington (1560–1612) cataloged 130 playbooks in his collection, including 15 titles by Shakespeare and most of Jonson's works (Furnivall); Edward 2nd Viscount Conway (1594–1665) owned 350 English playbooks, enough to make one scholar believe that Conway was buying playbooks on a "standing order" (Birrell, 123–24). Henry Oxinden (1608–1670) listed in his commonplace book 123 playbooks, most of which were printed before 1610. While Oxinden's playbooks were probably collected by someone before him, they nevertheless seem to have been part of an active library; an annotation in the list records the lending of *Roister Doister* and another playbook to Sir Basil in 1665 (Dawson, "Early"). Ralph Sheldon (d. 1684) owned 56 bound volumes of plays, perhaps as many as 560 individual titles (Birrell, 114). The Bridgewater House library, one of the largest seventeenth-century family collections, contained plays by Chapman, Dekker, Ford, Marlowe, Middleton, Shakespeare, and Webster.[29] Henry Hastings, the fifth earl of Huntingdon, added to his sizable library parcels of books that included Shakespeare's works in folio and "1 Maides Tragedy," as well as several proclamations. One of the more well-connected peers in Stuart England, Hastings purchased books and pamphlets valued at six pence or less.[30]

Playbooks also show up in smaller collections and in non-aristocratic collections. Jonson's *Works* is one of four volumes listed in the custody of Sir Richard Temple (1634–1697), while "Sheakspears plays" is one of six "in My Lady Temple's Custody" (Huntington Library manuscript STT CL&I, box 2). Frances Wolfreston (1607–1677) signed her name in ten Shakespeare quartos (Morgan), and a Cambridge physician listed several playbooks under the heading "pamphlets" in his library catalog, among which were Marlowe's *Edward II* and a *True Tragedy of Richard Duke of York*, which Pollard and Redgrave describe as a "mangled" version of *3 Henry VI* (F. R. Johnson, 91).

Hastings's purchases of cheap pamphlets and playbooks suggest the striking range of aristocratic book acquisition. As T. A. Birrell argues, seventeenth-century "reading habits are not stratified into peasant, bourgeois and gentry—gentry reading tastes were inclusive, and included the tastes of the peasants and the bourgeois" (113). Further, he points out that most extant copies of works of seventeenth-century popular literature have as their provenance gentry libraries (113). And indeed, at least one contemporary handbook on the furnishing of a library encouraged the prospective book collector to buy a range of works. Translated by John Evelyn as *Instructions Concerning Erecting of a Library* (1661), Gabriel Naudé's *Advis pour dresser une Bibliothèque* (1627) recommends that the reader collect all sorts of books because "there is no Book whatsoever, be it never so bad or decried, but may in time be sought for by some person or other."[31] Bodley, of course, would think that a person seeking a "decried" book had no place in his library.

As part of the effort to make a library as complete and useful as possible, Naudé advises his readers to supplement their collections with catalogs of other libraries' holdings, urging them to make transcriptions of

> all the Catalogues, not only of the great and most famous Libraries, . . . but also of the *Studies* and *Cabinets*, which for not being much known, or visited, remain buried in perpetual silence. (13–14)

Naudé's emphasis on private libraries suggests the richness of their holdings and their distinctiveness from "great Libraries." And certainly the case of Burton's bequest to the Bodleian indicates that a reader might find quite a different shelf of books in a private cabinet than in an institutional library.

Unfortunately, Naudé's description of the catalogs of these cabinet libraries as "not being much known, or visited" might also apply to their status for modern scholars. Records of private book holdings survive in many different forms, most of which have not received adequate scholarly attention: ownership stamps and signatures in extant books, references in journals and correspondence, passages in commonplace books, representations in portraits, accounts in biographies, and lists in probate inventories, household inventories, and library catalogs. Working primarily with this last group of sources—book lists—three scholars have done much to dig up what had threatened to "remain buried in perpetual silence." Sears Jayne locates and briefly describes 574 early private libraries, and Elisabeth Leedham-Green has produced a massive edition of 241 Cambridge inventories that contain books. Together, Leedham-Green and Robert Fehrenbach are editing *Private Libraries in Renaissance England* (*PLRE*), a project that makes available, both in bound volumes and in a database, annotated transcriptions of early modern book lists. By gathering previously published work in one place and greatly expanding upon it, *PLRE* should enlarge scholars' understanding of early modern book collecting and reading.

Despite the important contributions of each of these works, all three have biases that limit their usefulness in determining the place of drama in early modern libraries. The limitations to *PLRE* apply only to its current status: the editorial team is in the process of completing its survey of Oxford inventories, and as of August 1995, only inventories taken through 1576 had been entered into the database. Jayne, Leedham-Green, and *PLRE* (at present) all focus on Oxbridge collections, with inventories from the 1590s or earlier dominating the studies. Only a tiny percentage of early English drama had been printed before the 1590s; furthermore, scholarly libraries are unlikely to have held much drama during a period when English literature did not constitute a field of study. And, indeed, among the 4,188 titles currently listed in *PLRE* as having come from Oxford inventories, only 78 can be classified as drama, and all but one of these titles are in Latin or Greek. Even this one work of vernacular drama, an "English tragedie," is probably a translation of Seneca.[32] While Leedham-Green's *Books in Cambridge Inventories* has the advantage of stretching into the eighteenth century, only a handful of works of vernacular drama appears in her lists.

Even though very few playbooks show up in their studies, both Fehrenbach and Leedham-Green express the conviction that early modern libraries contained far more "riffe raffe" than they reveal (Fehrenbach in conversation, July 29, 1995; Leedham-Green, xiii). As Rous's failure to register each of Burton's playbooks obscures the presence of drama in the Bodleian, so too drama in private libraries may remain hidden from view. While issues of taste and decorum encouraged some bookowners to catalog their Coke but not their Shakespeare, the probate inventory system probably accounted for many more omissions. From 1521 on, a probate inventory upon decease was required by law, and from the 1520s through the 1590s, these inventories seem to have been conducted ordinarily with care and precision. After the 1590s, however, book lists in probate inventories become more cursory and far less detailed.[33] As it happens, during the period when scholars are most likely to find complete lists of book holdings (1521–c. 1590), almost no vernacular drama was in print.

While probate inventories may offer the most systematic way of determining the book ownership of large groups of people below the level of the gentry, they do not provide a full view of these collections, especially after 1590. Books, because of their low value, were often thrown together with other "household stuffes" or "goods in the study" (Clark, "Ownership," 98). The binding of a book figured significantly in its appraisal value; a phrase like "other books," therefore, may "conceal, among other things, a quantity of current vernacular literature not deemed worth the binding" (Leedham-Green, xiii).

Prices for individual playbooks typically ranged from two pence to eight pence, with folio versions of complete works costing far more. At a time when two pence was the usual minimum price for any printed work other than a broadside, playbooks were among the cheapest books available.[34] In general, such cheap books did not often survive long. Especially if their owners never bothered to have them bound, these books would have fallen apart easily, or they may have been discarded as mere ephemera (Clark, "Ownership," 103). The demand for paper meant too that cheap print was often converted to other uses in an early modern version of recycling (Spufford, *Small*, 48–50). When the bookish character in Glapthorne's play *Wit in a Constable* (1640) resolves to disperse all his books in order to become "new read" in love, his servant suggests giving them to a cook, who could use the "Rhemes of paper . . . to put under his bake meates" (B3). Even if a playbook or pamphlet did survive and was not immediately put to some such household use, most small books were of too little value to show up in probate inventories.[35] The absence of a title from an inventory, therefore, does not necessarily indicate the absence of a book from a collection.

Household inventories and library catalogs promise a more nearly complete view of book ownership. Less economically driven, these lists often document a much broader range of works than do the probate inventories, and they usually do so with a greater level of specificity. The book lists that document private holdings of "riffe raffe bookes" begin to reveal the status of vernacular drama in these libraries. Some catalogs show signs that vernacular drama did have a different status even from other works of English literature. The 1628 inventory of Sir Edward Dering's library identifies more than 628 books, among which are "27 playbookes . . . ten playbookes . . . 2 Allmanackes." With a few exceptions, Dering "very uncharacteristically . . . never names the author or title of the playbooks" in his otherwise meticulous catalog (Krivatsy and Yeandle, 141). Similarly, Frances Egerton, countess of Bridgewater, counted among her 241 books in 1633 several works of vernacular drama, including Jonson's *Gypsies masque* and *The New Inne*, Greville's *Tragedy of Mustapha*, "Diverse plays by Shakespeare," and seven other volumes of "diverse plays." These seven untitled volumes are specified not by author or title but rather by their bindings: "A booke of Diuerse plays in velum," "A booke of diuerse plays in leather," and "Diuerse plays in 5 thicke volumes in velum."[36]

Although one might easily argue that Edward Dering and Frances Egerton must have considered these playbooks as "lesser books" not worthy of careful bibliographical attention, Dering and Egerton seem otherwise to have been enthusiastic collectors of and participants in early English drama. Egerton performed in several of Jonson's masques at court, and her own children acted in Milton's *Comus*. Dering also was a great supporter of drama; his account books record many outings to the theater in London and small donations to masquers, and he seems to have staged private theatricals in his home. He was a voracious buyer of playbooks, purchasing as many as 159 playbooks in one two-month period in 1623 (Krivatsy and Yeandle, 141). Why, then, do Dering and Egerton pass so quickly over the drama in their collections? One answer is suggested by the other vague entries in these catalogs: Shakespeare's plays, French songs, and theological tracts are all listed in equally unspecific terms in Egerton's otherwise detailed catalog. They are linked here, as in other contemporary book lists, not by the cataloger's notion of their inherent value or ephemerality but by a set of material circumstances. The entries for Egerton's "Three Bookes of French Songes," "Three small Treatises of Divinity in one volume," and "Diverse playes in 5 thicke volumes" document books composed of several small works, for bookowners tended to bind slim quartos together, if at all, and early catalogers typically recorded only whole volumes, not individual titles. Indeed, it was a significant gesture to catalog quarto playbooks at all, given their physical slightness and low appraisal value.

Other large "Cabinet" libraries unequivocally reveal an interest in and inclusion of vernacular drama quite at odds with Bodley's disdain. In a family notebook, Sir John Harington listed the 130 plays that would have disappeared in an entry like "Diverse playes in 11 thicke volumes." Humphrey Dyson similarly recorded all of his book acquisitions, giving titles and prices for works as cheap as two pence, including three of Jonson's masques (F. R. Johnson). The catalog of Sir Roger Townshend's library, taken c. 1625, lists the titles of several small books and sensational pamphlets along with five English plays. Such a list, Fehrenbach argues, merely records what other bookowners like Edward Dering did not detail (81–82). That is, when we do get a full, seemingly complete book list, it includes much that Bodley would have classed as ephemera.

Along with the bibliographic details in catalogs, the handling, arranging, and dispersal of playbooks also provide a glimpse of the place of drama in these collections. While many playbooks were never bound, some bookowners, like Harington, did take care to preserve their quartos. Frances Egerton, as shown above, had her playbooks bound in leather and vellum. Bequests and reports of theft, which alternately prescribe or lament the dispersal of a collection, also indicate the value placed upon playbooks. In 1635, Richard Langhorne, a citizen and apothecary of London, divided his possessions: "I giue & bequeath vnto my vnckle Mr Thomas Eaton my greate guilte bible in folio, Item, I giue & bequeath to mr. Iohn Legatt My book of mr. Shakespeare's workes" (Honigmann and Brock, 5). Besides evoking the competition that Prynne sets up between Scripture and drama, this bequest suggests that one Londoner valued his Shakespeare folio enough to name and allot it individually. Similarly, the collector Frances Wolfreston took great care with the organization of her library, which largely consisted of popular works, many of which were playbooks. In her will, Wolfreston insists upon the maintenance of the integrity of her collection:

> And I give my son Stanford all my phisicke bookes, and all my godly bookes, and all the rest conditionally if any of his brothers or sisters would have them any tyme to read, and when they have done they shall returne them to their places againe, and he shall carefully keepe them together. (MORGAN, 200–201)

This attention to a system of organization—to the placing of books—suggests the hand of a bookowner who was both deliberate and knowledgeable. Playbooks, however, were not always dispersed in such an orderly way; two late seventeenth-century bookowners announce the theft of their books. Lady Mohun, in offering a forty shilling reward for the return of her stolen books, lists two volumes of drama among the dozen named books in her advertisement, and a 1687 inventory names several books that "are supposed to have been purloined, & embeazelled away": Bishop Hall's *Works*, four of Jonson's *Works*, and two Shakespeare plays (Honigmann and Brock, 243). The desire of both the thieves and the owners for these playbooks suggests that drama did seem "worth the taking" and "worth the hauing," perhaps not to Bodley but certainly to many early modern men and women.

Harington and Wolfreston and Egerton in their handling of their playbooks demonstrate that vernacular drama—if not yet granted the security it has found at the Folger Shakespeare Library—was beginning to find "rowme" in private libraries. So at odds with Bodley's prescriptions for his library, these collections point to the existence among the elite of two radically different conceptions of the category of literature. These conflicting constructions of literature also suggest a necessary distinction between private collections and public libraries, which were, after all, a new phenomenon in early modern England. Irrelevant for the private library, issues of access prompt tremendous social anxiety for Bodley. Unable to control how his readers proceed once they gain access to the books in the Bodleian, Bodley can only stand guard at the door, monitoring both the books and the readers that enter.

NOTES

1. Alternately called the University or Public Library by contemporaries, the Bodleian admitted visitors and "gentlemen strangers" but did not allow undergraduates or, for a time, Bachelors of Arts (Wheeler, *James*, xxi). Even so, this policy was unusual enough for Gabriel Naudé to name the Bodleian in the 1620s as one of only three European libraries "where one may freely enter and without difficulty" (88). For the criteria for admission to the library, see Bodley's letter to the vice-chancellor of Oxford (Wheeler, *Oxford*, #6).

2. When he first proposed restoring the University Library, Bodley referred to the space of the former library as proof of its existence: "where there hath bin heretofore a publike library in Oxford: which you know is apparant, *by the rome it self remayning*, and by your statute records" (Wheeler, *Oxford*, 4). From the beginning of the project, it seems, the space itself was central to Bodley's conception of a great library.

3. T. Kelly, 74. The earliest recorded town library had opened by 1557 at Ludlow, but like many town libraries established during the period, it was a church library. Even the Norwich library, while independent of both church and school, was designed "for the use of preachers" (T. Kelly, 70–76 and app. 2).

4. Philip, *Bodleian*, 6. For a fuller discussion of the history of Duke Humfrey's library, see Gillam.

5. For a thorough discussion of the furnishing of the Bodleian, see Sturdy. Bookshelves were still novel when Bodley had them installed in his library; his use of them served as a model for the designs of country house libraries (Girouard, 166).

6. Greg reprints these engravings (*Bibliography*, 2:plates cix, cx), as does Foakes, who provides a discussion of the images (*Illustrations*, items 128–29, 132–33).

7. Prynne also cites the figure of 40,000 printed playbooks in the Epistle Dedicatory with the explanation that "(as Stationers informe mee,) they being more vendible than the choycest Sermons." For a thorough and persuasive account of efforts to estimate the average size of early modern editions, see Blayney (*Texts*, 33–39). As Blayney argues elsewhere in this volume, many plays were probably produced in runs well under 1,250 copies. Prynne may have used a lower edition size—like 800 copies—if he counted pageants and masques as well as plays, for another sixteen "non-professional" plays were printed in 1631–1632. I owe the tallies of reprints during these years to conversations with Peter Blayney.

8. I am grateful to the staff of the Folger Shakespeare Library for allowing me to assemble and measure a shelf of all the plays listed by Greg (*Bibliography*) and Harbage (*Annals*) for the years 1631–1632.

9. Wheeler, *James*, 40, 86, 118, 203. Spanning the period from 1599 to Bodley's death in 1613, this series of 231 letters lays out Bodley's vision for his library, describing in detail his wishes for the formation and administration of the Bodleian.

10. Jean Howard offers a shrewd analysis of this list (5). In her very useful chapter on antitheatrical tracts (22–46), she discusses the rhetoric of "idleness" in one treatise as a response to "some real changes in social and economic relations in sixteenth-century England" (23–29).

11. For a concise overview of poverty and vagrancy in the sixteenth century, see Gurr (*Playgoing*, 53–54) and Howard (26); for a fuller discussion, consult Beier, especially *Masterless*, 40–47, on overcrowding in London.

12. Gurr, *Playgoing*, 53, 57; Mullaney, 21–22. In chapters 1 and 2 of *The Place of the Stage*, Mullaney develops his discussion of these suburbs or "Liberties"—the space outside the city walls and "in a certain sense outside the law" (22).

13. Prynne, \*\*3ᵛ. A character in Thomas Nabbes's play *Tottenham Court* similarly defines "learning for a gentleman" as "*Iohnson* and *Shakespeare*" and "Playhouses" (27).

14. A summary of this letter, dated January 21, 1638/39, appears in the *Calendar of State Papers*, 13:342. I am grateful to David Kastan for this reference. I quote here from *The Shakspere Allusion-Book*, which excerpts this section (Munro, 1:443).

15. The architectural historian Mark Girouard locates this shift at the beginning of the seventeenth century (166).

16. I owe this distinction to Peter Blayney (private correspondence, January 30, 1996).

17. Orlin, 182–89. Orlin persuasively argues that "the study not only inaugurated the experience of a private behavior but also nourished the apprehension of individual selfhood" (188). She defines this "apprehension" as "modern (male) subjectivity" (183), and the female characters she discusses are clearly locked out of the householder's study. Other women, however, do seem to have had access to similarly private spaces in the closely related book closet.

18. Girouard, 164; Folger Library L.b.550; Jayne, 127. Jayne attributes these books without explanation to George, mentioning the sisters' studies only in passing.

19. I am grateful to William Burns for this reference.

20. These items appear in John Dee's description of his library and studies (Roberts and

Watson, 196–97) and in the inventories of Sir William and Lady More (Folger L.b.550) and the earl and countess of Bridgewater (Huntington Library EL 8094 and EL 6503). William Sherman analyzes Dee's "living library" in chapter 2 of *John Dee*, which presents the early library as "privy" rather than "private," that is, "less asocial and apolitical than selectively social and political" (50).

21. Freke inventories more than 103 books in her closet, 82 of which are "putt into the deep deale Deale [sic] Box by the Fireside In my own Closett" (Freke Papers, vol. 1, British Library MS 45718, f91ᵛ-92). I am grateful to Jennifer Stine for sharing her microfilm copy of this account with me.

22. The infiltrators were four proclamations, a lone "Christian Almanacke," and a handful of plays (T. James, 406, 16).

23. Philip, Introduction, x. The agreement was printed in January 1611 (STC 16786.12). Under this agreement, the Bodleian acquired Shakespeare's First Folio, which is listed in the 1635 appendix to the 1620 catalog. The library's policy of selling off duplicates, however, meant that the 1623 Folio was sold when the Third Folio arrived (Clement, 273; Madan, Turbutt, and Gibson, 5). Bidding against Henry C. Folger, the Bodleian recovered its copy in 1906 for £3,000 (Craster, 179–81).

24. A *Monumental Columne* (1613), STC 25174, is recorded as *Elegie for Henry* in the catalog.

25. Bodley's letters to James document the closing of the deal with the Stationers' Company and his early frustration with delays in the depositing of books (205, 206, 217). The problem persisted, and in 1635, the librarian of the Bodleian sought the chancellor's intervention in correcting the negligence of the Stationers' Company (*Calendar of State Papers*, 9:65). For an overview of the relations between the Bodleian and the Stationers' Company, see Philip, *Bodleian*, 27–30.

26. The Latin original reads "in his porro, Comoediarum, Tragediarum, et Schediasmatum et Ludicrorum praesertim idiomate vernaculo aliquot centurias, quas propter multitudinem non adjecimus" (viii–ix). I have modified Kiessling's version only by translating "multitudinem" as "multitude" rather than "number."

27. Wheeler, *James*, 219, emphasis mine. See also 118–19, 203–4, 221–22.

28. Wheeler, *James*, 3. James took the hint: none of these books made it into the 1605 catalog of the library (Wheeler, 3 n. 4).

29. A "List of Books in The Bridgewater House Library" was probably compiled shortly after the Huntington Library's acquisition of the collection in 1917.

30. Bookseller's bills, 1638–40. Historical Manuscripts Commission, 389–90. Although she focuses on popular fiction rather than on playbooks, Margaret Spufford provides a pertinent discussion of small, cheap books in *Small Books*.

31. *Instructions*, 20. Roger Chartier discusses Naudé's treatise in chapter 3 of his *The Order of Books*, focusing on the books that Naudé deems indispensable to a good library. Chartier's book also serves as a useful introduction to the history of reading.

32. I am very grateful to Robert Fehrenbach for running several database searches for me and, more generally, for sharing his rich store of knowledge about early modern libraries.

33. For an overview of probate inventories and the methodological problems they raise, see Leedham-Green, xi–xiv, and Jayne, 9–15.

34. F. R. Johnson, 91–112. Johnson demonstrates the constancy of book prices, despite infla-

tion, between 1560 and 1635 (89). Blayney argues against the notion that six pence was "a standard—or even the average—price for play-quartos" (*Texts*, 391), and he provides a trenchant critique of Johnson in his essay in this volume.

35. Clark, "Ownership," 103; Spufford, *Small Books*, 45–50. In one survey of 1,500 probate inventories, only five noted cheap "little books" priced under six pence, all of which were copies for sale (Spufford, 48).

36. Huntington MS EL 6495. An annotated transcription of the catalog appears as an appendix to my dissertation (Brayman, "Impressions").

# PART II

*Early English Drama and Social Space*

CHAPTER 8

# Theater and Religious Culture

*Paul Whitfield White*

IN THOMAS RANDOLPH's comedy *The Muses Looking-Glasse* (performed in 1630), two overzealous dissenters, Bird, a feather man, and Mistress Flowerdew, a haberdasher's wife, visit the playhouse to peddle their wares to the assembled audience:

> FLO. See Brother how the wicked throng and crowd
>    To works of Vanity! not a nooke, or corner
>    In all this house of sin, this cave of filthinesse,
>    This den of spirituall theeves, but it is stuff'd,
>    Stuffed, and stuff'd full as is a cushion
>    With the lew'd Reprobate.
> BIRD. Sister, were there not before Innes,
>    Yes I will say Inns, for my zeale bids me
>    Say filthy Innes, enough to harbour such
>    As travell'd to destruction on the broad way;
>    But they build more and more, more shops of Satan[?]
> FLOWRD. Iniquity aboundeth, though pure zeale
>    Teach, preach, huffe, puffe, and snuffe at it; yet still
>    Still it aboundeth. (RANDOLPH, Sig. A2)

For most of this century scholars have cited dramatic episodes such as this one to illustrate the confrontational nature of relations between theater and religion in early modern England. Indeed, the main theme of those relations in the traditional critical narrative is conflict, with religious authorities and zealots engaged in a battle to suppress a popular pastime and the playing community fighting back by caricaturing religious types on the stage. Although studies of major playwrights such as Shakespeare and Marlowe have long recognized theatrical engagement with religious questions, the bias persists that religion had little or no significant representation on the "Renaissance English stage," partly because censorship prohibited it and partly because those who really took their religion seriously after the Reformation—the puritans—would have no part of it, except to voice their opposition and disgust.[1]

Certainly English religion in the wake of the Reformation did unleash anxieties and generate new ways of looking at the world that created the type of hostility and distrust exhibited by Randolph's buffoons, especially when faced with the emergence of a secular, commercialized theater enterprise. But this is only part of the picture. As scholarship of the last two decades particularly has shown, there were many English subjects of strong religious conviction, including those who may be legitimately called puritans, who saw the stage in very different terms. They ranged from those with a personal investment in playing—sponsors, playwrights, and players—to those who simply looked to the playhouse, the banqueting hall, and the village green for recreation. Moreover, while censorship measures did impose some restrictions on controversial religious subject matter, issues from ecclesiastical reform to personal religious faith were frequently represented and debated in plays.

In the discussion that follows, I will begin by taking a closer look at indigenous religious drama and its interaction with early Reformation attitudes toward and intervention in theater. We will then consider the changes within theatrical practice and Protestantism itself in early Elizabethan England that complicated interaction between theater and religion, paradoxically spawning both antitheatrical criticism and a drama of religious controversy. My final concern will be to consider the representation of religion in the mainstream "secular" drama extending through to the closing of the commercial London playhouses in 1642.

## Traditional Drama and the Early Reformation

The single most important event—or chain of events—to change the course of religious life and culture in early modern England was the Reformation of Henry VIII. The 1534 Act of Royal Supremacy established the king in place of the pope as the head of the English church, and the seizure of monastic properties, chantries, and church ornaments followed to destroy much of the institutional basis of Roman Catholicism. A full-scale propagandist campaign supported the new legislation, banning allegiance to Rome and adherence to its creeds and many of its seasonal rituals (Dickens, 106–221; Haigh, 105–202).

Yet first-generation Protestantism did not engage in a root-and-branch suppression of the drama and other popular pastimes. Much of what we today call traditional "religious drama"—the mystery play cycles, moralities, and saint plays—survived, many well into Elizabeth's reign. Some of these plays continued to espouse Catholic teaching on transubstantiation, the veneration of saints, and the cult of the Virgin, and were performed under parish, municipal, and academic auspices that remained sympathetic to pre-Reformation religion and sensibilities. Evidently as late as 1603 a traditional passion play was still being staged at Kendall in Westmorland, and we will never know how many were performed in recusant households like the entertainment at the home of the Catholic gentleman Sir John Yorke of Nidderdale in early 1609. There a controversial interlude of a visiting troupe depicted a Catholic priest and a Protestant minister, concluding with the preacher "being carried off by devils, amidst flashes of fire" (I. Lancashire, *Dramatic*, 234; Watt, 30–31; Greenblatt, *Shakespearean*, 121–22).

Better known today are the great mystery play cycles staged during summer holy days in towns of the north and southwest. They too preserved Catholic values and sensibilities before religious and economic changes caught up with them. The banning of the feast of Corpus Christi in 1548 undermined the religious occasion for the old cycles, and by 1580 those at York, Chester, Coventry, and Wakefield had ceased to be performed. Suppression by Protestant censorship is usually harnessed with the blame for this (Gardiner; Duffy, 579–82), and certainly the ecclesiastical Court of High Commission in the north, in some instances egged on by zealous Protestant preachers and their adherents, played a significant role. Yet it is equally important to recognize that the mystery cycles were intricately connected to the economic and cultural institutions of the towns that sponsored them, and consequently when the northern towns faced grave financial problems, along with the unraveling of their socioreligious guilds, as they did in the mid-sixteenth century, they could no longer afford the vast expenditures necessary to mount the cycle productions (Womack, 103–4; Bills; I. Lancashire, *Dramatic*, xxxi).

What's more, all the major cycles, some as early as Edward VI's reign, made an effort to expunge popish elements offensive to Protestant authorities and to revise play scripts to meet the demands of Reformation orthodoxy. In some instances local leaders may have felt pressured to do this to save a popular pastime and source of civic pride, but there is no reason to doubt that some local Protestants initiated the changes to reform a legitimate means of recreation and religious instruction. Certainly this was the case at Shrewsbury, where the Passion play was thoroughly Protestantized and attracted between ten and twenty thousand spectators in the 1560s, and in Kilkenny, Ireland, where a scaled-down version of a Protestant mystery cycle was staged in 1553 (Somerset, "Local"; Bale, 1:6–7).

Indeed, the evidence is clear that Protestant leaders appropriated the drama for propaganda purposes of their own. As Henry VIII's Reformation vicegerent of religion, Thomas Cromwell, organized state-sanctioned propaganda for the stage during the 1530s. He and his talented office of publicists recognized that in a nation that remained to a large extent illiterate, especially in those outlying regions where Catholicism was most firmly entrenched, drama communicated ideology effectively and entertainingly to the general public in concrete visual and oral terms. Since the institutions responsible for producing drama remained firmly intact after the Reformation, the Crown, with its many loyal officials strategically placed throughout the realm, could exercise some measure of control over the stage and exploit it, along with the pulpit and the press, as a means of drawing the people away from residual Catholicism and winning broad support for its Reformation policy (P. W. White, 13–15).

The players most active in performing Reformation drama appear to have been professional touring troupes under the direct sponsorship of the Crown and the nobility, as well as amateur players affiliated with the nation's academic institutions. Not surprisingly, the new generation of Protestant aristocracy, who richly benefited from the dissolution of the monasteries and had much to lose from a Catholic restoration, were active proponents of religious reform and used their household players to advance the cause of reform. No fewer than six members of Edward VI's Privy Council known to have supported Protestantism were patrons of acting companies recorded for performances in civic and ecclesiastical records across the realm. Moreover, the leading supporters of Protestant preachers and printers during the early years of Elizabeth's reign, the earls of Leicester and Warwick and the duchess of Suffolk, were also the patrons of the nation's most prestigious and widely traveled acting companies. Although the repertories of their troupes have been lost, the numerous Protestant interludes surviving from the period were clearly written for professional troupes of this kind and closely correspond in religious subject matter with the sermons and devotional writings sponsored by these Protestant noble patrons (P. W. White, 204, 56–66).

One major Protestant nobleman's troupe was Bale and His Fellows, which performed under the sponsorship of Lord Thomas Cromwell from about 1538 until Cromwell's death in 1541. The leader of this company, the reformer John Bale, wrote twenty-three plays (many, he said, for an earlier troupe patron, the earl of Oxford), and the five that survive (*King Johan, Three Laws, God's Promises, John the Baptist's Preaching*, and *The Temptation of Our Lord*) indicate that he assigned himself prominent acting parts in a troupe made up of five adult players. All of Bale's extant plays are modeled on medieval dramatic conventions and vigorously champion Cromwell's objectives for reform in the late 1530s when Bale's company of players is on record for three extensive tours to the provinces.

*King Johan* (c. 1538), for example, treats the Papacy as a foreign political institution that surreptitiously uses its clerical agents and ceremonies to gain dominion over the English state and overthrow divinely sanctioned monarchical authority. Recognizing the significance of visual images to Catholic authority (e.g., clerical vestments) and worship (e.g., the sacraments, relics, icons), Bale found his most effective weapon was to present those revered images before spectators only to discredit them by depriving them of their original sacred context, substituting a profane or diabolical one instead. Thus the Vice characters in *King Johan* parody genuflecting priests performing the rites of auricular confession and excommunication to expose popish priests as actors, their rites as good theater. Bale's plays reflect Crown fears that while the doctrine of papal supremacy had been legally dead since 1534, the religious and cultural foundation on which it rested was not. With the ever-present threat of invasion by Catholic powers on the Continent made more real by the solidifying of the Franco-Imperial Alliance of 1538, Bale's plays fulfill a mandate for propaganda against the Papacy to be stepped up in order to sway public opinion against Rome and reduce the risk of further seditious uprisings such as the Pilgrimage of Grace in 1535 (P. W. White, 12–41; Kastan).

Like other Protestant troupe dramatists, Bale was writing for the socially diverse audience that he and his players would have been expected to address while on tour. This was in line with the propagandist objective of Protestant leaders at court to disseminate Crown policy through print, preaching, and playing to all sectors of society (J. N. King, 48; Elton, 206). Yet Bale's plays provoked controversy and division among audiences, because most English subjects remained basically Catholic and even indifferent to reform during the Henrician Reformation (P. W. White, 29–30).

While Bale's plays reflect the anti-Catholic emphasis of Henrician Protestantism, which remained theologically undeveloped, later plays designed for professional troupes reflect the reception of Calvinism. Edwardian interludes such as *Lusty Juventus* (c. 1550) and *The Life and Repentaunce of Mary Magdalene* (c. 1550) preach a theology of irresistible grace and spiritual conversion, in contrast to the doctrine of works and free will found in the more traditional moralities and saints plays that supplied the dramaturgy for Protestant theater. Calvinism, especially as understood by returning Marian exiles in the late 1550s and early 1560s, accounts for other interludes such as *New Custom* (c. 1566) and *The Tide Tarrieth No Man* (c. 1575), which address the controversial issues of church vestments and ceremonies, and *Enough Is as Good as a Feast* (c. 1565), *The Trial of Treasure* (c. 1565), and *All for Money* (c. 1575), which reflect Protestant notions on divine calling and attack the acquisitive spirit and economic abuses of their London mercantile audiences.

Considering that the Reformation rode the crest of a population explosion (perhaps half of England's three million subjects were under the age of twenty around 1550 [Brigden, 37, 43]), it is understandable that much of the drama was addressed to and performed by the nation's youth, especially those enrolled in its academic institutions. At the numerous grammar and choir schools, many newly instituted by the regime of the boy king, Edward VI, headmasters such as Nicholas Udall, Ralph Radcliffe, Thomas Ashton, and Richard Mulcaster became some of the nation's most prolific and distinguished writers and directors of plays.

Drama theory in the academy, represented by the writings of the Continental reformer Martin Bucer, revived interest in classical models of dramaturgy and mixed humanist teaching with a Calvinist approach to the problems of raising and educating youth. *Nice Wanton* (c. 1550), *Misogonus* (c. 1560), and *The Longer Thou Livest the More Fool Thou Art* (c. 1560), among other plays, criticize the indulgence and indiscipline of Catholic parents in raising children naturally inclined toward wickedness, and enlightened adolescents are even urged to convert their parents to Protestantism. In *Jacob and Esau* (c. 1550) and *The Glass of Government* (c. 1570), one discerns a pronounced but unresolved tension between the religious doctrine of predestination and the reformative value of education. Academic drama generally allowed for considerably larger casts and more elaborate staging conventions than the troupe plays, but the exception may have been *The Longer Thou Livest*, by the schoolmaster/preacher William Wager, which contains doubling practices suitable for a small roster of privileged children educated in noble households (P. W. White, 111).

Both school plays and those produced at the universities of Oxford and Cambridge and the Inns of Court engage in more controversial subject matter. Two school plays were quite possibly directed against the Catholic administration of Mary I: the political message of the choir school interlude *Jacob and Esau* is that active resistance against reprobate authority is divinely sanctioned, while *Jack Juggler*, a grammar school play, contains a covert attack on transubstantiation and Catholic oppression. At Cambridge, the more radical and reform-centered of the two universities, drama courted controversy in 1545 with the apocalyptic morality *Pammachius*, and similarly warned against the dangers of popery and image worship some twenty years later in the biblical play *Ezechias* (1564) and an unnamed burlesque mocking the Catholic Mass, both staged before Queen Elizabeth. The queen was so outraged by the latter that she walked out in the middle of the performance. No less audacious were student productions at the Inns of Court, including the 1526 Christmas play *Lord Governance*, considered so seditious by Cardinal Wolsey that the author and some actors were jailed, while the leading player, Simon Fish, a known Protestant activist, reportedly fled to Tyndale's house on the Continent (P. W. White, 106–9).

## Theater and Antitheatrical Criticism in Elizabethan England

The use of drama to address religious issues continued through to the closing of professional playhouses in the 1640s, but following Elizabeth's accession, theatrical and religious practice developed in ways that complicated their interaction. Soon it would appear that more Protestant activists denigrated the stage than supported it.

The Elizabethan theater underwent rapid change during its first two decades. In the provinces, depleted funds, declining interest, and state-imposed censorship combined to reduce significantly the number of civic- and parish-sponsored productions, leaving it to touring troupes to supply the decreased demand for dramatic entertainment. In early Elizabethan London, however, the story was quite different. Public playing was transformed within the span of a decade and a half from an occasional form of recreation performed intermittently in rented halls, taverns, a few churches, and private rooms to a regularly scheduled event in permanent playhouses such as the Theatre (1576) and the Curtain (1577), each of which accommodated as many as three thousand spectators (Gurr, *Playgoing*, 22). This radical growth in the capital seemed overwhelming to the London City Council, whose minutes record distress over the risk of infection in crowded assemblies during plague time, of injury on account of collapsing scaffolds, and of behavior promoted in the plays themselves, such as outbreaks of public disorder and crime. Yet, these practical objections aside, religious convictions and interests fueled the highly publicized campaign by civic and ecclesiastical figures to suppress popular playing altogether. Ideological developments within Elizabethan Protestantism were beginning to change the way many thought about the stage as an effective, even morally acceptable, medium of religious instruction. Puritan leaders, dismayed by Sabbath-breaking citizens who thronged to theaters while their churches stood empty, emphasized preaching as the only acceptable means of proclaiming the gospel and teaching morality and doctrine. In London and throughout the provinces, nonincumbent preachers—or "lecturers," as they were more commonly called—were hired by city corporations and churchwardens, and in some instances funds that had previously been designated to pay for plays now went to cover the wages of the town lecturer.

Thus, by the 1570s, the Word dramatized, as opposed to the Word preached, came under serious attack. The use of "actors" to impart the Word was now considered by many an intolerable affront to the gospel message. This was part of the new ethical strain of the puritans, who looked to the theocracies of Calvin's Geneva and Bullinger's Zurich as models of the godly commonwealth. Moral "preciseness" also arose from a more literal and legalistic interpretation of the Bible; embellished dramatic accounts of scriptural stories were considered offensive, as was the use of bawdy and scurrilous language in treating religious topics. Certainly the earthiness of Bale's Vices now would be categorized as "filthie, lewde, & vngodlie," something, incidentally, that the old reformer would not contest, though he would see nothing wrong with representing it in a play (P. W. White, 169–73).

The Protestant attitude toward theatricality had always been ambivalent. Bale and his contemporaries never seemed to question the moral propriety of theater itself, but they routinely used the concept of theater negatively as a metaphor to expose the hypocrisy, deceitfulness, and spiritual emptiness of the wicked, which they usually associated with Roman Catholicism. Thus, the character of the Vice-as-popish-priest is explicitly compared to a player who outwardly signifies and pretends to be one thing (Christ-like and virtuous) when in reality he is something else (devil-like and worldly); his gorgeous attire, sacramental gesturing, and seductive speech are empty or misleading signifiers, which are as mesmerizing to unsuspecting sinners as the appearance and actions of stage players are to spectators in the theater. Early reformers did not seem to be troubled by the possibility that their critique of Catholicism's "theatricality" might raise disturbing implications about the theater itself as a reliable signifying system and, worse still, about their own Protestant religion put in Catholicism's place. Indeed, throughout the early modern period, this uneasy mixing of the theatrical and antitheatrical, of the iconic and the iconoclastic, is a feature of Protestant propagandist and mainstream "secular" drama alike (Siemon, *Shakespearean*; Barish, 132–54; Levine, 100–108).

Yet the contradictions here were not lost on antitheatrical moralists, who came down especially hard on religious drama, past and present, because it intermixed divine truth with idolatrous renderings of scriptural figures, especially God "pop- ishly conceived to be like an old man sitting in heaven in a throne with a sceptre in his hand" (William Perkins, cited in Watt, 136). The old comparison of popery to playing (which became ubiquitous in anti-Catholic polemic of all kinds) was now reversed by the antitheatricalists to become a comparison of playing to popery. Stage plays are "the bastard of Babylon" delivered directly from the papists to Protestant England, players the devil's own "professed Massepriests and Choristers," the "Play- houses his Synagogues" (Chambers, *Elizabethan*, 4:249; Prynne, 529). No sooner had the Reformation banished the Mass and restored the preaching of the Word than a new institution emerged to satisfy the idolatrous tendencies and enslave the affections of the unregenerate majority. Antitheatrical moralists such as Stephen Gosson and Philip Stubbes would have none of the sophistry of their play-defend- ing opponents that drama could transform spectators for the better. Even if a play *was* written and performed with the noble intention of teaching a moral lesson, the spectator would be too engrossed in carnal pleasure to consider vice objectively within the play's moral context. For human beings are weak, vulnerable sinners, who are plunged further into the wickedness to which they are already naturally inclined by attending plays (Gosson, *Playes*, C7r and D1r).

In *Playes confuted in five actions* (1582), Gosson moved from the position that professional playing is an unlawful vocation, since God called no one to make a liv- ing out of recreation, to the conviction that all acting, amateur or professional, is a form of lying: "In Stage Playes for a boy to put one the attyre, the gesture, the pas- sions of a woman; for a meane person to take vpon him the title of a Prince with counterfeit porte, and traine, is by outwarde signes to shewe them selues otherwise then they are, and so with the compasse of a lye" (E5r). In addition to deception, Gosson here suggests that theatrical impersonation impiously subverts one's God- given identity and place in the sexual and social order and counters the biblical mandate to imitate Christ in all things.

Antistage moralists questioned whether the constant role-changing habits of actors during working hours carry over into real life to have a destabilizing effect on their sense of self (Barish, 104). Moreover, for them, the gender-changing prac- tices of the theater illustrate the worst dangers of the actor's profession, for God never intended that boys should assume the identity of the opposite sex. Calvin was the first to mark this convention as an abomination and an incitement of whore- dom, invoking the Deuteronomic injunction "A woman shal not weare the apparel of a man: neither shall a man put on the garments of a woman" (*Sermons*, 773–74).

But we should avoid the impression given by recent criticism that transvestism generated anxiety among all serious-minded English Protestants. Calvin's playwrit- ing successor at Geneva, Theodore Beza, found the practice of boys' playing fe- male roles entirely appropriate, and just as the stage's detractors in early modern England cited Calvin, enthusiasts cited Beza. In *The English Gentleman* (1630),

Richard Brathwait refers to a dispute that took place between Genevan ministers over a young boy's impersonation of a woman in a play celebrating the league concluded between the cantons of Berne and Tiguris:

> In the end, it was agreed of all parts, that they should submit the determination of this difference, with generall suffrage and consent, to the authenticke and approved judgement of their *Beza*, holden for the very Oracle both of Vniversitie and Citie. This controversie being unto him referred, he constantly affirmed, that it was not only lawfull for them to set forth and act those *Playes*, but for Boyes to put on womens apparell for the time. Neither did he only affirm this, but brought such *Divines* as opposed themselves against it, to be of his opinion, with the whole assent and consent of all the Ecclesiasticall Synod in Geneva. (BRATHWAIT, 184)

Bale himself had earlier exploited the gender-changing convention to make a polemical statement about the sodomy of the Catholic clergy. In *Three Laws*, the transvestism of the male actor playing the old witch Idolatry is explicitly drawn to the audience's attention (Infidelitie: "What, sumtyme thu wert an he!"; Idolatry: "Yea, but now ych am a she") so that the subsequent fondling of "her" by the licentious monk Sodomy would demonstrate the homosexual practices of the monasteries (Bale, *Three Lawes*, ll. 425–26, 475–90).

The analogy of the priest as player, common in anti-Catholic polemic, dramatic and otherwise, exemplifies a linguistic exchange between religious and theatrical discourse that is further evident in a variety of Protestant-inspired prose works that regularly use metaphors, allusions, and rhetorical strategies drawn from the theater to express religious ideas and experiences. In an age that emphasized constant divine surveillance and intervention in human affairs, it was conventional to think of the world as "the Theatre of God's Judgements" (to cite the title of Thomas Beard's popular pamphlet of 1597), wherein the unregenerate, as spectators viewing a play, could observe and learn from God's punishment of the wicked and rewarding of the righteous. Thus in a moral pamphlet by Arthur Golding recounting the killing of one George Sanders by his wife's lover, George Browne, the murderer's evil acts and public execution are brought "into the open Theatre" of the world for the elect's spiritual benefit:

> when God bringeth such matters upon the stage, unto ye open face of the world, it is not to the intent that men should gaze and wonder at the persons, as byrdes do at an Owle. . . . His purpose is that the execution of his judgements should by the terrour of the outward sight of the example, drive us to the inward consideration of ourselves. (*Warning*, App., 226–27)

Not surprisingly, this story was brought into the "real" theater in the form of the homiletic tragedy *A Warning for Fair Women*. Calvin, who made the same analogy (and whose works Golding translated into English), also found theatrical language useful to explain predestination (*Institution*, 1.v.8), as did Sir Walter Ralegh in the opening of his *History of the World*: "God, who is the Author of all our tragedies, hath written out for vs, and appointed vs all the parts we are to play: and hath not, in their distribution, been partiall to the most mighty Princes of the world" (Ralegh, A3v). Theatrical images and devices are no less prevalent in those most puritanical of Elizabethan prose satires, the "Martin Marprelate" pamphlets, compelling Francis Bacon to protest, "This immodest and deformed manner of writing lately entertained, whereby matters of religion are handled in the style of the stage" (cited in Chambers, *Elizabethan*, 1:294).

### The Drama of Religious Controversy

The "Martin Marprelate" pamphlets return us to drama proper, and specifically the drama of religious controversy, for the public sensation that they generated in the late 1580s provoked a conservative backlash from professional dramatists such as Thomas Nashe and John Lyly, who wrote plays debunking Martin Marprelate and his puritan supporters (Dutton, *Mastering*, 74–80). Now the more zealous Elizabethan reformers, who had played the Virtues in such moralities as *New Custom* and *The Tide Tarrieth No Man* (both c. 1570), replaced Catholic priests as the new Vices and objects of ridicule. In one anti-Martinist morality, Divinity is brought forth "wyth a scratcht face, holding of her hart as if she were sicke, because *Martin* would haue forced her, but myssing of his purpose, he left the print of his nayles vppon her cheekes, and poysoned her with a vomit which he ministred vnto her, to make her cast vppe her dignities and promotions" (Chambers, *Elizabethan*, 4:232).

However, the anti-Martinist plays, reportedly performed at the Theatre and the Curtain, seem to have relied less on morality dramaturgy than on the secular tradition of folk plays, May games, morris dances, and carnivalesque rituals which the Marprelate writers themselves, not to mention Gosson and Stubbes, so loudly condemned. Thomas Nashe, following the precedent of depicting Martin Marprelate in "a *Maygame* vpon the stage," refers to a new play in the works in which "*Martin* himselfe is the Mayd-marian, trimlie drest vppe in a cast Gowne, and a Kercher of Dame *Lawsons*, his face handsomlie muffled with a Diaper napkin to couer his beard, and a great Nosegay in his hande." Despite the traditional transvestism of the May-game Marian (Hutton, 118), Martin's costume may well have been designed to mock puritan outrage at boys dressed up in women's apparel (Chambers, *Elizabethan*, 4:230–31).

It remains unclear to what extent the anti-Martinist plays received support from the episcopal hierarchy and other conservative leaders and to what extent they simply exploited popular interest in the ecclesiastical controversy. As in earlier times when the bishops themselves counted among them (see Wasson, *Records: Devon*, 466), Protestant stage patrons continued to exercise influence over the players they sponsored, but the commercialization of the theater now gave professional troupes and playwrights some measure of self-identity and empowerment to operate independently of state and church patronage. Certainly the anti-Martinist plays had become sufficiently scurrilous and acrimonious by the fall of 1589 for the Privy Council to order their suppression by means of a new licensing commission commanded "to stryke out or reforme suche partes and matters as they [i.e., the licensors] shall fynde unfytt and undecent to be handled in playes, both for Divinitie and State" (Chambers, *Elizabethan*, 4:306). This 1589 commission, made up of censoring officials appointed by the Archbishop of Canterbury, the lord mayor of London, and working in conjunction with the Revels Office and its master, has been cited as a turning point in Elizabethan stage censorship, after which few plays dealt directly, or even in allegorical fashion, with serious matters of religion. Yet, as Richard Dutton observes, the commission is not heard of again after 1589, the Revels Office resuming its central role in regulating the drama and tolerating some latitude in the treatment of religious issues, so long as Crown policy was not overtly challenged, especially in times of political crisis (the Marprelate controversy and the Essex rebellion being two examples) when public order was threatened (Dutton, 77–78).

What is clear is that the more radical puritans remained a popular satirical target of the playhouses right through to the 1640s, though most of the humor is at the expense of the socially marginalized religious sects that broke away from the national church and often settled in provincial towns and foreign cities (Holden, 94–144). Jonson's sour-faced hypocrites, Ananias and Tribulation Wholesome (*The Alchemist* [1610]), are Anabaptists from Amsterdam, and before we conclude that their names and that of his Banbury baker Zeal-of-the-land Busy (*Bartholomew Fair* [1614]) were invented only for comic effect, we should note that in the Sussex village of Warbleton during the 1590s nearly half the children were baptized with such names as Much-mercy, Obedient, and Zealous (Collinson, *Birthpangs*,149). Most of these figures are drawn from the lower classes, their manifest ignorance, biblical style of speech, austere manner of dress, and hypocritical revulsion at anything smacking of fun providing an easy source of derision.

In plays such as *Bartholomew Fair*, *The Family of Love* (1607), and *The Muses Looking-Glasse* (1630), the sectarians' lust, greed, drunkenness, and deviousness, barely hidden under an outer cloak of sanctity, seem to be exaggerated to please audiences. Typical of this, and also of "the Shee Puritan," as nonconformist women were called (see Earle, 96–98), is the famous scene in *A Chastemaid of Cheapside* (1613) where a group of female dissenters gets drunk at a christening. Like Richard Hooker (1:107), anti-puritan playwrights seemed to think women were particularly drawn to nonconformist religion, though (as depicted in the plays) they are no less easily seduced by young gentlemen who can mimic their pious cant. Nevertheless, heroines such as Mistress Plus in *The Puritan* (1607) and Mistress Purge in *The Family of Love* are strong and witty, if totally duplicitous, characters. Women often had leading roles in the sects, like the wife of the bellows-mender whom Mistress Purge heard preach in *The Family of Love*.

In some plays a clear distinction is drawn between hypocritical dissenters and true believers (e.g., in *The Atheist's Tragedy* the godly Calvinist Charlemont is juxtaposed to the hypocritical puritan Snuff). Yet in much anti-puritan satire on the stage one discerns a subtle attack on the more mainstream puritans, who sought further reform within the established church. Jonson links Ananias and Tribulation Wholesome with the agenda of the Presbyterians when in *The Alchemist* Subtle speaks of their "hope of rooting out the bishops, / Or th' Anti-Christian hierarchy," and the hysterical anti-Romanism, predestinarianism, and antitheatricality of Rabbi Busy and his brethren were shared by more than a few prominent conforming preachers. One was Richard Crashaw, who in a Paul's Cross Sermon of 1612 denounced *The Puritan*, in which two contemptible serving-men were named after London churches, one, St. Antholins, known for its zealous puritan parishioners (Seaver, 199).

Moreover, such anti-puritan plays as *A Merry Knack to Know a Knave* (c. 1592) and *The Pilgrimage to Parnassus* (c. 1597) debunk unlicensed preachers and other precisians associated with the Elizabethan Presbyterians for their devotion to the Genevan catechism, preaching against "good works," hostility to the arts, and tendency "to turn and wind the Scripture to [their] own use" (*Merry*, cited in Holden, 114). It may be this misreading of Scripture, especially as a means of gaining assurance of election, that Shakespeare satirizes in *Twelfth Night* when Malvolio "crushes" the text of Maria's letter to yield the meaning he so much desires—the special favor of Olivia; yet Malvolio's humiliation and punishment and his concluding vow of revenge may have been designed to raise questions about the strong-arm tactics of the government in suppressing dissent, however misguided and subversive it might be (Kendall, 212; D. Hamilton, 86–110).

Especially early in his career, Shakespeare shares the virulently anti-papal rhetoric of his playwriting contemporaries, most notably in his portrayals of the "scarlet hypocrite" Cardinal Beaufort (1 *and* 2 *Henry VI*) and the manipulative and self-serving Cardinal Pandulph (*King John*). This is no surprise, considering his links with such puritan-sympathizing patrons as the earls of Southampton and Pembroke (D. Hamilton, 20–29). Yet as Malvolio and perhaps also the overly "precise" Angelo in *Measure for Measure* demonstrate, Shakespeare also voiced considerable unease with the more extreme tendencies of puritanism.

Shakespeare's critique of puritanism was most controversial for his own day in the *Henry IV* plays, where that great comic worldling Falstaff was originally known as Sir John Oldcastle, named after the Lollard reformer executed by Henry V in 1417 for treason and heresy (Bevington, Introduction, 3–7, 22–23). The historical Oldcastle was glorified by John Foxe and other advanced Protestant reformers as a martyr who heroically defied papal authority and popish superstition. Significantly, Shakespeare follows Catholic and more conservative Protestant accounts of Oldcastle's life, and his depiction of Sir John's old-age debauchery and treasonable offenses seriously questions the hagiographic treatments of Foxe and others, which strained credulity to the limit by praising the old Lollard not merely as a model of Christian piety but as a loyal subject of the Crown as well. (History has shown that

Oldcastle, at the very least, was implicated in the great Lollard rebellion of 1414, for which he was convicted of treason.)

But if Shakespeare's use of sources suggests concern with the way some reformers represent (or, more properly, misrepresent) Protestant history, the satire seems to go deeper, for in jesting tones Sir John repeatedly speaks the language of the conscience-stricken puritan ("Monsieur Remorse" as Poins calls him [Shakespeare, 1 Henry IV, 1.2.106–7]), who alternately longs for and despairs of repentance (1.2.91–94; 3.3.1–10), mutters about hellfire to Bardolph, whom he likens to "the son of utter darkness," and fears he's "one of the wicked" and not called to grace (1.2.91; 5.1.128–29). It is not surprising, therefore, that while many contemporaries (including the queen, evidently) found Sir John endearing and amusing, some puritans of the period reportedly were offended by Shakespeare's characterization, and they, along with Oldcastle's Elizabethan descendants (the Cobham family), probably account for the name change to Falstaff (resulting in missed puns, irregular meters, and lost topical significance in the surviving text) and the apparent retraction in the epilogue of 2 Henry IV (see G. Taylor, "Fortunes"; Poole; Bevington, 1 Henry IV, 5–9).

What we know for certain is that Shakespeare's Henry IV plays provoked an effort to rehabilitate the Lollard reformer's saintly status in the rival Admiral Men's production of The True and Honorable History of the Life of Sir John Oldcastle, The Good Lord Cobham (1600), the Prologue of which alludes to Shakespeare's ignominious portrayal as "forged invention" (Oldcastle Controversy, 40). Following reformist chroniclers, Oldcastle is romanticized once again as an exemplary Protestant, and the play places particular stress on Oldcastle's patriotism at a time when the puritans' loyalty to the Crown was questioned by authorities (as it is in much anti-puritan satire). The play also demonstrates that ministers such as Crashaw cited earlier were not wholly representative of moderate puritan views of the stage.

Both Margot Heinemann ("Rebel") and Martin Butler (Theatre) have shown that English Protestants advocating further religious reform were heavily engaged in advancing their own views in the theater and were backed by powerful patrons. Sir John Oldcastle, in fact, is one of a whole series of what we might call "Protestant saint plays" modeled on accounts of exemplary Protestant reformers in Foxe's Acts and Monuments (popularly known as The Book of Martyrs), many performed by companies under the management of Philip Henslowe and patronized by Lord Howard of Effingham (Gurr, Playgoing, 148; Spikes). They include Thomas Cromwell (1600), When You See Me You Know Me (1605), Sir Thomas Wyatt (1604), and The Duchess of Suffolk (1624). Also in this Protestant tradition, though not history plays, are The Whore of Babylon (1606) and A Game at Chess (1624). As Heinemann says of these plays, "The central stage confrontation is between heroic Protestant individuals, victimized for conscience's sake, and rich, self-seeking, persecuting bishops (led by Cardinal Wolsey or by Gardiner, Bishop of Winchester, a scheming villain in play after play), who seek to persuade the monarch that his

most loyal subjects are traitors" ("Political Drama," 196). As in Bale's earlier iconoclastic drama, the perceived theatricality and image-centeredness of Catholic
power and authority are repeatedly suggested in these plays by means of the rich
vestments and "outward show" of the cardinals and bishops (often directly juxtaposed with their wicked speech and behavior), a point similarly made in the vest-
ment-stripping episode of Marlowe's *Edward II* (scene 1) and the appearance of
"Richard, aloft, between two bishops" (his "two props of virtue") in Shakespeare's
*Richard III* (3.7.96; 94 sd).

## Religion and "Secular" Drama

The Protestant saints play and similar drama are polemical and propagandist in
nature, in some instances commissioned, in other instances strongly encouraged,
by puritan patrons in positions of political power whose interests were being served,
among them the Jacobean lord mayors such as Sir Thomas Middleton (not to be
confused with the dramatist of the same name) and prominent noblemen such as
the earls of Southhampton, Pembroke, and Montgomery (Heinemann,
*Puritanism*, 258–83, and "Political"; D. Hamilton, 20–29). Although we have also
touched on aspects of religion (and religious controversy) in some plays of a more
"secular" nature, I would like to consider at greater length the question of what
interaction religion had with the mainstream drama, particularly the tragedies,
which offer a more complex account of the human condition and are more interested in pleasing than instructing audiences. Did religion figure in any significant
way in its composition, performance, and reception?

The answer to this question is unequivocally yes, since Reformation orthodoxy
was, by the midpoint of Elizabeth's reign, not merely the official doctrine of the
national church but internalized as a major feature of the national consciousness.
As Alan Sinfield asserts, "This orthodoxy hugely influenced the ideological field
within which [writers] produced diverse relations—of incorporation, conformity,
negotiation, disjunction, subversion, and opposition—between religious orthodoxy and other, divergent ideological formations" (Sinfield, 214). This is not to say
that unorthodox religion was insignificant. We know Catholicism oriented to some
degree the sensibilities of major playwrights—Shakespeare evidently in childhood,
Marlowe and Jonson in early adulthood, and some aspects of the occult were entertained in literary circles, at least during the 1580s and 1590s (Nicholl, 91–114,
191–201; Honigmann, *Shakespeare*, 114–25). Nevertheless, as the official religion of
Elizabethan/Jacobean England, Reformation teaching shaped the thinking and
the experience of the intelligentsia, including the large numbers of graduating
divinity students pouring out of Oxford and Cambridge and taking up influential
positions in the church, the civil government, and—as Marlowe and other playwrights demonstrate—the theater.

The prescriptions for religious belief and practice taught in the grammar
schools and universities, following the official Protestant articles, homilies, and

prayerbooks since Edward VI's reign, were thoroughly Calvinistic, and as such they radically undermined ways in which the Catholic Christianity of England's past (or to be more accurate, the way Protestants viewed it) perceived the self and its relation to God and society. Salvation of the soul was no longer achievable by the sinner's freely chosen participation in the sacraments provided by the church and mediated through its priesthood. The Catholic penitential system, along with other supposedly meritorious rites such as prayers to the Virgin, the saints, and their images, were now denounced as a massive, humanly devised fraud, which blocked rather than paved the way to salvation, and which the Papacy sanctioned to perpetuate its own institutions.

The practical consequences of this new Christian orthodoxy were far-reaching. Since the institutional apparatus of the Church could no longer help one "do" salvation, or at least combine external acts ("works") with belief ("faith"), one was driven inward to search one's soul for signs of divine grace and the stirring of faith. This enhanced introspective dimension of religious experience has led some scholars to argue that Reformation theology was "an instrument for the creation of self-consciousness, of interiority" in early modern England (Sinfield, 159; Rozett, 65–73). I would argue that it led to a great intensification of self-consciousness and interiority rather than contributing centrally to its creation, for as David Aers reminds us, the language and experience of the inner life and of autonomous selfhood had a long history in Catholicism, dating back at least as far as Saint Augustine's *Confessions* (Aers, 177–97).

The extent to which a new preoccupation with interiority existed in Protestant England depends on how widespread Calvinist-induced piety and soul-searching was at the time. There was sufficient interest in this sort of religious practice, at least among the "middling sort" and gentry in London, to flock to puritan sermons at Paul's Cross and elsewhere and to buy up large numbers of devotional, homiletic, and autobiographical writings addressing matters of conscience and assurance of salvation and the restlessness and anxiety, on the one hand, and confidence and comfort, on the other, that Calvinist theology generated (Rozett, 15–73).

The Protestant preoccupation, even fascination, with human sinfulness and divine retribution, with its accompanying anxieties and terrors, is recurrent in the tragedies of the period, most of which pay at least lip service to Fulke Greville's view that tragedy aims "to point out God's revenging aspect upon every particular sin, to the despair or confusion of mortality" (cited in Sinfield, 216). While this preoccupation is exemplified in such early incipient tragedies as *Enough Is as Good as a Feast* (c. 1565) and *The Conflict of Conscience* (1578), playwrights often took their lead from Seneca, whose themes of constancy and courage in the face of enormous suffering and the inevitable punishment of wicked deeds complemented and forcefully expressed Protestant moral and religious convictions. Where Elizabethan playwrights departed from Senecan Stoicism is in suggesting that God, not indifferent fate, determined the course of human events and that reliance on divine providence rather than reason (which was vitiated by the Fall) brought whatever solace could be attained in this world (Klink, 333; Sinfield, 222–30).

Calvinist pronouncements on providential retribution, universal human corruption, election, and reprobation are common in the major tragedies of the period and are often couched in language similar to that of the sermons, diaries, devotional tracts, and character books. Moreover, characters such as Faustus, Tamburlaine, Richard III, Macbeth, and the Duchess of Malfi, to name only the most prominent, exhibit patterns of behavior applied by contemporary theologians and moralists to the elect and the reprobate (Rozett; Wilks; Sinfield, 214–51).

A debatable question is *what happens* to religious rhetoric and representations of the self when fictionalized in the speeches and actions of the characters in these tragedies. This very much depends on how they are fictionalized and under what conditions. Muriel Bradbrook and Stephen Greenblatt have argued that religious discourse, when embedded in early modern drama, is transformed or (to use Greenblatt's expression) "emptied out" of its original meaning and effect (Bradbrook, *Rise*, 129–39; Greenblatt, *Shakespearean*, 94–128). Greenblatt explains how Shakespeare uses a religious source in *King Lear*—Samuel Harsnet's tract attacking Catholic exorcism—first to reaffirm Harsnet's claim that exorcism is an illusion, but then to suggest that perhaps religion itself is an illusion. Yet as Greenblatt admits, *King Lear* could conceivably have been read allegorically to support Catholicism, given the right staging and audience, which it might have found when it was performed by the same recusant troupe who staged the anti-Protestant polemic during Candlemas 1609/10 in the northern Catholic household of Sir John Yorke (*Shakespearean*, 121–22; Watt, 30–31). Be that as it may, reproducing religious discourse in "secular" plays could both subvert Reformation orthodoxy, as Jonathan Dollimore has extensively argued, and support it, and we risk reducing the plays by seeing them as primarily one or the other. Such popular domestic tragedies as *A Woman Killed with Kindness*, *A Warning to Fair Women*, and *Arden of Faversham* surely reinforced the conventional piety and religious values of the London middle-class who filled the playhouses to see them. Heywood's *A Woman Killed* (1603) was staged by Worcester's Men around the time this troupe and others managed by Philip Henslowe were promoting puritan religious interests in the city. The main subject of this play is adultery, specifically its effects on the marriage of John and Anne Frankford and on the spiritual condition of the adulterers, Anne and Frankford's friend Wendoll. As it turns out, the discovery of the affair and the subsequent punishment that Anne suffers (banished from her children and the household) become the occasion for Anne's religious conversion, worked out with the self-conscious soul-searching and remorse described in religious tracts and sermons. But whereas affliction and guilt for sin lead Anne to repentance, they serve only to drive the conscience-stricken Wendoll into despair and a sense of his own damnation: "Thus villains, when they would, cannot repent" (Heywood, ed. Van Fossen, 30 [6.52]). Heywood's play, of course, is not an overt exercise in Calvinist evangelism; the religious rhetoric of Anne and Wendoll is so interwoven into character and situation that it cannot be set apart as "message," and yet this may be more effective in reaffirming religious ideology than overt didacticism (see Heinemann, *Puritanism*, 15).

Other tragedies, however, may have evoked a more dissonant and questioning response from their audiences. *Tamburlaine* illustrates the notion, popular in the writings of Calvin and Elizabethan divines, that while bloodthirsty tyrants are condemned to eternal perdition for their wicked deeds, they carry them out in accordance with God's will and are thus used as "scourges" or agents of divine retribution (Battenhouse, 108). Yet if Tamburlaine presents the spectacle of the reprobate Other, to be shunned and judged, his expressions of self-confidence and aspiration (like those of Barabas in *The Jew of Malta*) often subtly parody the rhetoric of religious self-assurance and election found in contemporary sermons (Rozett, 146). The same holds true of Shakespeare's Richard III, although his sanctimonious utterances are hypocritical gestures to advance his quest for the Crown. Providential retribution appears no more rational and reassuring in *Richard III* than it does in Marlowe's tragedy. For if Richard has been chosen by God to be a scourge, does this not raise the more frightening possibility that he was doomed to this fate and incapable of saving his own soul? The mystery of *Richard III* is "that of the vessel and the reprobate instrument of God's wrath" and the questions, doubts, and fears that this perception of him raises evoke terror and perhaps metaphysical doubt (R. Hunter, 194).

God's retribution for sin is central to the enormously popular revenge tragedies. The dilemma posed by revenge is whether the righteous can be the instrument of God's wrath in avenging the murder of a family member. Reformation commentary, backing Elizabethan law, condemned revenge on the basis of the biblical injunction "Vengeance is mine, saith the Lord." The godly man, according to the Calvinist bishop Joseph Hall, bears the wrongs of others

> not out of baseness and cowardlinesse, because he dare not revenge, but out of Christian fortitude, because he may not . . .; victory consists in yeelding. . . . When crosses afflict him, he sees a divine hand invisibly striking with these sensible scourges: against which he dares not rebell or murmure. (J. HALL, 155–56)

This sermon rhetoric is faithfully reproduced in *The Atheist's Tragedy* (1607), subtitled *The honest Man's Revenge*, where *inaction* and resignation to divine providence are what distinguishes the explicitly elect Charlemont from his reprobate counterpart D'Amville. In other revenge tragedies, however, the rhetoric of the elect now speaks from the mouths of sympathetically portrayed avengers. In Marston's *Antonio's Revenge*, Antonio's commitment to avenging the murder of his father and Pandulphio's son is expressed in the language of religious vocation. The similar intermixing of Christian and classical terms to justify revenge in *The Spanish Tragedy* and *Hamlet* invites the audience to identify with revenge heroes and question orthodox Christian moralizing about revenge. For Hamlet, damnation may be the result of *not* acting out revenge ("And is't not to be damn'd / To let this canker of our nature [i.e., Claudius], come / In further evil?" [5.2.67–70]), although his reflections on special providence near the end (5.2.10–11, 217–20) suggest that seeking private revenge resists God's preordained course of events, over which he has no control.

In *Hamlet*, Claudius furnishes a succinct example of where the inefficacy of religious ritual in contributing to salvation in Reformation teaching intensified the split between the inner and outer selves in early modern England. Speaking the language of confession is not even close to being enough: "My words fly up, my thoughts remain below. / Words without thoughts never to heaven go" (3.3.97–98). Combine this recognition with belief in predestined depravity and reprobation (the latter, according to the preachers, is discernible in certain outward traits), and the result is the sort of spiritual anguish exhibited by Webster's Bosola in *The Duchess of Malfi*:

> a guilty conscience
> Is a black register, wherein is writ
> All our good deeds and bad, a perspective
> That shows us hell! That we cannot be suffer'd
> To do good when we have a mind to it!
> This is manly sorrow. (4.2.356–61)

Bosola's tragic course resembles that of other self-consciously damned protagonists: Faustus, Macbeth, and Giovanni in Ford's *'Tis Pity She's a Whore*. The self seeks meaning and favor through "merit," "service," sensual pleasure, or worldly achievement, but these failing, the reprobate come to believe what they have suspected all along: that such pursuits, as well as the tormented conscience and despair that follow, are signs of their own damnation. In *The Duchess of Malfi*, the conscience-stricken and self-divided Bosola is contrasted with the duchess, who also suffers, but for her, affliction and hardship are signs of "heaven's scourge-stick," which lead to spiritual self-assurance and a place in "the eternal church" (3.5.71; cf. J. Hall, 155–56, quoted above).

The most penetrating exercise in religious self-scrutiny in Renaissance tragedy occurs in *Doctor Faustus*. The play's tragic dimension is created out of the conflict between the two rival formations of selfhood that struggle for acceptance in the mind of Faustus. Faustus's rational intellect, his love for sensual experience, his ardent curiosity regarding the nature of things, and his belief in his ability to determine his own fate—these are ideals entertained by Marlowe and other bold Elizabethan intellectuals and expressed in the writings of Renaissance humanists from Pico and Ficino to Bruno (Bevington and Rasmussen, 10–11, 22–31). Many Elizabethan playgoers would not only have found such ideals highly appealing as they are exhibited in the magnificent character of Faustus but they may well have sympathized with Faustus's struggle to liberate himself from a religious conception of man as a depraved and helpless sinner. Yet by the end, Faustus comes to the full awareness of what he has feared all along: that the divinity he contemptuously dismissed embodies the truth. His vision of achieving God-like omnipotence and knowledge never materializes. His conjuring tricks in the Vatican are pitiable in comparison to what he sets out to achieve in scene 1 and make a mockery of his presumptions. But even more significantly, his belief in limitless free will to determine his destiny turns out to be a grand delusion. For all the time Faustus thought he was in command of his own fate, he was acting in accordance with the absolute will of God. Although the play ends with a reaffirmation of Reformation doctrine, it raises questions about the justness of that doctrine and about possible alternative conceptions of man and his destiny.

Written around 1590, *Doctor Faustus* has been cited by some critics as the last truly religious play of the age, after which state censorship prohibited the overt treatment of religion on the stage. This theory, I hope to have shown, is insupportable, if only by the fact that Marlowe's play remained one of the most popular playhouse works through to the closing of the theaters in 1642. In itself, it is a testimony to the continuing theatrical representation of Protestant orthodoxy, occultist practice, and libertine humanist reaction to religion throughout the early modern era.[2]

## NOTES

1. In early modern England, the term *puritan* was an abusive epithet for various groups of Protestant zealots both inside and outside the national church, but all so labeled privileged a personal, inward-looking religious faith centered on scripture-reading and shared dissatisfaction with the slow pace of reform within the church.
2. I would like to thank the students of my spring 1995 graduate seminar on Renaissance drama for many ideas in this essay, especially Deborah Mix and Margaret Reimer for specific points of detail concerning the Marprelate pamphlets and *The Puritan* respectively.

CHAPTER 9

# Wonderfull Spectacles: Theater and Civic Culture

*Gordon Kipling*

RICHARD MULCASTER describes Elizabeth I's entry into London in January 1559 as a collaborative drama performed by people, pageant actors, and queen. He repeatedly compliments both queen and people on their performances, admiring the people's portrayal of "earnest love" toward their new queen and her "ravishing" of them with her "louing answers and gestures." "If a man should say well, he could not better tearme the citie of London that time, than a stage wherin was shewed the wonderfull spectacle, of a noble hearted princesse toward her most louing people" (*Quenes*, 28).

Modern commentary only partially shares Mulcaster's enthusiasm for this "wonderfull spectacle." While a number of studies consider the political symbolism of the entry in detail, most seem embarrassed that this most important Tudor civic triumph had not yet adopted the neoclassical vocabulary of form that had been common on the Continent for half a century (Anglo, *Spectacle*, 344–59; Bergeron, *Pageantry*, 12–23; Frye, *Elizabeth I*, 24–54). In this vein, Roy Strong observes that "Elizabeth I's entry into London (1559) was a triumph for the Protestant Reformation and yet in style it was wholly a child of the preceding Gothic ages. . . . England had to wait until 1604 to have its first state entry in the Renaissance manner" (*Art*, 11).

Such a remark reflects a prevailing critical tradition best represented by the seminal work of Josèphe Chartrou. Examining the royal entry at what she perceives to be its period of transition, she briefly characterizes its vague "medieval" past as a series of processions enlivened only by religious tableaux and moral "divertissements" sponsored by the religious orders. Then, after the monks depart and the French invasions of Italy bring new inspiration to the civic triumph, Renaissance emblems and ideas begin to appear. In the end, she finds, French civic pageantry adopted an informing idea that she describes as "l'idée triumphal," and in so doing the royal entry became an art form worthy of serious study (9–10, 16–18, 26, 56–72). Following Chartrou's lead, modern commentary has continued to chronicle "the transformation of the royal entry into an antique triumph" (Strong, *Splendor*, 31).

This traditional critical approach has little to say about the two centuries of experimentation that gave purpose and meaning to these sophisticated civic dramas. If the earlier tradition is mentioned at all, it appears merely as a brief prologue to the swelling theme of the dazzling Renaissance festivals of the Medici, Valois, and Stuart courts. Almost without exception, modern writers find these shows interesting only when they cease being "medieval" in substance and begin to adopt classical ideas and political (rather than religious) imagery. The earliest pageantry offers only "a visual repertory of late medieval Gothicism little touched by the new forms of the Renaissance" (Strong, *Splendor*, 25; *Art*, 7–8). Such a viewpoint particularly marginalizes a study of the British civic triumph, since the majority of the most important monuments of the form remained products of the earlier tradition until the end of the Tudor period: Richard II's "Reconciliation" triumph (1392), Henry V's Agincourt triumph (1415), Henry VI's coronation triumph (1432), Henry VII's provincial tour (1486), Katharine of Aragon's London reception (1501), and the coronation triumphs of Anne Boleyn (1533), Mary (1553), and Elizabeth (1559). As a result, modern writers find themselves apologizing for the backwardness of these spectacles that seem to cling unfashionably to "Gothic" ideas while Continental triumphs routinely embraced the new neoclassical forms.

A new history of the civic triumph in Britain therefore needs to examine this earlier tradition on its own terms, with regard to ritual function, liturgical imagery, symbolic vocabulary, and dramatic form. In essence a dramatized inaugural ritual, this early tradition of civic triumph originated in the late fourteenth century, spread throughout Europe, and flourished in Britain until the end of the sixteenth century. With few exceptions, these civic dramas were almost always performed only upon the occasion of the king's inaugural entry into the city. They conceive of the king's entry into the city as a dramatic metaphor for his entry into his reign. Wickham thus describes the royal entry as a dramatized ritual of civic acclamation, a vehicle by which subjects might acknowledge "that the particular ruler is the representative in their midst, chosen by God for their own good as a figurehead and arbiter of justice." The early triumph, in his view, thus extended the ritual acclamation of the coronation out of the closed ritual space of the cathedral into open civic space, and it organized the presentation of the new king to his subjects by means of a procession through the streets, where the ritual acclamation could be "extended to a wider range of subjects than those privileged to attend the services in the cathedral" (*Early*, 1:54). Recent social anthropological analyses of the civic triumph both support and extend this view of the event as a dramatized inaugural ritual. Geertz, for instance, finds that such shows serve powerfully to "locate the society's center and affirm its connection with transcendent things by stamping a territory with ritual signs of dominance." Kings assert their authority by means of such shows; in performing the ritual of civic entry, they mark a city "like some wolf or tiger spreading his scent through his territory, as almost physically part of them" (Geertz, 125).

Few cities dramatize the king's entry in such overtly feral terms, of course, but for two centuries these "wonderfull spectacles" served British cities as ritual dramas of royal manifestation and civic acclamation. As drama, they required frankly mimetic performances from both ruler and citizens. Mulcaster thus notes that sovereign, people, and pageant actors all consciously performed roles to one another and that these roles were carefully scripted. As ritual, they drew their imagery, distinctive form, and purpose from the liturgy of the pre-Reformation Church. The performances were designed above all as acts of public worship. They constituted the orders of service in which a monarch was made manifest to his people, and the people in turn received their monarch through an act of ordered, public acclamation.

In its origins, perhaps, the civic triumph merely sought to make familiar ritual ideas more vivid by dramatizing them. Long before European cities began decorating their streets with pageantry, for example, they routinely imagined themselves transformed into another Zion, a celestial Jerusalem, whenever a king made a ceremonial entry. As Kantorowicz points out, "every city on earth preparing itself for the liturgical reception of one anointed, becomes a 'Jerusalem' and the comer a likeness of Christ" ("King's," 209–11; *Laudes*, 71). A London chronicler uses this traditional metaphor in describing the reception of Edward II and Queen Isabella (1308): "Then was London seen ornamented with jewels like New Jerusalem" (Stubbs, 152). By the end of the fourteenth century, however, London began to turn that metaphor into drama. In describing the "Reconciliation" triumph of 1392, Maydiston thus reports that the street decorations had transformed the city into "new heaven" (l. 62), and his detailed reports of the pageants erected in the streets show that the city was indeed attempting to represent itself as the New Jerusalem descending to earth at the coming of its Christ-king Richard.

The earliest civic triumphs—both in England and on the Continent—made extensive use of the liturgical imagery of Advent. The most common Latin term for *royal entry* was *adventus*, and such shows were usually performed upon the occasion of a king's formal inaugural entry into one of his cities. The pageants, which first began to fill the streets of British cities at the end of the fourteenth century, were an attempt to visualize and dramatize this metaphor. Early in Richard II's reign, London constructed two fairly modest New Jerusalem pageants for the coronation entries of first Richard himself (1377) and then Queen Anne (1382). On each of these occasions, the city placed an angelic castle with four turrets in Cheapside, so that the encounter between the royal visitor and the pageant might create a mimetic image of the entry of the Anointed One into the celestial Jerusalem. Beautiful maidens dressed in white scattered gold leaves and gold coins upon the royal visitors. Other angelic maidens offered them golden cups of red and white wine, which flowed from the sides of the structure. A mechanical angel atop the castle bowed and offered them a crown (Walsingham, 1:331; Withington, 1:128).

The "Reconciliation" triumph of 1392 represented an even more ambitious effort to transform the streets of London into the geography of heaven. The City stationed at least four pageants along the route of the royal procession, each depicting a celestial place populated by angels and saints. The first of the series stood atop the Great Conduit in Cheapside and consisted of a choir of singers costumed to look like one of the heavenly orders of angels. The Conduit ran wine instead of water, and the angels sang and scattered pieces of gold. The second pageant, the most technically ambitious of the series, took the form of a high, castlelike tower hung on ropes above the street. From this representation of the New Jerusalem "coming down out of heaven from God," a youth and a maiden, dressed as angels, descended to the street "enclosed in clouds . . . floating down in the air." While the youth offered a golden chalice of wine to Richard, the maiden presented the royal couple with golden crowns. At the Little Conduit, three orders of angels sat about the throne of the Almighty, singing and playing musical instruments. God Himself, played by a youth dressed in snow-white robes, sat above them, a light beaming like the sun shining upon him. Finally, a pageant set above Temple Bar depicted John the Baptist preaching in a wilderness. Beasts ran about, fighting, biting, leaping "as savage beasts do in the desolate forest." Saint John stood in their midst, dramatically pointing: Agnus et Ecce Dei. The pageants thus dramatized Richard's progressive reception into the holy city: he was first received by angels; then he encountered the holy city descending to earth; then he arrived himself before the throne of the Father, where he was finally identified by John the Baptist as a type of the Son (Maydiston; Kipling, "Richard II's").

London specialized in civic triumphs filled with celestial castles. From the first appearance of a single pageant in 1377 to Edward VI's coronation triumph of 1547, each London royal entry included at least one pageant representing the New Jerusalem. Often painted "jasper green," these structures imitated the Apocalyptic City of God, with its "light . . . like to a precious stone, as to the jasper stone, even as crystal" (Rev. 21:11).[1] John Carpenter accordingly describes the heavenly castle erected for Henry VI as a "castrum iaspertinum," which phrase Lydgate expands to "a castell bilt off iaspar grene, / Vpon whos toures the sonne shone shene" (643). Queen Margaret also found "the faire Citie of Jherusalem / Bisette aboute with many a precious gemme" awaiting her London triumph of 1445 (Kipling, "London," 23). In 1501, Katharine of Aragon reached the celestial Jerusalem at the Standard in Cheapside, its structure once again modeled upon Saint John's apocalyptic vision. God sat enthroned "full gloriously" in the Temple of God; surrounded by "ennumerable of angels singing full armoneously," he contemplated the twelve golden candlesticks of Revelation (Kipling, *Receyt*, 28, 136).

In their elaborate double triumph of 1522, Henry VIII and Emperor Charles V concluded their journey through the city before a pageant built atop the Little Conduit in Cheapside, "representing hevyn with son, moone & sterrys shynyng." This image of the City of God was filled

with angellys and with xij apostollys & . . . with the assumpcion off owr lady meru-
elous goodly conveyde by a vyce and a clowde openyng with Michael and Gabriel
angellys knelyng and dyuers tymes sensing with sensers and with voyces off yonge
queretters [choristers] syngyng psalmys and ympnys [hymns]. (WITHINGTON, 1:178)

The idea that civic triumph pageants ought to represent heaven was so well established in London that we find this expectation recorded in Henry VII's Household
Ordinances of 1494. When a queen should next be received into London,

at the Condit in Cornylle ther must be ordained *a sight with angelles singinge*, and
fresh balettes theron in latene, English, and ffrenche, mad by the wyseste doctors of
this realme; and the condyt in Chepe in the same wyse. (GROSE AND ASTLE, 1:303)

The entry of the king into the heavenly city often lent London civic triumphs a
distinctive formal coherence. In the show's early pageants, angels and saints sometimes descended from heaven to greet the king and sponsor his journey to the celestial city. A "sturdy champyone" awaited Henry VI at the gate of London Bridge to
defend his "estat riall" and foster him in becoming "Cristes champione" (Lydgate,
633). Saint Elizabeth, Saint Paul, and Mary Cleophas appeared on the bridge to
welcome Elizabeth Woodville into the holy city in 1464 (Wickham, *Early*,
1:330–31). Saints Ursula and Katharine descended from the "Courte Celestial" to
the bridge gate to "ayde, assiste, and compforte" Katharine of Aragon as she jour-
neyed through the city in 1501 (Kipling, *Receyt*, 13–14). The appearance of the heavenly castle was customarily postponed to the end of the triumph, so that the show
as a whole described the king's progressive entry into the heavenly city.

No London civic triumph more successfully martialed its pageants to turn city
streets into the symbolic architecture of heaven than did Henry V's Agincourt entry
(1415) (Taylor and Roskell, 101–13). Some made do with drapery canopies or box-
shaped "tabernacles" to suggest the dwellings of heaven. The throne of heaven
itself was merely an elaborate seat atop a tower of tabernacle niches, surmounted
by a sky-blue canopy held aloft by angels. At the foot of London Bridge, the decorated bridge gate served for the gate of the Heavenly Jerusalem. Two giant warders,
one bearing the keys to the city, guarded the entry to the "Civitas Regis Iustitiae,"
according to a legend inscribed on a wall. Several of the more ambitious pageants
clearly alluded to Saint John's description of New Jerusalem "like to a precious
stone, as to the jasper stone, even as crystal." The pageant at the drawbridge thus
featured turrets constructed of timber and "covered with linen cloth painted the
color of white marble and green jasper as if made of stones squared and dressed by
the handiwork of masons." An even more spectacular reflection of the glory of God
in the otherworldly masonry of heaven, a timberwork castle "adorned with graceful towers, pillars, and ramparts," stretched across Cheapside, permitting passage
by means of two arched gateways. Like the turrets on the drawbridge, "the covering of the castle was of linen fabric painted in colors to look like white marble and
green and crimson jasper, as if the whole work had been made . . . from squared

and well-polished stones of great price." A banner above the gateways identified it still further as a parish in the New Jerusalem: "Glorious things are said of thee, O City of God" (Ps. 86:3). Even the River Thames was pressed into duty to perform as one of the rivers of Paradise. Passing over the bridge, Henry found this banner flying from one of the jasper-stone turrets of the second pageant: "The stream of the river maketh the City of God joyful" (Ps. 45:5).

The drama forged by Henry's journey through London both acclaimed his famous victory and required him to offer thanks to God as the true author of his military feat. Just within the gates of the Heavenly Jerusalem, Saint George greeted Henry as England's patron. Wearing the martyr's crown ("laurel studded with gems sparkling like precious stones") and bearing a "triumphal helm" of saintly victory, he represented a spiritual version of the English king and conqueror. At the same station, a hierarchy of angels met the king, singing an anthem based upon the Palm Sunday greeting "Benedictus qui venit in nomine domini." Costumed in pure white robes, the angels presented faces that "glow with gold, their wings gleaming and their youthful locks entwined with costly sprays of laurel." At the next station, a company of prophets "with venerable white hair" greeted the king and sang Psalm 97: "Sing ye to the Lord a new canticle because he hath done wonderful things."

At the next pageant, the apostles, martyrs, and confessors welcomed Henry in heavenly communion. They presented the king with "round leaves of silver intermingled with wafers of bread" and served him with "wine from the pipes and spouts of the conduit," so that they "might receive him with bread and wine just as Melchizedek did Abraham." A "choir of the most beautiful young maidens, very chastely adorned in pure white raiment and virgin attire, singing together with tumbrel and dance, as if to another David coming from the slaying of Goliath" praised Henry, while a host of archangels and angels praised God. "Beautiful in heavenly spendour, in pure white raiment, with gleaming wings," they showered Henry with golden coins and leaves of laurel—symbols of heavenly grace—and sang the angelic anthem "Te deum laudamus."

To dramatize the gulf that separated Henry's mere earthly glory from heavenly glory, God appeared not in the form of an actor but rather as "a figure of majesty in the form of a sun . . . emitting dazzling rays" that "shone more brightly than all else." Around God's throne, when Henry finally reached it, more anthropomorphic "archangels moved rhythmically together, psalming sweetly" and accompanied by every kind of instrument. Having entered the "City of the King of Justice," Henry had at last come before the "Sun of Justice" itself. He found it to be exactly as Saint John had seen in his vision, for it "hath no need of the sun, nor the moon, to shine in it. For the Glory of God hath enlightened it . . . And the kings of the earth shall bring their glory and honor into it" (Rev. 21:23–24). Henry thus entered the New Jerusalem as one of the "kings of the earth" who bring glory and honor to God. As the chronicler observes, this pageant "concludes, in the same strain as the preceding ones, the tributes of praise to the honor and glory not of men but of God."

Entry into the New Jerusalem was prepared for in the early pageants for Henry VI's London triumph (1432) by staging a series of epiphanies in which the young king manifested himself as a type of the messianic king (Osberg, 219–20). To begin with, hosts of "virgins celestial" and "heavenly creatures" appeared to give the young king a series of symbolic gifts to acknowledge his Christ-like persona. Upon London Bridge, the goddesses Nature, Grace, and Fortune showered upon him their gifts of strength and fairness, science and cunning, prosperity and richesse. Seven "maydenys verey celestial" offered him seven doves, symbolic of the seven gifts of the Holy Ghost. Finally, seven other angelic maidens presented the seven pieces of symbolic armor that make up the "whole armor of God" (Eph. 6:13–18). At a "tabernacle of moste magnyficence" erected in Cornhill Street, Dame Sapience and the seven liberal arts bestowed upon the young king the blessings of wisdom, by means of which kings "moste of excellence" reign and "moste in ioye endure."

As these pageants evoked the gifts of the Magi, two others aimed at symbolic manifestations of Henry's messianic nature. Upon the Conduit in Cornhill, Henry thus encountered a symbolic image of himself as the messianic *rex iustus* as envisioned in a selection of "prophetic" psalms and proverbs associated with David and Solomon. Reflecting "the sentence off prudent Salamon" ("Mercy and Truth preserve the King, and his throne is upheld by Clemency" [Prov. 20:28]), a "childe of beaute precellyng [excelling]" sat regally between Dame Mercy and Dame Truth, with Dame Clemency hovering above "upholding" his throne. Because "justice and judgment are the preparation of thy throne" (Ps. 88:15), two judges and sixteen sergeants of the law attended the throne as the instruments of the king whose honor lies in the love of justice (Ps. 98:4). The pageant as a whole visualized "King David's" prayer, "Give your judgment to the king and your justice to the son of the king" (Ps. 71:1).

Passing from this symbolic manifestation of Henry's identity, the young king next effected his epiphany not just as a type of *rex iustus* but as a miraculous *rex christus* by staging a reenactment of the miracle at Cana. Along Cheapside, he found that the Great Conduit had metamorphosed into the central fountain of the restored earthly paradise. In an allusion to the miracle at Cana (John 2:1–11), his approach turned the Conduit's civic water supply into "the water of Archedeclyne [master of the feast]" (John 2:9). In fulfillment of Isaiah's prophecy, angelic maidens drew this Eucharistic wine with joy from the Fountains of the Savior (Is. 12:3), while Enoch and Elijah appeared in the heavens above to greet the young king. At the Cross in Cheapside, a pairing of genealogical trees provided a final manifestation of Henry's Christ-like nature at the very gates of the "castell bilt off iaspar grene," by portraying his lineage as akin to that of the Christ child. To the one side of the celestial Jerusalem grew a Jesse Tree; on the other, the intertwined trunks of two more trees rose upward from English Saint Edward and French Saint Louis to trace the royal lineage of Henry VI. The display identified Henry not only as heir to the crowns of both France and England but also as a messianic king, a Prince of Peace, whose advent promised to end the strife between the two realms.

The concluding three pageants of the show traced Henry's apotheosis as he progressively left the earthly paradise, ascended to the New Jerusalem, and entered into the throne room of the Trinity. In the earthly Paradise, trees burgeoned with fruit, and miraculous fountains of water turned to wine, while from the heavens above Enoch and Elijah looked down upon the scene, their gilded faces mimicking the angelic illumination of heavenly creatures. In the next two pageants, Henry himself seemed to ascend from the garden to the heavens, finally reaching the heavenly castle of Saint John's vision and penetrating to the very center of the New Jerusalem, for the last of the series of pageants staged his arrival before the throne of the Trinity just outside St. Paul's Cathedral (Lydgate, 630–48; Delpit, 245–48).

This selection of epiphanies was clearly tailored to the advent of a child prince. Dame Sapience appeared in part because the king was only a boy who must be lectured on the necessity of good schooling. Similarly, the actor portraying the enthroned king was chosen in part because he was of similar age to the king. But the young king's tender years cannot alone explain the abundant nativity imagery that filled the show from beginning to end. When the goddesses Nature, Grace, and Fortune bestowed their gifts upon Henry, they symbolically reenacted his birth. So, too, the genealogical trees that marked the king's admission into the Castle of Heaven were graphic symbols of both Henry's and Christ's nativities. The show included these pageants not simply because they were generally appropriate to a child king but primarily because the show as a whole aimed to dramatize the symbolic birth of the king to his people. Henry came to London for the first time just as Christ came to the world for the first time as a "childe off beaute precellyng." The show marked Henry's first formal appearance to the citizens of London after his coronations in England and France. As he moved through the streets, therefore, he was metaphorically born to his people and became manifest for the first time as their king.

It is important to understand that the show's nativity imagery was not merely conceptual but liturgical. The subjects and imagery of the pageants were drawn primarily from the liturgy that celebrated the advent, birth, and epiphany of Christ. Both the Jesse Tree pageant and the pageant of the gifts of the Holy Spirit derived from a passage indispensable to Advent: Isaiah's description of the messiah (11:1–5) as a flower springing forth out of the root of Jesse, while the sevenfold spirit of the Lord rests upon him. The many gifts offered by the various angels and personifications alluded to the gifts of the shepherds and the Magi at Epiphany. The same prophecy of Isaiah also described the future messiah as a *rex iustus*, who will judge with justice and reprove with equity (11:1–5), thus perhaps suggesting the pageant of the enthroned "childe of beaute precellying." Certainly many of the verses adorning the throne of justice pageant were drawn from the liturgy of Christmas and Epiphany (e.g., Ps. 71, an Epiphany psalm, and Ps. 88, a Christmas offertory). The "water of Archedeclyne," which miraculously turned to wine, is an Epiphany motif, and the same pageant also visualized the "Canticle of Isaiah" (12:3), which figured in the church's Christmas and Epiphany celebrations.

Many of the encounters that kings and pageant actors performed together in civic triumphs served as manifestations of the king's divinity. Pageant devisers invented a variety of techniques for staging such epiphanies, including symbolic allusion to the liturgy of the Epiphany season, and these became the most important dramatic devices in the repertoire of British civic pageantry. Since the liturgy of Epiphany celebrates three of Christ's epiphanies—the Magi, the baptism, and the wedding at Cana—and suggests many other prefigurations and types, pageant devisers found in it great scope for their ingenuity.

The Magi are suggested in every civic triumph that included the presentation of an epiphany gift. The mayor and aldermen, for example, traditionally presented the king with money and other gifts as a token of their submission and loyalty. The staged offering of a gift, like the gift of the Magi, symbolized the citizens' acclamation of the king and their faithful submission to him. As a reflection of this central act of submission sealed with a munificent gift, the Magi sometimes appeared in the city's pageantry to offer their gifts. At Aberdeen in 1511, according to Dunbar, the Magi thus "Offer to Chryst, with benygn reverence, Gold, sense, and mir, with all humility, *Schawand him king with most magnificence*" (135–36). Water turned to wine at the royal advent in almost every civic triumph, sometimes specifically alluding to the wedding at Cana. Trees of Jesse (sometimes accompanied by royal genealogical trees) bloomed everywhere.

But the most dramatically impressive epiphanies that could be offered by the civic triumph were stagecraft miracles. These enabled visiting kings and queens to manifest themselves as the elect of God by displays of divine prowess. Such a miracle enabled the New Jerusalem to descend into the streets of London to greet the advent of Richard II. In similar vein, when Henry VIII and Charles V made their entry into London (1522), a mechanical "Ile off englonde" sprang into life: "And att the comyng off the emprowr the bestys dyd move and goo, the fisshes dyd sprynge, the byrdes dyd synge reioysyng the comyng off the ij princes the emprowr and the kynges grace" (Withington, 1:177).

The civic triumph also achieved a manifestation of the king's messianic nature in a variety of other ways. Many pageants staged an epiphany of the king as a type of Christ the King by bringing the real king face-to-face with a pageant king seated in a throne of justice. Henry VI's encounter with a "childe of beaute precellying" on such a throne gained much of its force from its origin in Psalm 84—much used in the Christmas liturgy—which envisions the reconciliation of the Four Daughters of God upon the advent of Christ (Traver, 11–28). Still other triumphs engineer an epiphany by means of prophetic testimony. Prophets are frequently called in to "recognize" that the king is the Expected One, in the manner of an *ordo prophetarum*. During Prince Edward's entry into Coventry (1474), such testimony was provided by Jacob and his twelve sons, Saint Edward the Confessor, the Magi, Saint George, two prophets sensing him at the town cross, and the Children of Israel singing and strewing "obles" and flowers upon him (Harris, 2:390–93). Even nondescript characters might find themselves speaking in liturgical and prophetic voices when addressing royal visitors. A "Janitor" [porter] thus constructed his welcome for Henry VII out of a selection of antiphons used by the Church to announce that the ancient prophecies had been fulfilled in the advent and epiphany of Christ.

> Ecce advent Dominator, Domine,
> Et Regnum in manibus potestas & Imperium,

he began, citing the Church's familiar Epiphany antiphon, then continued with an Advent antiphon based on Haggai 2:8:

> Venit desideratus cunctis gentibus.
> To whom this Citie both al and some
> Speking by me, biddeth hertely Welcome. (LELAND, 4:192–94)

A kingly epiphany might even explicate the king's name. Philip of Spain accordingly found that his nature was best manifested in a display of the "foure moste noble Philips, of whose most noble actes and doinges we read in auncient stories" (Nichols, 147–48).

The four pageants devised by Henry Hudson, parish priest of Spofforth, for Henry VII's 1486 entry into York provide an especially vivid example of a civic triumph based exclusively upon staged epiphanies (Johnston and Rogerson, 1:139–43, 146–50). At each station, kings appeared to present symbolic gifts to the Tudor monarch. As with the Magi, this symbolic gift giving constituted an act of obeisance and feudal submission from a lesser to a greater monarch. At the first station the king demonstrated his messianic power by transforming "a world desolate" into a rose garden dominated by the Tudor Union Rose. At Henry's approach, "a roiall rich rede rose" and a "rich white rose" sprang up out of the desolate world to greet the monarch. All the other flowers in the garden thereupon "lowte and evidently yeue suffrantie" to the rose both white and red, and a crown—the first of Henry's symbolic gifts—descended from a heaven of "grete ioy and angelicall armony" to cover the roses. To complete this heraldic *blazon* of civic submission to the Tudor monarchy, Ebrauke, the mythic founder of York (Eboracum), took the stage to present Henry with the second of his gifts: the keys to the city. These gifts, Ebrauke pointed out, constituted an act of feudal homage from one king to another: "To you, Henrie, I submitt my citie, key and croune." Just as the "world desolate" had been transformed by the rose, so Ebrauke hoped that "the reame may recouer in to prosperity" by means of Henry's "aboundance" of grace.

A second epiphany awaited Henry above Ouse Bridge, where King Solomon sat in "a roiall troyne" surrounded by six other crowned kings "betokening the six Henries." As the seventh Henry approached, this council of kings performed a communal act of feudal submission, surrendering a "scepter of sapience" to Solomon, who in turn "submitting me vmbly," presented it to Henry as the third of his gifts. Solomon's presence at the head of this council of Henries is especially evocative. By virtue of his anointing and his wisdom, the son of David serves frequently as a type of Christ the King. By pressing Solomon into duty here as one of Henry's Magi, Hudson arranged for the anointed of the Old Law to pay his homage to this new Tudor *rex christus*. King David, in fact, awaited Henry at the next station to present him with the last of his symbolic gifts. In a pageant castle representing his realm of Jerusalem and filled with rejoicing Judaeans, David performed one last act of feudal obeisance. In recognizing Henry as the rightful lord of the city, he submitted to Henry his "swerd of victorie" as a token of York's acclamation of its king.

A final moment of epiphany concluded the show by demonstrating that Henry came to York not only as the feudal overlord but also as God's elect. The citizens apparently used their pageant for the Assumption of the Virgin from the York mystery cycle to manifest Henry's kingly legitimacy. Descending from the heavens of the pageant by means of its winching mechanism, the Virgin acclaimed Henry's advent. Although she was not precisely a Magus, she did bring the king the priceless gift of divine election. "My sone [i.e, Christ]," she reported, "as thy souueraigne hath the soothly assigned / Of his grace to be gouernor of his peoplez proteccoun." Moreover, she put herself at the king's service in her role as divine mediatrix, promising to pray continually for Henry: "I shall sew to my sone / to send you his grace." In his journey through the city, Henry thus encountered his Magi one by one and received from them the symbolic regalia: crown, keys, scepter, and sword. Each gift sealed an act of royal submission by means of which Henry was proclaimed the rightful king. This final pageant revealed him as the messianic king chosen by God to rule the English people. In the streets of the Yorkist capital, he was crowned king by his former enemies and acclaimed by the once rebellious citizens as the king chosen by God to rule them.

The civic triumphs considered so far have primarily been those staged for the entry of kings. In fact, queens' triumphs were equally important. Although they resembled kingly triumphs in some ways, they were conceptually distinct. Because of her gender and (until 1553) her inevitable status as consort rather than regent, a queen could not be received into a city as a type of Christ. Instead, to stage the civic triumphs of their queens, British cities exploited a distinctively female version of the royal entry with its own complex iconography, derived from the liturgy for the Assumption and Coronation of the Virgin. Consequently, queens, like kings, might also imaginatively ascend to the Castle of Heaven as they moved through city streets. The earliest queen's triumph on record, the London entry of Anne of

Bohemia (1382), thus merely reused the angelic castle that had featured in Richard II's entry five years earlier (Herbert, 2:217–18). But even though the queen's journey may seem superficially similar to a king's civic triumph, it imaginatively took the form of the Assumption of the Virgin Mary rather than the Advent of Christ. She therefore entered the city as Holy Mediatrix, bearer of Grace, Mother and Spouse of the royal Savior.

As the city's mediatrix, the queen traditionally identified herself with the citizens' interests, becoming their advocate before the king. As a sign of her willingness to sponsor her people, the queen symbolically "married" her realm at her coronation, becoming not so much the head of the body politic—the king claimed that role—as its patron and representative. In this way, she exercised an essential, distinctively queenly, power. If the king came to judge his people in the civic triumph, the queen came to mediate, bringing mercy beyond justice.

The citizens of London thus used the "Reconciliation" triumph of 1392 to cast Richard II's consort, Anne of Bohemia, in this familiar role, and she played the part superbly opposite Richard's rendition of the wrathful King of Justice (Maydiston; C. Smith). London staged Anne's manifestation as Virgo Mediatrix at Temple Bar amidst a presentation of gifts. At the same pageant, Richard's epiphany was celebrated not only by the pointing finger of John the Baptist, as we have seen, but also by the gift of a pair of altarpieces, while the citizens begged him to "be sparing of the ignorant even as that Heavenly King though unavenged was always forbearing to his enemies." As Richard left the stage, the citizens presented a similar pair of altarpieces to the queen, in whom they recognized a manifestation of the Virgo Mediatrix: "As often as you look upon these tablets, may you remember the people of the city and cause the king to be a friend to them." Under these circumstances, the gift becomes a contract; in accepting the city's gift, the queen must accept as well the role that the citizens would thrust upon her.

In the event, Queen Anne played her part to perfection, not only thanking the citizens for their gift but speaking in the authentic voice of the Virgo Mediatrix: "if there is to be peace ... it will be perfected through me." In a carefully staged scene in Westminster Hall, she again played Mary to Richard's Christ. Histrionically prostrating herself at the feet of the king, she interceded for the city in much the same way that the Virgin interceded for sinful mankind. When the king lifted her up, she explained:

> I suffer deeply for those citizens and for the city which has thus reverenced you and your household, and I steadfastly beg through Him by whom you bear love for me, if by love I bring anything worthy, that you would deem it worthy to spare the citizens who gave so willingly such magnificent gifts. . . . May it be acceptable now to return the city's ancient rights and to restore its liberties. (C. SMITH, 209–11)

Richard, of course, found he could no more deny Anne's mediation than Christ could deny Mary. In agreeing to her request, he invited her to take her place beside him on the Throne of Majesty, thus achieving a final epiphany as Queen of Heaven.

The queen's role as a bringer of grace finds full expression in the London entry of Margaret of Anjou (1456), which first staged the queen's epiphany as a bearer of divine grace and then dramatized her ascent to the Celestial Jerusalem as a type of the Queen of Heaven (Kipling, "London"). At the Bridge Gate station, the goddesses Peace and Plenty acknowledged her as a bearer of grace by welcoming her to London as "Causer of wealth, ioie, and abundaunce" and prophesying that "through youre grace . . . Pees shall approche" and "the reawmes two, Englande and Fraunce" shall achieve "rest and unite." At Noah's Ark on London Bridge, she was likened to the "Doue that brought the braunche of pees" as a "Tokyn and signe the Floode shulde cesse." According to Madame Grace, Chauncelere de Dieu, at the third station, her advent initiated "This tyme of Grace" in which "pees schall floure and fructifie." To others, she was a "Doughter of Iherusalem," a "Conueie of Grace," and a "Prenostike of pees." Each of the pageants thus contributed to a progressive epiphany in which Queen Margaret, like the Virgin Mary, became a Blessed Virgin "full of Grace."

The final three pageants traced the celestial assumption for which her abundance of grace had qualified her. The fifth pageant addressed her as the heavenly Sponsa whose "Grace in this lyf" had prepared her to join "Sponsus Pees the Kynge" in the "tabernacles highe" of heaven. At the Cross in Cheapside, she ascended "from vertu to vertu" to "the faire Cite of Iherusalem, / Bisette aboute with many a precious gemme." Finally, she came face-to-face with the Virgin Mary—"assumpt above the heavenly Ierarchie" and wearing a crown of twelve stars—who promised that Christ would also "crown her in blisse eterne" at the Day of Judgment (Kipling, "Grace").

The queen often played her most important role as a royal childbearer. In this way, she served the city she entered as both a divine mediatrix and a bearer of grace. In many more cases than can be the result of mere chance, the city received its queen for the first time only after she was pregnant. When Edward IV's consort, Elizabeth Woodville, entered Norwich in 1469, for example, she was pregnant with her second child. Pageants of the Annunciation and the Salutation, however, show that the citizens regarded their queen's *adventus* primarily as foreshadowing a princely nativity (Harrod). Similarly, when James IV's queen, Margaret Tudor, entered Aberdeen in 1511, she came as a scion of the old enemy at a time of increasing Anglo-Scottish tension. The three children so far born to her had all died within a year of birth, yet Aberdeen insisted on receiving her with images redolent of Advent and Epiphany that could only remind her forcefully of her duty to produce an heir (Dunbar, 16–18).

The same civic anxiety about royal succession explains the sometimes extravagant imagery in which the pregnant Anne Boleyn entered London (1533) to be offered a series of golden gifts in pageant after pageant (E. Hall, 800–802; Leland

and Udall, 373–401). These constitute, to be sure, epiphanies in which Queen Anne manifested herself as a "Queene most excellent, / Highly endued with all gifts of grace." But the gifts that London showered upon its new queen were not primarily given as a sign of homage, like the gifts of the Magi. As England bestowed these material, intellectual, and spiritual gifts upon its new queen, it expected another gift in return. They are thus a form of barter, or even (as one pageant expositor put it) "purchase":

> Wee the citizens, by you, in shorte space,
> Hope such issue and descente to purchase,
> Whereby the same faith shall be defended,
> And this cittie from all damages preserved.

In the pageant from which a child speaks these words, Saint Anne's children and grandchildren gathered, offering the queen an image of the fruitful and holy gift they expected from her. In a later pageant, three ladies cast wafers down upon the pregnant queen with this message written upon them: "Queen Anne, when thou shalt bear a new son of the King's blood, there shall be a golden world unto thy people." The confident wording of this scripture (which was also written boldly across the pageant) underlines the urgency of her people's expectations. The pageants clearly defined the queen's role for her: Virgo Mediatrix and Bearer of Heavenly Grace. The civic triumph expected their new queen to give them a royal child who would preserve the realm in the Christian faith. Such a gift, it is clear, would more than repay the gifts given her and justify her advent as queen (E. Hall, 801–2; Leland and Udall, 389).

The queen might enter the city and play the protagonist's role in her triumph, but the pageant always reserved a dominant role for her spouse as sponsor, author, and prime mover of the show, for such a role reflected his higher status. Kings, like Christ, *ascended* into heaven; queens, like Mary, had to be *assumed*. Queens' triumphs, as a consequence, often took pains to include epiphanies of the king from whom she derived her status and power. In these conditions, the consort queen often entered the city primarily as an agent in either her husband's or her son's epiphany.

In this spirit, various of the Nine Worthies, remarking that "your own souerayn lorde & kynge is present here," pointedly reminded Queen Margaret (Coventry, 1456) that they would "obey to you lady [and] youre persone prayse / and welcome you Curtesly" not primarily for her own sake, but "for the loue of your lege lorde Herry that hight" (R. W. Ingram, 32–33). The citizens of Aberdeen (1511) similarly confronted Margaret Tudor with a manifestation of James IV's chivalric glory in the form of a statue of the Bruce, the "nobill, dreadful, michtie campaign" (Dunbar, 16–18). Katharine of Aragon witnessed two such epiphanies. She first paused before a heroic image of her bridegroom, Prince Arthur—"a prince of all princes the very floure"— revealed as a reborn King Arthur riding a star-chariot in triumph through an enormous, turning zodiac wheel. At the very next station, she then approached a pageant depicting her father-in-law, Henry VII, as "Father of Heaven." A "Prelate of the Church" quickly proclaimed the kingly manifestation:

The Kyng of Heaven is like an earthly kyng
That to his sonne prepareth a weddyng.
And right so as oure sovereign lord, the Kyng,
May be resemblid to the King Celestial.

And to ensure that she would not miss the point, the citizens of London arranged for Henry to take a prominent standing just opposite the pageant, where he might both see and be seen (Kipling, *Receyt*, 26–31).

Encounters like these between queen and pageant actors served to dramatize the queen's powers of mediation. She stood symbolically between the two parties, occasioning manifestations of her spouse's glory to the people and pleading the people's case to her spouse. As she marched through the city, she enacted this role symbolically. At one pageant, her advent caused an epiphany of the king to occur, thus revealing her spouse's divine nature to them. The next pageant perhaps enlisted her support on behalf of the city by dramatizing her own powers of intercession.

Such role playing, of course, presupposes two conditions. On the one hand, because of her status as a consort, she brought with her the power to mitigate, sway, persuade, or stave off the awful judgment of the Lord on behalf of the city. On the other, the queen's role playing presupposed the city's sympathetic acceptance of a Roman Catholic view of salvation, in which the queen imitates the Virgo Mediatrix.

But what if these two conditions alter? What if the queen comes not as a consort but as a regnant queen? And what if the idealized role she plays—the Virgo Mediatrix—should suddenly appear to be compromised or corrupted by a change in religious belief? By the end of the sixteenth century, the Reformation and the appearance of queens regnant in both England and Scotland sharply challenged strongly gendered civic dramas. A city now had to define its relationship with a sovereign whom it found inconceivable to acclaim as Christ. Given the context of the Reformation, which both rejected the Marian model of queenly power and yet might reject the sovereign power of queens as a "monstrous regiment" (to use Knox's term), what are the idealized roles that citizens and sovereign might together achieve and acclaim in an inaugural drama, the better to define their respective political roles? What is the appropriate liturgy for the acclamation of a queen regnant? In the inaugural triumphs of the Tudor and Stuart queens, the drama of the civic triumph had to create an imaginative new political order for the first time, not merely acclaim the inherited political roles of an existing order.

As Susan Frye points out, Queen Elizabeth's inaugural civic triumph (London, 1559) was filled with anxieties about the new sovereign's gender. The citizens, she argues, constructed an entirely new idealized role for the queen. "Compliant, malleable, and grateful," Elizabeth entered London more to become the city's "metaphoric wife" than its sovereign king (Frye, *Elizabeth I*, 22–55). These housewifely traits, however, were similar to the traditional attributes of the Virgo Mediatrix, which consort queens formerly expected to play, except that the role had been drained of its specifically religious content, and the city had replaced the king as the virgin's *sponsa*. Reflecting the new Protestant and feminine regime, the show avoided most of the sacramental imagery of medieval sovereignty: no angels descended from heaven to crown the queen, nor did the queen ascend to the Castle of Heaven. Nevertheless, the show remained fundamentally conservative in its emblematic ideas. It preferred, wherever possible, to rehabilitate old images rather than to invent new ones.

These attempts to adapt old images to the service of a moderate Protestant regime appear throughout the civic triumph, even in those places where it seems most eager to distinguish itself from tradition. It often avoids the traditional emblems of sacramental monarchy, replacing these with careful citations of the Word. In many respects, however, it pours new wine into old bottles. A pageant at the Conduit in Fleet Street, for instance, staged an obligatory epiphany of the sovereign as a *rex iustus*. But instead of a messianic son of David seated on a throne, Elizabeth's entry cited the example of Deborah, who appeared seated beneath a palm tree precisely as described in Scripture. Neither anointed nor a son of David, she was no messiah. But, the pageant points out, she was "sent" to her people by God to be their judge. Emphatically, the pageant regards Deborah not as a messianic type to be embodied but rather as a scripturally sanctioned example of a female ruler: "a worthie president, O worthie Queene, . . . a worthie woman iudge, a woman sent for staie" (Mulcaster, *Quenes*, 53–55).

A pageant at the Great Conduit similarly sought to redefine the traditional image of the queen as grace bearer by careful evocation of Protestant scripture (Mulcaster, *Quenes*, 41–43). Eight children stood there upon an arch, symbolically "appointed & apparelled" to represent "the eight beatitudes expressed in the .v. chapter of the gospel of S. Mathew, applyed to our soueraigne Ladie Quene Elizabeth." As the queen arrived before the pageant, each child symbolically bestowed a blessing upon her. As in earlier triumphs, such an encounter served to establish Elizabeth's credentials as both a Holy Virgin full of Grace and a Bearer of Grace to her people. She received the eight beatitudes only to transmit them to her people.

But if this show adopted a traditional Marian persona for their queen, it also sought to rehabilitate that persona to suit a Protestant regime. Elizabeth came to London full of blessings, not Grace—perhaps a narrow distinction, but potentially an important theological shibboleth—and the pageant cited a particular Gospel passage rather than church tradition or patristic commentary to validate the emblem, thus clearly establishing the Protestant credentials of this rehabilitated image. The pageant carefully demonstrated that Elizabeth's entry was sanctioned by the Word, which manifestly "applyed" to her. In making her advent as a virgin full of blessings, Elizabeth thus ministered the world of God to her people.

Perhaps we see the show's essential iconographical conservatism most strongly in the most memorable pageant of the series, which conspicuously rehabilitates yet another of the former personas of the Virgin Mary—the Virgo Mediatrix—to suit the advent of a Protestant queen (Mulcaster, *Quenes*, 46–49). As Elizabeth approached the Little Conduit in Cheapside, she occasioned one of those miraculous epiphanies that had always been the staple of the civic triumph. Similar to the miracle wrought by her grandfather a century earlier in York, she transformed a "cragged, barreyn, and stonye" landscape into a garden, "fayre, fresh, grene, and beawtifull, the grounde thereof full of flowres and beawtie." She revived the single, desolate tree "all withered and deadde, with braunches accordinglye" that dominated the barren landscape so that it flourished as a "very freshe and fayre" bay tree. The inhabitants responded to the queen as much as the vegetation did. She thus also transformed a wretch named "Ruinosa Respublica" into a "freshe personage well apparaylled and appoynted" now "in state tryumphant" and renamed "Respublica bene instituta."

In previous triumphs, the mere advent of the messianic king would have wrought such a change. But this triumph required the queen to perform a mediatory act to accomplish this miraculous reformation. "An old man with a Sythe in his hande, hauynge wynges artificiallye made" emerged from a cave in a hill to greet the queen. He was Time, bringing with him his daughter, Truth, who held an English Bible in her hands and gave it to the pageant's expositor, who in turn "reached hys boke towardes the Quenes maiestie." This gift occasioned the central epiphany of the pageant, because the gift expressed the queen's personal motto: Veritas Temporis Filia. In order to complete the meaning of that motto, Elizabeth had to accept Truth's gift, and by accepting it, the queen necessarily performed a crucial emblematic action that revealed her nature as a Protestant ruler: she received the Word on behalf of her Reformed people. Only if empowered by the Word could the queen transform a landscape *sub lege* into a redeemed landscape *sub gratia*, for the Word, not the Catholic sacraments, was the true means of grace. The magically altered garden manifested the power of the Word, for only the Word offered in the English Bible had the power to reform the landscape.

The pageant required no further performance from Elizabeth to make its point. She had only passively to accept the epiphany gift and the pageant would manifest her nature to her subjects. Nevertheless, Elizabeth chose at this moment to play her part with relish. She "receiued the booke, kyssed it, and with both her handes held vp the same, and so laid it upon her brest, with great thankes to the citie therfore," actively cooperating with the role that the pageant prescribed for her. By her histrionic display, she demonstrated that she understood, approved of, and accepted that role. The Virgo Mediatrix had become the Minister of the Word.

Not all queens regnant were so sympathetically received, nor did they act their roles so expertly. A more radically Protestant establishment in Edinburgh inverted the traditional drama of the civic triumph as a means of rejecting their new sovereign, who was both female and Catholic. For the inaugural entry of Mary Queen of Scots (1561), John Knox's fellow citizens prepared a hellish *adventus* for its queen. As an act of scripted, communal liturgy, it invited popular repudiation rather than acclamation. To begin with, however, the show seemed deceptively to promise a celestial ascent according to the traditional pattern (Mill, 189–91; MacDonald, 109–10; Bergeron, *Pageantry*, 23–25). Angels sang to Mary "in the maist hevenly wyis" from scaffolds set high atop city gates. Saintly virgins "cled in the maist hevenlie clething" filled cups of wine for her from the streams that miraculously spouted from the town cross. A mechanical cloud opened to permit the descent of an angel, who presented Mary with two symbolic books—an English Bible and a Protestant psalmbook. These, the angel told her, she must "reade and vnderstande" if she were to succeed as queen, for they explained all the queen must know if she were to achieve an apotheosis into a Protestant heaven. But should Mary refuse the "perfytt waye" that these books described, the angel also warned that they showed how God "threatnes with his scurge and wand" all those "who the contrarie does wilfullie." The angel then reascended into his cloud.

This crucial pageant thus offered an epiphany gift that drew exclusive boundaries between sovereign and subject. The English Bible and psalmbook here symbolize an essential division between the ruler and her body politic, rather than corporate unity. The Protestant citizens, probably recalling the Londoners' similar gift to Elizabeth two years earlier, in fact offered these potent symbols because they knew their queen would refuse them. Only if Mary embraced her subjects' symbolic gifts to become, like Elizabeth, a Minister of the Word could she be acclaimed as the queen of this Protestant city. By rejecting the gift, she revealed herself as a Catholic and ungodly queen. Faced with this challenge, Mary attempted a diplomatic response: she directed one of her Catholic retainers to accept the gift for her. But she could not temporize. The moment had been designed as an epiphany, and her response to the offered gift would necessarily reveal her nature to those who watched:

> When the Bible was presented, and the praise thair of declared, sche began to frown; for schame sche could not refuise it. But she did no better, for immediatelie sche gave it to the most pestilent Papist within the Realme, to wit, to Arthoure Erskyn.

The second half of Mary's triumph proceeded to dramatize the "scurge and wand" with which God punishes those "who the contrarie does wilfullie." Mary, in fact, symbolically played into the hands of her enemies when she rejected the Bible and psalmbook that the pageant angel attempted to give her. As a consequence, the next pageant showed her "the terrible significations of the vengeance of God upon idolatry." In the pageant deviser's mind, the rebellion of Core, Dathan, and Abiron against the congregation of Moses, even as they were in the act of offering incense to God (Num. 16:8–35), constituted an Old Testament prefiguration of the damnable impiety of the Catholic Mass. Wooden effigies of Core, Dathan, and

Abiron were burned before Mary's face "in the tyme of their sacrifice," and a speech was made "tending to the abolishing of the mess," while a "priest in his ornaments reddie to say mass, made of wode" stood ready to be burned in the very act of elevating the Host. Though the earl of Huntly apparently "stayed that pagient," a final pageant nevertheless continued this foretaste of the fiery vengeance of the Lord upon idolaters by burning a spectacularly combustible dragon, probably the Beast of the Apocalypse. The civic triumph thus cast Mary in the role of the beast's mistress, the Whore of Babylon, who "shall be burnt with the fire, because God is strong, who shall judge her" (Rev. 18:8).

In dramatizing the queen's triumphant entry into hell instead of into some jasper-green castle of heaven, this civic triumph testified eloquently both to the persistence of a respected tradition to which pre-Reformation men and women had entrusted the organization of their lives and to the rejection of that tradition. Faced for the first time with a sovereign rather than a consort queen, the citizens of Edinburgh had no symbolic vocabulary to deal with the meaning of her advent. Since the Marian pattern was inappropriate, on both constitutional and religious grounds, these Protestant subjects of a Catholic queen designed a show that dramatized their rejection both of their queen and of the iconography that had given these shows their communal purpose and meaning for more than 150 years. She brought the city no gift of grace; no Jesse Tree proclaimed the imminent birth of an Infant Savior. Above all, she was no messianic sovereign come to rule her people. It was that very right to come to her kingdom as a type of Christ that the citizens rejected, and their rejection tells us a great deal about the seriousness with which citizens and sovereigns conceived of their roles and performed them to one another.

NOTE

1. All biblical quotations and citations in this essay are taken from the Douay Rheims version, which is a translation of the Vulgate, the text most often used by devisers of civic triumphs.

# CHAPTER 10

# The Theater and Domestic Culture

*Diana E. Henderson*

ALTHOUGH THEIR margins and powers changed radically during the sixteenth and seventeenth centuries, institutions such as the Church, the Court, and the City of London remain relatively easy to identify; by contrast, the exact parameters of domestic life defy simple geography. Familiar and socioeconomic relations shaped within homes remained powerful no matter where one moved, and the material consequences of marriages and domestic behavior made intimate relationships the very stuff of politics. Like its cousin popular culture, domestic culture both relied on theoretical hierarchies (husband-wife, parent-child, master-servant) and subverted those theories in practice. It existed in hundreds of households that were at best cognates rather than identical to one another, in many cases sharing little beyond the ideological authority of the father. The "householder" who presided over the homes of landowning or professional families was presumed to be male, benevolent, and in control. When represented onstage, the domestic order seldom bore out these presumptions.

As a generic label, *domestic* has most often been applied to tragedies involving characters within a family of less than royal birth whose downfall does not directly imperil the kingdom. Adams's classic study of the genre attributes to domestic tragedy a straightforwardly educational or "homiletic" intention. Plays deemed central to the domestic canon by these criteria include *Arden of Faversham* (pre–1592), *Two Lamentable Tragedies* (1594), *A Warning for Fair Women* (1599), *A Woman Killed With Kindness* (1603), *A Yorkshire Tragedy* (1605), and *The Witch of Edmonton* (1621). Many of these stories derive from historical incidents, and all are set close to home in time and place. Thus they invoke a second meaning of *domestic* that was current in the sixteenth century: its implied opposition to the foreign or strange. And yet here, too, theatrical representation works to undermine easy dichotomies, since such plays reveal strange dangers lurking within the local land-scape, including witches, foreigners, unruly servants and wives, and corrupt, tyrannical, or abdicating householders.[1]

During the nineteenth century, the heyday of a gendered ideology of separate public and private spheres, the generic tag *domestic tragedy* developed as a way of acknowledging these classically improper or "impertinent" plays (to borrow Orlin's apt phrase [246]). The category soon, however, became a way to dismiss such works as second-tier drama, in contrast to the tragic fall of princes; this created the illusion of a gaping gulf between kingly "public" and merely "private" stories in early modern England. For this reason, some contemporary critics suggest discarding the generic label completely, while others seek to honor particular plays above the putatively sensationalist pack.[2] These strategies, however, may discount the domestic perspectives (including those of women and servants) represented most vividly within such plays.

By contrast, attending to the social struggles in domestic drama allows an alternative understanding of Elizabethan theater. If one charts the development of the stage repertory from such origins as *Arden of Faversham* (nearly contemporaneous with *The Spanish Tragedy* and *Tamburlaine*, plays more conventionally cited as starting points), one immediately confronts anxieties about change that affected life at home and beyond: the rise of "new men," the displacement of tenant farmers, and uncontrollable women and servants. The focus turns from Senecan revenge and heroic drama derived from inherited stories and foreign climes back to the (devious) "motherwits" of domesticity more immediately reflecting the experience of the theater's audience. Invoking the domestic not only as a genre but as a culture encourages attention to the conflicts and material realities that recur in plays focused on local, contemporary home life, without separating them off as "other" to dominant stage practices.

While the home was certainly a site of hierarchical relations, it is not always clear who benefited from it as a power base. Whether at home or abroad, the master had to rely on his social inferiors for domestic order, making him vulnerable to their desires and managerial decisions; the stage repeatedly dramatized such tensions. Drama articulated the complicated emotions and attitudes within households, which among the privileged could include servants, retainers, and tenants, as well as blood relations and wards. Less often represented onstage were the many female-headed and single-person households that defied the ideological assumptions of church and state alike. By studying relationships between domestic ideology and stage practice on the one hand and between stage practice and historical evidence on the other, scholars are currently attempting to understand better the work of early English stages in shaping views of domesticity. Exploring the relationships between domestic culture(s) and theater thus becomes a dynamic form of attention.

Spurred by the new questions and insights of social historians, theater historians, and feminist and queer theorists, our understanding of the early modern home (and the homeless) is in the process of radical transformation. This essay replicates the development and current weight of work in the field, focusing predominantly on the reevaluation of the theoretical centrality of marriage and roles within the family, and gesturing more briefly at the crucial, emergent study of masculinities; master-servant relations; the complex variables of sexuality, class, and status; and the material conditions that shaped not only architecture but also the human inter-actions that took place within living spaces. The obvious danger in retracing a field's genealogy is to replicate its residual ideological biases; the compensatory logic of this representation is to provide a ground for understanding those biases and encouraging informed movement beyond them.

## Conjugal Bliss and Unruly Women

Domestic, and especially marital, ideology was inculcated prescriptively through classical tracts such as Xenephon's *Oeconomicus* and contemporary conduct man-uals such as William Gouge's *Of Domestical Duties*, as well as through the Church's *Homily of the State of Matrimony* and the law; it was also rendered onstage through fictional models such as *Patient Grissel* (Griselda being the infi-nitely patient "good" wife) and comic types such as shrewish city wives, hoarding uncles, and cuckolds.[3] Especially after the Reformation, the association of father and king, of home and castle, developed into a highly sophisticated analogical sys-tem. It included viewing the murder of a husband or master as "petty treason," while the father's murder of his child was regarded not only as infanticide but as "petty tyranny"; *Arden of Faversham* and *A Yorkshire Tragedy* use historical cases of those two crimes, respectively, to produce sensational entertainment as well as hortatory conclusions. The system of analogies allowed local, specific stories to be seen not (only) as luridly exceptional docudramas but as cautionary exempla revealing improprieties within the familial and social orders. On occasion, plays also encouraged sympathy for those who defied or suffered from the domestic status quo.

Conventionally, the career of a propertied "householder" began with a married man's establishment of his own home, thus giving the husband-wife relationship originary significance within domestic culture; at the same time, the wife became legally a *feme covert*, theoretically subsumed for the most part under her husband's identity. For all the post-Reformation talk of companionate marriage, household management was modeled not upon collaborative equality but upon monarchy. Moreover, marriages in moderately wealthy or noble households were most often arranged, motivated by material and social needs rather than personal desire. Nevertheless, economics and often love yoked together the subsequent fortunes of husbands and wives. Many a husband going off to pursue advancement would have reason to hope, as well as join *Henry V*'s Pistol to "command," that his spouse would "Let huswifery appear." The ironies of having to rely on a woman would have been clearer to an early modern audience; they boomerang comically in this fictional case. Thus despite much domestic and legal rhetoric, the home was not only the personal castle of the husband and master. Especially at times of (frequent) childbearing, it could become a space dominated by women, as well as being the dominant space for them, the place where they spent most of their lives.

It is therefore not surprising that among the earliest and most frequently represented domestic conflicts onstage is that between husband and wife—emphasizing the difficulty men had in upholding the religious and sociopolitical imperatives of female subordination. In the Chester cycle plays, Noah's wife becomes the comic prototype for all the unruly women who speak back to (here, quite literally) patriarchal authority. Her particular forms of rebellion include drinking and talking with her female friends; indeed, she values her "gossips" too much to leave them to die in the Flood. Noah finally enlists his sons' aid to carry their nameless mother against her will into the ark, a projection of idealized domestic space in which all the women are wives absolutely enclosed and controlled. But slapstick comedy does not undo a certain pathos for the drowned. As in the Brome Manuscript *Abraham and Isaac* (in which the mother is only a verbal presence but one repeatedly invoked by the anxious boy once his father begins to act strangely), the wife is located on lowly earth and associated with "natural" human bonds that are placed in dramatic opposition to the harsh, necessary Word of God the Father.

In Jacobean city comedies, concern about wives taking pleasure together unites with new economic emphases and the period's obsession with cuckoldry. Sometimes the mockery appears crudely, as in the Puritan women and gossips' eating, drinking, and urinating at the christening of Mrs. Allwit's adulterously produced child in Middleton's *A Chaste Maid in Cheapside* (1613).[4] Other times it combines with satire on privileged women's new aspirations to learning, as in the mockery of the "ladies that call themselves the collegiates" in Jonson's *Epicoene* (1609; 1.1.71–72). The few female friendships that are represented more positively onstage tend to be those less threatening to the male householder's control of his wife: those between confidantes before their courtship, or between a mistress and her waiting-woman. Even these bonds often have fraught or fatal consequences. Examples range from the petty insults between Helena and Hermia in *A Midsummer Night's Dream* to the deaths of Emilia in *Othello* and Diaphanta in *The Changeling*, and Paulina's loss of her husband in *The Winter's Tale*. Women's society outside the family constituted a challenge to the subsumption of the wife's identity by her husband, a challenge that the stage usually saw as a butt for satire or a threat to social stability.

Whether as compensation or as correlate, playwrights almost as often mocked the excessive worries of jealous husbands and chastised those who wielded their domestic authority too absolutely. Such "petty tyrants" were condemned even if the consequences of their actions fell short of murder. Some cases are ingenious in the ironic complexity of their narrative situation, showing virtuous women tempted unnecessarily by their husbands: the nasty Corvino threatens Celia with disfigurement in Jonson's *Volpone* (1606) if she refuses to prostitute herself; in Middleton and Rowley's *The Changeling* (1622), Isabella's husband, Alibius, confines her to their home in the madhouse he runs, where several suitors do in fact lurk in disguise. But the audacity and absurdity of these jealous husbands is hardly exceptional, whether in more directly "domestic" genres such as city comedy (Security the usurer in *Eastward Ho!* and his gulled counterparts in *Westward Ho!* and *The Family of Love*), or in romance (Leontes in *The Winter's Tale*), tragedy (*Othello*), and closet drama (Herod in *The Tragedy of Mariam*). While dramatizations throughout the period tended to evade the most local and direct form of indictment against domestic tyranny—there are disproportionately few English wife-murderers represented—the householder's misuse of his authority is a familiar trope.[5]

The gap between male views and "actual" female behavior provides one of the stage's central jokes as early as *The Second Shepherds' Play* of the Wakefield Cycle. After the rogue Mak complains to the shepherds about his lazy, shrewish consort, she deflates his rhetoric and (temporarily) saves his skin; it is Gill's idea to disguise Mak's stolen sheep as her baby, and her acting ability as a new mother suffices to mislead the shepherds during their first visit. Of course, she is thereby outdoing the comic villain and confirming stereotypes about women's deceitfulness and treachery, endorsed by the Church Fathers' interpretations of her biblical precedent, Eve. Moreover, the opening speech of the good second shepherd, Gyb, laments his loss of "will" in marriage and concludes with a litany of complaints about his conventionally sour, sharp-tongued, loud, huge wife. Because his rhetoric remains dramatically untested by subsequent events, the play finesses the question of whether misogynist discourse is simply male bluster. As such, the play provides a precedent for the mixed messages of many comic renderings of wives onstage.

Indubitably, the aggressive and contrary "shrew" became a stock source of dramatic comedy in the later sixteenth century. The type appears not only in ballads and the plays associated with Shakespeare's *The Taming of the Shrew* (*The Taming of A Shrew*; *The Woman's Prize*) but also in comedies as tonally diverse as John Heywood's interlude *Johan Johan* (Tyb), Jonson's *Epicoene* (Mrs. Otter), and arguably Dekker's *The Shoemaker's Holiday* (Margery Eyre is called a shrew, though her husband certainly outdoes her in verbiage and colorful insults—but as she repeatedly says, "let that pass"). In city comedies, assertive female characters became the target for concern about larger economic changes (elaborated below); however, the popularity of the type exceeds any single subgenre or displaced anxiety. Even in Chettle, Dekker, and Haughton's play putatively praising *Patient Grissel* (1600), a shrewish Welsh wife appears in the subplot. Indeed, as several of Shakespeare's later plays attest, characters based on the Griselda and shrew types often appear together, either as predictable opposites or, more interestingly, as a team (Desdemona and Emilia in the second half of *Othello*, Hermione and Paulina in *The Winter's Tale*). In this last variation on the theme, attention shifts away from policing the status quo through mockery of the female talker; instead, the shrew's transgression becomes a (temporarily) necessary corrective when husbands do indeed become "petty tyrants."

The comic limits of a husband's power in such a case are the subject of *The Woman's Prize* (c. 1611), John Fletcher's companion/response play to Shakespeare's *The Taming of the Shrew*. Here the shrew-taming Petruchio (after Katherina's early demise) finds himself outwitted by his second wife, Maria. She withholds not only sex but praise and any signs of concern for him, on the advice of a female "commander in chief" named Bianca—another version of the troubling "gossip." The women announce their gender rebellion by locking themselves indoors together and denying the men access. Thus they parody the only time women were fully sanctioned in taking over exclusive use of a major domestic area: during labor and the weeks of "lying-in" after birth. These disruptive women claim not only a chamber but a home, without first performing their crucial role as (in the words of the memorable "woman-hater" Joseph Swetnam) the "necessary evils" in reproduction.[6] As in Francis Beaumont's *The Knight of the Burning Pestle* (1607) and Middleton's *A Chaste Maid in Cheapside*, the romance plot succeeds only when a man unexpectedly pops up alive in his coffin, having feigned death in response to seemingly insurmountable obstacles. But in Fletcher's play, Petruchio does not arise in triumph; rather, he resurrects himself out of sheer frustration when even his death fails to move Maria. The wife's total control makes the ensuing happy ending seem even more serendipitous than is usual in comedy.

The shrew was a distinctly different type than the sexual transgressor—although their two kinds of unruly behavior were often elided in conduct books and stage plays, where any talkative woman was also presumed to be a "loose" one. Nevertheless, many "shrews" show no inclination to lasciviousness or sexual impropriety, and most such figures seem to be projections of male anxiety about controlling wives in particular. Indeed, Katherina in Shakespeare's *The Taming of the Shrew* (c. 1590–1593) begins as the rare unmarried shrew who would prove the rule, were she not so much more famous than the scores of shrewish stage wives. Before exploring the obsession with cuckoldry and female wantonness, then, it remains worth remarking that the currency of such "chaste shrews" undermines attempts to reduce fear of female speech to displaced sexual anxiety alone. So does archival evidence of sixteenth-century town life, which includes elaborate rituals of public shaming and punishment for "scolds" and the husbands who did not control them—a most notorious form of such discipline being the scold's bridle.[7] Independent speech and sexuality were both forms of female agency and, especially when practiced by wives, functioned as direct challenges to the patriarchal order of things.

In theory, the distinction between chaste and unchaste womanhood was absolutely crucial for establishing male identity and inheritance; in fact, it was much harder to police and define. The presumed life narrative for a woman was to inhabit sequentially three stages of life, named by relationship to her husband: maid, wife, widow. Opposed to this would be the improper life of a "whore," a term that could be applied to any woman with a sexual partner out of wedlock. (To cite a slightly more elevated example: the character dubbed a "Courtesan" by the protagonist Witgood in Middleton's A Trick to Catch the Old One [1605] has lost her virginity to him and slept with him alone.[8]) Negotiations between propertied families usually took place at the time of marriage to provide women with financial security through dowers or, more frequently, jointures; nevertheless, economic imperatives, if not desire, led most widows to remarry, complicating the three-stage model.[9] Nor was wedded fidelity universal. The Lawes Resolutions of Women's Rights proclaims: "All [women] are understood as either married or to be married and their desires [are] subject to their husband"—but it then adds that "some women can shift it well enough" (in Tilney, 6). The Elizabethan rhetoric praising "married chastity" tried to make wedded love sound as absolute a bodily state as virginity, but the need to rely on a woman's word for verification could make this sort of chastity seem a mystery, in something other than the religious sense.

While much domestic comedy and some tragedy derived from unwarranted male fears about women, just as many or more plays provided reasons for suspicion. Cuckoldry was a staple of popular comedy even before the English professional theater was fully established; it became an obsession, marking a key variation from the ancient New Comedy. John Heywood's rollicking Tudor interlude Johan Johan (c. 1520s?) presents the stereotypical triangle, descending from medieval satires against lascivious priests. Like Gill in The Second Shepherds' Play, Tyb is more ingenious than her husband. While she and the priest Sir Johan "eat pie," husband Johan Johan sits by the fire rubbing a candle to chafe the wax to fill the hole to mend the pail—the "candle" between his legs getting softer by the minute. When he finally explodes in violence, he only drives wife and priest together. Johan cannot win by asserting his domestic authority any more than he did by abdicating power to his wife, so he exits the playing space (imagined as being his own house) to prevent them from cuckolding him elsewhere.

Perhaps the most intriguing twist on the impotent husband occurs in Middleton's A Chaste Maid in Cheapside, in which the "wittol" Allwit willingly relinquishes access to, as well as control of, his wife, letting Sir Walter Whorehound into his home to worry about her behavior, father her children, and pay the bills. Characteristically blurring the line between propriety and absurdity, the playwright portrays sexuality as another form of labor—one with heavy financial burdens for men such as Allwit and Touchwood Senior, whose potency has become his curse. As in A Trick to Catch the Old One, Middleton also reveals the interchangeability of those putatively opposite categories wife and whore; he creates plots that allow a sympathetically etched "Dutch aunt" and a Welsh "lady" (courtesans who are thus doubly foreign to English domestic propriety) to become as respectably married as anyone else.[10] So much for the conduct books.

In Elizabethan domestic tragedies, the more serious treatment of "fallen" women creates odd shifts in tone. The most assertive such figure, Alice Arden, appears in a play that hovers perilously close to comedy, both because of her husband's resemblance to the comic wittol and because of the repeatedly foiled attempts to murder him by the hired ne'er-do-wells Black Will and Shakebag. For the majority of scenes, *Arden of Faversham* therefore seems unsure exactly where or how to place the blame for Thomas Arden's murder. Ultimately the domestic setting plays a crucial role in confirming that this is an egregious case of petty rebellion: Arden is killed, in his own home, when he has been displaced from the master's chair by Alice's lover, Moseby.[11] In two of Thomas Heywood's more sentimental tragedies of domestic betrayal, both Jane Shore (*Edward IV*) and Anne Frankford (A *Woman Killed with Kindness*) exude more pain than pleasure in their adultery, seeming quite literally to fall—or faint—into sin, passively and without choice. Trying to endorse the social order as benevolent while creating a sympathetic, penitent adulteress presented a challenge that Heywood resolves by muting the problematic existence of a woman's independent will. Similarly, in A *Warning for Fair Women*, Anne Sanders is virtually tricked into adultery and murder—by the bad advice, moreover, of yet one more version of the gossip, her false friend Anne Drury. Except for Alice Arden, none of these adulterous women seems to take much delight in disorder.

Jacobean adultery was more often staged as a calculating and sordid affair, a betrayal of domestic order. Suspicions about female sexuality and untrustworthiness mingle with the widespread disdain of women's "painted" faces; distrust of feminine surfaces permeates all sorts of public drama, ranging in tone from the delicate "Still to be neat" at the beginning of *Epicoene* to the vivid revulsion of Bosola in act 2 of *The Duchess of Malfi* (1614). Such castigation influences the ways female characters are viewed subsequently, making even necessary disguise, white lies, or playacting seem an indication of moral corruption: Bosola's speech, for example, subliminally "infects" the Duchess's next entrance as a secretly pregnant woman desiring fruit. In *The Changeling*, not only does the corrupt Beatrice-Joanna successfully counterfeit to pass a bizarre virginity test, but the common physical actions of the virgin Diaphanta whom she mimics—sneezing, laughing, and gaping—are thereby made to seem unnatural and ridiculous, as if all female bodies were inherently grotesque.[12]

Fears were not confined to the characters onstage: the presence of females in the audience drew fire from some stage practitioners as well as from antitheatrical divines. Public plays—especially domestic plays—were in danger of becoming "feminized." The boys' theater countered with satires aiming to discredit female spectatorship, as in Beaumont's *The Knight of the Burning Pestle*. The Citizen's wife is cheerfully mocked for pushing their apprentice Ralph into the play as hero, and also for her failure to discern the logic of the players' script: she adopts the wrong young suitor as her protagonist and castigates the comic spirit of the reveling Merrythought males. In each case, she condemns romantic extravagance because it threatens her "real life" sense of an interwoven domestic and commercial order. Beaumont uses a city wife's lack of discernment to make fun of those who expect art to imitate life exactly, as well as creating a travesty of public repertory plays that heroicize apprentices and merchants (*The Four Prentices of London, The Shoemaker's Holiday*). Gender thus functions as a convenient marker for other social differences.

Worries about women attending the theater went beyond their effect on it, to its effect on domestic culture. With women recorded as weeping for "fallen women" such as Jane Shore in Thomas Heywood's *Edward IV*, some claimed that plays would make wives unruly. Robert Anton's *The Philosopher's Satires* (1616) attacks theater for inciting women by showing them "Cleopatra's crimes"; he demands: "Why do our lustful theatres entice . . . Draw to the City's shame, with gilded clothes / Such swarms of wives to break their nuptial oaths?" (quoted by Heinemann, *Puritanism*, 34). In Thomas Heywood's *An Apology for Actors* (1612), the prolific author of domestic drama counters that theater led viewers to sympathize with the good and shun the bad, but even his comparatively straightforward plays do not encourage this pat a response. Perceptions as to the ideological impact of entertainments on home life clearly varied, then as now.

Often moments of misogyny and propriety exist in tension with complex social situations; the juxtaposition exposes paradoxes within domestic ideology. In *The Duchess of Malfi* and *The Changeling*, for example, both heroic and sinister female subterfuge has been prompted by male members of the household asserting their control over the women's marital choices. Plays of Mediterranean intrigue are thereby affiliated with more conventionally domestic tragedies, such as *The Miseries of Enforced Marriage* or *The Witch of Edmonton*. All these plays also reveal how quickly issues of male-female sexual choice expand into larger household matters, involving finances, social stability, and other familial and erotic relationships.

Indeed, focusing primarily on the marital bond runs the risk of privileging both the gentry and the relationship that has become most familiar in our own dominant culture. Strong cases have been made (in the wake of critical work by Sedgwick, Goldberg, Fineman, Montrose, and Hutson, among others) that obsessiveness about female chastity was itself a displacement of even more fundamental male rivalries: the male subject's primary determinants in locating himself.

### Family Matters

Most property was conceptualized as passing from male to male, with the body of a woman the necessary means for that transfer between generations. Focusing on her unreliability could deflect from worries about the dissimilarities between father and son or among brothers, worries that might undermine the logic of inheritance law. Conversely, material interests conspired against simple bonds of affection among male family members. The popularity of prodigal son plots testifies to this anxiety directly; from Gascoigne's *The Glass of Government* (1575) through Dekker's *The London Prodigal* (1604?) to Heywood's *The English Traveller* (1625) and Jonson's *Staple of News* (1626), the tension between blood ties and material interests provided a basic conflict for plays set in contemporary times. With similar frequency, hoarding uncles became a stock comic type that allowed sympathy for the younger generation—a less direct attack on paternal authority and the fact that kin were often less than kind.

Though Middleton's Touchwood brothers in *Chaste Maid* and the Piracquos in *The Changeling* provide counterexamples, bands of brothers repeatedly appear at odds on the early modern stage; it is usually a matter of the inheritance. In *As You Like It*, the murderous rivalry within two sets of brothers (the two dukes and the aptly named de Boys sons) initiates the plot and must be miraculously swept aside to allow a happy ending. *Much Ado About Nothing* presents maternal difference as a source of fraternal murderousness; Don John's loathing for his half brother is presented as if it were a motiveless malignity that accompanies bastardy, even though the negative social consequences of being illegitimate are painfully obvious. (The legitimate, elderly team of Leonato and Antonio in that play affirms that Shakespeare was not entirely obsessed with brotherly hate.)

Among the most disturbing representations of familial anxiety, in part because it is least grounded in material motivations, occurs in Shakespeare's *The Winter's Tale* (c. 1609). In his mad jealousy, Leontes undoes not one but all the relationships that establish his intimate identity: friend, husband, and father. Although the dramatic attention is focused upon the rupture between Leontes and his wife, Hermione, it is his brotherlike childhood friend and fellow king, Polixenes, whom Leontes wants to murder; the actual victim will be Leontes's own son, Mamillius. The Sicilian king thus disrupts "proper" self-displacement with his worries about the improper kind. Despite this overt irony, the play symbolically implies that, on some visceral level, all recognition of one's replaceability is equally painful. The moment when Leontes becomes irrational is nine months after his friend comes to visit, but it is also the time of life when his eldest (and, as it turns out, only) son is due to be "breeched." At the age of seven, boys were no longer to wear the undifferentiated dresses of children, instead acquiring the breeches that signified their entrance into a masculine world. Mamillius (whose very name may recall his mother's pregnant body) is clearly approaching the age for breeching, yet we see him instead telling Hermione a winter's tale—a kind of "old wives' tale." He does not separate from his mother until his anxiously tyrannical father—who calls him a "boy" rather than a "child" when instructing him to "go play" as his mother supposedly does—decides to force a more violent "breech." Again Leontes's actions parody the normative sequence within a socioeconomic system that demanded paternal displacement in order for the next generation to achieve full identity and inheritance. In attempting to hold on to his own sense of inviolability, the householder must destroy his intimates.

The bond between Leontes and Polixenes as surrogate brothers is finally restored, and their offspring repair the rupture created by the father's anxiety (though not before Prince Florizel's callous expectation of his inheritance from Polixenes feeds fears of filial ingratitude). Such deep affections between men, and the sociopolitical importance of male friendship, had a fundamental place within domestic culture and its representation onstage. The soldierly loyalties in *Much Ado*—not to mention those sincere and insincere bonds in *Othello*—are represented conventionally, as part of an alternative all-male ethos hostile to conjugal conclusions. More ambiguously, in *The Merchant of Venice* and *Twelfth Night*, male love is both threatened by and ultimately reliant on a heterosexual match for its sustenance. In the former play, the financial security and wit of Portia must rescue Bassanio and Antonio, respectively, and in the latter, Sebastian's marriage to Olivia leads to the freeing of his equally devoted, self-sacrificing Antonio from the imprisonment he risked for love. Marlowe's *Edward II* (1592) most provocatively suggests the complexity of erotic and political loyalties, in Edward's handling of his favorites; his marriage of Gaveston to his niece, which defies modern notions of a "one-and-only" love, seems satisfying to all parties and presents at least one temporary case of multiple, noncompetitive, erotic relationships.

Social advancement often relied on personal service, beds were routinely shared without the implication of sexual intimacy in inns and homes alike, and "sexual orientation" was not a recognized category. In trying to understand how these apparent differences interwove with seemingly familiar institutions such as marriage and with various forms of desire, we do well to be specific about our assumptions. Playwrights Beaumont and Fletcher were not alone in setting up a shared household as well as working collaboratively, but, as Jeffrey Masten reminds us, what they called "conversation" might be sexual whereas "intercourse" was just talk (Goldberg, *Queering*, 288 ff.). In a world where very little was private in our modern sense, emotional intimacy was often on display— especially at court, where it became a real-life drama signaling influence. Male friendship thus suggests a wide array of behaviors and emotions. As the different critical interpretations of Bray, Bruce Smith, Goldberg, Bredbeck, and Traub indicate, identifying "sodomy" and "homosexuality" with historical accuracy is a complex task. What we now call lesbian desire has been virtually invisible. In some cases, guests may well have been sexual intimates of household members; whether they were or not, the bond remained a fundamental one. In Thomas Heywood's *A Woman Killed with Kindness*, the villainy of Wendoll in violating the friendship of his host and provider, Master Frankford, is as deep a dishonor as is his sexual seduction of Frankford's wife, Anne.

One of Anne's punishments toward the end of *A Woman Killed* is to be deprived of access to her children. Although mother and child do not appear together earlier in this play—indeed, this dyad was infrequently shown on stage—such a separation is presented as devastating. As in *The Winter's Tale*, the unusual emphasis on this ruptured bond clearly makes the disintegration of a marriage a larger family matter. Family implied children; despite high infant mortality and little romanticization of childhood as a stage of life, offspring were crucial to the economic order, as well as being signs of honor, love, and posterity. Women could therefore spend virtually all of their childbearing years being pregnant (especially upper-class women who did not breast-feed). This did not necessarily mean that the family spent many years as a stable unit, particularly if (as often happened) a spouse died young and stepfamilies combined. Before they were teenagers, the children of aristocrats would be placed in service to other noble households or sent to school, while a much larger segment of young people (more than 10 percent of the total London population around 1600) became apprentices and serving-women. For children, then, home life could be dynamic, if not disorienting.

Absent or present, the mother was the parent culturally associated with childhood. Janet Adelman has detailed the ways in which specters of "suffocating mothers" haunt the men of Shakespeare's tragedies, and Deborah Willis has argued that the culture transformed such ghosts into witches.[13] Both as the source that contradicted male attempts at self-creation and as an apt site for displacing the other familial and social anxieties noted here, the mother bore an awful burden. She was placed in a position of subordination to her husband and eventually to the son she had earlier commanded; if she was an aristocrat, her ability to reproduce males was absolutely crucial, yet those sons could be removed by age seven, as blithely as when Oberon takes away Titania's adopted boy in A *Midsummer Night's Dream.*

Against this background, the heroic maternity of the Duchess of Malfi appears all the more remarkable. For all the limits and ironies of both the Duchess and Hermione in *The Winter's Tale* as monumentalized icons, these two characters, shown pregnant and with their children, serve as a complex counterimage to the parade of fickle, insatiate, shrewish, and smothering maternal images. Despite Bosola's sordid interpretation of the Duchess's "apricock"-eating, he is unwittingly witnessing a rare moment of domestic intimacy. The play is notable for emphasizing the details of family life, including the Duchess's concern for her child's cough when she is facing her own death. One discerns the emergence of that elusive, nostalgic, and remarkably powerful discourse that is now so cavalierly bandied about under the rubric of "family values." Webster venerates a domestic space even as he shows it to be impossible to sustain privately within an "unnatural" landscape of political and mental corruption.

That corruption, ironically, also derives from the Duchess's family: her birth family. Her brothers, the Cardinal and Ferdinand, forbid her to remarry, for reasons of power and greed (and in the latter case tortured, incestuous desire). They then murder all but her eldest son by Antonio. The play dramatizes one horrible variation on the familiar struggle of loyalties between birth and marital families, especially fervid among the nobility, for whom identity intermingled with pedigree. The logic of the Duchess's twin, Ferdinand, is taken a step further in John Ford's

*'Tis Pity She's a Whore* (1632). For Giovanni, the only desirable sexual partner is his own sister; that is the real pity. Nor does chastity serve as an escape: in less eroti-cized cases, the vulnerability of sisters as unmarried and hence powerless adult women within a family appears more starkly. Without even the qualified authority conferred upon a mother as parent and with no intimate bonds beyond her brother, Rachel Merry in Yarington's *Two Lamentable Tragedies* is imperiled by her sibling's independent actions. In this play based on a contemporary crime, the sis-ter of alehousekeeper Thomas Merry is unaware that her brother has committed murder within their home until he enlists her in its cover-up. Reluctantly, she adheres to domestic duty—and is executed as a result. Unlike strong-willed fic-tional sisters in similarly difficult straits (Susan in the subplot of *A Woman Killed with Kindness*; Isabella in *Measure for Measure*), Rachel Merry did not find a way to assert her own will. Stories based on actual lives, including those of Rachel Merry and the Duchess of Amalfi, often suggest that truth can be bleaker, as well as stranger, than fiction.

One female intimate was linked to an early modern family by milk rather than blood: the wet nurse, who in aristocratic homes could become as close to a child as were its parents. While the moderately privileged might send their infants away to a wet nurse for the first year of life, the very wealthy could hire the services of a woman for exclusive use, sometimes within or near their home. She could in fact become both the wet and the "dry" nurse who oversaw a child's upbringing. Such appears to be the case in *Romeo and Juliet*, in which we learn that Juliet was not weaned until the advanced age of three, and even then reluctantly; the Nurse, having lost her own family, stayed on to become Juliet's surrogate mother. In *A Chaste Maid in Cheapside*, the appearance of both wet and dry nurses indicates Allwit's desire to enjoy fully the status conferred by Sir Walter Whorehound's unusual forms of sup-port. In the wake of Gail Kern Paster's work directing attention to bodily particulars, the psychological impact of wet-nursing upon the stage's representation of children and family relationships is another topic ripe for further exploration. Links between such practices and the popularity of lost child and sibling plots derived from ancient romance remain hypothetical, though suggestive. Certainly the nurse's role in chil-drearing indicates the importance of attending to the effect of larger households that contained both blood relations and significant others, whether one is discussing the predominantly privileged subjects of theatrical fictions or their playwrights, many of whom came from more modest backgrounds.

## Housekeeping and Household Stuff

The most eminent sixteenth-century families sustained a large community that relied on their household. Among the merchants and businessmen of London, the household might similarly include apprentices, servants, and nurses as well as blood relatives. Then, as now, housekeeping also involved the actual care of a home, its maintenance and provision. All these aspects of domestic culture played a part on the early modern stage. Moreover, choices and changes in the use of the stage space gave emphasis to the representation of domesticity.

Early English plays represented both outdoor and indoor fictional locales. *The Second Shepherds' Play*, for example, presents what is imagined to be the interior space of a lowly home as the comedy's climactic stage location;[14] it shifts to this domestic space after the opening scenes in the shepherds' field and before the ritual denouement of a manger scene with the Virgin Mary. In so doing, the play epitomizes the dominant practice on early English stages, one at odds with both ancient theater and much bourgeois modern theater (in which the proscenium's imagined "fourth wall" is "removed" to reveal interiors only). Like the rhetoric of conduct books, such staging created a fluid movement eliding domestic and public action and promoted the habit of thinking analogically about the health of the local home and the emergent nation-state.

Michael Hattaway notes that the Jacobean Revels Office accounts indicate "that three-dimensional devices or 'houses' were frequently constructed for indoor court performances" and that companies probably used the same structures in public playhouses (*Elizabethan*, 38–39). Such stage "mansions" (sometimes representing outdoor constructions such as tents, other times containing domestic furnishings), like the "discovery" of upstage beds, could on occasion provide a visually specific reminder of what the fluidity of the open stage already allowed: frequent movement and interaction between—if not simultaneous scenes of—internal "private" or domestic space and external "public" space.

This practice represents the domestic as metonymically related to other social concerns. Whereas *The Second Shepherds' Play* uses scene juxtaposition in the service of religious typology, displacing comic parody with the analogous scriptural moment of Truth, later professional drama tends to employ this stage practice to create sociopolitical analogues and to reinforce the all-pervasive power of domestic ideology. Especially after the sixteenth-century ban on traditional religious drama, the dominant stage practice inclined toward imagining most scenes as "horizontally" linked in geographical space (by contrast, the craft cycles had ranged from Heaven to Hell and are fuzzier about the transitions between earthly locations). Thus homes and the movements between them became more focal.

In *The Taming of the Shrew*, the movement from Baptista's Paduan home to Petruchio's country house confirms that the marital traffic in women has succeeded, no matter how shoddy the wedding ceremony and how resistant the bride.[15] Even more important than the time spent at Petruchio's "taming school," however, is the subsequent movement back to Baptista's in two exterior scenes, during which Katherina submits to Petruchio's verbal and sexual will. First by naming the sun and moon as he commands (despite her empirical knowledge) and then by kissing in the street (despite her shame at doing so), Katherina reveals herself to have been subjectively "domesticated"; she is no longer simply Petruchio's prisoner or a resident in his house. The much-debated final speech at her sister's wedding is in this sense merely icing on the wedding cake. Katherina has already changed more than her hat to befit the dominant domestic order: she is Petruchio's Kate wherever she goes.

Even more comprehensively, movement among interior and exterior locales contributes to the ideological and narrative logic for Thomas Heywood's *A Woman Killed with Kindness*.[16] The symbolic use of space connects the main plot of Anne Frankford's sexual fall with the subplot of Charles Mountford's economic decline; both are narratives of exile and homecoming, in which the material realities of houses reflect their personal fortunes. By using these fictional locations to effect, the play mingles scriptural and socioeconomic "lessons." Anne's adultery with the houseguest Wendoll makes Frankford a stranger in his own home, vividly rendered when he pretends to be away in order to sneak back into his house, duplicate keys in hand, and catch the adulterers in his "polluted bed-chamber" (13.14). Because the Frankfords' own home has been corrupted, Anne must be sent away to another of her husband's properties. Her exile symbolizes both her estrangement and the inviolability of marriage. She cannot begin again with a new, penitent identity, nor can she sneak off, as Wendoll intends to do; and so she dies as Frankford's chastened wife.

By contrast, Charles Mountford's ill fortune begins on a hunting party at Chevy Chase, and his property is thus not the source of corruption but rather the pawn in Sir Francis Acton's plots to destroy him. When he and his sister, Susan, are reduced to living in a summer house, Mountford explicitly links his personal identity with the possession of this last physical sign of his inheritance. Partially confirming his fears, his relatives deny Susan's pleas for help once Charles is imprisoned for debt; the importance and inadequacy of aristocratic familial alliances become obvious. In a world in which kin—or at least "cousins"—can no longer be relied upon for kindness, economic self-sufficiency becomes all the more crucial.[17] Charles's outmoded code of honor pales before the greater wealth and clout of Acton, and only because of the latter's miraculous change of heart does the subplot avoid tragedy.

Within *A Woman Killed*, the power and transferability of property overwhelm old codes of honor and family stability, perceived as fading into a mythic past. The play thus epitomizes some common attitudes about the subject's growing need for self-reliance, portability, and privacy, emerging from the economic flux of the sixteenth century. The vast changes that transpired as a subsistence agrarian economy transformed into the urbanized market economy of the modern nation-state had been aggravated in England by changes in religion and the massive reassignment of Crown lands under the Tudors. As London, vagrancy, and inflation grew, so did the consciousness of a shift away from the provincial manor house as a locus of "housekeeping" for the surrounding community. By the seventeenth century, some prominent families appear to have abandoned country living entirely. In an age when enclosures, rackrenting, and other forms of tenant eviction increased suffering, some blamed the luxuries of London for undermining both economic and moral order. Even in plays that acknowledge domestic threats within the country-side, country gentlemen (not the nobility) who cherish the old ways are usually presented generously. Upstanding Old Carter in *The Witch of Edmonton* loathes London and luxury alike, whereas Sir Arthur Clarington epitomizes aristocratic corruption and the struggling Thorneys sacrifice honor to sustain their wealth.[18]

Some London playwrights occasionally acknowledged the inadequacy, if not the impossibility, of sustaining the old models of housekeeping. In *No Wit, No Help Like a Woman's* (c. 1613), Middleton parodies the gentry hospitality that could lead householders to financial ruin; and in *A Mad World My Masters* (1606), he mocks the ostentatious vanity of the landed gentleman himself, Sir Bounteous Progress. The stage more often vented its spleen upon Londoners who aspired to own country homes without helping the community. Another Middleton comedy, *Michaelmas Term* (1605), mocks the city businessman Quomodo for desiring a country seat; he is presented as egregiously overreaching beyond his proper geographical home. In Massinger's *A New Way to Pay Old Debts* (1625), the *nouveau riche* Sir Giles Overreach taints the world of a country household headed by the widowed Lady Allworth with her servant named Order; even in the 1620s, when the economic changes had become obvious, they seemed no less contemptible for their familiarity. Given that the good housekeeping of aristocrats usually involved nearly as much importation of London luxuries to their great houses as it did the purchase of local goods, the stage's condemnation of geographical fluidity among the populace has its unconscious irony as well.

*A Woman Killed* reveals a different threat to housekeeping—from the guest. Wendoll is a gentleman in financial straits, whose behavior toward his generous and friendly host baffles even himself. The play's biblical allusions imply that Wendoll is a (tame form of) motivelessly malignant serpent, although a modern analyst can find signs of latent resentment toward his wealthier friend. Especially with the greater emphasis on finances as a source of identity, such friendships between master and retainer were becoming more vexed; as Lena Orlin notes, the basis of male friendship was shifting "from virtue to interest" (166). Wendoll's escape after the crime—and especially his announcement that he will remake himself as a courtier—embody worries about increasing social mobility and the consequent opportunities to shift identity, like a stage player. As if to provide some consolation that all is not anarchy, Wendoll's nemesis is the faithful stablehand Nicholas, who vows to Frankford: "There's not room for Wendoll and me too / Both in one house" (8.51–52). With guests such as Wendoll (or Thomas Morsby, the real-life model for the murderous, adulterous guest in *Arden of Faversham*), one had to rely even more on the "help."

As Nicholas's role demonstrates, domestic culture involved not only blood relations and nurses but also those servants and retainers affiliated with the country house. The distinctions among serving-men and apprentices, house servants and stablemen, below-stairs maids and ladies-in-waiting complicate discussion of "master-servant" hierarchies; the topic demands more careful differentiation than can be undertaken here or than has yet been fully analyzed (Burnett). Shifts in these categories were also a source of anxiety, as medieval assumptions were displaced: apprentices and squires could no longer be expected to be (or not be) gentlemen. Amidst this flux, faithful servants such as Nicholas could provide a hero of their own for some in the theatrical audience as well as a consolation for their masters. Nicholas's city cousins are the apprentices of Simon Eyre's workshop in *The Shoemaker's Holiday*, similarly venerating their master.

Partially displacing the transgressive eroticism that both historical records and tragedy document, power struggles between male servants or apprentices and their mistresses provide a staple of comedy in *The Shoemaker's Holiday*, *The Taming of the Shrew*, and *The Woman's Prize*. Even more than the uncle/prodigal conflicts imagined in wealthier families, such battles both acknowledge domestic discontent and deflect it from the paternal householder. By contrast, the affection of the Citizen's wife, Nell, for her surrogate son, Ralph, becomes the cause of consternation for the players-within-the-play of *The Knight of the Burning Pestle*, disrupting their own narrative assumptions; it is also (unusually, for the stage) a bond between husband and wife, as the Citizen shares her affection for Ralph. Wife-servant friendship was more often presented as the source of serious anxiety. From *Arden of Faversham* onward, alliances of wives with servants, retainers, or guests raised the specter of domestic rebellion and even murder. As in *A Woman Killed*, to be a good servant to the master often required betraying the mistress.

The treatment of servants within the household becomes more than a laughing matter on the seventeenth-century stage. Greater realism and concern for female servants and ladies' maids in particular pervade certain Jacobean tragedies. In *The Witch of Edmonton*, the maidservant Winnifrede is initially tormented by her false assertion to Frank Thorney that he, rather than their master, was her first bedfellow; her pregnancy precipitates a marriage that becomes the ground for Frank's bigamy and subsequent murder of his other wife. Rather than vilifying or simply victimizing Winnifrede, however, the play endorses her turn from "a loose whore to a repentant wife" and sympathetically shows her struggling with competing duties. The waiting-woman Diaphanta in *The Changeling* shows less internal consciousness, one moment protesting the suggestion that she might not be a virgin, but then blithely volunteering to "serve" her mistress as a substitute in her bridal bed; nevertheless, when Diaphanta is murdered offstage as her "reward" for this service, her demise constitutes another callous crime by De Flores nearly as disturbing as his murder of her aristocratic "better," Piracquo. Similarly, although the Duchess of Malfi's waiting-woman lacks her mistress's dignity in facing death (an obvious signal of her less-heroic status), her witnessing throughout the first four acts gives her a choric importance. The major role given these serving-women is as "impertinent" in its way as is the genre of domestic tragedy itself—or as is *The Duchess of Malfi*—in creating heroic tragedy from a noblewoman's domestic choices.

While the decline and corruption of housekeeping provided fodder for domestic tragedies set outside London (in *The Yorkshire Tragedy*, as well as *A Woman Killed, The Witch of Edmonton*, and in certain senses *Arden of Faversham* and *The English Traveller*), the control of city households suggested comic themes. Perhaps in part this generic difference reflects the shift in energy, power, and goods from provinces to the capital; whereas the cost was great elsewhere, Londoners experienced both the difficulties and the exhilaration of socioeconomic change. A new type, the merchant householder as hero, appears in Dekker's *The Shoemaker's Holiday*, in which the romance plot involving nobility takes second place to the vigorous energies of Simon Eyre and his merry band of workers. Setting his play in the time of Henry V, Dekker still injects contemporary concerns about wars and foreigners into his domestic landscape; by having the foreign shoemaker actually be an English lover in disguise, however, the play avoids seriously confronting such differences. Less central to the action yet no less jovial are merchants such as Touchstone the goldsmith in *Eastward Ho!*, attempting to keep order amidst the rogues' gallery of prodigals, usurers, and apprentices that animate city comedy.

City architecture threw social classes and categories into close proximity, if not confusion. Rich London merchants lived on streets with alley tenements just around the corner. Nearby, courtiers' houses would be modeled after the internal courtyard pattern of Renaissance palaces. With the domestic space and garden located farthest from the street, merchants' homes were also their places of business; in many cases, the ground floor commercial area was dominated by women (hence the potential for actual resentment between wives and apprentices). Taverns, like shops, often grew out of private homes and were family-run; although balladeers would gender the alehouse a male space and the home a female one, such boundaries were in fact less absolute (as the Hostess in the induction to *The Taming of the Shrew* might have reminded Christopher Sly). The definition of what constituted a home remains itself at issue.

Dekker's mercantile heroes celebrate the sunny new possibilities of entrepreneurial capitalism; Ben Jonson balances that view with *The Alchemist*, in which con artists have taken over the master's house. The owner's escape from town to avoid plague may suggest aristocratic irresponsibility, but the scathing satire of greed, pride, and corruption embraces all classes.[19] The temptations of the flesh, as Sir Epicure Mammon's catalog of grotesque desires implies, were becoming more numerous and exotic within the domestic spaces of London.

While most Tudor homes were still dominantly medieval in their architecture, they were beginning to fill with new materials from abroad, the result of European expansion of trade and importation from Asia and the Americas. New dyes allowed greater variation in clothing, new foods enriched the diets, and new ornaments decorated the homes of those who could afford such luxuries. These visible changes, and the dissonant coexistence of residual with emergent cultures, no doubt aggravated many people's fears of a world turned upside down—the old ways lost, the new not yet integrated into a moral code. To live within a London tenement formed from a dissolved monastery and see city ladies in yellow-starched ruffs would be quite literally to sense a transition from a world dominated by religion to one dominated by the marketplace. Onstage, this shifting sensibility is evidenced by drama combining morality play allegorization with contemporary settings, as in *The Devil is an Ass* and *The Revenger's Tragedy*. Anxiety about material changes created many categories of "others" to scapegoat, among which was one form overtly linked to domestic culture: the metonymic blame of city and court wives for conspicuous consumption.

Aggressively acquisitive city wives inhabit Elizabethan and Jacobean comedies sympathetic to merchant-citizens (*The Shoemaker's Holiday*), as well as those performed by boys' companies at the "private" theaters (*The Knight of the Burning Pestle*; *Eastward Ho!*). Upbraided for her desire to marry an aristocrat as well as for her materialism, the merchant's daughter Gertrude in *Eastward Ho!* finds herself without the expected castle in the country—only a castle in the air. Given their own involvement in the upstart theatrical business, it was indeed ironic when city-born playwrights such as Jonson satirized those Londoners who aspired to social advancement. By focusing so much of the mockery on city women and their desire for fashions that defied old styles and sumptuary laws alike, dramatists deflected attention to a marketplace other than their own.[20]

Even in plays set beyond the city gates, concerns about class and consumption were often played out in terms of gendered domesticity. When the induction to *The Taming of the Shrew* ends and we find ourselves in Padua, we might think that the tinker Christopher Sly's concerns with his faded English pedigree have also faded. Boose's analysis of Petruchio as the upwardly mobile fortune-seeker proving his financial potency suggests otherwise ("*Taming*"). His shrew-taming vocabulary in fact derives from medieval words referring to class rather than gender tension. Similarly, Lena Orlin reveals how *Arden of Faversham* (uneasily and partially) subordinates a complex historical web of male indebtedness—including patronage relationships, town and church landholding, rents, fees, unhappy tenants, and more—to one primary focus of treachery: a wife's debasing affair with a steward who in turn aspires to material mastery. The play thereby rewrites the location of social threat away from Thomas Arde(r)n, who was in fact an upwardly mobile "new man" of wealth indebted to the Crown, rather than a longtime Kentish country "gentleman of blood" (as the character names himself).

Among the sixteenth-century "imports" into the domestic landscape were human beings; in addition to Dutch and Huguenot workers fleeing war and religious persecution, enough Africans had been brought to England to prompt Queen Elizabeth's 1596 proclamation expelling them.[21] Her action is indicative of English xenophobia at the time, deriving in part from fears of foreign competition among English workers and of foreign plots against this lone Protestant kingdom.

Scapegoating immigrants as a response to inflation and unemployment is sadly familiar; though these fears play a part in city comedies such as *Westward Ho!, An Englishman for My Money*, and *The Shoemaker's Holiday*, they are also held up to mockery. Perhaps more disturbing are the oblique cases in which the definition of the domestic comes to rely on its superiority to the foreign—even when distanced through a "romance" setting such as *The Merchant of Venice*'s Belmont.

In *Othello*, the presence of a domestic textile in a foreign frame, the common strawberry pattern on the handkerchief, symbolizes the unhinging of other familiar social givens: heterosexual relationships, the general as leader, the lord as Christian.[22] At the same time, the presence of this piece of women's work, and its crucial circulation among the three women in *Othello*, testify to another "subtext(ile)," which is not so much a threat to order as a critique of its injustices. And, of course, with Iago as the only "native" Venetian among the three leading male figures, the familiar itself is undone. It might well seem that there were, in Frances Dolan's words, "strange familiars" lurking everywhere. Nobody was safe at home.

The domestic ideology central to the public stage and to this article was directed primarily at those in the moderately privileged world of the gentry and merchants. Some aristocratic women in fact managed to avoid being confined to any of their numerous homes, much less "the" home; those at the other end of the social scale might have no home at all, and they could hardly afford to create gendered space—much less partake of new goods and services. Texts (especially literary ones) tend to preserve the voices and perspectives of those who dominate within society; we must supplement them with both historical data and our scholarly imaginations if we wish to hear more of the conversation. Female-headed households in *Gammer Gurton's Needle* may only be a schoolmaster's source of comedy or deflected anxiety, but it is also true that there were many female-headed households in town and city alike; historical study of Southwerk, the theater district itself, reveals that at least 16 percent of households were headed by a woman. The type of historical evidence we bring to bear when interpreting plays undoubtedly informs what types of domesticity we see represented, what gaps we notice, and how we value them.[23]

In discussing Middleton's tragedies, Margot Heinemann finds a "citizen atmosphere" in which "the imagery is practical and homely, imagery of workshop and counting-house, sewing and cooking" (187); the court women's "turn of speech often recalls the housewife" (188). As I have tried to convey through my mixture of exemplary cases, however, domestic concerns were not confined to a specific class, plot line, or genre. Heinemann also sees a new emphasis on the "tragedy of private life" as a sign of late Jacobean censorship of the directly political (144). But perhaps Middleton's work, like that of the theater itself, had been "domesticated" in a less escapist sense. In reaching beyond the palaces and pastoral landscapes of romance narratives into the realist mode, domestic drama partially anticipates the concerns that centrally occupy modern bourgeois culture. For nearly a century, the English public stage moved imaginatively from country home to city inn to madhouse to throne room. This mobility may be its most remarkable feature: while presenting a domestic culture in flux and in fear, the players and their audiences felt entitled to cross many threshholds, and to look at the conflicts inside.

## NOTES

1. Here and throughout this essay, I am especially indebted to the books of Dolan and Orlin.
2. See in Braunmuller and Hattaway, 109 ff., and in Hopkins, passim, respectively. Chartier, Fumerton, and Orlin discuss the complexity of defining public and private domains.
3. Among other influential treatises were the pseudo-Aristotelian *Oeconomics*; Cornelius Agrippa's *De sacramento matrimonii* (1526), Vives's *Instruction of a Christen Woman*; Erasmus's *Encomium matrimonii*; Heinrich Bullinger's *Christen State of Matrimonye* (1541); Dod and Cleaver's *Godlie Forme of Householde Government* (1598); and dialogues such as *The Flower of Friendship*, by Edmund Tilney. See Hutson, Klein, Orlin, and Wayne's introduction in Tilney. Space does not permit me to consider the impact of boy actors playing women, despite its potential to complicate the gendered representations discussed here.
4. See Paster's discussion of women as "leaky vessels" here and in *Bartholomew Fair*.
5. See Dolan for more detailed information on the law and historical cases.
6. Swetnam, 191, in Henderson and McManus. Unlike the similar action in *Lysistrata*, this rebellion is directly aimed at modifying the domestic order, not protecting it from an external threat.
7. On the historical treatment of scolds (including the arguments for believing that these instruments of torture were used at this time), see Boose, "Scolding"; M. Ingram; Underdown; and Kermode and Walker.
8. Valerie Wayne's forthcoming edition of the play for the Middleton complete works (Gary Taylor, general editor) will call attention to editors' perpetuation of such labeling, which elides mistresses with prostitutes.
9. Dowers set the widow's portion at a standard one-third of the husband's land held in fee simple during his life, whereas jointures (income from land held in joint tenancy by the couple, which was then held by the survivor until death) varied in amount, often being a tenth or more of the dowry paid at marriage by the bride's father to her husband or his family. See Wrightson, Prior, and Hanawalt, on the economics of marriage and widowhood. For more on women's historical conditions, see Amt, Amussen, A. Erickson, Houlbrooke, J. Kelly, L. Stone (*Family*), A. Wall, and Woodbridge.
10. Dekker's *The Honest Whore* both calls attention to the shiftiness of these categories and ultimately reasserts their importance.
11. In less-privileged sixteenth-century homes, there might be only one chair, the master's; wife and children would sit on stools or a bench. A woodcut from the Folger Library's 1563 *The Whole Book of Psalmes* (STC 2431) illustrates such a scene.
12. This scene mocks the greatest "domestic"—and Court—scandal of Jacobean England, the Essex divorce and Overbury murder. On painted ladies, see Garner, and on the grotesque body, see Stallybrass ("Patriarchal") and Paster.

13. Willis links witches with the desire for vengeance upon the phallic mother; see also R. Wilson, "Observations," and Kahn's key study of male and familial identity in Shakespeare. For a more benign example of women's conjuring, see *The Wise Woman of Hogsden.*

14. The play's narrative climax is the "discovery" of the lamb in Gill's crib; the religious ritual culminates with the adoration of the Virgin Mary and the Lamb of God.

15. See Gayle Rubin's classic essay on the traffic in women, quite obviously operative in the arrangements between Baptista Minola and Petruchio, whose only stated requirement for a wife is that she be rich. Among much excellent work on *Shrew* in relationship to contemporary domestic ideologies, see especially Boose, "*Taming*" and "Scolding"; Marcus, "Shakespearean"; and Newman.

16. For more on this topic, see my article and Orlin's detailed discussion (*Private*).

17. *Cousin* referred to any collateral blood relationship beyond sibling. Susan and Charles, in contrast to their cousins, are inseparable. Heywood simultaneously builds upon the morality tradition and modifies it; whereas in *Everyman* Cousin and Kindred desert first, only to be outdone in their treachery by Goods, here it is less apparent that material wealth is itself an evil. Sir Francis is finally moved by Susan's moral goodness, but money itself is not condemned except in its absence (tempting Wendoll and Charles to dishonor).

18. As its first scene (in which all the characters are speaking duplicitously) attests, *The Witch of Edmonton* is a complex and sometimes cynical play; thus Old Carter could be accused of provincial short-sightedness in preferring Frank to a gallant, even though in doing so he is honoring his daughter's choice. The energy and generosity of his comic speeches, however, suggest that the playwrights see him as a positive figure. For more on the architectural shifts and material conditions, see F. Brown, and Orlin, *Households.*

19. Ben Jonson's own escape from town, avoiding the plague in which his son died, may be implicated in this choice of framing device.

20. See Massinger's upholding of sumptuary hierarchy in *The City Madam* and Bruster's discussion of wittolry linked with the London theater as market.

21. See Newman, K. Hall, Stallybrass ("Patriarchal"), and Hendricks and Parker (including Jean Howard's discussion of *The Fair Maid of the West*) for more on the ways in which gender and class representation intersect with sixteenth-century conceptions of "race."

22. I am indebted to Susan Frye for information about the strawberry pattern as a marker of English textile work.

23. See Archer on the demographics of London at this time and McLuskie's helpful summation of many of the patterns and relations discussed here (*Renaissance*).

# CHAPTER 11

# Entertainments at Court

## Graham Parry

FESTIVITY IS the felicity of the court. If ceremony exhibits the glory of the court, and worship its decorous piety, festivals show the court united in pleasure. Costumed in the boldest conceits of fashion, the inhabitants of that favored little world gather to be entertained by whatever is most stylish, eloquent, and new. The provision of entertainments was always an important concern to the managers of a court, for these were the occasions to consolidate the affections of the foremost members of the realm by spectacles that gave expression to shared ideals and common loyalty. A privileged sense of being among the finest spirits of the age was the impression that many of these entertainments sought to transmit. From early Tudor times, theatrical shows competed with a range of eye-catching displays in festival periods at court, and it is perhaps a sign of the growing sophistication of the age that plays and masques eventually came to prevail as the most gratifying forms of courtly diversion. As they became central to the imaginative life of the court, these forms also acquired a significant element of political suggestiveness.

In the reign of Henry VII (1485–1509) and in the first years of Henry VIII, the preferred kinds of entertainment that enlivened the court calendar were pageants of an allegorical character, disguisings, and various types of military combats such as tilts, barriers (where knights clashed across a low palisade), and passages at arms, which often grew out of an initial debate between contesting forces and therefore had a semidramatic form. The acknowledged sources of these colorful, chivalric displays were the Burgundian court festivals of the fifteenth century, which influenced both court entertainments and civic pageantry until at least the middle of the sixteenth century. Tudor inventions rarely touched the heights of fantasy attained in Burgundy, but the ceremonies for the entry of Catherine of Aragon into London, and those at her marriage to Prince Arthur in 1501, were unprecedented in England and marked the full assimilation of the Northern European arts of secular celebration. Then were seen fantastically designed pageant cars for the entry of disguised lords, amorous tableaux suitable to a marriage, and a mobile display of two mounts, one green and flowery, the other sunburnt and studded with jewels, bound by a golden chain, representing England and Spain joined in amity. Feats of arms were continually enacted through the festivities, which concluded with a dramatic pageant in Westminster Hall, where a castle filled with beautiful women and singing children was pulled on by heraldic beasts, then accosted by a fully rigged ship that "sailed" into the hall. After a debate, the overtures of the sea adventurers were refused, whereupon a pageant of splendidly furnished knights flaunting their banners entered and made an assault on the castle, causing the ladies to capitulate. The evening ended with "divers and many goodly daunces" (Anglo, *Spectacle*, 98–103). The festivities were typical of their time, but they contain faint foreshadowings of the later masques. Spoken drama was notably absent from these revels, except for a brief debate of love.

Similar revels were characteristic of the early years of Henry VIII's reign, with an even greater emphasis on the military arts in order to display the prowess of the young king. A new note was struck on Twelfth Night 1512, when, as part of the entertainment, the king and eleven companions "were disguised, after the manner of Italie, called a Maske, a thyng not seen afore in Englande," as the chronicler Edward Hall remarked (E. Hall, 526; Anglo, "Evolution"). This appears to be the first use of the term *mask* to describe an entertainment, but in practice the event was fairly simple, for there was no action or plot, only an entry of royal and noble masquers to astonish and surprise. The novelty lay in the development of the entry, when the masquers danced with members of the audience and engaged in gallant exchanges with them. One should note Hall's comment that the disguising was "after the manner of Italie," for it was another example of Henry's importation of Italian fashions, as in architecture and decorative detail, the mark of a monarch eager to enlarge the cultural boundaries of his court. King Henry's active participation in the revels and in the chivalric displays mounted at his court were a singular feature of these shows, for it would not be until the reign of James I that royalty again appeared in prominently spectacular roles.

For the most part, however, Henry's court entertainments had a robustly native character, especially in their dramatic manifestations. Moralities and interludes were the favored forms when plays were required at court. Performed for the most part either during or after banquets, these plays enlivened the court year and were particularly frequent during the second and third decades of the century, when dramatic activity was most encouraged by the king. Henry VIII employed two companies of players, who were at liberty to travel the country when not performing at court, and he also had the services of the gentlemen and Children of the Chapel Royal, who were expected to show theatrical skills as well as musical ability. The interludes that these companies offered, such as Skelton's *Magnificence*, were

didactic in character, peopled with personifications or mythological or biblical figures, and often provided a commentary on spiritual, moral, or behavioral matters.

Court festivals declined during the 1530s, when the religious turmoil into which
Henry was leading the country dominated all minds. The succession of royal marriages did little to promote entertainments at court, and during the 1540s, as Henry
aged, he was distracted by futile wars against France and Scotland and by the continuing difficulties of Reformation. The court did not shine. The brief and stressful
reigns of Edward and Mary did not bring about a renewal of court life, and it was
only when Elizabeth was settled in her reign that the court began to revive as a stable and prosperous place with a regular calendar of entertainments under the control of a Master of the Revels. The festive season at Elizabeth's court usually ran
from the celebrations for her accession on November 17 through the days of Christmas, culminating in Twelfth Night, or Epiphany, the high point of the festival year,
with additional entertainments at Candlemas on February 2, and at Shrovetide
before the onset of Lent. These were the times when shows were most commonly
presented. The forms did not change greatly from earlier days, with pageants and
maskings, interludes, and occasional performances of Latin plays. The maskings
were especially enjoyed: the fancifully disguised masquers entered unexpectedly,
bursting into the hall, often bearing gifts for the monarch and chief guests, danced
prepared measures before the company, and then drew members of the court into
the dances. The favorite disguises were of picturesque foreigners: a Revels inventory
of 1560 lists among the sets of masquing garments in store at the beginning of
Elizabeth's reign Venetian Senators, Turkish Magistrates, Greek Worthies, Alba-
nian Warriors, Irish Kerns, and Turkish Women (Chambers, *Elizabethan*, 1:158 n).
We get a glimpse of one of these ebullient masques in *Love's Labour's Lost*, when
the French lords dance their entry into the ladies' camp disguised as Muscovites.
These entries were accompanied with music, and in some cases they had presenters who addressed the company; they are incipiently dramatic and point forward to
the fully elaborated masques of the Stuart era.

During Elizabeth's long reign, stage plays came to enjoy much greater prominence in court entertainments than hitherto. For many years the most active players were the boys' companies drawn from the Children of the Chapel Royal or from
St. Paul's School. These boy actors had been part of the court scene since the
beginning of the sixteenth century and were notable for their performances of
Latin plays, particularly the comedies of Plautus and Terence. In addition, they
presented the many Latin divertissements that were specially written for performance at court or college or grammar school: tragedies, comedies, and moralities.
The long vogue for this Latin drama was sustained by the importance of humanist
studies in schools and universities, as it promoted fluency in Latin and encouraged
declamation and the rhetorical graces, which were greatly valued in that humanist ethos. The children's companies also put on plays in English, but whether in
Latin or English, their delivery, one imagines, must have been highly stylized, a

specialized taste for which the court had a particular relish, for boy actors probably aroused teasingly odd responses with their bright, unbroken voices speaking of the affairs of the adult world.

In the middle of Elizabeth's reign, we find for the first time a body of drama written explicitly for performance at court. This was the work of John Lyly, designed in part for the boys' companies. Lyly, whose eloquence and stylistic graces had been copiously displayed in his prose romance *Euphues* (1578), fashioned his plays to suit the court taste of the 1580s. He excelled in fine speeches of love, philosophy, and compliment; he brought the amorous shepherds and shepherdesses of pastoral romance to Whitehall and Greenwich, he dramatized chivalric encounters, raised the noble figures of antiquity to speak English before a well-educated court, and time and time again fulsomely praised the queen. He provided theatrical settings for debates about the finer points of love, which had been the subject of sophisticated discussion at the Courts of Love in palaces and academies across Europe and which are best exemplified in Castiglione's courtesy book *The Courtier*. In *Sapho and Phao* we hear a debate between chastity and love; in *Campaspe*, between love and honor; in *Endimion* the claims of love and friendship are debated, and in *Gallathea* the strains between love and piety and self-preservation are explored.

Lyly's plays required a fair number of properties for their performance, as was usually the case with court entertainments, in contrast to works for the public theater. Scenes were set in rocks or forests, in caves or in pavilions; gods and goddesses glided down from clouds, or jerked heavenward in lifting devices. Plays and divertissements at court often had a dispersed setting, with the action moving around several parts of the hall. Lighting was another aspect of productions at court that was greatly appreciated by the spectators. Concealed lights, colored lights, patterns of light, but above all lights in large numbers contributed to the sense of the spectacular that was an important part of the experience of these entertainments. When Inigo Jones came to devise more intense and more magical illumination for his masques in the early seventeenth century, he could draw on the already wellestablished tradition of lighting effects from Tudor court performances.

With Lyly we encounter a theater whose primary intentions are to compliment the sovereign and praise and please the court. These plays could be presented in a public theater, but they would lack the tension and heightened allure that must have brightened their performance before the queen, whose presence gave a richer meaning to the action, and before a court whose taste for romantic fictions of antiquity and exquisite phraseology was being fully indulged. *Campaspe* portrays a great monarch, Alexander, enticed and beguiled by love, from which he finally turns away to devote his genius to the calls of heroic action and government. *Sapho and Phao* draws much closer to the queen. This Ovidian fantasy presents Sicilian Sapho as a royal lady engaged in amorous interchanges with the handsome ferryman Phao in passages of delicate and refined expressiveness as they explore the effects of love upon themselves, both subjectively and interactively. Venus and Cupid are entwined in the plot, which ends with Sapho freeing herself from the entanglements of love, disarming Cupid, driving out Venus (the patron of erotic love), and reasserting her position as the chaste adored ruler of Syracuse.

The figure of Sapho provides a link with Lyly's *Midas* (1588–1589), for she can be identified with the queen of Lesbos, who is portrayed as the inveterate enemy of King Midas, the golden monarch whose gold causes him nothing but misery and who is clearly associated with Philip II of Spain. *Midas* is a triumphalist play, rejoicing in the discomfiture of an overly wealthy monarch; the attention paid to Elizabeth on this occasion by means of a chaste, high-minded representative figure is relatively slight. *Endimion* (1585?) more than compensates for this neglect. The play contains a sustained note of adoration for Cynthia, the moon goddess, Queen of the Heavens, and a well-established type of Elizabeth. Lyly inverts the Ovidian story of Cynthia's love for the shepherd Endimion and has Endimion expressing his enraptured love for the unattainable Cynthia, the goddess who here appears encircled by a court of virtuous women. Dangerous and treacherous figures move on the outskirts of the court; they prevail over Endimion, who is charmed into an enduring sleep. Cynthia sees through the deceits and subterfuges of those envious of her and recognizes true worth even in eclipse. She awakens Endimion with a restorative kiss and bestows her approval, but not her love, upon him. Many phases of love are described, distress unfolded, and the consolations and rewards of love propounded, but the persistent theme is the glory of the chaste Cynthia.

The last years of Elizabeth's reign saw few entertainments specifically designed for the court; her preference turned increasingly to the plays of the professional London theater, which were brought to court and staged, we assume, in the old Banqueting House at Whitehall. The companies most frequently summoned to court were the Lord Chamberlain's Men, who included Richard Burbage, Will Kempe, and William Shakespeare among their players, and the Lord Admiral's Men under Edward Alleyn. Given the extraordinary quality of plays and performance currently available in London, it is hardly surprising that the queen chose to be entertained by the professional players or that shows in which spectacle was the chief interest declined.

With the new dynasty of the Stuarts, the court was transformed. A new cast of characters entered, younger, eager for pleasure, conscious of inaugurating a new age. Poets, scenting patronage on a lavish scale after the lean years of Elizabeth, hastened to acclaim King James as a second Augustus, a new Arthur come to rule over a united Britain, a Solomon whose wisdom and piety would attract the blessings of divine providence.

James took great pleasure in drama, and one of his early moves upon arriving in London was to take the Lord Chamberlain's Men under his direct patronage, so that they now became the King's Men. The frequency of their performances at court increased notably. Queen Anne was also an enthusiast for the stage, and she took over Worcester's Men and made them her own company of players. Anne was a culturally adventurous woman, who had a window onto a wider world via her brother Christian IV, king of Denmark, whose court was one of the more remarkable centers of late Renaissance Europe. From her brother's court she took into her own service, among others, the composer John Dowland and the designer Inigo Jones. The poets and men of letters who frequented her circle included Samuel Daniel, Ben Jonson, and John Florio. She employed the painters Robert Peake and Paul van Somer, as well as the Florentine architect and designer Constantino de' Servi and the French engineer Salomon de Caus, who came to further her plans for royal gardens in the mannerist style, with architectural amenities.

The queen's court, centered on Somerset House on the Strand, was the home of the aesthetic avant-garde in the first decade of the century, for she was a much more active and enterprising patron of artists than her husband, and it is not surprising that the most striking developments in court entertainments were initiated by her. She took charge of this area, and being relatively young (she was born in 1574) and having a number of high-spirited female companions as the nucleus of her social circle, she looked for a form of entertainment in which she and her friends could take the leading roles, so a new kind of masque was designed as a showcase for her talents. New for England these masques may have been, but they had been fashionable for some time in Italy, where Inigo Jones may have viewed them at the Medici court in Florence, or in Paris, which had a Medici queen.

The production of the first authentically new form of masque occurred in January 1605 as a result of the combined endeavors of Ben Jonson and Inigo Jones. Here for the first time was a full integration of text and spectacle, a fable that was a piece of high fantasy and royal compliment, and an action that revealed something of the mysterious powers of kingship. Set on a single stage, with music, song, and dance to amplify the action, with costume of unprecedented extravagance, with scenery and illusionistic effects, and novelty in lighting, *The Masque of Blackness* was a composite art form devised to honor the king and display the graces of the queen and her courtiers. Ben Jonson called it a "study of magnificence," proper to the courts of princes (Orgel and Strong, 1:90), and indeed its cost was so great that only a monarch had the means to sponsor such a spectacle.

The technical advances that made *Blackness* such an innovatory affair were introduced by Inigo Jones, here inaugurating a career as court masque maker that would continue up to 1640. Jones's early years were obscurely spent, but it seems probable that toward the end of Elizabeth's reign he lived for a few years in Italy, most likely based at Venice.[1] We assume that he passed some time at the Medici court at Florence, where the Grand Duke Ferdinand was patronizing a series of masques renowned for their technical proficiency and illusionistic splendor, created by the mannerist virtuoso Bernardo Buontalenti, who was an architect, engineer, and designer in the Vitruvian mode (Strong, *Splendour*, 169–209). These Florentine festivals seem to have provided Inigo Jones with the experience of stage mechanics and costume that enabled him to design and produce the masques for the Whitehall court, and we may remark that the most distinctive type of Stuart court entertainment, like its early Tudor predecessors, was the result of Continental influence infiltrating England. As Burgundy and the Habsburg courts provided the models for the Tudor festivals, so Florence and the Medici court lay behind the Stuart masque.

As the first essay in the technically complicated masque, *Blackness* was both revolutionary and rudimentary. Jones had a stage forty feet square set up in the old Whitehall Banqueting House, with a dancing area in front of the stage. There was full-perspective scenery for the first time, resulting in the illusion of great depth and space. Ben Jonson's printed account conveys an impression of harmonious beauty achieved by mechanical means: "an artificial sea was seen to shoot forth, as if it flowed to the land, raised with waves which seemed to move, and in some places to billow and break, as imitating that orderly disorder which is common in nature." Tritons and sea-maids sported amid the waves, and "two great sea-horses, as big as life, put forth themselves, the one mounting aloft and writhing his head from the other." "The masquers were placed in a great concave shell like mother-of-pearl, curiously made to move on those waters and rise with the billow; the top thereof was stuck with a chevron of lights which, indented to the proportion of the shell, struck a glorious beam upon them" (Orgel and Strong, 1:90).

The fable devised by Ben Jonson at the prompting of the queen lacked shapeliness. Queen Anne wanted a disguising to end the Christmas season and wished to appear with her ladies as blackamoors. Jonson feigned that they were the daughters of the Niger, the river of Ethiopia, who wished to clarify their beauty and who were told by an oracle to seek a sun shining in the west, which was the source of true beauty and which rendered perfect all who experienced his light. This sun is King James, illuminating the blessed isle of Britain. The masquers are revealed in their seashell, floating on the waves of the ocean by moonlight. They are wafted to Britannia, where they dance with delight at their arrival and are informed that with the passing of a year their beauty will be rendered perfectly fair.

For all the imperfections of *Blackness*, the basic pattern of the new form had been established: a single stage with scenery and scene changes; single-point perspective aligned to the king's chair of state; costumes of extravagant beauty; an action performed by professional actors; aristocratic masquers who are revealed at the climax of the action in a richly imaginative and illuminated setting; the main dance sequence, which has been carefully rehearsed; musical accompaniment, songs, and the concluding revels, in which the masquers involve distinguished members of the audience in dances that could continue for hours.

This elaborate spectacle was directed to the celebration of the monarch, for Ben Jonson ensured that the king was the essential point of reference in the masques, insisting that the royal presence exerted an influence over the action that revealed and illustrated some aspect of majesty. Thus the king could be represented as the source of Ideal Beauty, as in *Blackness*, or as the principle of Harmony, or Wisdom, or Heroic Virtue, whose secret yet benevolent operation on the nation or court could be made visible by the symbolic events of the masque. Under Jonson and Jones, the masque became a vehicle for celebrating the divinity of kings, and it was a felicitous coincidence that the most magnificent event of the court year usually took place on Epiphany, or Twelfth Night, for a god was indeed revealed among men and a succession of miracles occurred in the Banqueting House to suggest the presence of divinity in the person of the king. Not only the king but the whole court was "glorified," in Jones's word, by the action of the masque, for its leading members were displayed in a transfigured state, as demigods or powers or glorious heroes. With the final revels drawing in privileged spectators, the audience could associate themselves with the ideal qualities that were exhibited in the masque. Ideally, a finely executed masque could exalt the whole assembled company by music, spectacle, and royal praise.

Almost annually throughout the reign of James I, Jonson and Jones prepared a masque for the court, enlarging the scope and refining the technique each year. A significant early development was the addition of a preliminary anti-masque before the main masque, first provided for *The Masque of Queens* in 1609, when Queen Anne requested Jonson to compose "some dance or show that might precede hers and have the place of a foil or a false masque" (Orgel and Strong, 1:132). This opening device rapidly became a convention of the genre. Comedy was allowed a brief reign before the sublime movement of the main action began, or spirits of disorder were given license to appear before they were subdued or dispersed by the forces of the principal masque. In 1609, for example, a dozen witches went about their work of darkness in an infernal setting; they were identified as figures hostile to King James's policies and to the national well-being, for their leader proclaimed:

> I hate to see these fruits of a soft peace,
> And curse the piety that gives it such increase.
> Let us disturb it then, and blast the light. (ORGEL AND STRONG, 1:133)

Having performed a magical dance "full of preposterous change and gesticulation" (Orgel and Strong, 1:134), they were banished by a loud chord that marked the transition to the House of Fame from which the queens exercised their authority.

The anti-masque often enabled the virtuous powers attributed to majesty to be seen in active opposition to negative and disruptive agencies. It also enlarged the aesthetic scope of the masque, for "the spectacle of strangeness," as Jonson called the anti-masque, permitted wilder and more mannered dances, as well as an extended register of musical invention to accompany the antics of the subordinate characters. A distinct strain of the grotesque developed in the anti-masque over the years, appealing to a persistent trait in late Renaissance taste. These grotesqueries gave so much pleasure to the audience that they became disproportionately numerous in the 1620s and 1630s, threatening to steal the show from the principal masque.

Year after year the masques went on at Whitehall. Until 1613, the queen was the leading performer, dancing with her ladies in Jonson's *Masque of Beauty* (1608) (the completion of *Blackness*), *The Masque of Queens* (1609), Daniel's *Tethys Festival* (1610) for the installation of Prince Henry as Prince of Wales, Jonson's *Love freed from Ignorance and Folly* (1611), and Campion's masque for the wedding of the earl of Somerset and Frances Howard in 1613. The formal focus of praise was always the king, but recent criticism has drawn attention to the ways in which the queen's masques were asserting the worth of women in a male-dominated court headed by a patriarchal king.[2] *The Masque of Queens* in particular can be seen as a dramatization of female power, with its troop of militant queens famous for conquest, government, and the slaughter of husbands, who rode in triumph in their chariots around the Banqueting House stage before beginning their dances. Such gestures of feminine authority were in truth more spectacular than substantial, for the Jacobean court remained resolutely masculine in its power structures. The early masques did, however, give prominence to the spirited community of cultivated women who were associated with Queen Anne and helped to shape the distinctive identity of the queen's court.

The dominance of court entertainments began to shift away from the queen's control in 1610, when the heir to the throne, Prince Henry, began his stage career at the time of his investiture as Prince of Wales. As a youth of martial temperament, he mounted displays of armed combat that were reminiscent of the skirmishings and feats of arms that had been in vogue at the court of Henry VIII. He was allowed to devise the main entertainment for the Christmas season of 1609–1610, and he chose to preside over a festival of military character that would end not in the traditional dancing of the revels but in a passage at arms.

There was an antique character to his procedure: he issued a challenge at the Christmas feast to all worthy knights to prove their valor in a combat at court, and on January 6, 1610, *Prince Henry's Barriers* took place, preceded by a masque written by Ben Jonson, seemingly to Henry's specifications. The setting was the world of Arthurian romance, the theme the revival of chivalry by the prince. The prophet Merlin recalled the warlike deeds of England's kings and looked to Prince Henry to extend this record of valorous exploits. King Arthur is careful to advise that all his accomplishments must be for the glory of Britain and for the honor of King James, "and when a world is won, / Submit it duly to this state, this throne" (Orgel and Strong, 1:160). The presence of the prince causes the long-dormant figure of Chivalry to awaken, in the Portico of St. George, and then the Barriers (or combat at arms) commenced. A long sequence of fights with sword and pike ensued, gratifying to the prince and his companions, but probably less so to King James, who was always apprehensive at the sight of cold steel. But the evening was the prince's, and he used the occasion to declare that a new force was now in play: he had ambitions to conduct an aggressive policy on the international scene, and those who studied him knew he intended some venture that would champion militant Protestantism or the expansion of English influence abroad.

Prince Henry's star rose only briefly, for he died at the end of 1612, to universal consternation and dismay, puncturing the celebrations for the wedding of his sister Princess Elizabeth, which were just getting under way. The marriage took place on Valentine's Day 1613, after a brief period of mourning for the prince, and the masques that were played before the court on that occasion all had a political aspect that related to the Protestant alliance produced by the union of Princess Elizabeth of England with the German Elector Palatine. Prophecies of future empire were uttered at the end of Thomas Campion's *Lords' Masque,* and again in George Chapman's *Memorable Masque* as the princes of Virginia are drawn eastward to worship a true sun king in the person of James and discover a new age of gold dawning in Great Britain (Parry, "Politics"). A powerful masque of an apocalyptic character proclaiming the presence of the True Faith in Britain and the imminence of full reformation was canceled, presumably because of the death of Prince Henry, who seems to have been the sponsor of this spectacle (Norbrook).

After the eventful years of 1610–1613 (which saw the emergence of Prince Henry, his death, and the Palatine marriage), the entertainments at court settled down to a steady praise of the king. Ben Jonson effectively became the official masque maker from 1614 onward, creating a series of panegyrical fables. A fine example of Jonsonian invention is *News from the New World Discovered in the Moon* (1620), a witty entertainment in which the masquers were astral Jacobites, as the king was informed,

> a race of your own, formed, animated, lightened and heightened by you, who, rapt above the moon far in speculation of your virtues, have remained there entranced certain hours with wonder of the piety, wisdom, majesty reflected by you on them from the divine light, to which only you are less. (ORGEL AND STRONG, 1:311)

The chief masquer, Prince Charles, led his fellow spirits in a dance of adoration, and the masque concluded with the chorus pronouncing the name of James the name "of all perfection" and wishing that the lunar music of praise will mingle with the earthly music of the king's peace in a universal harmony.

The most unrestrained celebration of King James was the masque offered by Prince Charles on the king's birthday in June 1620. This was an exceptional event, for the masques were traditionally part of the winter season of festivity, and it was obviously intended as a mark of special esteem. Jonson and Jones devised *Pan's Anniversary,* an entirely pastoral entertainment in which James was typed as Pan, the god of all nature, the vital power in creation. The masquers were the priests of Pan, who enacted the rites of worship of their god. The songs of the Arcadians are termed hymns, and they praise Pan not only as the sustaining force of nature but also as the creator of the harmonious society of Arcadia. In the fulsome language of these paeans, Pan/James becomes indistinguishable from God the Father: "Pan is our all, by him we breathe, we live, / We move, we are" (Orgel and Strong, 1:318). Here more than anywhere, the divinity of the king is proclaimed in the ritual and language of the masque, and the tendency to absolutism that lay in the rule of the Stuarts must have been furthered by these ceremonies of uninhibited adoration.

A more noble and restrained depiction of the Stuart court was presented in 1622, when *The Masque of Augurs* was performed in Inigo Jones's new Banqueting House. To complement the thoroughgoing classicism of the architecture, Jonson chose a Roman setting for his fable and took the opportunity to show the court an idealized image of itself in Roman dress. The masquers were "a College of tuneful Augurs" who proceeded to foretell the glories of the reign of the British Augustus. They acknowledged the sublime wisdom of his authority and the benefits of his peace, and after the ritual dances, they interpreted the omens of state that promised an auspicious future to the Stuart dynasty. The character of the masque has an air of religious ceremony, imploring heaven for blessings and offering an assurance of secure government and national prosperity.

The Jacobean masque was an extremely versatile medium. It varied the terms in which the king was honored year by year and could range in mood from the gay to the grave to the sublime. It became an unofficial ceremony of state, a festive act of homage to a king who as James VI and I affected the style of "Emperor of Great Britain" and professed to be the medium for mysterious divine powers vested in him, and who as James Stuart enjoyed a play, relished a spectacle, and liked to watch the young men of his court dancing before him.

Charles I, who came to the throne in 1625, was a contrast in many ways to his father: more austere, restrained, courteous, and refined. He did, however, share his father's love of theater. Stage plays were regularly put on at court throughout his reign, usually in the theater that Inigo Jones designed at Whitehall, called the Cockpit-in-Court, the first proper theater in the palace. There, plays tailored to please court fashion were acted. The preferred dramatists were Massinger, Brome, Shirley, and Davenant. Refined in language, elegant in manner, these plays of love and political intrigue reflected the taste of the court for displays of conduct and expression that verged on preciosity. Queen Henrietta Maria too maintained an active interest in drama. In particular, she was fond of staging pastoral plays, sometimes in French, in which mannered scenes of courtship and romance were acted out in an atmosphere heightened by discourses on platonic love.[3] Like all the entertainments of the Caroline court, the distinguishing note was refinement—in language, ideas, and behavior, well suited to a reign when civility was assumed to be a source of strength.

During Charles's reign, the masque attained its fullest elaboration, and because both the king and the queen danced in these displays of power, the masques became more closely allied to royal policy than their Jacobean predecessors had been. Since all these shows belonged to the period of personal rule from 1629 to 1640, when Charles governed the country without Parliament, they tended toward propaganda, vindicating the king's policies and offering images of royal authority in a reassuring light. For financial and domestic reasons, the sequence of Caroline masques did not begin until 1631, when Jonson and Jones devised two festivals for the winter season, one for the king and one for the queen. Throughout the 1630s Charles and Henrietta Maria offered masques to each other as reciprocal state gifts: one would dance as principal masquer, and the other would be seated as principal spectator. Many of the masques celebrated the mutual love of the royal couple as the power that animated the nation and gave it a mysterious spiritual strength; as the decade progressed, the king's masques became increasingly concerned with displaying the benevolent effects of his autocratic rule. Presented before a court composed of the social and political elite, whose approval was essential to the conduct of state affairs (for these were the people who had to uphold the king's authority in the country at large), the Caroline masques needed to project an air of optimism and moral assurance in their annual statements.

Jonson's first masque for Charles, *Love's Triumph through Callipolis* (1631) set the tone for the decade: a celebration of the purifying presence of Ideal Love in Callipolis, "the city of beauty or goodness," a recognizable image of Whitehall, where Charles's court was centered. Jonson exploited the cult of platonic love fostered by Queen Henrietta Maria. "Love," he announced in the preface, "was wont to be respected as a special deity in court, and tutelar god of the place" (Orgel and Strong, 1:406). Under the pure and reforming influence of that love, all disordered and intemperate passions are banished from the court, after which the triumph of noble lovers occurs, led by the king as a Heroic Lover, possessed by a fine fury for the virtuous perfections of the queen, "who is the wonder of the place." They perform a dance of adoration before the queen, and then the scene transforms to display an emblem of Stuart concord, a palm tree of virtue, entwined with the roses of England and the lilies of France, surmounted by an imperial crown. This positive image of the court as a place of light, love, virtue, and altruistic power was an inspirational opening to the masques of the reign.

At this point occurred the regrettable quarrel between Ben Jonson and Inigo Jones over who was the more significant figure in the creation of a masque, the poet or the designer. Jonson felt he was responsible for the immortal part, the soul of the masque, because he furnished the invention and the poetry that coruscated with philosophic ideas; the designer only constructed the body of the work, an elaborate vehicle for the ideas, which functioned effectively for a day and was then no more. Undoubtedly Jonson was jealous of Jones's success and of his friendship with the king. Charles, in turn, did not respond as warmly to Jonson as his father had done, and temperamentally they were far apart. Jonson attacked Jones petulantly in poetry and around court, with the result that the king never commissioned another masque from him.

Jones became the dominant partner in the shows of the thirties, producing technical effects of remarkable virtuosity: scene changes became more numerous, colorful aerial journeys more adventurous, transformation scenes more breathtaking, and the lighting of the stage became more subtle and controlled. As one looks at the surviving drawings for the scenery of the later masques, with their imposing architectural vistas and their spacious rural views, all in deep perspective, one is conscious of looking at the work of a man completely in command of his medium. In these later works, too, the music became more sustained, with larger forces, and recitative was introduced as operatic tendencies developed.

The triumphal note that Jonson had struck in his first masque for Charles resounded down the decade. Charles worked closely with Jones and the poets in shaping the masques, and the fables reflect his preferences. It is clear that he favored the triumphalist mode, as the titles indicate: *Love's Triumph* (1631), *Albion's Triumph* (1632), *The Triumph of Peace* (1634), *Britannia Triumphans* (1638). Aurelian Townshend's *Albion's Triumph* cast Charles as a Romano-British emperor, Albanactus, whose capital city, Albipolis, was superbly realized by Inigo Jones in a series of monumental classical buildings. The gods go about their business above, and Mercury declares that Jove has decreed a triumph for Albanactus, a spectacle that will be

> mighty as the man designed
> To wear those bays, heroic as his mind,
> Just as his actions, glorious as his reign,
> And like his virtues, infinite in train. (ORGEL AND STRONG, 2:454)

A distant glimpse of the emperor in splendor is granted to the audience, but then an interlude intervenes, in which Publius, a common man, discusses the triumph with Platonicus, a philosophic idealist. Whereas Publius could see only a magnificent procession, Platonicus explains that the true triumph is visible not as military but as spiritual, a triumph of virtue and integrity:

> I have seen this brave Albanactus Caesar, seen him with the eyes of understanding, viewed all his actions, looked into his mind, which I find armed with so many virtues that he daily conquers a world of vices. . . . All his passions are his true subjects, and knowledge, judgement, merit, bounty and the like are fit commanders for such a general; these triumph with him. (ORGEL AND STRONG, 1:455)

Platonicus then observes that the inner meaning is always the important one in these public shows: "Outsides have insides, shells have kernels in them, and under every fable . . . lies a moral."

The audience, thus instructed, can now appreciate that Albanactus's triumph, which eventually takes place after a series of anti-masques of circus games, is one of moral grandeur. Charles is revealed in a stately temple, dressed in imperial costume, attended by fourteen consuls gracefully disposed about him. At the height of his glory, he is struck by Cupid, and the conqueror submits to love for Alba, the queen, who is viewing the masque from her chair of state. The dances are offered to her as rites of adoration. The scene changes to

> a prospect of the King's palace of Whitehall, and part of the city of London seen afar off, and presently the whole heaven open[s], and in a bright cloud [are] seen sitting

five persons representing Innocency, Justice, Religion, Affection to the Country, and Concord. (ORGEL AND STRONG, 1:457)

The Roman panorama transforms to London, dramatically suggesting that the finest aspects of high Roman civilization have now passed to Stuart England. Imperial promise is in the Whitehall air. Throughout the masque the rule of Albanactus/Charles is associated with a flourishing of the arts, especially poetry and architecture, and their best qualities seem to have been brought out by the public-spiritedness and moral integrity of the emperor. When love heightens the mind of the ruler and a consort of equal virtue joins him, the nation may truly feel that it enjoys the blessings of the gods. Such would seem to be the message of this masque to the English court.

A recurrent theme in the Caroline masques is the renovation of virtue, related to good government; always a spirit of love prevails, love both for the queen and for the country. Often the theme of moral reformation is imaged in some complementary scene of architectural beauty. *Albion's Triumph* shows the king's palace at Whitehall, where Charles had recently tightened up standards of behavior and reformed the organization of the court; *Coelum Britannicum* ends with a vision of Windsor Castle, the seat of the Order of the Garter, the institution dedicated to maintaining honor in England, whose statutes he had just reformed. *Britannia Triumphans* presents a prospect of the City of London dominated by St. Paul's Cathedral, which Charles had recently caused to be renovated as a sign of his care for the Church and evidence of his civic generosity. *Salmacida Spolia* concludes with a stupendous view of the Great City, Charles's ideal capital.

*Coelum Britannicum* was the most lavish of all the Stuart masques, and the one that played the theme of reformation most loudly and ingeniously. Thomas Carew invented the memorable fable: Jove has been so impressed by the high standards of conduct and morals at the court of Charles and Henrietta Maria that he has determined to reform Olympus on the Caroline model.

> Your exemplar life
> Hath not alone transfused a jealous heat
> Of imitation through your virtuous court,
> By whose bright blaze your palace is become
> The envied pattern of this underworld,
> But the aspiring flame hath kindled heaven;
> Th'immortal bosoms burn with emulous fires. (ORGEL AND STRONG, 2:571)

A strict new regime will now be imposed on Olympus: chastity will be the order of the day—and night; fidelity, temperance, and obedience will prevail. The most visible sign of change will be in the heavens: the old constellations that have eternized lust and violence will be unsphered, and in their place images of British Worthies, chief of whom is Charles himself, will be pricked out in the night sky. In a lengthy, complex, and beautifully composed masque (which still today reads better than any other masque text besides Milton's *Comus*), Carew paid a wonderfully flattering tribute to the Caroline court, made more impressive by Inigo Jones's confident designs and transformation scenes of striking originality. Skeptical thoughts about royal policies are expressed via the anti-masques and by the satirical figure of Momus, who makes some telling thrusts about the negative effect of some royal ordinances, but wit and good nature soften this licensed criticism.

Caroline court entertainments did acknowledge that all was not entirely well in the state, and the anti-masques sometimes acted as a container for political discontent. Opposition to the king was growing in the later 1630s, as resentment of his use of prerogative to tax and appoint and imprison increased and as dislike of his high-church policies mounted. Country mistrust of the court sharpened, and provincial gentry complained about the denial of their rights to counsel the king through Parliament. On the Whitehall stage, there was a tendency to represent this opposition as ill humors in the body politic that would be purged in time and with the success of the king's government. In Davenant's *Britannia Triumphans* (1638), for example, one of the anti-masques features leaders of popular rebellions in the past—John Cade, Jack Kett, and Jack Straw—as promoters of anarchy, but they are soon dispelled. By 1640, when serious opposition was gathering momentum toward a confrontation with the king, Charles attempted to make the New Year masque an appeal for understanding and conciliation.

William Davenant joined Inigo Jones, doubtless under the king's supervision, to create *Salmacida Spolia*, the last Stuart masque, as it turned out, and the one in which, uniquely, both the king and the queen danced. This is a masque that consciously attempts to deal with an emergency, and all the resources of spectacle and music are applied to vindicate Charles's personal government and present it as wise, benevolent, and in the best interests of the nation. The chief spectator was the queen mother, Marie de Medici, but the target of the masque was the court, where Charles hoped to persuade the most influential group in the land of his good faith. The theme was the king's secret wisdom in the conduct of government, a wisdom unappreciated by the populace but fit matter to reveal to a noble, educated audience. Charles cast himself as Philogenes, the Lover of his People, whose wisdom would defeat all those malignant spirits who envied his greatness, leading the country to unrivaled peace and contentment.

The curtain rises on a tempest with furies, who rage and vanish, to be replaced by the figures of Concord and the Good Genius of Britain, who descend into a peaceful landscape, fertile and well maintained, an emblem of Britain's prosperity under the Stuarts. They express their sorrow at the ingratitude of the people toward the wise Philogenes, who has striven so hard to improve the country. A series of anti-masque entries causes a long diversion. Then follows a scene that dramatizes the heroic exertions of the monarch on behalf of his people, showing a remote mountainous landscape, "which represented the difficult way which heroes have to pass e'er they come to the Throne of Honour," an image that illustrates the king's isolation at this stage of his career. The revelation scene exhibits the king installed upon the Throne of Honour surrounded by his masquing lords; beneath them lie bound captives and trophies of conquest. Here the fictions of the masque begin to strain credulity, for the spectators are offered images of a victory that has not occurred, a Platonic triumph that simply does not convince. A song that greets the king praises his forbearance in not crushing his enemies, for his wisdom knows their disaffection is a sickness that will pass; in effect, Charles's weakness is being represented as mercy. The queen and her ladies then descend from the heavens to add her love and virtue to Charles's power, and a final chorus asserts that sweetness and light will prevail. The masque was repeated in February 1640, a talisman to ward off gathering misfortune. Sweetness and light did not prevail, and the next change of the political scene brought in the Masque of War, for the hostilities of the Civil War began in August 1642.

Although court entertainments ceased with *Salmacida Spolia*, and the London theaters were closed by parliamentary ordinance in September 1642, the theatrical tradition was too vigorous to be suppressed by a change in the nation's political circumstances. Throughout the war years of the 1640s, and during the period of the English republic, from 1649 to 1660, there were outbreaks of performances in London as the prohibited companies found occasions to regroup and put on plays for appreciative audiences, until the soldiers moved in to stop them and confiscate their costumes.[4] The Stuart court dissolved, yet when Oliver Cromwell became head of state as the Lord Protector in 1653, a new version of court life developed around him. England may have become a republic, but Cromwell was effectively a prince and needed a court to sustain him in the exercise of the offices of state. Quite improbably, the masque revived under Cromwell, to heighten a state occasion. When the Portuguese ambassador came to London in 1653 to sign a treaty of alliance with Britain, he was regaled with *Cupid and Death* by James Shirley, who had composed one of the Caroline masques, *The Triumph of Peace*, in 1634. This Cromwellian masque had scenery, its music was composed by Christopher Gibbons, son of the famous Orlando, and by Matthew Locke, and its dances were performed by a company of gentlemen. The survival of the "Cupid" theme that had been fashionable at King Charles's court is particularly intriguing, for it suggests a continuity of taste from the 1630s into the 1650s. However, the Neoplatonism that once lightly colored the stories of Cupid has faded; now the action is played for its wit and the higher harmonies of the masque have gone. There is no attempt to glorify the state or to celebrate the mysterious power of the Protector. A novel feature of the musical style was the use of recitative throughout: one might infer from this development that as the masque in its revived form had shed most of the magical functions that belonged to a different social order, it was beginning to evolve toward a new secular genre, opera.

So it proved, for indeed, opera became the unexpected dramatic innovation of Cromwellian England. This minor miracle was achieved by Sir William Davenant, a remarkably resilient man, who, more than anyone, ensured the continuity of the theatrical arts from Caroline times into the Restoration (Edmond, *Davenant*). Under Charles I, Davenant had been a court poet, playwright, masque maker, and author of *Salmacida Spolia*, the last of the long run of Stuart court entertainments. Now he introduced opera, presenting it in a way that was acceptable to the authorities who disapproved of drama. He professed to be reviving a lost classical art form: "Entertainment by Declamations and Musick after the manner of the Ancients" (Davenant, *Works*, 341). His first full-scale production was *The Siege of Rhodes* in 1656. Davenant wrote the text, a story of love and honor in the French classical mode, set amid the conflict between the Turks and the Christians. John Webb designed the scenery, and the music was composed by Henry Lawes and Matthew Locke. Here, too, we may be struck by the cultural continuity from the old regime, for Webb had been Inigo Jones's assistant on the last masque, and Lawes had written the music for Milton's *Comus* and for a previous masque of Davenant's, as well as setting many songs by Cavalier poets. *The Siege of Rhodes* was extremely successful and was followed by two more operas that combined heroic drama with patriotic, anti-Spanish themes: *The Cruelty of the Spaniards in Peru* and *The History of Sir Francis Drake*. There are references to Davenant as Cromwell's Master of the Revels, an indication that there may have been more entertainment under Cromwell than is commonly supposed.

At the Restoration in 1660, it was Davenant, along with Thomas Killigrew, who received a royal warrant authorizing him to form a company of players and operate a theater. Killigrew's company performed at the Theatre Royal, Drury Lane, and Davenant's company, under the duke of York's patronage, played first at Salisbury Court and then at Dorset Garden. Davenant continued to write plays as well as managing his new company. It is principally because of Davenant, who had been born in 1606 and was probably Shakespeare's godson, that the theatrical experience of the Elizabethan and Jacobean stage was transmitted into the Restoration, and so became part of an unbroken dramatic tradition that continues to this day.

NOTES

1. The formative years of Inigo Jones are investigated in Harris and Higgott, 13–19.
2. See Lewalski, *Writing*, 28–43, for a view of Queen Anne's masques as a form of "subversive entertainment."
3. For Caroline court theater, see M. Butler, *Theatre*, 25–84; for the queen's involvement in drama, see Veevers.
4. Stage performances in London throughout the Civil Wars and the Commonwealth period are extensively documented in Hotson, *Commonwealth*.

# CHAPTER 12

# The Theater and Literary Culture

*Barbara A. Mowat*

IN 1942 C. J. Sisson published a brief account of "a volumi-
nous set of Star Chamber documents recording [the 1611] trial . . . for sedition"
of, among others, Sir Richard Cholmeley's professional players. "One of the principal charges against them," he writes, "was that of having acted a seditious play,
of Catholic purport, at . . . Gowthwaite Hall [in Yorkshire] . . . about Christmas
1609" ("Shakespeare's Quartos," 135). From Sisson's account of the Star Chamber records, we learn that Cholmeley's Players—a large, established provincial
acting company (136)—performed several plays for the 1609 Christmas season at
Gowthwaite as part of their extensive Yorkshire tour. The allegedly seditious play,
*Saint Christopher*, is no longer extant. But the repertory offered by the company,
as Sisson notes, is "of extraordinary interest" (137).

The Christmas play offered as an alternative for *Saint Christopher* was *The
Travailes of the Three English Brothers*, performed and printed in London in 1607.
And for Candlemas, as one of the players testified, "one of the playes acted and
played was Perocles prince of Tire, and the other was Kinge Lere" (138). That *Lear*
and *Pericles*, two relatively new King's Men plays, were performed in Yorkshire in
1609 is in itself interesting. More interesting is that all of these plays, according to
the various actors' testimonies, were performed from the printed quartos—from
books, that is, that had only recently appeared in London bookstalls, *Lear* having
been printed in 1608 and *Pericles* in 1609.

The actors' unanimous insistence that "these plaies which they so plaied" were
"played according to the printed booke or Bookes" and that "the booke by which
[they] did act . . . was a printed book, And they onelie acted the same according to
the contents therein printed, and not otherwise" (138) was testimony that, according
to Sisson, "amounted to a defence of the actors against any accusation of acting

unauthorized dramatic material" (140). As their leading actor, Richard Simpson, testified about their performance of *Saint Christopher*: "The play was suffered and permitted to be acted in other places, and there was no new addition or new matter put
into it but as was acted before in other places, and printed in the said book" (142). As
Sisson notes, "It is evident that in their eyes the use of a printed play as prompt-copy
was equivalent to a license from the Master of the Revels and gave them complete
protection" (142).

The story of the 1609 Christmas season at Gowthwaite Hall, where Cholmeley's
Players acted the printed quartos of several new London plays, provides a point of
entry into the very large and intricate topic of early English theater and literary culture. The topic is daunting in part because, in order to place early modern English
theater properly within the context of the literary culture of its time, we need to
know far more than we now do about that culture. For the purposes of this essay,
the term *literary* means, generally, that which was designed to be read, whether in
print or in manuscript, whether fiction or nonfiction, high culture or low culture.
A good case can be made for a less inclusive definition, but this larger meaning is
appropriate if one's interest is in the relationship between theater and that which is
"literary," in that early modern English theater itself ignores all the binaries just
mentioned. By drawing alike from ballads and Virgil, chapbooks and Seneca, theater transgresses the high-culture/low-culture binary that Ascham and others would
have set up. It ignores the fiction/nonfiction binary in that, while such writers as
Sir Philip Sidney made a distinction between "poetry" and "history," dramatists
drew on every variety of written and printed material, absorbing and dramatizing
Ovid's fables and Fabian's chronicles with equal respect—and disrespect (Mowat,
"Rogues"; Mowat, "Shakespeare's").

Our knowledge of early modern English literary culture—our knowledge, that is,
of that which was designed to be read and of the experience of readers—is slowly but
steadily expanding. We know something of the works read in the (Latin) grammar
schools and something therefore of the rich and complex impact of classical stories,
metaphors, and images on educated audiences (F. P. Wilson, "Shakespeare's," 19–20;
Baldwin, *Shakspere's*). We know something of the libraries of such book lovers as
John Dee and Ben Jonson, and—because Dee, at least, made his library available for
other readers—we therefore know something of the reading habits of literate
Londoners (Sherman, McPherson). We know a bit about the literary interests of
England's middling sort through Annabel Patterson's recent tracing of the construction and dissemination of Holinshed's *Chronicles*. And women's diaries, manuscript
miscellanies, and marginal jottings in early printed books are opening to us a fund of
information about reading and writing habits of the period (Grafton and Jardine,
Love, Marotti, W. Wall, Zwicker). As our knowledge grows—and despite the vast
amount that we do not (yet) know—we can say with some certainty that the theater
of the period was intricately, complexly interconnected with literary culture—as the
Gowthwaite Hall story with its printed quartos confirms.

An unexpected complexity in the relationship between theater and the literary is suggested in this story's bringing together performance with printed playtexts, which we tend to think of as designed for readers. The story of Cholmeley's Players reminds us that acting companies sometimes used printed plays as playbooks, a fact that David Bevington's *From "Mankind" to Marlowe* long since taught us but that we tend to forget. Bevington introduced us to the early history of the practice in the body of Tudor interludes and moralities "offered for acting"—that is, in Bevington's words, "printed with casting lists to indicate how many actors are required to perform the play" (5).

That this body of Tudor plays was printed with acting companies as a primary market is almost incontrovertible. Title pages of books in England in the early modern period were used to advertise books—posted separately as advertisements or placed on top of the printed sheets in bookstalls to attract passersby or browsers (McKerrow, *Introduction*, 88–94). The title pages of the Tudor plays "offered for acting" used eye-catching typography to highlight such words as *new* and *comedy* and contained such reassuring phrases as "eight men may easily play it." The title page of John Rastell's *Nature of the Four Elements* even includes instructions as to how an acting company, by leaving out much of what he calls the "sad [i.e., serious] matter as the messengers part and some of natures part and some of experiences part," might cut the play from a running time of an hour and a half down to three quarters of an hour, and "yet the matter will depend conveniently" (Sisson, "Shakespeare's," 131).[1] Since Rastell's own press printed this humanist interlude, the appeal to the acting market on the title page carries a double authority of printer and author and is a salutary reminder that the traveling company at Gowthwaite Hall in 1609 stood in a long and honorable line of players who acted from printed quartos.

The reminder is salutary in that it interestingly complicates the usual understanding of the relationship between early modern theater and early modern printed plays. Scholars tend to speak as if they imagine a play assuming physical shape first in a manuscript draft, then perhaps in a scribal copy of that draft annotated for production purposes, then embodied by the players in performance. This is presented as one line of dramatic transmission—i.e., from manuscript page to stage. A second line is then acknowledged, one that also begins with a manuscript (perhaps the original or perhaps the playhouse manuscript) that goes to the printing house, whence the play in printed form is offered to the reading public.[2] The Gowthwaite Hall story problematizes these presumptions by offering a disturbance of the assumed linear patterns.

Once one reflects on this particular disturbance—this blurring of the two lines of transmission and reversal of direction so that print precedes performance—one recalls other breaches and disturbances. One thinks, for instance, of the places where the conjunction of printed playtexts with performance leads to manuscript playbooks. Take, for example, the famous Dering manuscript of Shakespeare's *Henry IV* plays. All evidence indicates that the manuscript was copied by a scribe

from the 1613 quarto of *1 Henry IV* and the 1600 quarto of *2 Henry IV*, printed texts
that Sir Edward Dering marked up, abridging and otherwise revising for the copyist in preparation for a 1622 performance (which seems not to have taken place).
Dering, in marking up the quartos, introduced changes in the text that may indicate his own religious sensibility, along with alterations that seem to "reflect
Dering's recollection of London performances" or that "reflect regular stage usage"
(Williams and Evans, x–xi).

The seventeenth-century Folger manuscript of *Julius Caesar*, to take another
example, provides a text that traces back through earlier manuscripts to a copy of
the 1632 Shakespeare Second Folio in which the text of *Julius Caesar* had been
annotated for performance. Blakemore Evans argues that, while it is incontrovertible that the Folger manuscript indirectly derives from F2, much that we find in the
manuscript, with its interesting dramatis personae list, its 356 significant verbal variants that do not appear in any of the folios or any later printed text, and its eleven
omissions of passages, gives us "some indication of the actual text as it was presented on the stage during the middle seventeenth century" (Evans, "Shakespeare's," 410). One finds in the six seventeenth-century Douai Shakespeare manuscripts and in the seventeenth-century Folger manuscript of *The Merry Wives of
Windsor* comparable evidence of playtexts that have transmigrated from printed
texts annotated for performance into manuscript playbooks (Hedback; Evans,
"Douai"; Halliwell). The relationships among performance, playscript, and
printed text are thus more fluid, more disturbed, than scholars have tended to
imagine and describe them.

The Cholmeley Players' insistence, however, that "the book by which [they] did
act . . . was a printed book, and they only acted the same according to the contents
therein printed" indirectly confirms our initial sense of printed playtexts as designed
for readers—reminds us, that is, that printed plays, though sometimes incorporated
into the performance world, also had a primary existence in the literary world and
were subject to the rules of that world. Sisson's comment that for the Cholmeley
Players "the use of a printed play as prompt-copy was equivalent to a license from
the Master of the Revels" reflects his (and his contemporaries') belief that "a printed
play was one that had already been allowed to be acted in a London theatre. It had
received the licence of the Master of the Revels" (140). Richard Dutton's recent
study of the licensing of plays and books shows that the matter is more complicated
than Sisson had thought. Printed playtexts were, in fact, licensed or "authorized" for
printing in a different procedure from that which the manuscript underwent in
obtaining the Master of the Revels's "allowance to play." Like all printed books of
the time, printed playtexts, until circa 1607, were licensed for printing under the
authority of the bishop of London and the archbishop of Canterbury. Beginning
circa 1607, George Buc obtained the authority to license plays for printing. When
Buc later became Master of the Revels, he had the dual authority to "allow" a script
for playing and, in a separate act, to license a script for printing. (Thus the confu-

sion about the powers of the Master of the Revels and the status of the playscript as allowed for playing and/or authorized for printing.)[3]

The dual (legal) existence of the allowed/authorized play (i.e., allowed for performance, authorized for printing) often had interesting and complicating consequences. Ben Jonson's problems with the Privy Council about *Sejanus*, for example, may have arisen from either the play's performance or its printing; in the first case, the Master of the Revels may have been remiss in "allowing" the script for acting; in the second, the church authorities may have been careless in licensing it for printing (Dutton, *Mastering*, 15, 164).[4] The dual licensing procedure for plays also stands as a tangible reminder that early modern drama had distinct "radicals of presentation," to use Alistair Fowler's terminology (Lewalski, *Renaissance*, 4)—not so much "drama" versus "narrative" (two of Fowler's "radicals") as "performance" versus "print" or "playscript" versus "literature." As a script allowed for playing, a play was "theater"; as a licensed printed book, a play was itself a part of literary culture.

John Marston recognized this fact in apologizing for printing *The Malcontent*, claiming that it "afflict[ed]" him "that Scaenes invented, meerely to be spoken, should be inforcively published to be read" (Barish, 138). Samuel Daniel recognized the same fact in expressing his embarrassment that necessity had forced him to allow his *Philotas* to be performed, thus "making the stage the Speaker of my lynes" (Dutton, *Mastering*, 165). Ben Jonson, unembarrassed and unapologetic, took advantage of the drama's distinct radicals of presentation and, as Jonas Barish remarks, overturned the custom of printing dramatic texts that claimed to offer "authentic transcripts of what had been well received by audiences"; instead, he promised on the title page of his quarto printing of *Every Man Out of His Humor* to give the reader the play "as it was first composedby the AUTHOR B.I. *Containing more then hath been publickely spoken or acte[d]*. With the severall Character of every person." As Barish notes, "Jonson, clearly, is thinking of the play now as a reading experience rather than a theatrical experience, as a literary entity"; further, Jonson's publication of his plays as "Works" in his 1616 Folio lifts them "out of the turbulence of the public arena into the still silence of the page" and "appeals to readers over the heads of playhouse audiences." "The end result," Barish notes, "is to make the printed script rather than the live performance the final authority; the play moves formally into the domain of literature" (136–39).

In a certain sense, of course, neither printed script nor Ben Jonson was necessary in moving "the play . . . into the domain of literature," since plays in manuscript were valued as reading matter and therefore were a part of literary culture. Manuscript copies of plays were presented by actors to friends and patrons; professional scribes copied playscripts for patrons as well as for acting companies and printers (Werstine, "Narratives," 85–86; Love, 65–70). But the printing and selling of plays for readers made the boundary between theater and literary culture increasingly porous.

We see this porousness in, for example, the so-called poetomachia of 1599–1601, where satiric attacks of one poet on another moved between printed poems and the stage. A fictitious classical name assigned pejoratively to Ben Jonson in a published epigram, for example, became a character's name in a play, and Jonson, insulted by this stage representation of himself as pedantic poet-dramatist, retaliated by adding new scenes to his *Every Man Out of His Humor*—scenes that may have been performed at the Globe and that certainly appeared in the printed quarto (Bednarz, 1–5, 28). Comparable fungibility of literary matter and stage matter characterizes the Martin Marprelate controversy, in which Martin, the putative hero of the Marprelate pamphlets, is pilloried onstage, his theatrical representation in turn becoming part of the later pamphlet warfare (Poole).

Within this more complex context of theater and literary culture I would locate a second instructive feature of the Gowthwaite Hall Christmas season, namely, the presence in the Cholmeley Players' repertory of the play *Pericles, Prince of Tyre*, as acted from the 1609 quarto. This is a context in which theater scripts become literary entities and in which the movement between script and performance and print is interestingly recursive.

With regard to the performance of *Pericles* in Yorkshire, one notices, first, the unlikeliness of the *Pericles* quarto as a prompt copy. F. D. Hoeniger in his Arden edition of *Pericles* describes this quarto as "grossly corrupt" (1)—a reported text that is also badly printed, containing dialogue much of which Hoeniger calls "manifest nonsense" (li), stage directions that "are notable for their frequent omission" or that "are bare to the point of vagueness" (xxx), speech headings that are missing or that misattribute speeches, and "punctuation [that] . . . is frequently chaotic" (xxxi). The quarto, he writes, is characterized by a "very considerable number of gross errors, some of which have remained unsolved cruces" (xxxi). This is a precise description of the kind of text that twentieth-century wisdom would point to as unusable in the early modern playhouse, but testimony given under oath asserts that Cholmeley's Players performed their plays—including *Pericles*—"according to the contents therein printed, and not otherwise." This testimony may have much to teach us about our assumptions about acceptable early modern prompt copy.

More important than the odd fact that quarto *Pericles* served as an acting text is the fact that *Pericles* itself stands as a remarkable example, first, of the permeability of the theater/literary-culture boundary and, second, of the obvious dependence of theater on nondramatic literary culture. The sheer variety of *Pericles*'s early physical (theatrical, literary) forms makes it exemplary as a transgressor of boundaries. Contemporary references (in pamphlets, court records, and attacks by other dramatists) make it clear that, embodied in performance, *Pericles* was a remarkable stage success from about 1607 until the closing of the theaters in 1642 (Hoeniger, lxv–lxvii). In 1608 Edward Blount entered in the Stationers' Register "A book called The Book of Pericles Prince of Tyre." This formulation, coupled with the fact that the theaters were closed because of plague for much of 1608, leads scholars to believe that it was the acting company's playbook that Blount entered (Hoeniger, xxiii–xxiv). (Blount did not, for whatever reason, ever publish *Pericles*.)

In the same year appeared a book that reported the performed play of *Pericles* in the form of a novel. This was George Wilkins's "The Painfull Aduentures of Pericles Prince of Tyre. Being the true History of the Play of Pericles, as it was lately presented by the worthy and ancient Poet *John Gower*"—a title-page description that Wilkins supplements in his "argument," where he entreats the reader to "receive this Historie in the same manner as it was . . . by the Kings Maiesties Players excellently presented" (Muir). Finally, in 1609, a printer of tracts and other ephemera published a text of the play, noting on the title page that this was the play "as it was divers and sundry times acted by his Maiesties Servants at the Globe" and as it was written by William Shakespeare (Greg, "Introduction"). This 1609 publication, reprinted later that year and four more times before the theaters closed in 1642, is our only substantive text of the play. The play was not included in the First Folio.

There are many widely different stories that try to explain both the above facts and the few points of scholarly agreement about *Pericles* as it has come down to us—agreement, for example, that the play is deeply flawed and, most would say, only partially the work of Shakespeare, and agreement that there are many similarities and some notable differences between Wilkins's novel and the *Pericles* quarto. Each explanatory story, no matter what its premises and methodologies, finds itself having to posit a play that moved fluidly and recursively among the forms of print, script, and performance.[5]

The most elaborate scenario (supported variously by Kenneth Muir and Ernest Schanzer) would have it that in 1607 there existed a play about Pericles written by one or more unidentified playwrights; Shakespeare either saw the play performed by his company or he found it in manuscript, and he revised it. It was the earlier play—the ur-*Pericles*—that Wilkins saw in performance and reconstructed and published in his novel. The fact that there are Shakespearean bits in the novel is accounted for by proponents of this scenario by suggesting that Wilkins, while he was writing the novel, also attended a performance of the play as revised by Shakespeare, material from which contaminated his report of the ur-*Pericles*. But there is, as Kenneth Muir notes, "another complication." One or two passages in the 1609 quarto—which Muir sees as printing a reported reconstruction of Shakespeare's version of the play—read "as though they had been clumsily converted from [Wilkins's] novel" (xiv). Muir suggests as an explanation that although "both Shakespeare and Wilkins may have been borrowing from the source play, . . . it seems more probable that the reporters of the play or the compositors of Q [the quarto] made use of the novel to correct the copy" (xv). According to this narrative, then, behind the quarto text of *Pericles* is, first, a play in performance and/or in manuscript, followed by a Shakespearean revision in manuscript and performance, with the performance reconstructed in manuscript by one or two reporters and set into type by two or three compositors, with either the reporters or the compositors correcting their copy against the printed text of a novel that reported the pre-Shakespearean version of the play in performance.

Other narratives about the *Pericles* playtext work out less elaborate patterns and maintain stronger boundaries between forms. Hoeniger, for instance, has a single play onstage in 1608 composed by several playwrights, including Shakespeare, and reported in one form by Wilkins and in another by the reporter of the quarto. (As Hoeniger writes, "If the novel is only a very inferior and thus undependable report of the play, so is . . . the play's first quarto" [xliv].) Gary Taylor posits a collaboration between Shakespeare and Wilkins in writing the play (thus placing Wilkins's novel in an interesting position vis-à-vis the quarto) and posits several actors as the reporters for the quarto—actors who, in addition to drawing on their written parts and their memories, also obtained a copy of the part written out for the actor of Gower ("Pericles," 556–60). These versions of the story, though more straightforward than the first scenario sketched out, nevertheless reveal a play shifting fluidly from form to form—through scripts, revisions, performances, clumsy notes or hazy memories and actors' parts, into new manuscripts and final publication in two flawed printed forms—one a playtext, one a novel.

In its variety of physical embodiments and in the mysteries clouding the relationships among those embodiments, *Pericles* stands as an extreme example of the complex radical(s) of presentation of early modern drama. It exemplifies as well—perhaps more obtrusively than any other play of the period—the clear dependence of early modern theater on literary culture, on the book as source of the play's dramatic fiction, as authority, as that which, already disseminated in manuscript codex and in print, was brought to life (as they say) on the stage. From ashes ancient Gower comes "to sing a song that old was sung," a song that will both glad our ears and please our eyes, presenting a story that "hath been sung at festivals" and that "lords and ladies in their lives / Have read . . . for restoratives."[6] John Gower's own primary association is with literary and intellectual culture. His role as a major fourteenth-century English author is commemorated in the recumbent effigy over his grave in Saint Saviors Cathedral, which presents him with his head resting on a stone image of his three folio works, one of which—the *Confessio Amantis*, from which the Pericles story derives—looms large as a major early English book, printed by Caxton in 1483 from one of its many manuscript volumes, then printed again in 1532 and 1554.

Yet Gower as Prologue and Chorus is also a creature of theatrical tradition. Hoeniger traces the choral Gower most immediately back to Barnabe Barnes's *The Divil's Charter* (which, like *Pericles*, features the author of its source text as Prologue and Chorus) and to William Rowley, John Day, and George Wilkins's *Travels of the Three English Brothers*, in which Fame is the choral figure. Hoeniger links these 1607 figures directly to the Chorus of Folio *Henry V*—composed before Elizabeth's death in 1603—and indirectly to the vernacular saints'-play tradition (xix–xxiii). I find an even closer link between the Gower Chorus and the Poet who serves as Prologue and Epilogue to such miracle plays as the Digby *The Conversion of St. Paul*, who beseeches the audience for license to present the story "as the Bible gives us the information" and advises the interested that "Whoever wants to read the book, Acts of the

Apostles, there he can have the exact information. But as best we can, we shall briefly address ourselves to the story and . . . begin our play" (*Digby*, 27).

The Poet's double reference to the story in the book and the story in action becomes a triple reference in *Henry V*, where the act 5 Chorus alludes in rapid succession to the book from which the story is drawn, to himself as narrator, and to the play in performance:

> Vouchsafe to those that have not read the story
> That I may prompt them; and of such as have,
> I humbly pray them to admit th'excuse
> Of time, of numbers, and due course of things,
> Which cannot in their huge and proper life
> Be here presented. (5.Ch.1–6)

A similar triple reference appears in *Pericles* as:

> I tell you what mine authors say . . .
> What now ensues, to the judgement of your eye
> I give my cause. (1.Ch.20, 41–42)

The relationships among forms—among the written story, the chorus's narration, dumb show presentations, and full dramatic representation—are, throughout the play, at the heart of Gower's commentary. At one point, after apologizing for the improbabilities of enacted scenes—for the play's using one language, for instance, despite the several geographic locations "where our scene seems to live"—Gower foregrounds his own narration:

> I do beseech you
> To learn of me, who stands i' th' gaps to teach you
> The stages of our story . . . (4.4.7–9)

and then goes on to introduce a dumb show with the words:

> Like motes and shadows see them move awhile;
> Your ears unto your eyes I'll reconcile. (4.4.21–22)

And from beginning to end, the play self-consciously announces its own shifting forms, as narrative presentation gives way to dumb show and to full dramatic representation, and Gower reflects on the various modes of storytelling.

In this exceedingly bookish play, skulls and shields and faces all become books to be read, and the deeds of knights are likened to a "volume" needing no advertisement "in a title-page," "Since every worth in show commends itself" (2.3.2–6); but our attention is also repeatedly drawn to the theatrical and the spoken, to what is being presented for our eyes and our ears. *Pericles* thus forces on us an awareness of the complex nature of the stage play: a story become script become performance—the story here openly scripted from Gower's *Confessio Amantis,* and the script here so structured that the presentation bifurcates, with what we think of as normal dramatic representation splitting into choral narration for our ears and into motes and shadows for our eyes, then coming together again into what Gower interestingly calls "the text" (2.Ch.40).

*Pericles* is, of course, not alone in making obvious the relationship between the stage play and its bookish origins. In the sixteenth-century "interlude" of *Mary Magdalene*, for example, the Prologue identifies the play's source (its "Authoritie of Scripture") as "Written in the .vii of Luke" (Wager, ll. 58, 60), and the play includes a stage direction that reads: "Let Marie creepe vnder the table . . . and doe as it is specified in the Gospel" (l. 1742 sd). Only by consulting chapter 7 of the Gospel According to Saint Luke—or by remembering the words as read from the pulpit—would the reader of the printed interlude or the actor playing Mary know that "Mary" is here instructed to "wash Jesus's feet with her tears, wipe them with the hairs of her head, kiss his feet, and anoint them with ointment." In Shakespeare's *Titus Andronicus*, a schooltext copy of Ovid's *Metamorphoses* is actually brought onstage, where the raped, mutilated, and therefore mute Lavinia tells her story by using the stumps of her arms to find the page in Ovid that tells of the rape of Philomela, a tale that her molesters had earlier cited as the model for their reenactment of that story of horrors (Mowat, "Lavinia's").

More commonly, plays are less openly dependent upon books—or so it seems to twentieth-century readers. Marlowe does not have Doctor Faustus bring onstage the English Faust Book that his story dramatizes (*The History of the Damnable Life and Deserved Death of Doctor John Faustus*), nor does Lyly have Gallathea carry a copy of Ovid's *Metamorphoses*. Perhaps to an Elizabethan audience the dependence of these plays on their respective books was too obvious to require a physical stage prop. But whether or not playwrights expected their audiences to identify the books that their plays dramatized, it is abundantly clear that books provided the stuff that plays enacted. From the dramatized biblical texts that we call "mystery plays" and such "miracle plays" as the Digby *Mary Magdalene* through such early humanist plays as, for example, John Bale's *King Johan*, the (very) early English drama proclaimed its text-based origins.[7]

And as movable-type printing, translation, and classical learning expanded the boundaries of what Elizabeth Eisenstein calls the "Commonwealth of Learning" (xiii), playwrights absorbed an increasingly rich store of texts. Traces of those texts may be found throughout the corpus of early modern English drama. F. P. Wilson suggests that those traces would have been audible, and would have been heard with pleasure, in Shakespeare's theater: "We who are cut off for the most part from that great tradition in which Shakespeare was bred can realize only with difficulty how many thoughts and even images came to his audience with the pleasure not so much of discovery as of recognition" ("Shakespeare's," 20).

While we cannot know for certain just how audiences in early modern England heard the language uttered onstage, we can say confidently that when we place the extant texts of early modern plays among the other printed quartos and folios of the early modern period, we find in the pages of chroniclers, poets, pamphleteers, and romance writers many of the stories, ideas, and words woven into early modern playtexts.

That Ben Jonson should draw heavily on classical historians and poets does not surprise us, given his expressed love of the classics and his desire to compete with the past as Poet and Author (Helgerson). But Jonson is far from alone in making the stage a vehicle for embodied literatures. Indeed, his "translation" (as some pejoratively would have it) of Tacitus into *Sejanus* is matched, in its bookish dependence, by many of the plays of the supposedly unlearned "Swan of Avon." Not that Shakespeare is open about his bookishness. Most of his prologues and epilogues imply, in fact, that his plays depend on no authority other than the shaping fancy of the poet and the incarnation of that fancy in the (inevitable) mockeries of the stage (Mowat, "Shakespeare's"). *Pericles* is almost alone among Shakespeare's plays in announcing its literary background, citing its "authors" (i.e., those authorities on whom the story depends) and admitting that its tale is an old one "read" by long ago "lords and ladies." Yet while Shakespeare's other choruses speak as if their plays reflect a reality that has nothing to do with books, they are, in fact, just like *Pericles*, crafted from graven folio and quarto pages.

Many of Shakespeare's plays (like Marlowe's *Doctor Faustus* or *Edward II*) dramatize the plot line, the set of characters, and the specific confrontations present in a given piece of chronicle, a work of short fiction, a Greek romance, an Ovidian tale, or a chapbook. Shakespeare's *Richard III*, for example, transfers to the stage the pages of Thomas More's gripping and well-shaped biography of Richard III as it was printed in Holinshed's 1587 *Chronicles*, and in the process presents a new kind of history play; *Romeo and Juliet* dramatizes Arthur Brooke's narrative poem *The Tragical History of Romeus and Juliet* (published first in 1562, then reprinted in 1587); and *The Winter's Tale* transforms Robert Greene's novel *Pandosto* (printed in 1588, reprinted in 1607) into a powerful romance for the stage. Each of these plays reflects language and incidents from other books as well, but the plays as a whole can be considered dramatizations of particular literary works.

Other Shakespeare plays (like other plays by Jonson or Greene, or like Marlowe's *Jew of Malta*) instead weave together language, characters, and incidents from a variety of books. A *Midsummer Night's Dream*, for instance, which has "no identifiable narrative or dramatic source for the plot" (Barton, Introduction, 217), is crafted from at least a dozen identifiable printed books, plus several works that Shakespeare had to have seen in manuscript (*Midsummer*, ed. Brooks, lviii–xciv). The most significant of the printed books (i.e., those that left the most significant traces in the play) include the biography of Theseus in North's translation of Plutarch's *Lives*; Chaucer's *Knight's Tale* and his *Legend of Good Women*; Ovid's *Metamorphoses* (both in the original Latin and in Golding's English translation); Apuleius's *The Golden Ass*; Reginald Scot's *Discoverie of Witchcraft*, Spenser's *Shepheardes Calender* and Seneca's *Medea*.

Almost more impressive than the range of reading is the complexity of the inter-
weavings. Harold Brooks notes two "set pieces" that he calls

> striking examples of how Shakespeare weaves or fuses together material from a whole
> series of sources. The hunting-scene recalls from [Chaucer's] *Knight's Tale* Theseus'
> Maytime hunting at daybreak; and adds a reference to his having hunted in Thessaly,
> which comes from hints in Golding and North's Plutarch. . . . Titania's tale of devas-
> tation and dislocation is indebted not only to Seneca's *Medea*, but also . . . to . . . three
> appropriate episodes in Golding: the plague of Aegina, Ceres' curse, and Deucalion's
> flood. (lxxxvi)

And the play's representation of the character of Theseus, to take another kind of
example, is woven from texts both various and rhetorically and ideologically at
odds. Constructed from discourse expressing both sides of a current and heated
debate, the Theseus of *A Midsummer Night's Dream* re-presents Chaucer's "noble
duc," Plutarch's legendary military and sexual warrior, and Ovid's "most valiant
Prince"; at the same time, he is given powerful and memorable language that
expresses Reginald Scot's skepticism about, and scorn for, the very "antique fables"
that have created such fictional characters (Mowat, "Shakespeare's").

Even in the case of William Shakespeare, then, and even in a play that until
recently was considered "a matter of gossamer and moonshine, a charming trifle"
(Barton, Introduction, 217), the matter presented on the early modern stage had
absorbed and transmuted many a printed quarto and folio page (Mowat, "Rogues").
It is tempting to argue that the texts thus absorbed and transformed into playscripts
were thereby themselves disseminated, made available to the unlearned as to the
learned—to claim that thousands who would not have read the *The History of the
Damnable Life and Deserved Death of Doctor John Faustus* would have seen
Marlowe's *Doctor Faustus*; that Ovid, available in Golding's English but unavailable
to the nonliterate in any printed language, would have been widely known through
the plays of Lyly and Shakespeare. Margot Heinemann has recently argued that "the
influence of the drama has analogies with that of churches and preachers, at least
in London where the theatres were most active. Above all, it gave people—including the unprivileged and non-literate—images and languages to think with."
Indeed, she claims, theaters helped "to form the 'mentalities' to which they will later
appeal, not only at court and among the political elites but more widely among
London citizen audiences" (239).

It is unfortunately not possible to determine accurately the impact of theater on
early modern English audiences, and, as Leeds Barroll has cogently demonstrated,
it is easy to overstate that influence.[8] One could even argue that the transmission
of literary culture was an unintended side effect of the dramatizing of that culture,
in that the comic effect of, for example, Bottom's references to "Phibbus' car" and
of the mechanicals' mutilation of the Pyramus and Thisbe story assume an audience already well read in Ovid. But Jonas Barish is surely correct in noting that
both "adversaries of the stage" and its defenders alike "never doubted its hold over

audiences" (118). And it is indisputable that theater did, in fact, absorb and enact (and thus inevitably transmit) large sections of that vast field of discourse contained in written and printed texts.

The reciprocal effect of early modern theater on literary culture is less easy to demonstrate. There are a few examples of plays making their way back into other written or printed forms: a few letters, some journal entries, some ballads; pamphlet recollections of old Hamlet's ghost, of tigers' hearts in women's hides, and of devils appearing on the stage at performances of *Doctor Faustus*.[9] Anthony Chute's poem "Beawtie Dishonoured, written under the title of Shore's Wife" includes the line "He calls his *Kate*, and she must come and kisse him," recalling a performance of *The Taming of the Shrew*. Similarly, Harington's *The Metamorphoses of Ajax* cites "the booke of taming a shrew, which hath made a number of us so perfect, that now everyone can rule a shrew in our country save he that hath her" (Shakespeare, *Taming*, ed. Oliver, 32, 34). And Sir Edward Coke in 1606 included in his charge to a Norwich grand Jury a passionate "patriotic encomium" heavily influenced by John of Gaunt's "sceptered isle" speech in *Richard II* (Schwarz).[10]

But Wilkins's novel based on *Pericles* may be an unusual case of theater strongly entering literary culture under a new radical of presentation. The play *Arden of Faversham*, for example, seems to be the culmination of chronicle and pamphlet tellings of the Arden story rather than the trigger for new versions (except for one late ballad that seems to reflect the play); and Leeds Barroll, while reporting that Sir Edward Coke seems to suggest, in some apparent confusion, that *Richard II* was a dramatization of Hayward's 1599 *Life of Henry IV*, finds no indication that Hayward's book was influenced by the language or incidents in the play (Orlin, *Private*; Barroll, "New").[11]

Though playtexts were, then, only occasionally transformed into novels, chronicles, pamphlets, or (more often) ballads, they themselves clearly entered literary culture as manuscripts and printed texts. Having done so, they were accorded an equivocal status there—this despite the fact that classical dramas were certainly considered "literary culture" in the early modern period. Think, for example, of the fifteenth- and sixteenth-century editions of Terence, each folio page presenting a bit of text surrounded by learned commentary, that commentary in turn becoming the primary source for such works of literary criticism as Thomas Lodge's 1579 *Defence of Poetry* (Baldwin, *Shakspere's*, 333). Even the grammar school texts of Terence carry learned critical commentary in their margins (Baldwin; C. R. Thompson). Yet Thomas Bodley famously forbade printed plays and other such "riffe raffes" in the library at Oxford University (even though he included printed plays in his own private collections), and Ben Jonson was mocked for calling his plays "Works."[12]

John Pitcher indirectly suggests that what may be at issue here is conflicting attitudes not only about the nature of theater but also about print. In the context of his discussion of Samuel Daniel's expressed sensitivity to print (which Daniel saw as fixing and widely disseminating poetry or drama that Daniel preferred to hold in a less public, less final form), Pitcher raises once again the old question of why Shakespeare apparently never undertook to have his plays printed. He quotes Dame Helen Gardner's suggestion that Shakespeare "simply did not envisage a time would ever come in which people would read plays as they read and pored over poems, histories, and sermons," and he notes in response that by the late 1590s people were already reading "Shakespeare's plays in the unauthorized quartos, and . . . there are signs that certain Jacobeans chose to read them as books rather than see them in productions" (57–58). Since Shakespeare would surely have known that people were already reading his plays, Pitcher surmises that Shakespeare made a choice not to print. Perhaps, Pitcher suggests, "for a Jacobean writer to commit a play to print— or to refuse to—may have been an artistic as well as a social decision." Perhaps, he adds tentatively, "Shakespeare resisted the opportunity to print his plays simply because their passage into books, and into silent reading, away from the stage, might be in some ways inimical to his own creative and financial interests." "Perhaps [Shakespeare] guessed," writes Pitcher, "that his plays in print would be *literature*, letters in type addressing themselves entirely . . . to the imaginative faculty. What effects an edition of past plays might have on future productions at the Globe, and what audiences might want, and even how his writing might have to change in response, could well have been matters of concern to Shakespeare" (58).

Pitcher here returns us to the central questions involved in the topic of early modern theater and literary culture—namely, questions about the play's various physical forms (performance, script, print), about audience(s), about relationships between book and stage. I earlier used the *Pericles* quarto first as an example of the complicated ways in which performance might relate to printed texts of a play and then as an example of the less tangible relationship of the play to the book as source of the play's dramatic fiction.

Shakespeare's *The Tempest* suggests more-complicated interconnections. Like *Pericles*, *The Tempest* flaunts its dependence on the book for its production of spectacle—but *The Tempest's* books are part of the play's dramatic fiction and the spectacles they make possible are Prospero's (as somehow distinct from the dramatist's) magic shows. Just how Prospero's books yield spectacle is left quite vague, as is appropriate for books of magic. But the play clearly suggests a connection between, on the one hand, the magician, the book, and the illusory spectacle and, on the other, the dramatist, the book, and stage illusion. Shakespeare reads Ovid, Montaigne, Greek romances, and Virgil, and creates *The Tempest*; within the play, Prospero reads "books [he prizes] above [his] dukedom" and creates a scene of a disappearing banquet and a prophesying Harpy (re-creating a scene from the *Argonautica* by way of the *Aeneid* [Mowat, *Tempest*]) and a masque (modeled on masques presented in the court of King James).

The play suggests that there is something magic about the way books are transformed into living spectacle through the dramatist's art and suggests as well that the more subtle relationships between book and play, writing and performance, are worth our pondering. The prefatory poem by J.M.S., "On Worthy Master Shakespeare and His Poems," printed in the Shakespeare Second Folio (1632), acknowledges the dramatist's seemingly magic power, contrasting "What story coldly tells, what Poets faine / At second hand, and picture without brain, Senseless and souleless shows" with Shakespeare's gift of "a Stage / (Ample and true with life) voice, action, age," a stage on which Shakespeare has "kings his subjects, by exchanging verse / Enlive their pale trunks, that the present age/ Joys in their joy, and trembles at their rage."

The subtle dynamic between the written word and the stage presentation was obviously of interest to Shakespeare. David Schalkwyk has written compellingly about the embodiment, in Shakespeare's *Love's Labor's Lost* and *Twelfth Night*, of situations of Petrarchan address and reception normally found in the silent script or print of sonneteers (including Shakespeare himself). He shows that

> the material embodiment of a character onstage not only makes a response [to the Petrarchan address] necessarily possible but also forces us to read or hear silences *as such* and to enquire about the conditions of their enforcement, rather than pass over them unremarked. (405)

As we move with Schalkwyk through these plays and their material embodying of sonnet address and response, we begin to see the plays as serious reflections on sonneteering, as ways of approaching the complicated relationship between writing and performing.

One of the sonnets that Schalkwyk quotes suggests that Shakespeare, as dramatist/poet/actor, had given serious thought to this very relationship. The octave of his Sonnet 23 describes a would-be-sonneteering lover in the guise of a tongue-tied stage actor. To quote four of the eight lines:

> Like an unperfect actor on the stage
> Who with his fear is put beside his part . . .
> So I for fear of trust forget to say
> The perfect ceremony of love's rite.

The sonnet's sestet sets the poet's book in opposition to this stage actor, opposing the written word to the spoken word:

> O, let my books be then the eloquence
> And dumb presagers of my speaking breast,
> Who plead for love and look for recompense
> More than that tongue that more hath more expressed.
> O, learn to read what silent love hath writ.
> To hear with eyes belongs to love's fine wit.

The notion of books as "dumb [i.e., mute] presagers" that the beloved is to hear with eyes has seemed so nonsensical to editors that, beginning in 1725, most have

changed "books" to "looks," so that the line reads "O, let my *looks* be then the eloquence." If we accept the language of the 1609 quarto text of the Sonnets, we have
in this poem a wonderfully Derridean document in which writing attempts to substitute for the speaking breast and pleading tongue but is mute, silent, reminding
us of Plato's belief about writing—that it is a "mute, stupid simulacrum," a "cadav-
erous rigidity" (the descriptive words are Derrida's) as compared to the "vigor, richness, agility and flexibility" of the freely spoken word (Derrida, *Dissemination*,
113–15). But the actor, as the sonnet reminds us, does not speak freely. His speech
is, at best, citation; and, in this sonnet, the actor fails even to cite, since he forgets
his lines. The sonnet keeps distinct the actor and the dumb eloquence of the
graphic impression, sending the book directly to the beloved to be read. In drama,
such separation is not allowed—until the playscript enters the world of literary culture. Derrida defines writing by saying, "Writing is read"; in performed drama,
however, writing is spoken.

Early modern theater and literary culture can be seen as a site of complex interchange, where writing and speaking intricately interconnect. The interplay
between that which was spoken and done onstage and the written documents from
which those words and gestures issued is, in part, lost to us; equally lost is the interplay between that which was performed and the written and printed playscripts that
serve as "records" of those performances.[13] Remaining to us are the playscripts
themselves. Whether "dumb presagers" of the eloquent "speaking breast" of the
long-dead "actor on the stage" or silent, graphic, imprecise records of long-dead
performances, the extant playscripts represent our primary link with early modern
theater. At the same time, they stand as intertextual records of the literary culture
from which they were largely woven. And as we read them "again and again," we
realize that they stand as well as an important part of that literary culture, whether
they come to us in scribal transcripts or in garbled quartos or in massive folio collections. The relationship between early modern theater and literary culture,
which seems initially intriguing and complicated, finally collapses into a semi-
identity as the extant playscript absorbs the world of writing in which it developed
and becomes in turn an integral part of that world.

NOTES

1. The spelling here has been modernized. I follow Sisson in attributing the play's authorship to Rastell.
2. This description is, of course, an oversimplification, but that scholars do tend to think of
   the transmigration of the play in generally linear and categorized ways is, I think, accurate. The implications of such thinking are far-reaching. The presumption, for example,
   that the printed book is what stands at the end of one line of transmission of the playtext
   gets caught up in conventional notions of the printed book: the notion, that is, that "the
   book" is always at the end of the process and that the text, because it is printed, is therefore fixed. (Elizabeth Eisenstein, in fact, uses the term "typographical fixity" to help

explain some of the many impacts of the print revolution.) Again, the presumption that the printed text and the play-in-performance trace back to a common ancestor gives rise to a belief that both book and performance are witnesses to a text outside them, a text that scholars then try to discover somehow lying behind the print.

3. I am grateful to Peter W. M. Blayney for helpful conversations about this matter.

4. This way of stating the case assumes the identity of the script for playing and that for printing.

5. In order to focus on the physical forms of "Pericles" as performance, playscript, quarto, and novel, I am ignoring the additional complication of the influence on some or all of these forms of Laurence Twine's novel, *The Patterne of Painefull Aduentures*, printed several times between 1576 and 1607. As another, parallel example of the intricate and fluid relationships among theater and literary culture, one could profitably trace the relationships among Twine's novel and the other forms of the Apollonius story. Hoeniger mentions, for example, that the reprinting of Twine's novel in 1607 "may have been the immediate cause for the play [i.e., *Pericles*], or the play may have been the immediate cause for it." He goes on to say: "As Twine's novel is an indirect translation of the story in the *Gesta Romanorum* [the story that John Gower retells in *Confessio Amantis*, Shakespeare's primary source], some passages in the play that appear to be derived from Twine may in fact come from a different source" (xiv n. 2).

6. Quotations from *Pericles* are from Hoeniger. The lines quoted here are 1.1.1–8.

7. Near the end of *King Johan*, a character named Verity "offers what amounts to a formal documentation of Bale's portrayal of John" by citing nine historians. As Barry Adams notes, "As a diligent student of British antiquities, Bale was certainly in a position to utilize his formidable knowledge of historical writings in support of his hero." As supporters of Bale's view of John, Adams adds, this "catalog of witnesses is at best highly misleading" (26–27). Adams points out that Bale actually drew most heavily not on the texts that the play cites but on Tyndale and on the English prose Brut first published by Caxton in 1480 (25–38). The play's citing of the "excellent writers" on whom it depends, though it directs us to the wrong writers, nevertheless makes clear that it wants us to recognize its base in earlier historians.

8. Barroll argues against the widely held belief that the performance of Shakespeare's *Richard II* on the night before the Essex rebellion was designed to influence the London citizenry. In making this argument he writes: "If one looks beyond the locus that has been used to demonstrate the subversive value of Shakespeare's play, one finds other loci [specifically, John Hayward's *Life of Henry IV*] that add new readings of history. One could argue, in fact, that the Elizabethan authorities perceived in connection with the Essex plot a threat much more serious than acted plays: i.e., the printed book" ("New History," 452).

9. For a representative sample of the letters, journal entries, ballads, and pamphlet allusions to current plays, see Evans, "Records." For reports about devils on the stage at performances of *Doctor Faustus*, see Chambers, *Elizabethan*, 3:424.

10. Schwarz notes that Coke, "in his capacity as prosecutor" in 1601 of those connected with the Essex rebellion, twice referred to *Richard II*, calling it "the story of Henry 4th being set forth in a play, and in that play, there being set forth the killing of the King upon a stage" and suggests that Coke might, at that time, have read the quarto printing of the play (56).

11. Lena Cowen Orlin lists the "known redactions" of the Arden story, noting, "In *Arden of Faversham* is . . . completed a four-decade process of purging the story of its extradomestic elements." About John Taylor's mid-seventeenth-century statement that the murder was "fresh in memory," Orlin comments, "Plays rather than pamphlets probably kept the memories 'fresh' for Taylor" (64, 64–65 n. 106, 69 n. 110). I am indebted to helpful private conversations with Drs. Orlin and Barroll.

12. Sir Thomas Bodley wrote twice to Thomas James, first Keeper of the Bodleian Library, about his insistence that plays not be included among the library's holdings. The first letter (Wheeler, number 220) expresses his wish that James

> had forborne to catalogue our London bookes, till I had bin priuie to your purpose. There are many idle bookes, & riffe raffes among them, which shall neuer com into the Librarie, & I feare me that litle, which yow haue done alreadie, will raise a scandal vpon it, when it shall be giuen out, by suche as would disgrace it, that I haue made vp a number, with Almanackes, plaies, & proclamacions: of which I will haue none, but suche as are singular.

His next letter (Wheeler, number 221), which seems to be in response to a demurrer by the Keeper, is even more stern:

> I can see no good reason to alter my opinion, for excluding suche bookes, as almanackes, plaies, & an infinit number, that are daily printed, of very vnworthy maters & handling. . . . Happely some plaies may be worthy the keeping: but hardly one in fortie. For it is not alike in Englishe plaies, & others of other nations: because they are most esteemed, for learning the languages & many of them compiled, by men of great fame, for wisedome & learning, which is seldom or neuer seene among vs. Were it so againe, that some litle profit might be reaped (which God knowes is very litle) out of some of our playbookes, the benefit thereof will nothing neere conteruaile the harme that the scandal will bring vnto the Librarie, when it shalbe giuen out, that we stuffe it full of baggage bookes. . . . [T]he more I thinke vpon it, the more it doth distast me, that suche kind of bookes, should be vouchesafed a rowme, in so noble a Librarie.

13. See Dillon for a skeptical view of any one-to-one relationship between an extant text and an early modern performance.

## CHAPTER 13

# Theater and Popular Culture

*Michael D. Bristol*

### The Social Theory of Early Modern Popular Culture

During the night just before the Battle of Agincourt, Shakespeare's King Henry V tours the English camp in order to assess the morale of his soldiers. Muffled in his cloak to disguise his identity, the king encounters Pistol, one of Falstaff's old drinking companions from the Boar's Head Tavern. Pistol, surprised by the appearance of an apparent intruder, challenges the stranger.

> PIST. *Qui vous là?*
> K. HEN. A friend.
> PIST. Discuss unto me, art thou officer,
> Or art thou base, common, and popular? (4.1.37–38)

Pistol's question has a genuine urgency, since the answer will determine the exact bearing and attitude he will be obliged to assume toward this unknown person. The most salient of all social distinctions in his society is precisely that between an officer class, composed of gentlemen, and the larger popular element, composed of all sorts of ordinary people, from impoverished rural laborers to the wealthiest urban merchants. When the king identifies himself as "a gentleman of a company," Pistol should understand exactly how he ought to comport himself. His boast that he is as "good a gentleman as the Emperor" is a daring bid for recognition as an equal among fellow soldiers but probably marks him in the eyes of the king as base, common, and popular.

The social structure of early modern England was based on a highly differentiated system of rank, degree, and privilege. A complex social hierarchy assigned a traditional order of precedence to be observed on public occasions, and it determined both the division of labor and the allocation of authority. This hierarchy was stable but by no means static. The actual social practice of the period could accommodate considerable social mobility, both upward and downward, prompted in part by unusually dynamic economic activity. Despite the complexity of the social structure, however, and despite the many local instances of individual social movement, the distinction between gentlefolk and the common people articulated by Pistol remained fundamental.

The numerically small elite of gentlefolk in early modern England was entitled to enjoy a range of social and economic privileges that included a customary right to participate directly in political rule. The much more numerous popular element consisted mainly of private persons whose political vocation was to obey local magistrates and officers of the Crown. The elite was composed of all persons of "gentle birth," from the humblest mere gentlemen to the great lords. Obviously, such a group, even though small, might be very diverse in its interests and its political outlook. All gentlemen, however, whatever their wealth and status, were accustomed to enjoying social deference from "the inferior sort."

This rather straightforward situation was complicated by important divisions within the popular element itself (Holderness; Harrison, 113–84). Although ordinary people shared the fate of exclusion from gentle status, they were not on that account constituted as a homogeneous mass of "the unprivileged" with well-defined common interests. It is imperative to recognize the existence of a large and important group known as the "middling sort," which would include wealthy yeoman farmers and successful merchants, as well as the masters within the various craft guilds or livery companies (Archer; Rappaport). These individuals and corporations were themselves highly sensitive to issues of precedence and privilege. They were also accustomed to a significant exercise of political self-government at the level of civic administration. Many officials of the Crown were also drawn from this social constituency. Nevertheless, I would argue that this "middling sort" was necessarily included among the popular element, which it helped to define and to constitute.

The popular element in early modern English society, then, was not a working class in the modern sense, nor was it entirely unprivileged or economically oppressed in all respects (Thompson, "Patrician," 382–405). It was, rather, the complex ensemble of guilds, corporations, and local communities that carried out the tasks of actual production for the society as a whole. Although it could not accurately be characterized as a dominant culture, the customary practices and forms of expression of the base, common, and popular element of early modern society nevertheless constituted a majority culture. Since almost all of this cultural experience was produced by and for a local community, however, its concrete and particular forms of expression would exhibit a necessarily parochial character.

The popular element of the early modern period did, nevertheless, share certain values and cultural practices. The immediate hands-on relationship with the activity of economic life that marked people as base, common, and popular also distinguished them from the hereditary elite, who retained a right to bear heraldic arms and to style themselves gentle. The strong identification of the popular element with material life and productive effort gave rise to a heightened sense of local authority and proprietary right (Hexter). The various corporations and other local associations were animated by the conviction that they were entitled to benefit from the wealth created by their labor. Although the popular element was nominally excluded from the privilege of rule, they nevertheless exerted continual pressure on the hereditary elites through the weight of sheer numbers and through innumerable local contestations of surveillance, expropriation, and the nature of property rights.

The possibility of a meaningful popular resistance to domination by hereditary elites was linked to the accumulated power of the guilds, livery companies, and municipal corporations that regulated the various trades within the early modern economy. Guilds were voluntary associations of persons practicing a particular trade, who possessed a Royal Charter or license to practice and to regulate that trade (Black). Many of the important livery companies were of very ancient standing. The guilds were also hierarchical. Members were obliged to serve a term as apprentices before they were recognized as freemen and licensed to practice a particular craft. Regulation of the company was closely held by the settled master craftsmen.

Despite this hierarchy, the moral culture of the guilds was distinctive in its affirmation of the social principle of *Genossenschaftsrecht*, the idea of an association of equals or corporate entity based on voluntary initiative and fraternal solidarity (Gierke, 36–61). The municipal guilds and livery companies were brotherhoods claiming primary affective loyalty among their members. Well-established guilds could assert corporate authority and independence by virtue of their "ancient" or "aboriginal" character, although this "conservative" stand would at times lead to serious legal conflict with other kinds of authority. The right of citizens, however, to take the initiative, to assemble, and to constitute themselves as a corporate entity during the early modern period was based on much earlier precedent and formal jurisprudence.

The popular element thus had a distinct and well-ordered social existence, separate from the nobility and gentry who ruled over them. At the same time, however, the common people did experience complex forms of social dissonance among themselves, in addition to the chronic friction with hereditary elites. There are more or less permanent structural oppositions between rural and urban interests and, in addition, newer structural conflicts brought about by the introduction of new techniques and new sources of wealth. These oppositions were superimposed on traditional patterns of alliance and rivalry between particular guilds or between different towns and settlements.

There were also important informal associations that figured prominently in implementing popular cultural practices, particularly the "youth groups" or confraternities composed of apprentices or of young unmarried males (Capp; Davis, "Reasons"). Among the diverse social functions of these associations were the regulation of weddings and of sexual conduct (especially through the charivaris), organization and implementation of festive misrule, local defense, and popular justice (E. P. Thompson, "Rough"). The solidarity of these groups was often expressed in socially aggressive behavior, and they were often denounced for disturbing the peace. Despite the pervasive discord that characterized much of early modern popular culture, however, the guilds and community associations had developed strategies and cooperative resources for maintaining social continuity and for modulating but not eliminating social conflict.

Contrary to what earlier historical scholarship has always maintained, notions of hierarchy, subordination, and a "great chain of being" were not the only recognized tenets of social rationality at the time. The traditional corporate associations of early modern society gave rise to a distinctive set of social and moral principles based on mutual aid and reciprocity. Hospitality and feasting were important public manifestations of these principles. In the context of traditional popular culture, the practice of hospitality must be distinguished from the idea of occasional and purely discretionary entertainment. Hospitality was mandated by the ethics of an economy of expenditure. Seasonal feasts provided a form of compensation for agricultural laborers and apprentices. In addition, the practice of hospitality required that a fraction of surplus production be reallocated to the poor, the disabled, and the dispossessed.

The feasts of traditional popular culture were not, however, simple expressions of charity or social generosity. There was also a ludic element within early modern popular culture, expressed in various forms of transgression, social inversion, and excess. It was evidently customary for communities to invite a Lord of Misrule to preside over the participatory foolishness and disorderly conduct associated with certain seasonal feasts. Popular festive misrule was a travesty of the established categories of the social order that aimed at the temporary overthrow of hierarchy, domination, and privilege. It was much more, however, than a merely transient disruption of established ideological forms. Misrule interpreted social reality from the standpoint of the popular element itself. It substituted laughter for deference, collective participation for detached observation, and in general promoted the interest of material life and culture over against any abstract ideal of social harmony.

In the context of early modern England, the traditional forms of misrule characteristic of popular culture gradually came to be seen as a threat both to the established social order and to the personal hopes for the salvation of individuals. The vigorous antitheatrical literature of the period linked stage plays with a range of popular festive customs, including wakes, maypoles, and Lords of Misrule (Burke; Marcus, *Politics*). These customs promoted unruly passions and impiety and fostered habits of social disobedience (Hjort, 160–96). In this view, popular culture could be understood as a radically vitiated religion, a fragmentary set of dead ritual forms without any capacity to provide political, ethical, or social orientation. Unlike the true religion, the typical forms of popular culture produced a dysfunctional *anomie* in the form of individual profligacy or riotous crowd behavior.

## Popular Culture: Particular Forms

The traditional critique of popular culture stresses the ephemeral and shortsighted character of its aims, its orientation toward immediate gratification, and the triviality of its modes of cognition (Lowenthal, 15–18). Theodor Adorno, on the other hand, has recognized in the transgression and *anomie* of traditional popular culture an important "seriousness," the expression of a "rebellious resistance inherent within it as long as social control was not yet total" (85).

Adorno's intuition has been much more fully developed in the work of Mikhail Bakhtin on the popular traditions of Carnival and the Carnivalesque. Bakhtin maintains that the ludic and transgressive elements of popular culture actually constitute a valid knowledge of the social world. It is, furthermore, a mode of knowledge with a considerable history.

> The system of popular festive images developed and went on living for thousands of years. This long development has its own scoria, its own dead deposits in manners, beliefs, prejudices. But in its basic line this system grew and was enriched; it acquired a new meaning, absorbed the hopes and thoughts of the people. . . . Thanks to this process, popular festive images became a powerful means of grasping reality; they served as a basis for an authentic and deep realism. (BAKHTIN, *Rabelais*, 211)

The long-term continuity of popular culture is, in fact, the basis for its cognitive apprehension of social reality and, as well, the source of its contemporaneous practical significance. Popular festive forms contain the sedimented understanding of social relations accumulated over centuries. For Bakhtin, the tradition of Carnival finds its own literary and philosophical basis in the work of writers such as Rabelais, Shakespeare, Thomas Nashe, and Montaigne.

Carnival was observed throughout Europe during the early modern period, reaching its climax on Shrove Tuesday or Mardi Gras, just before the beginning of Lent. Traditionally this was a time of hedonistic excess and transgression. Carnival permitted and actually encouraged the unlimited consumption of special foods, drunkenness, and a high degree of sexual license, and it often led to street violence and civil commotion (Bakhtin, 196 ff.; Gaignebet and Florentin, *Le Carnaval*; Laroque, 96–103). The custom of masking and disguise made it easier for the participants to get away with violations of social order, and indeed it was typical of Carnival that social order was turned upside down.

Misrule, inversion, and travesty were typical of the Carnivalesque. A Carnival masquerade embodied an alternative set of rules for interpreting social reality. In these participatory celebrations, traditional religious and political symbols were combined with humble objects from the kitchen and the workshop, as well as with images of bodily functions, especially those relating to food and eating. In Breughel's painting *The Battle of Carnival and Lent*, the personification of Carnival rides on a wine barrel instead of a horse, and the combatants brandish cooking utensils instead of weapons. Various figures in Carnival's entourage wear articles of food or kitchenware on their heads—a kettle, a hat made of waffles—and Carnival himself is crowned with a meat pie that someone has bitten into (Gaignebet and Florentin, "Le Combat"). The comprehensive rethinking of the social world in terms of common everyday material and physical experience is central to the practice of "uncrowning"—the fundamental transformation downward of popular festive imagery. Here the kettle or meat pie takes the place of the crown or helmet as the "topmost" principle.

Although Carnival specifically refers only to festivities that immediately precede Lent, the typical Carnival experience of excess and social derangement was not limited to a single annual blowout. In fact, in early modern England many regularly occurring feasts shared the typical Carnivalesque features of material abundance, license, and social effervescence. In a further extension of the term, Carnival may also take in a class of social occasions held together by broad family resemblance—fairs, theatrical performances, public executions, and even spontaneous "social dramas."

Carnival in this broader sense is characterized by its negativity and in-between-ness. It is the liminal occasion par excellence, something that happens betwixt-and-between the regularly scheduled events of ordinary life. The combined sense of ambiguity and exteriority points to a further meaning for Carnival, not as a specific feast, a general type of celebration, or even a class of social occasions, but rather as a mode-of-being-in-the-world or mode-of-being-together-with-others. This is what Mikhail Bakhtin refers to when he describes Carnival as a second life of the people, with its own liturgy and its own system for the production and distribution of the good things of this life (255 ff.).

Shakespeare's Falstaff is undoubtedly the most vivid dramatic embodiment of Carnival. And in fact the ceremonial Battle of Carnival and Lent is an important structural pattern in the two parts of Shakespeare's *Henry IV*. Falstaff's corpulence, his excessive drinking and whoring, and his endless transgressions are all typical of the Carnivalesque spirit. His companion, Prince Hal, is a Lenten "stockfish" who regularly chastises Falstaff and encourages him to adopt more reverent, penitential attitudes.

But this is only one of many examples of a pervasive Carnivalization of dramatic form in early English drama. In Dekker's *The Shoemaker's Holiday*, festive misrule serves both to affirm the collective ethos of guild artisans and to regulate conflict among otherwise antagonistic social ranks. The mischief and clowning typical of Carnival are also predominant elements in serious religious drama, such as Marlowe's *Doctor Faustus*. Carnival is even manifested in tragedies, such as *Hamlet*, not only in the farcical possibilities of Hamlet's antic disposition, but even more fundamentally in the grim reenactment of the Battle of Carnival and Lent performed by Claudius and Hamlet respectively.

In Bakhtin's account, Carnival is very much more than just a particularly boisterous and extended holiday. For Bakhtin, Carnival expresses a fundamental truth about the world; its down-to-earth vocabularies, its affirmation of the body, its grotesque exaggeration and aggressive annihilation of all reified modes of legitimation in fact interpret the world in a more comprehensive, universal, and practical way than the official worldviews and serious philosophies of elite culture. Furthermore, the knowledge of the social world sedimented in Carnivalesque symbolic and participatory practice is available to the people as a resource in their defense of the everyday life-world against a colonizing political apparatus. Carnival may inform actual strategic deliberations aimed at correcting specific injustices or even structural alteration of the ensemble of social relations. Carnival both interprets the world and acts upon it, even when the participants cannot fully articulate what they are doing.

In addition to the traditions of hospitality and of Carnivalesque festivity, popular culture has a number of other equally important practices for the public expression of its characteristic values. Annabel Patterson has argued that the popular culture of early modern England was much more than merely festive or recreational activity. There was an important range of public ceremonial practices that articulated the traditions of communal life in a direct and politically self-conscious manner.

Among the more significant of these popular customs was the maintenance in various locations and at public expense of the city Waits, small groups of musicians who normally performed on wind instruments for the entertainment of city officials and for important ceremonial occasions. They often participated in civic processions, which were occasions for the assertion of civic dignity and pride. The mayor and other city officials, including members of the council, would parade in the city streets in full dress regalia to attend church services or government meetings. Processions would also be held on certain feast days, when the various guilds would participate, wearing their own characteristic liveries.

The Waits were particularly important for the observance of such seasonal events as the Christmas and Midsummer watches. These watches, or citizen musters, were in part historical commemorations of earlier violent conflicts; the watch expressed the city's capacity to maintain and foster social peace within its walls, as well as to repel hostile intruders (Connerton, 41–71). In Chester, for example,

the citizens retain an old Order, & Custome, which is this, allwayes on Christmas euen the Watch begin, & the Mayor, Sherrifs, Aldermen, & forties of the Common Counsell, goe about the Cittie, in triumph, with Torches, & ffire-workes. The recorder making a Speech of the Antiquity of her, founded by Gyants: On Misummer euen, the Giants, & som wild Beasts (that are constantlie kep for that purpose) are carr'd about the Towne. (CLOPPER, *Records: Chester*, 415)

Although the Waits enjoyed certain privileges and immunities within the city, the institution of the Waits was by no means strictly ceremonial. To the contrary, when they were not performing on behalf of the city administration, the Waits were frequently licensed to play for hire at the various guildhalls and in other venues. The Waits thus had an important entrepreneurial character as commercial suppliers of cultural goods and services, in addition to their official role in commemorative ceremonies.

The annual watches were also important as the occasion for the appearance of the giants. These giants were not fabulous creations of the literary imagination but rather homely and familiar, though oversized, artifacts maintained by local guilds to serve in the Midsummer shows. The obvious difficulty in talking about these giants is that, though large, they were not very durable and, as with so many other aspects of the popular culture of the early modern period, there is not an abundance of documentary material available for scholarly investigation. There are actually quite a few records of annual payments for "keeping Gyants," however, along with other items—coats for the giant, repairs, painting, and so on. The careful warehousing and maintenance of the giants suggests that within popular culture they were not the embodiment of social monstrosity or incivility, nor were they archaic memories of inimical previous inhabitants. The giants at Chester were honored as the founders of the city. These giants—probably constructed of wicker or other lightweight material—were contemporaneous favorites, crowd-pleasers, in the spectacles of popular culture. Taking good care of the town giant was in fact part of the overall practice of maintaining orderly collective life.

In the town records of Newcastle-upon-Tyne there are numerous entries for "the keeping Hogmagog" (Anderson, 26 et passim). A certain Thomas Pearson received an annual fee of six shillings, eight pence for this service, which passed, in 1568 to Robert Mould. At Newcastle these entries appear as one item in year-end accounts of expenses for the Midsummer show, expenses that also reflect the cost of maintaining the town fools. Hogmagog was probably the property of the common guild of the city of Newcastle; Pearson and Mould provided storage facilities during the year so that he was protected from weather and from possible vandalism.

The Newcastle records do not give any indication as to Hogmagog's size, but the cost of the materials needed to provide him with coats suggest that he must have been pretty big. Richard Withington, in his early study of English pageantry, documents records of giants upwards of fifteen feet tall. Storage and the provision of an appropriate wardrobe for such a figure would have been a complex and expensive responsibility for the keepers of the giant (Withington, 1:60 et passim). The expenses for the maintenance of the giant were met, at least in part, by an annual municipal subsidy, though the giants did not always belong to the common guild of a town. They were the property of individual guilds in some situations, and their annual appearance in civic pageants represented the prestige and authority of the guild that owned them.

In order to grasp the full implications of this peculiar institution, it may be useful to consider briefly the construction of the early modern pageant giant as a technical achievement. The initial problem in conceiving any piece of sculpture is getting it to stand up. When that sculpture is required to move through the bumpy, roughly paved streets of an early modern city, the standing-up problem is obviously compounded. The giant has to be both very light, so that it can be easily moved, and very stable, so that it doesn't topple over. In addition, this giant has to be decently clothed; in other words, oversize garments have to be fitted to the gigantic frame or armature without compromising the structural integrity of the engineering.

The anonymous craftsmen who built and maintained these artifacts obviously had whatever knowledge was necessary to accomplish this task. I would observe also that this was surplus technical knowledge, a level of skill over and above what was required, even for a master craftsman in a particular field. In the records for the city of Chester, there is an interesting hint about the division of labor required for the construction of a giant. The Chester giants were rebuilt, probably in about 1602, under the general supervision of John Wright and Nicholas Hallwood, of the painters guild. Their estimate of the work to be done is as follows: "We compute great hoopes dale bords Couper worke nayles size cloth bastbord paper for body sleves and skirts to be Cullered Tinsilld Arsedine" (Clopper, *Records: Chester*, 408).

It appears that the various aspects of construction were subcontracted to individual craft guilds and that final assembly was undertaken by the general contractors, Wright and Hallwood. The cost of a giant at the beginning of the seventeenth century was five pounds. It cost an additional ten shillings to hire the four men who carried the giant through the streets. Giants were traditional, even archaic figures, but the task of constructing a giant required a highly developed level of technical skill, as well as sophisticated administrative ability.

The ethical and political significance of the giants for popular culture is more difficult to summarize, but it is clearly connected with the social forms typical of the guild as an association of equals or as a corporate entity based on voluntary initiative and brotherhood. In one sense they must have resembled the corporate images of modern industrial companies—the Jolly Green Giant comes to mind here—except that the medieval and early modern guilds were very differently organized than are today's business corporations. Bakhtin's contention that the giant represented a collective entity is, roughly speaking, correct, except that the giants we are talking about represented not the "people as a whole" but rather a specific social agency with both economic and, we might say, moral modes of functioning. Like the Waits, however, the giants played an important role in representing the collective identity of a particular town or city, as well as in the annual commemoration of its history.

The city of Coventry had its own annual commemoration in the form of a dramatic entertainment known only as the Hock Tuesday play. The event was observed on the first Tuesday following Easter, a traditional festival of gender inversion. Evidently the play celebrated an important victory over the Danes, in which women played a significant role, and performances were apparently held in connection with visits by Queen Elizabeth in 1568 and again in 1575.

> Simon Cotton butcher maior 1574 & ended in 1575. . . . In his year the Queen came to Killingworth castle againe & recreated herself there xij or 13 daies. Att which time Coventry men went to make her merry there with there play of hockes Twesday & for there paines had a reward & venison also to make yem merry. (INGRAM, *Records: Coventry*, 271)

The impresario and leading performer was a certain Captain Cox, a mason who was evidently a gifted storyteller, widely acquainted with popular romances, ballads, and even literary narrative. The performance itself featured a mock battle between the Danes and the English. Though the Danes at first had the better of the conflict, in the end they were beaten down in triumph by the English women. The performers were then led into the great court, and the pastime continued with feasting, dancing, and some degree of unruliness (Ingram, *Records: Coventry*, 275).

Coventry was perhaps even better known for its annual cycle of religious drama, performed each year on Corpus Christi Day. The cycle at Coventry attracted audiences from all over England, although the cycles at York, Chester, and other urban centers were also very important. Livery companies assumed the financial burden for these performances; in addition, their members would participate both in preparing the mise-en-scène and in performing the various roles.

For complex reasons, these cycles were eventually discontinued; the Coventry plays were last performed in 1579. There was increasing pressure from church authorities to limit the role of the guilds in the organization of religious experience, especially since the cycle plays combined a form of religious devotion with the unruly and unpredictable aspects of popular festivity. In addition, the plays were becoming increasingly costly for the livery companies. Despite the disappearance of the cycle dramas, however, many of their dramaturgical and staging practices were preserved in the great professional theaters of late sixteenth- and early seventeenth-century London.

## Popular Culture and Theater: The Critical Tradition

The emergence of a professional theater as an independent, freestanding economic and social institution in early modern England was the result of a complex fusion of popular and aristocratic cultural traditions (Cohen; Weimann). Organized theatrical activity and amateur performances of various kinds were common among virtually all social groups and communities in early modern England. Many of the typical practices of popular festivity and of organized civic pageantry were carried over into the forms of theatrical practice. The popularity of the early English drama has been acknowledged from the time of the earliest professional theaters, although, as

I have already indicated, this was not always viewed as a positive or socially desirable state of affairs. The mixed decorum of the early theater, its "mingle-mangle" of disparate genres and literary conventions with rude and abusive clowning, as well as its resort to the idiomatic language of the popular element, was frequently criticized as both aesthetically deplorable and socially dangerous.

Beginning in the latter part of the eighteenth century, however, a substantially revised assessment of early modern popular culture began to be articulated. This reinterpretation was made possible by the antiquarian research of Bishop Thomas Percy, whose *Reliques of Ancient English Poetry* assembled the materials for the comprehensive study of early English drama. The broad reappraisal of popular culture was motivated in part by an interest in the dramatic writings of Shakespeare. Even the otherwise strongly conservative, neoclassically oriented Dr. Johnson recognized the importance of understanding an earlier popular culture for his 1765 edition:

> [Shakespeare] has more allusions than other poets to the traditions and superstition of the vulgar; which must therefore be traced before he can be understood. . . . If Shakespeare has difficulties above other writers, it is to be imputed to the nature of his work, which required the use of the common colloquial language, and consequently admitted many phrases allusive, elliptical, and proverbial, such as we speak and hear every hour without observing them. (*Johnson on Shakespeare*, 7:53).

For Johnson, the heterogeneity of Shakespeare's language, its wide-ranging familiarity with obsolete, common, and colloquial idiom, as well as with foreign languages, is something of an "embarrassment for the reader." Nevertheless, Johnson was astute enough to recognize that Shakespeare's use of colloquial speech was integral to his achievement as a writer of lasting value. As the compiler of the English dictionary, Johnson appreciated with perhaps unusual sensitivity that a language was an immense, shared resource, equally important for the unlearned and the learned, for the "common workmen" as well as the "critick." Shakespeare's works are, not incidentally for Johnson, a rich and varied printed archive of popular usage that continues to shape the language of everyday social interaction.

An even more vigorous defense of Shakespeare's "popularity" is articulated in Elizabeth Montagu's comparison of Shakespeare with neoclassical models. Her project is prompted in part by the attacks of Voltaire on Shakespeare as a rude, vulgar, and barbarous writer, ignorant of the most fundamental rules and standards for dramatic composition. For Montagu, however, the theater is a form of public entertainment that must be accessible to the broadest possible constituency. The "vulgarity" of theater, its ability to communicate effectively with the people, makes it particularly valuable in the formation of public opinion. On this view, Shakespeare's sympathy with traditional forms of popular culture and popular belief is central to his achievement as a dramatic poet:

> While there is any national superstition which credulity has consecrated, any hal-
> lowed tradition long revered by vulgar faith; to that sanctuary, that asylum, may the
> poet resort. . . . Our poet never carries his præternatural beings beyond the limits of
> the popular tradition. (MONTAGU, 176)

Voltaire had attacked Shakespeare as a drunken lout and argued that enthusiasm for this author's work was evidence of both a lamentable absence of cultural
standards among the English and their equally lamentable lack of aspiration
toward an enlightened social order (Voltaire, 4:502). Mrs. Montagu defended
Shakespeare as a great artist of the vernacular, capable of the fullest possible expression of the popular tradition.

Samuel Johnson and Elizabeth Montagu recognized the importance of popular culture in the works of Shakespeare very much against their better judgment.
Virtually everything distinctive in the Shakespearean oeuvre runs against the grain
of their critical principles and also against some of their deepest ethical and social
convictions.

A much more affirmative sense of the importance of popular culture for the
early English theater emerges gradually against the background of the larger and
more turbulent political struggles for democracy during the nineteenth century. In
1821, the French statesman and writer François Guizot analyzed the popularity of
the early modern theater in a wide political context:

> A theatrical performance is a popular festival; that it should be so is required by the
> very nature of dramatic poetry. Its power rests upon the effects of sympathy—of that
> mysterious force which causes laughter to beget laughter; which bids tears to flow
> at the sight of tears, and which, in spite of the diversity of dispositions, conditions,
> and characters, produces the same impression on all upon whom it simultaneously
> acts. . . . Dramatic poetry, therefore, could originate only among the people. . . . In
> order to produce its most magical effects, and to preserve, during its growth, its lib-
> erty as well as its wealth, it must not separate from the people, to whom its earliest
> efforts were addressed. (6)

Guizot's father had been executed in the Terror during the French Revolution,
and the son eventually became prime minister of France during the reign of Louis
Philippe, the Citizen King. When this regime collapsed, Guizot retired to England
and devoted himself to the study of history. His work on Shakespeare and popular
culture was part of his larger and more ambitious research agenda, which was to
understand the important social and cultural institutions that permitted the initial
growth and emergence of stable democratic institutions in early modern England.

The study of early modern popular culture has continued to be important for
the more specialized, professional scholarship of the twentieth century. E. K.
Chambers's comprehensive reference work, *The Elizabethan Stage*, gives considerable attention to various aspects of folk drama and other forms of popular culture.
Chambers is interested in this material mainly as an archival source that provided

raw material for the artistic achievements of later dramatists. In this view the popular tradition is described as an early or "naive" stage of the evolution toward the greater complexity of dramatic art achieved by the canonical writers of the Elizabethan and Jacobean stage.

Glynne Wickham, in his *Early English Stages*, has a clearer sense of the power and richness of early modern popular culture itself. That culture was collective, improvisatory, and oriented to the lived present:

> The idea of life in succession [is] opposed to disturbance and death through the lack of it. . . . No matter how cunning the machinery employed to operate these devices, or how sophisticated the allegorizing of the Bible, of Christian ethics, or of legendary modern history into dramatic *tableaux vivants*, all these ceremonies serve primarily to ornament a folk-ritual that at heart is concerned with survival, and thus with tomorrow rather than today. (3:53)

Wickham here draws attention to a substantive communal life that produces a popular tradition on its own behalf.

François Laroque, in his *Shakespeare's Festive World*, abundantly confirms the intuitions of Glynne Wickham. Laroque's exhaustive work on the calendar and on the schedule of seasonal feasts builds up a very complete picture of the traditional ceremonial and commemorative background for early English drama. What emerges from his study is an understanding of early modern popular culture as a knowledgeable community with its own social horizons, able to articulate both its sense of continuity and a comprehensive critique of the duly authorized social structure.

The most comprehensive synthesis of the relation between popular culture and the theater in the early modern period is the magisterial study by Robert Weimann, *Shakespeare and the Popular Tradition in the Theater*. Through an exhaustive review of an enormous volume of earlier scholarship, Weimann has demonstrated conclusively how much is known about popular culture in the early modern period and how energetically that culture contributed to the growth of learning, of art, and of political and social institutions. His analysis of the earlier traditions of folk drama and the popular religious cycles explains the importance of a range of formal devices, including fools, clowns, and devils, for the professional theaters. The discussion emphasizes the complex social unity achieved in the various forms of popularly based dramaturgy:

> Its audience was made up of every rank and class in society. . . . It was a multiple unity based on contradictions and as such allowed the dramatist a flexible frame of reference that was more complex and more vital to the experience of living and feeling within the social organism than the achievement of any other theater before or since. (WEIMANN, 174)

This complex unity was actualized in and through the organization of theatrical space. Weimann discusses the participatory character of the religious cycles and shows how this important social aspect of performance is reproduced within the public theaters. He identifies a special zone of immediate contact, the *platea*, that mediates between the privileged space of narrative representation or locus and the everyday world from which the audience is watching. This space is frequently occupied by clowns or by characters performing soliloquies. In this liminal region, the "multiple unity based on contradictions" is actualized through spontaneous and improvisatory dialogue between performers and their audience.

### Popular Culture and London Commercial Theater

It would be profoundly misleading to represent the popular culture of the early modern period exclusively in political terms, either as an idyllic community or as chronic and intractable struggle, conflict, and resistance. Nor can popular culture be adequately described exclusively in purely "folkloric" terms. A significant entrepreneurial and competitive dimension of the popular culture was apparent in the growing market for cultural goods, both in the rural fairs and in the urban center. This section will examine the relationship of these practices to the formation of a prototypical culture industry in the interstices of the urban economy of early modern London. Despite the well-known antitheatricalism articulated by certain religious authorities, the social and economic conditions of early modern London were actually favorable to the appearance of a commercially profitable theater.

By the time the first professional theaters were established in London, there was already a very lively market for a diverse range of cultural products and services. This market was able to provide many convenient alternatives to the more absorbing participatory forms of cultural experience associated with the traditional life-world of the livery companies. The growth of a consuming public for these products and services constituted a significant challenge to kinship affiliations and to the traditional bonds of great households, municipal guilds, and rural communes as the basis for social incorporation. Certainly the appearance of the cultural consumer marked off a new and specialized sense of "culture" as a sphere of activity distinguishable from the practical, moral, and religious imperatives of communal life.

The earliest permanently housed commercial theaters were established in London while Shakespeare was still a boy in Stratford. Considerable symbolic importance has been assigned to the simultaneous construction of no fewer than three new playhouses in 1576, but, as William Ingram's research makes clear, the events of that year were possible only on the basis of complex antecedent developments (INGRAM, *Business*, 119–50).

At least three distinct stages are evident in the early formation of show business. The first stage corresponded to the emergence of a number of more or less permanent repertory companies that provided a decent livelihood for their members by performing in rented spaces. The moderate success of these repertory companies evidently suggested the idea of capital investment in permanent infrastructure for a nascent entertainment business. In this crucial second stage, purpose-built playhouses were constructed to be leased on various terms to established companies. The investors and owners of such specialized commercial property would naturally proceed on the assumption that there was already a viable market for dramatic performances. The third stage in the development of this prototypical show business was what economists call "vertical integration," as the members of the repertory companies themselves invested in theater buildings and eventually even formed partnerships with booksellers for the distribution and sale of printed editions of selected plays.

Given the combination of surveillance by state power, hostility from the civic authorities in London, and religious antitheatricalism, the early playhouse projects would seem to have been ill-advised, if not downright suicidal. It is not clear why such apparently harebrained schemes would ever have been attempted, let alone how they could have survived and prospered. Certainly the well-documented social and cultural resistance to the theaters has raised the possibility that these ventures must have been widely interpreted as fundamentally subversive of the stability of the social order.

It is difficult to reconstruct from the very scanty evidence that has survived exactly what might have prompted such early entrepreneurs as James Burbage or John Brayne to invest in the construction of a building for the risky and possibly illicit purpose of staging plays. It seems highly probable, however, that their desire for a lucrative return on their investments was at least as important as any artistic aspirations they may have had or any political agendas they may have intended to pursue.

The evolution of a varied trade in cultural goods, which includes a specific demand for performance services, was not an abrupt emergence. The elaborate and possibly far-fetched scheme of earning a steady livelihood by charging admission to dramatic performances makes sense only within a large and well-developed money economy. James Burbage, John Brayne, and other speculators in the early days of show business had to assume that their potential customers would understand the basic idea behind what they proposed to offer. Even more basic than any of the purposes of playing in this context, of course, was the elementary notion of purchasing a commodity: "The citie of London standeth chiefly upon the traffique and intercourse of merchants and the use of buying and selling of their sundrie commodities" (*Breefe*, 21).

The circulation of cultural commodities by balladmongers, itinerant players, and mountebanks was, of course, already a well-established practice in the many towns and rural fairs all over England (Würzbach). These early and direct modalities of commodity exchange in cultural goods developed into the more complex and diversified forms of production and distribution typical of a rudimentary culture industry within the highly favorable social and economic environment of London.

Several factors account for the hospitality of London to an emerging trade in cultural commodities, specifically, for dramatic entertainments performed by full-time professional actors. London's familiarity with "the use of buying and selling of . . . sundrie commodities" has already been noted. But London also had a distinctive political culture, in which ideas of economic self-determination and the pursuit of economic advantage were well understood and carefully protected. The institutions of city government and of the livery companies that regulated trade were based on long-standing traditional privileges and prescriptive rights. By the end of the sixteenth century, these customary entitlements had been articulated as a strong claim for local self-government. In many ways the civic institutions of London at this time anticipated some of the typical features of the democratic, liberal, political culture that would emerge more fully during the eighteenth century:

> The manner of their government, whereat strangers do no lesse envie than admire seeing so populous a citie, conteyning by true estimation more then 500 thousandes of all sortes of inhabitants managed not by cruel viceroys, as is Naples or Millaine ... but by a man of trade or a meere marchant, who notwithstanding, during the time of his magistracie, carrieth himselfe with that honourable magnificence in his port, and ensignes of estates, that the Consuls, Tribuns or pretors of Rome ... never bare the like representation of dignitie. (*Breefe*, 15)

The virtual sovereignty of men of trade led to a situation in which certain limited rights of self-determination were not only recognized but strongly defended, mainly through litigation and precedent, but also through statutory law. In this environment there was a strong consensus that persons had a right to enjoy the benefits of property accumulated through their own labor. Brayne, Burbage, and the other early theatrical speculators were all themselves men of trade. Whatever objections might be raised to the idea of "harlotry players" on moral grounds, their right to dispose of their own capital assets would nevertheless be widely recognized.

At the end of the sixteenth century, London was the center of England's national economy and its primary link with the larger world economy. Its increasing importance as a growing center of that world economy was used to justify its claims for local autonomy in the form of exemptions from English common law and royal decree. The basis for these exemptions was that London institutions constituted a reservoir of practical and worldly knowledge that enabled its citizens to manage their own affairs for the larger benefit of the nation as a whole:

> Persons of needfull employment in the estate, have alwaies beene favoured in all their honest customes or prescriptions, and especially the Citizens of London, and the rather for the great presumption and opinion conceived of their experience, who being trayned by harde education, in great use of service and affaires and also by their travaile and traffique beyond the seas, by continuall negotiation with other Nations must needes (by all reasonable likelihoode) procure unto themselves great iudgement and sufficiency, to manage a political regiment in their citie, according unto that verse of the Poet Homer in the beginning of his treatise of wise Ulisses his adventures.

All travailers do gladly report great praise of Ulisses
For he knewe manie mens maners, and sawe manie cities. (*Breefe*, 13–14)

This sense that London is a cosmopolitan center would have been very auspicious for the prospects of cultural entrepreneurs like James Burbage. Despite the open hostility of the city authorities, the early theatrical speculators could count on a potentially large clientele already familiar with complex cultural negotiations in their everyday life. And of course the theater could provide a vivid, if only vicarious, experience of other cultures to a consuming public without the inconvenience and expense of actual travel. Individual cultural consumers might conceivably find particular plays distasteful on ideological grounds, but the larger principles of theatrical representation would pose no immediate challenge to their sense of social order. The citizens, apprentices, and foreign visitors in London during the early modern period were, of course, familiar with a public culture of spectacle and pageantry within a variety of social contexts. Dramatic performances were important in the social life of guilds, in universities, in aristocratic households, and in the popular festive traditions of small communities. These performances were intended as significant expressions of community solidarity and of the values of corporate life, and participation in this form of spectacle provided for a greatly enhanced experience of conviviality. The larger processions staged by the Crown, the lord mayor, and the great livery companies, on the other hand, were more frankly expressions of power and authority (Anglo, *Spectacle*; Orgel, *Illusion*; Tennenhouse). What was novel and perhaps threatening or disruptive about the commercial theaters could not have been the simple fact of theatricality itself. What the theaters were able to accomplish was the transformation of otherwise familiar performance practices into merchandise. To grasp the implications of this development, it is important to examine the notion of a "commodity" more closely.

A commodity is, of course, an article of commerce, usually exchanged with a view to purely economic advantage within the context of a money economy. Commodity exchange is typically an impersonal transaction among persons who are strangers to each other. Anthropological literature frequently distinguishes between commodity exchange and gift exchange in terms of their bearing on the spiritual and moral relations of the agents who participate in these two radically different economies (Cheal). In sixteenth-century usage, however, the term *commodity* had additional related usages of both expediency and convenience. The distinctive appeal of a commodity is this sense of a purely instrumental means for obtaining desired goods or amenities outside the complex networks of reciprocal obligation that prevail in a traditional community. Dramatic performance in the early modern commercial playhouse offered the commodities of spectacle, narrative, and conviviality without the time-consuming burdens of skilled engagement or social commitment that would be required to obtain these same goods in a social world organized by the ethos of gift exchange.

Theaters like the Globe or the Curtain were prototypical and paradigmatic examples of commodity exchange as this came to operate in the sphere of cultural goods and services. The public who paid for admission to these performances were enabled to enjoy these cultural goods at their pleasure as self-reliant consumers, without the time-consuming burdens of preparation and participation. Dramatic presentation in the commercial playhouses was no longer, strictly speaking, tied to the traditional schedules of the liturgical calendar or dependent upon the ceremonial life of guilds and on the patronage of great households, although the major repertory companies retained important links with powerful aristocratic benefactors. Nevertheless, commodity really was the bias of the show business world in the sense that theatrical incomes were independent of the social status of the paying customers.

The playhouses made performance available through direct purchase to a new social constituency of cultural consumers. Affiliation and identification with a corporate body gave way to the "exchange of equivalents" as the basic qualification for participation in a cultural event, and this conferred at least a temporary social equality on all consumers of the same product. The consumer had the added benefit here of enjoying a higher standard of performance, though this "higher" standard was accomplished by disengagement and alienation from direct participation in the creative process. Consumers were also, in a sense, undifferentiated; their only qualification was that they possess the price of admission. In a sense, then, the abstract, socially undifferentiated consumer of cultural services was the most important "invention" of the early modern theater.

The perceived danger of this social undifferentiation is prominent in many antitheatrical pamphlets. Fears connected with theatrical representation were connected to larger anxieties about independent sources of secular authority. Certainly with the acceleration of trade in cultural goods and services, authority became more discretionary or optional—a matter of money rather than of close embedding in the everyday practices and techniques of a traditional community with its patterns of solidarity, deference, and personal obligation.

The success of the theater as a freestanding cultural institution during the early modern period has traditionally been described in terms of the development of a fully achieved, durable public art form from folkloric practices, literary experiments, and a wide range of amateur forms of theatricality (Bevington, *"Mankind"*; Bradbrook, *Rise*; Weimann). But an important historical irony accompanies these developments. A less affirmative account might describe these events as the gradual alienation of traditional practices of narrative representation and performance from the diverse patterns of communal life in which they previously had been embedded. Participatory and communal forms of popular culture were already in decline at the time of the founding of the first professional theaters. The widespread commercial availability of cultural goods and services derived from the resources of popular culture almost certainly helped to accelerate the shift from direct skilled engagement in the production of cultural experience to the more passive habits of cultural consumption.

# PART III

*Early English Drama and*

*Conditions of Performance and Publication*

# CHAPTER 14

# Touring

*Peter H. Greenfield*

POPULAR LEGEND and theater history alike have portrayed touring the provinces as the players' last resort, a desperate measure taken only in times of plague in London or declining company fortunes. Taking to the road meant being at the mercy of uncertain weather and uncertain welcomes at the towns and aristocratic households where the company hoped to perform. Nor did previous success in the capital guarantee survival in the provinces, as Pembroke's Men discovered in 1593: forced to leave London by the major plague of that year, they found that their traveling expenses exceeded their gains; they returned to London, sold their wardrobe to cover their debts, and ceased to function as a company (Henslowe, *Diary*, ed. Foakes and Rickert [unless otherwise noted], 280). Itinerant players might escape the threat to life and property posed by highwaymen only to lose their liberty to local officials who considered the players themselves little better than roving vagabonds. Little wonder, then, that Hamlet asks of the players who visit Elsinore, "How chances it they travel? Their residence [in the city], both in reputation and profit, was better both ways" (*Hamlet* 2.2.328–29).

The dangers and hardships of touring were quite real, yet this traditional picture is a distorted one, born of antiprovincial bias and fed by the entertainment value of the more "dramatic" records of provincial performing, such as the fate of Pembroke's Men or the story of the "affray" at Norwich in 1583, when a scuffle at the gate of a performance by the Queen's Men ended with players accused of killing a man (Galloway, 70–76). Research in the provincial records, under the aegis of the Records of Early English Drama project, has yielded a great deal of new evidence of provincial performing and has prompted us to reexamine the place of touring in the life of the professional companies—and, indeed, of early English theater in general. Disputes with local authorities and payments "not to play" (or "to rid the town of them") have loomed large in theater histories, but such records make up less than 5 percent of the more than three thousand records concerning performance by touring companies during Shakespeare's lifetime. The remaining 95 percent of the records indicate that entertainers were allowed to play, were rewarded, or were otherwise successful (Somerset, "'How chances it they travel?'" 50).

Professional players expected to tour as a normal requirement of their occupation, not as an act of desperation. Even the great plague of 1592–1594, which caused the demise of Pembroke's Men and supposedly forced London companies onto the road, seems to have had less effect on touring than one would expect. Towns like Canterbury, Coventry, Leicester, Gloucester, and Southampton gave rewards to roughly the same number of itinerant companies during the plague years as they did for several years before and after. Nor did the identities of the companies rewarded change significantly through the early 1590s. Likewise, provincial records of visits by prominent companies like the Queen's Men, the Lord Admiral's Men, and the Earl of Worcester's Men reveal no increases in touring activity because of the plague.[1] Such companies ventured regularly into the provinces, even when they appeared frequently at court and had their own purpose-built theaters. In 1572 the Earl of Leicester's Men wrote to their patron asking him to grant them a license "to certifye that we are your houshold Servaunts when we shall have occasion to travayle amongst our frendes as we do usuallye once a yere" (Chambers, *Elizabethan*, 2:86). The construction of the Theatre in 1576 gave the company its own London home, yet produced no change in the pattern of annual tours.

## The Antiquity of Touring

Provincial touring in fact predated the construction of the first theaters in London by centuries. Though uncertainty about the precise meanings of Latin and English terms for entertainers makes it impossible to know exactly when the first stage players appeared, itinerant professional performers of some sort appear in many of the earliest extant records of towns and households. Minstrels (*ministralli, histriones,* and *mimi*) traveling under royal or noble patronage were rewarded as early as 1277 at Canterbury (Gibson), 1307 at Leicester (A. Hamilton), 1337 at Worcester (Klausner, 396), 1366 at Dover (Gibson), 1377 at Winchester (Cowling), 1388 at Shrewsbury (Somerset, *Records: Shropshire,* 127), 1393 at Gloucester (Douglas and Greenfield, 291), 1395 at York (Johnston and Rogerson, 9), 1428 at Southampton (Greenfield, "Records: Hampshire, Hertfordshire, Bedfordshire"), and 1446 at Ludlow (Somerset, *Records: Shropshire,* 74). Minstrels similarly entertained the households of the dowager queen Isabella at Hertford Castle in 1357 (Greenfield, "Records: Hampshire, Hertfordshire, Bedfordshire") and Elizabeth Berkeley at Berkeley Castle in 1420 (Douglas and Greenfield, 347). Later accounts from many places bear witness that minstrel troupes were seen frequently on provincial roads in the fourteenth and fifteenth centuries.

Whether these minstrels included plays in their repertoires cannot be known, but fifteenth-century provincial records do give indications of traveling dramatic performers, identified by their town of origin. Probably these players were amateurs, taking their performance to one or two places close to home. In 1425 two men from Shrewsbury were rewarded for *"ludentibus quoddam interludium"* [playing an interlude] for the household of Gilbert, Lord Talbot, at Blackmere, Shropshire (Somerset, *Records: Shropshire*, 354). The Cinque Ports frequently welcomed each others' players (or *"lusores"*) in the fifteenth century, as when the players of New Romney "played in the chirche" at Rye in 1474–1475 (Louis, "Records: Sussex"). They may have performed something like the passion play that New Romney revived in the 1560s, while a Saint George play is suggested by the payment that the churchwardens of Bishop Stortford (Hertfordshire) received for sending their dragon "made of hoopis & couered with canvas" to take part in a play at the village of Braughing a few miles away (Greenfield, "Records: Hampshire, Hertfordshire, Bedfordshire").

Town clerks use different terms for these local *"lusores"* or "players," and for the professionals touring under patronage until the last quarter of the fifteenth century, when some clerks begin to differentiate between minstrels and players having the same patron. While continuing to mention Lord Arundel's minstrels, the Hythe records also refer to *"lusoribus domini arundell"* in 1486–1487 (Gibson), while the "playares of my lord of Arundell" were rewarded at Dover in 1477–1478 (Gibson) and at Rye in 1481–1482 (Louis, "Records: Sussex").

The number of performing troupes on the road remained relatively constant through the sixteenth century, despite changes in nomenclature. The term *players* became more common in the sixteenth century, while strictly musical performers were usually designated *musicians* and the term *minstrels* appeared only infrequently. Players identified by their town of origin almost disappeared after Elizabethan statutes, the first issued in the year of Elizabeth I's accession, required touring companies to obtain a license from a noble patron. The number of noblemen's companies rose at roughly the same time, though there is no evidence that "town" companies simply found patrons. Even such events as the construction of purpose-built theaters in London (the Red Lion in 1567, the Theatre in 1576), or the great plague of the early 1590s, or James I's institution of a royal monopoly on patronage in 1603–1604 had little effect on the frequency of touring, which did not begin to decline noticeably until the second decade of the seventeenth century.

### Motives for Touring: Profit

Recognizing that touring had a long history and occurred with great frequency furnishes a new perspective on Hamlet's question: How chances it the players traveled so much and so regularly, if their residence in London was better for both reputation and profit? Playing in the capital certainly offered greater opportunities to increase the performer's reputation: London was much the largest city in the nation, and the court was nearby at Westminster. Profit, too, benefited from London's ability to provide much larger audiences, and therefore more income, than any provincial venue, while expenses on tour must have considerably exceeded those in "residence." Yet profit and reputation were the principal motives for touring. Provincial tours must have offered, if not substantial profit, at least financial survival to companies that undertook them, and if touring did little to enhance the artistic reputations of the actors involved, it might nevertheless do much for the political reputation of their patrons.

Most acting troupes must have at least broken even, since they returned to the provinces time and again. The disastrous fate of Pembroke's Men in 1593, though memorable, was rare. How much profit was to be made on the road is more difficult to assess. Expenses of touring would include room and board, plus food and stabling for any horses used for riding or pulling a wagon loaded with costumes and props. Around 1600, a shilling a day per man would seem to be the minimum a company could realistically expect to spend on tour, by forgoing horses and paying six pence for the evening meal and another six pence for a bed for the night. A small provincial company of six would thus have spent six shillings per day if on foot, twelve shillings per day if they hired horses, making their expenses for a week a minimum of forty-two shillings, but quite possibly as much as double that. A month on the road would cost about fifteen pounds (William Ingram, "Cost," 58–59). The larger, probably London-based companies of ten to fifteen would have had to meet expenses roughly double these figures.

Estimating income is harder, if not impossible. If the official rewards from civic authorities and heads of households supplied the players' only source of income, touring would indeed have been a futile enterprise. Extant records do not allow us to reconstruct even the official income from a company's entire tour. We do occasionally get enough information about a brief period to paint a reasonably complete picture, as in the case of a single week spent in the Midlands by Lord Berkeley's Men in 1584. October 7 found them at Nottingham, where they received five shillings (Coldewey, "Records: Nottinghamshire"); on October 10, at nearby Middleton Hall, they got ten shillings (Coldewey, "Records: Nottinghamshire"); on October 13 they had crossed into Derbyshire, where they were given only three shillings at Ticknall Hall (Wasson, "Records: Derbyshire"). The official take for the period of a week was thus a mere eighteen shillings, against minimum expenses of forty-two shillings if Berkeley's company—not a prominent one—had but six members and did their traveling on foot. The resulting loss of twenty-four shillings for the week would obviously have been a crippling figure if repeated throughout their time on tour.

Lord Berkeley's Men, however, probably did a good deal better than a twenty-four-shilling loss for the week of October 7–13, 1584. First of all, players could normally count on being fed and lodged when they performed in households. Pantry accounts of the duke of Buckingham's household at Thornbury for 1507–1508

(Douglas and Greenfield, 356–58) and of Francis Clifford's household at Londesborough for 1598 (Wasson, "Records: Derbyshire") reveal that players often got meals for two or more days, though they might receive only one reward. Presumably they were provided with beds as well. The advantages of performing in households were such that one traveling singer testified in court that he could maintain himself entirely by going "from gentilmans house to gentilmans house vpon their benevolence" (Somerset, *Records: Shropshire*, 280).

In addition to such reductions in expenses, the players derived further income — perhaps even the bulk of their income — from sources only hinted at by the official records. The best-known description of provincial performance is R. Willis's account of a play he saw at Gloucester:

> In the City of Gloucester the manner is (as I think it is in other like corporations) that when the Players of Enterludes come to towne, they first attend the Mayor to enforme him what noble-mans servant they are, and so to get license for their publike playing; and if the Mayor like the Actors, or would shew respect to their Lord and Master, he appoints them to play their first play before himself and the Aldermen and common Counsell of the City and that is called the Mayors play, where every one that will come in without money, the Mayor giving the players a reward as he thinks fit to shew respect unto them. (DOUGLAS AND GREENFIELD, 362–63)

This reward from the mayor would appear in the civic chamberlains' accounts, but it almost certainly did not represent the players' total "take" from visiting a town. Not every town allowed "everyone that will [to] come in without money," instead adding the official reward to an amount collected from the rest of the audience: at Leicester the chamberlains consistently recorded the amount of the reward as being "more than was gathered" (Hamilton, "Records: Leicester").

Furthermore, the "Mayors play" would not have been the only performance a company gave in a town. Willis speaks of the "Mayors play" as "their first play," implying that others would follow. In 1580 Gloucester's Common Council passed an ordinance that permitted the queen's players to perform three plays within three days, and players whose patron held the rank of baron or greater to play twice (Douglas and Greenfield, 306–7). At Norwich, the mayor's court books record that companies were licensed to play for periods from a single day to a week or more. Moreover, in a number of cases, the companies licensed by the mayor's court do not appear in the chamberlains' accounts as having received a reward from the city (Galloway, 109, passim). The Norwich records thus demonstrate what evidence from other locales only suggests, that the many records of touring performance we do have are only the tip of the iceberg, the majority of performances having gone unrecorded.

These unofficial performances may have involved collections at the door, as at the London theaters, or at the end of the performance, or both. The queen's players, at least, could command an admission fee, as we know from the description of the 1582–1583 "affray" at Norwich, which started when "one wynsdon would have intred in at the gate but woold not haue payed vntyll he had been within" and began to fight with the gatekeeper (Galloway, 72–73). Lesser companies may have had to rely on passing the hat, an uncertain means of ensuring one's livelihood, but for a talented group of actors, it could be a good deal more lucrative than the official reward. One suspects that, like Autolycus in *The Winter's Tale* or the rogues of Jonson's *Bartholomew Fair*, the players were adept at separating audience members from their money—and making them enjoy it.

Thus, while we cannot estimate how much individual companies might have made on the road, the unofficial and therefore unrecorded sources of income make profit a possibility. For the week in October 1584 mentioned above, Lord Berkeley's Men might have trimmed their expenses by half the usual amount, to perhaps twenty shillings, by spending three or four nights at Middleton Hall and Ticknall Hall, where their expenses would have been near zero. At the same time, the recorded income of eighteen shillings could have been augmented by rewards from other audience members when they performed in those households, from a collection or gate receipts when they played at Nottingham, as well as by takings from any unofficial performances they gave in that city. The twenty-four-shilling loss for the week that results from subtracting full expenses from the recorded rewards could just as easily have been a profit of similar size.

### Motives for Touring: Reputation, Patronage, and Politics

Hamlet is right that the players' principal concerns were "reputation and profit"; in fact, with the former came the latter. But the players' own reputations as actors were the least important kind of reputation where touring was concerned. In London, where audiences could compare the talents of several companies and choose between them, a troupe's reputation for performing excellence might be crucial to its success. On tour, however, reputation meant the reputation of the players' patron. In some places, the patron's stature might determine whether the players would be allowed to play at all. In 1582 Leicester passed an ordinance prohibiting performing by any entertainers "Except the Quenes maiestes: or the Lordes of the Privye Counsall" (Hamilton, "Records: Leicester"). How much a company could perform and how long they could stay might also depend on the patron. Gloucester codified what was common practice in other towns with its ordinance that allowed the queen's players to play three times over three days, players whose patron held at least the rank of baron to play twice over two days, and all other players to perform only once (Douglas and Greenfield, 306–7).

Often the size of the official reward reflected the size of the patron's power and influence. In 1582–1583 Gloucester gave thirty shillings to the queen's players, sixteen shillings, eight pence to those of the earl of Oxford, and a mere ten shillings to those of Lord Stafford. Civic officials made these distinctions based as much on a patron's local influence as on his standing in the national hierarchy. Lord Chandos's players received twenty shillings that year, more than Oxford's company did, recognizing that Chandos lived at nearby Sudeley Castle and had represented the county in Parliament. Thirteen shillings went to the players of Lord Berkeley, who had extensive holdings in Gloucestershire but resided at Caludon Castle outside Coventry (Douglas and Greenfield, 308). At Coventry in the same year Lord Berkeley's players were paid ten shillings, more than the six shillings, eight pence given to the earl of Worcester's players, yet less than the twenty shillings given to the players of the earl of Leicester, who was lord of nearby Kenilworth Castle, as well as an important national figure (R. W. Ingram, 298).

This careful differentiation among companies according to the importance of the patron shows that civic authorities thought of the players primarily as representatives of their patrons. Indeed, the patron's name is the one thing about a company of players that civic and household accountants nearly always recorded, in order to identify the purpose of monies paid out. (The names of individual players occur seldom in the documentary evidence, the names of the plays they performed even more rarely.) As Willis tells us, "when the Players of Enterludes come to towne, they first attend the Mayor to enforme him what noble-mans servant they are, and so to get license for their publike playing." Moreover, the players would be asked to give a "mayor's play" only "if the Mayor like the Actors, or would shew respect to their Lord and Master" (Douglas and Greenfield, 362–63).

In this show of respect for the patron, we can detect another of the major motivations for touring. If the patron's reputation helped to guarantee traveling players a welcome and a large reward, at the same time the players' travels helped to spread and reaffirm their patron's reputation. Whether patrons' conscious motives for sponsoring players were a love of the theater, a desire to follow fashion, or something else, patronage was an effective means of preserving and enlarging their influence, especially given the theatricality of power in sixteenth- and seventeenth-century England. Stephen Greenblatt argues that Queen Elizabeth was "a ruler without a standing army, without a highly developed bureaucracy, without an extensive police force, a ruler whose power is constituted in theatrical celebrations of royal glory and theatrical violence visited upon the enemies of that glory" (Greenblatt, "Invisible," 44). Because of this theatricality, the theater became "a prime location for the representation and legitimation of power" (Dollimore, Introduction to Dollimore and Sinfield, 3).

As a social event, a touring performance resembled a masque, in that it could serve its social function almost regardless of the content of the performance itself. The masque achieved its reaffirmation of the relation between sovereign and subject only partly through its emblematic text. At least as important was the concluding gesture, the ceremonial offering of the performance as a gift to the monarch. In accepting the gift, and then joining performers and audience in the concluding dance, the monarch acknowledged community with his or her subjects, represented by performers and audience, yet did so in a context that reaffirmed the monarch's position at the top of the hierarchical ladder. A performance by a touring company involved a similar exchange of gifts and reciprocal acknowledgment of the social hierarchy. The players' visit to a town functioned as a sharing of the patron's personal entertainment with the town or household and therefore as a gift, albeit one calculated to remind the city of the patron's influence. In return, by permitting the performance and giving a reward, the civic officials or head of household expressed recognition of the patron's influence over local affairs (Greenfield, "Professional"; Blackstone, "Patrons").

A touring performance also resembled a royal entry in being a dramatic event intended to remind both participants and audience of the hierarchical social relationships between them, and to act as a ceremonial, even ritual, reaffirmation of those relationships. While royal entries always enacted the town's acceptance of royal authority, they also frequently included a symbolic assertion of the town's sovereignty over itself (often granted by royal charter) and of town and monarch's need for reciprocal reliance. Similarly, while allowing the players to perform and rewarding them amounted to a recognition of the patron's influence and authority, requiring the players to obtain a license asserted the civic officials' authority over what happened within city limits. A whole tour would thus resemble a royal progress, with the players standing in for the absent monarch—or nobleman—as they moved around the countryside, advertising, spreading, and consolidating the power and influence of their patron.

This ability of touring players to serve as symbols of royal and aristocratic authority may have provided one of the primary motives for patronage of acting companies. The Tudor monarchs wished to stabilize the country and centralize power in their own hands, despite dynastic and religious upheaval. At the same time, the aristocracy was attempting to preserve its importance by using political influence to replace its traditional sources of power—military might and personal loyalty—which the Tudors had appropriated for the Crown (L. Stone, *Crisis*). So we should not be surprised to find that the monarchs all had players, and that their companies had the most extensive and consistent provincial itineraries. Nobles who aspired to royal or near-royal status themselves—Buckingham, Leicester, Essex—were also important patrons. Even a lesser aristocrat like Henry Berkeley might have political motives for retaining actors' services. He spent a great deal of time and money trying to regain possession of Berkeley Castle from the Crown (E. S. Lindley, 157–58; Smyth). Being patron to a company of players may have been a relatively painless way of increasing his influence both in the West Midlands and at court.

The great irony of dramatic patronage was that it involved employing as symbols of royal and aristocratic authority a group usually considered outside or at least on the margin of the social hierarchy and thus viewed as a threat to the social order. Without the license and livery of their patron, the players appeared to be masterless wanderers, the sort of men thought to be the greatest threat to the social order by aristocracy and civic magistracy alike. The players' visit to a town provided a temporary escape from the unchanging regimen of work, and of familial and civic duties, imposed by the social order. More dangerous was that the players themselves represented a life of constant festival, of freedom from the authority of master, guild, and city, of freedom to determine one's own time, movements, and actions. The players' appearance in town could hardly help reinforcing the desire of the powerless for such freedom, thereby arousing their discontent with the dominant social order, even though that discontent might be expressed only as temporary enjoyment of freedom, rather than in any concerted attempt to change their status. In a period of social instability and unprecedented social mobility, even temporary resistance could be perceived as a threat to the existing hierarchy.

Such perceptions may be the reason why aristocrats and urban leaders alike responded to players with repressive legislation. National statutes and local ordinances observed that players occupied a marginal position in the social order and so required them to have an aristocratic patron in order to tour and perform. The 1572 *Acte for the Punishemente of Vacabondes* ranked players lacking a patron with peddlers, tinkers, and petty chapmen as "Rogues, Vacaboundes and Sturdy Beggers . . . havinge not Land or Maister, nor using any lawfull Marchaundize Crafte or Mysterye" (Chambers, *Elizabethan*, 4:269–71). A statute passed in the year of Elizabeth's accession had given local officials the authority to require a visiting troupe to produce a license to be allowed to perform, and many towns reasserted this right in their own ordinances.

When the players came bearing the name of their patron, they became emblems of social hierarchy. As masterless wanderers, their social position resembled that of Falstaff's ragged charge of prisoners and the unemployed, "the cankers of a calm world and a long peace" (4.2.29–30). Yet, as Stephen Greenblatt points out, these "very types of Elizabethan subversion" become "the perfect emblem of containment" when Falstaff presses them "into service as defenders of the established order" ("Invisible," 30–31). Likewise, the players became emblems of contained subversion when their wandering and begging were institutionalized within the established order. The very qualities of the players' lives that held subversive potential became transformed into powerful symbols of contained subversion: the masterlessness of the wandering vagabond was cloaked in the livery that visually and obviously symbolized their master, while their freedom of movement mapped the lines of influence and interdependence that linked their patron with towns and other aristocrats within the web of the existing social order. Moreover, the begging that enabled the masterless men to maintain their position outside the social order was augmented, if not replaced, by the receipt of rewards given to the players in recognition of the power and influence of the patron for whom they acted as intermediaries.

In some cases, this symbolic value of players traveling under patronage was appropriated by local authorities—how consciously we cannot know. The sixteenth and early seventeenth centuries were a time of crisis for many towns, as surely as for the aristocracy. Many provincial towns suffered economic stagnation or decline, often because of the growing dominance of London, and at the same time they experienced a substantial increase in population, much of it immigration from impoverished rural areas. The result was widespread poverty, in some towns amounting to more than a tenth of the population in good years and as much as a quarter of it in bad ones (Clark, *Country*, 10). Social tensions grew as the gap widened between the poor and wealthier inhabitants, sometimes erupting in open conflict, as at Gloucester in 1586, when clothworkers rioted to protest merchants' shipping grain out of the city while the poor went hungry (Clark, "Ramoth-Gilead," 175).

In response, urban elites took steps to increase their control over public order. Some of these steps were legal, such as the ordinances regulating and even prohibiting playing issued by several towns. Like the sovereign, however, local authorities had limited power to coerce, so any legal measures they took were best accompanied by symbolic measures designed to engender "the civic deference necessary for effective government," as historian Robert Tittler describes it in *Architecture and Power*, his study of English town halls in the sixteenth century (122). Such symbolic measures included the building or rebuilding of the town hall, enlarging the ceremonial mace, and providing the mayor with a special chair of office (Tittler, 98–128). These ceremonial gestures helped to replace earlier communal ceremonies that had disappeared with the Reformation, including civic feasts, but especially the processions at Corpus Christi and Midsummer. The ceremony of those processions involved the entire population in a ritual affirmation of community, yet at the same time, the order in which civic officials marched, and the ceremonial garb they wore, advertised their position and authority. In fact, such ceremony largely constituted the social structure of the late medieval town (Davis, "Sacred"; M. James; Phythian-Adams, in Clark and Slack). By the late sixteenth century, Protestant resistance had eliminated much of this public ceremony, and increasingly oligarchic urban governments made their decisions closeted in the council chamber of the town hall (Clark and Slack, 21).

Towns responded variously to the threat to public order posed by visiting players. Some, like Leicester and Bristol, restricted the audience in the town hall to members of the council and must thereby have intensified social tension. Gloucester and other towns that allowed the players to give "a Mayors play, where every one that will comes in without money," instead found a way to promote order and social cohesion that we can see by returning to the analogy of the masque. The mayor plays a role at the performance analogous to that of the monarch at a masque. Even if the mayor is not specifically the subject of the performance, as the monarch is, the mayor's relationship to performance and audience is similar. The masque is both *for* the monarch and a gift *from* him or her to the audience. The giving and receiving at once reaffirm both the community of giver and receiver and the existing social distinction between them. The mayor's play works the same way, and all the more powerfully because —

like the masque — it happens in a space that itself symbolizes authority: the royal banqueting hall or the town hall. Tittler comes to a similar conclusion, arguing that
"civic authorities first encouraged a particular cultural activity [that is, performances
by traveling players] to relocate in the civic hall for what they saw as purposes of containment and regulation" (150).

The mayor's play resembles the masque in another important way. The
masque celebrates royal authority by imaging in the anti-masque the uncontrolled
forces subversive of the dominant order, thus legitimating the exercise of power by
the monarch to ensure the maintenance of order (Orgel, *Illusion*, 40). At the
mayor's play (as cultural performance), the forces of subversion were represented
by the players themselves, those wanderers who occupied a position outside, or at
least on the margin of, the Elizabethan social order. Yet the livery they wore made
their status as some "noble-mans servants" clear, and their performance of the
mayor's play made them temporarily the "mayor's men" as well. Performances in
aristocratic households could have much the same effect, with the players representing the reputations of their patrons but also of the head of household who
authorized the performance.

## Touring Circuits

The circuits that players traveled most frequently led east from London along the
Roman road to Canterbury and the Cinque Ports, northeast into the flatlands of
East Anglia to Ipswich and Norwich, north on the Great North Road to Cambridge
and all the way to York, and west to Bristol. A company might travel out from
London on one of these radiating spokes and back in on another, having taken a
connecting route like the one that led southwest from Leicester through Coventry
and Gloucester to Bristol.

Topography partly determined where the players went on tour: places close to
London were more often visited than those at a great distance, but ease of travel
also had much to do with where the players went and what routes they followed to
get there. Good roads were important, especially for companies traveling with a
cart loaded with props and costumes. Ashburton's location on the main road from
Exeter to Plymouth explains why players visited it but overlooked other, perhaps
more affluent, parishes. On the other hand, the height and ruggedness of the North
Downs discouraged companies from visiting Guildford and Farnham, despite the
fact that both towns lay on the old Pilgrims' Way from Canterbury to Winchester
(MacLean, "Players," 68–69). Players leaving Gloucester nearly always did so along
the Severn valley, south to Bristol or north to Worcester. To reach Oxford, about
the same distance from Gloucester, meant getting actors and their gear up the
steep Cotswold Edge. Companies often followed rivers like the Thames and the
Severn, which offered the gentlest gradients, and may even have taken to the river,
water travel being both easy and inexpensive. The frequency with which players
show up in the records of coastal towns also suggests that they were traveling by sea,

especially where inland roads were less dependable than coastal waters, as along the Dorset and Devon coasts.

Financial and perhaps political considerations often took precedence over topographical ones. The obvious route to Coventry, where itinerant companies were always welcome, would have followed Watling Street, the Roman road that ran northwest out of London. The extant records, though scanty, suggest that tours took less-direct routes to Coventry, swinging west through Abingdon and Oxford, or farther west through Bath, Bristol, and Gloucester. The speed and ease of travel offered by Watling Street could not outweigh the prospect of few and meager paydays, as the road touched few sizable towns between St. Albans and Coventry.

How lucrative a particular route might be depended partly on how many towns, households, monasteries, and other potential playing places lay on or conveniently near the principal roads on the route, and also on how receptive those places might be. Some towns welcomed players and rewarded them handsomely. Coventry rewarded several troupes annually without ever trying to prohibit or restrict playing, right through the 1620s and 1630s, when resistance to itinerant players had become widespread. Other towns gave fewer rewards and sometimes took great pains to establish civic control over players. Norwich, as the second-largest city in England, appeared to promise hefty paydays, and it is probably for that reason that civic authorities there regulated playing so carefully. As early as 1584–1585 Norwich began to pay companies not to perform, thereby denying them the important unofficial income. In 1588–1589 the civic assembly passed a ban on performing in that city, though it appears to have been short-lived, as the city then started to grant licenses to perform for specific periods, and to take action against troupes that outstayed their official welcome. Companies continued to come to Norwich, however, and if that city rewarded fewer troupes than the smaller Ipswich, the continuing attraction of the unofficial income to be had from Norwich's large population can be seen in the number of companies that tried to extend their visits there beyond the terms of their licenses (Galloway, 81, 91, passim; Somerset, " 'How chances it,' " 9). Smaller towns probably had better luck discouraging the players.

How receptive the mayor or abbot or aristocratic head of the household might be to a particular company was usually related to the magnitude of its patron's authority or influence in that locale. A minor example of the connection between itineraries and patrons' local influence can be seen in the travel patterns of the players of Lord Henry Berkeley. Of fifty-six known provincial visits of this company, seventeen occurred at Gloucester, Bath, or Bristol, towns that surrounded Berkeley's lands in southern Gloucestershire. Four more came from Bridgewater and Abingdon, still close to the lord's center of influence. Fourteen of the records concern Coventry and nearby Caludon Castle, Henry Berkeley's principal residence after 1590. A few records from Norwich and Ipswich probably reflect the circle of influence of the family of Berkeley's wife, Katherine Howard. Fewer than a third of the recorded appearances of Lord Berkeley's players occurred at places where the lord had relatively little influence. Furthermore, all of the visits to Gloucester, Bristol, and Bath occurred before 1590, but most went to Coventry after that date, reflecting Berkeley's having shifted his principle country residence from Yate Court in southern Gloucestershire to Caludon in that year.[2]

Other companies reveal similar parallels between their itineraries and the geographical spread of their patrons' authority and influence. The players of the Lord President of the Council in the Marches of Wales were most often to be found in the Marches, or in counties that their patron commanded as Lord Lieutenant (Somerset, "Lords President," 110). The Lord Warden of the Cinque Ports gave his name to a group of players who were very active in the 1540s and 1550s, but exclusively within the territory suggested by that name (Blackstone, "Circles"). As one would expect, the players of the reigning monarch ranged more widely than the entertainers of even their most powerful subjects. The one exception was the Earl of Leicester's Men, whose travels expanded with their patron's ambition to achieve royal stature himself.

## Repertory, Personnel, Playing Places

What was staged in this period, who staged it, and where it was staged are subjects discussed much more fully in other essays in this collection, but touring involves some unique features in every case. We know very little about what plays provincial audiences saw. Accounts and court records alike rarely mention the titles or describe performances. On the few occasions when they do, the titles and descriptions cannot be certainly linked to any extant play texts. The one extended description that we possess is R. Willis's account of a play called *The Cradle of Security*, which he saw at Gloucester in the 1570s. It clearly suggests a morality play or interlude

> wherin was personated a King or some great Prince with his Courtiers of severall kinds, amongst which three Ladies were in speciall grace with him; and they keeping him in delights and pleasures, drew him from his graver Counsellors, hearing of Sermons, and listning to good counsell, and admonitions, that in the end they got him to lye downe in a cradle upon the stage, where these three ladies joyning in a sweet song rocked him asleepe, that he snorted againe, and in the meane time closely conveyed under the cloaths where withall he was covered, a vizard like a swines snout upon his face, with three wire chaines fastned thereunto, the other end whereof being holden severally by those three Ladies, who fall to singing againe, and then discovered his face, that the spectators might see how they had transformed him, going on with their singing, whilst all this was acting, there came forth of another doore at the farthest end of the stage, two old men, the one in blew with a Serjeant at Armes, his mace on his shoulder, the other in red with a drawn sword in his hand and leaning with the other hand upon the others shoulder, and so they two went along in a soft pace round about the skirt of the Stage, till at last they came to the Cradle, when all the Court was in greatest jollity, and then the foremost old man with his Mace stroke a fearfull blow upon the Cradle; whereat all the Courtiers with the three Ladies and

the vizard all vanished; and the desolate Prince starting up bare faced, and finding himselfe thus sent for to judgement, made a lamentable complaint of his miserable case, and so was carried away by wicked spirits. This Prince did personate in the morall, the wicked of the world; the three Ladies, Pride, Covetousnesse, and Luxury, the two old men, the end of the world, and the last judgement. (DOUGLAS AND GREENFIELD, 363)

A few similar titles appear in the Bristol records of the same decade: "what mischief worketh in the mynd of man" and "the Court of Comfort" (J. T. Murray, 2:214–15). Provincial companies may have continued to offer such fare into the seventeenth century, but the major London companies must have brought Shakespeare, Marlowe, and Jonson to the rest of the country, though perhaps in versions cut to reduce the size of the cast. London companies on tour must also have cut their repertories to a few of their surefire favorites. They would have wanted to keep their cartload of costumes and props to a reasonable size and would also have had little chance to rehearse on the road. Since they gave only a few performances at each town or household before moving on, they did not have to provide a stream of new plays, as they did in London.

Touring companies as a rule had fewer members than their London counterparts. The Earl of Derby's Men numbered twelve when they played before the household of Francis Clifford at Londesborough in 1598, but other troupes mentioned in the same records had only six or seven actors (Wasson, "Records: Derbyshire"). Six may in fact have been a common size for a minor itinerant company, as *The Cradle of Security* clearly requires a cast of six, and the will of actor Simon Jewell states that he held "the sixth parte" of the company's investment in "horses, waggen and apparrell newe boughte" for a proposed tour (Edmond, "Pembroke's," 129). The visiting players in *Hamlet* provide fictional support for troupe size, as the stage directions for the dumb show that opens "The Mousetrap" indicate that the King, Queen, and Poisoner are accompanied by either "two or three Mutes" (Folio) or "some Three or Four" (Second Quarto), making a total company of between five and seven (3.2.8 sd). As David Bevington showed in *From "Mankind" to Marlowe*, extensive doubling of parts allowed companies of this size—the "four men and a boy" of the play within a play of *Sir Thomas More*—to perform most of the sixteenth-century repertoire (68–85). Some troupes were even smaller, especially in the waning days of provincial touring: in 1624 a group carrying a license from the Master of the Revels consisted of only three players and a minstrel (Douglas and Greenfield, 319–20). Even the major London companies may have reduced their numbers for provincial tours.

Touring players performed in many kinds of spaces, including the halls of noble households, churches, churchyards, streets, inns, private houses, and even a purpose-built theater—the Wine Street Playhouse in Bristol, opened around 1605.[3] The most common location for a touring performance, however, was the town hall. Accounts and ordinances from towns across the country indicate that when players performed with the permission of local officials, the first performance, at least, occurred in the town hall. Licenses granted to the King's Men in 1603 and Lady Elizabeth's Men in 1612 both specified town halls or moot halls as the places in which these companies were authorized to play (Chambers, *Elizabethan*, 3:209; Johnston and Rogerson, 538). Generally these were public performances in the main hall or public space, although there are indications that some towns restricted the initial performance to an audience of the mayor and council members, sometimes in the council chamber or other smaller space (Hamilton, "Records: Leicester"; Pilkinton, "Records: Bristol"). Stages were sometimes constructed for these performances at civic expense (Greenfield, "Professional," 84–89; Wickham, *Early*, 2.1:183–85; Southern, *Staging*, 329–48). Performances at inns, though less well attested, appear to have been fairly common, and usually took place indoors, rather than outside in the inn yard.

## The Decline of Touring

Provincial touring declined in the seventeenth century, having almost disappeared by the time Parliament ordered an end to all public performance in 1642. Coventry—the provincial town that most frequently rewarded touring companies—made payments to an average of six troupes a year in the 1590s, a figure that increased to eight in the first decade of the seventeenth century. From 1610 to 1619, however, the annual average shrank to four, then dipped further to only two per year in the 1620s and 1630s. Two companies received rewards in 1640, but they were the last at Coventry. Many other towns not only gave fewer rewards over this period but increasingly gave those rewards in lieu of allowing the players to perform, or as the records sometimes undiplomatically put it, "to rid the town of them."

The decline in touring took two forms: a substantial decrease in the number of different companies on the road and a decrease in touring activity by the companies that remained. The causes of the decline are harder to pinpoint, but the most important factors were the establishment of a royal monopoly on patronage of players and the strengthening of local authorities' pragmatic and religious objections to playing, coupled with their growing antagonism toward Crown interference in local affairs.

The royal monopoly followed closely on the accession of James I in 1603, as royal patents translated the players of the Lord Chamberlain, Lord Admiral, and Earl of Worcester into the King's Men, Prince Henry's Men, and Queen Anne's Men, respectively. In 1604, the statute against vagabonds was revised, withdrawing the right to license players from "any Baron of this Realme, or any other honourable Personage of greater Degree" (Wickham, *Early*, 2.1:335–36). In theory, then, only members of the royal household could act as patrons of players, a change whose effect could have been immediate and devastating: not only had James reduced the number of companies licensed to play anywhere, but limiting the companies to those that had their own London theaters ensured that the companies that remained were those with the least reason to go out on tour. Furthermore, provincial towns had legal cause to prevent nonroyal companies from playing, to deny them a reward, and even to lock them up as vagabonds.

In practice, however, some time elapsed before the royal monopoly achieved its full impact. The frequency with which itinerant players visited most provincial towns shows little change in the first five years of James's rule, nor do the identities of the visiting companies change, save those three that had gained royal patrons. By 1610 the effects of the monopoly began to appear. At both Norwich and Leicester, several companies enjoying royal patronage performed and received rewards, but all the companies with nonroyal patrons—those of Lords Berkeley and Chandos, and the earl of Arundel—were paid not to play (Galloway, A. Hamilton). That these towns still rewarded these noblemen's players, rather than locking them up, suggests the power of tradition and of the continuing importance of the players as carriers of their patrons' power and influence. Nevertheless, as a result of the Crown's actions in 1603–1604, some provincial towns began to recognize a distinction between players who had royal patrons and those who did not, a distinction that allowed them to prevent the latter from performing. Since official rewards alone could not sustain traveling players, the royal monopoly did eventually eliminate all other patrons, though it effected this indirectly by economic means, rather than by direct, legal ones. Early in James's reign, when only a few towns had begun to give rewards to prevent performance, a company could still survive on the road, performing where they got a friendly reception and making brief sorties into hostile towns to pick up their reward before moving on to greener pastures. As the number of friendly venues decreased, and the payments not to play grew, the financial squeeze gradually eliminated the companies without royal patrons, though a few of the companies survived by attaching themselves to another member of the royal household, or becoming a kind of shadow version—which appeared exclusively in the provinces—of an existing London company under royal protection. Eventually, even the royal companies suffered, for towns turned the tactic of paying the players not to play against those with royal patrons as well, when the nonroyal companies had disappeared.

The desire of local authorities to prohibit, or at least restrict, performing antedated the royal monopoly in many towns. Much has been made of the growing Puritan antagonism toward the theater during the Elizabethan and Stuart periods, but the motives of the local authorities—at least the motives they set down explicitly in the records—were as much pragmatic and economic as they were moral and religious. In 1580, a Gloucester ordinance limited the number of performances that players could give in the city, stating first that the council was moved to impose some restraint on the players because they "Drawe awey greate Sommes of money from diuerse persons." Concern for public morals does arise in noting that players "allure seruanutes, apprentices and iorneyman & other of the worst desposed persons to leudenes and lightnes of life," but then economics reappear, as the guild masters

who make up the council contemplate how playgoing encourages "the maintenance of idleness" among their employees, endangering their profits (Douglas and
Greenfield, 307). In the seventeenth century, the most common reasons for prohibiting performance were fear of plague and fear of damage to the town hall. The
threat of plague led towns to close their gates to all travelers, who might bring infection, while disruptions and damage in the hall obviously undercut any value the performance might have as symbolism of civic authority. While some places prohibited
playing entirely, at least at night, anywhere in the city—as Chester did in 1615
(Clopper, *Records: Chester*, 292–93)—others were mainly concerned with getting
the players out of the hall, and allowed inns as an alternative—as Southampton did
in 1620 (Greenfield, "Records: Hampshire, Hertfordshire, Bedfordshire"). As
Puritanism increased among urban elites, and their relationship with the Crown
deteriorated, touring players sometimes became pawns in the political struggle. In
1624 Norwich refused Lady Elizabeth's players permission to perform, claiming that
a letter from the Privy Council sympathetic to the city's prohibition of playing gave
the civic magistrates authority superior to the king's license carried by the players
(Galloway, 180–81). In general, those towns that were receptive to players in the
1620s and 1630s were those that also remained sympathetic to the Crown, but many
inconsistencies exist. Gloucester's mayor and justices rewarded players and watched
them perform in 1640–1641, only a year before the city's heroic resistance to the royal
army (Douglas and Greenfield, 328). Neighboring towns sometimes differed greatly
in their treatment of itinerant entertainers: Plymouth began to discourage visiting
players as early as 1600, while Dartmouth continued to reward them until 1634
(Wasson, *Records: Devon*, xiv, xx). Aristocratic households continued to offer the
most lucrative and comfortable tour stops well into the seventeenth century.[4] Still,
even Coventry, the most receptive town of all, gave its last reward to visiting players
in 1641 (R. W. Ingram, 447), and the Interregnum brought to an end the long tradition of players' touring the provinces.

NOTES

1. For Canterbury, see Gibson; for Coventry, see R. W. Ingram, *Records: Coventry*; for
   Leicester, see Hamilton; for Gloucester, see Douglas and Greenfield; for Southampton,
   see Greenfield, "Records: Hampshire, Hertfordshire, Bedfordshire." Data on provincial
   performances and touring patterns have been collected from all the published REED
   volumes and from unpublished transcriptions held at the REED office at the University
   of Toronto. I am especially grateful to the editors of the latter for allowing me to make
   use of their collections.
2. E. S. Lindley, 157–58. These figures on the travels of Lord Berkeley's company were compiled from J. T. Murray; R. W. Ingram, *Records: Coventry*; Somerset, *Records: Shropshire*;
   Douglas and Greenfield; Greenfield, "Berkeley"; MacLean's corrections of Murray's
   Bath transcriptions in "Players"; Gibson; Stokes; Coldewey, "Records: Nottinghamshire"; and Wasson, "Records: Derbyshire."

3. See essays in this volume by Wasson and Westfall for performances in churches and households. Open-air performances turn up infrequently in the records: the queen's players acted "in the Colledge Churche yarde" of Gloucester Cathedral in 1590 (Douglas and Greenfield, 311); performances in streets or marketplaces by itinerant troupes are mostly inferred from visual evidence. The full evidence for the Wine Street Playhouse will be published in Pilkinton's forthcoming "Records: Bristol"; see Pilkinton, "Playhouse."

4. Sir Richard Shuttleworth rewarded the players of Lords Derby and Stafford in 1616 and 1617 at Gawthorpe Hall, Lancashire (George, 176–77). Lord Wharton's players were paid by Sir Patricius Curwen at Workington, Cumberland, in 1629 (Douglas and Greenfield, 129). Lord William Howard rewarded unnamed companies of players at Naworth (Cumberland) as late as 1634 (Douglas and Greenfield, 143), while Thomas Walmesley welcomed Lord Strange's players to Dunkenhalgh Manor, Lancashire, in 1635–1637 (George, 210).

# CHAPTER 15

# "Cloathes worth all the rest": Costumes and Properties

*Jean MacIntyre and Garrett P. J. Epp*

THE PROFESSIONAL actors of early English drama, like their amateur counterparts in biblical cycle plays, were men and boys with some education but of "mean station," for the most part from families of artisans and shop-keepers (Forse, 14). Professional stage players, whether wandering provincial troupes or prosperous shareholders in London companies, were likely to be classed as "vagabonds and masterless men" unless they were enrolled among the servants of a nobleman and received his livery, a garment that identified their relatively humble status. Yet lowly actors commonly played beings of a higher order, from the saints and angels of the cycles to the kings and emperors of the Elizabethan stage.

This disparity between the actor's offstage status and the one he assumed on stage caused some uneasiness. Thomas More observed that "the losel [who] playeth the lord . . . when the play is done, he shall go walk a knave in his old coat" (Greenblatt, *Renaissance*, 26). The "Homily against Excess of Apparel" and the antitheatrical Philip Stubbes (1583) lamented that what clothing reported about class had become untrustworthy. Stubbes alleged the theater as a cause, for the "losel" often did not just play the lord on the stage; he hid his true status by wearing stage finery on the street and encouraging others to imitate him. In 1620, the author of *Hic Mulier* demanded whether excessive finery "be not as frequent in the demy-Palaces of Burgers and Citizens, as it is either at Maske, Tryumph, Tilt-yard, or Play-house" and the author of *Haec Vir* associated male effeminacy with "a Play house, or publique assembly" where the gallant preens in order to "cast himself amongst the eyes of the people (as an obiect of wonder)" (Baines, unpaginated). That is, outside the theater clothing was all too often theatrical, belying the God-given birth, status, or sex of Anybody, like the actor's costume.

On the stage, however, who and what an actor represents must be accurately conveyed, so that the audience can understand the play; if the play requires inaccuracies, this has to be made clear. Real apprentices defied London's rules about plain clothing to parade as gallants, but stage apprentices (as in 1 *Edward IV*) wore regulation coats and statutory flat caps; if they turned gallant like Francis Quicksilver in *Eastward Ho*, speeches and/or costume change on stage clarified their true status. In *Eastward Ho* and in *Coriolanus*, both written after the repeal of the Elizabethan statute requiring workingmen to wear "a cap of wool knit," the citizen is still known and mocked for his "flat cap." Philip Henslowe advanced money to Worcester's Men for "a sytyzen cotte & sleves" (Henslowe, *Diary*, ed. Foakes and Rickert [unless otherwise noted], 223), evidently a properly plain garment of the kind sometimes specified in the direction "like a citizen."

Whatever conventions of dress were violated by the vanity of the affluent and the social climber, on the stage the actor's costume normally placed his character in the right fictional class and occupation. Stage costume shows the social station or profession of each character in a play—king, queen, beggar, artisan, soldier, whore, priest—and often indicates occasion and/or activity, distinguishing the king-in-council in robe and crown from the king-at-war in armor, the artisan at work in an apron from the artisan on holiday in "best apparel." Costume gives body to imaginary beings like nymphs, fairies, gods, and devils, as well as ideas such as Pride, Knowledge, Liberality, and the like. Virtues such as Mercy in *Mankind* or Charity in *Youth* are often dressed as priests or friars; in Thomas Lupton's *All for Money*, Science is "clothed like a Philosopher," and Money has "the one half of his gown yellow and the other white, having the coin of silver and gold painted upon it."

Such ideas are made visible not only in the drama of personified abstractions called moralities, but also in more naturalistic dramas of human actions and character called histories, comedies, and tragedies—even without the presence of characters such as "Rumor, painted full of tongues" in the induction to 2 *Henry IV*. While showing a character's status in the social or economic sense, costume may simultaneously indicate his moral or psychological condition, as in the many variants on the Prodigal Son story, from the Tudor moralities of *Youth* and *Nice Wanton* to the Stuart *Eastward Ho*, *Timon of Athens*, *A New Way to Pay Old Debts*, and *The City Madam*. Fine clothes accompany the prodigal's "riotous living," which includes the sins of pride, gluttony, and lechery, while rags represent not only his poverty but also his remorse; new, usually simple or specifically penitential clothing, like the garment called Contrition given to the title character in *Everyman*, represent both improved condition and moral regeneration.

In biblical cycle drama, costume attempted to bridge the gap between a distant historical past and a very present theology through an ahistorical mix of costume styles. Records in England are generally too scant to support any conclusions on their own, but they suggest conformity with the practice of late medieval visual arts and with Continental parallels. Contemporary illustrations of processional tableaux, such as those of the 1594 Leuven Ommegange in the *Liber Boonen*, show the same sort of range in costume style as the manuscript illustrations for the biblical plays of Lille:

> Some of the costumes are fantastic clothing, a deliberate attempt on the part of the artist to create a sense of the exotic—the "otherness" and often the "orientalness" of the events depicted. Other costumes, however, reflect the fashions of the times. (SHEINGORN, 173)

The general rule would appear to be that roughly contemporary or old-fashioned costume was given to some minor (or invented) characters, but not to characters of high rank or "holiness"—the Apostles, Mary, and so on—or to any identified as pagan or in another sense alien—which could include any or all Old Testament characters (S. M. Newton, 70).

The large cast of the English cycles, as of Continental processions, employed multiple actors playing the same important roles. For instance, more than a dozen different actors may have played the Virgin Mary in any given performance of the York cycle; there were two dozen adult Christs. Recognition of a single important character depended largely on convention in costuming. A blue mantle made Mary immediately identifiable, much as in Hans Memling's painting *The Seven Joys of the Virgin* (1480; Alte Pinakothek, Munich); the pilgrims on the road to Emmaus might not at first have recognized the risen Christ, but the audience did—he wore red, as he conventionally did for his post-Resurrection appearances.

Religious iconography was not the only convention employed, however. Contemporary European Jews were often forced to wear visual identification of some sort, such as distinctive hats; stage Jews might wear strange, often conical hats. Jewish religious figures were in effect parodies of their Christian counterparts, as in the N-town *Passion*, where Annas was costumed as "a bishop of the hoold [old] lawe in a skarlet gowne, and ouyr that a blew tabbard furryd with whyte, and a mytere on his hed after the hoold lawe"; each of his advisers wore "a furryd cappe with a gret knop in the crowne," and his messenger was dressed "as a Sarazyn" (Spector, 26.164 sd). Herod was likewise a Saracen or Turk, or fantastically oriental. In Coventry and Chester, Herod, unlike other blustering tyrants, was played in a mask, which further emphasized his singular otherness—a visual counterpart to the verbal bombast mocked in Hamlet's advice, decades after the demise of biblical cycle drama, not to out-Herod Herod. Yet even the singular Herod was also multiple: at York, two different actors played Herod in separate pageants of the Magi and of the Slaughter of the Innocents, and this Herod was not explicitly distinguished from the Herod who mocked the adult Christ, at least in York. In Chester, this later Herod was masked, but the earlier Herod might not have been—the mask may have been used in the Trial pageant primarily to allow the same actor to play both Herod and Pilate (Twycross and Carpenter, 96)—a rare example of doubling in cycle drama.

While the various cycles shared certain costuming conventions, and even texts, there were certainly important differences between cycles. A difference in theological emphasis could mean a difference in costuming conventions. In Chester, Christ's face was gilded throughout the cycle, emphasizing his power and divinity; according to the Chester Smiths' records, even "litle God," the child Christ confronting the doctors of the church, had a gilded face and gloved hands, although nothing of the sort is alluded to within the text of the play itself. York's pageant of Christ and the Doctors is textually very similar but would have looked very different on stage, as the York plays as a whole stressed Christ's humanity and suffering. In York, God the Father wore a gilded mask, but Christ was very much the human Jesus.

Both in early traveling troupes of players and in the chartered companies of London's public theaters, a single actor generally played multiple roles, but costume still identified the character that an actor represented. Especially before companies increased in size in the 1580s, most actors played two, three, or more parts in every play. A changed costume meant the actor was a different character, unless the play said otherwise. This convention, incidentally, would have made the now-infamous "bed tricks" of plays such as Shakespeare's *All's Well That Ends Well* and *Measure for Measure* more convincing to a Renaissance audience—in effect, the costume was the character.

In *From "Mankind" to Marlowe*, David Bevington shows how methods of rapid costume change enabled small troupes to imply large numbers. Changes of costume allowed seven actors to play thirty-seven roles in *Cambises, King of Persia*. Such extensive doubling conditioned audiences to read the entry of an actor in a different costume as the entry of a different character. If the actor was required to change costume when his character embarked on disguise or deception, or achieved a new status, or altered his moral state, the playwright had to make clear that the character remained the same, whether by having the costume change take place on stage or by providing a verbal explanation. The Vices in *Respublica* and *The Life and Repentance of Mary Magdalene* don their disguises on stage while discussing their deceptive purpose. In *The World and the Child*, whenever World gives Child a new name, signifying his growing older, he also gives him new garments. Child thus visibly "grows" into Manhood, then exits with Folly and returns as ragged old Age. In *Impatient Poverty*, Poverty receives better clothes when renamed Prosperity and reenters in rags when, having wasted his substance, he has again become Poverty. In Shakespeare's *Love's Labours Lost*, Boyet ridicules the lords' imminent masquerade as Muscovites before they enter in disguises assumed offstage. In Jonson's *The Alchemist*, the tricksters don some of their disguises on stage, but also specify what disguise they will be assuming offstage while other action is going on. Whatever the play calls for, it must help the audience recognize a formerly seen character in different clothes.

Characters change costume on stage by removing outer garments, donning them, or, sometimes, exchanging them. Whether the change in a character's appearance represents a mimetic alteration or a symbolic one, the playwright must arrange a way to effect the change without impeding the progress of the play and without confusing the audience. In Shakespeare's *The Winter's Tale*, Perdita dons Florizel's hat while Florizel trades clothes with Autolycus, so they will not be recognized during their flight from Bohemia. In *Henry V*, King Henry borrows Erpingham's cloak, and when he puts it on, it is clear that others are not meant to recognize him; a borrowed cloak similarly hides the king's identity in Heywood's *Edward IV*. At the end of *Swetnam the Woman Hater*, the disguised Prince Lorenzo "throws off" layered garments, first those of an "old Shepherd," then those of an Amazon, to reveal his true royal identity. Much earlier, in the second Towneley Shepherds' play, the thief Mak makes his first entrance wrapped in a cloak, disguised as a yeoman; it is not clear whether the audience is supposed to be fooled for a moment, but the shepherds certainly are not.

Some disguisings relied more completely on stage convention: Henslowe's "robe for to goo invisibell" (Henslowe, *Diary*, 323) would have achieved the same basic effect as the net that the devil Titivillus used, more than a full century earlier, to make himself invisible to *Mankind*. Masks, too, were used as a form of disguise and to differentiate between roles. In the York pageant of the Last Judgment, the actor playing Deus speaks first as God the Father, then as God the Son; in each role he explicitly refers to the other. To make a visual distinction between the two roles, the actor simply needed to remove the mask worn for the part of God the Father— the use of a single actor economically indicates the unity of God, while the mask allows a necessary theological distinction.

Whenever an offstage costume change is required, the onstage action must last long enough to cover the time needed for the change. One function of double plots and seemingly irrelevant clown scenes is to supply the necessary time. Heywood, for instance, accommodates extensive costume changes in both plots of *A Woman Killed with Kindness* by having the actors belonging to each plot alternate long scenes throughout the play. Onstage fighting, processions, music, and dance all allow relatively flexible amounts of time for offstage costume changes. *The Tide Tarrieth No Man* specifically directs two characters to fight "to prolong the time" while the doubling player of a female role "maketh her ready" (Wapull, 1118 sd).

When a play's clothing cues are not accurate about sex or status, the audience can follow the play's action only if it is told that already familiar characters wear the changed costumes. This is the case, for example, when girls such as Shakespeare's Portia, Rosalind, Viola, and Imogen dress as men; when Fitzwater, a noble in Munday's *Downfall of Robert Earl of Huntingdon*, masquerades as a blind man; or when the title character in Chapman's *Blind Beggar of Alexandria* switches among his four identities as the beggar, a usurer, a count, and a duke.

Scripts distinguish between change for disguise and change for doubling parts: characters may describe their disguises in advance (Rosalind and Celia in

*As You Like It* 1.3, Viola in *Twelfth Night* 1.2) or identify themselves in some way when they reenter in disguise. Kent, entering at the start of *King Lear* 1.4, first says that he is in disguise ("raz'd my likeness"), then names himself ("banish'd Kent"), then reminds the audience of Lear's sentence on him in the first scene. Only after it is clear that the man disguised as a servant is an already known nobleman does the action proper of the scene begin. In the same play, Edgar announces his plan to disguise himself as Poor Tom (in 2.3) several scenes before he actually appears in his new costume, feigning madness (3.4); he maintains this disguise throughout that scene and well into the next before speaking as Edgar in one brief "aside" and the soliloquy that closes the scene (3.6). Few characters ever maintain so radical a disguise for more than one full scene, however, before somehow reminding the audience that they are indeed in disguise, thus avoiding potential confusion. In *As You Like It* (4.3), when Oliver reenters the plot, having been saved by and reconciled to his brother Orlando, it is clear that the audience is not supposed to recognize him immediately—he has been absent from the play for some time, the actor presumably doubling other roles, and he is now a changed man, with a new attitude and a new costume—but he reveals his identity well before the end of the scene.

The same concern for clear identification of characters holds when the character is undisguised but dresses inappropriately for his rank or activity. In *Woodstock*, the dandified King Richard and his own brothers berate Duke Thomas for dressing too plainly for his rank and so make it clear that the man in rustic frieze is of high station. In Cooke's *Greene's Tu Quoque*, the foolish servant Bubble inherits a usurer's fortune and orders a gaudy suit decades out of fashion, as shown by the title-page portrait of Thomas Greene in the role (Foakes, *Illustrations*, items 102–3). Duke Thomas's plain dress emphasizes his moral superiority to the king and his courtiers; Bubble's outdated overdressing declares his folly.

Plain garments worn by good characters, sumptuous by bad characters, conventional by wise characters, and fantastic by foolish characters signify or emphasize moral differences in many plays, from early morality plays such as *Mankind* (c. 1470) onward. Most costume changes in early traditional drama, however, have negative implications—a visible rendering of the doctrine that, since God is unchanging, changeability is itself a sign of ungodliness. Thus, in earlier morality plays, only Vices ever actually disguise themselves; for other characters, a change of costume usually means moral degeneration, as when Mankind's gown is made into a fashionably short, and progressively shorter, jacket. Unlike some other prodigals, Mankind does not receive a new garment to signify his repentance—the one evident example of a "good" costume change in moral drama.

Costume changes are, however, used increasingly in later commercial drama to indicate changes that have more to do with ordinary life than with abstract doctrine. A costume may imply a change in time or in offstage action and conditions. For instance, entrance "in his shirt" or "in his night gown" shows that a character is coming from or going to bed (Dessen, 71). Armor, besides its use in battle scenes, may indicate departure for or return from war, and boots and cloak (for women a cloak and the overskirt called a safeguard) indicate a journey. Properties are similarly used: when Orlando chases a shepherd offstage in *Orlando Furioso*, he returns carrying a leg, showing that he tore the shepherd to pieces.

Costume change may also help create or reinforce audience awareness of changed circumstance (finery for festivity, mourning for a funeral, as in *Much Ado About Nothing*), or of a change in a character's social status or occupation (Lacy in *The Shoemaker's Holiday* from soldier to shoemaker, Philip Harding in *Fortune by Land and Sea* from gentleman to servant, Wellborn in *A New Way to Pay Old Debts* from tattered "rogue" to gentleman). In Ulpian Fulwell's early Elizabethan morality, *Like Will to Like*, a stage direction reads, "Here entreth in Rafe Roister and Tom Tosspot in their doublet and their hose, and no cap nor hat on their head saving a nightcap, because the strings of the beards may not be seen" (Fulwell, 925), and the lines that follow indicate that the rest of their fashionable clothing, seen earlier in the play, has been lost at dicing. The costume change carries moral weight, but the staging itself is specifically naturalistic rather than symbolic. Nightcaps might seem awkwardly out of place, but they do serve to hide the more obviously unnatural strings on the beards.

Costume change on the modern stage is commonly naturalistic, signaling that time has passed or that characters' shown and unshown activities are changing: tennis costume yields to business suit and suit to nightclothes, even if the character never plays, works, or goes to bed on stage. Moral and biblical drama almost never does this, but during the sixteenth century, London commercial theater began to approach the modern usage, though often to make a specific point. The change was mostly gradual throughout the sixteenth century. More frequent changes of costume simply to show occasion, at least by major characters, became possible by the 1590s, when London companies settled in permanent theaters and began to increase their stock of costumes and properties. An enlarged stock let playwrights call for more costume variety in the course of one play. This variety trained audiences to expect costuming capable of more subtle and in general more "realistic" signals about what in the play was occurring.

In *Romeo and Juliet* (1594) Friar Lawrence tells Juliet that she will be clad in "best robes" to be carried to the tomb (4.1.109–12), which shows that she wears a different costume for her scenes en famille. But her father's feast in act 2 is an occasion for "best robes," so she is wearing them when she meets Romeo during the dance and plights troth with him in the "balcony" scene, and again when he finds her supposed corpse in the tomb. In this final scene Romeo and his servant Balthasar enter wearing the cloak and boots signaling travel. In a play whose more than thirty speaking roles required most of the actors to double two or more of them, costume change for any other reason had to be kept to a minimum in the interest of both economy and clarity (MacIntyre, 141–44).

Some twenty-five years later, in Fletcher and Massinger's *The Custom of the Country* for the same company, costume change shows multiple shifts in the status and fortune of many characters, including shipwreck, enslavement, illness, and mourning. Four characters assume short-term disguises, and one believed dead reappears so altered in looks that his mother fails to recognize him. The mother, a widow, first wears conventional weeds in a public scene, then enters "to bedward" in the loose robe called a night gown, then resumes the "public" garb, and finally appears in new clothes for her wedding. A rich lady wears at least two sumptuous gowns. One character is recognized by clothing as a Jew, others as Italian and Portuguese, two as physicians, several as sailors, and one as a bawd and witch who dons a "Magical Robe" on stage to conjure. For a single scene an old gentleman and his servants wear black mourning garb. Officers, guards, and a bravo are identified by clothing and hand-properties. *The Custom of the Country* needs more costumes than *Romeo and Juliet*, yet this play has fewer characters and doubles only the shortest of short-term roles. Clearly, the King's Men had more costumes in 1620 than they had as the Chamberlain's Men in 1594.

The same contrast in costume requirements appears between earlier and later plays belonging to other companies, though the nature of their costume stocks may differ. Plays performed at the Rose in the 1590s and at the Fortune and the Red Bull twenty years later, much like their guild counterparts in the two previous centuries, still needed devil suits and Turkish, Persian, Moorish, and other exotic outfits. These exotic costumes, however, were generally for plays about adventures in distant places and times, unlike the earlier biblical drama with its unhistorically oriental Herod; even "otherness" was now played with some attention to naturalism.

Plays set in contemporary England (a specialty of boy actors around 1600–1610, but in the repertory of all companies) were often centered on the young male fashion plates known as "gallants," frequently contrasted with "gulls," who tried to imitate them and failed. This meant steadily acquiring costumes in up-to-date styles for the gallants and demoting the out-of-style to the ridiculous would-bes. Fastidius Briske, the gallant in Jonson's *Every Man Out of His Humour*, appears in three successive costumes, and according to the fiction, the copycat Fungoso orders copies. This meant that the two actors shared two costumes, so the company needed four suits, Fungoso's dowdy first, Briske's fancy latest, and two fancy worn by both (MacIntyre, 175–77). The confusion between the disguised Viola and her brother, Sebastian, in *Twelfth Night* depends upon the use of two suits of identical or very similar "fashion, color, ornament" (3.4), but these at least could have been relatively plain. The title characters in Middleton's *Your Five Gallants* are really a used-clothing broker and four con-men, all dressed in finery from "the broking gallant's" stock to deceive their victims. Chapman's *An Humourous Day's Mirth* mocks preoccupation with finery, and so, probably, did his lost *Fountain of New Fashions*, on which the Admiral's Men spent between seventeen and twenty-two pounds in 1598, when a schoolmaster or an industrious artisan earned an annual income of about fifteen pounds.

Plays that satirized fashion, of course, demanded that the players possess au courant apparel; otherwise the satire would have been ineffective. The same was true in earlier morality plays, which used fashionable costume to identify characters who practiced fashionable vices: the Vice in Fulwell's *Like Will to Like* (1568) is named Nichol Newfangle, and the ruffian Tom Tosspot refers to his own wearing of "new-fangled fashions" (l. 238); a full century earlier, the play of *Mankind* included a character named New Guise. Both Newfangle and New Guise are also explicitly associated with effeminacy, as were the fashionable seventeenth-century gallants who were denounced in *Haec Vir* for preening themselves in the public theaters.

Costumes in current fashion could also be necessary to plays that had neither a satirical nor a specifically moral or didactic intent. Fletcher's late comedy *The Wild Goose Chase* (between 1621 and 1625), Shirley's *Hyde Park* (1632) and *The Lady of Pleasure* (1635), two comedies about urbanized gentry, and Brome's similar *The Weeding of Covent Garden* (1632) and *The Sparagus Garden* (1635), all set in fashionable parts of contemporary London, use current finery realistically to mirror the similarly dressed people in the audience. Jonson's *The New Inn* brings on a tailor who dresses his wife in the fine gowns that he makes before he delivers them to their purchasers. Massinger mocks aspirants to court fashion in *The City Madam*, whose three principal women, the wife and daughters of a London merchant, first wear up-to-date court styles above their degree and then are forced into servants' clothes below their degree. These plays realistically dress even nonspeaking characters, like the footmen who race in *Hyde Park*, in the clothes of their real-world counterparts.

Craft guilds regularly recorded expenditures for the storage of pageant wagons for the cycles, and for the repair of costumes, but the same few costumes and properties were generally used every year, with only occasional updating. In sharp contrast, Henslowe's 1598 inventory of the Admiral's Men's costumes and properties lists more than three hundred separate garments, including some stored "above in the tier-house in the cheast" and others "Gone and loste," among which some were located later (Henslowe, *Diary*, 317–19). The *Diary* also records many loans for new purchases both for particular plays and for "the stock." The London companies needed permanent storage before they could accumulate the necessary stock of costumes, and acting in purpose-built theaters did not guarantee such storage, since these were not at first the headquarters for one resident company but were rented now to one, now to another. The Queen's Men perhaps abandoned London because they could not secure a permanent base there, while the Admiral's Men (headed by Edward Alleyn) and the Chamberlain's Men (headed by Richard Burbage) may have owed success to their leading actors' being son-in-law and son, respectively, of Philip Henslowe and James Burbage, the theater owners, which made company tenancy secure.

Henslowe's records for the Admiral's Men show how costumes could accumulate automatically. Plays disappeared from the repertory, but whatever special costumes had been acquired for these plays were not discarded, even when not immediately usable, because they had value; they were retained for potential use in new plays or potential revival of old ones. Sometimes the existence of valuable costumes may have led to the purchase of additional parts for open-ended plays, like a second part for the expensively costumed *Carnowlle Wolsey*. The Admiral's Men produced four plays on the civil wars of France in 1598–1599, all of which could use the same distinctively French costumes. (One type of breeches was known as *French* hose.) Between 1617 and 1621, the King's Men produced at least three plays set in the Netherlands, which had to be costumed in the distinctive and well-known Dutch fashion, and between 1620 and 1625 they put on no fewer than eight plays calling for Spanish dress. Though topicality perhaps led a poet to set a play in the Netherlands or Spain, having costumes proper to those countries may have encouraged the company to accept further topical plays, as well as nontopical ones that could be set in Spain or Holland as easily as anywhere else.

Acting companies did not always own what they required for any given performance. On the other hand, some—perhaps many—actors owned playing apparel, if only for their own roles. Edward Alleyn inventoried an extensive stage wardrobe, identifying some garments by the roles in which he wore them, others "for a boy," probably his apprentice, some for roles (such as a suit for the fool Will Summers) that other actors would wear in plays that Alleyn owned. Henslowe loaned William Borne *alias* Bird money to buy himself "sylke stokens to playe the gwisse in" (Henslowe, *Diary*, 76) and "to Imbrader his hatte for the gwisse"(82), implying that Bird owned these garments. Alleyn and Christopher Beeston bought, sold, and perhaps rented out costumes, as did the haberdasher Thomas Giles and his competitor John Arnold, the Yeoman of the Revels in the 1570s.[1] So did the later Yeoman Edward Kirkham and his partner Thomas Kendall, from whom Oxford University rented numerous costumes to entertain King James in 1605. Various Cambridge colleges borrowed or hired a wide variety of costumes and properties for their plays to supplement their own valuable stocks; arms and armor, for instance, were borrowed from the town in 1545–1546 and 1547–1548, and from London in 1564 (Nelson, *Records: Cambridge*, 719). The Norwich Grocers had to hire an "angelles Cote" in 1557 and 1558, and no coat but "a Heare & Crowne for ye angell" in 1556 (Galloway, 43–44, 37). The Coventry Weavers regularly lent out their "players apparell" in the early seventeenth century—well after the last performance of the Coventry cycle in 1579 (R. W. Ingram, *Records: Coventry*, 352, 366, 370, 372).

Under repertory playing conditions, only a few costumes were reserved for a single role; to minimize capital investment, most costumes acquired for stock had to be usable in more than one play in the repertory, for the London companies as for earlier and smaller troupes. Much as a single woodcut could be identified on successive title pages as representing the character Everyman, Youth, or Hick Scorner, so too could a single costume serve to represent a succession of generic characters. Still, both Henslowe's and Alleyn's inventories show that some costumes were identified with particular characters—"Tamerlanes breches of crymson vellvet . . . Roben Hoodes sewtte . . . Tasoes robe . . . Longeshankes seute" belonging to the Admiral's Men, "daniels gowne . . . faustus Jerkin his clok" belonging to Alleyn (Henslowe, *Diary*, 322–23, 292–93). Most costumes in the inventories, however, are described only by style, color, and fabric. If a costume was bought for a new play, this is recorded; costumes not so identified were probably for the stock and must have been bought because they were likely to be usable in a number of plays.

According to Henslowe's records, the Admiral's Men bought many costumes from secondhand clothing dealers, pawnbrokers, perhaps including Henslowe himself, and original owners, including some company members.[2] Costumes for a new play that could not be so acquired were ordered from tailors. In 1600 a tailor received three pounds for making "sewtes" of the distinctive Polish cut "for the playe called strange newes owt of powland" (Henslowe, *Diary*, 135). Velvet, satin, and taffeta costing twenty-one pounds were bought to make the cardinal's robes for the lost *Carnowlle Wollsey* (1601).

Some plays evidently needed contemporary clothing not found on secondhand racks when needed, such as two taffeta gowns for Porter's *Two Angry Women of Abingdon*. For *A Woman Killed with Kindness* Henslowe paid twenty-two shillings to "the tayller for velluet & satten for the womon gowne of black velluet," perhaps to alter what must have been a very fine gown that the company had bought from Heywood for six pounds, thirteen shillings (Henslowe, *Diary*, 223); another tailor made a black satin suit for the play (Henslowe, *Diary*, 225); this may well have been the one first noted as on order for the lost *Black Dog of Newgate* (Henslowe, *Diary*, 224), which was also appropriate for Heywood's tragedy. But though costumes might be specially ordered to meet the requirements of a new play or a revival, nothing indicates that productions were designed as a whole, as in court entertainments, especially the Jacobean masque, and in the modern theater. Like the actors, costumes appeared on the stage "in repertory," and companies may even have decided to accept or commission a new play that could extend the use of a costly specialty like Cardinal Wolsey's robe.

Like costumes, properties often supply information: a crown and scepter identifies a king; an ax, an executioner; tools, a tradesman; a pack of goods, a peddler. A throne on a dais could be thrust out onto an Elizabethan stage to create a royal palace where there had been a battlefield; the York Mercers' inventory of properties for their pageant of the Last Judgment includes nine small red angels that joyfully "renne aboute in the heuen" when pulled by a cord (Johnston and Rogerson, 56). The Coventry Cappers' guild inventories include "adams spade" and "Ives distaffe" (R. W. Ingram, *Records: Coventry*, 334), and the same iconographic tradition that would have identified the primordial couple in the Cappers' representation of the Harrowing of Hell also helped define other characters: the distaff wielded by Noah's wife or Mak's wife, Gill, in the Towneley plays identifies both as types of Eve, as disobedient wives; Mankind's spade in the morality play identifies him with Adam, as well as indicating more mimetically that he is a farmer.

Samuel Rowland in 1600 refers to gentlemen imitating Burbage acting as Richard III "That had his hand continuall on his dagger," a mannerism that might indeed have a historical basis in Holinshed (Gurr, *Shakespearean*, 114, 210) but that is common also to Herod in the cycle plays and to a wide range of morality Vice figures. The difference is that Burbage and his imitators likely all had real daggers to work with; the Vice had a wooden dagger, signifying the inability of vice to harm the virtuous. In morality plays, stage properties increasingly have real-life reference but never lose their primary symbolic or iconographic significance.

In the professional London theater, properties are primarily implements for stage action, mimicking the real-life uses of objects in what Frances Teague calls "dislocated function" (17–18). That is, weapons are used in fights without intent to hurt, letters and books are read aloud without intent to inform, gamesters lay down cards or throw dice without winning or losing anything, candles, lanterns, and torches are carried and lighted on stage without need to give light (Dessen, 75–76), though the fiction of the play asserts the reality of what is done with the properties. Costume items like a cloak used in combat, a glove thrown in challenge, are nonce properties, and so are hats when used gesturally, as in Shakespeare's *Coriolanus*. Musical instruments when played for dancing or accompaniment to a song are not "dislocated," but the recorder that Hamlet uses to symbolize himself is, and so, in *The Roaring Girl*, is the viol that Moll Frith plays when she also makes it symbolize her unconventional lifestyle. When Truewit in Jonson's *Epicene* enters "like a post" after a horn sounds offstage, he is carrying the horn but does not blow it; it is "dislocated" on stage because the actor probably could not play the horn, though the horn sound is important for the scene once Truewit appears. Musicians were available, for later in the play trumpets and other loud instruments were to be sounded on stage.

Properties commonly pass between characters: purses and coins are given in reward or to pay for goods, letters are handed by sender to messenger or messenger to recipient, duelists may "change rapiers," in feast and tavern scenes servant characters fetch cups to drinkers. Most such interchanges contribute a sense of reality to whatever the actors are doing. Some, especially lights, may also symbolize the character's thoughts or feelings, much like the modern cartoonist's light-bulb representing "idea," or life itself—Macbeth's "brief candle" (5.4) might have been purely verbal, but when Othello comes into Desdemona's chamber to "Put out the light, and then put out the light" (5.2) he certainly carries a candle or lamp.

Some properties, and occasional costumes, created "special effects." Among these are the sword that seems to pierce the king's side at the end of *Cambises*, the arrows piercing Clifford's neck in Shakespeare's *3 Henry VI*, and the centaur's body in Heywood's *The Brazen Age* (Dessen, 16–18). Beaumont's *The Knight of the*

*Burning Pestle*, a Blackfriars parody of theatrical clichés, mocked the arrow-in property by having Rafe make a fifty-line dying speech "with a forked arrow through his
head" (5.303 sd). To flay the corrupt judge Sisamnes, *Cambises* calls for "a false
skin" (scene 5) under an outer costume and over a garment probably suggesting a
flayed carcass. Quite possibly this false skin was made of "white" or tawed leather,
like the "naked" suits of Adam and Eve as well as of Christ in various biblical
plays—actors rarely, if ever, were really naked on stage. In *King Lear*, Edgar as Poor
Tom wears only a blanket, but most "naked" characters entered "in their shirts,"
covered to the knees.

According to a stage direction in the Chester Last Judgment, blood flows visibly
from the wound in Christ's side—a spectacle repeatedly promised in the spoken
text, long before it actually happens (Lumiansky and Mills, 24.428 sd). The equivalent pageant at York is less spectacular and evidently does not require a false skin;
Christ instead wears what the Mercers' inventory of stage properties calls "a Sirke
[shirt] wounded" (Johnston and Rogerson, 55). In Shakespeare's *Julius Caesar*,
Caesar's mantle was probably two-sided, like the reversible gown of Avarice in the
Marian play *Respublica* and the "double cloaks" for villains that Jonson mentions
in *The Devil Is an Ass*: one side splendid for the scene in the senate, reversed to the
slashed and bloody side while he is hidden by his assassins, and held up to show
this side to the crowd at his funeral.

More than costumes, many of the 140 large and small properties listed in
Henslowe's 1598 inventory are linked to a specific play (Henslowe, *Diary*, 319–20).
"[F]rame for the heading in Black Jone," "cauderm for the Jewe," "syne for Mother
Readcap," "hecfor [heifer] for the playe of Faeton" and other "Faeton" properties,
and "dragon in fostes" probably mean that these were used only in the named play.
Other entries say for what character the property was intended: "Nepun forcke &
garland," "Mercures wings," "Kentes woden leage [leg]." The plays for which these
were bought are lost; Heywood's mythological *Ages* at the Red Bull a dozen years
later needed similar properties, many usable in two or more of the five. "[O]wld
Mahemetes head" and "Argosse head" (Henslowe, *Diary*, 319–21) suggest that property heads (among them those in *Edward II*, *Richard III*, and *Macbeth*) were got up
with wigs and beards like those worn by the actor of the beheaded character,
though they are unlikely to have been actor portraits.

Animals might be either costumed actors or properties, depending on what they
were supposed to do. Hobbyhorses, used in Dekker and Rowley's *The Witch of
Edmonton* and Fletcher's *Women Pleased*, hover between costume and property;
the Admiral's Men had one in 1598 (Henslowe, *Diary*, 318). In *Woodstock* a messenger rides a horse onto the stage, dismounts, and tells Duke Thomas to walk it.
This may be a two-man costume like the fabulous beasts ridden by the Magi in the
Leuven Ommegange, as illustrated in the *Liber Boonen*—two pairs of legs wearing
contemporary footwear are visible below the body of each beast. The "great horse
with his leages" listed as a property in Henslowe's 1598 inventory could also be such

a costume (Henslowe, *Diary*, 320), although it might be a wheeled horse—the mention of legs may indicate that no actors' legs would need to be substituted. The ass that lies down and speaks in the Chester cycle pageant of Balaam and Balack obviously requires an actor in costume; the Dog in *The Witch of Edmonton* is also a speaking part needing two costumes, one black, one white. Lance's dog in *Two Gentlemen of Verona* may have been a puppet like the "black dogge" of Henslowe's inventory (Henslowe, *Diary*, 312). *As You Like It* (c. 1599) calls for a deer carcass or its head; Fletcher's *The Prophetess* (c. 1620), for the carcass of a wild boar; the lost *Faeton* used a "hecfor . . . the limmes deade" and also "Faetones lymes" (Henslowe, *Diary*, 319).

While costume variety increased greatly between 1580 and 1642, the variety of properties did not noticeably expand, although the number used in plays increased with the years. Weapons, papers and books, musical instruments, drinking vessels, jewelry (often given as gifts or pledges), and money (both individual coins and bags or chests supposedly filled with money) were used throughout the period. The onstage use of these properties, however, was increasingly naturalistic. In Fletcher's *A Wife for a Month*, a "cabinet" containing Evanthe's letters and other keepsakes is rifled item by item on stage. "Shop goods" for plays set in London come into use from about 1600 onward. Heywood's *1 Edward IV*, the anonymous *Fair Maid of the Exchange*, Dekker's *The Shoemaker's Holiday* and *Honest Whore*, and his and Rowley's *The Roaring Girl*, among others, include scenes that require the display and purchase of wares and sometimes briefly mime their manufacture. These plays, normally taking the shopkeeper's side in confrontations with the upper classes, belonged to the companies at the Rose, the Fortune, and the Red Bull, which catered to a shopkeeping and artisan audience; shops and merchandise seldom appeared in plays at the Globe and Blackfriars, which aimed their appeal at "gentlemen."

Where properties and costumes are concerned, the courtly pastime of masquing has an uneven relationship with the professional theater. Some Elizabethan public theater plays incorporated imitations of entertainments like the Gray's Inn *Proteus* masque of 1594. In 1598 Henslowe inventoried "iiij torchberers sewtes" and in 1602 recorded the purchase of "maskyngsewtes antycke for the 2 pte of carnowlle wollsey" (Henslowe, *Diary*, 201). These were probably loose overgarments like the masquing suit used to muffle the kidnapped Thomas in *Woodstock*. After about 1608 imitations of the more elaborate Jacobean court masque appear in *The Tempest*, *The Maid's Tragedy*, *The Mad Lover*, *Women Beware Women*, and other plays, and for these companies needed to acquire, or hire, appropriate "maskyngsewtes." Especially during Fletcher's tenure as King's Men's playwright (c. 1610–1625), fanciful costumes copying court masque apparel became company necessities.

Hall's accounts of masquing at Henry VIII's court, and the revels accounts after 1545, show that these court entertainments always used specially designed garments.

The "device" for the masque determined the costumes: warriors, Turks, "Greek worthies," even cats and farmhands. Probably Revels tailors designed as well as made
the costumes, those for the masquers from rich materials, for their torchbearers and
musicians from complementary but less opulent fabrics or from old masquers' garments. Inigo Jones imposed Italianate design principles on the elaborately scenic
Jacobean and Caroline masques, some of which needed more than one hundred
costumes with their accompanying properties; Chapman's "Virginian" *Masque of
the Middle Temple and Lincoln's Inn* (1613) required more than two hundred specially designed costumes with suitable accessories for the anti-masquers, masquers,
musicians, actors, and attendants.

But Jones's design principles did not affect play production at the public theaters. In 1614, Henslowe and Jacob Meade contracted with Lady Elizabeth's Men
to supply them with a costume stock and required "ffower or ffive sharers" chosen
by themselves to consult them about buying further costumes and properties "for
their new plays" (Beckerman, "Philip Henslowe," 54). This indicates that neither
owners nor actors were thinking of designing and mounting each play separately.

In the 1630s the King's Men, chief purveyors of plays at court as well as speakers
and anti-masquers in court masques, may have enjoyed sanctioned access to used
masque costumes stored by the Revels Office. Their chief actor, Joseph Taylor,
became Yeoman of the Revels in 1639, and so had official charge of masque
apparel. But except for the masquelike black-and-white color scheme of *A Game
at Chess*, professional actors cannot be seen to design their productions on the principles of Inigo Jones. Reliance on a stock wardrobe meant that Jonesian harmonies
of cut and color would seldom be within reach for a professional company, even if
they had been thought desirable. In fact, Brome's gibe at the sumptuous staging of
John Suckling's court play *Aglaura*, "Scene magnificent and language high: / And
Cloathes worth all the rest" (M. Butler, *Theatre*, 189), indicates that one theater
professional of the 1630s thought such extravagant costuming was irrelevant to spoken drama. Brome's own plays could be costumed from stock garments, occasionally perhaps needing something new, as for the supposed Venetian courtesan in
*The Weeding of Covent Garden*.

Because fashion underwent major changes in cut and fabric in the 1620s, companies may have had to spend more money than before to update costumes for
plays set in the present. At the same time, revived plays and plays set in the recent
past could exploit Caroline nostalgia for Elizabeth and James by using "old fashioned" older costumes (M. Butler, *Theatre*, 189, 207, 253). Jacobean and Caroline
masques sometimes did the same; the text of Jonson's *Christmas His Masque* and
the designs for Shirley's *Triumph of Peace* call for figures dressed in Elizabethan
style, but Jones's extant drawings for the latter show that these were designed from
memory and newly made. That the public theaters produced few new plays in
comparison with their revivals of old ones may have resulted from perceived audience demand, but the ability to use existing costume stocks with minimal ongoing

replacement may have been one factor in their business decision to revive old plays rather than commission new ones.

For the sharers in Elizabethan men's companies, their costumes and properties amounted to their most important investment; the accumulated stock might have cost them more than their theaters cost to build—which averaged 673 pounds (Forse, 15). Through its record of loans for costumes and properties, *Henslowe's Diary* only hints at how much company capital was invested in them. When the Fortune Theatre burned in 1621, the building was not the company's loss but Edward Alleyn's; however, because "all their apparell and play-bookes [were] lost, . . . those poore companions [were] quite undone" (Chamberlain, 2:415). When their own theaters had been demolished after 1642, but while they still had costumes, the King's Men could play Fletcher's *A King and No King* in 1647 at the Salisbury Court and *The Bloody Brother* in 1649 at the Cockpit in Drury Lane (R. Bowers, *John Lowin*, 65–67). On January 1, 1649, soldiers raided the theaters:

> the players at the Red Bull, who had notice . . . were all gone before they came, and tooke away their acting clothes with them. But at Salisbury Court they were taken on the stage . . . and carried to White-Hall with their Players cloathes upon their backs. . . . They [the King's Men] made some resistance at the Cockpit in Drury Lane, which was the occasion that they were bereaved of their apparell, and were not so well used as those in Salisbury Court, who were more patient, and therefore at their releasement they had their cloaths returned to them without the least diminution. (R. BOWERS, *John Lowin*, 66–67)

Wright's post-Restoration account says that the soldiers "carried 'em away in their habits, not admitting them to Shift, to Hatton-house then a Prison, where . . . they Plunder'd them of their Cloths" (R. Bowers, *John Lowin*, 67). *The Wild-Goose Chase* was published in 1652 "for the . . . private Benefit Of John Lowin, And Joseph Taylor, Servants to His late Majestie," whose dedicatory epistle names their "miseries" and "necessities." The plunder of their costumes, not of the Globe and the Blackfriars, appears to have broken the King's Men, as their loss by fire had undone the "poor companions" at the Fortune twenty-five years before.

In his *The Seven Ages of the Theatre*, Richard Southern gives primacy to "the costumed actor" over theater buildings, stages, scenery, and scripted plays (65). Dramatic devils and goddesses, kings and artisans, clowns and melancholy lovers become who they are as much by what they wear as by what they say. Where they are when they speak makes relatively little difference: Coventry's Herod "ragis in the pagond and in the strete also" (l. 783 sd); the King's Men readily moved their repertory from one playing place to another. Costume differentiated actor from audience, whether on the street or on the stage. In some theaters, for a price, a few privileged spectators were allowed to sit on the stage. Dekker notes that a gallant sitting there gains "a conspicuous eminence . . . by which means the best and most essential parts of a gallant—good clothes, a proportionable leg, white hand, the

Persian lock, and a tolerable beard—are perfectly revealed," while he can "examine the play-suits' lace, and perhaps win wagers upon laying 'tis copper" (Dekker, *Gull's*, 99). Displaying his own costume while denigrating those of the actors, the gallant intrudes into their space, playing the part of Pride and risking a harsh critique of his performance from actors and audience alike.

Ben Jonson equated Inigo Jones's ostentatious dress with his overemphasis of the visual aspect of the masque, railing, "Your trappings will not change you. Change your mind: / No velvet sheath you wear, will alter kind" ("Expostulation with Inigo Jones," l. 25). Still, the "trappings" of theater mattered, especially in the masque. Masquers entered the performance space in fantastic garb that not even the most fantastical gallant would emulate; when they unmasked, revealing courtier, prince, or queen, and danced with partners in the audience, the illusion of the masque vanished, but it was re-created when the masquers retired into the "scene." On the other hand, while some of Inigo Jones's designs have survived, most of what we can now know of early English drama in general comes from texts of various sorts; the illusion that these texts represent has vanished along with the players' apparel.

## NOTES

1. Giles complained that Arnold was renting to Londoners of all classes masking apparel that belonged to the queen, and that he thus hindered Giles "of hys lyvynge herbye who havynge aparell to lett & cannot so cheplye lett the same as hyr hyghnes maskes be lett" (Feuillerat, 409).
2. Before 1580, the Office of the Revels on occasion gave players costumes worn for a court performance "in reward." Later acquisitions of masque and tiltyard array may be inferred, but this is undocumented until the 1630s.

CHAPTER 16

# Censorship

## Richard Dutton

THERE ARE as many ways of "reading" the censorship of the drama of the early modern period as there are of reading its plays. Consider, for example, the following statements, arranged chronologically, from seven critics, all writing in the twentieth century.

> What would the Elizabethan drama have been if it had been free from this supervision? Not materially different, I imagine, from what it was. . . . The Elizabethan drama was, indeed, essentially non-controversial. . . . It is difficult to imagine Beaumont and Fletcher, for instance, using the stage as a weapon in religious or political controversy; or, to take the most illustrious case of all, to think of Shakespeare as having been restrained by the censorship from entering the controversial arena. (GILDERSLEEVE, 135)

> A system existed to banish seditious, blasphemous, and other controversial subject-matter from the stage. . . . The most topical of all subject-matter, the relationship between Church, State and individual human being—the topic which had kept English drama so vividly in touch with life in the Tudor era—was the very subject matter which the whole machinery of censorship and control had been devised to license and suppress. And suppressed it most surely was. The decadence in Jacobean and Caroline dramatic writing which has so frequently been remarked and debated by literary critics is thus, in my view, due in far greater measure to the censorship (in the widest sense of that word) as exercised by early Stuart governments than to any particular failing in the writers themselves. (WICKHAM, *Early*, 2.1:94)

> The hypotheses so often and so solemnly advanced by many critics and readers of Tudor and Stuart plays about the dramatist's "advice to the Queen" or "protests against the law" or "assertion of his religious dissent" must be made either in igno-

rance of the powers of the Master of the Revels or in assumption of his incompetence or his venality. (BENTLEY, *Dramatist*, 149)

We find everywhere apparent and widely understood, from the middle of the sixteenth century in England . . . a system of communication in which ambiguity becomes a creative and necessary instrument. . . . There is a whole range of publishing in England that can better be accounted for by assuming some degree of cooperation and understanding on the part of the authorities themselves. . . . There were conventions that both sides accepted as to how far a writer could go in explicit address to the contentious issues of his day, how he could encode his opinions so that nobody would be *required* to make an example of him. (PATTERSON, *Censorship*, 10–11)

Yet the fact remains that during King James's reign as in Elizabeth's not one prominent poet or playwright was punished for libel. . . . Since nothing like the brutal mutilation of Stubbes under Elizabeth I or Prynne under Charles was ever meted out despite extreme provocation, I would conclude that it was almost impossible for a Jacobean dramatist to become a martyr for free speech. (FINKELPEARL, 124, 137)

It is salutary to recall, however, that all the plays of our period were written in the shadow of the censor and that no dramatist could unchain his thoughts from the agent of that most arbitrary and punitive instrument of state control. (CLARE, *Art*, 215)

The position of the Master of the Revels, jealously protecting court privileges as much as he sought to suppress "dangerous matter," made him as much a friend of the actors as their overlord. The stability that his office gave to the exchange of meaning in the early modern theatrical marketplace clearly played a part in fostering the unique vitality of the drama of the period. His "allowance" made for a range and complexity of expression on the social, political and even religious issues of the day that was remarkable, given the pressures on all sides to enforce conformity or repress comment altogether. (DUTTON, *Mastering*, 248)

The apparent contradictions in these accounts are not as difficult to reconcile as it may at first appear. In the first place, Gildersleeve, Wickham, and Bentley all write within the broad parameters of a traditional Whig view of history, in which "the development of the Tudor and Stuart despotism" (Gildersleeve, 1–2) is virtually an article of faith, is intimately associated with the fortunes of the drama, and can readily be blamed for various repressive, arbitrary, and probably venal practices that certainly restricted the free expression of the dramatists and may well (Wickham's point) have affected adversely the artistic quality of their work in other ways too. These commentators also write with a very positivist sense that a play means what it says it means, generally resist allegorized (much less deconstructive) readings, and—with the marked exception of Wickham—assume that dramatists as a species were apolitical and conformist, either prudentially or by conviction.

Patterson, Finkelpearl, and Dutton (the present writer) all write in the wake of the revisionist history of the second half of this century, which has redefined

"Tudor and Stuart despotism" by pointing to the diffuse and often competing sites of authority in early modern England and has reexamined key social practices—notably patronage and licensing—in ways that call into question simplistic charges of corruption and venality. They also all write in the wake of "theory"—and specifically at the moment when critics are applying that theory both to early modern texts and to the culture from which those texts derived. They have little difficulty accepting that language has a slipperiness that can be put to creative use, that dramatists in the sixteenth and seventeenth centuries understood as much and exploited the fact extensively (hardly any of them being apolitical or conformist), and that the bark of the regulations meant to control such matters was markedly worse than their bite.

It would be a mistake, however, to conclude that a "modern" view of censorship has simply superseded an older one. Clare's emphases, for example, are much closer to those of earlier writers, in finding early modern dramatic censorship both pervasive and repressive. Moreover, some recent critics have found the older formulations of censorship more congenial than revisionist ones. Jonathan Dollimore, for example, specifically relates his cultural materialist critique in *Radical Tragedy* to Wickham's view of censorship, making it part of a wider social picture in which "the dramatists fell foul of the law outside as well as inside the theatre; sedition, atheism, homosexuality and espionage are amongst the charges made against them" (24–25). Others again have found the debate between older, more repressive models of censorship, and recent, more liberal ones (a version, perhaps, of the long-running containment-subversion debate in Renaissance cultural studies), inadequately formulated.

We certainly need to take into account practices that go far beyond the vetting of specific playscripts. We need to consider all the pressures—of law, licensing, and patronage (the *multiple* manifestations of authority), as well as censorship more narrowly defined—that dictated who could and who could not perform plays, and under what specific conditions. And we need to start by recognizing just how integral plays and playing were to the way of life of the community, not only for entertainment but, more broadly, for self-display and self-definition. This was true everywhere, from the royal court and the households of the great Tudor aristocrats, to institutions like the universities and Inns of Court, to the great livery companies of the City of London, to the guilds and corporations of towns throughout the country, right down to the festive entertainments (like the Saint George, Robin Hood, and May King plays) that marked the turning of the year at the most local levels of community.

In such a context there was little inherent antipathy to, or suspicion of, drama as an activity per se. Nor was there any necessity for a centralized or comprehensive system of theatrical control; what was performed, and who performed it, were regulated by the local sponsoring authority, be that a group of aristocrats, clergymen, justices, mayors, dons, guild officials, or whatever.[1] Under normal circumstances the only reason for external intervention was if theatricals gave rise to riotous behavior amounting to a breach of the peace—which, for example, lay behind repeated attempts in the fifteenth century to ban or control mummings (Wickham, *Early*, 1:202 ff.) But two specific developments in the sixteenth century cut across what I have sketched in as a largely self-regulating situation, in which drama was a relatively uncomplicated element within the national culture. One of these was the Reformation, and the other was the growth of London to a point where it sustained professional theater at a wholly unprecedented level. Most of what we now call dramatic censorship during the period was addressed to containing problems arising from one or other of these separate, if overlapping, phenomena.

Most of the authors cited at the head of this essay are more concerned with the second of these issues than they are with the first. Glynne Wickham is the conspicuous exception. His study spans the whole period from 1300 to 1660, and one of his major themes is that the Shakespearean era is a late flourishing of a long, distinguished, and vigorous tradition. So he sees, with peculiar clarity, the effect of the Reformation on the religious drama and the very real curbs that were imposed, notably on the provincial cycles of mystery or (as he prefers) Miracle plays, of which he argues, "successive governments from 1535 to 1575 first undermined the Catholic stage by ridicule, censorship and threats and ultimately directly forbade its continuance" (*Early*, 1:117). The evidence of interference is quite undeniable. As early as 1532 references to the pope's control of the audience were removed from the proclamation of the Chester cycle. In the 1540s the Mary plays from the York cycle were not performed. In 1548 the Feast of Corpus Christi, with which so many of the cycles and other Catholic plays were associated, was suppressed in England. After repeated pressure from the archbishop of York, the Chester cycle was last performed in 1575. In 1576 the Diocesan Court of High Commission at York gave permission for the performance of its cycle, but stipulated that

> in the said playe no pageant be used or set furthe wherin the Ma[jest]ye of God the Father, God the Sonne, or God the Holie Ghoste or the administration of either the Sacrementes of baptisme or of the Lordes Supper be counterfeited or represented, or anything plaid which tende to the maintenaunce of superstition and idolatrie or which be contrarie to the lawes of God and [deleted] or of the realme. (WICKHAM, *Early*, 1:115)

With these conditions, as Wickham observes, the cycle was "censored out of existence." In 1579 the last of the cycles, that at Coventry, was "brought forth" for the last time. It was a process of slow attrition, which perhaps lasted until 1605, when the last recorded annual Corpus Christi play, at Kendal, was apparently suppressed (Douglas and Greenfield, 17–19).

What particularly exercises Wickham in all this is that he was writing when it was still widely held that the cycles, and other medieval forms of drama, were in decline by the mid-sixteenth century, with little popular support, and that the action of the authorities merely put an end to the slow withering. On the contrary, as he clearly establishes, the cycles flourished to the end, with increasingly spectacular scenic effects. It was demonstrably the case that national and ecclesiastical authorities sought variously to remove the Roman Catholic associations of this drama, and ultimately to suppress it altogether—a clear program of censorship. And in this they were acting against the clear wishes of town and city corporations, who sponsored the cycles when Church sponsorship lapsed with the Reformation, and the trades guilds who actually staged them. The mayors of Chester in both 1571 and 1574 were summoned before the Privy Council for allowing the cycle to be performed, the latter in direct defiance of the archbishop of York and of the lord president of the north.

The Reformation thus revealed just how fragmentary, in practice, was authority in Tudor England. While most people, most of the time, would defer to the monarch as sovereign, the exercise of power was localized and conditional upon particular circumstances. As far as control of the drama was concerned, church sponsorship of religious theater, before the break with Rome, contained local differences without apparent effort; after the break, different authorities—civil, ecclesiastical, local, national—ceased to pull in unison. This division of authority must largely explain why the censorship was so piecemeal and slow in working. Whatever may have been intended in Westminster, it took very nearly fifty years to eradicate the most conspicuous legacies of Catholic theater—the cycles—and even longer to stamp out lesser remnants like the Kendal play. It is commonplace to observe that Tudor governments had no standing armies, and only a limited civil service, with which to try to enforce their will. In the case of religious theater, even with the full machinery of the Church of England behind them, there were distinct limits to how much they could enforce, and how quickly.

The mystery cycles must have been particular targets precisely because they were so conspicuous and genuinely popular. There was, however, a much more relaxed attitude toward religious drama in more privileged contexts, such as at the court and in the universities; the prevailing orthodoxy normally set the standard, but judgments as to what was acceptable were clearly mixed. Before Henry VIII's break with Rome there are records of plays at court in which the "herretyke Lewtar" was a character; after the break there were plays guying certain cardinals. In 1537 Bishop Gardiner, Chancellor of Cambridge University (and never the most zealous of Protestants), was outraged by a performance of the scurrilously anti-Catholic play *Pammachius* at Christ's College, denouncing it as "soo pestiferous as were intolerable" (Wickham, *Early*, 2.1:62), though Thomas Cromwell was actively encouraging Protestant propaganda on the stage, and a play about King John, emphasizing his defiance of papal authority (possibly John Bale's *Kynge Johan*) was performed at Archbishop Cranmer's house in 1539. Catholic sympathizers reciprocated in kind, and between 1535 and 1540 "the acting of a religious interlude of St. Thomas the Apostle" gave rise to an "evil and seditious rising in our ancient city of York," as Henry VIII wrote to a justice of the peace there (Wickham, *Early*, 2.1:62–63).

Under Edward VI the war of stage words intensified to such an extent that a royal proclamation, dated August 6, 1549, ordered "those that be common Plaiers of Enterludes and Plaies, as well within the citie of London, as els where within the realme" not to "openly or secretly plaie in the Englishe tongue any kynde of Interlude, Plaie, Dialogue or other matter set furthe in forme of Plaie in any place public or private within this realm" for the following two months (Wickham, *Early*, 2.1:67). This was a blanket ban, designed to silence both overly ardent Protestants and Catholic apologists, to remove all possible provocation—a tactic to which governments resorted occasionally throughout the following century, notably at the height of the Martin Marprelate controversy (1589) when they banned plays supporting the bishops, as well as those opposing them; playing was also routinely prohibited whenever a monarch died. The maintenance of public order was always a prime concern, taking precedence when necessary over promoting the government's own views.

There were, however, two features of the 1549 proclamation that require further attention. It was by no means the first official mention of "common Plaiers," but it was one of the earliest documents to finger them as a potential cause of serious disturbance; and it was, I believe, the first implicitly to acknowledge that they represented a particular threat in the capital: "as well within the citie of London, as els where." The second point of note is that the ban was not, in fact, *total*. It carefully excluded plays not "in the Englishe tongue"—by implication those in Latin. There were similar exclusions in another proclamation (April 28, 1551). The latter was the first attempt to establish a centralized system to control playing, requiring scripts and performances to be approved by the Privy Council itself—in practice by the secretaries, including William Cecil, who had been involved in licensing printed texts since 1549 (P. W. White, 59). This arrangement probably did not outlast the reign, though the Privy Council was regularly involved in theatrical regulation for the remainder of the century; the fact that Cecil was its leading member for so long must have helped to evolve a stable policy in these matters.

A proclamation by Queen Mary (August 18, 1553) also excludes Latin plays from its proscriptions. The implication that such plays, in privileged contexts such as the court and the universities, were not to be subjected to the same restraints as those in the vernacular is intensely suggestive. I have suggested that drama was all-pervasive in early modern culture—and it was particularly important for the self-promotion and self-definition of the privileged classes. Where, as I have argued, power and thought were neither uniform nor monolithic (however much it may have suited monarchs and their ministers to pretend at times that they might be so), there was no apparent will to dictate what the various privileged audiences of the ruling classes—as distinct from those beneath them—could and could not see.

The clearest acknowledgment of this distinction (though also of the problems it posed in practice) occurs in a document that Queen Elizabeth drafted herself, in the earliest months (April 7, 1559) of her reign. In it she proposes the first universal and practicable system for the prelicensing of plays:

> The Queenes Majestie doth straightly forbyd all maner Interludes to be playde eyther openly or privately, except the same be notified before hande, and licensed within any Citie or towne corporate, by the Maior or other chiefe officers of the same, and within any shyre, by suche as shalbe Lieuetenauntes for the Quenes Majestie in the same shyre, or by two of the Justices of peax inhabyting within that part of the shire where any Shalbe played. . . . And for instruction to every of the sayde officers, her majesty doth likewise charge every of them, as they will aunswere: that they permyt none to be played wherein either matters of religion or of the governaunce of the estate of the common weale shalbe handled or treated upon, but by menne of aucthoritie, learning and wisedome, nor to be handled before any audience, but of grave and discreete persons. (CHAMBERS, *Elizabethan*, 4:263–64)

The queen may, in fact, have written this to appease foreign dignitaries who were complaining of theatrical insults to the pope and their Catholic monarchs, and it may never have been promulgated; there is considerable evidence that Elizabeth's own government actively promoted Protestant propaganda in the theater, against the spirit of these injunctions (P. W. White, 11). It remains, however, as clear a statement as we possess about the general understanding of the regulation of drama at this time.

"Matters of religion or of the governaunce of the estate of the common weale" are inevitably contentious subjects. Yet the queen herself conceded that these were not matters that may *never* be staged; she made an explicit exception for the privileged classes, both as authors and as audiences: "but by menne of aucthoritie, learning and wisedome, nor to be handled before any audience, but of grave and discreete persons." She thus erected what we may call a court standard of what is permissible, no longer tied to the linguistic exclusivity of Latin. And this court standard clearly fostered plays, like Sackville and Norton's *Gorboduc* (1561–1562), that, under the aegis of the Inns of Court (and the patronage of Robert Dudley), addressed such sensitive political issues as the need for the queen to marry and beget heirs or to nominate agreed successors, under the merest wisp of a fictional veil.

Such freedom of expression was clearly acceptable in privileged contexts. (Sackville, after all, was a rich courtier, ending his days as earl of Dorset and lord treasurer.) But as early as 1565 a pirated version of *Gorboduc* was printed; in 1570 an "authorized" octavo became available. The play thus passed from the privileged confines of its conception to be the property of anyone who could read, and it may well have been performed commercially, since there was no mechanism to prevent it. Professional actors could also disconcertingly pass from one status to another— from being vagabonds and masterless men, as in the Acts of 1572 and 1598, to being the liveried servants of aristocrats, and ultimately of royalty. The key element in stabilizing these multiple "translations"—keeping them within acceptable bounds and under the umbrella of royal authority—was the development of the role of the Master of the Revels.

Before 1581, the principal function of the Master of the Revels, an official in the lord chamberlain's department, was to provide suitable entertainment at court. In that year the existing master, Edmond Tilney, was granted a special commission, which significantly expanded his powers and, ultimately, his responsibilities. The commission authorized him:

> to warne commaunde and appointe in all places within this our Realme of England, aswell within francheses and liberties as without, all and every plaier or plaiers with their playmakers, either belonginge to any noble man or otherwise, bearing the name or names of usinge the facultie of playmakers or plaiers of Comedies, Tragedies, Enterludes or whatever other showes soever, from tyme to tyme and at all tymes to appeare before him with all such plaies, Tragedies, Comedies or showes as they shall have in readines or meane to sett forth, and them to recite before our said Servant or his sufficient deputie, whom we ordeyne appointe and aucthorise by these presentes of all such showes, plaies, plaiers and playmakers, together with their playing places, to order and reforme, auctorise and put downe, as shalbe thought meete or unmeete unto himselfe or his said deputie in that behalf. (CHAMBERS, *Elizabethan*, 4:286)

As W. R. Streitberger has demonstrated, the principal aim behind this commission was to support Tilney in his role of providing court entertainment and to do it as cheaply as possible, taking advantage of the growing numbers of professional actors now regularly in London—only five years after the erection of the Theatre ("On Edmond," 23; *Jacobean*, xxi). To exploit this resource to the utmost, he was given catchall powers over players. The provision that they should recite their repertoire before him was an extension of the earlier practice of Masters of the Revels who (like Philostrate in *A Midsummer Night's Dream*) would "peruse" and "reform" anything offered for court performance. Now he could require any and all companies to show him what they had on offer in this way.

It seems, then, that there was no deliberate intention to make Tilney the nub of a national system of dramatic regulation and censorship, though that is what eventually emerged from his commission. But the City of London authorities were fiercely opposed to court control, for they had their own ideas about regulating the theaters. As early as 1574 their Common Council passed an ordinance forbidding plays containing "anie unchastitie, sedicion, nor suche lyke unfytt and uncomely matter" and preventing the staging of any work in the city, "which shall not be firste perused and Allowed in suche order and fourme and by such persons as by the Lord Maior and Courte of Alderman for the tyme being shalbe appointed" (Chambers, *Elizabethan*, 4:273–76). There is no evidence that this ordinance was ever actually enforced, but the spirit of it—listing a whole string of unsavory activities associated with theaters, from the inveigling and alluring of maids to picking pockets and cutting purses—must have weighed with James Burbage when he built the Theatre just outside the jurisdiction of the city authorities, a precedent followed by virtually all of those who built new theaters in the next fifty years. Actors did, however, continue to use inn-yard theaters within the city limits until the practice was phased out in the last years of Elizabeth's reign.

Enforced or not, the ordinance tacitly set the city's authority against that of the court, since in May 1574 Leicester's Men received a royal patent authorizing them "to use, exercise, and occupie the arte and facultye of playenge Commedies, Tragedies, Enterludes, stage playes . . . aswell for the recreacion of oure loving subjectes, as for oure solace and pleasure when we shall thincke good to see them." This explicitly applied to London, as well as the rest of the kingdom, and was on the understanding "that the said Commedies, Tragedies, enterludes, and stage playes be by the master of our Revells for the tyme beynge before sene and allowed"; the officeholders to whom it was addressed were required "as ye tender our pleasure, to permytte and suffer them herein without anye yowre lettes, hynderaance, or molestacion . . . anye acte, statute, proclamacion, or commaundement heretofore made, or hereafter to be made, to the contrarie notwithstandinge" (Chambers, *Elizabethan*, 2:87–88).

The implication is plain. Leicester's Men had met resistance to their playing, very possibly in London; they had appealed to the court, very probably via their patron, Leicester, and this powerfully worded patent now gave them royal protection from all lesser authorities. The provision that the Master of the Revels should have "sene and allowed" their repertoire effectively meant that he had cleared it as fit to be performed before the queen. Who then could challenge his judgment? Eventually most of the "allowed" companies would have such patents, making the role of the Master of the Revels even more prominent in establishing their court-derived authority to play unhindered.[2] But this was some years in the future. Even after Tilney had been granted his special commission, we find the Privy Council (April 1582) requesting the lord mayor of London "to allowe of certain companies of plaiers to exercise their playeng in London, partly to the ende that they might thereby attaine to the more dexterity and perfection in that profession, the better to content her majesty."

The Privy Council deferred to what were by now usual objections to playing while there was plague in the city, or on the Sabbath. Moreover, against the risk that the plays might "containe mater that may bread corruption of maners and conversacion among the people," the council urged the city to "appointe some fitt persones who maie consider and allowe of such playes onely as be fitt to yeld honest recreacion and no example of evell" (Chambers, *Elizabethan*, 4:287–88). But nothing happened. As late as 1589, probably in response to the spilling over of the Martin Marprelate scandal onto the public stage, the Privy Council proposed setting up a Commission of Censorship, involving the Master of the Revels and others appointed by Archbishop Whitgift and the lord mayor of London, with swingeing powers of both censorship and punishment (Chambers, *Elizabethan*, 4:306–7; Dutton, *Mastering*, 77–78).

But this is the first and last we hear of the commission, which may never have functioned at all. It is almost the only time during the period that the Church is associated with censorship of the professional stage, yet Glynne Wickham seizes upon it, seeing all developments between 1575 and 1642 as a more systematic application of state control to the theaters, following through repressive processes begun with the Reformation (Wickham, *Early*, 2.1:75–79).[3] I contend that Tilney's evolving role derived from circumstances and motives entirely different from those prompting the control of earlier, religious drama. The Martin Marprelate affair was in some respects a brief throwback to earlier conditions, with Puritan dissidents substituting for Catholic ones, and that is doubtless why Whitgift was involved here. But Tilney's role was much more driven by the social and economic facts of a substantial commercial theater, and by a conflict of interests over its regulation between the court and city authorities.

Slowly but surely Tilney emerged as the sole regulator of the London stage. But he also emerged as its protector, as the lord mayor grimly acknowledged in February 1592 when he wrote to Whitgift, entreating his help in buying Tilney out of his office, as a prelude to eradicating the actors and theaters altogether. The matter was pursued but finally came to nothing (Dutton, *Mastering*, 78–80). The last crucial elements in determining the role of Tilney and his successors fell into place in 1597–1598, when the Privy Council was clearly beginning to worry about the succession to Elizabeth. First there was an outcry about a play by Nashe and Jonson, *The Isle of Dogs*, staged by Pembroke's Men at the new Swan Theatre; then the City Corporation petitioned directly for all the playhouses to be suppressed, and the same day (July 28, 1597) the Privy Council issued an order that all the purpose-built theaters should indeed be demolished. No one has ever satisfactorily explained why that order was not enforced, but it may have helped that Tilney could argue that the troupe (not having a regular London base) was not *his* responsibility and that it was the Surrey magistrates who should have ensured that the play was acceptable.[4] Certainly the outcome was that in February 1598 the Privy Council restricted playing in and around London to only two troupes, both patronized by its own members (the lord chamberlain and the lord admiral), both of whom were also cousins of the queen; and the companies were explicitly placed under the authority of the Master of the Revels. In 1600 these troupes were further restricted to a single playing place each (the Globe and the Fortune, respectively) and limited as to how many performances they might give.

This clear effort to contain as precisely as possible whatever threat the theater in London represented began to unravel almost as soon as it was instituted, with the revival of the boy companies, the Children of the Chapel Royal and Paul's Boys, whose freedom to perform derived from patents different in kind from those of the adult actors (though both were also subject to Tilney's authority). And in 1601 the earl of Oxford obtained the queen's permission for his men to play at the Boar's Head. But thereafter the situation stabilized and though companies transmuted, or came and went, London was served by four, or at most five, regular companies, all with fixed venues and (with a brief exception after the accession of James I) subject to the authority of the Master of the Revels. Their transfer to royal patronage after 1603, commonly still thought of as a sign of Stuart absolutism, was really only a logical extension of late Elizabethan policy. Legislation had progressively limited the privilege of patronizing a troupe of actors: in 1572 knights and gentry lost it; in 1598 justices of the peace lost the power to authorize performers in their own right; only the nobility could be patrons, thus tightly focusing the line of responsibility. But such patronage had itself been a source of dissension in the 1570s and 1580s, since there was theatrical competition between the grandees, especially for access to perform at court. The 1583 creation of the Queen's Men was partly an attempt to defuse that rivalry. The provisions of 1598 were an alternative strategy, as were arrangements under James I.

Of course, it is true that what Tilney was commissioned to do constitutes censorship, broadly defined. Actors who could not find employment with a patronized company either ceased to act or became subject to the vicious penalties for vagabonds and sturdy beggars; playwrights could sell their work only to a limited cartel of licensed performers (which Jonson, for one, clearly resented); even without more formal compulsion, it was inevitable that the licensed companies would pay disproportionate attention to the tastes of the court and the privileged classes. But alternatives could have been very much worse. The most positive outcome of these arrangements, for those actors and dramatists drawn within the privileged circle, was that their plays were largely subject to what I have called the court standard of what was acceptable. This was the regime that allowed dramatists like Marlowe, Shakespeare, Jonson, Webster, and Middleton to "hold, as 'twere, the mirror up to nature, to show . . . the very age and body of the time his form and pressure."

Very little survives to attest to the precise censorship practices of Tilney (who served in this role from 1581 to his death in 1610) or his successor, Sir George Buc (1610 till he went insane in 1621). Both of their office-books have been lost, but by the early 1590s, it is clear, the usual process was for the master to "peruse" a script (rather than see a rehearsal), insist on any changes he felt necessary, then append his "allowance" to the corrected version, which thereafter was the "allowed copy"—the only version to be used as the basis for performance. The "allowance" was to the company that was to perform the play, and it was entered as such in the office-book, rather than to the author or as constituting an open license. It thus served as a form of copyright, which must have helped to tie the actors into this structure of control.

One manuscript that shows Tilney at work in this role survives—*Sir Thomas More*—while two certainly show Buc's attentions—*The Second Maiden's Tragedy* and *Sir John Van Olden Barnavelt*, and three more may do so (Howard-Hill, "Marginal"). Collectively these show a careful attention to the scripts, often reinforced by hands other than those of the master himself, though possibly motivated by things he had said; the precise limits of a censor's influence are impossible to determine. Buc, for example, seemed to mark points of potential interest in pencil, then he went back through again and marked substantive issues in pen, occasionally making specific comments but often just leaving a cross in the margin, which may have indicated points he wanted to raise with the actors. Tilney's main intervention in *Sir Thomas More* was a strict note at the head of the play:

> Leave out the insurrection wholy & the Cause ther off & begin with Sr Tho: Moore at the mayors sessions with a reportt afterwardes off his good service don being Shrive [Sheriff] of London uppon a mutiny Agaynst the Lumbardes only by A shortt reporte & nott otherwise at your own perilles. E Tyllney.

Tilney insisted that all depiction of the anti-foreigner "Ill May-Day" riots be removed and replaced with the briefest of reports; his chief concern seems to have been public order at a time when London was again being repeatedly torn by anti-foreigner riots (Long, "Occasion"). Later, a scene in which More and the bishop of Rochester refuse to subscribe to Henry VIII's Act of Supremacy (though it is never explicitly identified as this) was also crossed out, so Tilney was clearly sensitive to the religious/political dimensions of the play. But it says something about the general tenor of his regime that he was prepared to try to make a play about a man whom many would have seen as a Catholic martyr playable, rather than simply ruling it out of court altogether.

Similarly Buc, with *Sir John Van Olden Barnavelt*, was faced with a play that touched on a number of sensitive issues—Arminianism, offense to a friendly neighbor state, the depiction of a quasi-royal prince, the execution on dubious grounds of a popular patriotic leader by a near-tyrannous government (where parallels with Ralegh were all too possible). Buc showed close attention to the text, worrying about the status of Prince Maurice of Orange (not precisely a monarch but in the process of becoming one) and about passages toward the end with provocative phrases about "all [Rome's] auncient freedoms," "all free speritts slain, or else proscribed," "the absolute rule of all," "this Government / chained to a Monarchie" and the extremely loaded admonition "you can apply this." With Prince Maurice, Buc apparently finally decided that enough was enough: "I like not this: neithr do I think that the prince was thus disgracefully used. besides he is too much presented": he wanted less of him shown, and proper respect. (In the furor over *A Game at Chess* it emerged that a specific injunction had been issued at some point to prevent the depiction of living Christian princes.) With the most provocative passages, there are clear signs that he did his best to redraft the offending lines before finally drawing a line through them all. Like Tilney with *Sir Thomas More*, Buc seemed to make a conscientious attempt to make playable a work that a more repressive regime would have found grounds for banning outright.

This is all of a piece with one of the most revealing entries from the office-book of Sir Henry Herbert. (Sir John Astley succeeded Buc when the latter went mad, but effectively sold his post to Herbert in August 1623.)[5] His entry, from January 1631, records: "I did refuse to allow a play of Massinger's because it did contain dangerous matter, as the deposing of Sebastian King of Portugal by Philip the Second and there being a peace sworn twixt the Kings of England and Spain" (J. Q. Adams, *Dramatic*, 19). Herbert refused to sanction the play, expressly because he deemed it hostile to the king's current foreign policy, yet five months later he licensed a play called *Believe as You List*, which was transparently a reworking of what he had earlier turned down (Dutton, *Mastering*, 97–99; Massinger, introduction). Massinger had merely transposed the action of the play from the recent history of Spain and Portugal to that of ancient Syria. But this was really no more than a fig leaf; the potential application of the play to current foreign policy was as apparent in the version sanctioned in May as it had been in that refused in January. The only difference was that a discreet veil of historical distance has been drawn over it, requiring an interested party (such as the Spanish ambassador) actively to draw parallels with the present rather than letting them speak for themselves. Incontrovertibly, Herbert knew that such parallels *would* be drawn, but he did not see it as part of his duty to police the intentions of authors or the inferences to be drawn by audiences, beyond points of specific provocation.

There is evidence of unusual specificity to show that people both could and did read plays as I have suggested here, in annotations by Philip, earl of Pembroke, to his copy of Chapman's *Byron* plays (Tricomi, "Philip"). Herbert drew significant analogies between the action of those plays and the careers of notable Englishmen, including Robert, earl of Leicester, the earl of Salisbury, and William Prynne. It remains highly likely that, when the play was staged in 1608, it outraged the English authorities because of its covert allusions to Essex, as well as antagonizing the French ambassador, who objected to the open affront to various French notables. Yet Pembroke took a longer view, involving figures both earlier and later. Prynne, of course, could never have been a target when Chapman wrote, but his reading was not circumscribed by a sense of the author's intentions. As very probably happened with Shakespeare's *Richard II*, the passage of time charged the play with unforeseen significance.

In such a context, no censor could hope to regulate what audiences might infer, and it seems that the Masters of the Revels did not even try. They drew the line when, as with the original version of *Believe as You List*, or *The King and the Subject* (see below), the implications were impossible to ignore and offensive to important people. They also tried to police how actors might point up a text that in itself was unexceptionable, as when in 1632, "In the play of *The Ball*, written by Sherley, and acted by the Queen's players, ther were divers personated so naturally, both of lords and others of the court, that I took it ill" (J. Q. Adams, *Dramatic*, 19). This was clearly also an element in the scandal of *A Game at Chess*, since the actors went to great lengths to decode Middleton's allegory for the audience, including acquiring Gondomar's own distinctive chair of ease. But even without such clues, as Pembroke's annotations indicate, audiences were quite capable of getting the point. The fact that Pembroke was Sir Henry Herbert's kinsman and, as lord chamberlain, his immediate superior, only underlined the limits of what could or would be policed.

What we see here is a working out of the principle behind the early Tudor special dispensation for plays in Latin, subsequently recast by Queen Elizabeth herself in terms of a court standard of what was permissible. Throughout the period, there was a predisposition to allow plays to be staged, under the right terms and conditions, rather than to seek to suppress them; restrictions may have been imposed when those in authority judged it expedient, but these were usually within circumscribed limits. The consequence, if not exactly the intention, of the office of the Master of the Revels was that it allowed the court standard to operate in the public theaters. Indeed, given the way his office linked the court and the commercial theater, in defiance of the city, it could hardly do otherwise.

This complex relationship is further attested in Herbert's careful handling of another Massinger play, provocatively called *The King and the Subject* (1638). Herbert insisted that the name be changed, but he was so worried by a passage clearly alluding to taxation without parliamentary approval that he referred it to King Charles himself, "who readinge over the play at Newmarket, set his marke upon the place with his owne hande, and in thes words: 'This is too insolent, and to bee changed.' Note, that the poett makes it the speech of a king, Don Pedro, kinge of Spayne, and spoken to his subjects" (J. Q. Adams, *Dramatic*, 22–23). If this is evidence that Massinger's freedom of speech was being infringed, it also shows that the infringement was remarkably circumscribed: Herbert records not only what the king insists be changed but *precisely* why, as a record (for his own future guidance) of where exactly the line has been overstepped. Provocative as the material clearly was, what was actually unacceptable needed clear demarcation. It is remarkable just how much could be said before the king himself judged it to be "too insolent." And even then, it was only "to bee changed"—there was no suggestion of Massinger's being punished for what he so clearly thought. There is, in fact, no record of any professional dramatist being taken to task for his beliefs, as distinct from causing offense to important individuals.

Charles I was equally relaxed in the only other instance in which we know he was involved in dramatic censorship, over Davenant's play *The Wits*. In 1606 Parliament passed An Act to Restrain Abuses of Players, to curtail the use of oaths in plays, and the Masters of the Revels seem to have enforced it fairly carefully, as we can often see in versions of a play licensed both before and after the act was passed (in the quarto and folio states of *Othello* and *Volpone*, for example). In this instance Davenant felt Herbert had been overly officious with his play, and he used his court influence to appeal, which resulted in the king and Herbert reviewing it together: "The king is pleased to take *faith, death, slight* for asseverations, and no oaths, to which I doe humbly submit as my masters judgement; but, under favour, conceive them to be oaths, and enter them here, to declare my opinion and submission" (J. Q. Adams, *Dramatic*, 22). Charles was scrupulous about not undermining Herbert's authority, but Davenant undoubtedly received special treatment here, as a result of his position. On the other hand, the whole incident is not atypical of the degree of give-and-take in the system as a whole.

The nature of the censorship regime I have outlined was, as Trevor Howard-Hill puts it, one in which the master's "relationship with the players although ultimately authoritarian was more collegial than adversarial" ("Buc," 43). That some plays did cause offense, and that actors and dramatists were on occasion imprisoned (and threatened with worse) thus needs to be explained. Two factors between them account for most of the familiar instances. One is the fact that the Master of the Revels was at most a middle-order court functionary, dependent for his position on the complex checks and balances of the patronage system under the Crown. His authority therefore depended to a degree on the political stability of the factions, alliances, and groupings that underpinned that system.

The stability of the court was most under strain when a reign was nearing its end. Because Elizabeth refused to nominate her successor, the tensions (including the Essex rebellion) were most intense in the last years of her reign, and much of the repressive attention to the theater that followed the *Isle of Dogs* affair can be ascribed to this. The peculiar scandal of *A Game at Chess* also reflects a breakdown of the usual political accommodations. James had vested so much power in Buckingham that when the latter challenged his foreign policy with Spain, the king himself was decisively isolated. Middleton rode the popular anti-Spanish wave with a provocative but veiled allegory, which Herbert "allowed" in the usual way. The actors then played it for all it was worth and got away with it precisely because of the king's literal and political isolation: he and the court, including Herbert, were out of town. Only when the Spanish ambassador protested, after nine unprecedented consecutive performances, did James finally hear of it, and the fury of his response was a reaction to the humiliating powerlessness it had exposed.

The other factor that accounts for so many of the theatrical scandals of the period—*Philotas, Eastward Ho, The Isle of Gulls*, the *Byron* plays, the Scottish mines play, and others—is the confusion of licensing authority that followed James's accession to the throne. By 1603 Tilney, by virtue of his position in the royal household, was the sole regulator and censor of plays in the London region. But the advent of a royal family with multiple households complicated the issue. In 1604 the Children of the Chapel Royal became the Children of the Queen's Revels, with a patent providing that noe such Playes or Shewes shalbe presented before the said Queene our wief by the said Children or by them any where publicly acted but by the approbation and allowaunce of Samuell Danyell, whome her pleasure is to appoint for that purpose. (CHAMBERS, *Elizabethan*, 2:49)

The company thus formed (its name changing repeatedly, though it always performed at the Blackfriars) staged many of the plays that caused offense, including Daniel's own *Philotas*, for which he was examined by the Privy Council.

It seems likely that Daniel lost his position as licenser because of this, but it is far from clear who took it over. *Eastward Ho*, another Blackfriars play, caused offense to the Scots at court, but what really exposed Jonson and Chapman to serious threats of mutilation was that the play proved not to have been licensed at all; a letter from Chapman to the earl of Suffolk suggests that he, as lord chamberlain, was needed to issue the license. When reincorporated as the Children of the Queen's Revels in 1610, their new patent (like that of the King's Men) mentioned no licenser. This may mean that they were self-evidently under the authority of the Master of the Revels, and perhaps had been for some time. But the successive theatrical scandals to which they had been party strongly suggests different standards, some of which may be laid at the door of Queen Anne herself. In 1604 the French ambassador wrote of the king "whom the comedians of the metropolis bring upon the stage, whose wife attends these representations in order to enjoy the laugh against her husband" (Chambers, *Elizabethan*, 1:325). Tacitly or otherwise, the queen's patronage may have sanctioned more provocative drama here than elsewhere (Lewalski, *Writing*, 15–43).

Whatever the case, the theatrical effect of tension in the royal family seems to have died down by the time Sir George Buc succeeded Tilney in 1610. That transition also ended another confused area of authority. In 1607 Buc began licensing plays *for the press*. Since 1586 all such licensing had been in the hands of the church Court of High Commission. In practice most licenses—without which the Stationers' Company was not supposed to sanction registration and publication— were granted by a panel of junior clerics. But the Bishops' Ban of 1599 called attention to the fact that some playbooks were slipping through without licenses— *Richard II* is a famous example—and attempted to close the loophole. It is not clear how Buc acquired the authority to license; he held the reversion to the Mastership of the Revels from 1603, but there is no good evidence that he ever served alongside Tilney. Tilney himself licensed only one play for the press (as distinct from for performance) after Buc had done so, but again his authority is not clear. There may have been competition between the two men, rather than cooperation.

In any case, when Buc succeeded Tilney, powers of licensing plays for the stage and for the press were finally vested in one man (though they were separate processes, for which he received separate fees). But it was a solution reached less by an authoritarian government determined to censor the theater than by the opportunistic evolution of the role of the Master of the Revels from a provider of court entertainment to the supervisor of the theatrical industry throughout the capital—and beyond. As early as 1600, there is a record in Norwich of "a Lycens made by Edmond Tylney esquire Master of the Revells for the shewinge of a beast called A Basehooke" (Galloway, 115). Tilney was exploiting the terms of his 1581 patent in a way almost certainly not foreseen when it was granted, and progressively expanding his income and authority.

In doing so, he exported the tensions seen earlier between the court and the City of London to the provinces. Certainly it is apparent that in Norwich by around 1620 the city authorities resented the privileges that actors claimed as part of their licenses. The city attempted repeatedly to buy off the actors for a flat fee, rather than allowing them to perform, and on other occasions officials challenged suspect licenses. The fact that some players' licenses were emanating from court without the authority of the Revels Office led the lord chamberlain in 1622 (William, earl of Pembroke, elder brother of Philip), to issue a warrant insisting that civic officials respect only licenses sealed by the Master of the Revels (Galloway, 188–89).

Problems nevertheless persisted. In April 1624 Francis Wambus and Lady Elizabeth's Men ran into a direct confrontation with the Norwich authorities, who refused to recognize their license, though it had the king's signature and the Privy Seal (Galloway, 180–83; Burt, " 'Licensed,' " 529–30). Wambus tried to make an issue of it, answering "that he would make tryall what he might doe by the kinges authority for he said he would play," and he was committed to jail. The following month, when

> Ellis Gest brought into this Court a lycence under the hand & seale of Sir Henry Hobart maister of the Revelles . . . they were not permitted to play But in regard of the honorable respect which this City beareth to the right honorable the Lord Chamberlyn and Sir Henry Hobart there ys given unto them as a gratuety xx s.
> (GALLOWAY, 189)

The entry concludes, "A Letter ys to be written to the Lord Chamberlyn touchinge players."

These events in Norwich perfectly illustrate why professional actors themselves should have found the evolving role of the Master of the Revels essentially a sympathetic one. It suited everyone—except the civic authorities who resisted the theater itself—that he should have the power he did. The court (insisting on the polite fiction that London actors were rehearsing against being called to perform there) was able to call on a reliable flow of high-quality, relatively cheap entertainment, while the actors whom the court patronized were also a measure of its own grandeur. Where acting had become a thoroughly commercial business, the master's license was a small but necessary overhead, and his interference with the actors' texts a small but necessary drawing of the line: it not only protected the actors from civic authorities but helped reduce tensions between acting companies themselves over performing rights.

In all facets of theatrical activity, the Master of the Revels represented stability, as much assurance as the early modern world could afford of licensed commercial freedom. And by applying a court standard of what was permissible to the texts he sanctioned, he made possible a more free—if discreetly veiled—discussion of "dangerous matter" than was ever openly admitted. He did, of course, represent an infringement of liberty, and it must be true that his presence prevented all manner of theatrical activity that might hypothetically have flourished without him. But, given the pressures exerted by the Reformation and the growth of London, the alternatives to a Master of the Revels could have been very much more repressive and very much less accommodating to the theatrical profession (as the Commonwealth ironically demonstrated). The link that the Master represented between royal power and commercial self-interest actually made him a peculiarly English figure of compromise, allowing in practice considerable freedom of expression, as long as it was exercised—and paid for— within the circle of his authority.

NOTES

1. This local regulation remained the norm in various areas of theatrical activity, such as civic pageantry. When Thomas Dekker encountered resistance to the line "Troy is now no more a city" in his contribution to James I's formal entry to the city of London in 1604, it is clear that his problem was the literal-mindedness of the civic worthies appointed to supervise the pageants, rather than an externally imposed censor. See Dutton, *Jacobean*, 9, 73.

2. A striking exception to patents invoking the authority of the Master of the Revels is the fact that he is never mentioned in any of those relating to the King's Men, though it is beyond dispute that they were subject to it; perhaps it was taken to be self-evident. See Dutton, *Mastering*, 157–59.

3. For an unusual late involvement of the Church in dramatic censorship, see Martin Butler, "Ecclesiastical Censorship of Early Stuart Drama," which discusses Jonson's *Magnetic Lady*, acted in 1632.

4. See Wickham, "Privy Council," for an explanation of why the order was not enforced, though I do not find the explanation entirely convincing.

5. Dutton, "Patronage"; Bawcutt, "Evidence." On the state of our knowledge of Sir Henry Herbert's office-book, see Bawcutt, "Craven Ord" and "New Revels Documents."

CHAPTER 17

# Audiences:
# Investigation, Interpretation, Invention

*Ann Jennalie Cook*

How is't possible to suffice
So many ears, so many eyes?
Some in wit, and some in shows
Take delight, and some in clothes.
Some for mirth they chiefly come,
Some for passion, — for both some;
Some for lascivious meetings, that's their arrant;
Some to detract, and ignorance their warrant.
How is't possible to please
Opinion toss'd in such wild seas?
— (MIDDLETON, *Works*, 4:281)

LIKE SO MUCH of theater history, the status of the audiences
remains a vexed issue — "Opinion toss'd in such wild seas." Part of the difficulty
derives from lack of evidence, part from inadequate interpretation of the limited
evidence available, and part from the subordination of evidence to preconceptions
about those who attended performances. To provide an overview without oversim-
plifying may be impossible in a single brief essay. Nonetheless, several broad, if
complicated, matters require consideration to develop even a preliminary understanding of this subject. First, the nature of the extant information needs some
assessment. Second, a discussion of aspects on which scholars agree must provide
a basis for the third and most controversial analysis — that of the disputed ideas
about the audiences.

Despite the continuing flow of discoveries by theater historians, the primary evidence for the audiences is a body of references at once contradictory and fragmentary. All the major investigations, from Alfred Harbage to Ann Jennalie Cook
to Andrew Gurr, have shared the same materials: legal records, diaries, sermons,
satires, letters, government orders, jokes, complaints, pamphlets, household accounts, poems, drawings, epilogues and prologues, prefaces and dedications, marginal notes, builders' contracts, reports of foreigners, the plays themselves. Most of
these data are gathered in the Malone Society *Collections*, E. K. Chambers's *The*

*Elizabethan Stage*, Gerald Eades Bentley's *The Jacobean and Caroline Stage*, and Glynne Wickham's *Early English Stages*, though accretions and revisions continue to appear.

In time, a good deal more light will shine on the period, particularly after the Records of Early English Drama (REED) all make their way into print. At the moment, audiences outside London (including those on the Continent) present the largest single area for further work. Dramatic activity at the Tudor courts of Henry VIII, Edward VI, and Mary has not yet received the scrutiny given to performances for Elizabeth, James I, or Charles I, nor does a systematic study of theatrical presentations to the livery companies and Inns of Court seem likely until REED's London volumes appear. Valuable research by Alan H. Nelson and others has dealt with spectators who watched university plays, yet more work on these audiences is also in order. While the emergence of professional companies and purpose-built sites for entertaining the paying public altered the dynamics between players and audiences that had prevailed from 1500 to 1570 or so, scholars need to determine the precise nature of that alteration. The evidence presently gives no definitive answers to many pressing questions, especially those related to the frequency of attendance, the sizes of audiences, the economics of playgoing, or the social composition of spectators at the large open-air houses. Since all written sources derive from those who had access to education, they perpetuate an inherent bias toward the centers rather than the margins of social power. Financial, architectural, archaeological, and other indirect testimony can partially correct the inevitable distortions of texts, but even the soundest inferences need to be offered with a degree of reservation.

Unquestionably people attended presentations in many different kinds of spaces from 1500 to 1650, and the professional players adapted to virtually any setting and to any set of spectators. Some drama aimed at small, exclusive audiences. Alvin Kernan points out that Shakespeare's company had at least 254 court performances between 1594 and 1612 (106), but they went to many different royal residences. Thus in the first Christmas season of James's reign, the King's Men played at Wilton House on December 2, 1603, but later gave five performances at Hampton Court when the celebrations transferred there (Barroll, *Politics*, 63, 67). All the Tudor and early Stuart courts expected diversions, not only during the holidays that lasted from Advent through Shrovetide but also on progresses and on special occasions, such as Henry VIII's Latin interlude for the French embassy on November 10, 1527, or the visit of Christian IV of Denmark in July and August 1606. The ever-parsimonious Elizabeth welcomed plays financed by her courtiers, though she also watched performances by the Children of Paul's and of the Chapel Royal as well as the adult Queen's Men. No such economy restrained the court of Charles I in its thirst for lavish masques.

In noble if not royal venues, the aristocracy routinely considered the drama a natural part of their existence. Suzanne Westfall has recently explored the roles of acting troupes, singers, and chapel performers in several aristocratic households, religious establishments, and other private venues during the early part of this period. She emphasizes the variety of presentations, their ties to special occasions and familiar stages, and their involvement in patrons' political agendas. The companies of Leicester, Oxford, Derby, and many other noblemen played to private audiences at estates throughout England. In 1600, Lord Clifford invited friends and neighbors at Skipton to see a play in his home at Londesborough (Wasson, "Elizabethan," 55), and in 1605 John Chamberlain attended a play at Sir Walter Cope's, where Chamberlain "had to squire his daughter about, till he was weary" (quoted in Cook, *Privileged,* 112). Countless other records attest to the practice of performing before such elite audiences both in the country and in London. In the city the lord mayor, Sir Edward Hoby, the earl of Southampton, and many other men of wealth and power provided dramatic fare for their guests.

Two entrenched areas of theatrical activity had always offered various kinds of theatrical pleasures—the schools and the Inns of Court. Studying grammar involved recitations from Plautus or Terence, while year after year the university community wrote, acted, and watched plays in Latin and eventually in English. According to some, the custom was deplorable.

> Who then most commonly doe compose their Playes? Idle branes, that affect not their better studies. Who are the Actors? Gentle-bloods, and lusty swash-bucklers, such as prefer an ounce of vaine-glorie, ostentation, and strutting on the Stage, before a pound of learning. . . . And who are the spectators? but such like as both Poets and Actors are, euen such as reckon no more of their studies, then *spend-all* Gentlemen of their cast sutes. (HEYWOOD, *Refutation,* C2)

Nonetheless, the popularity of the drama was so strong that Queen's College, Cambridge, set up its scaffolding annually for ninety years, and other colleges followed much the same pattern. Certainly both universities considered plays appropriate fare for the visits of sovereigns. As for the Inns of Court, London's legal institutions enjoyed productions by their own members as well as professional groups. *Gorboduc,* the first English tragedy in blank verse, was written by two Inner Templers, Thomas Norton and Thomas Sackville. Christmas revels featured Shakespeare's *Comedy of Errors* and *Twelfth Night* in the long history of drama at these prestigious enclaves.

Alongside such presentations for the few, however, were those that the larger populace could attend. Certainly Westfall's appendixes giving the sizes and movements of early Tudor player troupes (210–12, 216–19) indicate a wider range of audiences, as does Sally-Beth MacLean's work. So does the persistence of outdoor religious drama from the late fourteenth century virtually to the end of the sixteenth century, as well as traditional holiday revels. Playing locales included provincial guild halls, inn yards, churches, roofed "private" playhouses, and after 1576 the great open-air "public" theaters—in short, any place large enough to accommodate both spectators and a scaffold for acting. In London, the Bel Savage, Cross Keys, Bell, and Bull inns all hosted professional adult troupes by the 1570s, while at least one boys' company performed until 1590, with two available between 1577 and 1582. A country gentleman named William Darrell, for example, paid six pence to see the children at Paul's in 1589 (H. Hall, 211), and John Florio's *First Fruites* (1578) suggests going "To a playe at the Bull" (A1).

With the construction of permanent houses, however, performances eventually moved out of the inn yards and into a series of structures intended solely for paying audiences. In less than sixty years, seventeen theaters were built or rebuilt in London. Playgoers initially could go to the Theatre or Curtain to the north, a bit later to the Rose or Swan south across the Thames, and to the Boar's Head toward the east. Then a second generation of playhouses arose, with the Globe and Hope (mostly used for bear baiting) on the south bank, the Red Bull and Fortune north of London's walls. At the turn of the century troupes of children began performing within the city itself at Blackfriars and Paul's, where patrons could enjoy the comfort of a smaller roofed building. After Shakespeare's company replaced the boys at Blackfriars in 1609, spectators could see the King's Men inside during the long cold season and outside at the Globe from May to September. Other adult companies soon sprang up at Salisbury Court and Cockpit/Phoenix. Shortly before the closing of the theaters, audiences had a rather restricted choice among commercial playhouses—the open-air Red Bull and Fortune, the enclosed Salisbury Court and Cockpit/Phoenix, or the Blackfriars/Globe alternation.

Despite the wide variety of playing places, from about the 1570s onward, a sharp line divided audiences at the theaters, inn yards, or other profit-oriented venues from those at court, noble houses, universities, Inns of Court, and similar private locales. While the doors to private productions firmly shut out the general public, the commercial sites also shut out those in that public who did not pay to get in. At the public places, playgoers were customers; in the private places, they were guests. Public stages separated the paid professional performers from the paying onlookers; private theatricals could allow spectators to become actors or dramatists. Yet some members of the restricted audiences always invaded the spaces of popular audiences. From Edmund Spenser, teased in 1578 for attending "the Theater, or sum other paintid stage whereat thou and thy lively copesmates in London maye lawghe ther mouthes and bellyes full for pence or twoepence apeece" (Harvey, 68), to the four visits of Queen Henrietta Maria to Blackfriars in the mid-1630s, the elite could and did patronize drama outside their own circles. Drama within those circles, however, entertained only themselves. Thus, besides the variety of locations for performance that characterized the period, the fundamental split between exclusive and inclusive groups was also an important factor, as was the one-way traffic from the former to the latter.

Within virtually every theatrical setting, places were determined according to some hierarchical rationale, though the rationales might vary from one place to another. The best positions were not necessarily those with the best view of the actors but rather those where a spectator could be seen most prominently by the rest of the audience. The sovereign sat on a raised dais either centered before the stage at court performances or, at the universities, for instance, directly on the stage. Around but never ahead of the royal throne, onlookers watched both their ruler and the players from various areas in the rest of the hall. The proximity of spectators to the throne or to the other individuals of most importance depended upon status. Hence Trinity College set down regulations for placement and also for entrance when the chancellor of Cambridge University entertained foreign ambassadors on September 23, 1629. Among other rules, he decreed

> that noe Scholler vnder a Master of Arts doe presume to take any place aboue the lower rayle, or barr, either vppon the ground, or the side scaffolds. The space aboue the said barr vnto the stage with the scaffolds one [=on] both sides, to be for the Regents in their caps, hoods, & habits, & for the ffellow commoners; The space vppon the ground beyond the stage, & the scaffold aboue at the end of the hall, for non Regents, & Knights eldest sonnes. Yet soe, that they allsoe leaue the lowest seat of the said scaffold, at the end of the hall, with both the side scaffolds, which reach to the stage, for the doctors, & for such Courtiers, as shall not sit with the Chancellor, & the Embassador. (NELSON, *Early*, 40)

At the private performances, displacement from one's assigned status was unacceptable. When Queen Anna's brother, the duke of Holstein, took the seat intended for the Venetian ambassador at an entertainment in his honor, the offended guest left and the members of the royal family had to apologize in person (Barroll, "Locating"). A similar transgression occurred at the famous Gray's Inn Christmas revels of 1594.

> When the Ambassador was placed . . . there arose such a disordered Tumult and Crowd upon the Stage, that there was no Opportunity to effect that which was intended: There came so great a number of worshipful Personages upon the Stage, that might not be displaced; and Gentlewomen, whose Sex did privilege them from Violence, that . . . at length there was no hope of Redress for that present. The Lord Ambassador and his Train thought that they were not so kindly entertained, as was before expected, and thereupon would not stay any longer at that time, but departed, in a sort, discontented and displeased. (GREG, *Gesta*, 22)

At commercial locations, where placement depended on payment, money could overturn rank. According to the classic description of the system in the open-air theaters,

> There are different galleries and places . . . where the seating is better and more comfortable and therefore more expensive. For whoever cares to stand below only pays

one English penny, but if he wishes to sit he enters by another door, and pays another penny, while if he desires to sit in the most comfortable seats which are cushioned, where he not only sees everything well, but can also be seen, then he pays yet another English penny at another door. (PLATTER, 167)

Derek Peat points out the importance of recognizing that the audience surrounded the actors, so that they played to all directions, including the costly lords' room directly above and behind the stage. The Swan drawing, the Fortune contract, and many other documents reveal the presence of spectators here as well as in separate "roomes fitt and decent for gentlemen" (Greg, *Henslowe Papers*, 20). In both the public playhouses and the inn yards, the penny-groundlings stood about the stage, unprotected from the weather, while those in the surrounding galleries were covered by a roof. At the indoor theaters patrons sat directly in front of the stage and also on the sides and in galleries. Apparently the farther back in the hall one sat, the smaller the admission price. Yet here, too, the sections closest to the playing area were separated off and cost most. Sometime in the 1590s patrons began to pay very large sums for stools on the stage itself, from which vantage they, along with the performers, could enjoy the gaze of the entire house.

Within the theater people who paid only the minimum to stand in the yard automatically classified themselves as *"Peny Stinkards"* (Dekker, *Non-Dramatic*, 4:96), regardless of their social level, and Ben Jonson dismissed the fellows at the very back of the curved galleries at Blackfriars as "sinfull six-penny Mechanicks" (*Jonson*, 6:509). Conversely, a mere pretender to fashion could, for a price, buy fine clothes, wear a sword, and sit on a stool alongside true gentlemen.

> A Stoole and Cushion! Enter *Tissue slop*!
> Vengeance! I know him well, did he not drop
> Out of the *Tyring-house*? Then how (the duse)
> Comes the mishapen *Prodigall* so spruse,
> His year's *Reuenewes* (I dare stand vnto't,)
> Is not of *worth* to purchase such a *Sute*.
> (FITZGEFFREY, F2)

The audiences as well as the actors played to their mutual beholders. Inside these spaces every person with the price of admission could recapitulate what kings, peers, gentlemen, and scholars did simply by watching the performance of many of the same works shown in more exclusive settings. Yet that reenactment, tied as it was to economic stratification, enabled people to alter their culturally prescribed roles if they wished or could afford to do so. The theater offered socially transgressive possibilities to its spectators not solely in the content of the plays, nor even in the mingling of diverse social groups, but also in the opportunity to display a power denied elsewhere.

It goes without saying that no two performances and no two audiences were exactly alike. Outdoor venues had to contend with the weather but had the advantage of the sun for lighting. Indoor locations provided patrons with shelter from the elements but had the expense of torches and candles, along with the concomitant smoke and heat. Paying customers whiled away an entire afternoon, since the acting began at two or three o'clock and it took some time to reach the theaters. Because there was no reserved seating, at a new play or a really popular piece like *A Game at Chess*, "we must have ben there before one a clocke at farthest to find any roome" (Chamberlain, 2:578). In the winter months, audiences left performances lasting two hours or more to find the day slipping into darkness. By contrast, the exclusive private entertainments began after dinner, frequently lasting until one or two in the morning. While food and drink had to be purchased at the commercial houses, during the intervals refreshments were liberally provided gratis for guests at the royal palaces and noble halls.

In an age none too fastidious about hygiene, the breath of a "stinkard" or "the barmy jacket of a Beer-brewer" (Dekker, *Non-Dramatic*, 4:194; Marston, *Plays*, 3:234) may have been little worse than the odors emanating through silks and velvets, or the "Lock-Tobacco-Chevalier / Clowding the loathing ayr with foggie fume / Of Dock-Tabacco" (Buttes, P3). Understandably, many a thief would haunt "(places of more benefit) publick, & by your leaue priuat play houses," where he "thrusts and leeres / With haukes eyes for his prey" (Dekker, *Non-Dramatic*, 2:326; *Dramatic*, 3:17). Alongside plenty of respectable women, prostitutes *"spread their nets, where they are always sure for to catch their prey,* which they seldome misse at Stage-playes" (Prynne, 389–90; Cook, " 'Bargaines' "). Paying spectators bantered with the actors, blocked the view with their hats, jeered or left during plays they did not like, surreptitiously wrote down the best lines in their "Table-bookes" (Beaumont and Fletcher, *Works*, 10:71), cracked jokes and nuts, flirted, or went to sleep during the performance. In short, the action in the audiences competed with the entertainment on the stage.

The records indicate a looser atmosphere at commercial theaters than elsewhere, but any large gathering of spectators could produce disorder. The rules set down for Trinity College at a special performance reveal a familiarity with raucous reactions at such events, mandating "noe tobacco" nor "any rude, and immodest exclamations . . . nor anye humminge, hakeinge, whistlinge, hisseinge, or laughinge . . . nor any stampinge, or knockinge, or any other such vncivill, or vnschollerlike, and boyish demeanor" (Nelson, *Early*, 40). Even at court, the Lord Chamberlain had to use his white staff to keep order during performances. He broke it over the shoulders of Thomas May at a Shrovetide masque in 1634, "not knowing who he was" — a poet and a royal pensioner (Bentley, *Jacobean*, 5:1158). Most disturbances of this kind seemed to spring from high spirits, as at the Christmas revels at the Inns of Court, or from uncontrolled crowding. At Jonson's *Pleasure Reconciled to Virtue* of 1618, more than 600 crushed in (Edwards, 11). Christ Church accommodated " '810. without pressing' " (Orrell, *Quest*, 135), while at Trinity "above 2000 persons were conveniently placed" in the hall (Chamberlain, 1:587).

If such numbers were hard to manage in the private sphere, they presented even more problems in the public arena. Crowds of any kind provoked fear in a period when no organized police system existed and when officials had to deal with civil disturbances on a frequent basis. In London some ninety-six incidents occurred between 1517 and 1640—thirty-five of them between 1581 and 1602 (Manning, 187). These two decades saw a doubling of the city's population, crop failures with ensuing food shortages, rampant inflation that depressed the purchasing power of wages to the lowest level in English history, severe outbreaks of plague, and repeated alerts of impending Spanish invasion. With so much cause for unrest, the erection of playhouses specifically designed to attract large audiences alarmed those charged with maintaining order. In 1584 a series of incidents just outside the Theatre turned a gentleman's pirouette upon the body of a sleeping apprentice into a three-day rampage that swelled the unruly protesters into a gang of a thousand, bringing injuries to some and property destruction to others before the officials banned performances (Manning, 202–3; Malone Society, *Collections,* 1:163; Chambers, *Elizabethan,* 4:297–98). The throngs of people going to attend a theater offered cover for the mob who gathered to break into prisons and commit other depredations in 1592 (R. Wilson, "Mingled," 173–77). The lord mayor and aldermen routinely shut down playhouses whenever disorder threatened, as in the uprising of 1595.

In actuality, only two major disturbances took place inside the theaters. The first, in 1617, was one of the apprentice rampages that burst out periodically on Shrove Tuesday from 1606 to 1641.

> The Prentizes on Shrove Tewsday last, to the number of 3. or 4000 committed extreame insolencies; part of this number, . . . . making for Drury Lane, where lately a newe playhouse is erected, they besett the house round, broke in, wounded divers of the players, broke open their trunckes, & what apparrell, bookes, or other things they found, they burnt & cutt in peeces; & not content herewith, gott on the top of the house, & untiled it, & had not the Justices of Peace & Shrerife levied an aide, & hindred their purpose, they would have laid that house likewise even with the ground. In this skyrmishe one prentise was slaine, being shott throughe the head with a pistoll, & many other of their fellowes were sore hurt, & such of them as are taken his Majestie hath commaunded shal be executed for example sake. (BENTLEY, *Jacobean,* 6:54)

Yet it should be pointed out that "apprentices"—a loose term that could also include servants and was virtually interchangeable with "boy" (Manning, 192–93)—targeted taverns, brothels, Inns of Court, ambassadorial residences, and many other buildings during their holiday vandalism. Though rumor had it that they planned "to rase, and pull downe" the Fortune, Red Bull, and Phoenix the following year on Shrove Tuesday, another closure prevented such attacks (Bentley, *Jacobean,* 1:163). A brawl did break out, however, between some sailors and other spectators at the Fortune in 1626, leading to several arrests, while lesser incidents occurred there in 1611 and in 1614 and at the Red Bull in 1610, 1622, and 1638.

At the indoor theaters, one finds an occasional theft or quarrel but only one death—"George Wilson kild at y$^e$ play house in salesburie court" on March 1634 (Bentley, *Jacobean*, 6:99). Among patrons accustomed to wearing swords, insults could lead to injury. Lord Thurles, later duke of Ormonde, did not take it kindly when he mounted the stage and was asked by Captain Charles Essex not to block the view that he and Lady Essex enjoyed from their box.

> Wherevpon the lord stood vp yet higher and hindred more their sight. Then Capt. Essex with his hand putt him a little by. The lord then drewe his sword and run full butt at him, though hee missed him, and might have slaine the Countesse as well as him. (BERRY, "Stage," 165)

With a few exceptions, however, violent encounters between gentlemen occurred after the performances, not during them. For example, Sir John Suckling "waie layed M$^r$ Digby, that had formerly strook him, and, as he came from the play, he, with many more, set upon M$^r$ Digby; in which quarell Sir John Suckling had a man rune through, som say he is dead" (Braybrooke, 197). Similarly, Sir Peter Legh, "being at a play, . . . hurled a piece of tobacco-pipe at a man, thinking he had known him; but being mistaken, they fell out in words, and so challenged one another, and he was slain presently" in his duel with Valentine Brown (M. Butler, "Two," 93). Even among playgoers with considerable social status, nettled pride did not translate into fatal attacks inside the theaters.

In view of the volatile nature of any crowd, it is amazing that so few incidents are recorded for sizable gatherings, often taking place virtually every day, during a period that spans seven decades. Granted, on some holiday afternoons, "Nothing but noise and tumult fils the house," and when the players failed to please their unruly spectators, "the Benches, the tiles, the laths, the stones, Oranges, Apples, Nuts, flew about most liberally" (Gayton, 271). But such behavior did not represent the norm for theatergoers. According to Father Orazio Busino, chaplain to the Venetian embassy, who attended a tragedy at the Fortune in 1617, "the best treat was to see and stare at so much nobility in such excellent array that they seemed like so many princes, listening as silently and soberly as possible" (Bentley, *Jacobean*, 6:151). It is foolish to suppose that the actors always commanded rapt attention, for the evidence shows plenty of disruptive behavior, but audiences scarcely merited their detractors' characterization as "the refuze sort of euill disposed & vngodly people" bent on "mutinus attemptes" (Malone Society *Collections*, 1:78; Chambers, *Elizabethan*, 4:321). These people, at least ostensibly, had come to see a play and were prepared to pay for the privilege.

The perception of audiences as "the multitude" or "ten thousand spectators" (Peacham, *Thalia's*, "Epigram 94"; Nashe, *Works*, 1:212) does not indicate just how many could or did attend performances. Even at court or the universities, as indicated above, accommodation could range from several hundred to a couple of thousand or perhaps even more. For some public playing sites, especially the early inn yards, any estimate of capacity is problematic, and for houses like the Theatre or the Curtain, scholars can only speculate. According to Herbert Berry, the Boar's Head would hold 1,000, the Swan, Globe, and Fortune in excess of 3,000 (*Boar's*, 122). John Orrell further refines the Globe numbers to 3,350 (*Quest*, 137). The first Rose could probably take 2,000, the rebuilt house 2,425 (Leggatt, *Jacobean*, 12). Of the indoor theaters, Paul's held a modest 50 to 100 (Gair, 66–67), Blackfriars perhaps 900, with the rest somewhere in between.

However, the total number of playgoers at any one time depended on how many troupes were in residence in London, how many locations were available for playing, and the sizes of those locations. In 1584 the Queen's Men, apparently two companies with the best actors and dramatists divided between them, performed at all seven city venues as well as in the provinces, presumably to divert the prestige of noblemen's troupes into Elizabeth's hands. Yet the consolidation obviously restricted the public's access solely to these players and to the Children of Paul's and of the Chapel Royal. Similarly, when acting resumed in 1595 after the plague closures, only two houses — first the Theatre and the Rose, then the Globe and the Fortune — were licensed for the presentation of plays. By 1600 the number had increased to three. When such artificial constraints lifted, the theatrical enterprise expanded until it apparently exceeded demand. Thus after the return of boys' companies, about 1599, and the appearance of a spate of new playhouses in the years following, by 1617 the professional troupes had shrunk from five to four — a total of approximately 8,000 to 10,000 available places, depending on whether the King's Men were at Blackfriars or the Globe. In a city of perhaps 300,000 or more, audience capacity seemed to have reached its economic limit, i.e., maximum accommodation for about 3 percent of the population, with actual attendance considerably less.

Spaces available rarely translate into places filled. Philip Henslowe's *Diary*, along with other documents of the period, suggests that only holidays, new plays, or scandalous presentations could pack the playhouses. Apparently quality counted too, for "those which play best obtain most spectators" (Platter, 167). Novelty also had a strong attraction, not only in terms of first or revived productions but also with new companies and theaters. When the boys began performing in competition with adult troupes at the turn of the century,

Yfaith my Lord, noueltie carries it away
For the principall publicke audience that
Came to them, are turned to priuate playes
And to the humour of children. (*Hamlet*, [1603] E3)

Weather certainly affected attendance in an era termed the Little Ice Age (Cook, *Privileged*, 189). When *The White Devil* opened at the Red Bull in 1612, John Webster said it failed because "it was acted, in so dull a time of Winter, presented in so open and blacke a Theatre, that it wanted . . . a full and understanding

Auditory" (*Works*, 1:107). The harsh cold of 1607–1608 (Barroll, *Politics*, 159–60) may have prompted in part the move of the King's Men into the Blackfriars. Conversely, the more comfortable summer climate came just when many among the theaters' leisured clientele retreated from London into the country, especially toward the end of the period, so this seasonal custom may have had a balancing effect. Henslowe's takings averaged about half of the top amounts he collected (Henslowe, *Diary*, ed. Greg, 1:13–25, 27–28, 30, 42, 49–54), suggesting that on an ordinary day perhaps the playhouses drew about 50 percent of their total capacity.

The times when people did not see plays are as important to consider as the times when they did. There are no morning performances on record, and theater companies early on agreed to restrict their public offerings to the afternoon, though private presentations before exclusive audiences usually took place at night. Moreover, while some commercial troupes occasionally broke the ban on Sunday playing (Knutson, *Repertory*, 28; Rutter, 41; Berry, *Shakespeare's*, 13–14; Bentley, *Jacobean*, 7:10–15), James I resoundingly reaffirmed the order that no "Enterludes, Common Playes, or other like disordered or unlawful Exercises, or Pastimes, be frequented, kept, or used at any time hereafter upon the Sabbath-day" (Chambers, *Elizabethan*, 4:335). Charles I upheld the policy by reissuing his father's *Declaration of Lawful Sports*, which specifically excludes "Interludes" as suitable recreation for the common people on Sundays. With a few exceptions, the season of Lent also saw performances suspended (Bentley, *Jacobean*, 7:1–9; Barroll, *Politics*, 211–16).

Apparently forty weeks of playing per year made for a profitable enterprise, but a long sequence of plague closures could and did bankrupt companies. Leeds Barroll has shown that major shutdowns occurred from 1576 until the end of the century and that public theaters were dark for two-thirds of the time during the first decade of James's reign ("Social," 34–35; *Politics*, 173). Add to this record the orders to cease playing during periods of civil unrest or following royal deaths, and a rather patchy chronicle of performance emerges. Thus in October of 1605, Philip Gawdy may have been recording a fairly common experience when he wrote that he did not take his nephew to the theaters because they "are all put down" (Jeayes, 160). Since command performances at court and elsewhere, together with entertainments at the universities and the Inns of Court, took place only at special occasions or seasons, there would have been few periods when any spectator could count on seeing plays regularly.

There is general scholarly agreement on the many locations where audiences gathered, on the importance of the advent of purpose-built playhouses, on the assignment of places according to rank or price, on spectator behavior that ranged from the rapt to the raucous to the violent, and on the fluctuating attendance patterns. Consensus begins to break down, however, on the question of who patronized the drama. No one doubts the presence of both women and men at virtually all performances, though males in general and probably young males in particular seem to have constituted the most consistent playgoers. No one denies that the private venues offered entertainment to more elite groups, and the smaller, roofed theaters, because of their higher admissions (six pence versus one pence for the cheapest place), have always been regarded as oriented primarily toward a monied, if not necessarily an aristocratic, clientele. It is also widely acknowledged that after the closure of all playhouses in 1642, the covert activities during the next troubled years involved "young Lords, and other eminent persons," "Lords Ladies and Gentlewomen," "the Nobility and Gentry" (quoted in Cook, *Privileged*, 146).

Disagreement focuses on the composition of spectators at the large public playhouses. In 1941, Alfred Harbage's *Shakespeare's Audience* redeemed the spectators from Victorian contemptibility to working class respectability. His later work, pitting the proletarian moral soundness that gave birth to Shakespeare against the decadence of elitist tastes, heralded a whole series of dichotomies postulated in both the drama and its patronizers. Variously perceived as courtly, coterie, private, or sophisticated on the one hand and popular, public, plebeian, or unlettered on the other, the bifurcation can settle on locales of performance, types of drama, or levels of awareness within the same audiences. Thus Cook's *The Privileged Playgoers* argues for dominance of those with status, wealth, education, and/or achievement, though it never rules out the presence of many others at the commercial playhouses. Both Martin Butler's *Theatre and Crisis* and Andrew Gurr's publications insist on a socially elevated audience at the indoor houses and a far less prestigious citizen audience at the Red Bull or the Fortune, with the Globe attracting both sorts of people. The common element in all these conflicting positions is an agreement on some kind of social diversity, as well as the power of economic forces to stratify, include, or exclude potential customers. One looks in vain, however, for a reconciliation of the differing interpretations of the evidence.

The problem stems primarily from the difficulty of devising an appropriate description for the Tudor-Stuart society, especially during a volatile period of change. Richard Mulcaster sweepingly divides the population into two categories—"either gentlemen or of the commonality" (*Positions*, 198)—but others, such as Sir Thomas Wilson, Thomas Churchyard, Sir Thomas Smith, and William Harrison, make further distinctions among and within various levels. They struggle, as does the courtesy literature, to fix identity within a hierarchical structure that was itself in flux. Present-day designations of class merely import post-Marxian implications into a setting where they do not accurately apply. Nor do terms from the period itself simplify the matter. Is an artisan a hired laborer who has barely completed apprenticeship or a goldsmith with the vast wealth required to serve as alderman or lord mayor? Is an apprentice a gentleman's son or a child forcibly indentured by the Poor Law of 1597? What status has a Latin master earning a meager ten pounds a year, when an upstart player can amass a fortune large enough to buy a coat of arms or endow a college?

If the elitist connotations of the word *privileged* subvert its attempt to designate the tremendously varied levels of the upper portion of the population, then the word *citizen* is equally problematic. It would not include the apprentices, servants, or children of those men "free" of the city of London, nor any of the aliens, the unskilled workers, the discharged sailors and soldiers, the criminals, and the destitute who increasingly crowded into the English metropolis. Theodore Leinwand's recent effort to describe the "middling sort" finds the task as intransigent as his predecessors do. The important corrective here is that any label, whether it be *privileged*, *citizen*, or *middling sort*, refers to a heterogeneous rather than a homogeneous group of spectators.

Both the economics and the architecture of the commercial playhouses reflect this heterogeneity. The penny for standing room in the yard has perhaps distorted perceptions of costs at the open-air theaters. Not only did admissions double at new plays, but even for old plays, the outlay for most patrons doubled, tripled, and escalated to many times the initial cost. When the Hope opened, Ben Jonson allowed "any man to iudge his six pen'orth, his twelue pen'orth, so to his eighteene pence, 2. shillings, halfe a crowne, to the value of his place" (*Jonson*, 5:15) — prices in line with many other references (Cook, *Privileged*, 181–83). Moreover, the Fortune contract, as well as recent work on the Globe, shows that three to four times more square footage was allotted to the costlier space in the three tiers of galleries than to the pit (Orrell, *Quest*, 137; Cook, *Privileged*, 185–87). Investors always got their cut from takings in the galleries, and the enlargement of this area featured in the remodeling of the Boar's Head. Far from just offering comfort to a few favored patrons, the roofed portions of the house produced most of the profit. One must surely question Andrew Gurr's claims that "most of the audience stood for the performance in the yard surrounding the stage," that "the galleries were a bonus," and that "Burbage's priorities at his amphitheatres, including the Globe, favoured the mass of the poorest spectators" ("Theaters," 108; *Rebuilding*, 58, 59).

Too much evidence supports the presence of ordinary folk at the large public playhouses to suggest that they seldom attended. They came in droves on holidays, when everyone had liberty from work, but the companies seem never to have offered them new plays, which commanded doubled prices. Instead, "on Holy dayes, when Saylers, Water-men, Shoo-makers, Butchers and Apprentices are at leisure, then it is good policy to amaze those violent spirits, with some tearing Tragaedy . . . the spectators frequently mounting the stage, and making a more bloody Catastrophe amongst themselves, then the Players did" (Gayton, 271). Many observers all describe the convergence of "A thousand townesmen, gentlemen, and whores, / Porters and serving-men together" (*Pimlyco*, C[1]). Years after the theaters closed, the Fortune and the Red Bull would be recalled as "mostly frequented by Citizens, and the meaner sort of People" (J. Wright, 5). Yet save for holidays, when behavior hardly seemed like that of experienced or appreciative playgoers, attendance always depended on the availability of money and a free (or stolen) afternoon. Truant schoolboys and apprentices and servants, artisans not hired for the day, shopkeepers willing to forgo some sales, and anyone else with irregular hours of work could seek amusement from the players. The very existence of regulations that prescribed hours of labor or specifically forbade masters to allow apprentices to attend performances indicates that theaters did attract such individuals. It should be remembered, however, that the large numbers of the destitute, for whom a penny bought a loaf of bread but not much more, could seldom if ever spare a penny for the actors.

During the 1590s no public plays were available except at the large open-air theaters, so everyone with a taste for drama, rich or poor, went to these venues. Even after the roofed playhouses drew away the wealthier patrons, some who clearly had means and status continued to frequent the Fortune and the Red Bull. Among those involved in a 1626 fray at the Fortune was Lawrence Davige, a gentleman of St. Andrew's, Holborn, who was bound over for five pounds rather than the fifty pounds or one hundred marks charged the sailors and other plebeian offenders (Bentley, *Jacobean*, 1:266). Also at the Fortune, "certen gentlemen" suffered abuse at the hands of a couple of butchers in 1611, and while a yeoman wielded the knife at a 1614 stabbing there, Nicholas Bestney, "junior gentleman," was his victim (Bentley, *Jacobean*, 6:148). Gurr dismisses the 1621 visit of Sarmiento de Acuña, Count of Gondomar, and his diplomatic train at this theater as "a political act of ambassadorial self-display" (*Playgoing*, 70), though the Venetian entourage paid a similar visit in 1617. Even the report on the foray of Ambassador Antonio Foscarini to the sadly decayed Curtain in 1613 ridicules him for electing to stand in the yard with its "gang of porters and carters" because he would not pay "a royal, or a scudo, to go in one of the little rooms, nor even to sit in the degrees" (Orrell, "London," 171). The point here is not that the Venetian did not belong in public playhouses but that he did not choose a place commensurate with his social position. Several satirical works associate young gallants or visiting gentry with the Fortune, the Curtain, and the Red Bull, while the last theater's troupe accompanied a royal progress and performed at court in the 1630s. Though the Globe may represent a special case because of the preeminence of the King's Men, when it burned on June 29, 1613, the company did not abandon it in favor of Blackfriars but rebuilt it.

Other peripheral evidence cautions against presuming that most in the audience had only modest means, even at the large open-air structures. For boat hire across the Thames, reportedly "three or four thousand people" (quoted in Cook, *Privileged*, 191) daily paid a waterman from three pence to six pence so they could attend plays on the south bank. Food and drink sold in or brought to the theaters could easily cost more than the price of admission, as could the tobacco so often smoked there and the customary tavern dinner after the entertainment ended. Only the prospect of spectators with fat purses would have led whores and thieves to pay to get into the playhouses. The sale of pamphlets and printed plays at performances points toward literate theatergoers who could afford anywhere from two pence to two shillings to read the latest texts at leisure. Players routinely encouraged patrons to "arraign playes dailie" (Shakespeare, *Norton*, A3), and many did so, despite the expense.

How much patronage flowed from the more expensive, more exclusive locales to the less expensive, less exclusive ones depends on the interpretation of connections between the audiences and the offerings at the various playhouses. This issue has provoked controversy because some scholars tie particular types of plays to particular types of playgoers. They assume a limited taste, often derived from status, as well as an identification between the dramatic characters or situations and the spectators. To place in perspective the disagreements, which center primarily on the first half of the seventeenth century, one must look at what kinds of presentations played to what kinds of audiences in what venues. Even a casual glance shows that no single form survived unaltered from 1500 to 1650. The masquings of the early Tudors underwent a complete transformation into the elaborate productions of the Caroline era, though they continued to involve only the highest social levels at court and elsewhere. Similarly, other theatrical forms, notably Latin plays, restricted themselves almost entirely to educational settings.

Yet despite the changing fashions in offerings by the commercial companies, certain patterns indicate a shared taste for what became available. For example, all works performed by professionals at court seem to have played for public spectators as well. Leeds Barroll has connected Shakespeare's composition of new plays for James's court to times when they could be tried out first at the Globe "without any let or interruption" (*Politics*, 115; 125–26, 153–71). At a bare minimum, the practice shows that a royal gathering enjoyed the same kind of drama as did the audiences in London playhouses, in private homes, at Inns of Court revels, or on provincial tours. While adults apparently did not imitate the boys' early Lylyan drama, when children returned to the stage at the end of the century, they drew an eager patronage from the open-air theaters without having to create a new following. A Globe actor complains in *Poetaster* that "this winter ha's made vs all poorer, then so many staru'd snakes: No bodie comes at vs; not a gentleman" (*Jonson*, 4:255–56). The interconnections between play titles, such as *Satiromastix* and *Histriomastix*, or *What You Will* and *Twelfth Night, or What You Will*, not to mention the succession of gibes at actors and dramatists in the War of the Theaters, make no sense if many of the same patrons did not favor both kinds of companies.

After the boys lost the war, companies still seemed to compete for a shared audience. Roslyn Knutson, for example, has traced the way similar plays, often on identical subjects, rapidly appeared in one professional repertory after they proved popular in another (*Repertory*, 168–77). Certainly the King's Men got the lord chamberlain to prohibit the licensing of the rival version of *Doctor Lambe and the Witches* at Salisbury Court "till theirs [*The Witches of Lancashire*] bee allowed & Acted" at the Globe in July 1634 (Berry, "Globe," 213). Martin Butler and Andrew Gurr separate the plebeians at the Fortune and the Red Bull from the sophisticates at Blackfriars, the Cockpit/Phoenix, and Salisbury Court. Yet the same conservative revivals appeared at both kinds of houses, and playwrights creating new works for both "remained closely in touch with these older forms and voiced social and political sentiments much more traditional, popular and radical than obtain in the work of other elite-theatre writers," according to Butler (*Theatre*, 185). Similarly, Gurr must cope with the awkward fact that "the Red Bull . . . players transferred every few years to the Cockpit" (*Playgoing*, 174). In point of fact, dramatists and companies and repertories moved from one place to another throughout the final decades, as they had done before.

It would be amazing if spectators did not do so as well. Some, restricted by limited income, had choice only among the open-air playhouses, though in the summer they could see the King's Men perform works also presented to audiences at Blackfriars or to royalty itself. Others, motivated more by habit or display of status or convenience, might simply patronize the nearest playhouses. Still others made it a point to frequent every new work or to see popular performers or to return many times to favorite plays, regardless of locale. Weather or some other afternoon pleasure could always affect a choice. And if someone wanted to see a particular drama, say, *Doctor Faustus*, that playgoer had to attend the theater where and when the work was on the stage.

Moreover, preferences could change, so that as a boy Thomas Killigrew was happy enough to "go to the Red-bull . . . and be a devil upon the stage" so he could "see the play for nothing" (Pepys, 3:243–44), but as an adult he became a dramatist and staged masques at court. If the theories of fixed audiences at fixed locations sit uneasily with the possibility of such fluidity, then so does the insistence that certain kinds of plays appealed only to certain kinds of spectators. Lovers of *Tamburlaine* included "Gentlemen Readers," along with "peasants" and "ignorant gapers" (Levin, 53–54). Alexander Leggatt, writing about citizen comedy, observes that "while these plays are written *about* the middle class, they are not necessarily written *for* them" (*Citizen*, 4), and recently he says of the Jacobean public theaters that " 'popular' does not necessarily imply a particular social class; it implies a kind of taste" (*Jacobean*, 28).

Looking at the audiences of 1500–1650 is like looking through a kaleidoscope. With every shift in perspective, they assume a different configuration. Does one emphasize private or public, roofed hall or open amphitheater, elite or popular, early or late, provincial or metropolitan, persecutors or protectors, dissent or containment, decadence or morality? If, like Andrew Gurr, the viewer silently excludes from playgoing all but those who paid admission in London after 1576, then a distorted picture of the dramatic enterprise emerges, displacing the influences of education, private performances, and the court, not to mention the competing centers of civic, noble, and royal power, which affected the theater just as deeply as did the marketplace. And if there are sharp divisions among particular audiences, there are also continuities that unite them all.

# CHAPTER 18

# Rogues and Rhetoricians: Acting Styles in Early English Drama

*Peter Thomson*

IN THE SURPRISING second scene of *Twelfth Night*, the shipwrecked Viola turns for help to the Sea Captain who has brought her safely to Illyria:

> I will believe thou hast a mind that suits
> With this thy fair and outward character. (1.2.46–47)

A twentieth-century auditor, hearing "outward character," will experience briefly a sense of disjunction, even of oxymoron. Character is inward, a property of the psyche. There would have been no such sense of disjunction in an Elizabethan audience. The word *character* was most immediately associated with the formation of letters in writing or printing. The character is the visible symbol of a sound. It is something already formed. It may, of course, be subsequently deleted, but it is not plastic. It cannot transform itself, or be transformed, into another character, although, if it is badly formed, it may be confused with another character and so impede the clear reading of the text. In addition, the clearly readable character may be part of a lie, as Viola is aware. She prefaces her declaration of trust with the cautionary reminder that "nature with a beauteous wall / Doth oft close in pollution." But the character itself is initially neutral. It takes color only from its context in the word.

If we are to arrive at anything approaching a satisfactory set of speculations about early modern acting styles, we need to interrogate *character*. Twentieth-century actors, allotted a part in a Shakespearean play, are more likely to puzzle over the reasons for their acts in the play than over the acts themselves. The conduct of dramatic action is the allowed domain of the director; the actor's playground is the fictional character's psyche. Broadly speaking, the theme is still A. C. Bradley's and the orchestration Stanislavsky's. The honest modern actor—and actors are more consistently honest than directors—attempts to collude with the playwright on the common ground of a created subjectivity. The driving impulse of Stanislavsky's system was to bring the subjectivity of the individual actor into emotional alignment with the presumed subjectivity of the fictional creature. The dramatic character, rather than the dramatic action, became the habitual object of inquiry in the rehearsal space as well as in the classroom, a development flatly summarized by John Galsworthy: "A human being is the best plot there is" (47).

Theatrical approaches to sixteenth-century drama are increasingly, but still sporadically, assimilating recent shifts in cultural and theoretical perspectives. Meanwhile, for most actors, as well as for the unreconstructed spectator, character as subjectivity remains paramount. Actors will readily argue over what sort of person Ophelia *is* on the unspoken assumption that what she *does* (or fails to do) is Shakespeare's cryptic clue to her essential being. Though the actor may never be Ophelia, rehearsals operate excitingly within the dynamic of becoming. We can be sure that it was quite otherwise for Shakespeare and the Lord Chamberlain's Men.

By the time an Elizabethan company of players came together to begin the creative work on the staging of a new play, several processes were already complete. Often through the mediation of one of the leading players, the playwright (more commonly playwrights) had presented an outline plot and received an advance to convert that plot into a play. The manuscript, in either a single hand or several, had then been submitted, corrected perhaps to accommodate the criticism of the same leading player, and passed over to a scribe. In the best-conducted companies, the scribe (or scribes) had made not one but at least two fair copies of the manuscript. The first would become the property of the company, serving as what we would now call a promptbook: the second, to save further transcription, could then be cut up into individual "parts" and the scraps of speeches pasted onto a scroll, with short cues added. The first copy had, meanwhile, been delivered to the Master of the Revels to receive his license to perform. Any changes he required would need to be written in to the parts, either by the actor himself or by the playhouse book-keeper, if the parts had not yet been distributed.

Only when the parts had been assembled on their individual scrolls could the play conveniently be given its first reading by the company. There is some slender evidence in *Henslowe's Diary* that the Admiral's Men customarily conducted their first reading at the Sun Tavern in New Fish Street after their move from the Rose to the Fortune. Henslowe records a sizable payment to Robert Shaw to discharge his bill there on December 26, 1601 (Henslowe, *Diary*, ed. Foakes and Rickert [unless otherwise noted], 186). The first reading might well expose the need for further modifications. It would also have served some of the functions of a modern production meeting. The responsible member of the company would have noted any peculiar costume or property requirements. His task was to ensure that the physical demands of the play had been met in time for the scheduled first performance. At the end of the reading, each actor left with his part, his "character," in his hand.

If he dropped it between New Fish Street and his lodgings, the processes of rehearsal might be seriously delayed. From the perspective of the actor, a character in a new play or in an old play revived, before it was anything else, was a (mislayable) scroll.

No authoritative sources of information about the precise rehearsal practices of the early professional companies have survived. Peter Quince and the mechanicals of *A Midsummer Night's Dream* provide us with a famous parody, and there are inferences to be drawn from prologues and inductions, as well as from plays as various as *Hamlet* and Richard Brome's *The Antipodes*. But there is nothing to tell us how the individual actor set about interpreting his scroll. As Muriel Bradbrook first suggested (*Shakespeare*, 129), it is reasonable to read in Hamlet's admiration for the First Player Shakespeare's homage to Richard Burbage, but there is no suggestion that the Player (or Burbage) has so rehearsed as to *become* Aeneas:

> Is it not monstrous that this player here,
> But in a fiction, in a dream of passion,
> Could force his soul so to his own conceit
> That from her working all his visage wan'd;
> Tears in his eyes, distraction in's aspect,
> A broken voice, and his whole function suiting
> With forms to his conceit? And all for nothing!
> For Hecuba?
> What's Hecuba to him or he to Hecuba,
> That he should weep for her? (2.2.585–94)

It is the imitation of grief, not the imitation of Aeneas, that astounds Hamlet. Indeed, real grief would look and sound very different from this histrionic representation:

> What would he do
> Had he the motive and the cue for passion
> That I have? He would drown the stage with tears,
> And cleave the general ear with horrid speech;
> Make mad the guilty, and appal the free;
> Confound the ignorant, and amaze, indeed,
> The very faculties of eyes and ears. (2.2.594–600)

Unable to act out his own grief, Hamlet draws the attention of the audience to the First Player's ability to perform grief without feeling it. And yet we are here at a moment of great complexity in the evolution of acting styles. The First Player as Burbage as Aeneas is one kind of actor, but what of Burbage as Hamlet? On the platform stage of the Globe, the actor Burbage is simultaneously contemplating, criticizing, and practicing his craft; and, in doing so, he is highlighting Hamlet's subjectivity to the explicit exclusion of his own.

To conduct my argument in an orderly fashion, I need, at this stage, simply to pencil in a recognition that a significant step in the evolution of dramatic character can be traced in Shakespeare's work. My immediate concern is with rehearsal practices. Henslowe provides us with unadorned evidence about the time that might have elapsed between a player's receiving his pasted part and performing it. Like other companies, the Admiral's Men maintained several plays in repertoire, whilst relying on novelty to attract the maximum number of paying customers to the Rose. New plays were a commercial necessity, and there was a growing number of writers on hand to produce them as the sixteenth century advanced. The schedule for the staging of *Civil Wars: Part One* is not atypical. Thomas Dekker and Michael Drayton delivered the manuscript on September 29, 1598, and the play was given its first performance five weeks later, on November 4. Neil Carson has calculated that the preparation of the script—transcribing, correcting, partitioning—would normally take two weeks, although he has found examples of plays rushed into rehearsal after nine, six, and three days, presumably before preparation of the script was complete and certainly before it had been granted its license (73–74). By about October 12, then, *Civil Wars* was ready to be put into rehearsal.

But there is a snag. On October 21, the Admiral's Men opened another new play, *Pierce of Winchester*, in whose composition the industrious Dekker had the major hand. We must assume that *Pierce of Winchester* commanded the available rehearsal time in the week preceding its first performance. We should also note that the actors were onstage in one or other of the repertoire plays each afternoon, barring Sundays, and that it would have been too dark for convenient rehearsal, without hefty expenditure on candles, within two hours of the emptying of the playhouse. Nor does it seem likely that the actors went without a break from performing one play to rehearsing another. The mornings between October 22 and November 4, 1598, might have been available for the rehearsal of *Civil Wars*—and for the learning of lines as well as the assembling and testing of costumes and properties. On October 11, Henslowe recorded a loan of four pounds to the actor Thomas Dowton, "to bye divers thinges for the play called the first syvell wares of France," the same actor having borrowed six pounds for equally unspecified purchases three days earlier. This piece was evidently his responsibility (Henslowe, *Diary*, 98–99).

By November 3, Dekker and Drayton had completed the second part of the play, which opened on December 9. The authors received six pounds for each part, to be shared between them, and a further six pounds for a third part, completed by December 30. Even with the load shared, the composition of a five-act play in three weeks implies a kind of writing by numbers, a reliance on accepted conventions. To stage the same play after, at the most, twenty-four hours of rehearsal may suggest high efficiency, low expectations, or both. It would certainly have required an adherence to the shorthand of established staging conventions and a reliance on the authors to delineate with absolute clarity the distinct functions of the dramatis personae.

What I am here arguing is that it was by no means the priority of working playwrights to create a gathering of subjectivities—what later criticism would call "characters." Unless their roles were as clearly and finally defined as the characters written on the scroll by the scribe, the actors would be equally unable to read them. It was the material circumstances of the playhouses that conditioned the material of the plays, and the time available to the players was among the most important of all material considerations. It was, after all, the players who employed the playwrights.

The individual actor's first response to his scroll would more likely have been to commit it to memory than to rehearse it. He looked to the language for confirmation of the moral and social status ascribed to the role (more frequently, roles) he had been assigned. Given a clear understanding of the role's place in the pecking order of power, he could do most of the work alone. Hamlet's admired First Player need never have rehearsed the Hecuba speech. It is a rhetorical set piece in the tradition inherited and enhanced on the Elizabethan stage by Christopher Marlowe. All that is necessary for its carriage from memory through private recitation to performance is that his fellow players should know where to stand while he is speaking it; and such knowledge came easily at a time when the decorum of precedence intervened in every public occasion.

The cumulative impression, after a reading of hundreds of scenes in Elizabethan plays *as scenes*, is that very few of them would have needed to be rehearsed at all. Positioning in the great formal scenes is determined by precedence. Dialogues are conducted according to formula and can be rehearsed informally, not least as an aid to memory for the two players. Comic scenes are permitted the greater liberty of the clowns' physical, as well as verbal, improvisation. The onstage readjustment when additional characters enter is as much a matter of daily habit as of convention for a company that may be required to perform as many as six different plays in a week. It was the proud ambition of players to be perceived as trained craftsmen, members of a mystery. And, after all, it is only the apprentice carpenter who needs to rehearse making a table.

The great actor in every age has been distinguished by an uncommon ability to stretch the boundaries of the presiding conventions. It is a quality that Ben Jonson was striving to identify when he wrote his epigram to Edward Alleyn: "others speak, but only thou dost act." But Jonson's chosen verbs have lost whatever indicative force they may have had for his contemporaries. My supposition is that he was distinguishing between run-of-the-mill actors, whose speeches straightforwardly foreshadowed the ensuing action, and Alleyn, who seemed by the force of his personality to make it happen. Outstanding individuals do not, however, best represent the predominant acting styles of an age. They are more often esteemed in retrospect because they herald the shift in style that will become the norm of the subsequent age.

In the emergent professional theater of the late sixteenth century, players responded with commendable energy to the unprecedented challenges of a commercial enterprise. Some graduated from the small companies of touring household players, whose repertoire had no pressing need to grow at such a rate. Others, formerly unattached to a particular patron, were harried by legislation into membership of a licensed company. Still others remained where they were, generally distant from London, continuing to visit provincial centers of population and the homes of regional grandees. The number and significance of these companies, traveling often under the patronage of members of the lesser nobility, is only now being recognized. The impact on them of, and their impact on, the practice of the London companies remains obscure. They were, though, the nurseries of the first professional players, and the skills and customs acquired by their members established, in the turnabout of theatrical history, the ground rules of the drama that subsequent readers have found "great."

To advance a discussion of early modern acting styles, we must retrace some of David Bevington's steps from *Mankind* to Marlowe. The outstanding, and in some ways dangerously beguiling, description of a household company at work in the first half of the sixteenth century is that of Cardinal Wolsey's Men in the multiauthored play *Sir Thomas More*. This much-handled text was compiled early in the century's last decade and its authors' anxiety not to speak ill of the reigning monarch's royal father makes it a woeful sourcebook of political history. But the visit of the players, at the opening of act 4, is handled with unusual frankness. The writing does not invite the company performing *Sir Thomas More* to celebrate its own sophistication in contrast to the clumsiness of the presenters of the play-within-the-play, as Shakespeare's writing of A *Midsummer Night's Dream* might. Nor is there much evidence of an overarching intention to explore the poignant interaction of truth and illusion, as there is in *Hamlet*. Quite simply, the players arrive unannounced at More's house on a day when he is entertaining the Lord Mayor and his retinue. More accepts without question their claim to be the Cardinal's troupe (an openness discouraged by Elizabethan legislation) and finds their arrival timely. The main meal is drawing to an end in another room, and its aftermath, the banquet of sweetmeats, is not yet ready—an ideal time for an interlude. He asks what plays they have in their repertoire. The leader of the troupe names seven. And how big is the company? "Four men and a boy, sir."

More selects his play, *The Marriage of Wit and Wisdom*, discovers that the boy must play three parts in it but makes no inquiry about the amount of doubling required of the men, and welcomes in his guests who will compose the distinguished audience. There is then an awkward hiatus. The leader of the troupe, who will be performing the part of the Vice, asks for a brief postponement. They are short of a beard, and Luggins has run out to fetch one from Oagles. A beard is, of course, a vital property in a performance that calls for doubling and, especially, for quick changes. The historical Cardinal's Men would have come well supplied with beards, and the Elizabethan playwright is indulging himself here. Perhaps, though, he is also drawing our attention to the scrupulousness of this traveling troupe. Any old beard would surely suffice in the context of a one-off performance, but it is the *long* beard that Luggins has gone to find. More saves the situation by offering his own playfulness to the players. The occasion is one for pastime and good company, and the host steps in to extemporize the part of Good Counsel. The social interaction between Privy Councillor and players is marked by courtesy on both sides. (The patrons of the two leading Elizabethan companies were both Privy Councillors.) The whole scene is a nostalgic cameo, an idealized portrait of feudal hospitality from the viewpoint of a professional writer whose immediate task is to sell the commodity of a play to one of the middlemen of early capitalism.

The extract from *The Marriage of Wit and Wisdom* embedded in the play of *Sir Thomas More* engages four of the company. The unfortunate Luggins is denied his opportunity to perform when More is summoned to a meeting of the Privy Council before Luggins's first entrance. As was common, the leader of the troupe plays the corrupting Vice, a role that will receive particular attention later in this essay. A secondary player delivers the unimpressive prologue. His task here is to settle the audience. He will, presumably, play two or three clearly defined roles in the subsequent interlude—though not, as it turns out, today. He has already hurriedly laid out in sequence, in some convenient corner of the improvised performance space, the hats, cloaks, and beards that are the external aids to his immediate identification in each new role.

A younger colleague, perhaps already ambitious for a share in the leadership of the troupe, has the central part of Wit, for the possession of whose soul vices and virtues will do battle. He is required to enter "ruffling" (swaggering) and immediately to sing a song with the refrain "In youth is pleasure." His task is instantly to present an image of the handsome but naive young man. His manifest lustiness may, if he has the looks and some talent, elicit an exploitable response from some of the women in the room.

The boy has time to present only one of his three roles, that of Lady Vanity. Although the Vice has deceived Wit into thinking that this is Wisdom, there is no attempt to deceive the audience. Neither costume nor performance is ambiguous. The boy enters singing and beckoning seductively. Sir Thomas More recognizes the role immediately: "This is Lady Vanity, I'll hold my life. / Beware, good Wit, you take not her to wife" (4.1.211–12). The ductile Wit recognizes only the promise of pleasure. The dialogue of Wit and Vanity is openly sexual, an indication of the erotic currents generated by the boy-as-girl on the sixteenth-century stage. Sexual awareness is certainly an issue. This boy is not an innocent. As for Luggins, he, as you would expect from his name, is going to play most of the ungrateful parts. He is the company gofer, an essential if underrated member of the team.

In the Cardinal's Men, as in other known itinerant troupes, four or five players might have to carry up to twenty roles between them. They would also have to itemize and transport costumes and properties, make quick consensus decisions on appropriate staging in newly encountered nontheatrical spaces, and negotiate with those in authority at each different venue. To fall short in any of these areas would put at risk future invitations to play. Where hazards are so plentiful, teamwork is a necessity, and friendship a bonus. But acting, in its now-commonplace sense of self-transference, is not called for at all. The dramatis personae of surviving texts in what Bevington identified as a "popular" tradition incorporate instructions on the physical conduct of the player in their very names. The player's task is to suit gesture, movement, and vocal inflection to the name allotted.

The twentieth-century parlor game sometimes called Adverbs invites performance of this kind. The individual player's task is to enact the instructions embedded in the selected adverb (*sinuously; grudgingly; seductively*) with sufficient clarity to enable the onlookers to guess the word. To indulge in elaborate, individual interpretation is, in all likelihood, to fail in the purpose of the charade. Success, as for the sixteenth-century players, is achieved by an elimination of superfluous movements, distracting twitches, or false emphases: nothing approaching the neurotic fidget and mumble that led an exasperated Peter Ustinov to instruct a student of the American "method," "Don't just do something. Stand there!" (Thomson and Salgado, 102).

The need for each role to be clearly identified is, of course, intensified in a performance involving doubling. The old assumption that doubling was a necessary but unwelcome chore has been effectively contradicted, not least by Bevington's irresistible proposal that, in the original staging of *Mankind*, the player of the Vice, Tityvillus, doubled as his own major adversary, Mercy ("*Mankind*," 17). Doubling, in drama that relies on bold oppositions and instantly recognizable distinctions, is not a defect but a source of delight to the audience. It is, after all, not Dennis Price but Alec Guinness who makes the film *Kind Hearts and Coronets* memorable.

The view that gesture and speaking style on the stage should reflect the moral status of the enacted role stabilized performance throughout the first phase of the commercial theater. In the morally more slippery Restoration playhouses, social status came to provide a more consistent framework for actors in search of appropriate gesture, and there were, of course, precedents on the Elizabethan, Jacobean, and Caroline stage. But the social status of a role was, in clothes-conscious London, already signaled by costume, the visual feast provided by splashes of moving color in hierarchically significant silhouette on the platform stage.

Always conscious of the moral heat generated by the mere practice of their trade, Elizabethan players strove insistently to suit word to action and action to word, not in order to deceive an audience, but to communicate to it a morally colored narrative. What the audience expects of the actor of Hamlet is, of course, different from what it expects of the actor of Wit in *The Marriage of Wit and Wisdom*, but the differences in acting style record evolution, not discontinuity. There is no reason to suppose that the playwrights of the mid-sixteenth century, when they began to sprinkle historical, mythological, legendary, or fictional humans among such abstractions as Small Ability or Good Counsel, expected radical contrasts in the style of acting. The eventual outcome was a greater flexibility, but moral status remained the bedrock.

We can probably best understand how Burbage might have interpreted the "character" of Brutus, Hamlet, Othello, or Macbeth if we think in terms of "temperament." Renaissance inquiries into the perturbation of the human psyche discovered, with varying degrees of ingenuity, significant correspondences between physiology and behavior. Burbage might have read Timothy Bright's *Treatise on Melancholy* (1582) and almost certainly would have read Burton's extraordinary *Anatomy of Melancholy* (1621) had he lived a few years longer. The evolution I am here proposing is from an adverbial presentation of symbols of moral (or immoral) qualities—"characters" in an almost scribal sense—to a more subtle representation of temperaments in conflict with each other on the human stage. Even so, the expectation was much more that the player should make the temperament recognizable than that he should render it dazzling. It is not only the writing of Ben Jonson's *Every Man in His Humour* (1598), but also the play's extraordinary popularity, that helps to reinforce this stylistic point.

A distinction between presentational and representational acting is crucial here. The performers of early Tudor interludes stood in the unforgiving here-and-now to present to an audience human qualities at war with each other within a framing narrative. "Personation," which proposes that one whole human being (Hamlet, say) can be represented by another whole human being (Burbage), was an Elizabethan development that can conveniently be adduced from a chronological study of Shakespeare's plays. But even representational acting on the early modern stage addressed itself to the audience, allowing the player to slip easily, without performative disjunction, from dialogue to aside to dialogue to soliloquy. Audience and actors inhabited a shared space in the commercial playhouses of London, as they did in Sir Thomas More's house or the palace of Whitehall. The gradual linguistic shift from "player" to "actor" is culturally significant, but it does not carry us into a theater of illusion.

The idea of acting as if the audience were not there is a twentieth-century phenomenon, the outcome of Stanislavsky's spiritual and spirited inquisition of the proscenium arch. It is vital that we should recognize that presentational acting long outlasted the architectural division of actors and audience. Illusionism is dominant in the theater because it is the fad of the dominators. Conveniently for politicians, it is a fad that renders the theater largely innocuous. The early modern stage was, or was certainly felt to be, much more dangerous—a matter that I shall briefly address below. My present subject is presentational acting, the craft of *showing* that entitled Elizabethan players to present themselves as respectable tradesmen.

Some training in rhetoric would have helped, although there is only implicit evidence that such training ever took place. Critics with a primary interest in dramatic texts have sometimes proposed an acting style that prioritized speech in the public playhouses, and certainly audiences, in an era of widespread illiteracy, were habitual listeners. Knowledge of a new bylaw might depend on attentiveness to the pronouncements of the town crier, and an understanding of the terms of a settlement on the elocution of a scrivener. But contemporary comment on performance rarely mentions speech in isolation from action. Bulwer's impressive *Chironomia: or, the art of manuall rhetorique* (1644) carries a frontispiece showing two Roman actors instructing Cicero and Demosthenes in the art of pantomime, and this association of effective rhetoric with appropriate gesture had, by the time *Chironomia* was published, the authority of tradition.

The inference that sonorous speeches on the Elizabethan stage were accompanied by conventionally orchestrated shifts of posture is a reasonable one. It is less reasonable to stretch such an inference uniformly across a whole play. It cannot even be stretched across a whole part. The original actor of King Lear was not such a fool as to say, "Pray you, undo this button," as if it were part of the "Blow winds and crack your cheeks" tirade. What is striking about early modern drama is the variety of speech modes it contains. Suitable actions, where not indicated by explicit or implicit stage directions, were supplied by the versatility of the performer.

Doubling did not disappear with the increase in membership of the professional companies. If Cassius is given an uncomfortably early exit in act 3, scene 2 of *Julius Caesar*, it may well be to allow the actor time to change costume in preparation for his mutilation as Cinna the Poet. Such considerations have tended to discredit T. W. Baldwin's ingenious arguments for typecasting in Shakespeare's company. But Baldwin has a substantial point. A house playwright like Shakespeare writes toward the known strengths of his colleagues, and the busy actors, though unable to limit themselves to a single, favorite line of parts, would surely have had one. Although an actor might have displayed his versatility in *Much Ado About Nothing* by playing, with a lightning change in act 3, both Verges and Don John, there were other ways in which he might exploit his variety of skills.

The example of Augustine Phillips is instructive. We do not know when Phillips was born, and that he was a founder-member of the Lord Chamberlain's Men is only an assumption. He was certainly a leading member of the company through its glorious early years. It was he who took the responsibility for the contentious staging of *Richard II* in 1601, on the eve of the Earl of Essex's futile uprising, and his protestations of innocence at the subsequent arraignment are only histrionically convincing.

The terms of Phillips's will, proved on his untimely death in 1605, proclaim the intensity of his involvement with the company he served (Honigmann and Brock, 72–75). No fewer than thirteen of the Chamberlain's/King's Men are named beneficiaries, and an additional five pounds is to be shared among the hired men of the company. Particularly interesting are the bequests to two players whom he specifies as his apprentices. To Samuel Gilburne, he leaves two pounds *and* "my mouse Colloured veluit hose and a white Taffeta dublet A black Taffety sute my purple Cloke sword and dagger And my base viall." To James Sands, still serving his apprenticeship, he leaves two pounds *and* "a Citterne a Bandore and a Lute." For Gilburne and Sands, these gifts would have been of real professional value. Next to his part, an actor defined himself by his costume; and musical skills, instrumental as well as vocal, enhanced his attractiveness to employers and audience alike.

From the costumes in Phillips's possession, we can deduce that he played important roles—a purple cloak for Claudius, perhaps. From the properties, we know that he was a musician and might guess he was also an expert swordsman. Fencing with rapier and dagger was a spectacular alternative to fencing with rapier only. Laertes expresses a preference for it, and it was probably with rapier and dagger that he and Hamlet first skirmished on the London stage. Phillips, then, was actor, musician, swordsman. Given the courtly taste for "feats of agility," he had almost certainly been an acrobat in his youth and a graceful dancer throughout his career.

Nor is that all. An entry in the Stationers' Register on May 26, 1595, records the intention to publish "Phillips his gigg of the slyppers." The jig, more often a bawdy playlet than a dance, was a raucously popular afterpiece in Elizabethan playhouses. It was particularly relished by leading clowns, like Richard Tarlton and William Kempe, for the opportunities it provided for grotesque self-display and spontaneous contact with onlookers. Though rarely a solo piece, the jig was designed to feature a single performer. It is unlikely that Phillips would have written one and not performed the leading part in it. It is not merely fanciful, then, to picture an occasion in 1595 when Phillips, having just completed his role as Theseus in A Midsummer Night's Dream, reemerged in clownish disguise to perform his jig of the slippers. Such shape-shifting was the stock-in-trade of the versatile Elizabethan player.

We know, above all from the antitheatrical tracts of the period, that the shape-shifting of the players touched a nerve in the social commentators of Elizabethan England. At a visible level, there was the matter of costume. Legislators had endeavored, throughout the Tudor years, to regulate dress by the establishing of sumptuary laws, whose overriding intention was to ensure that the clothes people wore precisely reflected their station in society. The biblically condemned custom of cross-dressing boys and men in female roles was only the most sensational of the theater's sumptuary transgressions. Adverse comment on the inappropriate splendor of actors' apparel, outside as well as inside the playhouses, is a leitmotiv in Tudor moral outrage. It represented a threat to the certainties of hierarchy on which the preservation of power depended.

Several recent studies have drawn attention to the transgressiveness, latent or actual, of the practice of licensed acting. To the godly or the legalistic, the very act of licensing deception was a flouting of good order. As Jean E. Howard has recently argued, the defense of the stage even by its most distinguished apologist, Sir Philip Sidney, is "framed in terms which reveal fears of the usurpation of privilege by the unworthy, the elite's loss of control of the means of representing the real" (42). Sidney perceives hubris rather than transgression in the players' presuming to represent the real, and their conscious transactions, though always commercial, were only rarely transgressive. They measured their success in wealth and increased social access. Those, like Alleyn and Shakespeare, who rose to the ranks of the gentry, were exceptions. But there were many, like Phillips, who earned a place among the "middling sort," and many more who have vanished among the rogues and vagabonds. It was to the middling sort that, increasingly, they performed. The London playhouses, typically by their commercial assertiveness, were among the institutions that advanced the progress of an emergent English bourgeoisie.

There is an unresolved paradox here. Instability is as much the bugbear of the bourgeoisie as it is of those in authority over them, and yet, even at their least transgressive, actors advertise instability. If Hamlet can put an antic disposition on, he can also take it off. Identity in the playhouse is never fixed; nor is it, by analogy, in the world outside the playhouse. If a boy can play the queen or a master carpenter the king, what may the queen or king be playing? Although *"semper eadem"* was one of Elizabeth I's mottoes, it was well known that she was not "always the same." The histrionics of Elizabethan protocol are unmistakable. Performance was a major item in the queen's strategy for control. It was in the commercial interest of the players to sustain her authority; and yet, in playing the queen, the actor was unavoidably demystifying monarchy. The pervasive Renaissance image of the world as a stage is simultaneously a homage to the power of performances and a subversive pointer to the performances of power. A sense of himself as a metaphor cannot entirely have eluded the man who acted the part of Richard II on February 7, 1601. It did not elude Elizabeth I herself, as we know from her observation to William Lambarde: "I am Richard II, know ye not that?" (Chambers, *Elizabethan*, 2:326).

Persistently, actors mimed the ceremonies and spectacles of power for audiences who might otherwise never have seen them. Tudor grandees—Howards, Cliffords, Stanleys, Talbots—could see the deeds and misdeeds of their ancestors staged at court and know that they would also be staged in public. The players needed social skills and natural tact to negotiate a relationship with such contrasting constituencies. As well as threatening their livelihoods, failure would expose their professional liminality. There was never a shortage of holy watchdogs, eager to align actors with whores, the Devil and the Roman Catholic Church. And if there is some danger of aggrandizing the significance of the stage in the world order, we should remember that we owe that aggrandizing to contemporary commentators. Even James I, a much less willing actor than his predecessor on the English throne, looked to the playhouse for a simile of regal authority when writing *Basilicon Doron*: "A King is as one set on a stage, whose smallest actions and gestures, all the people gazingly doe behold" (*Works*, 181). In the 1599 edition, as Stephen Orgel has blisteringly noted (*Illusion*, 25), "skaffold" was preferred to "stage," grimly foreshadowing the climactic performance of Charles I's execution. Executions were always educational theater in embryo.

Most approaches to the early history of professional acting silently assume the primacy of tragedy, where the art of rhetoric most securely resides. But the playfulness of actors, both dangerous and delightful, was more naturally displayed in comedy. I began this essay with some cautionary comments on character and have proposed a gradual evolution of the word toward its currently received nexus of meanings. I shall end with a consideration of what Lesley Soule has termed the "anti-character."

Soule locates the anti-character in the quarrelsome relationship between the dramatic and the theatrical. The fictional dramatic character must always contend with the bodily presence of the actor, and "the anti-character becomes a paradigm of the dialectical nature of the actor-character relationship" (Soule, "Character," 218). It is a declared aim of illusionistic performance to obscure the distinction between character and actor, and there is a brittle assumption that the proper progress of acting has been in that direction. Phillips perhaps and Burbage certainly have been incorporated in what we may label that "orthodoxy." But several, predominantly comic, actors stand distinctively outside it.

Soule's exemplary anti-character is Rosalind in *As You Like It*, as created by the leading boy of the Chamberlain's Men: "a composite of fictional female and theatrical adolescent male" ("Character," 363). The flirtatious Lady Vanity of *The Marriage of Wit and Wisdom* would not be out of place in this composite picture, and Soule's nimble analysis of "Cocky Ros" at play in *As You Like It* goes some way toward restoring the virtually irrecoverable appeal of the boy-actor on the Elizabethan stage (Soule, "Subverting"). Never identifiable with the character he was presenting, he was nonetheless a mobile metaphor for female sexuality. If his performance was not, in itself, erotic, it triggered off erotic speculation among the spectators. Lesley Ferris's questions are relevant here: "Does the erotic rely on clear definitions of male and female? or is the blurring of distinctions its very source?" (9). The ambivalence of the concealed genitalia may have released the racing thoughts and neighborly whispers of the audience. In any event, the cross-dressed boy is insistently provocative, an actor implicitly interrogating his character and sometimes breaking out into open contradiction of it.

We do not know how the apprenticeship system worked in the Elizabethan theater. There was an evident distinction between choristers who might act and apprentice players who might sing; and there was probably more acrobatic training for the latter group. A charming entry in *Henslowe's Diary* records a loan to "the little tailor," at the appointment of the company, "to macke a payer of hosse for nycke to tembell in be fore the queen" (Henslowe, *Diary*, 186). The tumbling Nick was surely an apprentice to the Admiral's Men. But both choristers and apprentice players would have learned the rudiments of rhetoric and its associated gestures, both would dance and both be drilled in the protocols of precedence. There are many scenes in plays performed by the adult companies, almost all, in fact, that involve boys as *boys*, which shadow the relationship of apprentice to master. Such scenes further enforce the recognition that the boy-actor as anti-character was unavoidably metatheatrical. What seems certain is that his playfulness, the tendency of childish energy to burst through behavioral constraints, was not suppressed during his period of training.

The anti-character, when best pursuing the dialectical principle, stands midway between the play and the audience. The Clown may, at any moment, lose contact with the play altogether. His immediate antecedent is the Vice, an improvising marauder whose impulse is to create mayhem. To gratify that impulse, the Vice may collude with or threaten the audience. He has the Devil's charming confidence and an equal capacity to turn nasty if contradicted. It was, above all, Richard Tarlton who carried forward the presence of the Vice into the new drama of the commercial theater. When, in 1582, the Master of the Revels was instructed to select a company of twelve players to form Queen Elizabeth's Men, Tarlton's name was at the head of the list. When he died in 1588, the supremacy of the Queen's Men died with him. Cross-dressed in a jig, he was as grotesque and as abusive as Dame Edna Everage. Cast in a play, he remained Richard Tarlton, and was loved for it. He was all the more dangerous because he was popular. His ugliness defied decorum, and he rode with it. The intervention of a heckler was his feed-line. When an outraged woman threatened to cuff him, he agreed on condition that they reverse the consonants.

It does not matter whether this, one of his posthumously published *Jests* (1611), was ever said. It is enough that such put-downs were ascribed to him. They were part of his aura. It was neither possible nor desirable to constrain Tarlton, nor his famous successor Kempe, within a character. As late as 1638, Richard Brome is still prepared to celebrate a rogue-clown in the Tarlton tradition. Lord Letoy, in Brome's *The Antipodes*, has a "son" of Tarlton among his household players:

> one, that never will be perfect in a thing
> He studies: yet he makes such shifts extempore
> (Knowing the purpose what he is to speak to)
> That he moves mirth in me 'bove all the rest. (2.1.16–19)

The presence of such performers, for whom the label *actor* would be a misnomer, is a warning against any assumption that there was a single, uniform acting style on the Elizabethan stage. On the contrary, the professional theater accommodated a range of styles. Like all popular entertainment, it was not purist but eclectic. The aspirations of an Alleyn were quite other than those of a Tarlton, and if, as a surviving reference tells us, Kempe was prepared to be fobbed off with the part of Peter in *Romeo and Juliet*, it can only have been because he knew that his time would come in the post-play jig. The audience would have accepted no less. It wanted its money's worth.

Because the Vice stood so much closer to the audience than to the play, he cannot accurately represent the anti-character. When he is at play, the provocative dialectic of theater and drama is only sporadically in operation. But the commercial theater needed the crowd-pulling presence of those extraordinary performers who, in the itinerant companies, would have played the Vice; and the playwrights who created a national repertoire in the crowded last quarter of the sixteenth century were willing to accommodate him. For his Mephostopheles in *Doctor Faustus*, Marlowe borrows the Vice's function, with lightly written scenarios for improvisatory comic provocation. More startlingly, in *The Jew of Malta* he merges with Machiavelli in the disguise of Barabas. It is of some significance that the role of Barabas was probably first taken by Edward Alleyn. It gave him a fine opportunity to demonstrate the range and versatility of the professional player, as well, perhaps, as the Bottom-like possessiveness of the leader of a troupe. From Tamburlaine to Barabas is not a descent, but it is certainly a crossing of stylistic frontiers, and Alleyn, strong in the rhetoric of tragedy, was evidently attracted also by the demonic comedy of *The Jew of Malta*. In his prologue to the 1633 edition of the play, Thomas Heywood recalls Alleyn as both Tamburlaine and Barabas: "So could he speak, so vary."

But, as Bevington has hinted (*"Mankind,"* 83), the blending of Vice and human protagonist is at its most vivid in Shakespeare's Richard III. It is my contention that the reference was metatheatrically reinforced when *Richard III* was first performed (P. Thomson, *Shakespeare's*, 105–8). Only five years dead, Tarlton was not forgotten. Most of the audience would have seen him, hunchbacked and outstandingly ugly, easily imitated by a shape-shifting actor like, say, Burbage. This, surely, is the man who strides across the platform stage at the explosive opening of *Richard III* to declare himself a Vice:

> I, that am curtail'd of fair proportion,
> Cheated of feature by dissembling nature,
> Deform'd, unfinish'd, sent before my time
> Into this breathing world, scarce half made up,
> And that so lamely and unfashionable
> That dogs bark at me, as I halt by them;
> Why, I, in this weak piping time of peace
> Have no delight to pass away the time,
> Unless to see my shadow in the sun
> And descant on mine own deformity:
> And therefore, since I cannot prove a lover,
> To entertain these fair well-spoken days,
> I am determined to prove a villain. (1.1.18–30)

It is a fraught moment in the playhouse. Burbage as Tarlton as future king as Vice/Clown: the new drama encasing the old. The player is here addressing the audience directly, partly as Burbage, partly as Tarlton, and only partly as the Duke of Gloucester.

# CHAPTER 19

# Personnel and Professionalization

*W. R. Streitberger*

WHEN FYNES MORYSON wrote the *Itinerary* of his travels in 1617, he took special notice of the enormous popularity of London theater. He was impressed by the fact that London professional playing companies had their own theaters capable of seating thousands in performances held every day of the week except Sunday: "There be, in my opinion, more plays in London than in all the parts of the world I have seen" (C. Hughes, *Shakespeare's*, 476). English drama was far more widespread than Moryson's view suggested, for the opportunity to see plays was not confined to the public theaters of London. Between the time Shakespeare began his active career in the early 1590s and the closing of the theaters in 1642, there were about twenty professional companies that performed at one time or another in London, but there were well over a hundred of them on tour, performing plays all over England, as well as in Scotland, France, Holland, Belgium, Denmark, Germany, and even in Poland (Bentley, *Player*, 3–4). English companies also brought their plays to court for the revels—special performances before the king and queen, courtiers and ladies, and resident ambassadors and their entourages. Individuals at every level of society had the opportunity to see English professional companies that in Moryson's opinion "excel all others in the world."

The story of the development of these professional companies begins in the early fifteenth century when traveling players, who earned their livelihood all or in part from their performances, strolled the countryside in search of an audience. The productions of these professional players are to be distinguished from folk plays and the civic-sponsored mysteries that continued to be performed by amateurs in parts of England up through the early seventeenth century. They are also to be distinguished from the school and university drama written and performed by students principally for school audiences. Finally, they are to be distinguished from the drama, entertainments, and spectacles written and performed exclusively for the court. These distinctions cannot be urged too far, however, for professional players performed all over the countryside, in university towns, in the halls of the great houses of the nobility, as well as at court.

Some professional playing companies were independent, others were patronized by towns and by the nobility. Early companies were known by the names of their leading actor, by the community they represented, or by the names of the noblemen whom they served. The duke of Gloucester, the earls of Oxford, Essex, Derby, Northumberland, Buckingham, and Shrewsbury, and the lord of Arundel all had companies of players in the fifteenth century, and in the sixteenth century many more extended their patronage. Such patronage accomplished several goals at the same time. It ensured sophisticated performances in the revels given by the nobles in their great houses during the traditional feasts, developed their reputations as patrons of the arts, and extended their presence and influence among the boroughs and towns in which the companies performed. Patronage was also a means by which the behavior of traveling players could be controlled and so afforded the companies protection from local magistrates as well as serving as a recommendation to mayors and councilmen of the towns and villages in which they sought to perform. If the patron was influential enough, his company might be invited to perform at court, which would enhance both his and his company's status.

The extensive use of playing companies by the nobility for these purposes was no doubt one of the reasons that the royal family began to patronize them. When Henry VII created his own company of players in 1494, he set a precedent for the patronage of a royal company that would continue almost unbroken until 1642. Henry VII's original players performed regularly at court on state occasions and during the Christmas seasons, but they were essentially a household rather than a professional touring company. The members were bureaucrats and artisans who held positions in the royal household, and there are only a few records of their performances outside of the court. Prince Arthur's Players, however, were created as a professional touring company in 1495. His younger brother, Henry (later Henry VIII), who patronized the Lord Warden's company by about 1495 took over patronage of the prince's company after Arthur's death in 1502 (I. Lancashire, *Chronological*, 374, 389). Other members of the royal family patronized professional companies during Henry VIII's reign and again during James I's reign.

In 1515 Henry VIII restructured the King's Players into two groups, one consisting of the original players and the other of the new King's Players. The original players continued to perform at court each year until their retirement, sometime between 1521 and 1528. The new players were created as a professional touring company, and abundant evidence of their performances survives from the provinces. They were also invited to perform at court every year, often on the same bill with the original players. The creation of a royal professional company enhanced the king's image in the provinces and brought to court the kind of popular drama being played throughout the countryside, thus contributing variety to the revels. As players in this company retired, they were replaced. Called the Queen's Players under Mary and Elizabeth I, the company continued to tour and also performed at court in every year for which we have evidence until 1558 (Streitberger, *Court Revels*, 236–99).

Very few players during this period had backgrounds as entertainers. Of the four members of Henry VII's Players, one of them, John English, was a joiner who produced pageants and disguisings at court in 1501, 1502, and 1508, and another, Richard Gibson, was Yeoman Tailor and Porter of the Great Wardrobe, Sergeant of the Tents, and, later, deputy to the Master of the Revels. Many of the members of Henry VIII's Players were also new to the profession. John Young was a mercer, George Birch a courier, and George Mayler was a merchant tailor or glazier, but his professional status as a player is clear from a lawsuit over his agreement to take Thomas Arthur as an apprentice actor and to secure his employment as a member of the company (Chambers, *Elizabethan*, 2:80 n. 5, 81). Most players left their trades for an opportunity to join a prosperous company, and the trend continued throughout the period. James Burbage, former joiner and carpenter, became a player and a financier who built the first licensed permanent theater in the environs of London. A number of Shakespeare's colleagues in the Lord Chamberlain's–King's Men were members of London guilds: Robert Armin and John Lowin were goldsmiths, John Heminges was a grocer, and John Shank a weaver.

All of the professional troupes, regardless of who patronized them, were repertory companies—they kept a variety of plays in practice for performance. The plays used by early companies derived from a number of sources. Possibly some of their material was improvisational, based on set plots, ballads, or news. Anonymous popular playwrights supplied most of the playtexts that have survived, but humanists, such as John Rastell, John Heywood, and possibly John Skelton; propagandists, such as John Bale; and, later, university-educated men, like Thomas Preston, also wrote for playing companies. The scripts owned by the companies were important assets. In the early period they were difficult to obtain, and they were expensive. In October 1538, Lady Lisle wanted her agent in London, John Husee, to acquire a play on an ecclesiastical subject. Husee reported that they were "hard to com by" and they "be very deare, they askethe aboue xls. [40 shillings] for an Enterlude," an extraordinary sum in the late 1530s. Scripts were kept out of print until they were obsolete or until a company in desperation might be forced to sell them.

Information about the size and organization of the early professional companies derives from surviving playtexts and cast lists. Several texts from Henry VIII's reign indicate that some early companies were fairly small. *Mundus et Infans* (c. 1522), for example, has only five parts, which could be divided between two players. Surviving texts from the reigns of Edward VI and Mary indicate the need for four to six actors. While the early professional companies were small, their size began to increase in the reign of Elizabeth I. Two hybrid moralities dating from the 1560s, Robert Preston's *Cambyses* (c. 1561) and William Pickering's *Horestes* (c. 1567), are test cases for the development of the professional companies (Bevington, "Mankind," 60). Preston, a Cambridge scholar who attracted the queen's attention during her visit to the university in 1564, built his play on the model of a popular morality, but it includes historical characters and situations, offers political advice on the nature of monarchy, and contains classical elements. It was designed to appeal to a variety of audiences and was played in the counties, in London, and at court in 1560–61. The play has thirty-eight roles, which are divided among six men and two boys. *Horestes*, usually identified with the *Orestes* produced at court in 1567, is also aimed at an audience of courtiers as well as of commoners. Beneath a popular surface it contains political advice and classical material. The play has twenty-seven roles, divided among six players. *Horestes* and *Cambyses* illustrate not only the introduction of more-sophisticated subject matter in plays but also an increase in the number of parts for players.

The surviving texts of popular plays show a steady increase in length over the course of the sixteenth century, the corollary to which was a steady increase in the size of the companies performing them. Popular plays before Elizabeth I's reign average less than a thousand lines, a figure consistent with an average of between two and six players needed to perform them. Cast lists for longer plays dating from the 1560s and 1570s indicate that the average size of companies had increased to between seven and eight players. After the establishment of the theaters in London in the mid-1570s, nine to twenty players were needed when a company went on tour, and more than that for London performances. The increase in the number of players required to perform longer plays provided opportunities for employment in the profession. For the period 1590 to 1642, we know the names of more than a thousand players, but there were probably many more that we cannot document.

Another corollary to the increase in the length of plays in the later sixteenth century was that the doubling of roles had to be expanded. One of the first professional plays on record, the fifteenth century *Play of the Sacrament*, had twelve roles for nine players. During the first part of Elizabeth I's reign the ratio was more like three or four parts to one player. The tendency was in the direction of less doubling for the leading players and more doubling for minor players. Doubling was a century-old practice of the professional companies, which continued to be used in the commercial London theater.

Some plays written for early professional companies, like Bale's "fellows," evidence a fairly equal division of parts, suggesting equality among members of the company, but in most companies a hierarchy emerged over the course of the sixteenth century. Early companies were composed of a leading player and one or more subordinate players. In early popular moralities, like *Mankind*, the leading player usually took the role of the Vice character, and his fellows took the less demanding roles. The secularizing tendencies in drama later in the sixteenth century offered opportunities for other important roles. In *Horestes* and *Cambyses*, for example, the leading player portrays the principal human character rather than the vice, whose role fell to a supporting but important player. *Horestes* has roles for two leading adult players and a leading boy, and the rest of the nineteen roles are small parts. *Cambyses* also has roles for two leading players and two leading boys; the rest of the parts are fairly small and easily dividable among supporting players. These plays form a transition between the early moralities featuring entertaining Vice characters and the later drama and its great human characters like Hieronomo, Tamburlaine, Faustus, Richard III, and Hamlet.

Women did not perform in the professional companies or in the commercial London theater before the late seventeenth century. At court, and probably also in the great houses of the nobility, boys from the chapel enacted female roles on occasion, but there is no evidence from a pre-Elizabethan popular play that offers positive evidence for the presence of boys who enacted the roles of women (Bevington, "*Mankind*," 76). If possible, female and juvenile parts were avoided by early professional companies; if not, the parts were played by men. Professional companies began to employ boys by the 1560s. *Horestes* requires a boy to play both male and female roles. In *Cambyses* adult males play female roles, and the roles for a leading boy and a younger boy are segregated. Boy apprentices did go on later in the century to play women's roles, and some could continue playing these parts until they were between nineteen and twenty-one years of age.

The tendency in the composition of professional companies across the sixteenth century was in the direction not only of larger organizations capable of handling longer and more complicated plays but also of increasing the need for more personnel capable of playing leading as well as minor roles. By the 1560s and 1570s many companies had at least two principal players and several supporting players and boys. The growing distinction between leading and supporting players underlies the late-century hierarchy of master players and hired men in the commercial London theater.

While professional companies played throughout the country, a fair amount of theatrical activity was concentrated in London. Because of its density of population, London promised financial success on a large scale. It offered the possibility of developing much larger organizations than traveling companies could afford or find practicable, and it offered access to a variety of playing spaces. Evidence of temporary playing spaces in the environs of London survives from as early as the 1520s, when John Rastell built a stage at Finsbury Fields. The Almshouse at Rounceval had been used as a "playhouse" in 1531, and in 1557 a play was suppressed at the Boar's Head near Aldgate. In 1565, London "taverns, inns and victualling houses" are mentioned as places providing ready audiences where money was paid to hear plays, and in 1567 John Brayne, James Burbage's brother-in-law, erected scaffolding for plays at the Red Lion in Stepney.

Costumes and properties were also readily available. John Rastell sued his associate, Henry Walton, for hiring out his costumes to players, among them George Mayler, one of the King's Players. London mercers, like William Buttry, Christopher Milliner, and Thomas Gyles, who supplied some costumes and properties for revels at court and at the London houses of the gentry, were also a resource throughout the century. In 1572, Gyles complained that the queen's Yeoman of the Revels was damaging his business by hiring out costumes from the Office of the Revels inventory, some of them used by players (Feuillerat, *Office*, 409).

Over the twenty years from the early 1560s to the early 1580s, several specific political and economic developments conspired to offer a few of the professional traveling companies the essentials for establishing permanence in London: (1) companies were granted legal status; (2) opportunities surfaced for some of them to enhance their patrons' reputations by performances at court; (3) permanent playing spaces capable of accommodating large audiences were built; and (4) financial backing became available.

Early on, players were not officially considered to be part of a profession. Their activities were regulated by their patrons, and this system continued to be a key means of controlling their behavior and of restricting their numbers into the seventeenth century. But certain political events of the early- to mid-sixteenth century encouraged the Crown to take special precautions against seditious matter in plays and elsewhere. These events included the dissemination of Lutheran tracts, Henry VIII's divorce, his promulgation of the Reformation, his reversal of policy in the early 1540s, the accession of the Protestant Edward VI, followed by his Catholic sister, Mary, and then his Protestant sister, Elizabeth I—all in the space of thirty-five years. Plays critical of the king, his associates, or his policies occur at least as early as Skelton's *Magnificence* (c. 1519); plays treating topical religious subjects occur at least as early as Bale's polemical drama of the mid-1530s; and using the occasion of a play to incite rebellion occurred as early as Kett's rabble-rousing in Norwich in 1549.

The regulations that the Crown imposed on the drama and the injunctions it issued against players had their roots in ecclesiastical laws against the teaching of heretical doctrine and in civil laws against treason. Since players spoke in public, they fell under the laws and regulations governing censorship, and since they moved about the countryside, they fell under the ancient statute concerning vagabonds.

In 1527 Henry VIII revived the ancient statute regulating the number of servants that a peer could retain, and he repeated it in 1531, with explicit instructions to local authorities to punish idle wanderers (Chambers, *Elizabethan*, 4:260). Subsequent royal proclamations up to 1559 required licensing of books and plays, and there is much evidence of the Privy Council's active involvement in jailing offensive players and playwrights. Enforcement fell short of intention, and abuses by players continued to irritate all of the monarchs: Henry VIII considered using common players as galley slaves in the French campaign of 1542–44; Edward VI and Mary insisted on their own signatures on play licenses; and in 1572 Elizabeth I resurrected, once again, the ancient act for limiting the number of retainers and for the punishment of vagabonds.

The statute of 1572 required companies to be patronized by a nobleman or two judicial dignitaries of the realm. This latter provision was deleted from the further order of 1598, leaving only the great nobles with the stature to retain companies. The proclamation drove players to run for noble cover. James Burbage, a member of the Earl of Leicester's Men, wrote to his patron asking that his company be retained as "houshold servaunts and daylie wayters."

From the earliest notice of his company's existence until his death in 1588, Leicester lent support to his players, and on May 10, 1574, a patent under the Great Seal was issued to James Burbage, John Perkin, John Lenham, William Johnson, and Robert Wilson as principals in the company. The terms of this patent became a model for all those granted afterward to playing companies. It recognized the company as a legal entity, specified its privileges, rights, restrictions, and limitations, and stipulated that any plays would be "sene & allowed" by the Master of the Revels, whose ordinary job it was to select and to produce plays and other entertainments at court for the queen. In 1581 Elizabeth I issued a commission to her Master of the Revels, Edmund Tilney, to censor all plays for public representation and to license theaters and acting companies (Feuillerat, *Office*, 51–52). By the early 1580s, the Crown had an agent to oversee its interests, the nobility were the primary patrons of companies, and the professional companies were recognized as legal entities. The theater industry in London had become a legitimate institution.

The mayor and the Corporation of London had concerns nevertheless about the social problems caused by plays, which they had attempted to regulate on their own as early as the mid-1540s. By the mid-1560s official complaints began to be sent to the Privy Council, and this continued for close to thirty years (Chambers, *Elizabethan*, 4:266–67). Traffic congestion, the spread of disease, distracting the young from their work, profaning holy days, and providing the opportunity for criminals to practice their trade were among the social evils said to be encouraged by attendance at plays. The fact that theaters were built outside of the city's jurisdiction did not stop the mayor's continuing letters of complaint to the council, nor did it stem the tide of Puritan pamphlets objecting to plays and playhouses on moral grounds. The court's response to these complaints was to assume an increasingly protective role toward the companies.

The commercial London theater was also encouraged by a peculiar development in the queen's revels. Though the Queen's Players continued to perform in the counties, Elizabeth I chose not to use them in her court revels. She was the first monarch since Henry VII to extend a generous number of invitations to the playing companies of the nobility to entertain her. Such invitations, which began in the Christmas season of 1561, went to companies patronized by the most powerful and influential members of her court. Chief among these were Lord Dudley's (Earl of Leicester's) Men, the Earl of Lincoln's (Earl of Warwick's) Men, the Earl of Sussex's Men, and Lord Howard's (Lord Admiral's) Men. The practice continued until the early 1580s, connecting a few of the professional playing companies to the queen's revels and thus significantly elevating their status and leading to increased protection by the court.

When vacancies occurred in the ranks of the Queen's Players, Elizabeth I left them unfilled. In 1580, the last of the old queen's company, John Smith, died, and in 1583 Sir Francis Walsingham, Elizabeth's secretary, had Edmund Tilney select a new company of players for the queen, to be composed of the finest actors from the leading London companies; they were all appointed Grooms of the Chamber. This company included the famous actor Robert Wilson, and also John Lenham and William Johnson, all of whom came from the Earl of Leicester's Men. The new company also included John Adams and "the wonder of his time," the great comic actor Richard Tarlton, who came from the Earl of Sussex's Men. The creation of the new Queen's Men had the effect of making the playing companies of the nobility less sophisticated than that of the queen, as well as making it difficult for the lord mayor to object to public performances by his sovereign's company. The Queen's Men dominated Elizabeth's revels schedule until 1591, and they continued to play in London and in the counties until 1603.

Permanent places to play were developed in London beginning in 1576 when James Burbage, a former carpenter turned player, built the outdoor Theatre in St. Leonard's parish, Shoreditch. In the same year the Children of the Chapel began to play at Blackfriars indoor hall theater. These theaters were followed by others, including the Globe, the Rose, the Swan, and the Fortune, and other indoor theaters like Salisbury Court and the Cockpit. Over the course of the period, more than a dozen different playhouses were built or renovated. Many players who had or hoped to have employment in the industry moved into one of the two main theater districts. The largest was St. Savior's parish in Southwark, near the Globe, the Hope, the Rose, and the Swan theaters, and also near the Beargarden, the Clink prison, and the brothels. The other principal theater district was St. Giles Cripplegate parish, which included the Fortune, located outside the city walls. Companies paid theater owners rent for the use of their buildings, usually in the form of half of their gallery receipts.

Essential to permanent settlement in London was the financial backing to expand the companies' repertories, hire additional actors, commission new scripts, obtain and store costumes, and undertake a host of other expenditures that traveling companies had not encountered. Companies that could not afford to rent a theater or buy costumes, properties, or scripts turned to a financier like James Burbage, or Francis Langley, or—the most famous of them—Philip Henslowe. Henslowe was a substantial landholder who was financing the Southwark Beargarden in 1594 under a license from the Master of the Royal Game, eventually securing a transfer of the joint mastership to himself and to his son-in-law and business partner, Edward Alleyn. A theatrical entrepreneur who apparently enjoyed his work, Henslowe was mainly concerned with the Rose and the Fortune theaters, where the Lord Admiral's Men were his most important tenants. Apart from paying rent on this theater, the company had to pay for scripts, properties, garments, and licensing fees to the Master of the Revels. From 1597 Henslowe regularly met these payments and debited the sums advanced to a running account with the company. He had good relations with the poets and actors, who were frequently in debt to him for small loans, and on occasion he lent the money needed to buy a share in a company and accepted installment payments on it. He died a wealthy man in 1616 and left his papers to Edward Alleyn. It is from those papers that much of our information about the operation of London companies in this period derives. While London promised fame and financial success, those results were not guaranteed. The sheer number of professional companies struggling for survival in the late sixteenth and early seventeenth centuries is striking, but even more striking is the rate at which companies failed. In such an unstable market, it was commonplace for players to move from one company to another. Any number of events might cause a player to move. Internal dissension, the death of a patron, or financial hardship might break up a company, leaving a number of actors in search of new positions. The death of a principal member of a company necessitated replacement, and in such cases players might move from one company to another. While touring could be profitable, it also could produce financial strain. Most London companies were too large to travel, and changes in personnel could occur when companies went on tour. Lord Strange's Men wrote to the Privy Council in 1591 or 1592, arguing that their company was so large that traveling in the country "wilbe a meane to bringe vs to division and seperacion." As a result of debt, difficulties with patrons or authorities, theater landlords, or a variety of other problems, many companies were driven to disband. Often enough they re-formed under different patronage or different management, only to repeat the cycle.

The formation of the Lord Chamberlain's Men in 1594 illustrates part of the pattern. Henry Carey, Lord Hunsdon, Lord Chamberlain (1585), had patronized companies in the 1560s and in the 1580s, but the personnel of the company that assembled in 1594 as the Lord Chamberlain's Men and that was later patronized by his son, George, also Lord Chamberlain (1597), was formed out of the reshuffling of company personnel in the early 1590s. Three of the men who would join this company had worked together on the continent. William Kempe, one of the most famous Elizabethan clowns, was with the Earl of Leicester's Men in the Netherlands in 1585, and in the following year he was performing at the Danish court in Elsinore with Thomas Pope and George Bryan. Kempe returned to England, but Pope and Bryan got appointments as player-entertainers at the court of the Elector of Saxony in Dresden, where they remained in 1587. All three were reunited in London several years later at James Burbage's Theatre.

In 1590 Burbage's Theatre was home to a large joint enterprise of former players for the Lord Admiral's and Lord Strange's Men, who had gotten into difficulties with the authorities the previous year. The Lord Admiral's Men was suppressed by the lord mayor of London for performing plays that the Crown's censor, Edmund Tilney, "misliked," possibly having to do with the Martin Marprelate controversy. Lord Strange's Men shared their fate, and later that year many of the personnel of both companies were performing in 2 *The Seven Deadly Sins*, at the Theatre (Greg, *Dramatic*, 19). Along with Kempe, Pope, and Bryan, seven others who would join the Lord Chamberlain's Men performed in this play: Augustine Phillips and his apprentice Christopher Beeston, Richard Cowley, Henry Condell, John Duke, William Sly, and James Burbage's younger son, Richard.

In May 1591 a quarrel erupted with James Burbage over his withholding play-house receipts, and some of the players, led by Edward Alleyn, moved to the Rose, Philip Henslowe's theater in Southwark. Alleyn took part in financing and running the company at the Rose with Henslowe, whose records show that they performed regularly from 1592 to 1594 (Henslowe, *Diary*, ed. Foakes and Rickert [unless otherwise noted], 87, 136). In 1594, a number of these players re-formed themselves as the Lord Admiral's Men and went on to perform the most popular plays of the day—Marlowe's *1 and 2 Tamburlaine*, *Doctor Faustus*, *The Massacre at Paris*, *The Jew of Malta*, and others, all starring Alleyn, the most admired actor of the era. Around the same time, another group of these players re-formed themselves as the Lord Chamberlain's Men.

Some of the personnel who would join the Lord Chamberlain's Men had followed Alleyn to the Rose in 1591. Pope, Bryan, Kempe, Phillips, Cowley, and Heminges did, where they remained in the Lord Strange's part of that company. But not all of the players who performed in 2 *The Seven Deadly Sins*, went to the Rose. Richard Burbage, who could not have been pleased by Alleyn's disagreement with his father, appears to have joined the Earl of Pembroke's Men. This company experienced serious financial difficulties on tour in 1593 and were forced to sell their costumes and, it appears, some of their plays as well (Greg, *Henslowe Papers*, 40). Burbage then became a principal sharer in the Lord Chamberlain's Men.

Several theories about how Shakespeare came to join the Lord Chamberlain's Men have been advanced. The Earl of Pembroke's Men had some of his plays in its repertory, so it is possible that Shakespeare was a member (Chambers, *Elizabethan*, 2:130, 198), or he may have been one of the new Queen's Men, John Heminges's former company. The Queen's Men needed an actor when they performed at Stratford in 1587, and by 1593 the company was faltering.

While we cannot exactly place Sly, Duke, and Condell, after their performances in 2 *The Seven Deadly Sins*, or Shakespeare certainly at all, we know that of the twelve members of the Lord Chamberlain's Men in 1594, ten played at Burbage's Theatre in 1590 as part of the joint Admiral-Strange enterprise, and the eleventh,

Heminges, was traveling with Lord Strange's Men in 1593. The Lord Chamberlain's Men, then, was formed from a reshuffling of personnel in the wake of serious difficulties in at least three companies—Admiral's, Strange's, and Pembroke's—which included problems with the censor and the lord mayor, an argument with James Burbage over playhouse receipts, and the financial disasters that afflicted two companies on tour in 1593.

While the means by which the Lord Chamberlain's Men was formed in 1594 illustrates the pattern by which companies broke up and re-formed, that company's later career was wholly atypical. Immediately after its formation, the Lord Chamberlain's Men began to appear in court revels before Elizabeth I, and it continued to appear every year until her death in 1603. Along with the Lord Admiral's Men, who also appeared frequently at court, the Lord Chamberlain's Men became one of only two licensed companies to perform in London during this period. These special considerations are due in part to the fact that both companies were patronized by Elizabeth's cousins, who were also high officials in her government, but it is also clear that both companies had significant reputations for their performances.

When James I came to the throne in 1603, he immediately took over patronage of the Lord Chamberlain's Men, making them the King's Men, and Prince Henry took over patronage of the Lord Admiral's Men, making them the Prince's Men. This established a pattern for patronage by members of the royal family. The king's cousin and heir presumptive, Lodovic Stuart, patronized a company beginning in 1604; Queen Anne took over the Earl of Worcester's Men in the same year; the duke of York patronized a company beginning in 1608; Lady Elizabeth did so in 1611, and her husband, the Elector Palatine (or Palsgrave), took over patronage of the Prince's Men after Henry's death in 1612. While the proliferation of playing companies under the patronage of the royal family was reminiscent of the situation at Henry VIII's court, the implications for the commercial London theater were quite different. Of the enormous number of professional companies operating, only a few of them—those patronized by James's family—were licensed to play in the commercial theaters of London. And of those few, the only company to enjoy a continuous existence from the mid-1590s until the closing of the theaters in 1642 was Shakespeare's, the Lord Chamberlain's–King's Men.

After the professional companies became legal entities in the 1570s, their organization became guildlike, but there are some important differences between the companies and the London guilds. Unlike the guilds, the companies had no central organization, no court system, and no regulations that governed all of them. They had no hall and certainly did not have the social prestige of the ancient guilds, like the Goldsmiths or the Mercers. The companies also used different names for their ranks. Each professional company was organized into a hierarchy of sharers, hired men, and apprentices. Within each, the master players were generally named in the company's patent as the legally responsible members. They are called "sharers" because they shared the costs of producing plays and the receipts of the theater after every performance, as well as the fees for court performances.

The group of sharers in a company selected new patented members, sometimes from their own employees, called hired men, or from other patented companies. New sharers had to pay in order to cover their part of the company inventory of costumes and playtexts. This buy-in fee could be reimbursed after a sharer left, or it could be paid to his widow after his death. The price of shares varied. A share in the Lord Admiral's Men in 1597 was worth fifty pounds. A share in Queen Anne's Men in 1612 was valued at eighty pounds. The income on a share in the King's Men in 1634 was one hundred eighty pounds for one year (Chambers, *Elizabethan*, 1:352). Sharers' duties varied, but as principal members of the company they rented the playhouses, purchased costumes and properties, hired stagekeepers, prompters, wardrobe keepers, musicians, and minor players. They regulated the affairs of the company, on occasion fining or dismissing members for breach of contract, and they performed the principal roles in plays.

Some sharers were the most popular performers of their time. Edward Alleyn of the Admiral's Men and Richard Burbage, Nathan Field, and Joseph Taylor of the Lord Chamberlain's–King's Men had reputations as great tragedians, and Richard Tarleton of the Queen's Men and William Kempe, Robert Armin, and John Shank of the Lord Chamberlain's–King's Men had reputations as comedians. But a good many sharers never achieved a reputation for their performances. There is no evidence that William Shakespeare, Henry Condell, John Heminges, or Christopher Beeston were ever distinguished players.

One of the main duties of the sharers was to purchase or approve new play scripts for the company. Plays were still an expensive and regular drain on company resources in the late sixteenth century, and London repertory companies needed a constant supply of them. Henslowe's records show that in 1594–1595, for example, the Lord Admiral's Men performed a total of thirty-eight plays, of which twenty-one were new. A two-month summer tour in 1595 was followed by forty-two weeks of playing, in which they performed thirty-seven plays, nineteen of which were new. In 1596–1597, they performed thirty-four plays, of which fourteen were new (Henslowe, *Diary*, 21–27). The Lord Admiral's Men were using roughly one new play every two weeks until the year 1600.

The demand for plays contributed to collaborative writing, and four or five poets might work on a single project. Henslowe kept a staff of writers on retainer to produce scripts or to update, touch up, and alter plays that he bought for the companies he financed. He paid Ben Jonson, for example, who wrote for many different companies, to make additions to Thomas Kyd's *The Spanish Tragedy*. In 1598 another of Henslowe's writers, Thomas Dekker, helped write sixteen plays, for which his total payment from Henslowe was thirty pounds. Henslowe was paying five pounds for a play bought outright at this time, but by the 1630s Richard Brome was being paid twenty pounds a play. What has survived into our own time from this period is probably only a small proportion of the total output. Thomas Heywood, poet and actor who wrote for Henslowe in 1598 and for Queen Anne's Men from 1605 to 1619, claimed to have been associated with the writing of 220 plays.

When sharers contracted with a poet to write plays for the company, he was expected to write only for the company that hired him and to provide a fixed number of plays a year. Poets did not hold a copyright in our sense of the word; plays were the property of the companies that bought them. Companies fortunate enough to have the talent could turn to their own members for new plays. Shakespeare wrote an average of two plays a year during his active career, and various others of the Lord Chamberlain's–King's Men wrote plays for the company. Sharers assembled to read new plays and to pass judgment, a task that would have required a great deal of their time and energy in the late sixteenth century. In the early seventeenth century, as the number of plays owned by the companies increased, their need for new ones dropped off. At Charles I's court sixty-four out of eighty-eight plays staged were old (Streitberger, *Jacobean*, 89–150). By the 1630s the King's Men owned all of Shakespeare, nearly all of Beaumont and Fletcher, and most of Massinger, Middleton, and Jonson (Bentley, *Jacobean*, 1:108–34). They commissioned few new plays in that decade. The declining demand for novelty coincided with the rising status of plays from popular entertainment toward more serious literature. Collections of plays were now beginning to be published in expensive editions like the Jonson folio (1616) and the Shakespeare folio (1623).

Just as the number of sharers varied from company to company, so did the number of hired men, so called because they were paid a weekly wage rather than a share in the company profits. In December 1624, the King's Men employed at least twenty-one of them. Hired men sometimes had to post bonds to guarantee their stay with the company. Their duties varied. Most were employed as musicians, prompters, stagekeepers, wardrobe keepers, or gatekeepers, but all could be called on to fill in minor roles when needed. The name of Tawyer, belonging to one of the men hired by the King's Men in 1624, appears in a stage direction of the folio text of A *Midsummer Night's Dream*. He was pressed into service to play a trumpet while leading in Bottom and his fellows in a scene in the fifth act.

A few of the hired men were employed as actors. In productions by the King's Men between 1626 and 1632, from one to four hired men were assigned roles in plays. At the lowest level, hired men were paid little more than artisans. In 1597 Henslowe hired William Kendall at ten shillings a week for playing in London and five shillings for the country (Henslowe, *Diary*, 269). But wages varied according to the company's profits and prosperity, and no one was paid when the theaters were shut down, as they often were during outbreaks of the plague. Some hired men eventually became sharers. Of those employed by the Lord Chamberlain's–King's Men, John Duke, John Lowin, Alexander Cooke, William Eccleston, John Underwood, Thomas Pollard, William Penn, and John Honeyman all became sharers in this or in other London companies.

At the lowest level of company organization were the boy apprentices. Some of these boys came from the children's companies, which flourished in London as commercial enterprises after 1576. Behind the appeal of such companies lay a centuries-long tradition of performances by choirboys and at least fifty years of performances by grammar school boys. Such performances by skilled boy players were appreciated at all levels of society. The Children of the Chapel Royal performed at least one play at court in every year for which we have evidence from 1517 throughout the early reign of Elizabeth I. The Children of the Chapel Royal at Windsor, the Children of Paul's, and others were also invited often to perform at Elizabeth's and at James's court. In 1576, the Children of the Chapel moved into the Blackfriars indoor theater as a quasi-commercial venture under the direction of Richard Farrant, deputy of William Hunnis, Master of the Children of the Chapel Royal. By 1584 the Children of Paul's had set up operation under the direction of Thomas Giles, Master of the Children of the Chapel at Windsor. Later, in 1629, Richard Gunnel and William Blagrave were licensed to train boys as players to supply the professional companies. It is possible that Lady Elizabeth's company and Beeston's Boys also performed this function, but it is unlikely that they could have trained the number of boys needed. Most of the training went on within the professional companies themselves.

Boys were apprenticed to individual sharers, rather than to the company itself, for a period of several years. They received board, room, clothing, and training. We know little about the methods used to train them. The number of boys in each company varied. There were fewer roles for boys than for men. Plays dating from the later part of the period had approximately four to six women's or juveniles' parts that boys might play, but doubling was common. Boys did not receive a salary, but when they were hired by one company from another or from a financier to perform, their rate was less than that paid to hired men. Henslowe charged three shillings a week in 1600 for the use of his boy, James Bristow (Henslowe, *Diary*, 167). After their apprenticeship boys might be taken on as hired men, or in some instances as sharers. Nathan Field (former boy player at St. Paul's Grammar School), John Underwood and William Ostler (former members of the Children of the Queen's Revels), and Nicholas Tooley (apprentice to Richard Burbage), all became sharers in the King's Men, and Christopher Beeston (apprentice to Augustine Phillips) went on to become a wealthy theatrical financier. But such success stories were the exceptions (Bentley, *Player*, 238).

The evidence we have for casting is small compared to the large number of plays produced, and most of the evidence dates from late in the period. Major roles were generally assigned to sharers and less important parts to hired men and apprentices. On the other hand, some sharers, like Shakespeare, seem never to have played major parts, and in perhaps two dozen plays the longest parts appear to have been played by boy apprentices—as, for example, Portia in *The Merchant of Venice*,

Rosalind in *As You Like It*, and Helena in *All's Well That Ends Well*. Still, this is a very small minority of the approximately six hundred to seven hundred plays produced in the later period. Promptbooks and plots show players taking more than one role and in several instances four or more, making it highly unlikely that minor characters would be individualized.

What we know of the sharer system and the careers of individual members suggests that fairly distinct roles were recognized. New sharers usually took on the roles of the players they replaced. When Joseph Taylor replaced Richard Burbage in the King's Men in 1619 he took over several of Burbage's parts (Nungezer). Robert Benfield joined the company in 1615, probably to replace William Ostler, and took over his part as Antonio in *The Duchess of Malfi*. Leading comic roles appear to have gone regularly to the resident comedians—William Kempe, Robert Armin, John Shank—but there is no clear evidence of typecasting. The question of whether or not playwrights wrote with specific players in mind is still an open one. Some plays—Shakespeare's for the Lord Chamberlain's–King's Men, for example—were probably written with the expectation that certain players would perform certain parts. But evidence of the conditions under which most scripts were produced is sketchy. Casting was probably a matter of convenience, though major tragic and comic roles would ordinarily go to the sharer with a reputation for them.

Earlier in the twentieth century scholars were convinced that only boys rather than adult males played women's roles, but the evidence is controversial. The name of Robert Pallant appears in the cast list of *The Duchess of Malfi* (c. 1613–1614) quarto as playing the doctor and doubling as Cariola. Pallant had been acting since *2 The Seven Deadly Sins*, in 1590, and he went on to become a member of Queen Anne's and a few other companies. Chambers, Bentley, and all those following them believe the reference is to a younger person, also named Robert Pallant (Chambers, *Elizabethan*, 2:331; Bentley, *Player*, 259). In the Ralph Crane transcript of *Sir John van Olden Barnavelt* (1619), "Nick" is assigned the part of Barnavelt's wife. Greg and those following him think the reference is to the young Nicholas Underhill (Greg, *Dramatic*, 273; Bentley, *Jacobean*, 1:74, 2:601–2). Others identify this "Nick" as Nicholas Tooley, one of the Lord Chamberlain's–King's Men who was acting as early as 1592, and who would have been in his forties when he played the part in 1619 (Forse, 90). John Shank is clearly assigned the role of the waiting-woman, Petella, in Fletcher's *The Wilde Goose Chase*, and Anthony Turner is listed as playing a "kitching" maid in a revival of Heywood's *1 A Fair Maide of the West* (Bentley, *Player*, 256–58, 275). But even this evidence is problematic, for Turner, a sharer in Queen Henrietta's company, has only five lines, and Shank is not assigned any.

That boys played women's roles provided one obvious objection to the theater for Puritan pamphleteers of the period, who condemned cross-dressing as immoral and ungodly. William Prynne was concerned about those comely youths . . . wholly consecreated to the stage (the Devil's Chapel as the Fathers phrase it) where they are trained up in the School of Vice . . . to the very excess of all effeminacy, to act those womanish, whorish parts which pagans would even blush to personate. (171–72)

The causes and effects of boys playing women's roles in the theater have received much attention by critics in our own time. On one end of the spectrum, cross-dressing is thought of as virtually identical to transvestism and has become a departure point for investigations of sexual identity and misogynistic and homoerotic tendencies in Elizabethan society (Orgel, "Nobody's," 13). On the other end of the spectrum, cross-dressing is thought of merely as a theatrical convention, much like that in contemporary Japanese Kabuki theater (Hyland, 1–8; Forse, 82).

The affairs of the professional companies were complicated. Hundreds of costumes had to be ordered and paid for; theater rents had to be paid; plays had to be commissioned, paid for, and licensed; and fees had to be paid to the Master of the Revels, not only for licenses but also for various privileges. Court and private performances had to be arranged and payments collected; transportation to the palaces and great houses had to be arranged; liveries had to be received and distributed; men had to be employed and paid; properties had to be collected; rehearsals and other meetings of the company had to be scheduled; tours into the countryside had to be arranged and financed; and playbills had to be printed and distributed.

These administrative tasks were taken on by one or two of the sharers, who may have been called in the records *steward, chief, warden, governor, leader,* or *master.* Originally these duties were performed by John Heminges for the Lord Chamberlain's–King's Men; after 1630, Joseph Taylor and John Lowin assumed responsibility for them. After Christopher Beeston left the Lord Chamberlain's Men, he did the same job for Queen Anne's Men, then for Lady Elizabeth's Men, Queen Henrietta's Men, and for Beeston's Boys. Edward Alleyn did it for the Lord Admiral's and the Palsgrave's Men.

To be a shareholder was to be a businessman involved in a demanding operation that had a substantial turnover of expenses and income. The sums of money involved were astronomical by the standards of the day. In 1600, the estimated annual income for an artisan was about 15 pounds (Forse, 16). In the same period the Rose cost 816 pounds to construct, the first Globe 600 pounds, and the Fortune 600. Ongoing costs were also high. In 1635 upkeep of the Globe and Blackfriars ran 100 pounds a year, in addition to 36 pounds for licensing fees. Costs were high, but so was income. In 1597 the Admiral's Men's gallery takings alone were averaging 20 pounds a week (Henslowe, *Diary*, xxxv), and by 1635 Blackfriars was yielding 700 to 800 pounds a year and the Globe a little less.

Despite the sums of money involved, there are few success stories concerning either the companies or individual players. Most companies folded, and most players barely eked out a living. Those few who prospered were the exceptions, mainly those with financial interests in the business side of the companies. As a result of his partnership with Henslowe, Edward Alleyn was able to retire from acting before he was forty, to purchase the manor of Dulwich for 10,000 pounds, to build the College of God's Gift on the manor, and to spend about 1,700 pounds a year maintaining his household and his foundation. This was an enormous amount of money, and Alleyn was as wealthy as many of the peers of the realm.

James Burbage was a joiner and actor when he borrowed money to build the Theatre in 1576, an enterprise that he left to his sons, Cuthbert and Richard. Richard died in 1619 worth a fairly substantial 300 pounds a year in land, about the same amount Shakespeare was worth at his death in 1616. Thomas Pope, Augustine Phillips, Henry Condell, and John Heminges were also well off at their deaths. They all belonged to the most successful and the only stable company in the period. The Lord Chamberlain's–King's Men was one of only four companies to be consistently licensed to play in London from the Privy Council decree of 1598 until the breakup of the companies when the theaters were closed by act of Parliament on September 2, 1642. Further, several members of this company— including Burbage, Shakespeare, Heminges, and Condell—owned shares in the company's two theaters. Such ownership was not common, and it helps account for their financial success.

With financial success for some came a desire for social status and respectability. Alleyn married a daughter of John Donne, dean of St. Paul's, in 1623, and it appears that he was hoping for a knighthood, like the one that Jonson was supposed to have been offered by King James I. The self-conscious pretensions of Burbage, Henslowe, Pope, Phillips, Cowley, Heminges, and Shakespeare to be numbered among the ranks of the gentry are attested by their applications for, or their assumption of, coats of arms. Others received appointments at court. George Bryan received a royal appointment as Yeoman of the Wardrobe and Joseph Taylor as Yeoman of the Revels. Philip Henslowe obtained an appointment as Groom of the Chamber at court in 1592, and in 1603 he became Gentleman Sewer of the Chamber to James I. He acted the part of pillar of the Southwark community, serving as vestryman of St. Savior's parish in 1607, churchwarden in 1608, and governor of the free grammar school in 1612. While it is possible to be condescending about such aspirations and achievements in an age in which knighthoods as well as coats of arms were almost literally for sale, there is evidence that the status and reputation of players and companies rose during the period. The general attitude toward players and the profession was by no means the same in the early 1640s as it had been in the early 1540s.

Within a short time of their establishment in London, the playing companies produced celebrities—men who came from nowhere but achieved more fame than many leading figures of government. Richard Tarlton, member of the Queen's Men in the 1580s, was a playwright, a composer of ballads, a drummer, a tumbler, and a Master of Fencing (Bradbrook, Rise, 162–77). He became famous as a comedian in the 1570s and 1580s. Jestbooks published after he died kept his reputation for wit and extemporaneous performances alive for a century.

Robert Wilson, a member of the Queen's Men also noted for his wit, was famous as an author. He was with the Earl of Leicester's Men in the Netherlands in 1585–1586, when he played with William Kempe, possibly the first player of Falstaff. Kempe, who had some part in every play in the Lord Chamberlain's Men's repertory, is also known to have played Peter in *Romeo and Juliet* and Dogberry in *Much Ado About Nothing*. Kempe was famous for his outrageous popular stunts, such as his nine-day jig from London to Norwich. His successor Robert Armin was a playwright as well as a singer and a comedian. For Armin, Shakespeare wrote the part of Feste in *Twelfth Night* and the Fool in *King Lear*. John Shank became the principal comedian for the King's Men between 1613 and 1629.

By 1600 Edward Alleyn of the Admiral's Men and Richard Burbage of the Lord Chamberlain's Men had achieved significant reputations as tragedians. Alleyn, born in 1566, was the son of a London innkeeper. By the time he was sixteen, he was a member of the Earl of Worcester's Men, a leading London company, and by 1592 he had earned a reputation for his interpretation of the roles of Tamburlaine, Faustus, and Barabas in Marlowe's plays, and the role of Orlando in Greene's *Orlando Furioso*, and other similar roles. Through his business partnership with Henslowe, Alleyn rose to a position of unparalleled prosperity, and early in the seventeenth century he devoted all of his time to business affairs, including his interest in the Lord Admiral's Men (Bradbrook, *Rise*, 194–207). Richard Burbage, the younger son of James Burbage, was two years younger than Alleyn. Richard was a member of Alleyn's joint Admiral-Strange venture at his father's theater in 1590, but by 1594 he was the leading actor and major shareholder in the Lord Chamberlain's Men, where he is credited with the roles of Richard III, Hieronomo, Hamlet, Othello, Lear, and Ferdinand in *The Duchess of Malfi*. His name appears on all Lord Chamberlain's–King's Men's plays for which lists survive between 1599 and 1618. Burbage died in 1619 at fifty years of age, and Nathan Field, who joined the company by 1616 and who rivaled Burbage as a great tragic actor, died only four months after him. The King's Men was successful in finding replacements and continued to the end of the period to be home to the most famous serious actors—Joseph Taylor, John Lowin, and Elliard Swanston—as well as to the leading comic actor—John Shank.

A number of other factors contributed to the rise in status of players. After 1574, they no longer fell under the acts against rogues, vagabonds, and masterless men, although Puritan polemicists continued to regard them as such. The London companies and a number of provincial companies had licenses, patents, or charters that formally made them members of the court or some noble household and that specified their rights and privileges. By the 1560s, professional companies were regularly invited to perform at court, and the number of invitations increased throughout the period. Such patronage by the court enhanced the status of certain companies.

Early in the period, plays were regarded as ephemeral entertainment and, when printed, were issued in cheap quartos. In 1616 Jonson's collected works were published in an expensive folio edition, which included his plays and the cast list of the comedians and tragedians who had played the principal roles. The success of the Jonson folio was followed in 1623 by the publication of the folio edition of Shakespeare's plays. The publication of plays in individual quarto editions now began to bear dedications to persons of importance, like William Camden, Lord Aubigny, Lady Wroth, the earl of Pembroke, and the earl of Montgomery. Tracts on players and the theater, like Thomas Heywood's *An Apology for Actors* (1612) and Nathan Field's "Letter to Mr. Sutton, Preacher at St. Mary Overies, 1616," drew, in the former case, on classical and, in the latter, on biblical learning to defend the profession (Bentley, *Player*, 9–10). Alleyn's act of piety, the foundation of his College at Dulwich, was made conspicuous by a reading of the deed before a gathering of officials in London, and the civic accomplishments of other successful players tended to enhance the status of the profession as a whole. There is also anecdotal evidence of personal relationships suggesting that the reputation of players rose. Sir Philip Sidney became godfather to Richard Tarlton's son, and when Richard Burbage died in 1619, William Herbert, who was the earl of Pembroke, lord chamberlain of the royal household, and one of the brothers to whom Shakespeare's first folio is dedicated, stayed away from court because he could not endure to see a play "so soon after the loss of my old acquaintance Burbadg" (Nungezer). The fact that one of the leading peers of the realm who was also one of the highest-placed officials at James I's court could be personally moved by Burbage's death suggests that attitudes toward players had changed substantially. We are certainly a long way here from Henry VIII's attitude in 1542, when he was thinking of using common players as galley slaves.

# CHAPTER 20

# Playwrighting:
# Authorship and Collaboration*

*Jeffrey Masten*

> They vsed not onely one boord, but one bedde, one booke (if so be it
> they thought not one to many). . . . all things went in cōmon betweene
> them, which all men accompted cōmendable.
>
> JOHN LYLY, *Euphues* 1.199

SHAKESPEARE AND Fletcher; Fletcher and Beaumont; Fletcher
and Massinger; Field and Massinger; Fletcher, Field, and Massinger; Greene and
Lodge; Norton and Sackville; Marlowe and Nashe; Marlowe and Kyd?; Porter,
Chettle, and Jonson; Wilson, Munday, Dekker, and Drayton; Dekker, Jonson, and
Chettle; Chettle, Dekker, Haughton, and Day; Dekker and Webster; Munday,
Drayton, Webster, Dekker, and Middleton; Jonson, Chapman, and Marston; Day,
Rowley, and Wilkins; Dekker and Middleton; Middleton and Shakespeare?; Hey-
wood and Rowley; Field and Daborne; Field, Daborne, and Massinger; Daborne
and Tourneur; Middleton, Massinger, and Rowley; Middleton and Rowley; Rowley,
Dekker, Ford, "&c"; Rowley, Dekker, Ford, and Webster; Rowley and Fletcher;
Jonson and another; Dekker and Ford; Brome and Heywood; Kyd and Jonson;
Chapman and Shirley; Hands A, B, C, D, S, and Tilney, the censor . . .[1]

By beginning a discussion of authorship and collaboration in early English
drama with this list, I mean to emphasize that much of the drama of this period was
written by more than one person, produced through collective forms of making—
even if most of the drama we now customarily read, stage, film, watch, and teach
is associated with the singular figure of Shakespeare. Playwrights in early modern
England did write alone (though we will need to return to what the term *alone*
means in this culture), but more often they wrote with another playwright, or with
several others, or revised or augmented scripts initially produced by others. G. E.
Bentley, in his comprehensive study of commercial playwriting in this period,
notes that "nearly two thirds" of the plays mentioned in the theatrical manager
Philip Henslowe's records "are the work of more than one man" and argues that "as
many as half of the plays by professional dramatists in the period incorporated the
writing at some date of more than one man" (*Dramatist*, 199). Studying the Rose

theater, Neil Carson finds that "collaborated plays accounted for 60 per cent of the plays completed in the Fall-Winter 1598, and an astonishing 82 per cent in Spring-Summer 1598" (57). While I would emphasize the necessarily approximate nature of such figures, they nevertheless suggest that collaboration was the standard mode of operation within the early modern English theater, not a problem to be confronted only after considering singularly authored plays.

An essay like this might thus proceed to set out the facts of playwriting—which playwrights wrote which plays (together or separately) and, within collaborative plays, who wrote which scenes—and then initiate a discussion of this evidence, moving toward a cultural history of collaboration. Indeed, one might argue that my initial list begins to do precisely that. One of my contentions here, however, is that *as* (not simply *after*) we read the evidence of "playwrighting" that survives, we must thoroughly reconceptualize our default notions of singular authorship, collaboration, intellectual property, originality, imitation, and even "the individual" in the modern sense (R. Williams, *Keywords*, 133–36; Stallybrass, "Shakespeare")—in short, the making of lists that divide up intellectual property and its owners.[2] These ideas now typically inform and organize the study of literary history, but retaining them in the study of the early modern theater (and early modern culture more generally) risks *de*forming our analysis of this culture and its textual production.

In this essay I begin instead by presenting one of several *possible* avenues toward rethinking textual production in early English drama on more collective grounds; I then reread the conditions and conventions of authorship and collaboration within this context. Throughout, I attempt to demonstrate that the writing of scripts for the professional theater with which this essay is predominantly concerned cannot be separated from specific material discourses and practices of the culture that surrounds (and absorbs from) the theater, the complexly interrelated "physical" and "social" spaces with which this *New History* begins.[3]

## Conversation

In the sixteenth and seventeenth centuries, the word *conversation*, along with the related terms *converse* and *conversant*, had a much more complex aura of meanings than it has for us today. The oldest meaning of *conversation*, from the fourteenth century onward, is living in a place or dwelling among a group of people, as in the question that the *Oxford English Dictionary* locates in 1483, "where conuersest thou?"[4] or the 1611 Authorized Version's use, "For our conuersation is in heauen" (Philippians 3:20, Holy Bible T3), a usage for which the 1881 Revised Standard Version tellingly substitutes "citizenship." A related obsolete meaning of *conversation* is: "The action of consorting or having dealings with others; . . . commerce, intercourse, society, intimacy." As Valentine says of his friend Protheus in *The Two Gentlemen of Verona*: "from our Infancie / We haue conuerst, and spent our howres together" (Through Line Numbering [TLN] 712–13).

Some other related meanings circulating in the seventeenth century were one's "Circle of acquaintance, company, society" and "behaviour, mode or course of life." Indeed, according to the period hard-word lists and translation dictionaries, these were the most prominent seventeenth-century meanings of the term: John Bullokar's *English expositor* glosses "*Conuersant* [as] Vsing much in ones company" (E2ᵛ); John Minsheu's *Guide into the Tongues* defines *converse* as "*accompanie, or associate much or often*" (95); and John Florio translates the Italian "Conuersatione" as "*conuersation, societie*" (*Worlde*, 85). Add to this the related sense that is now the *only* meaning for *conversation*, beginning around 1580: "Interchange of thoughts and words; familiar discourse or talk"—what Tourneur called in 1609 "Conversation (the Commerce of minds)." One specialized meaning that persisted at least until the end of the sixteenth century is related, through the persuasive quality of familiar discourse: conversation as conversion, what Coverdale, translating the Acts of the Apostles in 1535, called "the Conuersacion of the Heythen."

Thus far I have neglected an important resonance of this word, the meaning that the OED dates from the early sixteenth century as "sexual intercourse or intimacy." This meaning remains in circulation until just after the emergence of the term *sexual intercourse*, which seems to take its place around 1800 (Fleming, 160). There are important differences between early modern *conversation* and modern *sexual intercourse* that I am not able to examine here, but consider these appearances of conversation-as-intercourse: Richard III's condemnation of Lord Hasting's "Conuersation with Shores Wife"; a clearly sexualized 1649 discussion of "a conjugall conversation"; and, most succinctly, a 1646 usage that makes these two terms synonymous/exchangeable : "converse or copulation."

Sexual conversation is often figured as illicit or explicitly condemned, at least when it refers to what we would now call heterosexual relations. In *Richard III*, Hastings's severed head is displayed onstage as recompense for his "conversation with Shore's wife." Conversing with Palamon in *The Two Noble Kinsmen*, Arcite illustrates this problematic:

> We are young and yet desire the waies of honour,
> That liberty and common Conversation
> The poyson of pure spirits; might like women
> Wooe us to wander from. (21)

The passage suggests that one kind of conversation—between kinsmen—must ostensibly be protected from other kinds of conversation: "common conversation," conversation among/across social classes; and cross-gender conversation, associated with "liberty" and promiscuity. *Conversation*, in this and other instances, seems always potentially to register transgression; a 1656 sermon demonstrates this in its insistence on the condoned nature of the intercourse: "They may *lawfully* converse together as man and wife" (my emphasis). The problem for early modern culture is the uneasiness (in both senses) of imagining the possibility of an equitable conversation between the heterosexes—as well as the ostensible problem of effeminization through heterosexual practices (Orgel, "Nobody's," 14–15). In 1615, George Sandys writes of men "Enfeebled with the continual conuerse of women," and Florio, translating Montaigne's essay on friendship, outlines the misogynist ideology that I take to be widely held in the period:

> the ordinary sufficiencie of women, cannot answer [the] *conference* and *communication* [of male friendship] . . . nor seeme their mindes strong enough to endure the pulling of a knot so hard, so fast, and durable. (MONTAIGNE, 91)

In contrast to this pejorative portrayal of the impossibilities and dangers of cross-sex communication, the discourse of male friendship inscribes a model of the exchange of discourse and even identities based in a notion of equitableness. Defining *acquaintance*, Richard Brathwait writes of friends who are "in two bodies individually incorporated, and no lesse selfely than sociably united," friends who "shew[] the consenting Consort of their minde" (Brathwait, frontispiece). Montaigne/Florio emphasizes this other, sanctioned mode of male conversation as well, and the text suggests a conversation that is both the exchange of ideas *and* homoerotic intercourse, if we keep in mind the promiscuous signification of the word *will* in seventeenth-century English as sexual organ and desire (Shakespeare, ed. Booth, 466):

> [Friendship] is I wot not what kinde of quintessence of all this commixture, which having seized all my will, induced the same to plunge and loose it selfe in his, which likewise having seized all his will, brought it to loose and plunge it selfe in mine, with a mutuall greedinesse, and with a semblable concurrance. (MONTAIGNE, 93)

All these terms associated with the exchange of discourse and ideas are also insistently *spatial*. Etymologically, a semblable *concurrence* is a running together; to *converse* is to dwell or live together; *conversion*, "A turning from euill to good" (Bullokar, E2ᵛ); to *converse* is also to turn about, to reverse course and discourse (*OED*; W. Wall, *Imprint*, 33–34). Speaking of space, these terms situate our study of textual production at a complicated nexus of interrelated discourses: dwelling among; interchange between; commerce, society, intimacy; sexual intercourse; conversion.

### Shuffling

> When J was first suspected for that Libell that concern'd the state, amongst those waste and idle papers (which J carde not for) & which unaskt J did deliuer vp, were founde some fragmentes of a disputation toching that opinion affirmed by Marlowe to be his, and shufled with some of myne (vnknown to me) by some occasion of our wrytinge in one chamber twoe yeares synce. (BROOKE, 104, editorial notations not reproduced)

These words, in one of the few texts we can closely associate with the playwright
Thomas Kyd, are from his letter—somewhat frantic in tone, befitting someone
who has recently been tortured by order of the Privy Council—written to Sir John
Puckering, the Lord Keeper and a member of that council. Kyd's words in this letter are usually read as evidence that he and Christopher Marlowe lived together
during the time that both were writing plays for Lord Strange's Men, among other
companies; as Jonathan Goldberg somewhat chastely puts it, Kyd was Marlowe's
"fellow playwright and sometime roommate" ("Sodomy," 78).

For the purposes of this essay, I do not want to efface the probability that Kyd
and Marlowe lived together, but I do want to notice that the evidence emphasizes
Marlowe and Kyd's *writing* arrangements as much as their living or sleeping
arrangements: their pages get "shufled," Kyd says, on "some occasion of our wry-
tinge in one chamber." Kyd is at some pains to separate himself and his papers from
Marlowe, but, rather than discounting this evidence as the tattle-taling of a terrorized early modern subject (though it is certainly also that), I want to point out that
implicit in Kyd's letter, the story he circulates because it is believable to Queen
Elizabeth's secret service, is the story that the papers of playwrights get "shufled"
together. This is also the assumption of, for example, the title page to *The Spanish
Tragedie,* the only play attributed to Kyd in the period; early seventeenth-century
editions describe the play as

> Newly corrected, amended, and enlarged with new Additions of the Painters part, and
> others, as it hath of late been diuers times acted. (1615 edition)

These may or may not be the "additions" to this play, also known as *Jeronimo,*
for which Philip Henslowe recorded payment to Ben Jonson in 1601–1602:

> vnto bengemy Johnsone
> Lent^ at the a poyntment of E Alleyn ⎫
> & w^m birde the 22 of June 1602       ⎪
> in earneste of a Boocke called Richard ⎬ x^ll
> crockbacke & for new adicyons for    ⎪
> Jeronymo the some of . . . . . . . . . ⎭
>     (GREG, *Henslowe Papers,* 1:168, 149).

But for our present purposes (the shuffling of playwrights' papers) it makes little
difference—indeed, the question's indecidability further illustrates the point.[5] As
the manuscript of *Sir Thomas More* complexly suggests, early modern playwrights
were far less interested in keeping their hands, pages, and conversation separate
than are the twentieth-century critics who have studied them (McMillin,
*Elizabethan*). This, indeed, has been the problematic of early modern English
playwrighting for the twentieth century, for we are confronting material, as I argue
in detail below, that largely resists categories of singular authorship, intellectual

property, and the individual that are central to later Anglo-American cultural, literary, and legal history.

In thinking about Marlowe and Kyd as playwrights writing together, we could start with the hands of the documents in question, since, unlike the manuscripts of most plays from this period, these manuscripts exist, and include: one signed letter from Kyd to Puckering, one apparently unsigned letter from Kyd to Puckering, and some pages of what Kyd calls "some fragmentes of a disputation toching that opinion affirmed by Marlowe to be his." The "fragmentes" are in an entirely "different" hand, an italic hand, an observation that at first seems to support Kyd's implication that they are Marlowe's. But looking more closely, we can also notice that the hand of the disputation, the italic hand, is also the hand *Kyd* uses, in the signed letter, for emphasis (the word *Atheist*) and for Latin quotations, e.g., from Cicero on friendship (Brooke, 56). Keeping in mind that one signature is all that apparently [otherwise?] remains of Marlowe's handwriting, and remembering too that Thomas Kyd, if he is the Thomas Kyd we think he is, was the son of a scrivener, is thought briefly to have followed his father into that trade (Edwards, xviii–xix), and could, as we see in his letter, write with multiple hands, we have a number of questions to ask: Whose hand is whose? Are the fragments, already a quotation from an earlier printed theological tract, also written out *by* Kyd *for* Marlowe? How do we read the ambiguity of Kyd's syntax: "some fragmentes of a disputation toching that opinion affirmed by Marlowe to be his, and shufled with some of myne"? Are the papers, or the opinion in them, or *both* "affirmed by Marlowe to be his"? How closely does Marlowe's opinion touch the disputation? How closely do Marlowe's opinions touch Kyd's? What has been shuffled?

I do not favor bringing out the paleographical evidence as if it could answer these questions, or as if these are the right questions to be asking in the first place.[6] We should notice that these questions, which seem to be called up by the evidence itself and seem also to be very much like our own default questions about the authorship of collaborative Renaissance plays (who wrote which pages?), are actually questions formulated by the intervention of power into this collaborative chamber. In the words of the Privy Council order that eventuated in the arrest of Thomas Kyd, the civil authorities were ordered

> to make search and apprehend every person . . . to be suspected [in this matter], and for that purpose to enter into all houses and places where any such may be remaining. And, upon their apprehension, to make like search in any the chambers, studies, chests, or other like places for all manner of writings or papers that may give you light for the discovery of the libellers. And after you shall have examined the persons, if you shall find them duly to be suspected, and they shall refuse to confess the truth, you shall by authority hereof put them to the torture in Bridewell. (BROOKE, 55)

Separating the authorship of the Kyd/Marlowe papers, though apparently Kyd's idea at this juncture, is a strategy produced in reaction to the state and the state's regulation of an apparently extra-theatrical matter. It does not seem to have occurred to Kyd to mark with such precision the authorship of anything else he wrote. The same holds for Marlowe.

I want to think about Marlowe and Kyd's relation (and thus the relations of early modern playwrights more generally) in terms that are both less anachronistic in resisting "solving" questions of "individual authorship" and less on the side of a certain mode of state power, by looking instead at the language of male friendship that pervades these documents. To be sure, Kyd's discussion of friendship with Marlowe (usefully dead) is entirely in the negative. Though he discloses that they have shared one chamber and an unnamed patron for whose company they both wrote plays, he also refers to Marlowe distantly as "this Marlowe." And Kyd's repudiation of Marlowe, when it comes, could hardly be more emphatic:

> That J shold loue or be familer frend, with one so irreligious, were verie rare, when Tullie saith *Digni sunt amicitia quibus in ipsis inest causa cur diligantur* which neither was in him, for person, quallities, or honestie, besides he was intemperate & of a cruel hart, the verie contraries to which, my greatest enemies will saie by me. (BROOKE, 104, emphasis added)

And yet: when we read this passage within the constellation of meanings that surround male-male friendship in this period, Kyd's repudiation becomes more complicated. The quotation from Cicero's "De Amicitia," or dialogue on friendship—"they bee worthye of Frendshippe, in whom there is good cause why they should be loued," reads a contemporary translation (T. Newton, E2)—is straightforward enough, implying that Kyd and Marlowe were never friends, because Marlowe was not worthy. But the quotation derives from a section of the dialogue on the ending of intimate male-male friendships that *have* existed: "There is also somtimes (as it were) a certain calamity or mishap in the departure from frendes" (Newton, E1).

Read in relation to Cicero's dialogue, the letter denying friendship seems suddenly suffused with, haunted by, a dead friendship. "That J shold loue or be familer frend, with one so irreligious, were verie rare," Kyd writes, and Cicero's text uses the same word, *rare* (*rara*), in an exclamation directly following the line Kyd recites, to describe the "rare class" (*rara genum*) of friends worthy to be loved, and then again to amplify on this rarity: "It is a rare thing [*rara genum*] (for surely al excellent things are rare [*rara*]) and theris nothĩg harder, then to finde a thing which in euery respect in his kinde is throughlye perfect" (Newton, E2). "All excellent thinges are rare" declares the marginal gloss on this sentence in the contemporary translation, and in this context, Kyd's rare love or familiar friendship with Marlowe begins to look not only rare (unusual) but also rare (valuable, excellent).

Read through the classical text that it prominently cites, Kyd's letter is haunted by Marlowe in another sense as well, for Cicero's dialogue, often called "Laelius on Friendship," stages a conversation in which several interlocutors question Laelius on his feelings of grief upon the death of his close friend Scipio. Kyd, writing a few days after Marlowe's death, repudiating his acquaintance with "this Marlowe," quotes a classical dialogue on friendship in which the central figure speaks of his grief for the death of a close friend. Given Kyd's allusive writing practice elsewhere in the letters to Puckering, we might read the recourse to classical quotation as itself a marker for, inscription of, a kind of male relation in this context: Marlowe, Kyd writes, "wold report St John to be our saviour Christes Alexis J cover it with reverence and trembling that is that Christ did loue him with an extraordinary loue" (Brooke, 107). To cover it with reverence and trembling is to discover an allusion to Virgil's homoerotic eclogue; extraordinary love (*rara genum?*) is made to speak Latin, and Kyd's denial of love and friendship with Marlowe, written in Latin, begins to speak another language, that of male-male conversation. (What is covered by reference to Tullie?)[7]

Walter J. Ong argues that the learning of Latin itself functioned as a male puberty rite in English culture, separating the men from the boys and the women; the reading of Latin, particularly Cicero, was an everyday part of male education during the period. While at Cambridge, Marlowe and his fellow students attended "a rhetorick lecture, of some p[ar]t of Tully, for the space of an houre," every afternoon at three o'clock (Hardin, 388); Kyd's education at the Merchant Taylors' School was similar in method and content (Freeman, 6–10; Siemon, "Sporting"). Cicero is built into the structure of, and central to the rhetoric of, the everydayness of male relations in this era. These are some of the cultural meanings of Kyd's reference to Cicero; even as the letters to Puckering deny close acquaintance or conversation with Marlowe, they inscribe it, in terms that both Goldberg (*Sodometries*, 63–81) and Bruce Smith (81–93) have further identified as the homoerotic classical pastoral.[8] These are *conversation*'s intersecting spaces: "Come *live with me* and be my love," Marlowe writes elsewhere, precipitating reply poems from other men, shuffled in numerous commonplace books and manuscripts, "And we will *all the pleasures* prove" (Marlowe, "Passionate," 2:537).[9]

The covering and uncovering of male relations in this case plays the line Alan Bray has identified between sodomy and male friendship in this period ("Homosexuality"), and the larger problem in these letters (including the related, more famous testimony of Richard Baines in the same case) is one of keeping separate the languages of male relations.[10] Baines too says Marlowe associated Christ and Saint John the Evangelist, though he does not "cover it with reverence and trembling," writing instead that Christ "vsed him as the sinners of Sodoma" (Brooke, 99). For Baines the problem is to remain outside Marlowe's discourse of male relations, even as he announces its persuasiveness; he testifies

> that this Marlow doth not only hould [these opinions] himself, but *almost into every Company he Cometh* he perswades men to Atheism ... as J Richard Baines will Justify

> & approue . . . and *almost al men with whome he hath Conversed* any time will testify
> the same. (BROOKE, 99, my emphasis)

Marlowe's conversation is potentially *conversion*, the "Conuersacion [*to*] the
Heythen"—and again can be read over into other modes of conversation: "If these
delights *thy mind may move*; / Then *live with mee*, and be *my love*" (Marlowe,
"Passionate," 2:537). Such conversation must be marked as both irresistible (and
thus threatening to the state) and not fully successful (thus allowing Baines to testify as one not "perswade[d] . . . to Atheism").

Kyd's attempts, too, to separate himself from Marlowe's papers, person, and circle of conversation face the same problem: to disclose an intimate knowledge of
Marlowe and at the same time to disavow acquaintance, intimacy, conversion:

> Ffor more assurance that J was not of that vile opinion [of atheism], Lett it but please
> your Lordship to enquire of such as he *conversd* withall, that is (*as J am geven to vnder-
> stand*) with Harriot, Warner, Royden, and some stationers in Paules churchyard, . . .
> of whose consent *if J had been*, no question but J also shold haue been of their con-
> sort. (BROOKE, 105, my emphasis)

To link *consent* and *consort* so emphatically is dangerous ground for Kyd, who
has already admitted consorting with Marlowe, and the closeness of Richard
Brathwait's later phrase ("consenting Consort") serves as a reminder of the continuing strength of that linkage within the discourse of male friendship—even if,
in Kyd, it appears here under negation ("as J am geven to vnderstand . . . if J had
been").[11]

Though I have dwelt on Kyd's remarks about Marlowe, I want to make it clear
that I see them as representative of early modern dramatic collaborative and
domestic practice only in the discourses they employ under negation—only in the
disclosures they make that seemingly oppose their expressed intent of distance
from, rather than proximity to, Marlowe. But place Marlowe and Kyd, writing in
one chamber, next to Aubrey's recounting of another pair of playwrights living and
writing near the theater:

> There was a wonderfull consimility of phansey between [Francis Beaumont] and Mr.
> John Fletcher, which caused the dearnesse of friendship between them. . . . They
> lived together on the Banke side, not far from the Play-house, both batchelors; lay
> together . . . had one wench in the house between them, which they did so admire;
> the same cloathes and cloake, &c., between them. (AUBREY, 1:95–96)

This passage sanctions what Kyd is eager in his circumstances to avoid (but discloses anyway): a portrayal of a collaborative male friendship that is reflexive and
imitative. As I have argued elsewhere ("Dads," 303–4), Aubrey's account emphasizes the playwrights' doubly reflexive "consimility of phansey"; his description suggests the theatricality and perhaps indiscernibility of playwrights who wear the
same clothes and cloak, not far from the playhouse.

In Aubrey's account we may thus see the interpenetration of modes of "living" and identity with modes of performance, acting, and writing. In his essay "Of Friendship," Francis Bacon writes, "where a Man cannot fitly play his owne Part: If he haue not a *Frend*, he may quit the Stage" (116), and it is worth recalling, through Bacon's metadramatic vocabulary, that a number of the dramatists cited above, among them Shakespeare, Jonson, Armin, and Rowley, were also active as actors, playing *as well as writing* others' parts. The wills of the players—documents that inscribe relations of fellow-ship among the "sharers" in the company and apprenticeship (itself a kind of pedagogy or convers[at]ion)—often produce such a shuffling and sharing of clothing, roles, and other properties:

> Item I geve and bequeathe to my ffellowe william Shakespeare a Thirty shillinges peece in gould. . . . Item I giue vnto Samuell Gilborne my Late Aprentice the some of ffortye shillinges and my mouse Colloured veluit hose and a white Taffety dublet A blacke Taffety sute my purple Cloke sword and dagger And my base viall.
> (HONIGMANN AND BROCK, 73, editorial notations not reproduced)

Around the theaters in early modern England, this accumulating evidence suggests, there was a complicated culture of male relations that we have only begun to unearth and analyze—a culture characterized by co(i)mplicated identifications and by (simultaneously) collaborative living and writing arrangements.[12] And even funeral arrangements, for it seems Fletcher and his friend and collaborator Massinger were buried in the same grave. "Playes they did write together, were great friends," Aston Cokain, another playwright, says. "And now one Grave includes them at their ends" (186).[13] I am arguing, in short, that we cannot begin fully to understand the practice of playwrighting, collaborative *or* singular, until we see it as enmeshed in, located within, *conversant* with (in the earlier senses), other material practices and discourses: the language and everyday conduct of male-male relations (and not incidentally in the largely male theater, the exclusion of women from most of these relations); the languages and conduct of domestic relations, which included men living, working, and sleeping together (Bray, *Homosexuality* and "Homosexuality"; Goldberg, *Sodometries*, 79); and the languages and conduct of textual relations, the ways in which this culture produced texts.

### Evidence

Let's return to the list of playwrights with which I began. This gathering does not aspire to be comprehensive, or complete, or exhaustive, nor could it be—a result of the kinds of evidence we possess.[14] I do not mean that the evidence is lamentably incomplete; rather, it has seemed so for certain modern purposes. The kinds of evidence we have customarily desired for discussing the authorship of Renaissance plays (e.g., who wrote what lines of what play) may never have existed, because it may not have mattered to those who recorded the evidence we have, and/or because it did not matter in the same way, or with modern standards of "accuracy."

The list at the beginning of this essay, for example, is in part compiled from evidence recorded in the theatrical manager Henslowe's papers. Henslowe records payments made to playwrights for the completion of plays, advance payments for plays to be delivered later, installment payments for parts of plays, and payments made for revisions and augmentations of plays (Henslowe, *Diary*, ed. Greg; Bentley, *Dramatist*, 200–206; Carson, 54–66). These payments are registered alongside Henslowe's records on the purchase and circulation of other theatrical commodities: props, costumes, building materials. (This is not to mention the intercollation of records that seem to us to occupy the space of *household*, rather than *playhouse*, economics: personal loans and expenditures, Henslowe's memoranda to himself, recipes for medications, ways "[t]o know wher a thinge is $y^t$ Js stolen" [1:33], the recording of significant dates like the wedding of his stepdaughter, aphorisms [Carson, 5–13].) We learn from Henslowe that plays were sometimes parceled out for writing by acts, but we learn little about which playwrights wrote which acts and instead learn much more about the economy of the payment system: the value of particular kinds of contributions, the rate of payments for parts of plays, the value of revision and "additions," the frequency of revision, etc. Even from someone as concerned as Henslowe is with property—with accounts and things stolen—there is no accounting of *intellectual* property in our terms.

Henslowe's papers emphasize that the terms in which playwrighting was discussed were fundamentally economic; they concerned the attributed value of kinds of labor in/for the playhouse, and they remind us that playwrights were employees of acting companies who produced scripts that became the property not of the "authors" who produced them but of the companies that produced them onstage. The playwright Richard Brome's contracts with the Salisbury Court players—requiring that Brome write three plays a year, deal exclusively with this company, probably supply prologues, epilogues, and new scenes for revivals of older plays, and forgo printing "his" plays without the company's permission—illustrate this in detail, and Bentley's evidence suggests that other professional dramatists and companies observed these same strictures (*Dramatist*, 111–44).[15] Collaboration and authorship, then, from the perspective of Henslowe's papers and other theatrical records, are not about the precise attribution of intellectual property but about the allocation of labor, and (co)laborers.

The other main body of evidence for authorship and collaboration is the ascription of plays to writers in print, typically on title pages of printed plays in quarto format. But this evidence, too, is not simply to be weighed within a modern paradigm of facticity or fiction. Early modern title pages of printed playtexts do not simply deploy authors' names as we now do; the appearance of playwrights' names on title pages must be seen as part of a network of figures that appear on play quartos and authorize a text, most notably the acting company and patron. Playwrights' names, when they do appear (and they do so much more regularly in the 1620–1640s than at the beginning of this period), function as a kind of printer's device, a selling point for a playtext, like the recitation of memorable events of the play's plot ("the obtayning of *Portia* by the choyse of three chests"), the advertisement that the text is presented "[a]s it hath beene diuerse times acted" by a particular acting company ("the right Honorable my Lord Chamberlaines seruants"), performing at a particular theater ("at the Globe on the Banck-side"), or for a particularly noteworthy audience ("As it vvas presented before her Highnes this last Christmas"), or with a particular audience reaction ("with great applause").[16] Printed ascriptions of authorship are thus implicated in the economics of printing, the vendibility of certain printed features, including names, and often the posthumous fame of the playwright(s). Title pages suggest that, first, ascriptions of authorship were not essential data for inclusion in published plays (Masten, "Beaumont," 337–39); second, the notion of complete, "accurate" authorial ascription was not one to which this period necessarily subscribed ("William Rowley, Thomas Dekker, John Ford, &c." [*Witch of Edmonton*]); and third, there was no stigma attached to printing a play as *either* collaborative *or* singlehandedly produced.

The emergence of single-volume collections of plays in folios — particularly *The Workes of Beniamin Jonson* (1616) and *Mr William Shakespeares Comedies, Histories & Tragedies* (1623) — might seem to deviate from the practice I have described, organized as they are around a particular playwright. If quarto playtexts highlight a network of figures associated with playmaking — actors, audiences, printers, sometimes (and increasingly) writers — this situation does begin to change contemporaneously with the publication of plays in the folio format. As a number of recent studies have shown, folio volumes rearranged and reconstituted this network of figures and began to organize plays around a central authorial figure. Studies by Stallybrass and White, Loewenstein, Timothy Murray, and others on the Jonson folio, and by Blayney, de Grazia, and Marcus on the Shakespeare folio, have suggested the immense amount of cultural work involved in converting texts written for the theater (with the writer[s] at the very least decentered, the initial but by no means the controlling producer[s] of meaning) into volumes that could organize texts under a singular authorial patronymic.[17] But while these folio collections do work in a new mode, it is likewise clear from these volumes that the construction of dramatic authorship in the early seventeenth century is no fait accompli in 1616 or 1623. Recent critical studies have emphasized the tentativeness of this new mode of organization — its reliance on earlier models of classicism and patronage (Jonson) and its continued dependence on the network of figures associated with the theater, patronage, and the publishing house (Shakespeare). The folio as a form continued to be a site of contestation, a complicated (de)construction site, well into the 1660s and 1670s, as the Beaumont and Fletcher folios (1647, 1679) and the Margaret Cavendish folios (1662, 1668) demonstrate (Masten, "Dads").

To resist the notion that dramatic authorship becomes an accomplished fact with the publication of early seventeenth-century collections is to resist the common critical assumption that authorship is a desire in the minds of authors that pre-exists its articulation; the appearance of "authorship" in the Jonson and Shakespeare folios of 1616 and 1623, respectively, is said to give voice to something always-already present—the presumptive human desire to possess what one has written. Authorship, in this paradigm, does not come into being so much as it is at long last given articulation; the term I have used, *emergence*, is not fully appropriate either, if it is taken to imply that authorship comes out from within some interior, anterior space. This may be the assumption of Loewenstein's description of Jonson's "bibliographic ego"; likewise, a careful sentence in Marcus's reading of the Shakespeare folio—"the construction of a transcendent, independent place for art was a project that empowered seventeenth-century authors and opened up a whole range of new possibilities for their lives and work" (*Puzzling*, 30)—holds within it the assumption that "Authors *wanted* to be recognized as individuals with their own identifying attributes" (29, my emphasis).

Recent work on these materials has, however, begun to argue that "seventeenth-century authors" did not exist independently of their construction in the textual materials we read and that, to the extent that there appears to have been a desire for authorship, that desire is itself related to the textual articulation of authorship elsewhere.[18] Second (and following from this), since early seventeenth-century dramatic folios did not simply voice already present desires, they also did not simply bring forth authorship in the apparently immutable and timeless form familiar to us today. Questions posed by the Beaumont and Fletcher folios—Are Beaumont and Fletcher collaborating playwrights? Are they a single "author"? Are they collaborating "authors"?—suggest that the viability of the author as the paradigm of textual production in drama was still very much open to question in 1647. Far from being an accomplished event ("the birth of the author"), authorship continued to be negotiated in relation to the collaboration that prevailed earlier in the century; conversely, collaboration was also rewritten in relation to the emerging regime of the author, and the urgency of knowing the lineage of plays and parts of plays—an urgency that has since prevailed in literary-historical treatments of these texts—was brought into being.

The term *lineage* is no accident, for—just as collaboration can be situated at the complicated intersection of homoeroticism, male friendship/conversation, and domestic relations—authorship emerges inseparably from discourses and practices now viewed as distinct: reproductive, textual, political, dynastic. Rereading tropes of filiation and consanguinity in the preliminaries to the first Shakespeare folio, de Grazia writes that "the 1623 preliminaries work to assign the plays a common lineage: a common origin in a single parent and a shared history of production" (*Shakespeare*, 39). And it is worth recalling that, far from being a simple, ungendered, and unambiguous signifier for *writer*, as it now is, the word *author* continued in this period to inhabit a complex network of meanings, including: "person who originates or gives existence to anything"; "The Creator"; "He who authorizes or instigates; the prompter or mover"; and "One who begets; a father, an ancestor"

(*OED*; Gilbert and Gubar; Said; Grossman, 1–2). In addition to the modern mean-ing ("the composer or writer of a treatise or book"), *author* could also mean "the person on whose authority a statement is made; an authority, an informant." The translators of the 1611 Authorized Version write to James I that they "offer [the book] to your MAIESTIE, not onely as to our King and Soueraigne, but as to the princi-pall moouer and Author of the Worke" (Holy Bible, A2ᵛ). *Author* had also at one time meant "one who has authority over others; a director, ruler, commander"—a meaning that resonates in the translators' words as well.

All of these meanings—some of which are still residual in words like *authority*, *authorize*, and *authoritarian*—enter English at about the same time and continue to circulate during the early modern period. In this context, it is not possible to say, for example, that paternity was simply a "metaphor" for authorship (Gilbert and Gubar; Grossman, 239), for which is the tenor here and which the vehicle? This discursive fact, along with the male-male languages and practices associated with collaboration in and around the theaters, may begin to explain the almost entire absence of women writing drama in a period during which they wrote, sometimes prolifically, in other genres; notable exceptions are Elizabeth Cary's probably unperformed, anonymously published *Tragedy of Mariam*, and Mary Wroth's unpublished but possibly privately circulated and performed *Love's Vic-tory*.[19] Margaret Cavendish's collections of plays, published much later in the sev-enteenth century, are indeed attempts to insert her work into a rhetoric of author-ship that, as the nexus of meanings above suggests, made the participation of women seem oxymoronic (a female "creator"? "father"? "begetter"?), or revolu-tionary (a female "authority"? "commander"?).

The notion of the author is thus multiply contingent. First, the author is impli-cated in, evolving with and out of, a number of culturally resonant discourses (paternity and reproduction, patriarchal-absolutism, classical authority). And sec-ond, as Foucault suggested and as recent work has helped to document, the author is a historical development—an idea that gradually becomes attached to playtexts over the course of the seventeenth century, registered in the increasing appearance of the term in the playtexts' printed apparatus in quartos and folios.

Another category of evidence that suggests authorship's contingency is the emergence of booksellers' catalogs of printed plays in the mid- and late seventeenth century. Edward Archer's 1656 catalog advertises itself as

An Exact and perfect CATALOGUE of all the PLAIES that were ever printed ; together, with all the Authors names ; and what are Comedies, Histories, Interludes, Masks, Pastorels, Tragedies. (MASSINGER, *Old Law* [some copies], a1; GREG, *Bibliography*, 3:1328–38)

Running to sixteen pages and 622 titles, this catalog groups plays alphabetically by title and includes a column of letters noting genre and a column that sometimes attributes authorship. The catalog appended to *The Careles Shepherdess* (reprinted in Greg, *Bibliography*, 3:1320–27) is a title list with less frequent notation of authorship.[20]

Many authorial identifications in the Archer list now seem to us to be "incorrect" ("Hieronimo, both parts . . . *Will.Shakespeare*"); some plays whose authorial attributions now seem noncontroversial are not identified with authors (*Doctor Faustus, Troilus and Cressida*); and, judged in relation to other evidence, collaborations are often simplified (the only collaborators identified as such are Beaumont and Fletcher). But, again, to read the evidence of these catalogs for the factual identification of authorship or authorial shares, as Greg does, is to mistake their function ("Authorship Attribution").

Unlike the modern, author-organized *Short Title Catalogue*, the seventeenth-century catalogs are organized to facilitate locating plays by *title* (rather than by author); to the extent that they engage authorship, the catalogs seem not as interested in consistency with even the other available printed attributions as they are in producing an interest (in the literary and the economic senses) in plays associated with recognizable names. Playwrights' names emerge into print as a way to create desire for volumes available for purchase in several London bookshops around 1656: "And all these Plaies you may either have at the Signe of the *Adam and Eve*, in Little Britain; or, at the *Ben Johnson's* Head in Thredneedle-street, over against the Exchange" (*Old Law*, a1). That this catalog, one of the first to attempt the large-scale attribution of early English drama to authors, should be sold at the sign of a playwright's head reminds us, first, that dramatic authorship emerges from the publishing house and only indirectly from the theater and, second, that authorship in its emergence is as much about marketing as about true attribution. To revise Foucault's question: *Where* is an Author? In the bookshop.[21]

### Individuation

That the categories of evidence available to us (theatrical records, printed title pages, book lists) sometimes conflict, overlap, and/or do not fully agree suggests that there is a systemic ambivalence[22] about the division of authorship in early English drama, an ambivalence that many modern critics have sought to ignore — or, indeed, to reverse. The critical approach that has prevailed for much of this century has emphasized: the isolation of discrete authors writing alone;[23] the analysis of a developing, individuated style over the course of an authorial career, rather than the mutual inflections of style(s) among collaborators, or the existence/emergence of a (play)house style, what Aubrey might call a "consimility of phansey"; the organization of the dramatic canon into a series of authors' "complete works," rather than the less anachronistic canons that might be organized around acting companies or years of the repertory; the publication, performance, and teaching of, especially, Shakespeare, as separate from "his contemporaries."

Traditionally, criticism has viewed collaboration as a subset or aberrant kind of authorship, the collusion of two otherwise individuated authors whom subsequent readers could[24] discern and separate out by discovering the traces of individuality (including handwriting, spelling, word choice, imagery, and syntactic formations) left in the collaborative text. The study of collaboration has sought to reverse a collaborative process of textual production—to make collaborative playtexts conform to an authorial model by separating them into smaller units ostensibly identified with particular single playwrights.

The work of Cyrus Hoy, the most influential example of such studies, attempts to separate out the collaborators in the Beaumont and Fletcher canon on the grounds of "linguistic criteria"; there is, however, a recurrent conflict in Hoy's project (and others that have followed it [Lake, *Canon*; MacD. P. Jackson; Hope]) between post-Enlightenment assumptions about authorship, textual property, and stylistic individuality, and the evidence of the texts under analysis. Hoy wishes "to distinguish any given dramatist's share in a play of dual or doubtful authorship" by applying a "body of criteria that, derived from the unaided plays of the dramatist in question, will serve to identify his work in whatever context it may appear" ("Shares I," 130). His studies thus begin by presuming singular authorship ("unaided plays") and proceed to collaboration (tellingly glossed as "dual or doubtful"). Furthermore, his results assume that a writer's use of *ye* for *you* and of contractions like *'em* for *them* is both individually distinct and remarkably constant "in whatever context."

These assumptions are challenged by evidence Hoy himself adduces. Problematically, as Hoy realizes, "there is no play that can with any certainty be regarded as the unaided work of Beaumont" ("Shares I," 130),[25] and he admits that "Beaumont's linguistic practices are themselves so widely divergent as to make it all but impossible to predict what they will be from one play to another" ("Shares III," 86). Beaumont's presence will thus be ascertained as that which remains after Fletcher, Massinger, et al. have been subtracted. Further, because he finds *The Faithful Shepherdess*, though "undoubtedly Fletcher's own," linguistically at odds with his other unaided works, Hoy omits it from his tabulation of evidence establishing Fletcher's "own" distinctive style ("Shares I," 142).

Whatever the other problems of method and evidence, this deliberate omission seriously undermines Hoy's project and alerts us to the theoretical issues inherent in using evidence of "linguistic preferences" and "language practices" in the pursuit of essential, stable identities ("Shares I," 130). These terms, indeed, may expose a problem now more fully legible through the lens of sexuality theory: Is Fletcher's style chosen or innate? an act or an essence? Are his practices preferred or (and?) performative?[26] Jonathan Hope's recent attempts to detect writers by correlating syntactic variants with birth region and age within a rapidly changing circa 1600 linguistic environment likewise fail to account for the transformation(s) of a writer's linguistic practices over time or in relation to particular social, generic, and/or collaborative circumstances, or for the performativity of linguistic practices, particularly as registered in drama. Like Hoy, Hope also omits *The Faithful Shepherdess* from his Fletcher sample (14, 75).

The results of Hoy and others are, furthermore, rendered problematic by the frequency of revision in these texts and the mediation of copyists, compositors, and their "linguistic preferences" between Hoy's hypothetical writers' copy and the printed text he actually analyzes.[27] This is even to leave aside the broader nexus of collaboration in these plays that this essay has largely ignored by concentrating on playwrights—the participation of: composers of music; actors revising scripts in ways that may or may not have eventually registered in the texts we have (Loewenstein, 266; Masten, "Beaumont," 344–45, 350; Jenkins, 62–63); acting company book-holders (Long, "Bookkeepers") and copyists (Howard-Hill, *Ralph Crane*; J. A. Roberts; Shakespeare, *Tempest*, ed. Orgel, 56–61); audience desires in the context of the theater as a market enterprise ("Beaumont," 339–40, 348–49). Additional questions about linguistic methods arise when we consider the complexities at the outset of collaborative writing itself, which may have included "prior agreement on outline, vetting of successive drafts by a partner, composition in concert, brief and possibly infrequent intervention, and even a mutual contagion of style as a result of close association" (Beaumont, *Knight*, ed. Zitner, 10).

The last item in Zitner's series highlights the extent to which he remains in Hoy's paradigm, in which one writer's healthy individual style must be protected from infection by another's. The presumed universality of individuated style depends on a network of legal and social technologies specific to a post-Renaissance capitalist culture (e.g., intellectual property, authorial copyright, individuated handwriting [Woodmansee; Goldberg, *Writing Matter*]). Furthermore, the collaborative project in the theater was predicated on *erasing* the perception of any differences that might have existed, for whatever reason,[28] between collaborated parts.

Moreover, writing in this theatrical context implicitly resists the notion of monolithic personal style that Hoy presumes: a playwright im/personates another (many others) in the process of writing a playtext and thus refracts the supposed singularity of the individual in language. At the same time, he often stages in language the *sense* of distinctive personae, putting "characteristic" words in another's mouth. What Hoy says of Beaumont might well apply to *all* playwrights in this period:

> His linguistic "preferences"—if they can be termed such—are, in a word, nothing if not eclectic. . . . it is this very protean character which makes it, in the end, quite impossible to establish for Beaumont a neat pattern of linguistic preferences that will serve as a guide to identifying his work. ("Shares III," 87)

A more detailed critique of linguistic attribution studies might investigate the extent to which, for example, Hoy's specific linguistic criteria (the pronominal forms *ye/you*) are, as the *OED* suggests, actually class-related differences—the extent to which they reflect not an individual's linguistic preference but rather a subject inscribed in and constituted by specific, culturally variable, linguistic practices. (This is an issue of some complexity, for *ye* rather than *you* may announce the writer's inscription in class-coded language and/or may be the writer's ascription of that language to characters within the text.) Or a further critique might consider the methods and evidence Hoy uses to produce a layered composition (Beaumont revising or revised by Fletcher; Massinger shuffling the papers of Beaumont and Fletcher) out of a two-dimensional printed document. I cite here some of the general problematics of Hoy's work because it has become the standard model for twentieth-century considerations of collaboration. While more recent work on collaborative texts has ostensibly made progressive improvements and sought new methods, it remains susceptible to many of the points raised above, and Hoy usefully illustrates the distinctly modern notions of individuality and authorial property underlying these considerations (Lake, *Canon*; MacD. P. Jackson). The individuating aims and, I would argue, the problems of stylometric analysis are parallel to those of linguistic studies.

 The individuation model of collaboration has had significant effects not only within attribution studies but, more widely, on the editing and publication of early English drama—especially in "complete works" volumes and series—and on syllabi, curricular requirements in literature and theater programs, and performance schedules. Even an edition like the forthcoming *Collected Works of Thomas Middleton*—which is especially inclusive of collaborative playtexts and attentive to the centrality of collaboration in the early modern theater and in Middleton's career—attempts to identify parts of plays with particular playwrights, using linguistic attribution. More seriously, *The Plays and Poems of Philip Massinger* is overwhelmingly given over to plays "of sole authorship," including only two of Massinger's collaborations.[29] Complete works editions of Shakespeare routinely omit *The Two Noble Kinsmen*; only in its third generation has the Arden series included this play. A more extreme version of this methodology is the printing, in both the Riverside and the Oxford editions, of only the ostensibly Shakespearean passages of *Sir Thomas More*, the manuscript of which encodes the most evidence of collaboration and revision of any surviving play from the period (Wells and Taylor, 889–92). Collaborative texts thus are made to submit to an editorial apparatus founded on singular authorship, their "authorial problems" solved, before reading and interpretation are permitted to proceed. The effects of the individuation model extend to the MLA citation procedure followed in this volume; the method of citing texts parenthetically by "author" only uncomfortably accommodates the materials that we are here studying and, at least for the uninitiated reader, gives a falsely concrete sense to an only emergent notion of authorship.[30]

## Authorship

I myselfe readinge mine owne woorkes, am sometime in that case, that I thincke *Cato* telleth the tale, and not myselfe.

—THOMAS NEWTON, translating Cicero, writing to his friend Atticus, in *The Booke of Freendshippe* (NEWTON A2$^v$, A3)

To be sure your stile may passe for currant, as the richest alloy, imitate the best Authors
as well in Oratory as History.
— HENRY PEACHAM, *The Compleat Gentleman* (44)

This essay has argued that we need to reconceive our sense of how collaboration
functioned in the early English theater—as a mode of writing and as a discursive
practice embedded in other discourses and practices of the period. This reconcep-
tualization will have significant effects on texts that we customarily think of as having been written by one playwright, working "alone." Our approach to writing
"alone" in this period must be reconceived historically to account for a range of
practices, including:

1. A pedagogical practice that emphasizes imitation over what we call originality (Quint; Greene); the copying and translating of classic models, methods, styles
(Goldberg, *Writing Matter*; Pittenger); renaissance over naissance.[31]

2. A rhetorical grammar that serves as a deep structuring device—a handbook
for the reproduction and dissemination of style that is ideally not individuated
(Parker, *Literary*; Trousdale, *Shakespeare*).

3. Practices of the hand writing that, as Goldberg argues, resist rather than disclose (modern notions of) the individual, inscribing instead the indivisibility of
master and pupil, king and secretary, the "manual" and the hand. Further, indivisibility at the level of the letter is not separable from other practices that I am separately enumerating; "[t]ranslation," Goldberg remarks, in a way that is illuminated
by our reading of Kyd writing Cicero, "extends well beyond the writing exercises
that filled the notebooks of grammar school children, for the proprieties that mark
the hand are also behavioral paradigms for structures of decorous and refined
behavior" (*Writing Matter*, 42–43).

4. A corresponding notion of the "individual" subject that, within certain identifications of social class, gender, nationality, and race, emphasizes similarity and
continuity over individuality in the modern sense (Whigham; R. Williams, *Keywords*; Stallybrass, "Shakespeare").

5. An approach—in early modern culture generally and particularly in the theater—to the replication and dissemination of what we misleadingly call "source"
material that cannot be accounted for within modern notions of intellectual property (T. Murray, 70; Goldberg, "Speculations"). I mean to describe here a writing
practice that is agglutinative and appropriative in its approach both to texts outside
the theater and to other plays (see Mowat, "Theater," in this volume). Our terms
for these practices (*appropriation, borrowing, citation, parody, plagiarism,* etc.) all
imply a modern regulation of intellectual property that was only emergent in a
period that lacked, but did not see itself as lacking, authorial copyright.[32]

6. A tradition within the theater of ongoing revision, deletion, and "additions,"
whether by the "original" playwright (Ioppolo; Urkowitz, " 'Well-sayd' "; Taylor and

Warren) or by others. (In this sense, two *Lears* and, though the realization has been resisted, three *Hamlets* are the rule, not the exceptions; Henslowe's papers, however, suggest that we cannot restrict revision, as the cited critics have, to a singular playwright revising his own work.) The modern critical model of authorial development that dwells upon "date of composition" and first editions (to construct, say, the chronological arrangement of Shakespeare's plays in modern editions) obscures the extent to which a play revived and reprinted could exert a continuing influence on the "original" playwright himself, as well as other playwrights watching, acting in, or revising the play. Revision may furthermore figure a *complication* of the authorial self—rather than disclose its ongoing unity of intention (McMillin, *Elizabethan*, 153–59).

7. The effects of a collective writing practice even on plays written in isolation. To what extent does Beaumont before or after his death function within Fletcher's "individually" written plays? To what extent are the collaborations of Beaumont and Fletcher, or Shakespeare and Fletcher—in practice, content, style—transmitted into the work of Massinger? And to Field and Middleton and . . . ?

What might it mean, then, to write "alone" in such a context? Turning our normative paradigm on its head, we might hypothetically ask whether notions of aberrancy were attached to the 18 percent of the textual production produced *merely* single-handedly for the Rose theater in 1598 (Carson, 57); was it perverse to write "alone" in this context? Peacham's writing instructions are a kind of answer, a reminder, even as he invokes "Authors," of the distance of this culture's sense of style and individuated production from that of our own culture. Like currency (related etymologically to *discourse*), Peacham's gentlemanly style circulates, and is an alloying of genres and authors, a collaboration of what's "currant" and what's past/passed.

## Extended Conversation

Not so common as commendable it is, to see young gentlemen choose thē such friends with whom they may seeme beeing absent to be present, being a sunder to be conuersant, beeing dead to be aliue.
—LYLY, *Euphues*, 1:97

By way of a conclusion that is more prolegomena than solution, I want to return to Thomas Kyd, for a reconstrual of the dynamics of conversation, collaboration, and writing "alone" may have something to say about the other bits of evidence that survive about this playwright—his writing, sleeping, and living arrangements. The bits are scarce and fragmentary, but I want to suggest that they speak in the discourses we have been analyzing—and speak more resonantly than in a critical discourse that seeks to deliberate the facticity of Kyd's life and "settle" the authorship of his texts.

• The texts that we can associate with Kyd are collaborations (counting *The Spanish Tragedie* as such, as it was seen in the period) and translations, most relevantly, his translation of Garnier's tragedy *Cornelia* (published 1594). At his most heteroglossic, as in *The Spanish Tragedie*'s "play of Hieronimo in sundry languages . . . set down in English," Kyd is both collaborator and translator. Add to this Hieronimo's Latin speech at the end of act 2, citing an editor's gloss: " 'A pastiche, in Kyd's singular fashion, of tags from classical poetry, and lines of his own composition' (Boas). There are reminiscences of Lucretius, Virgil, and Ovid" (Edwards, 44). But what do *singular* and *fashion* mean in Kyd's shuffling context?

• Another example of Kyd as translator that converses in the discourses we have analyzed is a 1588 volume identified by the initials T.K. Kyd—with his waste and idle papers, his pages and fragments shuffled unbeknownst to him—would have the Privy Council think he was no great housekeeper, but evidence suggests he is the T.K. who translated Tasso's *Padre di Famiglia*, a book T.K. calls, in English, *The housholders philosophie. Wherein is perfectly described, the true oeconomia of housekeeping.* Conversation: interchange of words or ideas; dwelling in a place. . . .

• *The Spanish Tragedie* had an afterlife not only in its continual revision, revival, and republication but also in *The Spanish Comedy*, also apparently known as *Don Horatio* and *The Comedy of Jeronimo.* This play was a sequel or prequel to the now more famous *Tragedie* (Henslowe, *Diary*, ed. Greg, 2:150), and Henslowe's records show that it was performed frequently in repertory with the *Tragedie* ("*Jeronimo*"), for example, on March 13–14, 1591; March 30–31, 1591; April 22 and 24, 1592; and May 21–22, 1592 (*Diary*, ed. Greg, 1:13–15).

Another related title, *The First Part of Jeronimo* (published 1605), may be the same play as the *Comedy*, or a revision of it. In either case, it registers the continuing popularity of "Kyd's" Jeronimo play(s)—whether or not Kyd participated in its composition at some point (Freeman, 176–77).

Add to this the circulation of *The Spanish Tragedie*, later subtitled *Hieronimo is mad againe*, in other plays through allusion, emulation, parody, etc. Hieronimo's act 3 lament for his dead son, for example—

Oh eies, no eies, but fountains fraught with teares,
Oh life, no life, but liuely fourme of death:
Oh world, no world but masse of publique wrongs. (1592 edn., E1ᵛ-E2)—

is replayed tragicomically at the end of Middleton-Massinger-Rowley's *The Old Law* (1618?). The play's Clown learns that, as a result of a law's repeal, he will lose a two-to-one bet (his "venter"/venture) because he cannot have his old wife put to death and marry a new wife on the same day:

Oh Musick, no musick, but prove most dolefull Trumpets,
Oh Bride no Bride, but thou maist prove a Strumpet,
Oh venter, no venter, I have for one now none,
Oh wife, thy life is sav'd when I hope t'had been gone. (K4ᵛ)

We might then say that Kyd's collaborations continue after his death, if we are willing to acknowledge that playwrighting is a continuum in this culture that includes diachronic collaboration—the writing of several playwrights on a playtext at different times (revision) and the manifold absorption and reconstitution of plays and bits of plays by playwrights writing later. Hieronimo is mad, again and again.

*The Old Law's Spanish Tragi*-Comedy may remind us once more of problematic questions that the individuation model of playwrighting asks but is hard-pressed to answer: Who shuffled these papers? Whose "linguistic practices" or "preferences" does the Clown's speech register: those of Middleton? Massinger? Rowley? Kyd? (Marlowe?) A murderous/witty Clown, perhaps written in part by a playwright who also played clowns (Rowley), speaking in the voice of a mourning father who is both player and playwright, written by the two-handed son of a scrivener? What linguistic analysis will sort this out?

• Unlike Massinger and Fletcher, recorded in Cockayne's poem as lying in a single grave, Kyd had a solitary burial (Freeman, 38). But he is figuratively interred with Marlowe in another poem that takes up the question of the burial of playwrights, together or apart—Jonson's poem on the dead Shakespeare in the 1623 First Folio:

> *My* Shakespeare, *rise; I will not lodge thee by*
> Chaucer, *or* Spenser, *or bid* Beaumont *lye*
> *A little further, to make thee a roome:*
> *Thou art a Moniment, without a tombe,*
> . . . . . . . . . . . . . . . . . . . . . . . . . . . . .
> *That I not mixe thee so, my braine excuses;*
> *I meane with great, but disproportion'd* Muses:
> *For, if I thought my iudgement were of yeeres,*
> *I should commit thee surely with thy peeres,*
> *And tell, how farre thou didstst our* Lily *out-shine,*
> *Or sporting* Kid, *or* Marlowes *mighty line.* (JONSON, "To the Memory," 9)

There is a hint here, in the appearance of "sports" (erotic slang in the period, not unrelated to the term's more theatrical meanings [*OED*]) and the pun on *kid/goat* (a figure of playfulness, wantonness, even lechery)[33] of another Kyd that we have not seen in his terrorized letters to the Privy Council. What has *this* Kyd written? "Sporting Kid" seems no allusion to *The Spanish Tragedie* or *Cornelia*, though perhaps to *The Spanish Comedy*; Jonson's gloss must also be set alongside Dekker's, "industrious *Kyd*" (K4v)—an evocation suggesting that Kyd's shape may change more than we have yet reckoned, for "industrious" does not seem fully appropriate to Kyd's currently slender canon.[34]

Unlike Cockayne's burial poem, Jonson's is a poem *against* mixing, *against* collaboration—a poem performing the separation of Shakespeare from his acting company and fellow playwrights, urging him toward a singular apotheosis. But even Jonson (greatly invested in this process of singularization, whether in this folio or his own) does not keep Kyd and Marlowe separate. His "*sporting* Kid" is lodged with Marlowe; they are written together, if not writing together, conversing in one line.

Reading "Closure and Enclosure in Marlowe," Marjorie Garber has analyzed a thematics and formal poetics of enclosure in Marlowe's writing that she finds epitomized, for example, in familiar lines from *The Jew of Malta*:

And as their wealth *in*creaseth, so *in*close
*In*finite riches *in* a little room. (GARBER, 20)

If we follow Garber's reading in seeing spatial homologies in the little room, the line, and Marlowe "working within the confines of the tiny Elizabethan stage" (21), we can, by reading Kyd writing with Marlowe, see that the confines of the chamber, the collaborative stage, and *Jonson's* line may enclose or disclose *several* playwrights, writing together. In a word, *conversation*. "[C]ome *Gaueston*, / And share the kingdom with thy deerest friend," reads some fragment of a letter Marlowe shuffled in a play (*The troublesome raigne*, A2). Or is the play shuffled into this letter, with which "it" begins? The little room, the collaborative early English playhouse, and the "oeconomia of housekeeping" in these related houses, may enclose and include discourses and practices we are only beginning to reckon.

### NOTES

* Thanks to Will Fisher, Jay Grossman, Karen Newman, Eric Wilson, and audiences at MLA 1994 and Brown University for comments and suggestions; to Eric Wilson and Marco Torres for research assistance; and to Johns Hopkins University Press for permission to reprint some words that they own in the section "Individuation" (Masten, "Beaumont").

1. This list is largely a redaction of Bentley's chapter "Collaboration" (*Dramatist*, 197–234), gathering information from title pages, Henslowe's papers, and the Stationers' Company Register. On the list's (non)comprehensiveness, see my section "Evidence" below. On Hand A et al., see McMillin, *Elizabethan*; on "Shakespeare and Middleton?," see Middleton, *Works*, ed. Taylor; on "Chapman and Shirley," see Bentley, *Dramatist*, 224–25; on "Jonson and another," see Orgel, "Text." Orgel's article, to which I am indebted, was the first to recognize the larger implications of Bentley's work on playwriting. I'm grateful to Jay Grossman for imagining the list.

2. In the remainder of this essay I deliberately use *OED*'s nineteenth-century "nonce-word" *playwrighting* in order to gesture toward three overlapping senses: (1) toward the process of writing for the theater (playwriting); (2) toward the identity category of being or acting *as* a playwright (what Bentley calls "The Profession of Dramatist"); and (3) through the word *wright*, toward the sense that the process of writing and rewriting plays was a craft, and a labor (cf. *shipwright*, *cartwright*).

3. This essay treats texts written for the professional theaters and does not engage theatrical writing (e.g., masques) produced in other locations.

4. Definitions and examples derive from the *OED*, unless noted.

5. Discussion has focused on whether the published additions are "characteristic" of Jonson. That additions/revisions might cohere more with the play under revision than they would disclose the "characteristic" hand of their writer is one of the present essay's corollaries. On Jonson and *The Spanish Tragedie*, see Siemon, 553 n. 2; Edwards, lxvi–lxvii.

6. My resistance to paleographic evidence as a conduit of (modern) identity is indebted to Goldberg, *Writing Matter*.

7. "The Romaine *Tullie* loued *Octauis*," says Morti·ner Senior in his catalog of "mightiest kings" and "their minions," "[a]nd not kings onelie, but the wisest men." (Marlowe, *The troublesome raigne*, D1)—signaling what Tullie's name may have referenced for Marlowe, Kyd, and others in their culture, whatever the "actual" relation of Cicero and Octavius.

8. Smith distances Cicero's dialogue from homoeroticism (36, 40–41), but see Smith, 84, and Goldberg, "Sodomy," 79, for bedfellows reading "De Amicitia."

9. Bowers attempts to strip away the collaborative history of this text, eliminating "non-Marlovian," "spurious" stanzas, but on the poem as implicated in networks of circulation, imitation, and response, see Marotti, 167, and W. Wall, 189–90.

10. On Baines, see Goldberg, "Sodomy,"; Fisher.

11. The period meanings of *consent* and *consort* are closely related and overlap with meanings of *conversation* and *converse* discussed above (*OED*).

12. See Baldwin's attempt to map the residences of members of the King's Men (*Organization*, 148–61).

13. For a more detailed analysis of the burial, see Masten, introduction to *Textual Intercourse*.

14. The list does not represent all *available* evidence; I have, for example, emphasized the best-known playwrights, while also suggesting that playwrights now forgotten often collaborated with those now canonized.

15. See also Dekker's comment (attributed, within a dream narrative, to Nashe): "being demaunded how Poets and Players agreed now, troth sayes hee, As Phisitions and patients agree, for the patient loues his Doctor no longer then till hee get his health, and the Player loues a Poet, so long as the sicknesse lyes in the two-penie gallery when none will come into it" (Dekker, *A KNIGHTS Coniuring*, L1).

16. Quotations are from the following Shakespeare title pages, respectively: *The most excellent Historie*; *The Tragoedy of Othello*; *A Most pleasaunt and excellent conceited Comedie*; *The Late, And much admired Play*; *A Pleasant Conceited Comedie*; *The Two Noble Kinsmen*.

17. To group these studies is *not* to say that they agree, especially on the question of who organized the texts under an authorial rubric or how that idea came into being. On Jonson, see also Brady and Herendeen.

18. For example, Jonson, the figure around whom so much discussion of the emergence of dramatic authorship revolves, was not dependent on the commercial theaters after 1602 and did not function as an "attached or regular professional" (Bentley, *Dramatist*, 31–32).

19. This is not to say that these dramas were not influenced by, or influences upon, public-theater plays. On Cary, see Ferguson; on Wroth, see Lewalski, *Writing*, 296–307.

20. The "Kirkman" list of 1661 (reprinted in Greg, *Bibliography*, 3:1338 f.) places an author col-

umn first but continues to group the plays alphabetically by title; authorship is thus marked more prominently than in the earlier catalogs, but title is still the organizing principle.

21. The playwright's head sign arrives on the scene *after* the closing of the theaters. I appreciate Peter Blayney's assistance in attempting to trace (thus far unsuccessfully) Jonson's Head prior to 1655–1658 (Plomer, 148).

22. Bentley writes: "a title-page statement . . . tended, as a number of examples show, to simplify the actual circumstances of composition" (*Dramatist*, 199). I argue that we cannot prioritize this evidence in this way, as if Henslowe's papers provide "actual circumstances," while printed ascriptions are mere representations. Both sets of evidence are mediated and provide no transparent access to "the actual."

23. E.g., the dust jacket of Hope's recent *The Authorship of Shakespeare's Plays*, which pictures Shakespeare, writing alone in a (nineteenth-century) study.

24. Or *must*: "Scholarly investigation of the *authorial problems* posed by collaborative drama is . . . a *necessary precondition* to critical and aesthetic considerations of such drama" (Hoy, "Critical," 4, my emphasis). Cf. McMullan, 149.

25. This uncertainty extends to the other playwrights of the period, and linguistic study often relies on external evidence to anchor its "unaided" samples, while aspiring to adjudicate the truth or falsehood of other evidence that comes from identical sources (e.g., title pages)—a selective practice that often relies upon and eventuates in the canon as already received.

26. On the performativity of sexuality and gender, see, for example, Judith Butler.

27. Hope acknowledges that "any expectation of textual integrity, or purity, in early Modern play-texts"—by which he apparently means an unmediated authorial transcript—"is misplaced" (4–5), but his study then largely ignores this issue.

28. McMullan's interpretation of this phrase as referring to *authorial* differences is apparently the central point of his critique of an earlier published version of this sentence (154).

29. The collection's rationale for inclusion is inconsistent: the canon seems to be defined by printed attributions to Massinger during or immediately after his lifetime, but one such play is excluded (*Old Law*); another collaboration is excluded because it has been previously edited (*Virgin Martyr*).

30. "[A]lphabetize entries in the list of works cited by the author's last name or, *if the author's name is unknown*, by the first word in the title," write *The MLA Style Manual's* collaborators (Achtert and Gibaldi, 102), suggesting that there is always an author, though some have not yet become known.

31. Rambuss's discussion of letter-writing and vocational manuals like Day's *The English Secretary* suggests that my numbered categories above must be seen as related and overlapping (30–48).

32. More "emergent" for some playwrights than for others, e.g., Jonson—with his manifold citations, marginal annotations, and early use of *plagiary* (and related words) to apply to texts. See Loewenstein.

33. Cf. "Leaping like wanton kids" (*FQ* 1.6.14.4, Spenser, 81). Adjectivally, *kid/kyd* also meant "well-known; famous; notorious" (*OED*).

34. For a reading of "incongruities" in *The Spanish Tragedy* that also takes off from Jonson's naming and then traces conflicting figurations of style and *sprezzatura* in the play, see Siemon. Siemon's reading goes some way toward demonstrating the multi-valency of

Kyd's writing in *The Spanish Tragedy,* and shows in particular its possible relation to pedagogical practices at the Merchant Taylors' School; my point is to assert Kyd's polyvocality as not simply characteristic of Kyd but as implicated in the larger circles of collaborative playwrighting. Cf. Greene's famous description of Shakespeare: "an absolute *Johannes fac totum.*"

# CHAPTER 21

# The Publication of Playbooks

*Peter W. M. Blayney*

FOURSCORE AND several years ago, Alfred W. Pollard told a memorable tale. He had realized that while each of Shakespeare's plays printed in quarto presented its own unique textual problem, one group of them (which he dubbed Bad Quartos) preserved texts of a kind quite distinct from the remainder (which he therefore called Good Quartos). He had also noticed that while some of the plays were first published by the men who first registered them at Stationers' Hall, others were not, and some were not registered at all. Imagining that he could distinguish two different kinds of "irregularity" in the registers, and that the differences coincided with the different kinds of text, Pollard constructed a narrative to explain the phenomena. It was, in fact, rather more than a mere narrative. Rejecting the prevailing view that virtually all play quartos were surreptitious piracies that the players had been powerless to prevent, Pollard offered a stirring melodrama in which Good players, with occasional help from Good stationers, struggled against a few Bad stationers and usually won.

Most experts today recognize that the story owed far more to Pollard's vivid imagination than to any real evidence. It remains true that the five quartos he described as Bad resemble each other more closely than they resemble any of the fourteen he called Good. But comparatively few of his notions of what constitutes "irregularity" in the Stationers' Registers have survived closer examination, and some of the scenarios he devised for individual plays—most notably *Hamlet*—are not even self-consistent, let alone plausible.

But no matter how flimsy the narrative has proved when subjected to scholarly scrutiny, as a story it has proved all too durable.[1] Like a folktale, it continues to surface in whole or in part in most introductory accounts of the relations between the early theater and the book trade. And so the old, unfounded myths persist: that acting companies usually considered publication to be against their best interests; that some publishers were so desperate to satisfy their eager customers that they would acquire plays by any dishonest means; that if a stationer failed to register a play he was probably trying to conceal its origins; that if he registered it but failed to publish, he was probably acting on behalf of the players to forestall piracy by someone else.

What keeps the story alive is, I suspect, a reluctance to question the principal fallacy on which it depends. That same false assumption had, in fact, supported the earlier narratives before Pollard borrowed it. Literary scholars are predisposed to assume that their own attitudes toward highly valued texts were shared by the public for whom those texts were first printed. It is therefore usually taken for granted that plays in quarto—especially *important* plays in quarto—must have sold like hot cakes. Editors who venture a guess at the size of the first edition of their chosen play almost always aim implausibly high: perhaps 1,500 copies, or perhaps 1,250; rarely, if ever, 1,000 or below. A publisher lucky enough to acquire a play, we have been repeatedly told, would confidently expect a quick profit. Everything depends on the axiom that the demand for printed plays greatly exceeded the supply—which happens to be untrue.

### Supply and Demand

Before Elizabeth came to the throne in 1558, the drama had made virtually no impact on the English book trade. A few early printed plays have undoubtedly been lost, and others may have been reprinted more often than we know—but Greg's *Bibliography of the English Printed Drama* lists fewer than thirty pre-Elizabethan plays printed in English. During the 1560s and 1570s there was a noticeable increase, but in neither decade did the number of new titles reach thirty.

For the sake of analysis I shall divide what might be called the Age of the English Printed Play into three twenty-year periods: 1583–1602, 1603–1622, and 1623–1642. The first of those periods (the last two decades of the reign of Elizabeth) saw the first printing of 117 works qualifying for inclusion in Greg's *Bibliography*. The second period (the first two decades of the reign of James I) is represented in Greg by 192 works, and the third (from the First Folio to the closure of the theaters) by 251.

Not all those works, however, are what we would usually call *plays*, and it takes quite a stretch of the imagination to consider Sidney's *Entertainment at Wanstead*, included among the items appended to editions of the *Arcadia* in and after 1598, as a "playbook" in any realistic commercial sense. I shall therefore subtract all masques, pageants and entertainments, closet and academic plays, Latin plays and translations published as literary texts, and shall consider only plays written for professional public performance (by both adult and juvenile companies). Thus adjusted, the number of new plays published in each of the three periods defined above is respectively 96, 115, and 160.[2]

In the two decades before the accession of James I, then, the average number of new plays published each year was 4.8. In the next two decades it was 5.75, and in the last two decades before the theaters were closed, exactly 8.0. For the same three periods, the chronological index to the revised *Short-Title Catalogue* (Pollard and Redgrave, 3:331–405) lists an average of just under 300, just under 480, and a little over 600 items per year respectively.[3] Not all those items are books, and many of the books are reprints rather than new titles—but it should nevertheless be obvious that printed plays never accounted for a very significant fraction of the trade in English books.

Those figures do not, of course, necessarily reflect demand alone: it could be argued that what they show is how well the players succeeded in withholding their scripts from the press. On the question of supply and demand, the Stationers' Registers provide evidence that is less equivocal. The following table shows the number of plays first registered in 1585–1604.

| PERIOD | PLAYS | PERIOD | PLAYS |
|---|---|---|---|
| 1585 | 1 | 1596 | 0 |
| 1586 | 0 | 1597 | 2 |
| 1587 | 0 | 1598 | 3 |
| 1588 | 0 | 1599 | 3 |
| 1589 | 0 | 1600 (Jan.–Apr.) | 3 |
| 1590 | 3 | May 1600–Oct. 1601 | 27 |
| 1591 | 3 | 1601 (Nov.–Dec.) | 2 |
| 1592 | 3 | 1602 | 4 |
| 1593 (Jan.–Nov.) | 3 | 1603 | 1 |
| Dec. 1593–May 1595 | 27 | 1604 | 5 |
| 1595 (June–Dec.) | 4 | | |

The most notable features are the two eighteen-month periods during which no fewer than fifty-four plays were registered—as compared with a total of forty in the remaining seventeen years.

If we look at the publication history of the plays registered *outside* the two peak periods, we find that thirty-four (85 percent) were printed in either the year of registration or the following year. Three of the remainder (7.5 percent) were printed within three years of registration, two were newly registered by others six years after (and apparently in ignorance of) the original registration and printed accordingly, and only one (2.5 percent) was never printed. For the plays registered *during* the peak periods, though, the proportions are distinctly different. Only thirty (56 percent) were printed before the end of the following December (1595 and 1601 respectively). Seven others (13 percent) were printed within five years of registration, and one after fifteen years; three were newly registered and printed after eleven, twenty-three, and thirty-eight years respectively, and eleven (20 percent) were never printed. Shortly after each peak period there was a brief but noticeable slump: in 1596 no plays were registered and only two printed; in 1603 only one was registered and two printed. It is difficult to escape the clear implication: in each period plays became available to the book trade in such quantities that the market was temporarily glutted.

The cause of those two flurries of activity is not difficult to guess, but the myth of the reluctant players has tended to obscure the obvious. Even Pollard drew what appears to be the only plausible conclusion—that on each occasion the acting companies themselves offered an unusual number of manuscripts for publication—and suggested that the first peak period was connected with the closure of the playhouses during the plague of 1592–1593 (*Shakespeare*, 9–10; *Shakespeare's Fight*, 41–42). But his suggestion that the players were motivated by financial hardship is less compelling, partly because the peak period happened *after* rather than during the closure and partly because the sums involved would have been relatively small.

Tradition has offered two explanations for the supposed reluctance of acting companies to allow their plays to be printed. One is that they feared losing their exclusive acting rights: that once a play was in print, any other company could perform it.[4] But as Roslyn L. Knutson has shown elsewhere in this volume, the London companies seem for the most part to have respected each other's repertories, printed plays included, so there is no obvious reason why any company should have feared otherwise.[5] The second explanation is even less credible: that the sale of printed texts might itself reduce the demand for performance. For that theory to work, the market in printed plays would have to have been lively enough, and the plays themselves deadly enough, to create so many hundred disappointed readers in such a short time that their collective absence from the playhouse was noticeable. I know of no evidence that any player ever feared that those who bought and read plays would consequently lose interest in seeing them performed.

For Pollard, the fact that the first flood of registrations did not begin until the playhouses reopened in late 1593 was a minor difficulty, evaded by implying that there would usually have been quite a long delay between the sale and the registration of a manuscript. To use his own words, "they had been sold by the players during the time that the theatres were closed and were now being registered as they were got ready for publication" (*Shakespeare*, 9). If we assume that the players thought of performance and publication as mutually exclusive alternatives, it would indeed seem likely that the closure, rather than the reopening, caused the glut. But if we decline to make that assumption, there is a perfectly plausible reason why the reopening itself might have prompted the players to flood the market with scripts. The strategy is known today as "publicity," or "advertising."

What initiated the second peak period is uncertain. Pollard suggested that it was a Privy Council order of June 22, 1600, that restricted both the number of playhouses and the frequency of performances (*Shakespeare*, 10)—but the beginning of the 1600 landslide can be very precisely dated to the last week of May. Whatever the immediate cause, on this occasion there can be even less doubt that the initiative came from the players.[6] On May 27 the printer James Roberts went to Stationers' Hall and provisionally registered a Chamberlain's play (now lost) called *Cloth Breeches and Velvet Hose*. Roberts held the monopoly for printing playbills and was therefore in frequent contact with the playhouses. But although he occasionally acquired plays and registered them (in most cases only provisionally), after doing so he usually sold them to other stationers rather than taking the financial risk of publishing them himself.

Having written out the registration ("provided that [Roberts] is not to putt it in prynte Without further & better Aucthority" [Arber, 3:161]), the Stationers' clerk, Richard Collins, did something unprecedented. He turned to the beginning of the register, wrote the heading "my lord chamberlens mens plaies Entred" at the top of a blank flyleaf, and made a brief entry below it: the date, Roberts's name, and the title of the play (3:37). When Roberts provisionally registered a second play two days later, after writing the registration itself Collins turned back to his list and made a second entry below the first. As it happened he did not use the flyleaf again until August and never continued the list in its original form—but what is significant is that he started it at all. Its purpose was probably to keep track of an expected string of provisional entries, so that whenever the required "Aucthority" for one of the plays was produced, he could use the list as a finding aid. But even its precise purpose is relatively unimportant: what matters is that on May 27 Collins heard something—presumably from Roberts the playbill printer—that made him expect the imminent arrival of enough Chamberlain's plays to make a list desirable. As things turned out, only eight of the plays registered during the second glut belonged to the Lord Chamberlain's Men—but the significance of the list and its heading lies not in the outcome but in the expectation. The single play that Roberts brought in on May 27 was correctly recognized as the first of many.

What I have shown so far is that although comparatively few new plays were published each year, at least twice the supply conspicuously exceeded the demand. But there is more to the question of popularity than the annual number of new works in a genre, and we need also to look at the frequency of reprinting. Once more, however, the facts bear little resemblance to the myth. Of the 96 plays first published in 1583–1602, only 46 (just under 48 percent) were reprinted inside twenty-five years.[7] The percentage is slightly higher for the plays of 1603–1622 (58 out of 115, or just over 50 percent), but in 1623–1642, when the number of new plays per year reached its peak, the number reprinted inside twenty-five years fell back to 46 out of 160, or less than 29 percent. And if an increased number of new texts led to a sharp decrease in the rate of reprinting, it would seem that the overall demand had not greatly increased.[8]

Of the plays that did reach a second edition, a few went through a respectable series of reprintings. Judged by the number of editions inside twenty-five years, the eleven best-sellers were the following:[9]

| PLAY (AND YEAR OF FIRST EDITION) | EDITIONS IN 25 YEARS |
|---|:---:|
| Anon., *Mucedorus and Amadine* (1598) | 9 |
| Marlowe, *Doctor Faustus* (1604) | 8 |
| Kyd, *The Spanish Tragedy* (1592) | 7 |
| Shakespeare, *Henry IV, Part 1* (1598) | 7 |
| Shakespeare, *Richard III* (1597) | 5 |
| Shakespeare, *Richard II* (1597) | 5 |
| Heywood, *If You Know Not Me, Part 1* (1605) | 5 |
| Daniel, *Philotas* (1605) | 5 |
| Suckling, *Brennoralt* (1642) | 5 |
| Anon, *How a Man May Choose a Good Wife* (1602) | 5 |
| Fletcher, *Philaster* (1620) | 5 |

One point worth making is that if I had included closet and academic plays, Samuel Daniel's *Cleopatra* (1594) would have ranked second (it reached its eighth edition seven years more quickly than did *Doctor Faustus*) and Thomas Randolph's *Aristippus* and *The Conceited Pedlar* (jointly published in 1630), fourth. That would have pushed Shakespeare firmly out of the top five—whether to sixth or seventh place would depend on how the Randolph plays were counted. *Cleopatra* was never published singly and could be purchased only as part of a collection of Daniel's verse. What that means is that the professional stage produced only a single play—*Mucedorus*—capable of outselling Daniel's verse. It is also worth noting that Shakespeare's best-selling work, *Venus and Adonis*, outsold his best-selling play by four editions.

Just in case a final emphasis is needed, let us now compare that list with the performance of some nondramatic best-sellers. The first seven are counted from the date of the first extant edition, and the last four from the editions of 1583.

| WORK (AND YEAR) | EDITIONS IN 25 YEARS |
|---|:---:|
| Sorocold, *Supplications of Saints* (1612)* | 10 |
| Dent, *The Plain Man's Pathway* (1601)† | 16 |
| Dering, *A Short Catechism for Householders* (1580) | 17 |
| Smith, *The Trumpet of the Soul* (1591) | 17 |
| Dent, *A Sermon of Repentance* (1582) | 20 |
| Parsons, *A Book of Christian Exercise* (1584) | 27 |
| Bayly, *The Practice of Piety* (1612) | 36 |
| *The New Testament* (English versions published separately from 1583) | 34 |
| *The Holy Bible* (Bishops' and Geneva translations from 1583) | 63 |
| *The Book of Common Prayer* (from 1583) | 66 |
| Sternhold and Hopkins, *The Psalms in English Meter* (from 1583) | 124 |

* The first and tenth of the surviving editions describe themselves as the third and twenty-second respectively.

† The sixteenth surviving edition describes itself as the nineteenth.

It is therefore safe to conclude that few early modern stationers ever imagined that the best way to make a quick fortune was to wrest—honestly or otherwise—a play or two from the supposedly protective clutch of an acting company. A demand for printed plays certainly existed, though it was far from insatiable, and a stationer lucky enough or clever enough to acquire the right play at the right time could make a satisfactory profit. Andrew Wise, for example, struck gold three times in a row in 1597–1598 by picking what would become the three best-selling Shakespeare quartos as the first three plays of his brief career.[10] But few of those who dealt in plays enjoyed comparable success. If a printer published a new play for himself, he would expect to break even and begin making a profit when about half the edition had been sold. If he paid someone else to act as wholesale distributor, his higher costs would have taken correspondingly longer to recover. The great majority of plays, however, were published by booksellers,[11] and a bookseller would normally have to sell about 60 percent of a first edition to break even. Fewer than 21 percent of the plays published in the sixty years under discussion reached a second edition inside nine years. What that means is that no more than one play in five would have returned the publisher's initial investment inside five years. Not one in twenty would have paid for itself during its first year—so publishing plays would not usually have been seen as a shortcut to wealth.

## Publishers and Others

At this point it is necessary to define a few key terms. Some of the common misconceptions about the procedures and economics of publication stem from confusion about exactly who was responsible for what. To avoid that confusion we need to use the words *printer* and *bookseller* more precisely than they are often used—more precisely, indeed, than they were sometimes used by the stationers themselves.

The *printer* of a play was the person who owned the type and the press, and whose workmen set the text and impressed its inked image onto the paper. The printer, in other words, physically manufactured the book—and did so in a small factory called a *printing office* or *printing house*. Most printers spent most of their time manufacturing books for others. A typical customer brought in a text, paid to have several hundred copies of it printed, and then took them away. In a transaction of that kind the printer bore no more responsibility for procuring or marketing the text than does a photocopier. Sometimes, indeed, it can be salutary to remember the similarities between a printing house and a copying machine: a text, a heap of clean paper, and the required payment were inserted at one end, and the paper emerged from the other end with the text on it. It is rarely appropriate to hold the machine responsible for the supposed origins of the text it reproduced.

In a few of the larger printing houses the premises probably included a *shop*: a room or annex fronting on the street, from which books were retailed. In such cases it is important to keep the separate functions of the two parts of the premises carefully distinct. Most printers did not retail books to the public, because most of what they printed was not theirs to sell—and a potential reader in search of a book would go to a bookshop, not a printing house. In the early records of the trade the word *shop* always and exclusively means a place where books were sold to the public. Since the modern American *print shop* tends to blur what is sometimes a crucial distinction, it is a term best avoided in historical contexts.

A *bookseller*, obviously enough, was someone who owned or worked in a retail bookshop. But while we can pertinently refer to "the printer" of a playbook,[12] there was no such thing as "the" bookseller, and it is therefore necessary to deal briefly with another widespread fallacy. Throughout his career, Greg never gave up the search for new and improved ways of determining who owned the copyright of a printed play at any given time. As part of this quest he spent some time trying to devise what might be called a "calculus of imprints"—a set of rules for interpreting the various forms of wording found in imprints and colophons.[13] Unfortunately, his discussions of the matter were marred throughout, and partly invalidated, by his belief that any bookseller identified in an imprint was the book's exclusive *retailer*.[14] The assumption was a traditional one, but Greg did more than anyone this century to entrench it.

The primary purpose of an imprint was the same in early modern England as it is today: to inform *retailers* where a book could be purchased *wholesale*. Since virtually all wholesale distributors were also retail booksellers, a potential customer who knew about the imprint might correctly deduce that the distributor's shop would be the one most likely to have copies in stock—but that was merely incidental. Several of Greg's own books were published by the Clarendon Press. We do not therefore conclude that anyone wishing to buy a copy had to go to Oxford, nor should we imagine that the only shop in London selling the first edition of *King Lear* was that of Nathaniel Butter. The goal of whoever handled the wholesaling of a book (either its publisher or a chosen agent) was to sell as many copies as possible, and that meant selling them to as many of England's hundreds of *bookshops* as possible. The idea that anyone could benefit from restricting retail sales to a single shop in a single city is nothing less than absurd.

Any bookseller could buy and sell any book. If we confine our attention to new books published in London,[15] a bookseller who belonged to the Stationers' Company could buy them at loosely controlled wholesale prices from other Company members. Alternatively, a bookseller who had published a book of his or her own might take the shortcut of exchanging small batches with other publishers.[16] Neither London booksellers who belonged to other companies nor booksellers from outside London were entitled to the same wholesale rates,[17] but they could buy books at the usual London retail price discounted by three shillings in the pound (G. Pollard, "Sandars," 15). No bookseller, of course, could stock every book that came out—many undoubtedly specialized in books of certain kinds and would tailor their stock to suit their preferred clientele. But although there were probably disapproving booksellers who declined to stock plays at all, any playbook could otherwise have been sold in any shop.

Between the printer and the booksellers stood the prime mover. The person who acquired the text, paid for several hundred copies of it to be manufactured, and sold them wholesale, was the *publisher*. It was the publisher, not the printer, who decided that the text should be made public and who would eventually make a profit if it sold well enough during his lifetime. And by the same token, it was the publisher whose investment was at risk if the public declined to buy the book.

There are two reasons why it is sometimes difficult to keep the terminology precise. The first is that the early modern book trade had no separate word for what we now call a publisher. Once an edition had been printed, the business of distributing it consisted of selling books — and the stationers evidently felt little need to distinguish between selling books wholesale to retailers and selling them retail to the public. Furthermore, when publishers discussed their activities in prefaces, they generally used the word *print* in the sense of "cause to be printed." The formulaic heading, "The Printer to the Reader," was therefore commonly used by publishers who were not strictly speaking printers at all.[18] And if the publishers themselves could interchangeably call their enterprise "bookselling" and "printing," modern scholars who use the words imprecisely have some excuse.

The other complicating factor is that publishing was not usually thought of as a profession. There were certainly some early stationers who published so frequently that they probably considered publication to be their principal activity — but they were few in number. Most books were published by stationers whose daily trade was bookselling; a few were published by stationers who were also printers. For most of them publishing was a form of speculation, undertaken to augment their regular income rather than to replace it. Since virtually every early modern publisher was also either a bookseller or a printer, it is hardly surprising that the three words are sometimes confused — but even when two of the roles were played by the same person, it is important to keep them distinct.

Whatever his or her regular trade, then, the person who paid for a book to be manufactured was its publisher. If the manuscript had been illicitly obtained, or if any rules of the Stationers' Company were evaded or broken, the responsibility lay with the publisher — not with the printer. In the comparatively uncommon event that the publisher's trade was printing and he manufactured the book for himself, that responsibility was his only by virtue of his role *as publisher*. As printer, he was responsible only for the quality of the printing. If we want to investigate the text of a play — the relationship between what the typesetter saw in the manuscript and what appears on the printed page — we need to study the printer. But if our concern is the source of the manuscript, the reasons why *that* play was published *then*, or the supposed attitude of the players or the playwright to the fact of publication, we must focus not on the printer but on the publisher.

If the publisher had a bookshop of his or her own, that shop would usually be the source of wholesale distribution, so the publisher's name and address would usually appear on the title page. But if a book was published by someone who lacked the facilities for storage and distribution (a printer, or a journeyman bookseller with no shop of his own), that publisher would need to find a bookseller willing to handle the wholesaling. The imprint on such a book would usually announce that it was "to be sold" by the bookseller in question—meaning "to be sold wholesale." It could, of course, be sold to the public by any retailer in England (or elsewhere) who was willing to order one or more copies from that distributor.

### Varieties of Manuscript

Every now and then a particular play would become a cause célèbre, either by virtue of unusual popularity onstage (*Tamburlaine, The Spanish Tragedy,* or *Pericles*) or because it fell foul of the authorities (*The Isle of Dogs, Eastward Ho,* or *A Game at Chess*). On such occasions one or more stationers might have approached the playwright or the players to ask whether they could buy a text for publication. If the company made it known that a particular play was on offer (or as in 1594 and 1600, a selection of plays), a stationer with a few pounds to invest and nothing more promising in sight might take the hint and approach the playhouse. But since the overall demand for plays was unimpressive it is likely that many of those that saw print were offered to, rather than sought out by, their publishers.

The nature of the manuscript offered to the press would depend largely upon its source. After the first edition was printed, the publisher would usually keep that part of the manuscript on which the authority to publish and the license to print were recorded. What happened to the rest of it might depend on how extensively the printer's workmen had marked or mishandled it—but the person from whom it had been bought would not usually have expected it back. In special cases, such as some of the plays included in Jonson's *Works* in 1616 or the First Folio of Shakespeare in 1623, a supplier might have lent a printer a manuscript instead of surrendering it, but that was not the usual practice. So if a play still in repertory was offered to a publisher by the players, or by the playwright himself with their consent, the manuscript supplied would not usually have been "the allowed book" then being used for performance.

One possible manuscript, if it still existed, would be the one from which the allowed book had itself been copied. That might often have been a late draft or "final" copy in the playwright's own hand: what the playhouse scribe Edward Knight called "the fowle papers of the Authors" when he had to copy the extant manuscript of *Bonduca* from them because "the booke where by it was first Acted from" had been lost (Greg, *Shakespeare,* 107). Or if the current version of a revived play had evolved so much that a new copy had been prepared and allowed, the publisher might have been given an obsolete promptbook. Alternatively, if the players declined to part with any of their existing manuscripts, it would not have cost very much to have one of them (probably the allowed book itself) transcribed.[19] If publication was the playwright's own idea, to which the players had merely consented, he might conceivably have copied out a playhouse manuscript himself. Or, as in the case of Jonson's *Sejanus*, he might have prepared a revised version especially for the press.

Sometimes, though, the person who tried to sell a play to a publisher might have no direct connection with the playhouse at all. A manuscript mislaid by a company might be innocently found by someone else; a player might borrow a manuscript and copy it for a friend; the company might collectively commission a scribal copy for presentation to a patron or benefactor. Any kind of manuscript that left the playhouse for any reason might conceivably be copied, more or less expertly, and each new exemplar might itself be transcribed. It is unlikely that there was a very flourishing trade in manuscript plays before the theaters were closed in 1642—that many circulated in manuscript at all, or that there were many copies of those that did—but extra-theatrical manuscripts certainly existed, and they were sometimes sold to stationers. How closely they resembled their playhouse ancestors would depend on the number and skill of the intervening copyists, and it may often be difficult or impossible to deduce the full history of the manuscript underlying a printed text (supposedly characteristic features that survive in print could equally have survived prior transcription). But whether or not we can accurately distinguish one from another, any kind of manuscript playbook that can conceivably have existed could conceivably have found its way into print.

The possible sources I have considered so far have one thing in common: direct descent by transcription, though in varying directions and at varying removes, from an ancestral manuscript actually penned by the playwright. There was, however, another kind of manuscript that could, and sometimes did, come into a stationer's hands. After the closing of the theaters had changed the nature of the trade in plays, Humphrey Moseley spent some time collecting copy for the Beaumont and Fletcher Folio of 1647. In his address to the readers he explains how diligently he sought out good, full-length texts of which the playwrights themselves would have approved. Then, anticipating the kind of response that his claim still sometimes evokes, he continues:

> One thing I must answer before it bee objected; 'tis this: When these *Comedies* and *Tragedies* were presented on the Stage, the *Actours* omitted some Scenes and Passages (with the *Author's* consent) as occasion led them; and when private friends desir'd a Copy, they then (and justly too) transcribed what they *Acted*.
>
> (GREG, *Bibliography*, 3:1233)

Greg, borrowing both the quotation and the associated term "private transcript" from Sidney Lee, assumed that Moseley meant the kind of manuscripts that Greg called private transcripts—texts copied out on behalf of the company, by either the playhouse scribe or the playwright himself, for presentation (*Shakespeare*, 152–54). In other words, he interpreted "they . . . transcribed what they *Acted*" as "the company . . . made a fair copy of the promptbook." That seems to me to be a forced and legalistic reading, far more characteristic of Greg than of Moseley.

As I understand the passage, Moseley is expecting someone to object (because "everyone knows") that plays were usually and markedly abridged for performance, and that when actors made copies for their friends they wrote down what had been spoken onstage. No texts of that inferior kind, he boasts, will be found in *his* book. What he seems to be referring to, then—texts of a kind so familiar that someone is bound to bring them up unless he forestalls the objection—are performance texts written down by actors who took part in them. The quality of such texts would vary greatly (both from each other and from scene to scene within a single text), depending on the infinitely variable circumstances of their origins. If the actor responsible was able to copy from the allowed book, dutifully omitting every passage marked for omission in the current performance version (which might itself vary from revival to revival), his text would be visibly shorter than most printed plays. If he had to copy it partly or wholly from memory, those parts of the performance he had least opportunity to observe might prove extremely difficult to reconstruct and might emerge noticeably garbled. What Moseley has been trying to tell us since 1647 is, I believe, the commonplace and innocent origin of the kind of text that Pollard called a Bad Quarto—but we have been too busy chasing imaginary pirates to listen.

### Acquiring Copy

At this point it will be useful to switch from general statements to the particular actions of an imaginary stationer—a bookseller by trade—who has just been offered a manuscript play and is tempted to buy it.[20]

Before deciding, such a stationer will probably want to know whether the vendor is entitled to sell it. He would not question the right of a company of players to sell a text they had bought from a playwright; nor, in all probability, would it occur to him to doubt the right of a playwright to sell a play that he had written.[21] He might perhaps be wary if someone with no visible theatrical credentials were to offer him what was clearly a playhouse manuscript—but it is unlikely that he would question the right of the friend of an actor, or the friend of a friend of an actor, to sell a manuscript of whatever kind Moseley really meant. Modern notions of literary property simply would not apply: what is being sold is a manuscript, not what we now call a *copyright* (an eighteenth-century word for an eighteenth-century innovation).

The nearest equivalent to copyright in early modern England—and the resemblance was only distant—was the publishing right conferred by the Stationers' Company on its members. Neither the author of a text nor the owner of the paper on which it was written had the right to publish it, so neither of them could sell or grant that right. If a stationer acquired a text written by someone important, or someone whose friendship might benefit him, he might have had the self-interested courtesy to offer the author the opportunity to write a dedication or an address to the readers. But he was under no legal obligation to do so, and it was not unknown for a stationer to admit quite openly that a book was being published without its author's knowledge or consent (Bennett, 1558 to 1603, 22–26; 1603 to 1640, 62–63).

Having satisfied himself that the transaction will be legal, my stationer has to set a price. We have, unfortunately, no direct evidence at all for the customary payment for a publishable playbook—or, indeed, for any comparable manuscript—because there is only one early modern writer of minor works for whose earnings we have written testimony. Richard Robinson, a translator and editor active in 1576–1602, has left a detailed account of the publication of his nineteen works, for each of which he notes the licenser, the publisher, the format and the number of sheets, how much the dedicatee gave him for the presentation copy, and how much "benefit" he made by selling copies to others (for a full transcript, see Vogt). If Robinson was typical, all that a minor author usually received from a publisher was twenty-six free copies of the book: one to present to the dedicatee in the hope of a handsome reward, and twenty-five to sell at inflated prices to his friends.[22]

But Robinson's books were all either compilations or translations, and it may well be that cash payments were more common for original works.[23] Furthermore, Robinson usually hoped to make more from his dedications than from the sale of benefit copies. While a playwright might sometimes have hoped to persuade both a dedicatee and his own friends to reward his creativity, nobody else who sold one of his plays to a stationer would have had quite the same expectations. Only five of the playbooks first printed in 1583–1602 contained dedications (5 percent). In 1603–1622 the number rose to twenty-two (19 percent), and in 1623–1642, after the Jonson and Shakespeare collections had helped to increase the respectability of printed plays, it soared to seventy-eight (58 percent).[24] Despite the late surge, though, in the overall totals for 1583–1642 playbooks with dedications remain firmly in the minority (31 percent), so those who sold them for publication would usually have hoped for a more direct reward.

In *The Second Part of the Return from Parnassus* (c. 1601), an author is shown offering a manuscript to the printer and publisher John Danter. Danter observes that he lost money on the author's previous book and that some authors pay *him* to print their work—but he nevertheless offers "40 shillings and an odde pottle of wine" (Leishman, 247–48). In the preliminaries to his *Cynthia's Revenge* (1613), John Stephens speaks of authors who "gape after the drunken harvest of forty shillings, and shame the worthy benefactors of *Hellicon*" (STC 23248, sig. A2ᵛ), while in *The Scholars' Purgatory* (1624) George Wither deplores the fact that a stationer need never pay a reasonable fee to a qualified scholar, "Seeing he cann hyre for a matter of 40 shillings, some needy *Ignoramus* to scrible vpon the same subject" (STC 25919, sig. I1ᵛ). Whether or not those three quotations adequately support the frequent claim that two pounds (forty shillings) was the *usual* payment for a small pamphlet,[25] they remain the best evidence we have.

My imaginary stationer, however, is not dealing with a book of the kinds implied by Stephens, Wither, or the *Parnassus* playwright: he is considering a play, and is well aware that the odds are against a second edition during his working lifetime. However many copies he decides to commission, he will need to sell more than half of them before breaking even. Provided that he can sell the whole edition, then the more he invests, the more he will eventually profit—but the longer it will be before that happens. For an acceptable profit margin he will need to keep his cost per hundred copies within sight of one pound. If he is prepared to risk an edition of 1,200 copies or more, he can reasonably afford to pay two pounds for the manuscript. If he prefers to put less capital at risk but is nevertheless confident that the book will be reprinted at least once, he can accept a reduced profit on the first edition and make up for it with the second—in effect, spreading the one-time cost of the manuscript across two editions. In this case, however, the stationer decides that his confidence extends no farther than a single edition of 800 copies. A rough calculation persuades him that while he can just about afford to spend two pounds on copy for the book, that sum has to include *all* the costs of copy—including the price of having it perused and allowed before printing as the regulations require. The vendor was hoping for more, but eventually agrees to an outright sale at the price of two pounds minus the cost of having the manuscript properly allowed by the authorities.

### Authority

Before a book could legally be printed, certain requirements had to be met. In 1930 Greg suggested that there were essentially three requirements, and that the Stationers called them *authority, license,* and *entrance,* respectively (Greg and Boswell, lxix–lxx). In fact, the Company usage of those words changed over time. Before 1637 there were only two requirements, and before the 1620s neither *license* nor *entrance* usually meant quite what literary historians usually mean by them.

The first requirement was originally called *authority* or *allowance*: the approval of a text by a representative of either the church or the state. Authority of one kind or another had been officially required of every new printed book since the 1530s. During the first half of Elizabeth's reign the rules for allowance were defined by article 51 of her *Injunctions* of 1559 (Arber, 1:xxxviii). That regulation was effectively replaced in 1586 by a decree of Star Chamber, which remained in force until superseded in turn by a new Star Chamber decree in 1637 (Arber, 2:807–12; 4:528–36). Each formulation differed in detail, but each placed the principal authority in the hands of the bishop of London and the archbishop of Canterbury.[26]

But although each enactment, and each of the frequent official reminders of its existence, insisted that *every* book should be seen and allowed, it seems unlikely that even the authorities themselves expected total compliance. Books that could offend nobody—books of mathematics, gardening, or cookery; funeral sermons in praise of uncontroversial dignitaries—were often published without authority, and no stationer is known to have been punished for failing to have an inoffensive text perused and allowed. The purpose of the regulations was to prevent the publication of unacceptable material and to justify the punishment of anyone who overstepped the line. If an unauthorized book caused offense, the perpetrator could be punished for failing to have it properly allowed, but noncompliance seems otherwise not to have mattered.[27]

Plays were allowed for the stage by the Master of the Revels, but a license for acting was evidently not acceptable for the press. Until the end of 1606 plays were usually allowed for printing by the same ecclesiastical authorities who allowed books of all kinds—occasionally the bishop or archbishop, but more often one of the prebendaries or chaplains to whom they delegated the task. In late 1606 Sir George Buc, who had secured the reversion of the Mastership of the Revels in 1603, was apparently also granted the sole right to allow plays for the press, and for several years thereafter virtually all plays that were authorized at all were allowed either by Buc or by his deputy.[28] Buc continued to authorize plays for the press after he finally succeeded Edmond Tilney as Master in 1610, but after 1612 neither he nor his successors in office held that right exclusively, and the ecclesiastical authorities started allowing plays again in 1613.

Exactly where my imaginary stationer will take his manuscript for perusal, then, will depend on the date. What he will have to pay for the service is equally uncertain, because the cost of allowance is yet another subject about which we know very little. In 1598–1600 Tilney charged 7s. to license a play for performance (Henslowe, *Diary*, ed. Greg, 2:113–16). The price apparently rose to £1 during Buc's tenure of the office (1610–1622), and by 1632 Sir Henry Herbert was charging £2 to license a new play and £1 to relicense an old play for revival (J. Q. Adams, *Dramatic*, 17–18). If Herbert's practice can be taken as suggesting that a second perusal always cost less than the first, then allowance for the press may usually have been cheaper than licensing for the stage. But it is equally possible that the rates were essentially unrelated to the price of a Revels license, and were determined by whatever rules governed the fees paid to the ecclesiastical authorities. One of the three books about which we have information is hardly comparable: Fulke Greville's *Certain Learned and Elegant Works* (1633) is a small folio of ninety-seven sheets, for the allowance of which Henry Seile paid Sir Henry Herbert £1 in cash plus books to the value of another £1 4s. (J. Q. Adams, *Dramatic*, 41; Greg, *Bibliography*, 3:1068–69). In the same year, however, Seile paid Herbert only 10s. to authorize Cowley's *Poetical Blossoms* (1633), which was printed as a quarto of eight sheets (J. Q. Adams, *Dramatic*, 41; STC 5906), and thirty years earlier Thomas Pavier had paid 10s. to an unidentified censor for authorizing a small newsbook that was printed as a quarto of four sheets (Greg and Boswell, 85; STC 7434). Perhaps, then, it is not unrealistic to suggest that my imaginary stationer eventually pays 30s. for the manuscript and 10s. to have it allowed for the press.

## License

The second requirement was originally called *license*. Before the 1620s the Stationers' Company clerks rarely used that word as a synonym for *authority*,[29] and when they did so it was usually in the unspecialized sense of *permission* rather than as a technical term.[30] But in the great majority of its appearances in the Stationers' early records (including more than two thousand book entries before 1590), the word *license* meant the *Company's* permission to print—which was something fundamentally different from authority. When a publisher sought a license from one or more of the three elected officers (the master and wardens), the question of whether the manuscript had been authorized was certainly taken into account. If it had not, or if the officers considered the signatory to be of inadequate rank, they could (and often did) license it on condition that it should not be printed until "further," "better," or simply "lawful" authority had been obtained.[31] Alternatively, they might license it on condition that if any trouble arose, the publisher would take full responsibility.[32] Or they could agree with the publisher that the book could offend nobody, and license it without authority.

Given that license was sometimes refused because a manuscript had not been authorized, the concerns of the Company officers sometimes coincided with those of the authorities. If they let too many offensive books slip past them, they could themselves be held accountable. But censorship was neither the sole nor even the main purpose of license, which could be (and sometimes was) withheld from manuscripts that had been lawfully perused and allowed.

The Company's license originated as an expression, embodiment, and constant reminder of the powers it had been granted by charter in 1557. When the charter was sealed a new set of rules came into effect, one of which was that no new book should be printed without the Company's permission. For that permission—that license—a small fee was charged. For the first few years a licensed book had to be actually printed before ownership of the "copy" could be claimed, but during the early 1580s the rules were modified so that license and ownership were conferred simultaneously (G. Pollard, "Early," 254–59).

There are two essential differences between the ownership of a *copy* and the later concept of *copyright* that make it unwise to use the words interchangeably. The first is that the right to a copy, being conferred by and existing only within the Company itself, could extend no farther than the Company's jurisdiction. Unlike copyright, it was not a generalized right to an intellectual property: the publisher of a book had no control over any form of dissemination (acting, public reading, manuscript copying, etc.) other than publication in print. But if in that sense it was a more restricted privilege than copyright, in another way it was more comprehensive, because the protection it gave extended far beyond the limits of a specific text.

What distinguished printing from most other manufacturing industries in early modern Europe was not merely that it relied on mass production, but that each part of a book was mass-produced in turn. It was necessary to print the whole edition of a book before the first copy could be sold: necessary, therefore, to put a substantial investment at risk before beginning the process (which often took years) of recovering it. The owner of a copy had not only the exclusive right to reprint the text, but also the right to a fair chance to recover his costs. He could therefore seek the Company's protection if *any* book—not necessarily a reprint or plagiarism of his own copy—threatened his ability to dispose of unsold copies of an existing edition. Thus the license granted to Mulcaster's *Positions . . . for the Training up of Children* (1581) was to be void if it contained "any thinge preiudiciall or hurtfull" to Ascham's *Schoolmaster* (most recently 1579), Thomas Adams twice claimed that Hopton's *Concordancy of Years* (1612 and 1615) infringed his right to Grafton's *Brief Treatise* (most recently 1611), and George Thomason tried to block the publication of Dugdale's *History of St. Paul's Cathedral* (1658) on the grounds that Daniel King "hath written vpon y$^e$ same subject" in his *Cathedral . . . Churches of England and Wales* (1656).[33] And when the publishers of Gervase Markham's various books on animal husbandry started accusing each other of infringement, Markham was persuaded to sign a promise "Neuer to write any more book or bookes to be printed, of the Deseases or cures of any Cattle" (W. A. Jackson, *Records*, 86, 95; Arber, 3:679).

When Millington and Busby tried to license Shakespeare's *Henry V* in 1600, therefore, the wardens would not have cared about either the authorship or the "Badness" of the text—but they would have required the consent of Thomas Creede, who had published (and printed) *The Famous Victories of Henry the Fifth* in 1598. Creede presumably did consent, on condition that he be hired (and therefore paid) to print the rival play. Shakespeare's *Taming of the Shrew* and *King John* could not have been included in the First Folio without the consent of the owners of the anonymous *Taming of a Shrew* and *Troublesome Reign of King John*—and the theory that the Folio publishers could have circumvented Henry Walley's right to *Troilus and Cressida* merely by printing it from a different manuscript is quite untenable.[34] Given the deliberate imitation in the later title it is unlikely that Butter and Busby could have published *King Lear* (1608) without the consent of the owner of *King Leir* (1605), and one possible reason why Edward Blount left *Pericles* unpublished after registering it in 1608 may be that he failed to reach an agreement with the publisher of George Wilkins's novel, *The Painful Adventures of Pericles* (1608), which explicitly describes itself as "The true History of the Play of *Pericles*." The right to a copy was not at all the same thing as copyright—and it was problems of infringement, rather than of censorship, that the Company's license was intended to regulate.

During the first quarter-century after the charter, the Company's fee for a license was determined by the projected size of the book—three sheets a penny, with a minimum of fourpence (W. A. Jackson, "Variant"). In or around March 1582 the fee was standardized at sixpence for a book and fourpence for either a ballad or a small pamphlet. During the next few years the lower fee was phased out, and apart from a handful of scattered exceptions in 1588–1591, after 1587 all licenses cost sixpence.[35] The wording of book entries before 1588 clearly indicates two important facts: that the purpose of each entry was to record a payment, and that the payment was not for the entry itself (as has sometimes been suggested) but for the license.[36] When the granting of a license and the conferring of ownership were combined in the early 1580s, what we call a *register entry* became the entry of record that *proved* ownership. But it also continued to serve its original purpose of recording that the license fee had been paid.

Needing a license, my imaginary bookseller brings his authorized manuscript to Stationers' Hall and seeks out one or both of the wardens. Had the play not been authorized they might well have questioned him about the contents before deciding, and had they foreseen possible conflicts of interest with other publications they would have either recommended or required him to negotiate with any potential rivals. But in this case the manuscript has been properly authorized, and nobody in the room can think of any existing book that might be jeopardized by it. The wardens therefore sign it as near as conveniently possible to the authority.[37] Those signatures constitute the stationer's license: the act of signing simultaneously makes the play his officially recognized "copy" and grants him permission to have it printed. Before he does so, however, he will first pay the small debt he now owes to the Company.

### Entrance

According to Greg, a third requirement had to follow authority and license. He based that belief on a record of 1597 that describes a printer's offense as printing a book "disorderlie w<sup>th</sup>out aucthoritie lycence and entraunce." Ever in search of rules from which ownership could be unambiguously deduced, Greg interpreted "entraunce" as securing the right to a copy by entrance "in the register book of copies," and took the wording as proof that the ordinances required registration (Greg and Boswell, lxix, 57). But in a later study he showed that roughly one-third of the books published during the period were not registered (Greg, "Entrance, Licence," 3–7; *Some Aspects*, 68; for more recent statistics, see Bell), and he never squarely confronted the difficulty of reconciling that fact with the idea of compulsory entrance. Leo Kirschbaum, however, argued that the sheer numbers proved that entrance cannot have been required. Suggesting that after 1586 *entrance* and *license* became synonymous (61–74), he showed that scores of unregistered books were assigned by their original publishers to others with the approval of the Court of Assistants (the governing body of the Company). Not only did the court evidently accept that each assigner owned something assignable, but not one assigner was ever punished for having failed to register such a copy. That, argued Kirschbaum, proved that the act of publication itself established ownership of a copy, and that registration was therefore not a requirement.[38]

Before 1605 only two stationers were fined for printing without "entrance" alone. To Kirschbaum that proved that entrance could not have been mandatory; to Greg the fact that the fines were imposed at all proved the opposite. He also claimed that there were "many" cases in which entrance was "mentioned, along with absence of authority and licence, as part of the offence" (*Some Aspects*, 69). More specifically:

> Disorderly printing is repeatedly defined as being "without authority and entrance" or "without aucthoritie lycence and entraunce," from which it is at least possible to argue that entrance was one requisite of orderly publication. ("Entrance and Copyright," 309)

To be charitable, that is an exaggeration. This debate took place before the later court records were published, and Greg knew of only three examples of the first phrase. The second is unique: never before, and not again until 1621, were the words *license* and *entrance* explicitly linked in a comparable way (W. A. Jackson, *Records*, 135).

One of the two fines for non-entrance in fact undermines Greg's case. In 1602 Edward Allde was fined 6s. 8d. "for printinge a booke without entrance Contrary to thorders" (Arber, 2:835). But immediately afterward Thomas Pavier was fined twice as much "for causing Edward aldee to print the same booke contrary to order." Pavier was therefore the publisher and Allde only the printer—and while it might have been reasonable to fine Allde for printing a manuscript that he could see was unlicensed, nobody would have expected him to guess that a visibly licensed copy had not been registered. Registration was a matter concerning Pavier alone—so no matter what the record actually says, Allde was fined for printing the book without *license*. And if "entrance" does not mean *registration* in that instance, we can hardly pin much faith on its precise meaning in the other. When we turn to the three instances of printing without "authority and entrance," the weakness of Greg's position becomes even more obvious. To argue that the phrase was a precise legal definition of the offense is necessarily to imply that *license* had been granted—in which case the absence of ecclesiastical authority was presumably the fault of the wardens who had failed to require it.

During the 1580s the clerk, Richard Collins, evidently began to think of an entrance as essentially the same as the license it recorded. He sometimes had to note that if certain conditions were not met, "this license shall be void." In August 1586 he wrote "this entrance" instead, and, after using the old formula once more on the next page, made the change permanent (Arber, 2:336, 390, 438, 451 [*license*]; 450, 452, 454, 455, 477, etc. [*entrance*]). In November 1587 appeared an even more significant change: for the first time a copy was "entered" (as distinct from licensed, admitted, allowed, assigned, granted, or tolerated). The first five entries in which that word was used were all conditional upon further authority, but by the end of 1588 "Entered . . . for his copy" had established itself as the standard wording. By the turn of the century *entrance* and *license* had become interchangeable in other contexts too. In March 1602 the court ordered that any ballads not brought in before the next meeting "to be entred according to order" would be forfeited (Greg and Boswell, 85). Although Greg cited that order in support of his theory ("Entrance and Copyright," 309), it signally fails to demonstrate that "entred" meant *registered*. More than a year elapsed before the next item described as a ballad appeared in the register,[39] so it was apparently possible to have ballads or books "entred" without having them registered.

Later fines for printing without "entrance" include other examples in which the word demonstrably means *license*, either because a publisher and printer were fined for the same transgression or because the offense was described by one word when the fine was imposed and by another when it was paid.[40] By the 1620s there had been further changes in usage. As the censoring authorities began to describe their own activity as "licensing" rather than "allowance," the clerk (now Thomas Montfort) began to follow suit (W. A. Jackson, *Records*, 155, 213, 234, 260), and in 1621 we encounter fines for printing without "license [formerly *authority*] or entrance [formerly *license*]" (135, 466). So while Greg was right that something called *entrance* was mandatory, he was wrong in assuming that the word meant *registration*.

Kirschbaum correctly recognized that the censors' *authority* and the Company's *license* were distinct, but wrongly assumed that their purpose was identical (namely censorship). He therefore suggested that when the Star Chamber decree of 1586 mandated authority for all books, license became no more important than registration and could safely be ignored (64–65). Supposing that license would usually have been recorded when obtained at all, he inferred that the surviving record is essentially complete: that if a book was not registered, it was probably not licensed either. The main difficulty he overlooked is that even if *license* and *entrance* were synonymous, the fines for omitting one or the other prove that *something* was mandatory, under whichever name.

Evidence from another source disproves both theories. In 1617 several senior stationers testified in Chancery about a disputed assignment of copy, and their testimony clarifies several important points (Sisson, "Laws," 15–19, especially 18). Kirschbaum was right that a stationer could only assign a copy to which he had legal title, but title could not be acquired without Company license. And while registration was certainly part of the customary and recommended procedure, it was not yet mandatory in 1617. The witnesses agreed with a document of 1620 (cited by both Greg and Kirschbaum) that an entry in the register was "the commun and strongest assurance yat Stationers haue, for all their copies" (Arber, 3:39). Such an entry of record was, indeed, the *only* unquestionable evidence of ownership—but it was not the only *possible* evidence, nor was it a requirement. The Company license—which the witnesses described variously as assigning, confirming, or ratifying ownership—was mandatory, but registration was not.

There is, in fact, evidence in the registers themselves that the same was true in and before the 1590s. The two most explicit entries were cited by Chambers as long ago as 1923 (*Elizabethan*, 3:172 n. 4), though neither Greg nor Kirschbaum seems ever to have addressed them. The last entry for the financial year 1585–1586 is a note that "master warden barker brought in about iiij⁵ moore which he had Receved for copies yat were not brought to be entred into the book this yere" (Arber, 2:448). In the summary account for 1592–1593, the total received "for lycensinge of Copies this yeare as by the Clerkes booke appeareth" is followed by a separate item: "Receaved more for Seauen Copies which haue not ben broughte to be entred in the booke" (1:559). There are a few other clues pointing in the same direction,[41] but those two entries alone demonstrate unequivocally that paying for a license without registering the copy was not only possible and legal but openly accepted.

A few years after the Chancery suit we find the first evidence that the rules may be changing, when in September 1622 the court orders

> that noe Printer shall print anie booke except the Clarke of the Companies name be to it to signifie that it is entred in the hall Booke according to order. (W. A. JACKSON, *Records*, 149)

That seems clear enough—though it should be noted that it stops short of commanding every publisher to register every book. The order had no visible effect on the number of books printed without registration during the 1620s, and a total of five fines ostensibly for printing "without entrance" in the next fifteen years does little to suggest vigilant enforcement (171, 471, 224, 478). Perhaps the clerk was allowed to sign the copy when the license fee was paid, whether or not the book was actually registered. Not until the Star Chamber decree of 1637 was it unambiguously ordered for the first time that every book printed thereafter "shall be first lawfully licenced and authorized . . . and shall be also first entred into the Registers Booke of the Company of Stationers" (Arber, 4:530).

The reason why I have discussed this matter at such length is that no aspect of the Pollard mythology has generated as many inane conspiracy theories or as much free-range guesswork as the question of entrance and the registers. Every amateur who learns that a given book was not entered feels free to infer some kind of skullduggery. Stationers who avoided the register, we are told, must have been trying to hide something—even though in many cases they put their names on the printed title pages. It is rarely specified from whom the supposed secrets were being concealed; seldom realized that the Stationers' records were so far from the public domain that even the Court of Chancery had to make do with certified transcripts of the entries on which the case of 1617 depended (Sisson, "Laws," 18). And if the publisher of a suspected text was unsporting enough to register it anyway, the entry is likely to be scrutinized for signs of supposed "irregularity"—which are easy enough to imagine if one knows nothing about the range and idiosyncrasy of the records.

Certainly before 1622, and probably until 1637, a stationer was not required to spend money on an entry in the register. An entry was an insurance policy: paid for, it provided the best possible protection, but the price had to be weighed against the risk. Authority was officially compulsory, but in practice the Company officers could decide when it was or was not required. License was mandatory, and the Company punished evasion whenever it was detected. But entrance was voluntary, and its absence is *never* sufficient reason for suspecting anything furtive, dishonest, or illegal.

My imaginary stationer is either an optimist (hoping that his play will do well enough to attract thoughts of piracy) or a pessimist (anticipating unspecified problems of infringement), and so decides to register the copy. When he goes to the clerk's countinghouse, therefore, he not only pays the license fee (as he is anyway required to do) but pays for a register entry as well. The clerk has a Company salary, but that is paid "ouer and besydes the duties of entries apperteyninge to his office" (W. A. Jackson, *Records*, 1). His salary covers what he does for the Company as a corporation, such as keeping the court minutes and the accounts of the wardens and renters. The "duties of entries" that he also receives are personal fees for any entries that benefit individual stationers.

The clerk's fees were paid directly to him, and were not recorded in the ledger because they were not part of the wardens' account. For many of his services we know only what the fees were raised to in 1697 (Stationers' Hall, Court Book F, fol. 259$^r$: R. Myers, *Records*, reel 57), but there are two clues to the earlier entrance fee. First, in 1620 it was ordered that John Legate junior should have his father's copies entered to him. The license fee for the forty-two copies in question is recorded in the register as twenty-one shillings, or the expected sixpence each—but the court had ordered Legate to pay "the fees due to the house viz$^t$ x$^d$ a Copie" (Arber, 4:45–46; W. A. Jackson, *Records*, 130). Second, sometime in the mid-1670s the clerk John Lilly was thinking about replacing the written rules and ordinances that had perished in the Great Fire. The nearest piece of paper to hand was a folded copy of a court order of 1672, so on the outside of it he jotted down three notes under the heading "Copie of By-Laws."[42] The first of those notes confirms the implication of the Legate entry: "For y$^e$ entrance of copies 6$^d$ paid to y$^e$ Company & 4$^d$ to y$^e$ Clerke."

It will therefore cost my imaginary stationer tenpence to register his copy: sixpence to the Company for the license and fourpence to the clerk for penning the entry.[43] He can now rest assured that his ownership is unchallengeable—unless, of course, when the clerk reads out the new entries at the next court meeting (Sisson,

"Laws," 16, 18), someone present realizes that another stationer has a prior claim. In the case of this imaginary play, though, no such problem will arise.

### The Publisher's Costs

Having satisfied all the applicable regulations, the stationer now needs to choose a printer. If he is an experienced publisher he will already have formed more or less regular associations with one or more printers, which will narrow the choice—but there are anyway no more than two dozen printing houses in London,[44] some of which would refuse the job. Neither the Royal Printer nor the Law Printer ever prints plays, and the one printed before 1637 by the Eliot's Court Press (which has close associations with the Royal Printer) is distinctly out of character.[45] There are also commercial printers who never print plays, probably because of Puritan sympathies—notably Thomas Dawson (printing in 1577–1620), Thomas East (1567–1608), Richard Field (1588–1624), and William Jones III (1616–1643). Since my imaginary stationer is more interested in economy than quality he will automatically rule out the few printers in London with fairly high standards of craftsmanship, of whom the best not already named are Henry Denham (1563–1589) and his successors Peter Short (1590–1603) and Humphrey Lownes (1604–1630). Without necessarily going to the opposite extreme—perhaps Ralph Blower (1595–1619) or Simon Stafford (1598–1613)—he will presumably choose from among the more competent of the lower-priced printers. He will probably try to pick one who has printed at least a few plays before, and who can therefore anticipate the special problems inherent in the genre.[46]

Having made his choice, and having confirmed that the chosen printer can fit the job into his schedule, the stationer will hand over the manuscript for an estimate. If he has strong ideas about typography and layout he will explain his preferences at the outset, but otherwise will leave such matters to the printer's professional judgment. He will hardly need to specify a format unless he wants something other than quarto, which will otherwise be the automatic choice for a single play. It is equally obvious that he will be supplying paper of the smallest of the common sizes ("pot" paper, named after the watermark most commonly found in sheets of that size), measuring somewhere between fifteen inches by eleven (38 x 28 cm.) and sixteen by twelve (41 x 30 cm.). He does, however, need to tell the printer that the edition is to consist of 800 copies.

The printer's first task is to estimate the number of sheets of paper that will be needed. Had the play been unusually short he might have decided to set it in type of the size called english,[47] but the usual choice for a play is the rather smaller size called pica.[48] Knowing that the publisher is particularly concerned about costs, the printer will choose what he considers to be the largest page-area practicable for a pot-paper quarto. To this particular imaginary printer, that means 39 lines excluding the headline (38 lines of text plus the direction line used for catchwords and signatures), set to a measure (line length) of 42 ens.[49]

The printer can now begin the process known as casting off (or counting off) the copy—calculating how much text will fill each printed page, and marking the manuscript accordingly. If he had been dealing with a work written entirely in verse, marking off each page would have been as simple as counting 38 lines. A prose work would not have been quite so easy to mark up: he would have had to adjust a composing stick to the required measure and set one or more sample lines in order to ascertain the ratio between manuscript and printed lines. But so long as he made proper allowance for variations in the size of the handwriting, and for paragraph breaks, chapter headings, and the like, an experienced printer could usually cast off prose without undue difficulty (Moxon, 239–43).

In this case, however, the text is a play that contains both verse and prose, so the printer will have to keep switching from one method to the other. In verse passages, and in prose dialogue consisting mostly of very short speeches, he can simply count the lines, but each longer prose speech will have to be measured. He may also have to make decisions about stage directions written beside the text rather than in it: should any of them be centered, and should there be space above or below? Can an exit share a line with the end of a speech, or should it have a line to itself? And in prose passages he will have to remember that speech prefixes, although written to the left of the text, will be indented in the printed page, and must therefore be allowed for in the first line of each speech.

Having decided to allow the equivalent of fifteen lines on the first page for an ornament and the head title, the printer finds that the text occupies nearly sixty-nine pages. Although this play resembles the majority in having no other preliminary matter, it will have a title page.[50] Allowing for that page and the blank page backing it, the text will begin on page 3 and end on page 71—the recto page of the thirty-sixth leaf. In a quarto, each sheet of paper is folded to produce four leaves (eight pages), so each copy will consist of nine four-leaf gatherings, or nine sheets.

We have no direct evidence for the rates paid for composition by London printers at the beginning of the seventeenth century. In Cambridge a century later the "standard" rate for setting uncomplicated prose in either english or pica worked out to a little less than 4d. per 1,000 ens (McKenzie, *Cambridge*, 1:77–80). Early London rates were probably somewhat lower, especially in a printing house of the kind under consideration. Furthermore, the pages of a verse-and-prose play contain less text—more marginal space and less visible type—than do those of a prose work, so the printer might well offer a slightly lower rate for mixed text. My imaginary printer therefore will pay the compositors at a rate of just over 3d. per 1,000 ens. He would not express it like that, because rates for composition were quoted by the sheet or the forme (one side of a sheet), but each full sheet contains 13,104 ens, and he will pay the compositors 3s. 4d. (40d.) per sheet.[51] The first and last sheets each contain one blank page, and the number of ens in the title page and head title is considerably less than in the equivalent area of pica text. But the practice at Cambridge was to pay the contracted rate for all sheets regardless (McKenzie, *Cambridge*, 1:79), and the same was probably true in London. The total payment to the compositors for set-ting the type will therefore be £1 10s.

My imaginary printer does not run the kind of establishment that would keep a full-time press corrector on the payroll. Whenever he prints a book that requires the attention of a specialist—a text in a foreign language, perhaps, or one contain-ing many special symbols or numerical tables—he hires one. Most of his books, however, are proofread either by one of the compositors or by the master printer himself.[52] In Cambridge at the beginning of the eighteenth century, correction was invariably charged at one-sixth the cost of composition, no matter who actually did the correcting or what special skills were needed. Correction at the Cambridge University Press was undoubtedly more thorough, conscientious, and expert than in the lower-priced London printing houses a century earlier—but the very inflex-ibility of the Cambridge rate suggests a long-established trade custom. The printer of the play will therefore charge 5s. for correction, even if he does it himself.

Presswork rates are slightly better documented than are those for composition. They are usually quoted by the week (six days), the day (sometimes ten hours, sometimes twelve) or the hour—but it should be noted that the word *hour* had a special meaning. When two men were working at press, printing one side of a *token* (250 sheets) was called an *hour*, no matter how long it actually took (Moxon, 344, 484–85). One hour therefore equals 250 impressions.

On the day on which he became free of the Stationers' Company in 1631, William Gay contracted with George Purslowe to work for a year at the rate of 8s. a week (W. A. Jackson, *Records*, 221). He was to print (up to) 3,000 impressions a day, so his rate per hour was to be 1.33d. The Gay contract is unique in having been recorded in the Court Book, and since the wages are the lowest on record, Gay may have been working off some kind of obligation. In 1592 Benjamin Prince, having contracted to print 2,500 impressions a day for John Legate in Cambridge, was dismissed for failing to do so. Prince was one of at least three Legate pressmen who were paid at the rate of 10s. a week, or 2d. an hour (McKenzie, "Notes," 100–102). Rates in Cambridge a century later were higher—rarely less than 3d. an hour, and often more—but the rate of 2d. an hour is also recorded at Oxford dur-ing the seventeenth century (McKenzie, *Cambridge*, 1:85–86). My imaginary printer therefore will employ two pressmen at that rate, paying a total of 4d. an hour for presswork.

The printer's estimate will be his price for supplying 800 complete copies of the book to the publisher. In order to do so, he will have to print rather more than 800 copies of each side of each sheet. At least one proofsheet will have to be printed and corrected for each forme. If a copy of that forme is compared with the proof while the press is running and is marked for further stop-press correction, that sheet too will be discarded if it is no longer clean enough to be put back in the heap. Various accidents may spoil one or more impressions, and if a sheet already printed on one side is spoiled it will usually be too late to print another copy of the first forme. In addition to anticipating wastage, the printer will have to allow either one free copy or a corresponding payment of "copy-money" to each workman who works on the book (McKenzie, *Cambridge*, 1:74–75; W. A. Jackson, *Records*, 148; Arber, 4:22). In a documented case of 1600, when printing an edition of 1,000 copies Thomas East laid an additional twenty-five sheets on each heap (Dowling, 370–71). In an arbitration of 1635 the Stationers' Company ordered that no more than "Two quires vpon an heape" should be laid on for extras (Arber, 4:22). The size of the heap was not specified, but the preceding article limited the number of impressions that could usually be printed from a single setting of type to 2,000, so it would appear that the norm was one extra quire for every two reams, or one extra sheet for every forty sheets. The printer will therefore add twenty sheets to each heap of 800.[53]

To print both sides of 820 sheets the pressmen must pull 1,640 impressions, or six hours (1,500) plus an additional 140 impressions. In eighteenth-century Cambridge presswork was charged only in whole hours (McKenzie, *Cambridge*, 1:89), so a press crew would have been paid the same for 1,640 impressions as for 1,750. On the assumption that the same rule applied a century earlier, each pressman will be paid 1s. 2d. (14d.) for seven hours' work on each of the nine heaps, and the total cost of presswork will be £1 1s.

Adding the costs of composition, correction, and presswork, the printer expects to pay his workmen a total of £2 16s. That sum, however, does not include his overhead and profit, for which there is a standard markup of 50 percent.[54] The total printing costs to be paid to the printer by the publisher, then, can be summarized as follows (with an additional column giving the sums in pence only for the sake of those unfamiliar with pre-decimal currency):

|  | £ | s | D | (PENCE) |
|---|---|---|---|---|
| Composition (3s. 4d. per sheet) | 1 | 10 | 0 | (360) |
| Correction (one-sixth of composition) |  | 5 | 0 | (60) |
| Presswork (2s. 4d. per sheet) | 1 | 1 | 0 | (252) |
| Total wages | 2 | 16 | 0 | (672) |
| Markup (50 percent of wages) | 1 | 8 | 0 | (336) |
| Total printing costs | 4 | 4 | 0 | (1,008) |

The printer therefore submits an estimate of £4 4s. to the publisher—who has meanwhile been seeking out a suitable stock of cheap paper.

Writing in 1622, the Cambridge printer Cantrell Legge claimed that the price of printing paper used in London varied from 3s. 4d. a ream for "the lowest" to 5s. 6d. a ream for "the finest" (25). The context, and his unqualified statement that a quire consists of twenty-four sheets, suggest that Legge meant specifically pot paper as distinct from crown or larger sizes. Dutch paper, and most French paper in the smaller sizes, was sold in quires of twenty-four sheets, but most Italian paper and the larger sizes from France came in quires of twenty-five sheets (Gaskell, 59). The paper used in the 1596 edition of Foxe's *Book of Martyrs*, nearly twice the size of pot paper, was rated at 7s. a ream.[55] Legge also limited his remarks to book paper, which had to be of better quality than the cheaper paper that was often used for single-sided printing: a regulation of 1612 prohibited the printing of ballads on paper costing less than 2s. 8d. a ream (W. A. Jackson, *Records*, 54). But even if Legge's context was deliberately narrow,[56] he was focusing on exactly the kind of paper my imaginary stationer would choose. I shall therefore assume that he has located a source of acceptable paper at 3s. 4d. a ream.

As it left the paper mill tied up with cord, a ream consisted of twenty quires, each folded in half. The two outer quires, which would usually have been somewhat damaged by the cord by the time they reached the printer, were made up of more or less defective sheets. The purchaser could therefore count on no more than 432 "perfect" sheets in each ream—although the cording quires would usually yield at least a few usable sheets whose defects were sufficiently minor to ignore. What the stationer expects to receive back from the printer is 800 copies of a nine-sheet book: a total of 7,200 printed sheets, or the equivalent of fifteen reams. To produce those sheets the printer will actually print enough for 820 copies, or 7,380 sheets. If we assume that the average ream supplied by the stationer will yield 450 usable sheets, he will need to supply at least 16.4 reams—or 16.5 to be on the safe side. At 3s. 4d. a ream, the cost of the paper is therefore £2 15s.[57]

The stationer's overall direct costs (excluding storage and other overhead not yet incurred) can now be added up.

|                          | £ | S  | D  | (PENCE)   |
|--------------------------|---|----|----|-----------|
| Copy and authority       | 2 | 0  | 0  | (480)     |
| License and registration |   |    | 10 | (10)      |
| Paper                    | 2 | 15 | 0  | (660)     |
| Printing                 | 4 | 4  | 0  | (1,008)   |
| Total                    | 8 | 19 | 10 | (2,158)   |

At only twopence short of nine pounds, the total is slightly higher than he had hoped—but remains within acceptable limits. That these figures are realistic estimates can be confirmed in various ways. In his account of production costs in 1622, for example, Cantrell Legge suggests that the typical combined cost of paper and printing in London ranged from 8s. to 13s. 4d. a ream (25). The complete edition of 800 copies contains fifteen reams, and the cost of paper and printing is £6 19s.

(1,668d.). The cost per ream is therefore just over 9s. 3d. (111d.), which is near the lower end of Legge's range. Had the stationer risked a larger edition—say, 1,200 copies at the same rates—the price per ream would have been almost exactly 8s.

At this stage in a real transaction the printing itself would begin. Space will not permit me to follow the play step by step through the printing house, and the mechanics of hand-press printing can anyway be studied in more or less detail elsewhere.[58] The compositors and pressmen must therefore be left to earn their wages offstage.

### Expected Profits

When the printer has completed his task, he will deliver the books to the publisher *in quires* (or *in sheets*). Each copy will consist of nine printed sheets in the right order and similarly oriented, folded in half. The folded copies will have been pressed flat in heaps of suitable size (in this case probably one hundred or two hundred copies), and tied in bundles with a blank sheet of waste paper (from the cording quires) protecting each end. There should also be another bundle containing all the odd printed sheets left over after the required number of complete copies (including the printer's "overplus" copies) were gathered and collated. And if the agreement between the printer and stationer so requires, all the unused paper (mostly defective sheets) will also be returned.

What the stationer has to do with the books now is to sell them, and before he can do so he needs to decide on a wholesale price. Once again, we have little direct testimony about customary rates—but there are enough clues to support an informed guess, even though one of the most important pieces of evidence has usually been misinterpreted. On January 19, 1598, the Court of Assistants ordained that no new book set in either pica or english and lacking illustrations should be priced at more than a penny for two sheets, and no book set in brevier or long primer (smaller sizes) at more than a penny for a sheet and a half (Greg and Boswell, 58–59). In his study of book prices in 1550–1640, Francis R. Johnson concluded that the average prices throughout the period seemed to be fairly consistent with those figures. But although the actual prices recorded in Johnson's study form a useful body of evidence (94–112), his conclusions were distorted by his belief that the 1598 ordinance was intended to regulate *retail* prices. He therefore usually assumed that any significantly higher price included the cost of a binding—and so it is hardly surprising that his adjusted "averages" coincide fairly closely with the figure toward which he nudged them.[59]

Virtually everyone who has ever cited the 1598 order has, like Johnson, overlooked the obvious, namely that the prices it was intended to control were *wholesale*, not retail. The booksellers of London made their living by marking up the price of the books that they passed on to the public—and the more they marked it up, the better the living they made. The Stationers' Company can have had no conceivable motive for wanting to limit the income of its members by siding with their customers against them; the Company *was* its members, and prospered as they prospered. The Court of Assistants was concerned to protect Company members from each other, but had neither reason nor the right to step between them and the source of their income, namely the book-buying public. It ought therefore to be clear that the purpose of the regulation was to prevent stationers from exploiting each other instead of their customers.

The ceiling imposed by the ordinance was intended to curb excessive profiteering and must necessarily have allowed for an acceptable profit margin, even on books whose production costs were at the very top of the "normal" range. According to Cantrell Legge (25), the cost per ream of the best London printing in 1622 was 13s. 4d. The wholesale limit of a penny for two sheets (£1 per ream) would allow a 50 percent markup on those costs—and as we have seen, that was the standard rate claimed by printers for overhead and profits. My own analysis of wholesale and retail prices has led me to conclude that a margin of 50 percent was considered acceptable at each stage in the proceedings: that it was customary for retailers as well as printers, and that a publisher would often—perhaps usually—determine the wholesale price of a first edition in the same way.[60]

At £8 19s. 10d. for 800 copies, the unit cost of the play is just under 2.7d. Marked up by exactly 50 percent, a single copy would wholesale at 4.05d.—close enough to 4d. for the difference to be insignificant in a batch of less than a dozen. The stationer will therefore set the wholesale price at 4d. When sold unbound by a retailer who paid that price, the play will retail at 6d. a copy—a typical price, though by no means invariable.[61]

I know of no way of determining the relative demand for printed plays inside and outside London, so at this point I must resort to uninformed guesswork. For the sake of argument I shall therefore assume that my imaginary publisher will (eventually) sell 40 percent of the edition wholesale to other members of the Company, 50 percent at a higher rate to non-Stationers both in London and elsewhere, and 10 percent at the retail price directly to the public.

By long-established custom, any Stationer who bought a *quartern* of copies (twenty-five) was given one copy free of charge (Greg, *Companion*, 133; Greg and Boswell, 22; W. A. Jackson, *Records*, 34)—although it is unclear whether that meant twenty-six for the price of twenty-five or (more probably) twenty-five for the price of twenty-four. In this case, though, the point is almost certainly moot, for it is hardly likely that any retailer would buy that many at once. If a typical bookseller who dealt in plays at all had typically bought them in batches of twenty-five or more, any publisher whose play was ordered by thirty or forty such booksellers (and there were more than thirty bookshops in St. Paul's Churchyard alone) would have sold his whole stock within weeks—which rarely happened.

Let us therefore suppose that over the years the publisher will sell 320 copies to members of the Company at 4d. each (a margin of 48.3 percent) for a total of £5 6s. 8d. (1,280d.). The 400 copies he will sell to non-Stationers will be priced at the usual London retail price discounted by 3s. in the pound (G. Pollard, "Sandars," 15), or 85 percent of 6d. He can hardly sell single copies for 5.1d. each, but if he sells them in batches at the rate of five for 2s. 1½d. (a margin of 89 percent) they will return £8 10s. (2,040d.). Of the remaining 80 copies I shall suppose that he gives 5 away for various reasons (as gifts or bribes, but probably not as quartern copies) and sells 75 in his own bookshop for 6d. each. His margin over cost will be 122.4 percent, and the return will be £1 17s. 6d. (450d.). By the time he has sold the whole edition it will have returned £15 14s. 2d. (3,770d.). If he had no overhead at all, that would mean a total profit of £6 14s. 4d. (1,612d.), or 74.7 percent over cost. But if the play took ten years to sell out (which, it should not be forgotten, would be distinctly better than average) the publisher would have to subtract the cost of storing the unsold copies. Even if he had so many other projects in hand that he could reckon storage at less than 18d. a year and subtract only the odd 14s. 4d., that would bring the total profit down to £6 (1,440d.) and the margin to 61.8 percent.

If, then, the stationer who published this hypothetical play was lucky enough to sell all 800 copies in ten years, he would recover his original investment plus storage costs to date after almost exactly six years, while for the remaining four years he would make a profit of £1 10s. a year. According to popular myth, "London stationers were of course aware that a six-penny quarto edition of a single play . . . was practically certain to make a handsome profit" (Hinman, x). In fact, London stationers knew better—and if the real profit margins make it difficult to understand why a stationer would bother to take the risk at all, we should remember that during the sixty years on which I have focused it was, on average, only half a dozen times a year that anyone *did* bother.

What made the venture worth the risk was the chance that a well-chosen play would merit a second edition during its publisher's lifetime. Even though the odds were against it, many publishers were willing to gamble at least once that their sense of the market was above average—and more than a few gambled successfully. If a play did sell out, the speed at which it had done so would determine the size of the second edition. If it took several years to sell, the publisher might well hold the next edition down to the same number of copies as before, or even fewer. If it had sold quickly, and the demand showed no sign of fading, he might risk a larger edition—say 1,200 or even 1,500 copies.[62] The big difference would be that his costs would no longer include the price of the manuscript, authority, license, and registration. If he commissioned a second edition of 800 copies at the same rate as before, having established 4d. as the wholesale price for this play, he would continue to ask it—but instead of the original profit of 48.3 percent on wholesale copies he would now make 91.8 percent—or, from an edition of 1,200 or 1,500 copies, respectively 121.2 percent or 138.3 percent. His profits on copies sold outside the Company and on those he retailed himself would also be correspondingly higher, so while the first edition made a total profit of nearly 75 percent over the direct costs, another edition of 800 copies would make 126 percent. Similarly, a second edition of 1,200 copies would make about 161 percent, or one of 1,500 copies, 181 percent. There would still be a delay before that edition broke even, the profits would still take time to accrue, and the sums involved would still be far from huge (on a reprint of 1,500 copies at the same rates, the total profit would be a little under £19 less overhead). But the return from a second or later edition would adequately justify the original risk.

### Bookshops and Their Customers

Until copies of the play reached the bookshops they would remain in quires. Most booksellers who bought a batch would have at least some of them turned into something more closely resembling books, although few copies (if any) would be actually bound. The basic minimum would be to fold each sheet in four and to stack them in order as if for binding, to take a bodkin and stab three or four holes through the whole stack about a quarter-inch from the spine fold, and to stitch through the holes with packthread—essentially the equivalent of side stapling. Each successive pair of leaves in the stitched copies would be joined along the top; the bookseller might or might not bother to have the folds opened. Some might choose to have the folded sheets put in a paper wrapper before stitching; if so, the paper might be plain but defective white paper from a cording quire, or a piece of coarser wrapping paper—sometimes natural brown or gray, but more often blue. Whether or not there would be a charge for that service (or alternatively, whether there would be a small discount on a copy sold in sheets) would be up to the individual bookseller.

The bookshops themselves were more substantial buildings than the kind of market stalls, booths, and kiosks that have sometimes been imagined.[63] Like most commercial buildings before street numbers were introduced in the eighteenth century, they were identified by pictorial signs,[64] and like most other kinds of shop, they could be identified as shops by their distinctive exterior fittings. Below each working window was a hinged wooden counter called a *stall, stall-board,* or *shop-board,* that could be closed up like a horizontal shutter across the lower part of the window. Another, larger board formed a sloping roof to protect the stall and its contents from the weather. This was called a *penthouse* or *pentice* and may sometimes also have been hinged, closing down across the upper part of the window at the end of the day. When a bookshop was open, it could be recognized not only by the books displayed on the stall but by the title pages fixed to all suitable surfaces.

Many customers would do most of their browsing outside, but in all except the smallest shops there was more stock, and room to inspect it, inside. All the early bookshops of which descriptions and surveys have been found were at least two stories tall; some of those in St. Paul's Churchyard had four stories plus garrets, were more than forty feet deep, and had frontages ranging from thirteen feet to nearly thirty. The early modern book trade was not the primitive cottage craft that some have imagined, hawking its meager wares from open-air market stalls. It was an advanced industry of mass production, with a well-developed national infrastructure for distribution and marketing. And while the trade in printed plays was only a relatively insignificant part of it, bookselling (especially in London) was a lucrative and flourishing business.

When the occupant of one of those shops bought a batch of large books, or of fat books in small formats, he or she might well decide to have a few copies plainly bound in either vellum or calf. The larger the book, the more likely it was that *most* copies would be bound before sale. Customers who wanted a special style of binding could either commission it from the bookseller or buy the book unbound and take it to a favored binder. But pamphlets and other books as slim as most play quartos would usually be sold without bindings, and few purchasers would want them bound individually. Those who bought such books regularly would wait until they had what they considered to be a suitable number, and would then have them bound as a single volume.

The question of who actually bought printed plays is yet another about which we know comparatively little. It is true that we know the names of several collectors whose libraries contained substantial numbers of plays, either because many of their books have survived with identifiable ownership marks (Robert Burton, Edward Gwynn) or because lists of their purchases (Sir Edward Dering) or catalogs of their collections (Sir John Harington, Henry Oxinden) have been preserved.[65] Those libraries, however, are known because they were atypical. Some owners of smaller collections may also have inscribed or marked their books in recognizable ways, and if the major research libraries ever pool their provenance files we may learn the names of many men and women who collected on a small scale. But names alone will tell us little; what we want to know is not what they called themselves but what kind of people they were.

One rather general clue is provided by typography. During the closing decades of the sixteenth century roman type displaced blackletter as the usual design for books of many kinds, and by 1600 most works still usually printed in blackletter tended toward one of two extremes. The more old-fashioned typography was evidently considered to confer a kind of antiquarian dignity on serious and conservative works such as lawbooks, chronicles, and lectern-size Bibles.[66] It was likewise favored for official documents such as proclamations and statutes, and the hornbook from which children first learned their alphabet was also customarily printed in blackletter. For fairly obvious reasons, though, roman type (or italic) was preferred for Latin, and the basic Latin school text, Lily's *Grammar*, was therefore printed in roman. This fact apparently led the book trade to associate roman type with a higher level of literacy and education than blackletter. Works aimed at the barely literate—at those who had learned their hornbook but had not graduated to Latin—were usually printed in blackletter: jestbooks, works for the instruction and improvement of the young, certain kinds of sensational news pamphlets, and above all, ballads.[67]

In the first decade of the sample period, 1583–1592, nine out of the twenty plays (45 percent) were printed in blackletter, but in 1593–1602 the proportion dropped to ten out of seventy-six (13 percent). One play was printed in blackletter in 1603, another in 1604, and the last three (all printed by William Jaggard for Thomas Pavier) in 1605. For what the evidence is worth, the preference for roman type suggests that the publishers of plays were aiming more at the middle class than the working class. That is not to say that they thought of plays as appealing *only* to the educated reader; the significance is more that they did *not* perceive them as belonging to the same market as jestbooks and ballads.

For one other clue we can turn again to Humphrey Moseley's preface to the Beaumont and Fletcher Folio of 1647. The rise of Puritanism in London during the 1630s and the closure of the theaters in 1642 had undoubtedly changed the trade in printed plays, and Moseley's assumptions in 1647 may not apply to 1583–1642. But he offers a particularly interesting reason for having limited the volume to plays that had never before been printed. To have included reprints would have increased the size of the collection,

> And indeed it would have rendred the Booke so Voluminous, that *Ladies* and *Gentlewomen* would have found it scarce manageable, who in Workes of this nature must first be remembred. (GREG, *Bibliography*, 3:1233)

An unqualified "must be remembred" might have been simple gallantry, but "must *first* be remembred" suggests that Moseley envisaged a readership in which women outnumbered men.

## Conclusion

It is not uncommon for an introductory guide, handbook, or companion to the study of early modern English drama to include an essay on the publication of plays, and shorter discussions are often found in the textual introductions to editions, especially collected editions. Such essays sometimes include a brief and fairly accurate summary of how compositors and pressmen actually set and printed the text of a play. Otherwise, though, they typically either include or consist of some version of the Pollard myth. Greedy publishers (usually mistaken for printers), impatient to make a quick fortune from the insatiable demands of hordes of eager play collectors, therefore spend much of their time conspiring with disaffected bit-part players. Having procured an illicit text they carefully conceal their involvement from the private ledgers of the Stationers' Company—while nevertheless proclaiming it on the printed title page. The confidence with which such fictions are asserted is not always directly proportional to the writer's knowledge of the book trade. And what is rarely discussed at all, even by those familiar with the word, is *publishing*.

What I have tried to do in this essay, then, is to focus on the neglected subject of publication. There was rather more to publishing a play than deciding "What my customers really want is *Love's Labor's Lost*,[68] so I must procure them a text." I have therefore tried to show what had to happen both before and after a playbook was actually printed: what factors had to be considered before the first type was set, and what the publisher had to do after the printer delivered the finished sheets; how much a first edition would have cost, and how much profit it might have made. It is necessarily true that in the absence of direct testimony about the publication or printing of any specific play, the account I have offered above is not much less conjectural than was Pollard's. The difference, however, is that I have tried to make sure that every single guess is consistent with the most nearly related sources of documentary evidence I could find—albeit from different times, places, and circumstances.

I realize, of course, that my own conjectures, and the imperfectly reverent attitude of my imaginary publisher toward dramatic texts, may be found unacceptable, and that others may wish to offer alternative scenarios. I have therefore done what I can to make it difficult for future theorists to evade one inescapable fact about printed plays—namely, that they were not the best-selling moneyspinners that so many commentators have evidently believed they *should* have been. Any hypothesis that ignores that fact, whether it be a generalization about the trade as a whole or a theory about the publication of a particular play, can safely be ignored in return. Far more is known today about the early modern book trade than Pollard knew—and it is about time we left 1909 behind.

NOTES

1. Neither the traditional nor the new elements in Pollard's tale have escaped challenge, and many of his contemporaries made their reservations clear (Chambers, 3:183–92; Albright, 217–87; etc.). But those who shape the popular imagination usually find fiction more memorable than fact.

2. My exclusions agree for the most part with the classifications in Harbage's *Annals*, 3d ed. In borderline cases I have considered whether the printed book appears to be aimed at the buyers of less equivocally professional and public plays. *Cornelia* and *Summer's Last Will and Testament* are therefore included because of their authorship, *The Wit of a Woman* because of its title page, *The Second Part of The Cid* because the first part had been publicly acted, etc. I have included most university plays in English, excluding only a handful that are clearly not aimed at the "typical" buyer of plays (such as *Sicelides: A Piscatory* and *Work for Cutlers*).

3. The figures were determined by counting items in every fifth year from 1584 and calculating the intervening years from the average number of items per line.

4. In some accounts a more tangible fallacy is found. It is therefore worth noting that the present-day concept of literary property, which includes the rights to both publication and performance, simply did not exist in early modern England. Neither "right" existed in law, and neither the stationers nor the players imagined that they had any authority over each other's professional activities.

5. Neither of the two early comments usually adduced as evidence is either explicit or trustworthy. The anonymous epistle prefixed to *Troilus and Cressida* in 1609 suggests merely

that the unidentified "grand possessors" of the play might have preferred to keep it unpublished. But a manuscript had been provisionally registered six years earlier by James Roberts, who had then (characteristically) declined to publish it. So neither the motive nor even the *identity* of the "possessors" is beyond doubt—and if the play had never yet been considered worth performing in public, I cannot see why we should imagine that the players feared competition.

In an epistle to his *English Traveler* (1633), the ever-complaining Thomas Heywood claims that some of his plays "are still retained in the hands of some Actors, who thinke it against their peculiar profit to haue them come in Print" (Greg, *Bibliography*, 3:1222). The context, however, is an explanation of why his plays have not been collected and published as *Works* (the rest can be summarized as "Many have been lost" and "I have no interest in having them printed"), and Heywood is an unreliable witness. The indifference to publication that he professed in so many printed epistles is no more credible the year after he published the fourth and fifth of his *Ages* plays (the two-part *Iron Age* [1632]) than in the address he prefixed to the first of them (*The Golden Age* [1611]). He may well be right that some players in 1633 did not want *others* to sell their property to the press—but we cannot ascertain their reasons without more and better testimony.

6. Gary Taylor has suggested that the resumption of playing by the Children of Paul's, and the consequent increase in competition, might have created a perceived need to advertise.

7. That is, counting the year of publication as year 1, before the end of year 25.

8. If we express the annual number of new plays as a percentage of the annual number of items listed in the chronological index to the *Short-Title Catalogue*, the mean figures for the three periods are 1.6 percent, 1.2 percent, and 1.3 percent respectively. The first figure is distorted by the lower rate of survival of nonliterary books of the sixteenth century. Once again, therefore, the general impression is of a demand that was low but fairly constant.

9. Each of the last two reached its fifth edition in nineteen years, so they rank equal tenth.

10. In 1600 Wise trod more carefully and shared the risk of his next two plays with William Aspley, even though one of them was the sequel to a best-seller. Once again he showed either extraordinary luck or an enviable instinct for the trade—because neither *Much Ado About Nothing* nor *Henry IV, Part 2* was reprinted for twenty-three years.

11. Approximately 74 percent in 1583–1602, 88 percent in 1603–1622, and 91 percent in 1623–1642.

12. Like other printed books, playbooks were sometimes farmed out in sections to two or more printing houses (Blayney, *Texts*, 1:31–32, 49–52), but even in a shared book it is appropriate to refer to "the printer" of each section.

13. See in particular his "Entrance, Licence," 14–22; *Some Aspects*, 63–89; and *Bibliography*, 4:clxi–clxix. An *imprint* is a statement on a title page giving details of publication: the place and/or date, and often the names of one or more of the stationers responsible. A *colophon* is a similar statement placed at the end of a book.

14. In his first discussion of imprints ("First Folio," 130–34), Greg admitted that other bookshops would "probably" have stocked a copy or two (133). But by the time he published his first detailed analysis ("Entrance, Licence," in response to Shaaber), he no longer acknowledged that possibility.

15. The present separation of the trade in new books from the trade in used books is comparatively recent. Early modern booksellers sold books of all kinds: new, nearly new, used, and antiquarian; homegrown and imported; printed, manuscript, ruled, and blank. Many also sold other things, some related to the book trade (paper, parchment, and cardboard; pens, ink, and wax) and some not.

16. It is sometimes suggested that exchanging books acquired at cost saved money—which is economic nonsense. In a fair exchange, one batch of books worth a given sum at retail prices would be traded for a batch of different books worth exactly the same. It was immaterial how much either party had paid for his own batch: each started and finished with goods of equal value. What was increased by trading was not overall profit but the rate of turnover. While it might take several years to sell five hundred copies of a single title, ten copies each of fifty carefully chosen titles might be sold in a matter of weeks.

17. Any freeman of London had the right to retail virtually any commodity except certain controlled perishables (principally food and drink). All London booksellers were subject to the regulatory authority of the Stationers' Company, but they did not have to belong to it.

18. A few publishers even insisted on imprints claiming that their books were printed "by" them rather than "for" them.

19. The Dering manuscript of *Henry IV* is an abridgement of both parts, prepared before February 27, 1623. At 1½d. per sheet for thirty-two sheets, which included the equivalent of four rewritten sheets, the copy cost Dering a total of 4s. (Yeandle, 224). If London prices were comparable, a play of average length could have been copied for between 2s. and 3s.

20. Although stationers' widows were automatically free of both company and city in their own right, and some had very successful careers, between 1541 and 1666 no women were either apprenticed or freed as stationers. Of the 371 plays I have used for statistical analysis, only four were published by women (three by Joan Broome and one by Anne Wilson)—so my imaginary publisher is male.

21. The players, however, might disagree. Three playwrights (Barrey, Drayton, and Mason) were parties to the Whitefriars contract of 1608, which provided that no sharer should publish any of the company's plays. Richard Brome's 1635 contract with the Salisbury Court company similarly forbade him to publish his plays without the company's consent (Albright, 239, 235).

22. Robinson seldom asked a dedicatee in advance, and some of his chosen benefactors were neither impressed nor grateful (Vogt, 631, 635, 637–38, and 644–45). He was aware that selling copies to his friends was also an imposition: after one patron was unexpectedly generous, he noted that "his liberality . . . kept mee from trubling my frendes abrode for one whole yeares space afterwardes" (636).

23. But William Prynne's only payment for his massive antitheatrical diatribe, *Histriomastix* (1633), was thirty-six free copies (Greg, *Companion*, 278).

24. In this case the percentages are of playbooks rather than plays, because several plays were printed in pairs or larger collections. Some paired plays have separate dedications, but the dedication to the Shakespeare First Folio belongs neither to each of the plays in the book nor to any one of them. The numbers of play*books* in each period are 93, 114, and 135 respectively.

25. John Stephens's reference to "the worthy benefactors of *Hellicon*" might suggest a dedicatee's patronage rather than a publisher's payment, and in 1612 Nathan Field more explicitly identified 40s. as the expected gratuity for dedicating a play (STC 10854, sig. A3$^r$). The most generous rewards received by Richard Robinson for dedications were 60s., 50s., and 40s. (twice each).

26. The *Injunctions* named other ecclesiastical and civil authorities but required that "the ordinary of the place" of printing always be included; the Stationers' charter of 1557 had effectively restricted English printing to London (Arber, 1:xxxi), thirteen of whose parishes were under the authority of the archbishop rather than the bishop. The decree of 1586 required both that every book be allowed in accordance with the *Injunctions* and that it be seen by either the bishop or the archbishop; that of 1637 specified various kinds of books that could be allowed by others and then placed the bishop and archbishop at the head of the list of authorities who could allow "all other Books."

27. In the three years before March 1596, only 20 percent of register entries claimed authority. After a stern warning from the High Commission (Stationers' Hall, Liber A, fol. 67$^v$: R. Myers, *Records*, reel 71), the percentage for the next three years was an improved 48 percent, and during the three years after the "Bishops' Ban" of June 1599 (Arber, 3:677–78) it soared to 63 percent.

28. See Dutton, *Mastering*, especially 148–62. It should, however, be noted that there were more than two exceptions "between 1606 and 1615" (150) and that John Wilson was not a member of the Stationers' Company (149). Plays allowed by others were registered in January 1607 (Owen Gwyn), June 1607 (Edmond Tilney), February 1607, May 1608, and June 1610 (all John Wilson), February 1613 and January 1614 (both Gervase Nid), and May 1614 (John Taverner jointly with Buc).

29. In June 1588 the archbishop appointed a panel of what we would now call licensers, and when the clerk recorded the order he identified the topic in the margin as "Licensinge of Copies"—but the word *license* is not used in the order itself (Greg and Boswell, 28–29).

30. As when Robert Waldegrave enrolled an apprentice, Henry Denham had a fellow stationer arrested, and Edmund Bollifant left a Court meeting, in each case "without lycence" (Arber, 2:848, 850, 861).

31. For a selection of variously worded examples (including three uses of "license"), see the entries transcribed by Greg under the dates May 27 and 29, 1600; October 24 and November 11, 1601; February 7, 1603; February 12, March 2, and June 26, 1605; March 12 and May 13, 1606 (*Bibliography*, 1:15–21).

32. Arber, 2:388 (Charlewood), 411 (White), 620 (Wright); 3:91 (Shaw), 126 (Bishop), 138 (Adams), 397 (Jaggard), etc.

33. For Mulcaster/Ascham, see Arber, 2:390; for Hopton/Grafton, see Blayney, *Texts*, 1:293–94, 297; for Dugdale/King, see Stationers' Hall, Court Book D, fol. 29$^v$ (R. Myers, *Records*, reel 56).

34. Suggested by (inter alia) Greg, *Shakespeare*, 448–49. See also Blayney, *First Folio*, 17, 21–24.

35. By the late eighteenth century the "VJ" still written beside each entry may have become an empty formula. Whether or not it still denoted a payment of sixpence, it made its last appearance on June 10, 1785 (Stationers' Hall, Entries of Copies 1774–86: R. Myers, *Records*, reel 7).

36. Most entries before 1583 (and some thereafter until 1590) record the sum as "Received" for a stationer's "license" either "to print" or "for printing" a specified book (more than 1,500 examples before 1590). The next most common formula, introduced in 1576, is "Licensed unto him" and the name of the book (more than 700).

37. Two surviving examples, each showing both the signed authority and the licensing signatures of the wardens, are reproduced in Blayney, *Texts*, 1:260, 270.

38. In support of this theory, Kirschbaum cited another myth: "Scholars . . . must explain why, except for at most five or six instances between 1586 and 1640, the Master, Senior Warden, and Junior Warden never entered a book during their year in office" (65). No explanation is needed, because the statement is not quite accurate. For "at most five or six," read "274."

39. Arber, 3:234 (May 18, 1603). It is uncertain whether the "sonnett" (209), the "songe" (220), or the "thinge in verse" (230) registered during the intervening months would have fit the Company's definition of a ballad, but it is hardly likely that any of them was registered in pursuance of the order.

40. W. A. Jackson, *Records*, 443 (Okes and Archer, 1609), 68 and 455 (Allde, 1614), 467 and 471 (Jones, 1621), 171 and 472 (Okes, 1624), etc.

41. In the account for 1582–1583 there is a payment of 6d. from Thomas East "for A copie he ough for" but apparently never entered (Arber, 1:497); under December 6, 1588, there is a note of 12d. "Receiued for ij copies by master Denham [*the junior warden*]" (2:510); an undated note on a flyleaf records that Richard Jones has printed a book called *Polyhymnia* (by George Peele, 1590: STC 19546), and that "master warden Cawood hath Receaved vj^d/ but it is not entred" (2:36).

42. Stationers' Hall, Supplementary Documents, series I, A.1.viii (R. Myers, *Records*, reel 97). This item is both misdescribed and misnumbered in R. Myers, *Stationers'*, 85. Despite the headnote to Folder 1, the order is a manuscript; item *via* has been misnumbered "vii," and items vii–x are consequently misnumbered "viii–xi"; the order ("ix"), enacted on March 14, 1672 (Court Book D, fol. 197^v: reel 56), forbids the piracy of law books; it has no connection whatever with the series II item noted beside it.

43. He, or his assistant, would hold the pen; Greg's claim that some of the entries in the 1580s and 1590s were written by the entering stationers is false. Of the three entries he reproduced to support that view ("Some Notes," 379), the first and third are in the same hand, and the marginal names do not resemble the signatures of the stationers themselves.

44. The precise number varied between 21 and 24, depending on the date.

45. The play is *Bussy D'Ambois* (1607). The revised STC conjecturally attributes *The Whore of Babylon* (1607) to the same press, but it was printed by Robert Raworth.

46. For example, plays required unusually large supplies of periods (for the numerous short speeches and abbreviated speech prefixes), question marks (more common in dialogue than in expository prose), italic capital E's (for entrances and exits), etc.

47. In modern terms, 13 point. Twenty lines of english measure 92–93 mm; one inch contains approximately 5.5 lines. Showing a high tolerance for ambiguity, early printers also used *english* to mean blackletter ("gothic"). When used first (english italic) the word denotes the size; when used second (pica english) it means the style.

48. Modern 12 point: 20 lines measure 82–83 mm; one inch contains approximately 6 lines.

49. An *em* is the body-height of the type; an *en* is half an em. A measure of 42 ens is therefore equal to the depth of 21 lines: in this case, 86–87 mm.

50. The wording of the title would often, perhaps usually, be decided by the publisher.

51. Now may be a good time to explain to those unfamiliar with early modern English currency that twelve pence (12d.) equals one shilling (1s.) and that twenty shillings (20s., or 240d.) equals one pound (£1). While it is misleading to compare wages before and after the Industrial Revolution, in terms of its power to purchase basic necessities (such as bread) the pound in 1600 can be considered the equivalent of between 100 and 200 U.S. dollars in the mid-1990s.

52. A few textual scholars still cling to the long-discredited hypothesis that plays were not usually corrected at all before the presswork began. That belief, however, has never been accepted by anyone with practical experience of hand-press printing. See Blayney, *Texts*, 1:189–205.

53. Additional copies of the first sheet would also be printed so that title pages could be displayed outside bookshops or on posts in public places—but I do not know how many extra titles were usually printed.

54. The markup therefore accounted for one-third of the price charged *by* the printer and was traditionally known as a *third*, or as *the printer's thirds* (McKenzie, *Cambridge*, 1:153, 2:8–28, and "Printers," 34 n).

55. Greg and Boswell, 51; the size is either small royal or large demy. A ream contained ten quires, therefore either 480 or 500 sheets.

56. Legge's purpose was to complain about what he considered to be the excessive profits made by the English Stock of the Stationers' Company, so it was in his interest to estimate costs as low as possible. Since Legge's figures have sometimes been mistaken for *typical* London profit margins, it is perhaps worth noting that the whole point of the English Stock was to increase the margins by cutting out one layer of middlemen.

57. The paper costs almost as much as the total paid in wages. If nothing had to be spent on copy, the cost of the paper in a book printed by its publisher could (as is often noted) equal or exceed half the prime cost. But by the time the costs in this case have been marked up by printer, publisher, and retailer, the paper will account for less than 14 percent of the retail price. Not even the publisher's *total* costs would equal half the bookshop price.

58. For a condensed account, see Gaskell, 40–56 and 78–141. For greater detail from the horse's mouth, see Moxon, 191–320.

59. Other flaws in the analysis include Johnson's conscious inclusion of wholesale prices from Edinburgh on the grounds that "the wholesale price in Scotland approximates so closely to the retail price in London" (88) that he is supposed to be investigating rather than presupposing. His understanding of the roles of printers, publishers, and retail booksellers also seems confused, as when he speaks of books as being sold retail "by the publisher" (86) at prices decided by "the printers" (93).

60. Marked up by 50 percent, the 1598 limits would translate into maxima of 0.75d. a sheet for plain text in pica and english and 1d. a sheet for brevier and long primer. The *average* retail prices would be fairly close to the wholesale maxima—and that conclusion is quite consistent with the actual prices recorded by Johnson.

61. The belief that all play quartos always cost 6d. is another common fallacy. If produced at the same rates as my hypothetical quarto in editions of 800 copies and marked up as suggested, the retail prices of four selected quartos would have been as follows: *A Yorkshire*

*Tragedy* (four sheets) 3.42d., *A Midsummer Night's Dream* (eight sheets) 5.53d., *Richard III* (twelve sheets) 7.57d., and *Every Man out of his Humor* (seventeen sheets) 10.16d. The only recorded prices paid for Shakespeare plays before 1623 are 5d. for the 1600 quarto of *2 Henry IV* (Bartlett and Pollard, 30) and 8d. for the 1595 octavo of *The True Tragedy of Richard Duke of York* (3 *Henry VI* [F. R. Johnson, 91, 109]).

62. William Ingram has drawn my attention to a lawsuit of 1623 concerning two books printed by Nicholas Okes for Thomas Walkley in 1622 (Corporation of London Records Office, MC.1/38/38). Only 800 copies were printed of the first (and only) edition of STC 10599, but the second edition of *Philaster* (after the first had sold out in two years) consisted of 1,500 copies.

63. The information in this paragraph and the next is condensed from Blayney, *Bookshops*.

64. Or occasionally by their proximity to some landmark. It is sometimes suggested that bookshops identified themselves by the signs of adjacent taverns (e.g., Allen and Muir, xxii), but the idea that if a building had a sign, it was probably a tavern, is purely anachronistic.

65. For Dering, see Fehrenbach and Leedham-Green, 1:137–269, especially 141; for Harington and Oxinden, see Greg, *Bibliography*, 3:1306–17.

66. All editions of the Bishops' translation, appointed for use in churches in 1568–1610, were in blackletter. The earliest editions of the Geneva version (1560–1577), intended primarily for private study, were in roman; thereafter, while all the octavos remained in roman, more than half the larger editions (quarto and folio) were in blackletter. The first edition of the King James version (1611) was in blackletter, as were all subsequent large folios and more than half the quartos. The smaller folios, octavos, and duodecimos were all in roman.

67. These remarks concern only books or broadsides in which the main text is in blackletter. It was also commonly used as a contrasting design for emphasis or for other special purposes. Many works of religious controversy, for example, print the Protestant commentary in blackletter (english), the text of the Catholic adversary in roman, and quotations from elsewhere in italic.

68. Published 1598, reprinted in collection 1623 (sixteen years after the first publisher had died).

# CHAPTER 22

# Patronage and the Economics of Theater

## Kathleen E. McLuskie and Felicity Dunsworth

IN 1615 John Cocke's satiric description of "a common player" asserted that "howsoever hee pretends to have a royall Master or Mistresse, his wages and dependence prove him to be the servant of the people" (Chambers, *Elizabethan*, 4:255). Cocke's statement could be taken as a paradigmatic description of the state of the early modern theater in 1615. It suggests that the theaters were financially autonomous and functioned in a market in which entertainment, in the form of play performances, was sold. The playing companies played in the name of royal and aristocratic patrons, but these connections were a hangover from an older mode of theatrical production and had only symbolic significance in the theatrical markets. Cocke's simple opposition between patronage and commerce, however, glossed over the wide variations among players (boy players, adult players, hired men, and sharers) and left open the economic question of how the theaters were financed in the first place: how the players' "wages and dependence" were connected to the sale of performances. It provided no comment on the connection between the *social* relations of patronage and the *economic* relations of a fully commercial theater.

In the twentieth century, versions of Cocke's account have been reformulated, linking plays to the market, via the market in plays (Bruster, Agnew). This thematic connection between a market economy and the renaissance of English drama has been variously used by those of different political persuasions, to validate market economics as the only begetter of cultural supremacy, to denigrate the writers of this period as the apologists of a repressive economic order, or to locate in literature the subversion of the dominant relations of production. The resulting "poetics of the market" (Bruster, 11) seems the more persuasive for being corroborated and endorsed by early modern writers. Whether they deplored or admired the market, commentators on theater were clear that it was fundamentally changing the social relations in which they worked. In Dekker's *Gull's Hornbook* the Muses had turned to Merchants, in *Bartholomew Fair* the theater audience was urged to temper its judgment to the price of the seats, and in numerous prologues and addresses to the reader, audiences were addressed as consumers of the latest product in a competitive market.[1]

Given the elegant symmetries of this model, it seems perverse to disrupt it with an irritable reaching after fact. It must be recognized, however, that ideological appropriation of the concept of "the market" was as much a feature of its early modern deployment as of its more recent use. The triumphalist welcome given to Eastern Bloc countries as they entered the "world market" may seem the antithesis of the anti-acquisitive complaints of Jacobean satirists, but the two uses have similar effects. They smooth over the difficult and contradictory processes of economic change; they reify market institutions into smoothly humming machines to which everyone has access; above all, they interweave economic with moral discourse (Appleby). For in spite of their apparent contemporaneity and insistence on novelty, early modern accounts of the market were embedded in traditions of complaint and satire that extended back to the Middle Ages and beyond. Dekker's *Gull's Hornbook* brings alive the London scene through the detail of its social observation, but it also enacts an old-fashioned pageant of the seven deadly sins, in which conspicuous consumption and the bustling markets of early modern London are presented as the modern masks of Lechery and Sloth (77).

The longevity of tropes that connected the market to immorality reduces their value as evidence of precisely located economic activity, but they also reveal the absence of an autonomous discourse of economics. Statements that modern disciplinary divisions would locate with economics, statements about wages, prices, investments, and surpluses, were tightly bound in with other discourses of social analysis: questions about the proper use of money, questions about work and idleness, questions about the just price for staple commodities and the distorting effects of luxury.

Writing to Sir Christopher Hatton in 1591, his private secretary, Cox, deplored the fact that

> we should suffer men to make professions and occupations of playes all the yere long whereby to enryche idel loyterers with plenty whyle many of our poore brethren lye pitifully gasping in the streates, ready to starve and dye. (CHAMBERS, *Elizabethan*, 4:237)

Like many of the complaints about contemporary theater, this one offered no necessary *economic* connection between the alleged affluence of players and the poverty of others. In the statement about the relative wealth of players and the rest of the poor population, we find, behind the discourse of economics, a cultural statement about the appropriate social place for playing. Playing, in Cox's view (and in those of many others) was a matter for holidays, for seasonal festivity, not for "all the yere long." He looks back nostalgically to a time when the players' custom "was only to exercise their interludes in the time of Christmas, beginning to play in the holidays and continuing until twelfth tide, or at the furthest until Ashwednesday," and associates this golden time with perfect patronage, when players performed "without exacting any money for their access, having only somewhat gathered of the richer sort by the churchwardens for their apparel and other necessaries" (Chambers, *Elizabethan*, 4:237).

Playing "all the yere long" was seldom possible for early modern theater companies, not least because of plague, but that was not to Cox's point. Nor is it to his point that commercial playing in which actors thought of themselves as involved in a trade and employed the necessary commercial transaction required to mount their productions had existed since at least the beginning of the century.[2] Antitheatrical writers tended to exaggerate the affluence and success of players in order the more forcefully to contrast their low social status with their undeserved wealth. Indeed, Cocke's satiric contrast between the "royall Master or Mistresse" of patronage and the "wages and dependence" of commerce is itself an attempt to denigrate players and deny them the social status that they might claim from their association with royal or aristocratic patrons. Questions of patronage and commerce, in other words, were part of a rhetoric of cultural politics rather than the material of social analysis.

Even when specific sums of money are mentioned, the economics of theater was inextricably entangled in the discourses of social differentiation. In the Praeludium to *The Careless Shepherdess*, for example, three members of the audience discuss the play they are to see. Their discussion causes Thrift, the citizen, to conclude that he cannot be pleased with the fare on offer:

> And I will hasten to the money box
> And take my shilling out again
> I'll go to the Bull, or Fortune and there see
> A play for two pense with a Jig to boot.
> (BENTLEY, *Seventeenth-Century*, 35)

Thrift's references to a "shilling" and "two pense" provide some evidence that by 1635 the costs of theatergoing had increased from the penny for a public theater place that Platter and others had noted in 1599 (Gurr, *Playgoing*, 15–18). The sums mentioned are contradicted, however, by the reference to "two shillings" in the prologue to Habington's *Queen of Arragon* (1635) or Jonson's gibe at the "sinful *sixpenny* mechanics" in the induction to *The Magnetic Lady* (1632). What is equally important is that Thrift's preference for a cheaper entertainment is connected to theaters that had become bywords for artistically conservative theater relying on variety and display. Inexpensive entertainment, low social status, and reduced aesthetic value had become locked in a discursive circle from which empirical evidence is difficult to extract.

The connections between the economics of theater, the social status of its consumers, and the aesthetic value of its products were, however, most delicately balanced, and the balance changed over time. The moral rhetoric of antitheatricalists was replaced by the discourses of commodity exchange, which were further modified by an address to social and aesthetic value. By the turn of the seventeenth century, playwrights seemed to accept that their patrons were the paying audience in the theater and replaced the rhetoric of morality with one that, like Thrift, assumed a freedom of consumer choice. The epilogue to Fletcher's *Valentinian* announces, "We have your money and you have our wares," and the prologue to Habington's *Queen of Arragon* seeks a contract with the audience "Ere we begin that no man may repent / Two shillings and his time" (Hazlitt, 327).

In adopting the language of commodity exchange and consumer choice, the playwrights identified the relationship between players and audience as one between producers and consumers, untrammeled by social considerations. The economics of theater made it imperative to include as wide a paying audience as possible, and as Dekker points out in *The Gull's Hornbook*, the financial transaction made the theater available to anyone who could afford the price of entrance. Nevertheless, the social dimension of these economic relations could not so easily be effaced. As each new wave of theater practice attempted to secure its own market niche, the discursive connection between taste and social status became more important. When the boys' companies reopened the hall theaters in Paul's and Blackfriars, for example, they traded on a kind of exclusivity, promising their audiences that they would not be pasted to "the barmy jacket of a beer brewer." They would be offered the latest in sophisticated drama, as compared to the "musty fopperies of antiquity" provided by their competitors in the public theaters (Marston, *Plays*).

There was, of course, an economic dimension to these distinctions in that the price for a seat in the hall theaters was considerably higher than that of the public amphitheaters, but the marketing impact of innovation and exclusivity was clearly significant too. Moreover, the language in which they were expressed drew on a further entanglement of connections between price and value and social status. "Stale fare" and "musty" products are also pejorative terms for bad food and are only one example of the intersection between the aesthetic and nutritional discourses of taste. Theater could thus be seen as both a staple necessity and one whose price and value could be as acceptably comparable as in the highly regulated markets for food.

The regulation of food markets and prices was necessary, however, precisely because of the instability of economic relations in a period of high inflation (Archer, 202–3). The economic relations of theater, which offered not simply a commodity or service but a complex mix of social status and artistic pleasure, was all the more difficult to define or even to understand.

## Guerdon and Remuneration

One of the most complex of the economic relations of theater was between the players and those who financed them. Companies of players were established by "sharers," who put money into the operation, but they were often described (as in Cocke's statement) as the "servants" either of their patron or of their public. Being a servant, however, involved more than an economic relationship, for its patterns of payment complicated the connection between commodity and price. In *Love's Labours Lost*, for example, Costard evaluates Armado's three farthings against Biron's shilling, both paid for the same service of delivering a letter and each called by different names:

> Now will I look to this remuneration—O, thats the Latin word for three farthings. Three farthings—remuneration. "What the price of this inkle?" "One penny" "No, I'll give you a remuneration." (3.1.133–37)

He translates money into market terms, asking Biron how much carnation silk ribbon may be bought with "remuneration." When Biron, in turn, pays him for carrying another letter, he calls the reward a *guerdon*, and Costard is quite clear which is the more valuable:

> Guerdon! O sweet guerdon!—better than remuneration, elevenpence farthing better. (3.1.166–67)

Costard finds himself in much the same situation as the servants of noble and gentry households whose remuneration consisted of a mix of wages, gratuities, gifts, board and lodging, and livery. These different categories of payments together made up the economic value of service, but their proportions could not be counted on, nor were they paid in relation to tasks performed or services rendered.

For players, only indirectly connected to a patron's household, a similar connection may have obtained. It has certainly been used to explain gaps in the records, as Paul Whitfield White explains:

> For the company to defray its expenses and make a basic living from playing, would have required far more bookings than the surviving records indicate . . . the travelling players performed most of the time not in towns but at noble households where they could be assured of several good meals, safe lodging and sizeable remuneration [*sic*] for playing. (26)

As late as 1636, and long after the King's Men was a thriving company owning two theaters, each of its players was receiving a royal allowance of cloth for a cloak and a cape every second year at Easter (Bentley, *Jacobean*, 1:90). The *cost* of these payments is often noted in the records, but their economic *value* (as a proportion of turnover, a contribution to actual costs, as compared with other gifts disbursed or payments made) is harder to ascertain. Traditional bonds between powerful aristocrats and their clients were being commuted into cash payments during the course of the seventeenth century (Peck). Nevertheless, the relationship between patron and client was seldom reducible to an instrumental set of profits and advantages in the form of money or even influence.

The Records of Early English Drama (REED) investigations have begun to indicate that patronage was important to playing companies not only through payments in kind, which remain unrecorded, but through a patron's more general influence in a local area.[3] The common council of Gloucester, for example, made provision in 1580 that the first play performed there by a visiting company should be a special performance before the mayor and "the Aldermen and comon Counsell of the City." At that performance "everyone that will comes in without money, the Mayor giving the players a reward as hee thinks fit to shew respect unto them" (Greenfield and Douglas, *Records*, 252).[4] The payments, in other words, were not for a service or a commodity but were part of the extended network of social relations involving players, local authorities, and the patrons who were influential in the area. Similar payments might be made to players *not* to play, whether because of plague (Somerset, "Lords," 103) or for more antitheatrical reasons, and on the occasions when companies attempted to play without licensing, their behavior was drawn to their patron's attention.

Though the patron/client relationship was often idealized in contemporary comment,[5] having a patron was never a guarantee of financial success in the uncertain world of early modern theater. Much more frequently, the formation, amalgamation, and reforming of companies seemed to take place without reference to the patrons at all (Gurr, "Three"). During the difficult plague period of 1592–1593, when the movement among companies seems especially hard to trace, Pembroke's Men, according to Henslowe's gossipy letter to Alleyn, were forced to abandon their tour:

> they are all at home and hauff ben this v or sixe weackes for they cane not save ther carges wth travell as I heare & weare fayne to pane ther parell for ther carge.
> (HENSLOWE, *Diary*, ed. FOAKES AND RICKERT [unless otherwise noted], 280)

The fact that Pembroke's Men were playing in the name of an important courtier—and, indeed, had played at court during the 1592–1593—season did not save them from collapse.

For as far as the royal court was concerned, companies of players were merely another of the groups that provided for its complicated and expensive needs. Performances at court were organized by the Office of the Revels. Under Edmund Tilney the office went through a bureaucratic streamlining similar to that involved in other areas of court purveyance, which gradually moved from direct purchasing for the royal household to a set of contracts with suppliers (Woodworth; Chartres). Tilney discovered, like many a modern manager, that it was cheaper to franchise others to provide services than to provide them in house. The increasing frequency with which playing companies appeared at court may have been an effect of noble patronage. It may have also been due to "the simple economic fact that it cost only one third the sum to employ a company of public players for the royal pleasure than it cost to stage a masque" (Gurr, "Three," 161).

The need to supply the court also seems to have had the same disruptive effect on playing companies as it had on the purveyors of food. In 1583, the best players from existing companies were taken to form the Queen's Men, with devastating effects on the groups that lost members. In 1594 Lord Hunsdon seemed to be proposing a similar scheme when he moved, with his predecessor as lord chamberlain, the lord admiral, to establish their two companies with sole rights to play in London (Gurr, "Three"; McMillin, "Queen's"). Twice in just over a decade, aristocratic patronage had acted to undermine rather than to protect the interests of the companies of players. The patron's role was partly to provide economic opportunities for his favored servants; it was also to act as a powerful courtier, manipulating the players for his own ends.

## Economics and Control

For the courtiers involved in patronage of theater, the playing companies that played in their names were the instruments of patronage as much as the patrons' direct clients. When Lord Hunsdon was considering the office of lord chamberlain, he was told that the office would entail "the preferment of sundrie to her Maiesties service" (Stone, "Office," 282), though on balance it was felt not to be an especially advantageous move. This preferment, at least in the early years of his tenure, did not include providing favorable conditions at court for his own company of players; it had more to do with the potentially lucrative business of licensing playing places—lucrative because it would involve payments from those who wished to avoid the restraints imposed.

In giving his players, and the lord admiral's, rights to act in the city, the lord chamberlain was also establishing his authority over playing in the city as well as at court. Ingram has described how the city authorities resisted requests from courtiers to award patents for licensing playing places, as for other functions that the city thought more properly to be its own business (*Business*, 125). In this regard, the City of London was enacting a more protracted and powerful version of the tense relationship that can be read behind the mayor of Gloucester's gracious comments on players and their patrons noted above. In "giving the players a reward as hee thinks fit to shew respect unto them," the mayor was making a statement about his own status and the status of his town. He was indicating his right to patronize (in both senses) the players and the patron in whose name they played. In the case of the Gloucester authorities, this was made explicit through their attempts to codify and regulate the terms in which respect for patrons was to be measured against their own need to be seen controlling public activities in their town. They agreed to allow performances of three plays in three days to queens' men; two plays in two days for barons'; one play on one day for those below the rank of baron who are nonetheless authorized to play. The players were not allowed to play at night nor in private houses "without express licence of Mr Maior" (Douglas and Greenfield, *Records*, 307).

The city fathers have often been regarded as intrinsically hostile to playing and their regulation of theater as a combination of philistinism and political repression. As William Ingram's systematic analysis of the minutes of the Common Council shows (*Business*, 130–33), however, regulating the players was not at the top of the council's agenda. It appears only sporadically alongside more pressing concerns that had to do with the complex daily business of running the city. When the question of playing did arise, as in the act of 1574 regulating the inn yards in which plays could be performed, the details of the act show that the city authorities were as concerned to keep order and to raise income by regulation as they were to suppress theatrical activity. They were also acting to preempt courtly interests in the same matters. The innkeepers were accordingly hung round with requirements to post bonds for the good order of their premises, put up plays for scrutiny and permission to play, and make themselves responsible for the matter that was eventually performed.

The question of regulation was also a question of economics, since every "layer of permission meant more fees and more hassle" (Ingram, *Business*, 131). Furthermore, the act included the requirement that every innkeeper be required to pay an open-ended tax, assessed by the mayor "to the use of the poore in hospitalls of the Cittye or of the poore of the Cittye visited with sicknesse." In a characteristically complicated maneuver, the city fathers had discouraged a civic nuisance and also ensured that its continuance would solve another city problem: the need to fund the expensive former monastic foundations, which provided poor relief for the city. It only remained to add the final brilliant administrative device of requiring Christ's Hospital, one of the principal beneficiaries of this funding, to collect the fines!

## The Local Economy

The connection between the economics of poor relief, taxation, and the regulation of playing in the city show that patronage and the economics of theatrical production were built into the wider experience of economic existence in the early modern period. Between the action of playing and the remuneration by the playgoers lay strata of social relationships that complicated the rates of pay or the costs of providing the service. The city's brilliant coup of making those responsible for disorderly playing venues contribute to supporting the poor intertwined a social relationship with an economic arrangement. In doing so, it gave real meaning to the discursive connection that had been made between inappropriately wealthy players and the "poore brethren (who) lye pitifully gasping in the streats, ready to starve and dye" (Chambers, *Elizabethan*, 4:237).

The connection between successful players and their obligation to the poor was also made in 1600 in a petition to the Privy Council from the inhabitants of Finsbury. They asked the council to tolerate the Fortune theater, on the grounds that its owners "are contented to give a very liberall porcion of money weeklie towardes the releef of our poore" (Rutter, 184). The rhetoric of the petition was familiar enough, but its meaning needs to be questioned. A theater would have been assessed for poor relief like any other establishment in a particular parish. A petition to the Privy Council drawing attention to the fact suggests that someone was turning antitheatrical rhetoric on its head in order to gain support for the new business venture. The prime suspect, according to Carol Rutter, was Philip Henslowe (Rutter, 184–85).

Henslowe had, after all, been implicated rather closely in the watermen's petition, which appealed to the lord admiral to rescind the Privy Council's restraint on playing at the Rose. Lord Strange's Men had asked to be allowed to continue playing at the Rose, which would provide "a greate releif to the poore watermen" who ferried affluent north bankers to the theater; the watermen themselves were mindful of the "muche helpe and reliefe for us oure poore wives and children by meanes of the resorte of suche people as come unto the said playe howse"; and the Privy Council warrant that restored the right to play also noted that "a nomber of watermen are therby releeved" (Rutter, 63–66).

There may have been instrumental intent in the organization of the watermen's petition, but the interdependence of theater and other commercial concerns was real enough.[6] Like any increase in commercial activity, theaters contributed to the local economy not only through increased taxation for poor relief but also by providing employment for a range of related trades. Philip Henslowe's account book lists his dealings with carpenters, wood merchants, ironmongers, painters, and thatchers for the building and the upkeep of the Rose (Chambers, *Elizabethan*, 2:408).

As well as the building trades, the theaters employed craftsmen like the "littel tayller" who was given "tafetie & tynsell to macke a payer of bodyes for a womones gowne to playe allece perce" (Henslowe, *Diary*, 73). The costume makers were sometimes very specialized, like "Goodman Freshwater," who supplied "a canvas sewt and skenes" for a stage dog for the Worcester's Men season at the Rose (Chambers, *Elizabethan*, 2:239). Sometimes, like Richard Edwards, a tailor dwelling in the parish of St. Dunstans in the West, they supplied such routine, but still expensive, items as "four felt hats with hatbands" (Ingram, "Playhouse," 210).

The range and extent of the commercial activity involved in making theater— the trade in playbooks and costumes, props, and "stuffes"—required business acumen and ready money, but once again, the commercial and the social were intertwined. The recurring names recorded in lawsuits and arguments are a reminder that though all the activities recorded were commercial, they remained part of a face-to-face economy, often involving kin networks, such as those traced by Ingram between the family of Peter Street, who built the Globe and Fortune theaters, and the Burbage family, also joiners living in Southwark. Like other early modern businesses, the theater economy worked through "the essentially personal conception of credit upon which private trading was based" (Everitt, 116).

It is important not to sentimentalize these kin networks as emblems of preindustrial harmony. The lawsuits that provide much of our information about the working of early modern theater reveal the acrimony that these arrangements often caused. They also reveal changes in the ways in which those relations were conceptualized. Players' wills, for example, in their bequests to neighbors, provision for the poor, and support for the next generation provide evidence throughout the period for the web of connections between theater people and the communities in which they lived. In these wills, economic bequests speak for social relations, and social relations provide insight into economic circumstances.

Simon Jewell, for example, was an actor with Pembroke's Men, and his will included bequests to his fellow players and the prompter at the Globe. He left Eme Scott his livery coat, raising the possibility that livery clothes could be used outside their formal functions; and he left Roberte Nicholls "all my playenge thinges in a box and my velvet shewes." But Simon Jewell also used his will as, literally, a final account. He lists money owed to him, as well as bequests, and arranges, among other things, for his outstanding rent to be paid. The sums of money owed and to be disbursed are complicated, but they indicate that Jewell assumes that his share of the company's finances belongs to him:

> due to me the said Simon Jewell from my fellowes for the share of apparell the somm of thirteen pounde six shillinges, eight pence. Item more due unto me from my fellowes the sixth parte of thirtie seven pounde which amounteth to six pound three shillinges fouer pence and have paid my share of horses, waggen and apparell new bought. (HONIGMANN AND BROCK, 58)

They suggest that the sharers were dividing the costs of the enterprise among them equally; that the company owned the apparel, horses, and wagons required for the tour jointly; but that an actor as an individual also owned "playing thinges," such as those Jewell left to Nicholls.

The business of sharing in theater companies is complex and cannot be generalized from one company or time to another. Comparing the practice in a number of different situations leads Ceresano to conclude that "a share was, most precisely, a combined interest in time, skill and capital, valued more in the preservation than in the selling, at which time it was worth whatever a player could get for it" (242). Nevertheless, it is interesting to contrast Simon Jewell's sense of his economic relations with those that prevailed some ten years later, when Worcester's men began their season at the Rose.

The equitable Pembroke's Men arrangement implied in Jewell's will, though it may have been common throughout the sixteenth century, did not provide adequate finance even for a tour in 1592–1593. By the end of the century, conditions in

London were even harder, in part because the conflict over the licensing of playing places had made it more difficult for companies to find anywhere to play in London. When Worcester's Men returned to London in 1602 with a season at the Boar's Head Inn, the new venture was not a success. Worcester's patronage had ensured that his company received permission to establish another playing venue in London, even though the number of companies had been restricted to two, but he evidently did not provide the financing to make the venture successful. For that the company needed Henslowe's loan system, which allowed a company to borrow capital in advance of production in order to ensure that his theater had a tenant. Henslowe provided Worcester's Men with a "total of £234. 11s 6d" (Chambers, *Elizabethan*, 2:228) to commission writers, including Dekker and Heywood, and to buy and order costumes: the company moved to the Rose (Rutter, 200).

There was nothing new about the owners of playhouses commissioning writers.[7] The extent of Henslowe's involvement, however, illustrates the rather different interest that a playhouse owner had in keeping his playhouse occupied. Players linked in cooperative companies had the advantage of flexibility: the possibility of regrouping or disbanding and selling their playbooks and costumes to recover their loss. For the playhouse owner who was looking for a return on investment, it was vital that his house be occupied, even if he had to advance the money that would make that feasible. Given this relationship, it was hardly surprising that the playhouse owners sought to tie the players more firmly to their houses (Bentley, *Dramatist*, 111–12). During 1597–1598, over a period of nineteen months, Henslowe records a series of contracts between himself and individual players. Rutter suggests that since "Henslowe signed all the witnesses' names" the actors may have been acting without company authorization. By these contracts, the actors pledged to play in Henslowe's house and "in no other a bowte London publickeley yf he do with owt my consent to forfet unto me this some of money." The sum of money bonded was forty pounds (Rutter, 119).

Henslowe may have felt the need to protect his interest formally, because the actors concerned had defected earlier in the year to Francis Langley's new, unlicensed theater, the Swan. Langley, who had operated sharp practices in a number of commercial areas, had bound the players with bonds of one hundred pounds on the understanding that he would provide three hundred pounds' worth of properties and costumes (Ingram, *London*, 190). Langley's theatrical adventure turned out to be a disaster, not least because the players became involved in the scandal over *The Isle of Dogs*, which caused Nashe to flee and Jonson to land in jail. Langley tried to sue the actors for their bonds, and the resulting lawsuit saw the relations between playing and investing in theater turned into competing economic equivalents. Langley accused the actors of reneging on payment to the tune of three hundred pounds, and they countercharged him with withholding costumes that belonged to the company, and even of converting "the same to his best profytt by lending the same to hyre" (Rutter, 125).

Langley's involvement suggests that by the 1590s the theater was being seen, with some justification, as an investment that could provide substantial return. Ingram points out that Henslowe's earnings of about "£2 per performance between July 15 and July 30 1594 . . . easily equalled the yearly income from a newly built tenement. A great many tenements would be needed to bring in £450 in one year" (*London*, 113). Of course, 1594–1595 was an unusual year: there were no interruptions to playing from plague or restraint, and only the expected closure during Lent. It was also a time when the Lord Admiral's Men were led by the most famous actor in England, Edward Alleyn. Moreover, Henslowe was making regular payments to the Master of the Revels and had a repertory that, in spite of its modern reputation as transgressive, did not attract the adverse attention of the authorities.

Other investors in theater were not so successful. The Theatre, for example, was built as a collaborative venture between James Burbage and his brother-in-law, John Brayne, a grocer. According to the lawsuit in which their heirs were subsequently embroiled, Burbage had to persuade Brayne to enter the deal with "swete and contynuall persuasions." As Berry has observed, however, Burbage went on to make himself and his children "people of substance," while Brayne lost everything in the joint theatrical venture (Berry, "Shylock," 188). The reasons for Brayne's loss have been variously identified and could be seen as part of the swings and roundabouts of profit and loss to be expected in a market. Theater historians' accounts of the extended and complex litigation involved in Brayne's and Burbage's dealings around the theater suggest, however, that the passage from investment to earnings in the period was far from smooth.

The initial arrangement seems simple enough. Both Burbage and Brayne were to use the profits from the Theatre to repay the costs of the building; Brayne was then to get back the extra money he had put in, and subsequent income was to be divided evenly among them. While the debts were being paid, Brayne was to receive income of ten shillings a week and Burbage eight (Ingram, *Business*). But none of this happened. Instead there is a story of a pawned lease, arrests for debt, and a series of ad hoc arrangements, all unreliably described by the opposing parties in the depositions.

Other accounts of investment in theatrical ventures suggest a similar degree of muddle. When Lording Barry attempted to float a new theater venture at White-friars in 1607, he began with a flurry of borrowing, which raised £120. None of the money was repaid. The lease of the theater was sold on to another group: what became of the "Playe boyes" whose "diet" was paid for during October 1607 remains unknown (Ingram, "Playhouse"). Similarly, the arrangements for the administration of the Red Bull resulted in a lawsuit involving not only shares sold on to another party not involved directly in the theater but also the sale of the right to act as "gatherer" (collector of admission charges) in the theater (Wallace). Since this information comes from litigation, it is hardly surprising that it highlights the complications and confusions attendant on investment in theatrical affairs. It indicates the difficulties involved in analyzing the economics of theater in terms of money taken and money made.

It also suggests that, by the turn of the century, investment in theater was moving out of the hands of playing companies whose work contributed directly to its operations. When Simon Jewell made provision for the money from his share of Pembroke's Men to be used to pay his rent, he was, in effect, trading in his share, though in a very simple and direct way. Francis Grace's will, proved in 1624, made the more complex provision that "the benefitt of my share which is to continew for two yeares after my decease shalbe disposed in this manner to the payment of my debtes as farr as the two yeares profitt of it doth come to" (Honigmann and Brock, 130). As the Brayne/Burbage case showed, such provisions were easier to write down than to execute. Grace's wishes do, however, suggest that a theatrical "share" was becoming thought of as a currency with an established and recognized value independent of its function as part of a division of theatrical resources, including labor.[8]

This changing conception of the value of a theatrical share was put to the test in the case of Susan Baskervile (Chambers, *Elizabethan*, 2:236–38). Susan's first husband, Thomas Greene, was "one of the principall and cheif persons" of Queen Anne's company. When he died, his widow expected to receive eighty pounds, as well as thirty-seven pounds that he had given the company for "diuers necessarie prouisions." She expected this not because it was the value of his investment but because George Pulham, another company member, who had died shortly before Greene, had received forty pounds as a "half sharer." Pulham's money, however, might have been given as part of the custom and practice of playing companies, which had for a long time made payments to widows on the death of their members. Susan Greene/Baskervile did not get her money, and she appealed to Viscount Lisle, who as chamberlain of Queen Anne's household, was felt to have some control over the players. He proposed that Susan should receive a half share in the profits until the debt was paid but evidently had no authority or inclination to enforce this, since she only ever received six pounds.

In spite of her difficulties with the company, Susan and her new husband, Baskervile, continued to invest with them. Between 1615 and 1617 they made separate settlements with the company in which sums of money (£57 10s. and £38) were to be set against daily payments (1s. 8d.; 2s.) "for every six days in the week where in they should play" during the lives of the creditors and their children. The complexities of this case leave a number of puzzles: were the sums put forward loans that the Baskerviles might expect to be repaid, or were they investments in which the couple would have to take their chance on profits? The provisions for pensions is equally puzzling. If the Baskerviles' new investments of £57.10 and £38 were repaid at the rate of 1s. 8d. and 2s. per day, respectively, they would have been repaid in just over three years. The repeated attachments of this provision to various lives suggests that they were not investment in the modern sense but harked back to an older form of social relationship, in which members expected to be looked after for life.

In any event, the company did not pay. By the time the case had trundled through the courts, it was ten years since Greene had died, the company had moved to a different theater and was a slightly different group of men, some of whom felt they had no responsibility for agreements made before they joined. To complicate matters still further, the Court of Chancery ruled that the agreement was "unfitt to be releeued or countenaced in a courte of equitie," whether, as Chambers suggests, because it was made by players, or because they were in the wrong court.

In an additional twist to the Baskervile story, the players alleged that Mrs. Baskervile was in league with Christopher Beeston. The players claimed that Beeston was responsible "at that tyme and long before and since" for the "managing of their whole businesses" (Chambers, *Elizabethan*, 2:238), so he must have had some involvement in the affair. But the division of responsibility between the financier and the players for a company's resources, especially when debts were involved, was fluid and inexact.

By the second decade of the seventeenth century, it was becoming a matter for conflict. The control that financiers exerted over players' affairs was perhaps the corollary to financial support, but the players were beginning to have mixed feelings about their dependence upon people not directly involved in playing. In 1615, the players of Lady Elizabeth's Men put together a document outlining their grievances against Henslowe over the years from the spring of 1613. According to their account, Henslowe had so complicated the relations of debt to him and so confused the combination of commodities, apparel, playbooks, and cash that formed their financial dealings with him as to put their continued viability as a playing company entirely at his disposal. He had also so exploited the changing relationship between bound servants and wage labor among the nonsharer members of the company as to transfer their allegiance from the company to himself. The Lady Elizabeth's Men was licensed by a patent of 1611 to play (formulaically) "in and about our Cittie of London in such usuall howses as themselves shall provide, And alsoe within anie Towne Halles, mootehalles, Guyld halles, Schoole hoses or other convenient places . . . &c &c" (Chambers, *Elizabethan*, 2:248–50).

By 1611, playing in guildhalls and moote halls was not without its problems (Blackstone, "Patrons," 129), though the company is first located playing across the breadth of the country (Bath in 1610 and Ipswich in 1611). The "usuall howses" in the city of London, however, were owned by entrepreneurs, and it was in order to play in one of Henslowe's houses that the company entered into a bond of £500 with him.

Lady Elizabeth's Men was made up of a motley assortment of players from the Admiral's, the King's, and the duke of York's companies, but at least one player came from the former Queen's Revels Company, a company of boy actors. By 1613, when complaints against Henslowe begin, the company had been filled out with others from the former Queen's Revels Company (including Nathan Field), and Henslowe was in partnership with Philip Rosseter, who had taken on the Queen's Revels in 1609 and moved them to Whitefriars. The boys' companies had evolved from the choir schools, but during their brief period of fashionable—not to say scandalous—success they had developed as "commercial companies hiring their dramatists and guided no longer by a single master but by a board of directors banded together in accordance with strictly business principles" (Hillebrand, 267). The business principles seem to have included a more exploitative relationship between the entrepreneurs and the players, perhaps an inevitable situation when the players were children. They echoed the economic relationship of bonds and contracts that Langley had employed in the Swan venture and were different from the loans with which Henslowe financed Worcester's Men in 1602. It may have been that the change in Henslowe's practice was, as Carson suggests, "the result of long and bitter experience dealing with irresponsible (or indigent) players" (34). It is equally possible that he was keeping up with Langley's business practices and helping to establish them in theatrical circles.

In the "Sharers Papers" of 1635, a similar conflict between actor and theater owner was still at issue, even in the King's Men, where the sharers owned the playhouse. Three players from the King's Men petitioned the lord chamberlain to be allowed to buy shares in the company. The actors, they claimed, received only the taking from the outer doors and half of that from the galleries and boxes. From this they had to meet the playing expenses of poets and costumes, the wages of hired men and boys, and all the day-to-day theater expenses. The shareholders, on the other hand, were responsible only for the rent and upkeep of the building and could sublet other parts of the property to meet their costs. The division between the owners of a building and the performers of the plays, which fueled the grievances against Henslowe and the players' suspiciousness about Beeston, seem to apply in this case too. The petitioners' objection was partly at the restrictions against their joining in this more lucrative side of the business, but their economic concerns were put in terms of an objection to the activities of a particular individual, John Shank. Shank had not been one of the original company, nor an heir of an original member, but had simply bought his shares. In the players' view he had therefore the least right to "reape most or the chiefest benefitt of the sweat of their browes, & liue upon the bread of their Labours" (Bentley, *Dramatist*, 1:45). Shank countercharged that each petitioner had made £180 out of playing in the previous year. But the money was not the only point. What the players were objecting to was a perceived change from the cooperative venture of playing, in which "share" meant literally "shared labor," to an economic organization in which shares were a currency of investment. Their appeal to the lord chamberlain also harked back to an older form of social relations in which important people in a local community could be called upon to settle disputes. It was a model of the relations between patronage and commerce, which had been superseded by an economic system of contracted returns on investments.

The "Sharers Papers" provide potentially one of the fullest accounts of the economics of play production. They suggest that the day-to-day costs of playing in 1635 amounted to £3 a day or £900 to £1,000 a year; they assert that the six housekeepers share 12s. a day to the eight players' 3s.; they also offer the incredible suggestion that a player could make £180 a year. Since this information came out of conflict, the figures and the extrapolations that scholars make from them are unreliable; what they tell us most clearly is the terms on which the conflict was conducted. Those seem to have been the residual terms of an ideology opposed to exploitation, which was curiously, but quite predictably, at odds with the organization of the contemporary theatrical economy.

Every historian knows that any route taken through the forest of documentation involves exclusions that arise from a thesis, if not a larger view of the world. We should, however, become especially suspicious both when the path taken follows the tracks of contemporaries too firmly and when it speeds down the superhighway of a modern historiographical teleology. The view that the economics of theater moved from a system of patronage to one of commerce follows both of those roads. For the early modern antitheatricalist, it fed nostalgia for an ordered, coherent community; for the modern historian, it fits the grand narratives of modernization and commercialization.

The evidence around which this essay is organized does not dissent from this general view. But it also draws attention to other, complicating factors. It suggests that the increased control of playing in London was as much economically as ideologically motivated, and it had important economic effects. It made the costs of theatrical production higher and provided the opportunity for the owners of theater buildings, through their hold on theatrical finances, to establish a more exploitative relationship between financiers and players. In this economic relationship, there was limited scope for patronage, which was therefore replaced, even for court performances, with a system of regular fees.

The evidence also shows that the economics of dramatic production cannot be isolated from other social relations. As late as 1636, the King's Men were being paid £20 a week from the king's "princely bounty" to tide them over during a long plague (Bentley, *Jacobean*, 1:53). It was as much as they would have been paid for two court performances, but it was not presented as payment. More speculatively, if Henslowe had been a nobleman, would it have been called patronage or commerce when he rescued the players from the Admiral's Men from the Langley debacle, or paid to get writers out of prison, or paid for the dinner when the company was about their agreement?

The evidence for the ascendancy of commerce is similarly contradictory. It is in the nature of the historical records that there should be more evidence of the break-down of commercial relations than of their smooth operation. Nevertheless, the lawsuits over theaters, the cases of grievance against both playing companies and financiers, and the frequent confusion about who was responsible for debts suggest that the infrastructure of commerce was barely ready to support a "culture indus-try." The early modern theater, like most consumer commerce of the time, was small in scale and London-based but in regular trading contact with the provinces, regulated by both civic and state authorities and often disrupted for the purposes of court provision (Kerridge). In other respects, however, the market for plays was *not* comparable with the market for commodities. The product, play performances, was not a commodity, in that there was not a stable method of production (it could involve a variety of producers; it could be produced from scratch; it could be recy-cled and adapted), and there was a highly unstable relationship between product and price. The same play could be produced in a number of different venues at dif-ferent prices, and in the provinces companies were sometimes paid as much for not playing as for a particular performance.

Moreover, the commercial relations of the early modern theatre were only indirectly related to the plays that it produced. While the Queen's Men was embroiled in the Baskervile case, the company was also building the popular repertory that gave the Red Bull its special reputation. While Lady Elizabeth's Men were smouldering with resentment at Henslowe, they were performing *Bartholomew Fair* and *A Chaste Maid in Cheapside*. In the early years of the Brayne and Burbage agreement, however, when the playing companies in Lon-don should have required around "a hundred or so different playscripts each year to satisfy the demands of their spectators," barely five or six plays have survived for any given year, and the bulk of these were performed at court or in the universi-ties (Ingram, *Business*, 120).

Our sense of the relations between the drama and the original conditions of its production often rests on the similarities between the economics of theater and the dramatization of economic relationships in the plays. The early modern theater excelled in representing itself: the combination of metatheatricality in the imagery, the frequent representation of playing in the dramatic narrative, and enough con-temporary references to suggest authenticity, all create an irresistibly suggestive (and often repeated) model of the stage. There is, as always, a gap between the smooth, artistically satisfying conceptualization of social change and the much slower and more muddled and contradictory pace of change in institutional struc-tures and social relations. It is in this gap that meanings can be made. What the meanings are will depend on how the writer theorizes the relations between money and artistic freedom, between economic and ideological relations, between the his-tories of the past and the present. These are subjects that go beyond, but are nev-ertheless implicated in, patronage and the economics of theater.

NOTES

1. I have described this process and the response of playwrights to it in McLuskie, "The Poets Royal Exchange." This essay is an extension and a corrective to that one.
2. See, for example, evidence of payment for plays in the REED volumes. See also Coldewey, for evidence of a paid "director" being brought in to oversee a city entertainment.
3. Blackstone discusses the extent to which patrons' names commanded respect and the extent to which they were challenged by local authorities.
4. See also Greenfield, "Professional." The extent to which players gathered money at separate performances is under discussion among REED editors.
5. See, for example, Cox's idealized description of the conditions of playing "in ancient former times"(in Chambers, *Elizabethan*, 4:237). This nostalgia is not restricted to early modern commentators. Bergeron argues that "systems of patronage . . . remained intact" until the closing of the theaters ("Patronage," 294), and Leah Marcus claims that King "James was far and away the most lavish supporter of the drama" (*Politics*, 61). Evidence of payments made to playing companies suggests that by the Jacobean period there was a standard fee of £10 for a Court performance (Bentley, *Jacobean*, 1:passim). The patronage of individual *dramatists* was different from the patronage of theater.
6. Compare John Taylor the Water Poet's much more extensive defense of his fellows under the same circumstances in 1614. Taylor's position was complicated by the fact of his own commercial involvement in the sale of his pamphlets.
7. In 1572, the Dutton brothers, who were financing players, "entered into a contract requiring one Rowland Broughton of London" to supply them with some eighteen plays over the course of the next thirty months (Ingram, *Business*, 140).
8. This aspect of Grace's will is discussed in Ceresano. John Shank's will also deals with the trade in shares, and he is eager that the full value of his share should be passed to his widow (Honigmann and Brock, 186–89). See also Bentley, *Jacobean*, 1:46–47.

# CHAPTER 23

# The Revision of Scripts

*Eric Rasmussen*

TIME'S GLORY, according to Shakespeare, is "to blot old books and alter their contents." A similar tribute could be justly bestowed on the dramatists of the early English theater. Henslowe records numerous payments to his itinerant playwrights for "mendynge" and "altrynge" scripts, as well as for "new adicyones." Every extant dramatic manuscript from the period shows signs of revision. Some of the most significant early English plays — *The Spanish Tragedy, Doctor Faustus, Hamlet, The Malcontent, King Lear, Othello,* and *Every Man in His Humour* — exist in two distinct textual versions. The standard reference work on revision, for most of the past quarter-century, has been Bentley's chapter on the subject in *The Profession of Dramatist in Shakespeare's Time.* Much has happened, however, since Bentley wrote in 1971. In addition to useful surveys of play revision during the period (J. Kerrigan, 195–217; Ioppolo, 44–77), studies of revision in Shakespeare's plays have appeared and have begun to multiply like Falstaff's men in buckram. This recent profusion of textual scholarship continues to refine our understanding of the multifarious ways in which revision was conceived and carried out in the early English theater.

One such conception belongs to the mechanicals in A *Midsummer Night's Dream.* In the woods outside Athens, where the players assemble in order to "rehearse most obscenely," they agree that rehearsal implies revision; when problems emerge during their first run-through of *Pyramus and Thisbe,* Bottom eagerly proposes "a device to make all well" and demands that the resident dramatist, Peter Quince, revise the script. Every play in the early English theater must have been revised to some extent during rehearsal, as companies met with difficulties that could not have been foreseen in the written text. In *An Apology for Actors* (c. 1608), Heywood writes of plays being "rehearsed, perfected, and corrected before they come to publike view" (Chambers, *Elizabethan*, 4:252). Textual scholars have always assumed that the book of the play would be "altered and revised during the practical tests of rehearsal" (Bowers, *On Editing*, 111).

The most obvious resources for information about the nature of the revision of scripts are the dozen or so extant manuscript playbooks from the period.[1] The cautionary work of Paul Werstine, William B. Long, and Marion Trousdale, however, has amply demonstrated that many of the traditional assumptions about the book of the play that was used by the prompter or book-keeper in the early English playhouse were based on an editor's idea of what a playbook would or should have looked like, rather than a careful examination of the playbooks themselves. Consequently, these assumptions often do not square with the empirical evidence. I wish to focus here on the way that revision was carried out in the playbooks and on the use we can make of these manuscript revisions in evaluating apparent revisions in printed texts, especially Shakespeare's.

Many of the surviving playbooks are more or less heavily cut, while few lines, if any, are added. In other cases, additional passages are written out on separate sheets or slips and inserted into existing playbooks that remain otherwise unchanged. Still other manuscripts exhibit a complex interplay of subtraction and addition. Textual scholarship has tended to concentrate almost exclusively on the authors responsible for these revisions. But I would suggest that the question of authorship can never be satisfactorily resolved and that the emphasis on agency has for too long deflected our attention from an equally important issue—the motivating factors behind the revision of scripts.

## Theatrical Cutting

Early accounts of theatrical cutting appear on title pages and in prefatory matter to printed plays. As Chambers observed, "opportunity was afforded on publication to restore passages which had been 'cut' to meet the necessities of stage production" (*Elizabethan*, 3:192). The title page of the longest printed play quarto from the period, *Every Man Out of His Humour* (1600), credibly claims to print the play "as it was first composed by the Author B.I. containing more than hath been Publikely Spoken or Acted." Similarly, the title page of *The Duchess of Malfi* (1623) offers "the Perfect and exact copy, with diverse things printed that the length of the play would not bear in presentment." In the 1640 edition of *The Antipodes*, Richard Brome asserts that "you shall find in this book more than was presented upon the stage, and left out of presentation for superfluous length (as some of the players pretended)." Humphrey Moseley's preface to the 1647 Beaumont and Fletcher Folio explains why his printed versions of the plays may differ from private transcripts of the performed versions: "When these Comedies or Tragedies were presented on Stage, the Actours omitted some Scenes and Passages (with the Authour's consent) as occasion led them. . . . But now you have All that was Acted, and all that was not."

From these four accounts, we can reach two preliminary conclusions about the nature of theatrical cutting: (1) scripts were often deemed to be too long and were cut in order to reduce overall playing time; and (2) the players, not the playwrights, were the motivating force behind the cutting. Moseley's reassurance that the playwrights acquiesced to the alterations is countered by the strong sense that Jonson, Webster, and Brome are vindicating their art by restoring passages in print that were cut in the theater.

Early editors assumed that plays were indeed cut in order to shorten performance time but disagreed about the agents responsible. Johnson (1765) contended that the end of act 4, scene 7 in *Lear* was "omitted by the author, I suppose, for no other reason than to shorten the representation" (Furness, 305). But Malone (1790) responded, "It is much more probable that it was omitted by the players, after the author's departure from the stage, without consulting him" (Furness, 305). Two hundred years later, the question of agency has yet to be resolved, and the debate has been further complicated by new questions about the purpose of the cuts. Critical attention has focused, in particular, on the significant differences between the Quarto and Folio texts of *Hamlet* and *King Lear*. Q2 *Hamlet* has 230 lines that do not appear in the Folio; Q *Lear* has 285 lines that are not in F. These textual variants were long regarded as revisions made in the theater in order to meet "the exigencies of the stage" (Greg, *First Folio*, 107). Within the last two decades, however, a growing number of scholars have argued that these variants represent Shakespeare's own artistic revisions (Honigmann, Ioppolo, Taylor, Urkowitz, Warren, Werstine). These studies have, in turn, sparked calls for a return to the traditional view that differences between Quarto and Folio texts represent "cuts of necessity for performance" (Bevington, "Determining," 510) that "may be traced to normal kinds of alterations in the promptbook" (Knowles, 118).

Much of this debate revolves around the figure of a mythic book-keeper. In Dover Wilson's imagination, this book-keeper is "experienced," "businesslike," "competent" (32); others see a book-keeper who is rather simple, even stupid, "a moron" (Honigmann, "Shakespeare's," 157). If we buy in to the myth of the simple book-keeper—one who would have had little theatrical insight and would have cut only material that was obviously and painfully dull—it will appear easy enough to differentiate cuts made by the book-keeper from those made by the author. Gary Taylor concludes that "Shakespeare must be presumed responsible for all the Folio excisions" in *Lear* because

> the major Folio excisions . . . like the heavy abridgment of 4.2, can hardly have been
> dictated by hack-theatrical considerations . . . those who attribute other Folio cuts to
> a stage-manager's impatience with static poetic narratives should feel some discomfi-
> ture in having to assign the excisions in 4.2 to the same anonymous philistine. The
> heavy abridgment of 3.6 should embarrass conflationists even more. Not only is the
> omitted material 'dramatic' in the simplest sense; it also largely consists of speeches
> from Edgar and the Fool . . . [who can] hardly be characterized as likely targets for a

stage-manager's blue pencil; nor does the mad trial in particular recommend itself as the victim of a Jacobean impresario's surgical depredations. ("*King Lear*," 418)

When Taylor later observes that the "excised passages consist almost entirely of explicit moral commentary" (434), one is left to wonder why he regards them as "'dramatic' in the simplest sense." In any case, although Taylor claims not to believe in "the theatrical bogeymen of the editorial imagination" (450 n. 154), it is absolutely necessary to his project that he posit a book-keeper with these philistine inclinations. As Taylor himself admits in a footnote, an intelligent book-keeper would interfere with the case for attributing all of the cuts to Shakespeare, since "anyone concerned about success at [the] aesthetic level would be indistinguishable from the author" (450 n. 154).

Other editors have reached similar conclusions. G. R. Hibbard claims that the cuts in *Hamlet*

> can hardly be the work of the book-keeper. . . . The informed understanding of matter that is far from easy, the critical sense that distinguishes between what is dramatically indispensable and what is not, together with the unerring ear for the rhythm of the line—all these abilities, so evident in the cutting, forbid any such deduction and point, instead, to Shakespeare himself as the exciser. (SHAKESPEARE, *Hamlet*, ed. Hibbard, 107)

Taylor and Hibbard may be right, but they begin by assuming the thing to be proved—that it would be impossible for a book-keeper to make sensible cuts. If we are to make valid claims about the "likely targets for the stage-manager's blue pencil" or what "can hardly be the work of the book-keeper," we ought to have an informed understanding of how book-keepers actually worked or, more specifically, of the ways in which passages were cut in the extant dramatic manuscripts.

The manuscript of *The Second Maiden's Tragedy* (B.L. MS Lansdowne 807; 1611), the only extant playbook of a play performed by the King's Men when Shakespeare was an active member of the company, is arguably the one theatrical document that is most directly relevant to a discussion of the possible cutting of Shakespeare's plays. The cuts marked in the *Second Maiden's* playbook are similar in many respects to the apparent cuts reflected in the Folio text of *Hamlet* and dissimilar from those reflected in Folio *Lear*. In the Folio texts of *Hamlet* and *Lear* (both of which may derive at some remove from manuscript playbooks), the distribution of cuts within the five-act structure is nearly identical:

| HAMLET | | | LEAR | |
|---|---|---|---|---|
| Act | Lines Cut | | Act | Lines Cut |
| 1 | 44 | | 1 | 35 |
| 2 | 0 | | 2 | 5 |
| 3 | 26 | | 3 | 90 |
| 4 | 90 | | 4 | 114 |
| 5 | 44 | | 5 | 36 |

Given the concentration of cuts in the third, fourth, and fifth acts, it would appear (if we take the early accounts of play cutting at face value) that the cuts were made in order to shorten each play by abbreviating the second half.[2] But these similar results were achieved by very different methods. In *Hamlet*, lines are generally cut from the middle of long speeches (see 3.4.53–85, 3.4.159–82, 4.1.38–45, 4.7.65–89, 4.7.94–105, 4.7.109–25). Two of these speeches were originally more than twenty lines long, and two were originally longer than thirty lines. Three of the cuts leave half-lines or metrically defective full lines (3.4.167, 4.7.80, 4.7.99–101).

The *Second Maiden's* reviser also generally marked cuts in the middle of speeches (2.1.76–92, 2.1.111–53, 2.1.154–65, 2.3.34–52, 2.3.53–62, 3.1.231–55, 5.2.20–34, 5.2.193–212). The majority of the cuts are made in lengthy speeches, four of which were more than twenty lines in the original and one of which was originally more than forty lines. As in Folio *Hamlet*, the *Second Maiden's* cutting leaves several half-lines dangling (2.1.88, 2.1.156, 2.3.45, 2.3.59, 3.1.232). The *Second Maiden's* reviser only twice simply deleted the end of a speech (3.1.215–21 and 5.2.38–47).

By contrast, in *Lear* lines are generally cut from the ends of speeches (1.2.140–47, 3.1.6–15, 3.1.17–42, 4.1.55–62, 4.2.29–67, 5.1.19–33; ed. Muir), and, following the same principle, larger cuts simply remove the conclusions of scenes (3.6.95–113, 3.7.97–105, 4.7.85–97). Not one of the speeches cut in *Lear* is more than twenty lines long, even though there are several speeches of twenty lines or longer that could have been cut but were not: Edmund's soliloquy at the opening of 1.2, Edgar's at the opening of 2.3, and Lear's speeches at 2.5.266–88 and 4.6.110–33. The *Lear* reviser trimmed. The *Hamlet* and *Second Maiden's* revisers performed surgery.

The type of "internal cutting" found in both Folio *Hamlet* and the *Second Maiden's* playbook is the method still used by directors when they must shorten a text—especially when the cuts are thrust upon them by pragmatic considerations such as those that Peter Hall encountered when he directed *Hamlet* at the National Theater in 1976:

> There is enormous pressure on me from my colleagues not to do it as I want to, full-length. We simply can't afford it, they say. Overtime and the impossibility of matinees, with the consequent loss of revenue, would put another 50,000 on the budget. So what am I to do? I don't want to *interpret* the play by cutting it. (P. HALL, 176–77)

As Hall notes, any attempt to shorten a play risks involving the reviser in an act of interpretation. When Hall must make cuts simply because a play is too long, he tries to avoid interpretation by making "internal cuts." From the full text of both parts of *Tamburlaine*, for instance, Hall says that he "managed to lose 25 minutes, but only by chipping within speeches" (254). As Stanley Wells points out, this type of cut is generally "practical rather than interpretive" (*Royal*, 9).

The cuts in the *Second Maiden's* playbook are similar to Hall's but noticeably different from the apparent cuts reflected in Folio *Lear*. The method of cutting in

*Lear* resembles that performed by newspaper editors who assume that their reporters have structured their articles in a "pyramidal form" (most important information first, least important last) and so cut from the end if the story needs to be shortened. Obviously, dramatists do not write according to these rules. Certain principles of closure absent from the journalist's work are nearly always present in the playwright's: fifth acts are frequently more important than fourth acts; the climax of a scene may be more essential than the opening. One cannot simply cut from the end of the play, or a scene, or even a speech with any assurance that a passage's structural position indicates its relative significance.

The various methods of cutting in *Hamlet, Lear,* and the *Second Maiden's* manuscript may be traces of different revisers with different working habits, but we cannot conclude that one type of cut necessarily points to a revising author and that another points to a non-author. Once we have recognized the formal resemblances between the cuts in *Hamlet* and those in the *Second Maiden's* playbook, we can no longer be confident that the cutting of *Hamlet* "can hardly be the work of the book-keeper" (Shakespeare, *Hamlet,* ed. Hibbard, 107), unless we are prepared to argue that the *Second Maiden's* cuts could not have been made by the book-keeper either. And given the manifest differences between the methods of cutting in *Hamlet* and *Lear,* how likely is it that Shakespeare alone was responsible for the cuts in both plays?[3]

The standard procedure for identifying authorial revisions, however, is to examine not the methods of cutting but the nature of the material cut. The central insight of revisionist criticism (and what may be its most lasting contribution to the study of Shakespeare's texts) has been the discovery that scattered textual variants are often interrelated. The careful and sensitive readings of Michael Warren and Steven Urkowitz revealed that many of the Quarto/Folio variants in *Lear* occur in speeches by or relating to Albany and Edgar. Taylor noticed that the Folio text of *Lear* removes all references to French participation in the final conflict. Building upon an overlooked essay by Nevill Coghill, Honigmann showed that the Quarto/Folio variants in *Othello* are thematically related in their concern with sexuality. Werstine pointed out that the Q2/F variants in *Hamlet* affect Laertes's role, and alter Hamlet's relationship to Claudius. These formal patterns are frequently offered as substantial evidence that the revisions must be Shakespeare's (Werstine is the lone exception). But the discovery of thematic links between the passages marked for excision in an extant playbook must give us pause.

The editor of the *Charlemagne* playbook (B.L. MS Egerton 1994; c. 1600) concludes that the cuts in the manuscript were made by the book-keeper, "no doubt with the object of shortening the play," but goes on to observe that the majority of the 240 deleted lines describe the influence of fortune on human affairs (Walter, vii). Once we recognize the existence of this thematic pattern among the particular passages marked for omission, the distinction between pragmatic theatrical cutting and literary revision begins to blur, and we must either rethink our ideas about the agent responsible or perhaps abandon as untenable the notion that we can distinguish cuts made by an author from those made by a book-keeper.[4]

### New Additions

On February 3, 1602, Henslowe paid four playwrights in full for "the boocke called the second pt of the blacke dooge." Shortly thereafter, the company began to prepare the play for the stage: on February 15, Henslowe notes that the "tyreman for the company" bought some "black satten . . . to macke a sewt for the 2 pte of the blacke dogge." At some point during the early stages of production it became apparent that the script still needed some work. On February 21, 24, and 26, Henslowe made small payments to dramatists for "adycyones for the 2 pte of the blacke doge" (Henslowe, *Diary*, ed. Foakes and Rickert [unless otherwise noted], 223–24). Henslowe frequently refers to the task of revision as mending or altering: Chettle was paid for "the mendynge of the firste pt of Robart hoode" (101) and for "the altrynge of the boocke of carnowlle wollsey" (175); Dekker received four pounds "for mending of the playe of tasso" (206). What seems implicit in the use of "mending" is that there was something wrong with the play that needed to be fixed. And, indeed, many manuscript additions were often intended to remedy specific theatrical problems. Scott McMillin has demonstrated that an added scene in the theatrical plot of *The Dead Man's Fortune* was probably a late insertion designed to serve a pragmatic theatrical purpose. "Without the insertion, the sub-plot actors would have appeared in the scene preceding the conclusion. With the insertion . . . the sub-plot actors would have gained time to dress for their doubled roles in the conclusion ("Plots," 240 n).

Additions written out on separate sheets or slips are found in surviving manuscript playbooks from throughout the early modern period, from *King Johan* (Huntington Library MS HM 3; c. 1538) to *The Queen of Corsica* (B.L. MS Egerton 1994; c. 1642). Many of these additions appear to have solved difficulties in staging or problems in casting. Anne Lancashire has shown that the added soliloquy on addition slip 47 in the *Second Maiden's Tragedy* manuscript was inserted in order to provide a desirable break between scenes in which the same characters exited and immediately reentered (206). There are a number of similarities between this *Second Maiden's* addition slip and the twenty-one-line soliloquy on addition slip 3 in the manuscript of *Sir Thomas More* (B.L. MS Harley 7368). In both plays, someone has added the name of an actor in the margin next to the pasted-on slip, indicating perhaps that the addition slips in both were added after the play had been cast (Rasmussen, "Shakespeare's," 22–23). Peter Blayney suggests that addition 3 was added to *More* "when the play needed expansion" ("*Booke*," 67), but the primary motive behind the addition may have had more to do with problems of casting. These would include difficulties arising from the practice of theatrical doubling.

Since the publication of Bevington's *From "Mankind" to Marlowe*, we have known that many early English plays were specifically constructed to facilitate the doubling of roles. Given the doubling possibilities inherent in the structure of the revised version of *More*, a company of eighteen actors (thirteen men and five boys) could perform the play.[5] Some of the role changes required for such a performance would be fairly quick: the actor playing the Second Officer in scene 7 would have to double as Randall in scene 8. The amount of time that it would take an actor to change costumes is a matter of some debate. David Bradley claims that "even in late Morality Plays an actor very rarely if ever changes identity in under twenty-seven lines of dialogue" (*Ignorant*, 21). Bevington, on the other hand, finds thirty-eight instances in Tudor popular drama of character changes covered by twenty-five lines or fewer, but cautions that the precise amount of time depends upon the nature of the roles and the complexity of the costume change ("*Mankind*," 91). The Officer/Randall change in *More* is a particularly difficult one because the actor had to appear not only as Randall but as Randall disguised as More. McMillin notes that the change is "covered by twenty-two lines" and concludes that this would afford a sufficient amount of time (*Elizabethan*, 78). What McMillin fails to point out is that the lines in question are the lines of addition 3. The soliloquy was apparently inserted into the manuscript for exactly the same reason that soliloquies were used in the earliest English drama: to provide time for a costume change.[6]

Along with adding new material to a finished script before the first production, playwrights might write additions for later revivals (see Knutson, "*Henslowe's*"). In the simplest cases, large chunks of text were grafted onto an existing play that otherwise remained largely unchanged. These supplementary passages are generally referred to as "new additions" on the title pages of the expanded texts: *The Spanish Tragedy* (1602): "Newly corrected, amended, and enlarged with new additions of the Painter's part, and others"; *The Malcontent* (1604): "Augmented by Marston. With additions played by the King's Majesty's servants. Written by John Webster"; *Mucedorus* (1610): "Amplified with new additions"; *Faustus* (1619): "With new Additions"; *A Fair Quarrel* (1617): "With new additions of Mr. Chaughs and Tristrams Roaring." So, too, Henslowe refers to "adicyons" in his payments to the authors of the revisions: "bengemy Johnsone . . . for new adicyons for Jeronymo" (Henslowe, *Diary*, 203); "Bvrde & Samwel Rowle for ther adicyones in docter fostes" (206); "thomas deckers for new A dicyons in owldcastelle" (213).

Often taking the form of new scenes, the additions are generally of substantial length: those to *The Spanish Tragedy* are 54, 10, 45, 185, and 49 lines long; *The Malcontent* contains a new 130-line induction and added passages of 42, 17, 44, 14, 31, 21, 62, 116, 55, 29, and 15 lines; *Mucedorus* includes a prologue, epilogue, and three new scenes; the addition to *A Fair Quarrel* forms a single 223-line extension of the fourth act.[7] The new additions are often comic: the Birde-Rowley additions in the B-text of *Faustus* enlarge the farcical scenes; the additions to *Mucedorus* expand the clown's part and include Mouse's encounter with a bear; the bitter clown Passarello is created in the additions to *The Malcontent*; Rowley's additions to *A Fair Quarrel* amplify the part of the plump clown Clough (see J. Kerrigan).

From a theatrical viewpoint, there are some obvious advantages to additions that could be incorporated into the existing playbook and the players' roles with minimal effort. A more thorough revision would almost certainly necessitate a new playbook and the preparation of new parts. As Greg notes, "We may safely assume that the sort of textual revision that would force the book-keeper to provide and the actors to learn a complete new set of parts would not be popular in the theater" (*Editorial Problem*, 42). Taylor, however, contends that "the opportunity to advertise the play as 'with new additions and revisions'" would compensate "for the trouble involved in preparing a new prompt-book and new actors' parts" ("*King Lear*," 428).

In any case, the insertion of fresh scenes and passages was the easiest and most efficient expedient for providing a revised version of a play. Sir Henry Herbert's receipts from his tenure as Master of the Revels (1622–1642) indicate that this was a standard method of revision during that period: "For adding of a scene to The Virgin Martyr" (J. Q. Adams, *Dramatic*, 29); "For allowing of a new act in an ould play" (32); "An ould play, with some new scenes" (36). There is also the testimony of Brome, who listed as one of his duties as playwright for the company at Salisbury Court that "he hath made divers scenes in old revived plays" (Haaker, 305). Apparently, a few passages added to an old play could produce a new play. Herbert records an instance in which he allowed a company to "add scenes to an ould play, and give it out for a new one" (J. Q. Adams, 37). Fletcher's *The Lover's Progress* (1623) was revised by Massinger in 1634 and retitled *Cleander*. In the prologue, Massinger asserts that he has retained some of Fletcher's original and added some new material: "What's good was Fletcher's, and what ill his own" (prologue.24). Heywood combined parts of his *The Golden Age* (1611) and *The Silver Age* (1613) to create *The Escapes of Jupiter* (c. 1624).

Additions may have been written to keep pace with current theatrical trends. Anne Barton offers an attractive theory for the genesis of the additions to *The Spanish Tragedy*. In 1601, Henslowe was faced with the new vogue of psychological revenge tragedy—*Hamlet* at the Globe and *Antonio's Revenge* at Paul's—but the only revenge play in the Nottingham's Men's possession was *The Spanish Tragedy*, which "now seemed psychologically perfunctory" (Barton, 15). So Henslowe commissioned Jonson to update the play by injecting some psychological realism, and Jonson wrote the additions that expand Hieronomo's grief and derangement. Similarly, in the 1620s Dekker rewrote some scenes from his *Noble Spanish Soldier*, a revenge tragedy of 1604, to create a fashionable tragicomedy, *The Welsh Ambassador* (Hoy, *Introductions*, 140).

The induction to *The Malcontent* gives some insight into the motives for and occasion of revision. Marston originally wrote the play for the Children of the Queen's Revels at Blackfriars, and it was later acquired by the King's Men. In Webster's induction, the players discuss the acquisition and the changes they have made:

SLY: I would know how you came by this play.

CONDELL: Faith, sir, the book was lost, and because 'twas pity so good a play should be lost, we found it and play it.

SLY: I wonder you would play it, another company having interest in it.

CONDELL: Why not Malevole in folio with us, as Jeronimo in decimo-sexto with them? They taught us a name for our play, we call it *One for another.*

SLY: What are your additions?

BURBAGE: Sooth, not greatly needful, only as your sallet to your great feast, to entertain a little more time, and to abridge the not-received custom of music in our theater. (INDUCTION, 70–81)

Apparently, the original version contained too much music for the tastes of the Globe audience. Once the music was cut, the additions were needed "to entertain a little more time." Michael Scott has argued, perhaps too ingeniously, that there were other considerations as well. In Marston's original play, the boy actors mimicking Machiavellian policies, sexual ingenuity, and the pride of courts would have been inherently grotesque. When the play was performed by adult actors, however, the fierceness of the satire would have been lost. The addition of a bitter clown, the further exaggeration of Bilioso's sycophancy, and the expansion of Malevole's part were needed to compensate for "those elements which the play necessarily was in danger of losing by its transference from the one theater to the other" (Scott, 103).

### Complex Revision

Several plays exist in two printed texts that exhibit more complex revision than simple addition or subtraction: the 1601 quarto and the 1616 folio versions of Jonson's *Every Man in His Humour,* the 1607 and the 1641 versions of Chapman's *Bussy D'Ambois,* and the 1606 and 1633 versions of the fifth act of Heywood's *2 If You Know Not Me You Know Nobody.* The revisions of both *Every Man in His Humour* and *Bussy D'Ambois* were apparently made on printed quarto copies of the original plays (Jonson, ed. Herford et al., 3:294; Brooke, lxii). As such, the revisions probably postdate the first performance. Heywood's revisions of *2 If You Know Not Me You Know Nobody* can be confidently classified as postperformance because the revised passages rely heavily on a source, Abraham Darcie's summary of the Armada forces published with Camden's *Annales* in 1625, that appeared two decades after the play was originally staged (Heywood, ed. Doran, xiv–xv).

In the revision of *Every Man in His Humour,* which may have been undertaken specifically for publication, Jonson shifts the scene from Florence to London, renames the characters, enlarges the play with topographical references and contemporary allusions, and alters the punitive nature of the ending. The 1641 revision of *Bussy D'Ambois* is somewhat less extensive, although the title page claims that the text was "much corrected and amended by the Author before his death." Albert Tricomi suggests that Chapman revised *Bussy D'Ambois* so that it could be produced in tandem with its sequel, *The Revenge of Bussy D'Ambois.* Tricomi argues that the revised version deliberately intensifies Bussy's uncontrolled passions and impudence in order to set Bussy in marked contrast to his wiser and more learned brother Clermont in *The Revenge*; the revision makes Tamyra most lustful, intensifying the contrast to the virtue of the countess of Cambrai; and the revision opens up the final act in order to lead more naturally into the sequel (Tricomi, "Revised," 262).[8] The 1633 revision of *2 If You Know Not Me You Know Nobody* is confined to an expansion of the Armada scenes in the fifth act.

The revision in each of these three plays is characterized by small excisions, additions, and verbal changes in nearly every line:

2 IF YOU KNOW NOT ME YOU KNOW NOBODY

Now noble souldiers rouze your hearts like me,
To noble resolution: if any heere
There be that loue vs not, or harbour feare;
Wee giue him libertie to leaue our Campe
Without displeasure. (1606; 2631–35)

Now Countrey-men, shall our spirits here on Land
Come short of theirs so much admir'd at Sea?
If there be any here that harbour feare,
We giue them liberty to leaue the Campe,
And thanke them for their absence. (1633)

BUSSY D'AMBOIS

When the most royall beast of chace (being old,
and cunning in his choice of layres and haunts)
Can neuer be discouered to the bow
The peece or hound: yet where his custome is
To beat his vault, and he ruts with his hinde (1607; 3.2.152–56)

When the most royal beast of chase, the Hart
(Being old, and cunning in his lairs and haunts)
Can never be discover'd to the bow,
The piece or hound: yet where (behind some queich)
He breaks his gall, and rutteth with his hind. (1641)

EVERY MAN IN HIS HUMOUR

That I would have you do; and not to spend
Your crowns on everyone that humours you.
I would not have you to intrude yourself
In every gentleman's society,
Till their affections or your own desert
Do worthily invite you to the place. (1601; 1.1.60–65)

'That would I have you do; and not to spend
Your coin on every bauble that you fancy,
Or every foolish brain that humours you.
I would not have you to invade each place,
Nor thrust yourself on all societies,
Till men's affections or your own desert
Should worthily invite you to your rank. (1616)

John Kerrigan points to the two distinct types of play revision—simple additions and more complex revision—and argues that this distinction can be used to distinguish non-authorial revision from revisions that were made by the original playwright:

> The available evidence strongly suggests that when, in the early seventeenth century, one man of the theater overhauled another's play, he cut, inserted, and substituted sizable pieces of text without altering the details of his precursor's dialogue. Revising authors, by contrast, though they sometimes worked just with large textual fractions, tended to tinker, introducing small additions, small cuts and indifferent single-word substitutions. (196)

Bentley also claims that the "usual practice" was for additional passages to be written by someone other than the original author (Bentley, *Dramatist*, 236). Although this was clearly sometimes necessary because the author was no longer with the company that was reviving the play, or because the author had died, it is by no means a hard and fast rule. Kyd and Marlowe, for example, were both dead by 1602, when Nottingham's Men left the Rose, moved into the newly built Fortune, and revived several old plays as showcases for Edward Alleyn, who emerged from retirement to inaugurate the new playhouse (Knutson, "Influence"). The additions to Middleton and Rowley's *A Fair Quarrel* are almost certainly Rowley's (Holdsworth, xiv–xv, xliii; G. R. Price, xiii–xiv, 111–12). Moreover, linguistic and stylistic tests suggest that half of the additions to *The Malcontent* are also authorial (Marston's) and half are Webster's (Lake, "Webster's," 158).

Kerrigan's second claim does not hold either: non-authorial revisers would often tinker with the text they were revising. Birde and Rowley did a fair amount of tinkering with *Faustus*, introducing a host of single-word substitutions (Rasmussen, *Textual*, 76–89). And one of the many hands that worked over the *More* manuscript, Hand C, made numerous small verbal changes:

> I, *I must haue thee* proude, or else thou'lt nere
> be neere allyed to greatnesse: obserue me *Sir.*
> The lerned Clarke Erasmus is arriu'de
> within our English Courte, *this day* I heare,
> he feasteth with *an* English honoured Poett
> the Earle of Surrey, and *I know this night*
> the famous Clarke of Rotterdame will visite

Sir Thomas Moore, therefore Sir, *act* my *parte*.
(Munday's original 741–48; emphasis added)

*tis fitt thou shouldst wax* prowd, or ells thoult nere
be neere allied to greatnes. observe me *Sirra*
the Learned Clarke Erasmus is arived
w^th in o^r english court. *Last night* I heere
he feasted w^th o^r honord English poet
The Earle of Surrey. and I *learnd to day*
the famous clarke of Rotherdam will visett
S^r Thomas moore, therefore sir *take* my *seat*
(Addition 4, 6–13)

The two types of revision—the addition of sizable new scenes and more complex, intricate revisions that often involved hundreds of minor changes—were apparently employed both by original authors and by others. I would suggest that, contra Kerrigan, differences in form cannot be used to distinguish authorial from nonauthorial revisions.

Textual scholars have meticulously counted hundreds of single-word substitutions and verbal changes in revised plays. Peter Ure notes 228 points at which the revised text of *Bussy D'Ambois* differs from the original. The champions of Shakespearean revision cite the numerous variants between the Quarto and Folio texts: Stanley Wells counts "850 verbal variants" in the texts of *Lear* ("Once and Future," 8); Coghill finds "about a thousand minor variations" in the texts of *Othello* (165). Such calculations take no account of different types of variants in individual plays.

A comparison of the first half-dozen variants in the texts of *Lear, Othello,* and *Bussy D'Ambois,* however, reveals that the types of variation are decidedly different:

LEAR: kingdomes/kingdom (1.1.4)
    equalities/qualities (1.1.5)
    into/to (1.1.20)
    Liege/Lord (1.1.34)
    we will/we shall (1.1.35)
OTHELLO: you/thou (1.1.2)
    has/hast (1.1.2)
    And in conclusion/(omitted) (1.1.15)
    chosen/chose (1.1.17)
    toged/tongued (1.1.25)
BUSSY D'AMBOIS: incessant/continual (1.1.5)
    forging/forming (1.1.8)
    our tympanous statists/men merely great (1.1.10)
    powers/wealth (1.1.20)
    glad/fain (1.1.25)
    world/earth (1.1.31)

In the Shakespearean texts, the variants appear to be little more than minor modifications in grammar or compositorial slips. In *Bussy D'Ambois*, each variant reading is a different word, often synonymous with the reading it has replaced (*forging/forming* is the only variant that might be a compositorial accident). The *Lear* and *Othello* variants may represent intentional revision. But we have to acknowledge that, at least in this small sample, the variation in *Lear* and *Othello* is clearly different in kind from the variation found in other revised playtexts.

## Modern Editing of Revised Texts

The editorial interest in distinguishing between revisions made by the author and those made by others is grounded in the principle first advanced by McKerrow, and subsequently refined by Greg and Bowers, that an edited text should include all revisions made by the author and exclude any revisions made by others: book-keepers, censors, and subsequent revising authors (McKerrow, *Prolegomena*, 12–14). The classic formulation of the method for distinguishing authorial from non-authorial revisions is Greg's "Rationale of Copy-Text." Greg suggests that when dealing with a revised text, the editor should ask

> 1) whether the original reading is one that can reasonably be attributed to the author, and 2) whether the later reading is one that the author can reasonably be supposed to have substituted for the former. If the answers to both questions are affirmative, then the later reading should be presumed to be due to revision and admitted into the text, whether the editor himself considers it an improvement or not. (54)

Despite Greg's warning that an editor should not base this decision upon a personal evaluation of the variant readings, his criteria for identifying authorial revisions rely entirely upon interpretation. Consequently, the interpretation of revisions is seldom divorced from the question of the authorship of those revisions. There are, for instance, readers of *Bussy D'Ambois* who find the revised version superior. Peter Ure claims that the revisions

> are successful in developing more powerfully the intention of the original or in abolishing harmful ambiguities and inelegancies in expression . . . there are changes in forms of address designed to sharpen irony or accuracy (like the use of the royal "we") as well as minor expansions in the dialogue for the sake of consistency or clarity of situation. (261–62)

Other readers clearly prefer the original version:

> I am persuaded that the original *Bussy D'Ambois* is very much superior to the more familiar second play: superior poetically, theatrically, in terms of character development, in its psychological realism, and in the clarity with which it transmits a tragic vision. (R. P. ADAMS, 144)

Difficulties arise, however, when an interpretation of the relative merit of revisions influences the attribution of authorship. The danger of this subjective procedure is obvious: what a given critic likes is authorial; what the critic does not like is non-authorial. "It cannot, I think, be denied that some lines peculiar to B are very good indeed . . . in other words . . . we *must* accept some of the revision as Chapman's work" (Brooke, lxiv). "The reviser . . . was perhaps less skillful in dramaturgy and poetry . . . Chapman should not be held responsible for the changes in his text which tend to destroy much that is best in his work" (Sturman, 187, 201). The arguments for and against Shakespeare's authorship of a revised version of *Lear* are similar. If the Folio variants are "obtuse mistakes and misconceptions," then "the person responsible for editing and revising the Q text was not Shakespeare" (P. W. K. Stone, 114). If, however, the variants represent "careful revision by a theater artist," then they must be "Shakespeare's own" (Urkowitz, *Shakespeare's*, 16–17, 129).

While much recent scholarship has concentrated on the authorship of revisions, some textual scholars have begun to challenge the traditional view of authority itself. Jerome McGann contends that the "hypnotic fascination with the isolated author" has resulted in a failure to recognize the "collaborative or social nature of literary production" (122, 125). James McLaverty states the case more strongly:

> It cannot be the editor's job to riffle through his texts discarding passages suggested by friends and conjecturing what the author would have written if he had been a hermit. If this were his role, all Pound's excisions from *The Waste Land* would have to be restored and Wordsworth's suggestions for the "Ancient Mariner" deleted. (137–38)

The traditional view, however, does not assert that the act of literary creation is necessarily private, nor that it is adulterated by any social influence. Editors are not interested in who initiated the revisions, but in whether or not the author approved of them. Textual critics attempt to determine "which revisions made or suggested by others . . . were fully accepted by the author in the spirit of active and welcome collaboration" and to distinguish them from "those revisions that the author appears to have accepted grudgingly or been forced into accepting" (Tanselle, "Historicism," 23–24).

The shortcomings of the theoretical principles for dealing with revision are revealed when one tries to apply them to the actual revisions in a manuscript playbook. For an editor to "select only those variant readings which he estimates are true revisions, while rejecting those which he believes to be unauthoritative" (Bowers, "Current," 61 n. 7) would seem to be easy enough when working with a manuscript in which the agents of each revision can be identified (for example, by different inks and handwriting styles). But this is not always possible. In the playbook of Henry Glapthorne's *The Lady Mother* (B.L. MS Egerton 1994; c. 1635), we can trace the revising process with some precision: (1) the play was initially copied out by a scribe, probably working from the author's foul papers; (2) Glapthorne then went over the manuscript making corrections and a few additions; (3) the scribe or book-keeper made further corrections and added stage warnings; (4) the manuscript was submitted to the censor, William Balgrave, who made a few revisions (changing "buttock" to "bacside" and "Recorder" to "Iudge" or "Iustice" throughout); (5) the manuscript then underwent a thorough revision by Glapthorne in which several passages were deleted; (6) the scribe or book-keeper then made the changes dependent on the censor's reformations (Brown, vi–xii).

Despite clear demarcations of revising agents, an editor confronting this mass of revision might well ask, "Is there a text in this manuscript?" Is it possible to include all that is Glapthorne's while excluding all changes made by the scribe, book-keeper, and censor? What is the editor to do, for example, with authorial revisions made after censorship? In the wake of the censor's changes, Glapthorne cut one fifty-line passage and bridged the gap left by the cancellation with the interpolated line "stay, stay, by your leaue mr Iustice." In referring to the character as "mr Iustice" rather than "Mr Recorder," Glapthorne is deferring to the censor. Despite the fact that the change was made *by the author*, should the editor emend the line to "by your leave Mr Recorder," on the grounds that this is what Glapthorne would have written if he had been able?

Once the editor has determined that a work exists in two versions, the McKerrow-Greg-Bowers tradition dictates that the final authorial version of the work should be presented to the reader. McLaverty expounds upon the theoretical reasoning behind this predilection for the final authorial version:

> The editor chooses the final version not merely because he respects the author and wishes to give him the final say, but because he believes there is one overall intention or conception running through the various versions of the work and realized in the final version. (130)

If, however, the revised text represents a "thorough reworking of concept and texture," then the editor is to treat the original and the revised texts as independent units; as such, the two versions "require parallel texts or separate editions" (Bowers, "Remarks," 38). The standard examples are Henry James's thorough revision of his early novels for the New York edition and Wordsworth's lifelong revisions of *The Prelude*. There are parallel text editions of *Every Man in His Humour*, of the A- and B-texts of *Faustus*, of act 5 of 2 *If You Know Not Me You Know Nobody*. And there are now separate editions of Quarto and Folio *Lear* and of the *Faustus* texts as well.

This profusion of parallel texts and separate editions raises an important question: how much (or how little) revision is needed to produce a new version? How are we to distinguish between drafts and versions? Do the author's foul papers constitute a completed version, or are they merely preliminary to the preparation of the book of the play? If both an author's foul papers and the playbook were printed—as may have been the case with the Quarto and Folio texts of *Lear*, *Othello*, *Troilus and Cressida*, and *Hamlet*—should we grant the Folio text priority as the final version, or must the two texts stand independently as separate units? (The Oxford editors give priority to the Folio texts of *Hamlet*, *Othello*, and *Troilus*, but print both texts of *Lear*.)

Perhaps we need to make a distinction between texts that are drafts—preliminary to a final version—and texts that should be regarded as versions. Preliminary drafts, as Dr. Johnson observed, can be fascinating:

> It is pleasant to see great works in their seminal state, pregnant with latent possibilities of excellence; nor could there be any more delightful entertainment than to trace their gradual growth and expansion (407).

Few editors would consider preliminary drafts to be individual versions of the work. Drafts are regarded as curiosities, early stages of the final version, analogous to an artist's "study." Renaissance masters frequently made dozens of preliminary drawings—sketches, studies, and more elaborate *modellos* and cartoons—before executing the final work of art. These drawings are of interest as steps in the process by which the work of art came into existence; they are viewed as necessarily preliminary to the final version and invariably titled "Study for. . . ." The intractable view of studies as preliminary begins to strain, however, when one acknowledges that by the time Raphael reached the cartoon stage, "nearly all of the creative work was already done . . . no essential changes were subsequently made at the painting stage" (Gould, 9). By contrast, a perplexed art historian considering Cigoli's "preliminary" studies for the *Martyrdom of St. Stephen* candidly writes, "The most enigmatic aspect of this series of drawings is that none of them especially resembles the final design of the painting" (Spalding, 296). Should Raphael's cartoons be considered final versions? Should Cigoli's drawings be considered preliminary?

Clearly, art historians and textual critics need a method to distinguish preliminary drafts from finished versions. Peter Shillingsburg contends that the difference is temporally determined:

> A version is a coherent whole form of the work as conceived and executed by the author within a limited time. . . . Variants (other than corrections of errors) produced at significant intervals of time belong to subsequent versions, rather than being drafts. (49)

Shillingsburg's theory allows an author to take periodic breaks while in the process of composition, but an author who resumes work on a draft after a week, a month, or a year (whatever is longer than "a limited time") is no longer at work on the same draft but is creating a new version. I would suggest that we cannot distinguish between versions and drafts solely on the criterion that a certain amount of time has elapsed. As Tanselle notes, "It is obviously possible for authors to make consistent sporadic revisions late in life, and the timing of revisions is therefore not itself the key" ("Editorial," 199).

A second criterion for classifying works as separate versions seems to be grounded on some idea of extensive or "thorough" revision. But Hans Zeller intelligently points out that we cannot "decisively distinguish two versions by quantitative criteria, which might demand that the variants should exceed a certain number" (228). Zeller sees a literary text as analogous to a speech act, and contends that *any* amount of variation creates a new version: "A version is a specific system of linguistic signs, functioning within and without, and authorial revisions transform it into another system . . . in principle a new version comes into existence through a single variant" (240). Tanselle agrees with Zeller in principle, but argues that "in practice, editors are not going to regard each version as necessarily a separate work" ("Editorial," 198). Tanselle defines two types of revision: vertical revision, which changes the purpose, direction, or character of a work; and horizontal revision, which intensifies, refines, or improves a work. Employing these two types, Tanselle offers a "rationale" for distinguishing those instances of revisions that are to be edited as separate works from those that are not:

> If revisions do not spring from the same conception of an organic whole as the original version manifested (what I have called vertical revisions) then they produce a new work, even though the actual number of new readings is small; if revisions are attempts to develop and improve the original conceptions (what I have called horizontal revisions), then they do not produce a separate work for practical purposes, regardless of the number of changes involved. ("Editorial Problem," 198)

McLaverty has criticized Tanselle's formulation, pointing out that "there is no satisfactory principle of division . . . it is not clear what constitutes a change of purpose, conception, or direction" (133). As an alternative, McLaverty contends that the act of publication confers the status of a separate version: "Each version the author decides to publish should be regarded as a separate utterance" (130). The criterion of publication, however, is of limited use for editors of early English drama, since publication was often outside the playwright's control and showed no deference to his "authority."

Practical application of these textual theories is never simple. Are the differences between the two texts of *Faustus*, for instance, significant enough to give an editor warrant to publish, and a student reason to read, both versions? In 1910, Tucker Brooke presented the A-text in its entirety, but relegated the B-text, in bits and pieces, to an appendix. In the wake of Greg's rehabilitation of the B-text in 1950, Jump (1962) and Bowers (Marlowe, *Works*, ed. Bowers, 1973) reduced the A-text to fragments and confined it to the appendices of their B-text editions. In the last decade, the A-text has enjoyed a return to favor, and it is the B-text that languishes in the appendix of Roma Gill's 1990 edition.

When David Bevington and I set out to edit the play for the Revels series, we were faced with the combined pressures of an editorial tradition which dictated that we choose one text or the other and a university press that would clearly have been much happier had we done so. We began by assuming that the majority of the B-text revisions (most probably those "adicyones" for which Henslowe paid William Birde and Samuel Rowley in 1602) simply extend some of the comic themes already found in the A-text; these additions apparently represent attempts to develop and improve those parts of *Faustus* that had proved popular in the theater, without altering the essential character of the original play. If the only difference between the two texts were these added scenes, then the B-text would not need a separate edition. Our initial plan, then, was to edit only the A-text, with the B-text additions in an appendix.

As our work on the edition progressed, however, we discovered more complex and interrelated patterns of revision that represented a thorough reworking of concept and texture, significantly altering the direction and character of the tragedy, particularly its religious and political ideology. The fundamental differences between the original and the revised version proved so compelling that we abandoned our plans for a single-text edition. Both versions of *Faustus* were read and performed in the early English theater. Time's glory may be to blot old books and alter their contents, but in our view (and ultimately in our publisher's view as well), the time had come for a reading edition of both texts, unblotted and unaltered.

## NOTES

1. Occasionally, printed play quartos were marked up, apparently to serve as playbooks in the theater. Examples include the University of Chicago copy of the 1598 quarto of *A Looking-Glass for London* (Baskerville); the British Library copy of the 1607 quarto of Edward Sharpham's *The Fleire* (Leech); and the recently discovered annotated quarto of *The Two Merry Milkmaids* (L. Thomson).

2. Modern directors also tend to cut the second half of Shakespeare's plays. J. W. R. Meadowcroft points out the "progressively increased cutting . . . towards the end of *King Lear*" in the RSC production directed by Trevor Nunn and John Barton in 1976 (84).

3. See Werstine's arguments for revision in *Hamlet* and against it in *Lear* ("Textual").

4. The Revels editor of *The Second Maiden's Tragedy* manuscript offers an important caveat: "It is not possible . . . to attribute the corrections according to the nature of the alterations made . . . manuscripts of the period show . . . that individual correctors did not necessarily make only one kind of change in a manuscript. The censor, for example, might make a technical or a literary correction; the author might censor his own work; the scribe might do theatrical revision or literary alteration" (*The Second Maiden's Tragedy*, 10–11).

5. For the methods of determining a "minimum cast," see Greg's *Two Elizabethan* and Gary Taylor's *Three Studies*.

6. Bevington points out that in *Mundus et Infans* (1508) a dramatic monologue "repeatedly occupies the interval required for the brief costume changes of player two" ("*Mankind*," 120).

7. Bentley incorrectly asserts that the printer of *A Fair Quarrel* "prints the new material as he has evidently received it, on additional pages bound in at the end and not distributed through the play, as it would have been when acted by Prince Charles's Men" (*Dramatist*, 244). In fact, a supplemental quire of three leaves was sewn in between the original H3 and H4 leaves at the end of act 4. A blackletter direction, apparently inadvertently printed, reads, "Place this at the latter end of the fourth act." The 223-line

addition was not intended to be distributed throughout the play, but forms one continuous scene.

8. Honigmann argues that *Troilus and Cressida* was revised for a similar reason: "There is textual and other evidence that *Troilus and Cressida* was to have ended with Troilus's death, a plan abandoned when the play was almost completed, when it was decided to keep Troilus alive for the sequel" ("Date," 47).

# CHAPTER 24

# The Repertory

*Roslyn L. Knutson*

A Note of all suche bookes as belong to the Stocke, and such as I have
bought since the 3d of March 1598.
(HENSLOWE, *Diary*, ed. Foakes and Rickert, 323)

tragedy, comedy, history, pastoral, pastoral-comical, historical-pastoral,
tragical-historical, tragical-comical-historical-pastoral
(*Hamlet*, 2.2.397–99)

A PLAYING COMPANY was known by the offerings in its reper-
tory. Advertisements on the title pages of quartos suggest as much: "Tamburlaine
the Great . . . as . . . shewed upon Stages in the Citie of London. By the right honorable the Lord Admyrall, his seruantes"; "The Troublesome Raigne of John King
of England. . . . As it was (sundry times) publikely acted by the Queenes Maiesties Players"; "Fair Em the Millers daughter. . . . As it was sundrietimes publiquely
acted . . . by the right honourable the Lord Strange his seruants"; "Blvrt Master-
Constable . . . As it hath bin sundry times priuately acted by the Children of Paules."[1]
    Theater historians have used the collective offerings of a company to determine
its commercial success, a success in turn measured by the character of the playgoers who allegedly attended the shows. Behind the assumption of repertory appeal
is the belief that audiences were drawn by literary aspects of the plays, such as complexity of images, consistency of narrative, and psychologically plausible characters. Moreover, because scholars used to focus primarily on Shakespeare, the repertory was formerly a way to privilege the Lord Chamberlain's–King's Men and
denigrate other companies.
    Consequently, old narratives of theater history are full of disparaging judgments
about the repertories of companies not associated with Shakespeare. For example,
R. B. Sharpe, evaluating the Lord Admiral's Men's offerings at the Rose and the
Fortune, asserted that the repertory was "aimed . . . at the tastes of the *older*, less
sophisticated, more middle-class types" (19). To G. E. Bentley, both the Fortune
playhouse and the Red Bull were places of "uncultivated audiences and vulgar
fare" (*Jacobean*, 6:148). Curiously, though, scholars had trouble making similarly
negative judgments about the boys' companies; perhaps persuaded by apparent evidence that the Children of Paul's and the Children of Queen Elizabeth's Chapel

enjoyed enormous popularity around 1599–1603, theater historians lumped the Chamberlain's Men with other adult companies as temporarily displaced in play-goers' affections. Alfred Harbage, attempting to explain the rivalry for audiences that allegedly ensued, asserted that the contrasting repertories at the men's play-houses (i.e., the Globe and the Fortune) and those of the boys' (i.e., Paul's and Blackfriars) were "symptomatic of deep-seated tensions, involving class antago-nisms, rival moral philosophies, and, in a fashion, even the issue of ancients *versus* moderns" (*Rival Traditions*, 90).

The repertory, therefore, has mattered very much as a means of ranking com-panies in a hierarchy of excellence. It still matters in this way; theater historians continue to differentiate one company from another by their offerings and to draw conclusions about the quality of their dramatists and the audience appeal of such fare. But with the generally heightened interest among scholars in the culture of early modern England, we are finding it useful to explore the repertory as a per-spective on the economics of playing, cultural attitudes, and commercial relations in the playhouse industry. This shift of focus enables us to consider individual plays within the spectrum of offerings across lines of company and playhouse in a given time frame. It also invites consideration of the London playhouse world holistically as a theatrical enterprise with principles of cooperation and decorum that fostered the welfare of its members and protected the industry against its critics among the clergy and civic officialdom.

To assemble repertory lists for companies before the 1590s and after 1603, the-ater historians must rely on documents such as title pages of quartos, records of activities at Court in accounts of the Chamber and Revels Office, allusions in con-temporary literature, and the known work of dramatists with company affiliations. All too frequently, such documents provide the title of the play or the site of the performance without providing also the name of the company that owned and staged the play. In 1567–1568, for example, the Revels accounts give the titles of eight plays presented at Court during the winter and the names of five companies that performed, but the companies are not matched with the plays. In that same year (1567), from an entry in court proceedings of the Worshipful Company of Carpenters, we learn that a play called *Samson* was performed at the Red Lion, a newly constructed playhouse at Mile End, but the company is not named (Marsh, 95). Two plays were published in 1567—*The Interlude of Vice* and *The Trial of Treasure*—but the title pages of the quartos do not advertise the company owners.

In the 1580s it gets easier to make lists. One reason is that John Lyly wrote plays for the Children of Paul's during these years, and many of his plays were published advertising that connection. Another is the prominence of the Queen's Men, formed in 1583; when printed, their plays often bore an advertisement of the com-pany owners on the title page. Also, the accounts of the Chamber and the Revels Office are reasonably detailed for the 1580s. In 1585 the Revels accounts name four plays performed by the Queen's Men. An even more detailed set of records survives from 1579–1581, in which clerks of the Revels Office entered the titles of at least seventeen plays, each matched with one of five different companies.

After 1603, the title pages of quartos frequently carry an advertisement of the company owners and/or the dramatist. Court records remain an invaluable source of repertory information. In 1611–1612, for example, the Revels accounts give the titles of twelve plays, matched with the companies giving the performances; in 1612–1613, the Chamber accounts provide the titles of twenty plays performed by the King's Men, two performed by the Prince's Men, two performed by Lady Elizabeth's Men, and four performed by the Children of the Queen's Revels.

Between 1592 and 1603, theater historians rely on the record of playhouse activity known as *Henslowe's Diary*.[2] This document, a book of accounts kept from February 1592 to March 1604 by Philip Henslowe, owner of the Rose playhouse on the south bank of the Thames, enables us to construct data-based discussions not only of the repertory but also of repertory management.[3] Edmond Malone received Henslowe's accounts from Dulwich Library officials in time to squeeze transcribed selections into his monumental *Plays and Poems of William Shakspeare* (1790), and the value of these records as a source of material evidence about the Elizabethan repertory system was immediately and widely acknowledged.

Unfortunately, Henslowe himself acquired a bad reputation in the nineteenth century, and scholars were reluctant to apply the management principles in the diary to companies throughout the playhouse industry, least of all to the hallowed Chamberlain's–King's Men. In 1845 J. P. Collier called Henslowe "an ignorant man . . . [who] kept his book . . . in the most disorderly, negligent, and confused, manner" (Henslowe, *Diary*, ed. Collier, 15). In 1890 Frederick Gard Fleay asserted that the diary showed "the selfish hand-to-mouth policy" that guided the Admiral's Men, supposedly rivals of the Chamberlain's Men, and it showed why the Admiral's Men failed "in spite of the excellence of many of their plays and the genius of their authors" (118).[4] For too long a time, opinions were based on this mixture of venom and prejudice. Encouraged, however, by a judicious new edition of the diary by R. A. Foakes and R. T. Rickert in 1961 and the commonsense application of Henslowe's data to Shakespeare's company by Bernard Beckerman in 1962, theater historians today consider *Henslowe's Diary* the most comprehensive and reliable source of information available on the playhouse industry. Of course, we continue to refine interpretations of its data in coordination with other documents of playbook ownership, that is, advertisements on the title pages of quartos, lists of plays performed at Court, dramatists' company affiliations, and the like.

In the *Diary*, Henslowe recorded the day-to-day business operations of several adult London companies, 1592–1604, primarily the Admiral's Men. For the five-year period from February 19, 1592, through November 5, 1597, his entries occur in the form of playlists that carry dates of performance, titles of plays, and sums of money. From October 21, 1597, to May 9, 1603, the entries occur in the form of payments for playbooks, properties, and apparel. Henslowe did not make entries of expenditures when he was keeping playlists or entries of playlists when he was entering payments for books and apparel; consequently, there are not complete, matched sets of playlists and expenditures for offerings at the Rose and the Fortune. Nonetheless, Henslowe's records provide data on both the practice and the economics of the Elizabethan repertory system.[5] The playlists address questions such as the number of plays a company offered in a month, season, or year; the calendar of playing dates; the pattern of stage runs; and the commercial returns of one offering relative to another. Both the playlists and entries of expenditures address issues of economics and a company's commercial strategies.

Below is a section of *Henslowe's Diary* for September 1594 (Henslowe, *Diary*, ed. Foakes and Rickert [unless otherwise noted], 24), some three months into a residence of the Admiral's Men at the Rose that was to last until the summer of 1600, when the company moved to its newly built Fortune playhouse with Henslowe as partner. It will serve here as a sample of the kinds of information available in the playlists.

| | | |
|---|---|---|
| 2 of septmber 1594 | Rd at the Jew of malta | xxiijs vjd |
| 3 of septmber 1594 | Rd at Tasso | xxxxvjs |
| 4 of septmber 1594 | Rd at phillipo & hewpolito | xxijs |
| 5 of september 1594 | Rd at the venesyon comodey | xxxvjs vjd |
| 6 of septmber 1594 | Rd at cvtlacke | xjs |
| 7 of septmber 1594 | Rd at masacar | xvijs vjd |
| 8 of septmber 1594 | Rd at godfrey | xxxxs |
| 9 of septmber 1594 | Rd at mahemett | xxxvs |
| 10 of septmber 1594 | Rd at galiaso | xxvs |
| 11 of septmber 1594 | Rd at bellendon | xxiiijs vjd |
| 12 of septmber 1594 | Rd at tamberlen | xxxxvs |
| 13 of septmber 1594 | Rd at phillipo & hewpolito | xxs |
| 15 of septmber 1594 | Rd at the venesyon comedy | xxxvjs vjd |
| 16 of septmber 1594 | Rd at the Rangers comodey | xvs |
| 17 of septmber 1594 | ne — Rd at palamon & arsett | ljs |
| 18 of septmber 1594 | Rd at tasso | xxvijs vjd |
| 19 of septmber 1594 | Rd at phillipo & hewpolyto | xiiijs vjd |
| 20 of septmber 1594 | Rd at godfrey | xxxs |
| 21 of septmber 1594 | Rd at mahemett | xxviijs |
| 22 of septmber 1594 | Rd at the venesyon comodey | xxvs |
| 23 of septmber 1594 | Rd at bellendon | xvjs vjd |
| 24 of septmber 1594 | ne — Rd at venesyon & the love of & Ingleshelady | xxxxvis |
| 25 of septmber 1594 | Rd at masacar | xiiijs |
| 26 of septmber 1594 | Rd at cvttlacke | xiijs |
| 28 of septmber 1594 | Rd at tamberlen | xxxjs |
| 29 of septmber 1594 | Rd at galiaso | xvijs |
| 30 of septmber 1594 | Rd at docter ffostose | iijli xijs |

Fifteen different titles are offered in this schedule of twenty-seven playing days. The pace, though rigorous, is normal: the Admiral's Men offered between thirteen and sixteen plays per month in fifteen of the thirty-four months of their tenure at the Rose between June 15, 1594, and July 18, 1596. In comparison, at the beginning of seasons or during months of sporadic performances, the Admiral's Men usually offered about seven different plays. For the year to which the above month of entries belongs, that is, for June 15, 1594, to June 25, 1595, Henslowe names about thirty-five plays. Under ideal conditions, that number was probably tops for repertory size. But conditions were rarely ideal. Still, even in the shortened playing year of 1596–1597 (October–July), the Admiral's Men gave performances of twenty-nine different plays. Since disruptions of the playing year distort figures, the seasonal repertory may be a better measure of repertory size. In the autumn that includes the September 1594 records (August–November), the Admiral's Men staged twenty different plays. It is therefore logical to assume that during a given season— whether autumn, winter, or spring—an adult company had between one and two dozen plays from which to choose for a given day's performance.

As the sample above indicates, the Admiral's Men gave twelve performances in twelve days; after a day off, they gave another twelve performances in twelve days. W. W. Greg, who was sure that Henslowe got dates wrong, corrected the entries to eliminate Sunday performances.[6] As a result, Greg gave the players more breaks— at least four days off a month—than they apparently gave themselves (in fact, Henslowe's accounts imply that the players would perform nonstop if conditions permitted). Greg was persuaded to eliminate Sunday playing by the declaration of bans in Privy Council orders such as one issued on June 22, 1600. He believed that the bans were enforced; most theater historians today believe that the bans would not have been so frequently repeated if they *had been* enforced in the first place.

Yet there were times when the players did not play. The Privy Council order of June 1600, which apparently restrained Sunday performances, called for bans during Lent and an outbreak of plague. *Henslowe's Diary* documents a partial observance of the former. In Lent of 1595 and 1596, the Admiral's Men gave a few performances past Ash Wednesday, then ceased until Easter Monday; in 1597 they gave sixteen performances during Lent. Evidence in the diary of breaks resulting from plague are complicated by a habit of summer touring. Even though no restraint was issued in the summer of 1595, the Admiral's Men did not play at the Rose from June 25 to August 25; likewise, in 1596 they did not play from July 18 to October 27. Entries in the diary for the spring of 1603 illustrate the raggedness of interrupted playing but do not make clear whether plague, or a restraint because of the death of Queen Elizabeth and the accession of King James I, or some other kind of official intervention caused the playhouses to be closed. Henslowe's entry of payments for playbooks and apparel on May 9, 1603, carries this heading: "Begininge to playe Agayne by the kynges licence" (Henslowe, *Diary*, 225). But after a payment for *Jane Shore*, Henslowe's entries stop, without comment on the cause. They resume nearly a year later with a single entry on March 14, 1604, when Henslowe "Caste vp all the acowntes frome the begininge of the world vntell this daye," concluding his diary of playhouse expenditures (209).

The first play to be repeated in the weekly offerings in the sample above is *Philipo and Hippolito*, now lost, its dramatist(s) unknown. Its initial performance had taken place two months before (July 9). Counting that debut, it had received eight performances by September 4; it received two more in September, and it was retired on October 7. In all, *Philipo and Hippolito* received twelve performances in a four-month run. The pattern of its scheduling—performances within a week of one another at the beginning of the run, stretched to separations of two or three weeks toward the end—is a standard one for new plays. *The Venetian Comedy* and *Tasso's Melancholy* fit the pattern, with one common variant: the final performance, as if an afterthought, is separated by more than two months from the previous offering. The pattern is also standard for revivals. *The Massacre at Paris*, new in 1593, was given ten performances over four months during its 1594 revival.

A few plays, no doubt because of their spectacular audience appeal, were given runs unusual in length and number of performances. *The Wise Man of West Chester*, which the Admiral's Men introduced in December 1594, was given sixteen performances in just seven months. By its retirement in July 1595, after twenty months in production, it had received an extraordinary twenty-nine performances. A play in revival might also be given a remarkably long stage run; *1 Tamburlaine* received fifteen performances over sixteen months, from August 28, 1594, to November 12, 1595. Some plays, it seems, were never really retired. *Doctor Faustus*, introduced in the sample month above on September 30, stayed in production over twenty-nine months and received twenty-four performances. When the Admiral's Men needed to open the Rose on short notice in the fall of 1597 and also to absorb the newly acquired players from the Earl of Pembroke's Men into their company, they turned again to *Doctor Faustus* (October 11–19).

While the Admiral's Men were playing twelve plays in twelve days, they were rehearsing a new play, *Palamon and Arcite*, which they introduced on September 17. When he entered the title "palamon & arsett," Henslowe recorded the figure "ljs" in the right-hand column, that is, the sum of 51 shillings, the largest such sum in the month's lists. He also wrote the letters "ne" to the left of the play title. A short week later, the company introduced yet another "ne" play, apparently named "The Love of an English Lady" (ultimately to be called *The Grecian Comedy*). This proximity is unusual; more typical of the playlists is the introduction of plays marked "ne" at intervals of two or three weeks. For example, *Tasso's Melancholy* and *The Venetian Comedy*, which had been introduced in August as "ne," were scheduled two weeks apart. W. W. Greg determined that Henslowe's sums, as a rule, represent a half-share of the gallery receipts for the day, which he also determined to be Henslowe's payment for the lease of the playhouse. Greg puzzled over the meaning of "ne," and subsequent theater historians have continued to wrestle with the problem.[7] All agree that the occurrence of "ne" and high receipts are not coincidental. Most also agree that "ne" is a sign of a play new or marketably new and that the receipts are high because attendance at the opening of a play was a fashionable activity.

New plays were obviously valuable commodities. On June 26, 1594, at the opening show of *Galiaso*, which the Admiral's Men had played six times by its two September showings illustrated in the sample passage above, Henslowe recorded the sum of £3 4s. ("iijli iiijs"), the equivalent of 64s., or 768d. By the time it was retired after a show on October 25, Henslowe had collected receipts averaging 28s. 6d. over its nine performances. Henslowe's share of *Galiaso's* receipts might have been profit, but the Admiral's Men had to subtract the cost of the playbook and the expenses of apparel and properties from their share. Henslowe did not record expenditures of this kind until 1597, at which time he stopped providing playlists.

But even though the two sets of records do not match up, we get an idea of the company's expenses by looking at its payments for apparently comparable plays, 1597–1603. As E. K. Chambers suggested, the most common price for a playbook was about £6 (*Elizabethan*, 1:373). This was the cost of *Mother Redcap* in December 1597 and *The Boss of Billingsgate* in March 1603. The Earl of Worcester's Men paid the same rates for their plays, as illustrated by the payments of 60s., 30s., and 30s. to Thomas Heywood for *The Blind Eats Many a Fly* (December–January 1602–1603). The players might have used apparel and properties already in stock in the tiring house for a new play, or they might have had to buy new things. Henslowe's records show no new expenses specifically for *Mother Redcap* or *The Boss of Billingsgate*, but when the Admiral's Men acquired the two-part *Black Bateman of the North*, for which they paid a combination of £7 and £6, they paid another £8 for "divers thinges" (June 13, 14, 1598). Henslowe's records also do not show that Worcester's Men bought apparel and properties for *The Blind Eats Many a Fly*, but after paying Heywood £6 in 1603 for the playbook of *A Woman Killed with Kindness*, they laid out 73s. for "A womones gowne of black veluett" (February 5) and 10s. for "the blacke satten sewt" (March 7). The top range of expenses for new plays is probably illustrated by the costs to the Admiral's Men of the two-part *Cardinal Wolsey*: the playbooks cost a total of £14, including some revisions; the apparel cost £50 11s. In addition to expenses for the playbook, apparel, and properties, companies paid the Master of the Revels 7s. per play to license it for performance. Henslowe occasionally recorded such payments, as in the payment of 14s. for a license for the two-part *Robin Hood* (March 28, 1598).

It was less expensive to revive a play from stock, and the receipts might be as high as those for new plays. At some time between May 1601 and November 1602, the Admiral's Men revived five plays from the September 1594 repertory, and Henslowe's records show the kinds of expenses they incurred. *The Jew of Malta*, in revival in September 1594, had returned an average of 23s. per performance to Henslowe at that time. When it was revived in 1601, the Admiral's Men spent 100s.

for "diver thing*es*" and another 10s. to "the littell tayler" for "more thing*es*" (May 19). *Tasso's Melancholy* had been in its maiden run in September 1594; it received twelve performances over nine months and returned an average of 30s. per performance to Henslowe. The Admiral's Men paid Thomas Dekker 20s. for alterations to the playbook on January 16, 1601, and another 60s. the following winter for more changes (November 3, December 4). In 1601, for the second revival of *Mahomet*, the Admiral's Men spent £3 12s. 4d. on apparel (August). Also in 1601, for the second revival of *The Massacre at Paris*, the Admiral's Men laid out a total of £7 14s. 6d. for new apparel, and they bought the playbook from Edward Alleyn for £2. For the 1602 revival of *Doctor Faustus*, the Admiral's Men apparently did not buy new apparel or properties, but they paid William Bird and Samuel Rowley the sum of £4 for revisions to the playbook (November 22).

By far the least expensive repertory offering was the play's continuance past the eighth or ninth performance. A "typical" stage run, whether for a new play or a revival, appears to be one in which the play was performed eight to twelve times over four to six months (Knutson, *Repertory*, 33). By the eighth performance, therefore, the company probably had recovered its costs of production and even made some profit. Plays such as *The Wise Man of West Chester*, which enjoyed a run of twenty-nine performances over nineteen months, and *A Knack to Know an Honest Man*, which received twenty-one performances over thirteen months, brought in much more than overhead. Their success compensated for apparent failures. One such failure might have been the "ne" play *Julian the Apostate*, which received three performances in less than a month in April and May 1596 and returned on average 29s. to Henslowe.[8]

Henslowe's entries of receipts for *The Wise Man of West Chester* and *A Knack to Know an Honest Man* in 1595–1596 show that continuations from one year to the next served several commercial functions. One was to fill out the offerings while the new plays of the season were being rehearsed. This function is most obvious in the fall of 1596–1597. *Valteger*, the first new play of the season, was not ready until December 4, 1596; therefore, from the opening performance of October 27, 1596, until the debut of *Valteger*, the Admiral's Men kept eight plays from the repertory of the previous year in production, even though their receipts to Henslowe fell below 10s. on numerous afternoons. Old plays had yet another function: they could be scheduled on holidays, when attendance was usually high regardless of the offering. In the September 1594 sample above, the receipts of *The Love of an English Lady* (renamed *The Grecian Comedy*) slipped to 15s., 10s., and 4s. on its performances just before its offering on December 26 (Saint Stephen's Day), one of the best holidays commercially at the Rose. On that date, the aging play brought a comparatively large return of 46s. to Henslowe.[9]

In addition to showing the economics of new, revived, and continued plays, the September 1594 playlist illustrates several commercial strategies in the selection of offerings. One is the mix of comedies, histories, and tragedies. Within each of these genres, Henlowe's entries of play titles suggest additional variety in subject matter and formulas. The comedies in September 1594 show this diversity. Three of the plays—*Philipo and Hippolito, 1 Godfrey of Bulloigne*, and *Palamon and Arcite*—appear to have been heroic romances; *The Venetian Comedy* and *The Love of an English Lady* (later, *The Grecian Comedy*) probably were built on love plots. In the playlists and payments for playbooks in *Henslowe's Diary* generally, such comedic forms as pastorals, folk plays, craft plays, and moral plays are common; there are also examples of a coy bawdry (e.g., *A Toy To Please Chaste Ladies*), mythology (e.g., *Cupid and Psyche*), fortune hunting (e.g., *The Widow's Charm*), domestic virtue (e.g., *Patient Grissil*), and domestic vice (e.g., *The Triplicity of Cuckolds*). Two of the plays in the September 1594 repertory by Christopher Marlowe represent different configurations of tragedy: *The Jew of Malta* is a villain-revenge play, and *Doctor Faustus* is a moral tragedy. Elsewhere in Henslowe's playlists, a common form is the domestic crime play (e.g., *The Tragedy of Thomas Merry*).

The remainder of the September 1594 offerings have some claim to the category of history play. *The Massacre at Paris* and *Mahomet* tell of foreign politics and bloody conquests. *1 Tamburlaine* and possibly *Cutlack* focus on larger-than-life warriors. *Tasso's Melancholy* was probably a moral biography. *Belin Dun*, set in the time of King Henry I, was one of many chronicle plays named by Henslowe. Perhaps its appeal was the focus it shared with several plays in the diary on the world of criminals and masterless men, for its title character is "Bellin Dun the firste thief that ever was hanged in England" (according to the entry of the play in the Stationers' Register, May 17, 1594). In *Henslowe's Diary* generally there are plays based on real and mythological history (e.g., *Jugurtha, Aeneas and Dido*), Bible story (e.g., *Abraham and Lot, Judas*), and pre-Roman as well as contemporary sixteenth-century British history (e.g., *Mulmutius Dunwallow, Cardinal Wolsey*).

The play of *Mahomet* in the September 1594 sample illustrates yet another strategy of the company repertory: the duplication of popular subject matter by way of similar plays. A canard of old theater histories is that players guarded their playbooks from printing in order to keep other companies from acquiring their properties and presenting them on rival stages. In fact, companies left one another's repertory holdings alone. Under certain circumstances, a play might become available legitimately; for example, players from disintegrating companies might carry playbooks with them into newly formed companies. Presumably this is how the Admiral's Men acquired the two parts of *Tamar Cham*, which had been owned by Lord Strange's Men in 1592. Or players switching from one company to another might have taken a few playbooks with them. Martin Slater sold five playbooks back to the Admiral's Men after he left the company in 1598 (Henslowe, *Diary*, 89, 93), but he might have kept others.

For the most part, however, instead of getting a printed quarto or pirating a playbook from another company's stock, companies bought a new script on the same or a related popular subject. For example, instead of buying and playing Shakespeare's *Richard III* when it became available in quarto in 1597, the Admiral's Men acquired their own play on Richard III, *Richard Crookback*, from Ben Jonson (now, sadly, the play is lost). Instead of appropriating the two-part Queen's play of *The Troublesome Reign of King John* as printed in the 1590 quarto, the Chamberlain's Men acquired their own version of the story from Shakespeare. Three companies—Earl of Derby's Men, Earl of Sussex's Men, and Pembroke's Men—played *Titus Andronicus* before the Chamberlain's Men acquired it in 1594 (according to the advertisement of company ownership on the title page of the 1594 quarto); however, after that acquisition, none of these three is known to have played it, even though two of them were often touring after 1594 and therefore possibly beyond the reach of the new owners in London.

That duplication, not theft, was an acceptable way of competing with other companies' successful material is suggested by an incident concerning a possible clone of *The Spanish Tragedy*. Though in production somewhere by 1587, *The Spanish Tragedy* first turns up in theater records on March 14, 1592, in the playlists of Strange's Men in *Henslowe's Diary*, along with a forepiece heretofore unknown and also not marked "ne" ("spanes comodye donne oracioe," or *The Spanish Comedy*, February 23). *The Spanish Tragedy* turns up again in *Henslowe's Diary*, this time without its forepiece, in the offerings of the Admiral's Men in January 1597. The company still owned the playbook in 1601–1602 when Ben Jonson was paid perhaps as much as £4 for additions. But in 1604 Shakespeare's company, the King's Men, acted as if *they* had owned *The Spanish Tragedy*, and they were outraged that the company at Blackfriars had stolen it from them. They advertised this outrage in a new induction to *The Malcontent*.

In that induction, the King's Men's own players raise the issue of company ownership of a playbook. William Sly asks Henry Condell, "I would know how you came by this play," to which Condell replies, "Faith, sir, the book was lost, and . . . we found it and play it" (ll. 70–72). As the players have been hinting that *The Malcontent* had been played at Blackfriars by the Children of the Queen's Chapel, Sly presses further: "I wonder you would play it, another company having an interest in it" (73–74). Condell fires back, "Why not Malvole in folio with us, as Jeronimo in decimo-sexto with them: They taught us a name for our play, we call it *One for another*" (75–77). But what *Jeronimo* are the King's Men claiming that the boys stole? Was it a copy of the quarto of *The Spanish Tragedy*, printed at least three times before 1603? Had the Chamberlain's Men (now the King's Men) acquired a copy from Strange's Men, as the Admiral's Men apparently did, and had they offered their own production of the playbook since 1594? Or did they have a clone, which turns up by the name of "Hieronimo, both parts" in the playlist printed by Francis Archer in 1656? There is not sufficient evidence on which to base more than a guess that the "stolen" *Jeronimo* was the exclusive property of the King's Men, that is, an "original" variant of the Hieronimo story. Nonetheless they clearly believed that the children's company had violated the protocol by which companies considered one another's playbooks off-limits. They also clearly believed it appropriate for them to call attention publicly to the boys' company's offense.

1 *Tamburlaine* and 1 *Godfrey of Bulloigne* in the September sample from *Henslowe's Diary* illustrate the extension of the principle of duplication by way of sequels, serials, and spin-offs. The prologue of Marlowe's 2 *Tamburlaine* explains the commercial logic of its composition: "The general welcomes Tamburlaine received, / . . . Hath made our poet pen his second part" (ll. 1–3). Audiences demanded more of their favorite heroes' adventures. Soon dramatists were inviting that demand. The dramatist of *Selimus* concludes the play with the prompt that "If this first part Gentles, do like you well, / The second part, shall greater murthers tell."

Henslowe's records indicate that the two parts of a play were often scheduled on consecutive playing days. For example, Strange's Men played *The Spanish Comedy* on March 13, 1592, as prelude to the introduction of *The Spanish Tragedy* on the next day. Thereafter, the pair were played consecutively on March 30–31 and May 21–22. The Admiral's Men revived 1 *Tamburlaine* on August 28, 1594, and gave it seven performances up to December 17. On December 19, with no play scheduled on the intervening day, the players introduced 2 *Tamburlaine*. Thereafter, on all six of its showings, the Admiral's Men scheduled the second part just after its first part (or just after by a day). Henslowe's entries show that the first part of a serial was often scheduled by itself, but the second part was commonly played in tandem with the first part. The second part of *Hercules* was scheduled consecutively with the first part for six of its eight performances in the spring of 1595.

The payments for several plays in Henslowe's records, 1597–1604, imply that sequels were sometimes planned from the start and sometimes afterthoughts. *Sir John Oldcastle* was conceived as a two-part play: at its first entry in the diary, Henslowe recorded payments of £10 "for the first parte of the lyfe of Sr Jhon Ouldcasstell & in earnest of the Second Parte" (Henslowe, *Diary*, 125). In contrast, the payments for *The Blind Beggar of Bednal Green* imply the pattern of an afterthought: some eight months after having paid Henry Chettle and John Day 110s. for the playbook of *The Blind Beggar of Bednal Green*, the Admiral's Men began a series of payments to William Haughton and John Day for part 2. Despite the demand by playgoers, second parts seem to have been less successful than their parent plays; for example, the second part of *Seven Days of the Week* received only two performances in one month (January 1596), while the first part received twenty-two performances over eighteen months (June 1595–December 1597).

The impetus behind the spin-off is nowhere better illustrated than in the evolution of payments for the second part of *The Blind Beggar of Bednal Green*. On January 29, 1601, Henslowe recorded a payment of 40s. to the dramatists "in earnest of A Boocke called the second parte of the blinde beager of bednowle grene with thomme strowde" (Henslowe, *Diary*, 166). Thereafter he entered payments under the title of "The Second Part of Tom Strowd." On the heels of this second part, the Admiral's Men began paying for a third part, which was called "The Third Part of Tom Strowd" from the start. There is support in legend as well as fact for spin-offs featuring popular characters. An example is the birth story of *The Merry Wives of Windsor* (advertised to readers and perhaps also to playgoers as "A Most pleasaunt and excellent conceited Comedie, of Syr John Falstaffe"). Supposedly, Shakespeare wrote it to please Queen Elizabeth, who asked for a play of Falstaff in love after she had seen *1 Henry IV*.[10]

In the climate of recent theoretical movements that emphasize the cultural context of plays, theater historians are looking within and across lines of company ownership and giving new attention to repertory items that share such issues as politics, international trade and exploration, social governance, gender and sexuality, labor, religion, science, and/or domestic relations. We are hampered, of course, by the fragmentary nature of the evidence and the paucity of surviving plays. Nonetheless, a knowledge of the repertory enables us to consider ways in which plays apparently related by subject matter and chronology (not by dramatist and company) provide insight into values and attitudes in early modern England.

The potential of the repertory as a component of cultural studies is illustrated by *1 Tamburlaine* in the offerings of the Admiral's Men in September 1594. Within the confines of the repertory of the Admiral's Men, Marlowe's play invites comparison with the two-part *Tamar Cham*, of which nothing remains but a transcription of the theatrical "Plot" for part 1. (The "Plot" in this case is an outline of entrances, exits, and casting assignments.) The *Tamar Cham* plays, based on the legendary exploits of a Tatar warlord, were a kind of spin-off of the elder *Tamburlaine* plays. The Admiral's Men appear to have played the two-part *Tamar Cham* as substitute *Tamburlaines*, in that they revived 1 and 2 *Tamar Cham*, in May and June of 1596, just six months after they had retired 1 and 2 *Tamburlaine*, in November 1595. There might have been another such pairing after the opening of the Fortune playhouse. Although Henslowe does not record a revival of the *Tamburlaine* plays after 1595, his inventory of 1598 shows that the Admiral's Men kept Tamburlaine's coat with copper lace and crimson velvet breeches in stock. Henslowe implied a revival of the *Tamar Cham* plays by recording the Admiral's Men's purchase of the playbook from Edward Alleyn on October 2, 1602.

Across the boundaries of company ownership, the *Tamburlaine* plays invite comparison by way of parody. In 1598–1599 the Chamberlain's Men offered *2 Henry IV*, which alludes to Tamburlaine by way of Pistol's comic rant, and it was probably still in production at the newly built Globe in 1599–1600.[11] Ben Jonson created another Tamburlainian *miles gloriosus*, both terrifying and comic, for the stage at Blackfriars in 1601. In *Poetaster*, the railing Captain Tucca, like Pistol, declaims in fragments of old plays. Thomas Dekker appropriated the character of Tucca to rail at Jonson in *Satiromastix*, which was played by two companies in 1601, the Chamberlain's Men at the Globe and Paul's Boys at Paul's.

*1* and *2 Tamburlaine*, as well as the two-part *Tamar Cham*, illustrate another feature of repertories within and across the boundaries of playing companies: a fascination with travel, exploration, maritime commerce, and the exotic peoples discovered in the course of such risky business. Not long after the Levant Company was formed in 1581 to facilitate trade with Turkey and the eastern Mediterranean world, plays appeared on the English stage with characters (often tyrants) from the Levantine world. In the wake of Marlowe's *Tamburlaines* in the repertory of the Admiral's Men were *Selimus* and *The Turkish Mahomet and Hiren the Fair Greek*, probably in the repertory of the Queen's Men (1588–1592); *Soliman and Perseda*, probably in the repertory of Pembroke's Men (1593); and *The Battle of Alcazar*, the property of the Admiral's Men. Called "Mahomet" in *Henslowe's Diary*, *The Battle of Alcazar* belongs to a cluster of related plays on North Africa, including also Strange's Men's "Muly Mullocco" (1592). *1 Tamburlaine* raises the subject of captivity, which frightened as well as fascinated playgoers. Tamburlaine, anticipating his battle with Bajazeth, emperor of Turkey, brags that he will free "Christian captives" enslaved in chains on galleys (3.3.47), then subdue the "pirates of Argier, / . . . the scum of Africa" (3.3.55–56), who prey on merchants and mariners.[12]

Othello had exploited a romanticism in the dangers of conquest when he wooed Desdemona; when he catalogs his adventures before the Venetian Council, which include his having been "sold to slavery, . . . [and] redemption thence" (1.3.140), he wins their approval also. In the years after *Othello* was onstage at the Globe, Thomas Heywood and William Rowley's *Fortune By Land and Sea* was offered at the Red Bull playhouse by Queen Anne's Men; one plot of the play concerns the pirates Clinton Atkinson and Thomas Walton. The Admiral's Men had acquired *The Siege of Dunkirk* in 1603 as a vehicle for Edward Alleyn in the role of pirate. At some time after 1609, Robert Daborne capitalized on the continuing popularity of such tales for *A Christian Turned Turk* (Q1612), a moral biography of John Ward and Simon Dansiker.

*2 Tamburlaine* extends the global reach of travel lore; two of Tamburlaine's puissant kings, Techelles and Theridamas, exchange war stories from distant lands where they have seen wonders such as Prester John, the Amazons, and dancing devils. In 1592 Strange's Men had a play called *Sir John Mandeville*, also no doubt full of marvels. Othello recounts adventures that exposed him to cannibals, the Anthropophagi, "and men whose heads / Do grow beneath their shoulders" (1.3.147), and Trinculo and Stephano discover a monstrous man-fish (*The Tempest*). For African exotica, however, no play in this period is likely to have exceeded the first part of *Tamar Cham*, which was staged at the Rose playhouse by Strange's Men in 1592 and by the Admiral's Men in 1596. The play itself is lost, but the surviving Plot is sufficient to suggest an unmatchable display of real and fabulous aliens. On parade in the final scene are pairs of Tatars, Geates, Amazons, "Nagars," olive-colored Moors, cannibals, hermaphrodites, Boharians, pygmies, Cryms, Cattaians, and Bactrians (Greg, *Henslowe Papers*, 148).

A curiosity among early English playgoers about exploration, conquest, maritime commerce, and contact with indigenous peoples no doubt lay behind the acquisition of *The Conquest of the West Indies* by the Admiral's Men in the summer of 1601. But views on the discovery of new worlds were complex, as plays of the early 1600s illustrate. In *Eastward Ho!* by Ben Jonson, George Chapman, and John Marston, Sir Petronel Flash and an assortment of mariners and adventurers plan a Virginia voyage. Seagull, the captain, conveys one colonialist attitude when he imagines that the virgin land waits impatiently until they arrive to "share the rest of her maidenhead" (3.3.14–15). Different views are illustrated by the perspectives of Gonzalo and Prospero in *The Tempest*. Engaging the utopian discourse of his time, Gonzalo rhapsodizes about the commonwealth he would create had he "plantation" of the island and "were the king on't" (2.1.146, 148). Politically there would be no magistrate, and thus no treason; occupationally, all men would be idle, and thus no "use of service" (154). Prospero's interaction with the inhabitants of the island has led to a less utopian, more stratified society. Prospero rules; Ariel and Caliban serve. Prospero has taught Miranda to define morality in sexual terms; consequently, Caliban is stigmatized as a creature incapable of "any print of goodness" (1.2.355). Although Caliban lacks an education in political science, he nonetheless understands that he, who "first was [his] own king," has been co-opted to enslave himself (1.2.344).

In addition to *Tamburlaine*, the September 1594 sample of plays in the repertory of the Admiral's Men contains *Doctor Faustus*, which evokes a set of cultural attitudes and beliefs on science, magic, and religion. After December 2 when *The Wise Man of West Chester* was introduced "ne," the Admiral's Men often scheduled it in coordination with performances of *Doctor Faustus*, almost as if the two were a pair.[13] In July of 1597, the company revived *The Wise Man of West Chester* along with an old play called *The Witch of Islington*, and by October *Doctor Faustus* was back in production. This coordination implies the blurred lines between folklore, science, and magic, as well as between the comedic activity of matchmaking and the tragical result of temptation. In the years before 1594, other companies had had friar plays, or magician plays, in repertory. According to its title-page advertisement (1594), *Friar Bacon and Friar Bungay* was owned by the Queen's Men. It apparently had a sequel, *John of Bordeaux*, which belonged to Strange's Men in 1592 (McMillin, "Ownership," 250–51), and it shared similarities as well with *John a Kent and John a Cumber*. Sussex's Men owned *Friar Francis* in January 1593.

*Friar Bacon and Friar Bungay* illustrates the comedic role of magicians as matchmaker. Friar Bacon allows Lacy to gaze into a magic glass and witness a meeting between Friar Bungay and Margaret in which she confesses that she loves Lacy. At the Theater in 1594 the Chamberlain's Men contributed *A Midsummer Night's Dream* to the offerings of magical matchmaking. At the Globe in 1602 they contributed *Merry Devil of Edmonton*, in which Peter Fabell, a Cambridge don, supposedly helps his former pupil, Raymond Mounchensey, steal his beloved from protective custody in a nunnery and bed her in a nearby inn. Promising disruptions of nature, Fabell merely changes the alehouse signs so that the parents do not catch the lovers in time to prevent the betrothal from being consummated.

Perhaps coincidental with a run of *The Merry Devil of Edmonton*, the Admiral's Men took "the playe of bacon" out of stock and on December 14, 1602, paid Thomas Middleton 5s. to write an epilogue for it "for the corte" (Henslowe, *Diary*, 207). Perhaps not coincidentally, the Admiral's Men paid William Bird and Samuel Rowley £4 on November 22 of the same year to revise *Doctor Faustus*, presumably for revival. The King's Men had yet another variant of the magician-as-matchmaker in *Robin Goodfellow*, the title Dudley Carleton gave to a play performed at Hampton Court on New Year's night 1604; ballads about Robin Goodfellow narrate his success in rescuing a young woman from her lecherous uncle and delivering her into the hands of her lover.[14]

The demonic in *Doctor Faustus* had repercussions in the repertories across company lines as well. Peter Fabell, the "merry devil," begins where Faustus ends, with a summons to hell. By tricking the devil's messenger into a magic chair, however, Fabell negotiates another seven years of mischief-making. In *The Devil's Charter*, a play in the King's Men's repertory in 1606–1607, the motif of the occult turns back toward tragedy. In the opening dumb show, Roderigo Borgia seizes the papacy with the help of devils; Faustus-like, Borgia dismisses the spirit "*in most vgly shape*" but receives those dressed in "*robes pontificall*," signing their contract with blood drawn from his vein (ll. 44–45). As Alexander VI, Borgia uses the study as a site of wickedness. From there he plans murders and conjures visions of demonic power. He is in that study, poisoned inadvertently by his own hand, when the devils come to claim his soul. As the playlists in *Henslowe's Diary* illustrate repeatedly, companies often duplicated popular features of their own plays. In terms of the treatment of magic and damnation, *The Devil's Charter* had been anticipated in the repertory of the King's Men by *Macbeth*, which was introduced new in 1605–1606.

*Macbeth* was in revival five years later in the spring of 1611 when Simon Forman (himself an intriguingly theatrical figure) saw it at the Globe during the same spring when he saw *Cymbeline*, *The Winter's Tale*, and a play he called *Richard the 2*. Forman was a physician and occultist. When he was not otherwise occupied having sexual relations with his female patients, manufacturing a pedigree for himself, or predicting the future, he attended plays.[15] That spring he went to the Globe and saw the four offerings in the repertory of the King's Men. Forman's entries in his personal diary show that he was excited by the element of prophecy and the supernatural in the plays he saw. He commented on the "3 women feiries or Nimphes" in *Macbeth*, as well as on the ghosts and "prodigies seen" in connection with Duncan's death; on the sleeping potion taken by Imogen in *Cymbeline*; and on the truth of the oracle and the Puck-like identity of Autolycus in *The Winter's Tale*.[16]

But Forman was particularly struck by the unjust treatment of a wise man in *Richard the 2*. In language seething with outrage, he records an episode in which John of Gaunt, after having sought the advice of a prophet, has the man hanged in order to keep that prophecy secret: "But I sai yt was a villaines parte, and a Iudas kisse to hange the man for telling him the truth."

Although the repertory has only recently begun to receive appropriate attention as a medium of cultural study, theater historians have long considered it a primary feature of competition among playing companies in London. The best-known narrative of company rivalry by way of repertory offerings is usually dubbed "The War of the Theaters." This so-called war is supposed to have begun in 1599–1600 when the playhouses at Paul's and Blackfriars were reopened with companies of boy players. According to the narrative, the "little eyases" passage in the folio *Hamlet* marks this escalation in the competition for playgoers, a competition that the boys' companies — being "now the fashion" — temporarily won. Ben Jonson allegedly refers to a continuation of the same phenomenon in *Poetaster* (1601), when the player Histrio complains that "this winter ha's made vs all poorer, then so many staru'd snakes: No bodie comes at vs; not a gentleman, nor a —" (3.4.328–29). In the alleged War of the Theaters, the companies are said to have fought for a larger market share by adding the newly invented comical satire to their repertories.

Scholars, however, by focusing on only one kind of play in the companies' repertories, have confused the so-called war with a genuine instance of heated debate among dramatists in 1601. This confrontation, termed a *poetomachia* by Thomas Dekker (one of the participating dramatists), broke out on London stages with the production of Ben Jonson's *Poetaster*, which was first played at Blackfriars in mid-1601. In that play, Jonson champions the poet Horace, whom scholars have seen as a self-portrait. At the same time, Jonson ridicules the poet-pretender Crispinus, and he sneers at the grubby existence of common players through a collection of characters including Demetrius, Histrio, and Captain Tucca. Theater historians have identified Crispinus as John Marston and Demetrius as Thomas Dekker. Though Jonson denied that he was pointing at specific people (*Poetaster*, "To the Reader," ll. 83–84), some of his fellow playwrights decided that he needed to be answered. The result was Dekker's *Satiromastix*, in which Horace is publicly humiliated and forced to forswear his aberrant behavior. *Satiromastix* was played at the Globe and at Paul's playhouse, and it caused aftershocks as far away as a stage at Cambridge, where *2 Return from Parnassus* was played. After *Satiromastix* was staged, Jonson withdrew from the battlefield, conceding the quarrel and consoling himself with an occasional grenade of insults and self-defensive posturings in his prefaces, conversations with friends, and appeals to the reader of his *Works*.

In addition to being confused with the *poetomachia*, the War of the Theaters, based on rival repertories, lacks credibility because the boys' companies did not rely solely on satire. As Michael Shapiro has demonstrated, Paul's Boys (the Children of Paul's) and the Children of the Queen's Chapel at Blackfriars had a much broader variety of fare available (180–232). The offerings of Paul's Boys in 1599–1603 illustrate a variety that matches up quite well with the repertories of the adult companies, their supposed rivals. Among the boys' new repertory pieces at their reopening in 1599 was *Antonio and Mellida*, which was joined within months by *Antonio's Revenge*. Together the plays represent several features of the men's repertories: the fashion of revenge tragedy and the duplication of story matter into two-part plays.

The most obvious parallel would seem to be the pairing of *The Spanish Comedy/The Spanish Tragedy* in the repertory of Strange's Men in 1592–1593; the Admiral's Men were playing *The Spanish Tragedy* in 1597–1598. The Chamberlain's Men might have been playing their mysterious two-part *Hieronimo* or *Jeronimo*, which the King's Men publicly reprimanded the Children of the Queen's Chapel in 1604 for having stolen. In terms of duplicate story matter, however, the most obvious parallel was *Hamlet*, introduced at the Globe sometime in 1599–1600 and thus coincidental with the run of the two-part *Antonio* plays at Paul's playhouse.

The other offerings of Paul's Boys at the time of the War of the Theaters were a mix of moral plays, mythological pastoral drama, and love comedies. *The Contention Between Liberality and Prodigality* was an apparent throwback to the heyday of the moral interlude. Not only does the text mix abstract characters such as Vanity, Vertue, Equity, Tenacity, Money, and Fortune (as well as Liberality and Prodigality) but it is also structured to accommodate a company small by the standards of 1599 (ten or twelve players could easily double the twenty-eight roles). The repertories of the Admiral's Men and the Chamberlain's Men show that the moral play was a feature of adult company offerings also: the Admiral's Men played *Fortunatus*, and the Chamberlain's Men played *Cloth Breeches and Velvet Hose* in the winter of 1599–1600. At the playhouse at Paul's, the boys' company staged *The Maid's Metamorphosis*, a Lyly-esque pastoral; meanwhile the Admiral's Men were offering plays with mythologically suggestive titles such as *The Arcadian Virgin*, *Truth's Supplication to Candlelight*, and *Golden Ass and Cupid and Psyche* (all lost).

Paul's Boys also staged *The Wisdom of Doctor Dodypoll*, *Jack Drum's Entertainment*, *What You Will*, and *Blurt Master Constable*, which are a hodgepodge of comedic formulas with the pairing of young lovers as common denominator. Several have remote parallels with plays in the repertory of the Chamberlain's Men. *The Wisdom of Doctor Dodypoll*, for example, has a pastoral episode with an enchanter that evokes Ganymede's story of a forest magician in *As You Like It*. *Blurt Master Constable* has a touch of city comedy from a clown plot of the constable and his watch not unlike Dogberry's fellows in *Much Ado About Nothing*. *Jack Drum's Entertainment* makes fun of old, rich, lecherous lovers as well as husbands foolish enough to test their wives' fidelity, faintly reminiscent of *The Merry Wives of Windsor*. The only surviving comical satire in the repertory of Paul's Boys is *Satiromastix*, which dilutes the untrussing of Horace with a folktale plot in which the king claims the maidenhead of the bride. With this repertory offering, however, Paul's Boys could not vie for playgoers at the Globe in any normative sense of rivalry because *Satiromastix* had been performed there first by the Chamberlain's Men.

Using an old-fashioned scholarly approach to the repertory based on literary merit, theater historians might argue that the Chamberlain's Men were the better company in 1599–1603 because Shakespeare's plays are better than Marston's. Or, using an old-fashioned approach based on class and clientele, they might conclude that Paul's Boys were the better company because young gallants supposedly preferred the *Antonio* plays to the fare at the Fortune or the Globe. But an approach more consistent with current theater history is to consider the repertory as a product of a growth industry in 1599–1603. New playhouses were being built (the Globe and the Fortune); nearly new ones were being enlarged (the Boar's Head); several old ones were still in use (the Curtain, the Rose); and some that had formerly been closed were reopened (Paul's, Blackfriars). Despite the repartee among a few plays in 1601 about which playhouses were in fashion, the companies in business during these years continued strong. They did so for the same reason that companies had flourished since the 1580s, if not before: the number, variety, and economy of repertory offerings. The playlists in *Henslowe's Diary* imply that a company could make back its costs on a given production in less than four months and on fewer than a dozen performances. By recycling apparel such as cloaks, hose, and gowns, and properties such as crowns, beds, and coffins from one offering to another, a company could mount thirty or more productions without much overhead. It could revive old plays, often with no more investment than the 5s. cost for a prologue and epilogue. If another company scored a hit with a new play on a popular subject such as Henry V, Richard III, or the prodigality of young heirs, the company could acquire a duplicate and make money on the story also. Much more, then, than a measure of literary talent and audience taste, the repertory is one context in which the study of an individual play, an eventful year, a significant cultural issue, or the dynamic of commerce in the drama of early modern England may be studied.

NOTES

1. Greg, *Bibliography*, 1:171, 178, 192, 300.
2. Because of the superior evidence on repertory practice in *Henslowe's Diary*, I focus in this essay on 1592–1603. Yet I believe that the claims I make for the function of the repertory as the prime commodity of the company, as a vehicle of cultural commentary, and as a measure of industrywide norms in the tastes of playgoers are applicable throughout 1500–1650. I believe this because the concept of repertory acquisition and marketing seems to me to be one of the most stable features of the Elizabethan playhouse world. Companies change patrons; their membership changes; the plays themselves in the repertory change. But the concept of variety in subject matter and dramatic formula does not seem to change, and the desire to give playgoers more of what they like does not seem

to change. For company repertory lists after 1616, see Bentley, *Jacobean*.

3. Henslowe kept records of more than his playhouse business (for example, his expenses in remodeling the Rose in 1592 and his pawnbroking operation); but for the purposes of this essay, references to *Henslowe's Diary* and Henslowe's records are references to the playhouse accounts.

4. The illogic here—dispraise of Henslowe, praise of the repertory of the Admiral's Men, yet their repertory can attract only vulgar playgoers—is a common one in repertory studies before 1960.

5. Users of data in the diary should exercise caution. Titles of plays are not always clear, as in the apparent evolution of *The Love of an English Lady* into *The Love of a Grecian Lady* into *The Grecian Comedy*. The apparent cancellation of a play after one performance, as in the case of *The Merchant of Emden*, might not mean that the play was unpopular (after all, it seems to have brought Henslowe 68s.). The dates of some entries are puzzling, making some offerings appear to be double bills, as in the confusions of August 5–10, 1594, when eight plays are listed for six calendar days.

6. Henslowe, *Diary*, ed. Greg, 2:324–26. Collier also challenged Henslowe's dates, calling the accounts disorderly "as respects dates in particular" (Henslowe, *Diary*, ed. Collier, xv). Examining Greg's revisions, Foakes and Rickert challenge the premise that Henslowe's dates "should provide an accurate record from day to day," suggesting that such clerical care does not fit "the character of the entries and the character of Henslowe himself" (xxix).

7. Henslowe, *Diary*, ed. Greg, 2:128–29, 132–36. Neither has anyone satisfactorily solved the conundrum of the accounting form adopted by Henslowe in January 1597 (see Henslowe, *Diary*, ed. Foakes and Rickert, xxxiii–xxxvi).

8. Much of the data in *Henslowe's Diary*, interpreted superficially, suggests that many plays were failures. I address the issue of short runs in "Puzzle" and that of partial payments for plays in "Commercial."

9. Other lucrative holidays were Allhallows (November 1), Saint John's (December 27), Holy Innocents' (December 28), New Year's (January 1), Epiphany (January 6), Candlemas (February 2), Shrove Monday and Tuesday, Ash Wednesday, and days during Easter Week and Whitsun Week.

10. John Dennis first told the story of the queen's command in the epistle to *The Comical Gallant* (1702); Nicholas Rowe repeated it with the embellishment about Falstaff as lover in the biography of Shakespeare included with *The Works of Mr. William Shakespear* (London, 1709). This biographical sketch ceased to be merely a "good story" and became fact by being repeated in subsequent eighteenth-century editions.

11. Pistol's lines are as follows: "Shall Packhorses / And hollow pampered jades of Asia / Which cannot go but thirty mile a day / Compare with Caesars, and with cannibals / And with Troiant Greeks?" (2.4.162–64). The entry of a book called *The Tartarian Cripple Emperor of Constantinople* at Stationers' Hall on August 14, 1600, provides further evidence of the cloning of *Tamburlaine*.

12. For further discussion of repertorial features of Mediterranean plays, see Knutson, "Elizabethan Documents."

13. For implications of this coordination, as well as the relative profits from the plays, see Knutson, "Influence," 271–273.

14. Carleton spoke of the performance to John Chamberlain in a letter dated January 15, 1604 (Lee, 53). E. K. Chambers, representing an opinion of his time that plays with similar characters and similar titles were the same play (not, as I argue, duplicates or clones), identified *Robin Goodfellow* as *A Midsummer Night's Dream* (*Elizabethan*, 4:118).

15. For Forman's nontheatrical occupations, I am indebted to Traister.

16. Quotations from Forman's diary are taken from Shakespeare, *The Riverside Shakespeare*, ed. Evans, 1840–41. Superfluous punctuation has been silently removed.

# CHAPTER 25

# Plays in Manuscript

*Paul Werstine*

MANUSCRIPTS OF early English plays have occupied the labors of editors and scholars since the eighteenth century, but it was not until the twentieth century that any systematic efforts were made to classify, edit, and disseminate these materials. One individual, Sir Walter Wilson Greg, may be credited with having established the study of early modern drama in manuscript as a field of rigorous scholarly inquiry, with his 1931 two-volume work *Dramatic Documents from the Elizabethan Playhouses: Stage Plots, Actors' Parts, Prompt Books*. Greg's work as general editor for the Malone Society, from its founding in 1906 to 1939, was equally crucial to the definition of this branch of study. While much tribute is also owed to Greg's successors as general editors of the society, it remains the case that Greg's work was decisive in formulating the questions that have directed the study of early modern play manuscripts.[1] I emphasize our debt to Greg so strongly at the outset of this essay because so much of what follows will take issue with the direction that Greg set; in spite of that, I believe it important to insist how much one depends on Greg's work even in calling his presuppositions into question.

In a 1926 article, "Prompt Copies, Private Transcripts, and the 'Playhouse Scrivener,'" Greg began to develop what is still accepted by many present editors as *the* general theory of the production and reproduction of early modern plays in manuscript. In Greg's later formulations, in *The Editorial Problem in Shakespeare* (1942) and *The Shakespeare First Folio* (1955), this theory appears to be grounded upon an objective survey of extant dramatic manuscripts. As the present essay will show, however, by relocating Greg's writing in its historical context, Greg's theory is both logically a priori, by his own admission (*Dramatic Documents*, 1:195), to any survey of the manuscripts and chronologically prior to his own limited survey of them in *Dramatic Documents*. Greg's haste to produce a general rational theory grew out of his struggles both with his longtime rival Sir Sidney Lee and with his longtime friend and sometime collaborator A. W. Pollard (and the latter's disciple J. Dover Wilson). Insofar as editors and scholars continue to labor under the influence of Greg's theory, they continue to evade the complexity exhibited in the range and diversity of the extant manuscripts and instead reproduce under the guise of general theory the ad hoc rhetorical strategies developed by Greg to counter equally ephemeral observations by his contemporaries.

Present-day scholars thus face an important choice. On the one hand, there is what I have called Greg's "general theory," which reduces a dispersed heterogeneity of manuscripts to the linear simplicity of his narrative, colonizing the manuscripts to make them serve as the sites of clues to the nature of the lost manuscripts that once lay behind plays now available only in printed texts—most especially the plays of Shakespeare. On the other hand, there is the irreducible historical messiness of the actual manuscripts, which disrupts the conceptual tidiness, the orderliness of classification, and the economy of hypothesis that Greg so successfully championed.

## Greg's Dramatic Documents *and After*

From the perspective of the present, *Dramatic Documents* is easily mistaken for an objective and inclusive survey of its field. Yet Greg was attractively modest about the scope of his undertaking. He divided his project into three: in the first part, he attempted to include reference to all the relevant actors' parts of which he had knowledge;[2] in the second, all the theatrical "plots";[3] and in the third, some of the manuscript playbooks. From this last category he excluded "all early drama—miracles, morals, interludes—all academic plays, masques, and Court entertainments, and lastly literary compositions of the closet drama type."[4] He called his "classified list of extant manuscripts . . . a rash venture which must plead for leniency on the ground of its being a first attempt" and indicated that his concern was "with plays written for production on the regular public stage before the outbreak of civil war closed the theatres" (1:191).

Some omissions from Greg's *Dramatic Documents* seem the consequence of time and space. Published in 1931, just a year before the opening of the Folger Shakespeare Library in Washington, Greg's work could not record the extensive holdings of that library, holdings that had been disappearing without trace into Henry Clay Folger's vaults for decades before the library's completion. Greg could, for example, only list in the barest fashion the contents of the great Lambarde Collection and describe its disappearance at auction (1:366–67). Its preservation in the Folger Library would not be announced to British scholars until 1934 (Boas); a number of the Lambarde manuscripts were discussed by R. C. Bald in the decade following publication of Greg's survey (*The Lost Lady, The Inconstant Lady, Hengist*, and, in his *Bibliographical Studies, Beggars Bush* and *The Womans Prize*). At the time he published *Dramatic Documents*, Greg could not list several other plays at the Folger that arguably fall within the bounds of his attempted survey: A *Dialogue betweene Pollicy and Piety* (Tricomi), Robert Wild's *The Benefice* (the only manuscript of which Greg could record is a fragment at the British Library), *Boote and Spurre* (R. S. Thomson), *The fary knight* (Bowers), *The Partial Law* (Dobell), *July and Julian* (Dawson).

Other omissions from *Dramatic Documents* may indicate, however, that Greg would not have consulted the Folger's holdings even had he had the opportunity. He never visited the Huntington Library in San Marino, California, with its substantial holdings in manuscript drama; he seems not even to have examined manuscripts in such locations as Alnwick Castle, north of Newcastle, where *John of Bourdeaux* and *The Wasp* are to be found. Had he seen *The Wasp*, he surely would have recognized, as its Malone Society editor later did, that that manuscript showed clear signs of use in the theater, and he would not then have misclassified it (Lever). The rather narrow range of Greg's search for materials may be gauged by his listing of the manuscripts of William Cartwright's *The Royal Slave*. Greg lists only the British Library manuscript of the playtext; his discussion makes implicit reference to another British Library manuscript (Egerton 2725) containing only the play's prologues and epilogues. Yet twenty years later, G. B. Evans could record the existence of no fewer than three other manuscript texts of the whole play (two in England—but not London—one of these at the Bodleian Library, Oxford, and one in the possession of the duke of Bedford; one at the Folger Library), and Evans also indicated that a fourth additional manuscript, the Heber, was once reported but had since dropped from sight (167, 869).

The limits of Greg's search have had important consequences for our understanding of transcription of plays: because Greg did not look far beyond London, he found few manuscripts of any single play (except *Game at Chesse*, which R. C. Bald had, conveniently for Greg, edited in 1929[5]), and so he used his foundational study in the service of the then already existing presumption that normally there never had been many manuscript copies of any single play. The implications of this view (considered below) have shaped discussion and editing of early modern drama throughout the rest of this century. In spite of evident shortcomings in Greg's search, a salutary effect of publication of his *Dramatic Documents* was to arouse interest in extending the search. The upshot was finally, in 1940, the list of "Extant Play Manuscripts, 975–1700: Their Location and Catalogue Numbers" in Alfred Harbage's 1940 *Annals of English Drama* (252–64). While Harbage's list aims laudably at inclusiveness, it is bare of any description of the extant materials.[6]

### Promptbooks

Greg's own classification and analysis of manuscripts are as historically conditioned as was his search itself. His classification appears to be threefold. Class A contains what he calls "prompt books proper," or transcripts of them. He opposes these manuscripts to Class B, manuscripts "prepared for some private purpose." Distinctions break down in Class C, "a rather miscellaneous collection," which is somewhat in disarray because of the incompleteness of Greg's work (1:191). In Class C Greg has grouped manuscripts of which he has little knowledge (like *The Wasp*) with others that interested him, even though sometimes they were outside the announced limits of his study (like the fragmentary manuscript of George Wilde's *The Lovers' Hospital* in the Lambarde Collection, a collection whose contents Greg was at pains to list even though Wilde's play is academic drama, acted at St. John's College, Oxford, and even though Greg excluded another manuscript of the same play, entitled *Love's Hospital*, located in the British Library).[7] In view of the disorganization of Class C, one suspects that Greg's chief purpose in classifying the manuscripts this threefold way was to isolate the ones that have signs in them of their theatrical provenance.

Greg's classification of manuscripts enabled him to intervene decisively in the academic debates of his day. By establishing a class of "authoritative playhouse manuscripts," no matter how diverse the members of this class might be, Greg could stigmatize as ahistorical and drive from the field the characterization of such texts offered by his longtime academic rival Sir Sidney Lee, who, in 1902, had claimed that the distinctive marks of these copies were complete division into acts and scenes, stage directions, scene locations, and lists of the roles in the plays (Lee, quoted in Greg, "Bibliographical History," 274). Greg's identification of particular manuscripts as "prompt copies" enabled him to deploy empirical investigation of them against Lee's speculations. It was Greg's ambition to ground his Class A of "promptbooks" securely in history by demonstrating that in the theatrical industry of the broadly defined "Elizabethan" period, such manuscripts as those in Class A were already recognized as a distinct class with their own distinctive name. They were, said Greg, called *Books*, as in, for example, "The Book of Iohn A kent & Iohn a Cumber" or "The Booke of Sir Thomas Moore," the actual labels inscribed on the vellum wrappers in which these two Class A manuscripts have been preserved. Greg said that *Book* was the contemporary signifier for the signified referred to in modern theatrical parlance as the *promptbook*.

Unfortunately for Greg's position, it, like Lee's, is ahistorical, triply ahistorical. First, the term *Book* was not, as Greg argued, reserved for a manuscript of exclusively playhouse provenance. When Philip Henslowe, the theater owner, recorded in his *Diary* that he had "lent vnto the companey the 30 of marche 1598 30 *shillings* in full payment for the boocke of goodwine & his iij sonnes," Henslowe quite evidently was using the formula "the book of" to refer to a manuscript that the company was just then buying, a manuscript that had as yet no playhouse provenance (Henslowe, *Diary*, ed. Foakes and Rickert, 88). It cannot be assumed, then, that Greg's distinction between his Class A (promptbooks) and his Class B (extra-theatrical manuscripts) is a historically grounded distinction, since members of the "Elizabethan" theatrical community could use the same formula (*the Book of* _____ ) for manuscripts in each class.[8]

Second, Greg purported to identify the *Book* of "Elizabethan" times with the term *promptbook* first used in 1809 to refer to "copy of a play prepared for the prompter's use, containing the text as it is to be spoken, and directions for its performance" (*OED*); by using this anachronistic term, he implied that there are certain universal or transhistorical features of playhouse manuscripts that can be recovered through purely rational inquiry, without respect for the differing historical conditions of "Elizabethan" and nineteenth-century playhouses.

Finally, in a third repudiation of history, Greg idealized the ahistorical term *promptbook* by scrutinizing manuscripts that he had already classified as "promptbooks" to determine if they met certain purely aesthetic criteria that he assumed must always have characterized "promptbooks." He was concerned about the "extreme untidiness" of the *Launching of the Mary* "promptbook" and dismissed it as "exceptional"; he did the same with the famous *Booke of Sir Thomas Moore* when he wrote that it "would have needed a good deal of tidying up before it could have served as a prompt copy" (1:200). Greg is driven by these aesthetic criteria to postulate the following as the norm for the *Book* or "promptbook": a unique manuscript inscribed in a single hand and a single ink to include not only the playtext but also the theatrical annotations. But this norm is an ideal one: Greg observes that no such "promptbooks" have come down to us.[9]

Thus Greg empties out the category "promptbook" by elevating it to ideal status. Anyone with experience of nineteenth- or twentieth-century promptbooks knows that Greg's stipulations of tidiness are merely ideal and were rarely, if ever, in force for theatrical manuscripts, even in these later periods. By this stage in his analysis, Greg not only had transcended history altogether but also had flatly contradicted the identification of the term *Book* as uniquely referential in the "Elizabethan" period to "promptbook": the *Booke of Sir Thomas Moore* cannot both be labeled a "*Booke*" by theatrical personnel of its own time and, at the same time, not be acceptable as a *Book* according to the standards, as Greg constructs them, of those very personnel.

### Greg Versus Pollard

The explanation for Greg's self-contradiction, like the explanation of his construction of Class A ("promptbooks"), is historical and located in the academic debate of his era. It lies in his need to set his words not only against those of his old enemy Sir Sidney Lee but also against those of his friends and sometimes collaborators Alfred W. Pollard and J. Dover Wilson in a polite academic contest to assert his own narrative of the production and reproduction of drama in manuscript against their narrative. Pollard and Wilson's narrative elevated such "Books" as *Moore* and *The Launching of the Mary* to the status of master examples of the kind of manuscripts from which plays may well have been put into print; thus it was very much in Greg's interest to deny such status to these "Books." Hence his concentration on their putative untidiness, which, for him, disqualifies them from even being "Books" ("promptbooks" in his sense), let alone normative examples of "Books." The development of this contest between Pollard and Wilson, on the one hand, and Greg, on the other, is worth examining because the hypothetical dramatic manuscripts generated by Greg in the course of this debate ("promptbooks" and "fowle papers") have exercised greater influence over subsequent textual criticism and editing than have any of the actual manuscripts that Greg attempted to classify.

Greg began writing about the transmission of early modern English drama from manuscript to print before Pollard did. At that time neither Greg nor any of his contemporaries entertained much hope of being able to identify the kind of manuscript that might lie behind an early printed text of a play—even of the most prized of plays, the Shakespeare plays. In 1902 Greg declared simply, "We lack evidence sufficient to decide the question" ("Bibliographical History," 283).

Pollard, in his initial speculations about what kind of manuscripts lay behind Shakespeare's printed plays, worked closely with Greg. In 1909, Pollard purported to have found a means to trace the manuscripts behind Shakespeare's plays to origins either inside or outside the playhouse.[10] Pollard divided the earliest printed quartos of Shakespeare into two classes, the "good" (deriving from playhouse manuscripts) and the "bad" (not deriving from playhouse manuscripts) depending on whether they had been properly "entered" in the Stationers' Register (the document in which the stationers [or publishers] recorded ownership of copyright for books). He tried to show that there were procedural irregularities in the entrance for each of the so-called "bad" quartos, but that the "good" quartos had, at least for the most part, been correctly entered. He inferred that the Stationers denied copyright in plays to the publishers of the "bad" quartos because these publishers did not obtain their manuscripts from the actors' companies whose property, Pollard said, the plays were; in contrast, for Pollard, the "good" quartos, properly entered in the Register, offered "good" texts based on manuscripts that publishers had legitimately purchased from the acting company that owned them.

Pollard's attempt to construct his distinction between "good" and "bad" quartos upon Stationers' Register entries has been repeatedly invalidated—some "bad" quartos are properly entered, some not; some "good" ones are, some not (Chambers, *Elizabethan*, 3:186–87; F. P. Wilson, *Shakespeare*, 22–24). Pollard's implicit vesting of the acting companies with copyright in plays has also been invalidated; copyright, in this period, belonged to publishers, who were under no obligation to secure any mythical "right" to print a play from the acting company that owned it (Kirschbaum). Paradoxically, Pollard's conclusion that manuscript copy for the "good" quartos must have come directly to the printers from the actors has been widely accepted, despite the scholarship just cited that reduced this conclusion to no more than a bald assertion.[11]

Pollard and Greg came to differ from each other in the way that they exploited this credulity (which they called "optimism" [Pollard, *Shakespeare*, v–vj]) about play manuscripts' necessarily going directly from playhouse to printing house. In

Pollard's view, it would have run counter to the interests of a company ever to duplicate an authorial manuscript through scribal transcription—since the company would then have to protect two manuscripts rather than just one. Instead, said Pollard, the company would send the authorial copy to the censor; after it was returned the company book-keeper(s) would annotate it as the "promptbook." Then when the company had no more use for the play as a stage vehicle, the authorial copy as censored and as annotated by the book-keeper(s)—there was, in this narrative, no other copy—would be sold to a publisher who would have it put into print.

Pollard supported his narrative with reference to a few actual manuscripts in the British Library, each inscribed in the hand of a known dramatist, each annotated by a book-keeper with directions for performance, some also bearing the marks and/or license of the Master of the Revels. These manuscripts are *Believe as You List, The Launching of the Mary, Moore, John a Kent,* and *The Captives* (*Shakespeare's Fight,* 55–83). The kind of manuscript postulated in this narrative acquired the name "continuous copy." This narrative held sway throughout the twenties as J. Dover Wilson elaborated it in his editions of the Shakespeare comedies, interpreting every irregularity in their printed versions as an opportunity to imagine some rehandling of the "continuous copy" in which each play was thought to have been uniquely preserved prior to its printing.

To displace this narrative from its dominant position, Greg was concerned to deny any representative status to the playhouse manuscripts cited by Pollard. Thus Greg devoted space in *Dramatic Documents* to dismissing them as special cases. He pointed out that *Believe as You List* is a rewrite by Massinger of a play originally about Spanish and Portuguese politics, to which the Master of the Revels had objected. Greg also argued that *Moore* is a heavily revised play that may never have been acted, that *The Launching of the Mary* is a manuscript that the censor had licensed but for which he had demanded fairer copy, and that *The Captives* is written in an allegedly illegible hand, with the "prompt" notes intermixed with the dialogue, and bearing no license (198–203). Greg was no doubt justified in denying normative status to these manuscripts, but his justification lies in the disuniformity evident in the extant playhouse manuscripts, which defy the imposition of any norm.

Yet Greg was interested not in acknowledging such disuniformity but in enforcing his own normative narrative upon the various materials. In doing so, he privileged a single manuscript, *Bonduca*—or, to be more precise, he privileged his interpretation of the circumstances surrounding the inscription of *Bonduca*. Transcribed for a patron by Edward Knight, who had been a member of the King's Men since at least 1624 (Bentley, *Jacobean,* 1:15), the undated manuscript of *Bonduca* by John Fletcher, major dramatist for the King's Men until his death in 1625, is, to my knowledge, unique among early modern dramatic manuscripts for containing within it some account of its origin. Arriving at the beginning of act 5 in his transcription, Knight briefly summarized the contents of two scenes and part of a third that he said were "wanting." He then went on to explain "the occasion why these are wanting here. the booke where by it [i.e., *Bonduca*] was first Acted from is lost: and this hath beene transcrib'd from the fowle papers of the Authors wch were found" (90).

It is upon this note that, beginning in 1926 (five years before he published his survey of dramatic manuscripts in *Dramatic Documents*), Greg erected what has come to be the master narrative of the manuscript transmission of playtexts.[12] According to Greg, Knight recovered Fletcher's "fowle papers," minus two foolscap sheets containing the missing scenes, from the company's "archives" of plays, since that is where Knight would have searched for "the booke where by it was first Acted" ("Prompt Copies," 156). From this reading of Knight's note, Greg concluded that it was the general practice of acting companies to demand from dramatists not only fair copies of plays but also the "fowle papers" from which these were transcribed; in this way, according to Greg, companies could guard against the double sale of plays by playwrights and would have in reserve some copy of a play in case "the booke where by it was first Acted" should go missing, as apparently happened in the case of *Bonduca* and a couple of other plays (*The Winter's Tale, The Honest Man's Fortune*).[13] Extending this narrative, Greg also imagined that an acting company would be most ready to part with these "fowle papers," rather than any fair copy, if and when the company chose to put a play in print (*Editorial Problem*, 102 ff.). If the company behaved in this manner, of course, modern readers would have the singular advantage of being able to read the printed plays of Shakespeare and his contemporaries in the confidence that all that stood between the reader and the dramatist's "fowle papers" was a mere printer. Greg defined "fowle papers" as a "draft" containing "the text substantially in the form the author intended it to assume though in a shape too untidy to be used by the prompter" (*Editorial Problem*, 31), or "the text of a play substantially in its final form" (32). Greg then went on to list characteristics likely to distinguish printed plays based on such "fowle papers" from those printed from his other major category of dramatic manuscripts, namely, "promptbooks" (*First Folio*, 110–14).[14]

### Foul Papers

Despite the highly rational integrity of Greg's narrative, it in fact exceeds the documentary evidence upon which it purports to be based. First of all, as E. K. Chambers told Greg (*Dramatic Documents*, 195–96 n), Knight says nothing about where he found Fletcher's "fowle papers," and so Knight's jotting in *Bonduca* offers no support for Greg's speculation about a general practice of playwrights' depositing their "fowle papers" in acting companies' "archives." Greg also assumes that Fletcher's foul papers must originally have contained the whole of the play known to Knight, even though Knight invokes the explanation that he is copying "fowle papers" solely for the purpose of accounting for a lacuna in his transcript. That is, while Knight's usage of authorial "fowle papers" associates the term with a text that is incomplete in relation to the text of a theatrical manuscript, Greg's appropriation of the term associates it with the "final form" of the play as "the author intended it." For Greg to grant that a play might not achieve its final form until it had passed beyond the author and into the playhouse, as Knight's words may suggest was the case with *Bonduca*, would be to deny the author's individual creation of that form.

As a counterbalance to Greg's assumption, notice needs to be taken of the documentary evidence that indicates how the composition of plays could and did issue from collaboration between playwright and players, rather than from playwright alone. (In cases of such collaboration—which, for all we know, may have been as frequent as the single authorship postulated by Greg—there never would have been a manuscript that conformed to Greg's normative conception of "fowle papers," that is, a manuscript wholly the author's work—as author, not copyist of his/her individual creation—and nothing but the author's work.) On April 4, 1601, Samuel Rowley, writing as a player, a member of the Admiral's Men, told theater-owner Henslowe that "he had harde fyue shetes of a playe of the Conqueste of the Jndes [by Day, Haughton, and Smith] & J dow not doute but Jt wyll be a vere good playe[.] tharefore J praye ye deliuer them [Day, Haughton, and Smith] fortye shyllinges Jn earneste of Jt" (Greg, *Henslowe Papers*, 56). It would seem from this note that sometimes the linear model of playtext transmission from author to players that Greg assumes in his construction of "fowle papers" ought to give way to one in which playwrights consulted with players in the course of composition. Nashe's account of the company's role in the composition of *The Isle of Dogs* assigns the players an even larger role in the process: "I hauing begun the induction and first act of [*The Isle of Dogs*], the other foure acts . . . by the players were supplied" (McKerrow, *Nashe*, 3:154). The Privy Council supports Nashe's version in that it records having imprisoned a member of the acting company who was "not only an actor but a maker of parte of the same plaie" (5:31 n).

Without regard for such documents as these, and without having developed in *Dramatic Documents* any class of manuscripts entitled "fowle papers," Greg nevertheless sought in his later writing to ground his notion of "fowle papers" in extant manuscripts. In both his *Editorial Problem in Shakespeare* (1942) and *The Shakespeare First Folio* (1955), he cited what he alleged to be three extant examples of "fowle papers." One is a complete manuscript, Heywood's *The Captives*, that Greg had classed as a "promptbook" in *Dramatic Documents*—that is, as the opposite of "fowle papers" in his binary system—even though, as I have noted, he had doubts that *The Captives* was legible enough to be a "promptbook." Greg's second example of "fowle papers" is "most" of the fragmentary additions to the *Moore* manuscript, another example of what Greg, again with some reservations, had classified as a "promptbook." The third example is a single partial leaf at the Folger Library that provides what appears to be a variant text of a few lines printed in *The Massacre at Paris*.[15] Examination of these manuscripts indicates the irreducible recalcitrance of extant manuscripts to the ideal category "fowle papers."

Commenting on *The Captives* in *Dramatic Documents*, Greg stated his belief that the manuscript was Heywood's first inscription or "fowle papers": "I see no reason to believe that behind the extant manuscript there need be fouler papers" (1:203). At the same time, however, he had to acknowledge that it bore "no obvious or at least indubitable evidence to mark it as foul papers ... no more 'blotting', interlining, or alteration than many which we naturally accept as fair copies" (1:202–3). The fact that *The Captives* manuscript is also annotated copiously in another hand with production notes forced Greg to classify it as "promptbook." This single manuscript threatens to swallow up in itself all of Greg's distinctions and categories.

To force it out of the category of "promptbooks" and into that of "fowle papers," Greg concentrated in *The Editorial Problem in Shakespeare* and *The Shakespeare First Folio* on the illegibility of the hands in which it was inscribed (*Editorial*, 30), a "vile hand that must, one would suppose, have made it useless to the prompter" (*First Folio*, 109).[16] Yet, one of Greg's successors in the office of general editor of the Malone Society, Richard Proudfoot, has written that "Heywood's hand is perfectly legible, with practice" (Hill, 98). In another reevaluation of Greg's findings, E. A. J. Honigmann has compared Heywood's inscription of *The Captives* to Heywood's transcription of *The Escapes of Jupiter*, which cannot be "fowle papers" in Greg's sense of a draft because it is almost entirely a reproduction, with some revisions, of scenes from Heywood's earlier plays *The Golden Age* and *The Silver Age*.[17] The likenesses in transcriptional errors between *Escapes* and *The Captives* lead Honigmann to conclude that the latter, like the former, is largely, if not entirely, a "fair copy" (200–206). The history of reception of *The Captives* raises a serious question whether an extant manuscript can be subjected to the rigors of Greg's purely rational (rather than empirical) categories.

The reception history of the *Moore* manuscript, which contains in some of its "Additions" Greg's second alleged extant example of "fowle papers," is similarly vexed with respect to his idealized classifications of authorial drafts and playhouse transcriptions. The questions of just which handwriting in *Moore* is that of an author freely composing his "foul papers," which is that of a known author transcribing his or another's composition, and which is that of a mere theater scribe and/or player devoid (in the implicit literary class system) of creative talent are all issues that have not yielded consistent answers to those scholars who have taken them up. In his 1911 Malone Society edition of the play, Greg divided the manuscript into two major parts; the first part he called—misleadingly, as will shortly become evident—"the original." It is a discontinuous text of some thirteen leaves, all inscribed in a single hand, and annotated by the censor, Sir Edmond Tilney, as well as by two, or possibly three, of the hands that Greg identified in the second major part of the text, the Additions. These six Additions consist of eight more leaves, which are either interleaved in the "the original" or pasted onto leaves of "the original." The Additions are inscribed in five different hands, two or three of which appear nowhere in "the original." The hand of the censor, Tilney, is nowhere to be found in the Additions.

At first, in 1911, Greg confessed to the difficulty of determining whether the thirteen surviving leaves of "the original" were inscribed in the hand of their author or in that of a scribe; on the basis of one particular error in the transcription ("fashis" for "fashiõ"), he opted for an anonymous scribe that he designated "Hand S" (for scribe) (xvi). The next year, 1912, Farmer published his facsimile of the manuscript *John a Kent*, which is inscribed in the same hand as *Moore* and which is subscribed with the known dramatist Anthony Munday's name. In 1913, Greg reversed himself and declared that he had been misled in declaring Hand S to be that of a scribe.

History makes it far from clear whether Greg was right in 1911 or in 1913. After all, Munday was a man of many parts, an "actor . . . poet, spy, journalist, recusant-hunter, pamphleteer, playwright, pageant-poet, antiquary, translator, citizen, and draper" (Byrne, 225). The Munday of the *Moore* manuscript may then have been an author of the play, as Greg said in 1913; or, closer to what Greg thought in 1911, Munday may have been a member of an acting company copying a play, since Munday is reported to have "ruffle[d] upon the stage" (Chambers, *Elizabethan*, 3:444).

Comparable instability has beset identification of the function of the hands that inscribed the Additions, some of these hands also being found annotating the "original" (Hands A–E in Greg's designation). Take Hand B, for example, the handwriting that Greg thought in 1911 to be that of the principal author of both "the original" text of *Moore* and the majority of the Additions. His method was elimination: Hands S and C he regarded as scribal; Hands A, D, and E he regarded, on undisclosed stylistic grounds, as the authors of only what they inscribed. In favor of Hand B's authorship of the play were two factors: (1) his handwriting, Greg thought, was too rough and illegible to be a copyist's, and (2) Greg's copyist, Hand C, is to be found transcribing a few lines first written by Hand B. Then, in 1923, Greg suggested that Hand B bore a "considerable resemblance" to Heywood's (Pollard, *Shakespeare's Hand* 44 n), an identification supported by Tannenbaum in 1927. Greg's suggestion that Hand B is Heywood's, an identification that would endorse the view that lines in Hand B represent free composition ("fowle papers"), has been favored by several scholars, including Harold Jenkins (*More*, ed. Greg 1961, xxxvi) — but it was not endorsed by Greg himself, who refused to grant that it was "at all adequately established" ("Reviews," 210), or by J. M. Nosworthy, who fiercely resisted it on palaeographical, orthographical, and stylistic grounds ("Hand B," 50). Recently Eric Rasmussen has endorsed and modified Nosworthy's hypothesis that Hand B is, instead, an actor's; for Rasmussen, Hand B, once thought by Greg to be that of the play's principal author, may instead be that of a book-keeper copying lines improvised by an actor. (For a fuller account of the indeterminacy of function of the various Hands in *Moore*, see Werstine, "Close Contrivers.")

Greg's choice of the *Massacre at Paris* fragment located at the Folger Library as his third and last extant example of "fowle papers" seems desperate. The provenance of this irregularly shaped partial leaf is unknown, a circumstance perilous for the erection of any scholarly conjecture, especially in light of the existence for well over a century now of a increasingly lucrative market for forgeries of documents alleged to have been associated with Shakespeare and his contemporaries. The leaf bears no sign of free composition: not so much as a single letter, let alone a word, has been erased (that is, crossed out), and so there has been absolutely no revision either *currente calamo* or afterward. There are also none of the other stigmata that, according to Greg, mark "fowle papers." Instead, for example, of a variety of designations for the same character-role, such as are supposed to appear in "fowle papers," the speech prefixes are exactly the same as the names in the stage directions and are completely uniform. The handwriting, unlike that of *The Captives* or of Hand B in *Moore*, is immediately legible. This handwriting bears no resemblance to that of the single signature ever attributed to Marlowe; yet if the fragment is to be "fowle papers" the handwriting would have to be that of the play's "author" (Alton). Such is the "optimism" inspired by Pollard and Greg that many, though not all, twentieth-century scholars and editors have accepted the fragment as authentic (Adams; Nosworthy, "Marlowe"; Oliver, lviii-lix; Marlowe, *Complete Works*, ed. F. Bowers, 1:358).

## On the Other Side of Rationalist Excess

Greg's influence has produced some crippling and far-reaching contradictions in the editing of early modern drama in the latter half of the twentieth century and in the continuing study of early modern dramatic manuscripts. By providing what purports to be a general theory of the production ("fowle papers") and reproduction ("promptbooks") of early modern drama and by conveniently listing the allegedly distinctive features of each of his ideal categories, Greg empowered generations of editors to carry out their task without ever having to engage the fierce particularities of the extant manuscripts. Thus generations of editors have been able simply to reproduce Greg's judgments and arguments from *The Editorial Problem in Shakespeare* (1942) and *The Shakespeare First Folio* (1955) with greater or lesser acknowledgment of indebtedness to these works (Long, "Stage-Directions"). Even the recent Oxford edition, for all its pretensions to having subverted the editorial tradition, is uncritically enthralled by Greg's general theory (Wells and Taylor, passim, but esp. 12–14, 145–47). When, however, an editor sets aside this theory and examines the extant manuscripts themselves instead of relying on Greg, the editor is confronted with the radical indeterminacy of identifying what kind of manuscript may lie behind a printed dramatic text. Shakespeare's *Comedy of Errors*, for example, is supposed to be the paradigmatic case of a text printed from author's "fowle papers"; it was made to serve that role when Greg's friend R. B. McKerrow made his famous—but purely rational, rather than empirical—"Suggestion Regarding Shakespeare's Manuscripts" (Werstine, "McKerrow's 'Suggestion' "). But when one brings to the study of the *Errors* text both the discoveries of analytical bibliography about the First Folio, in which it was printed for the first time, and consultation of actual dramatic manuscripts, then the identification of the manuscript behind *Errors* becomes irreducibly problematic, rather than as simple as McKerrow's rational construction claimed to make it (Werstine, "'Foul Papers,'").[18]

In *On Editing Shakespeare* (1955), Fredson Bowers issued an important challenge to the hegemony of Greg's general theory that had narrowed the range of possible manuscript copy for printed texts to a choice between "fowle papers" and "promptbooks." Bowers listed thirteen possibilities in all and promised that research already in progress might well turn up more (11 ff.). Bowers's possibilities, like Greg's, were developed rationally, rather than empirically, although there is an empirical basis for some of them among the extant manuscripts. Reviewing Bowers's book, Greg objected to this multiplication of hypothetical printer's copy and invoked Occam's razor in defense of his restriction of the possibilities to "fowle papers" and "promptbooks." However, Occam's razor, it is to be remembered, gives preference to the theory that provides the most economical explanation for *all* the observable phenomena. Since Greg's general theory fails to cope in any meaningful way with the extant dramatic manuscripts in their variety and disuniformity, it cannot be preferred, according to Occam's razor, to any theory that multiplies hypotheses toward the objective of including such variety.

Early modern dramatic manuscript study is an exciting field that is expanding in several directions, with genuinely novel discovery—including discovery of new dramatic manuscripts—remaining an always present possibility. The 1992 offering of the Malone Society, for example, was the hitherto unknown manuscript play *Tom a Lincoln*. T. H. Howard-Hill has recently drawn attention to a half-dozen previously undiscussed dramatic manuscripts located at the Warwickshire Record Office and in Arbury Hall, Nuneaton (constituting the canon of the amateur playwright John Newdigate III) ("Another"). The most exciting of recent discoveries may be that of the scholar-adventurer William P. Williams, who in 1977 unearthed the Castle Ashby manuscripts of plays by the Interregnum dramatist Cosmo Manuche. A partial list of these had been inscribed by Thomas Percy, the compiler of *Reliques of Ancient English Poetry*, in his interleaved copy of Gerard Langbaine's *Account of the English Dramatic Poets* (1691). Percy mentioned nine titles; Williams found thirteen, three in multiple drafts.

But new discoveries are still all too likely to get swallowed up in Greg's master narrative, especially because finding a convincing example of "fowle papers" seems to have become a kind of Grail quest (Werstine, " 'Foul Papers,' " 67–75). For example, in discussing the Newdigate manuscripts in 1980, Howard-Hill gave pride of place to just one of them—the manuscript play that he titled *Glausamond*. He nominated this manuscript as the earliest extant example of "fowle papers." His claim can be justified within the parlance of the "Elizabethan" period, where the term *foul papers* refers to any manuscript of which there is also a "fair copy," and there is in Arbury Hall, Howard-Hill reports, a "fair copy" of the play in the author's hand. Yet Howard-Hill's "foul papers" manuscript play *Glausamond* is not "fowle papers" in Greg's sense of the term, according to which *fowle papers* are a "draft" containing the "text substantially in the form the author intended it to assume." As Howard-Hill himself indicates, the play was "extensively rewritten" and "substantially revised and enlarged" in the author's "fair copy" before it was transcribed in the British Library scribal manuscript, its third and last version, the one titled *Ghismonda* by its editor, H. G. Wright ("Boccaccio," 24, 28).

And so the quest for Greg's "fowle papers" was still afoot on Good Friday 1985, the date of the discovery of the fragmentary Melbourne manuscript (consisting of just four pages) by Felix Pryor. Writing in 1988, Hammond and Delvecchio argued that these four pages are the only example of "fowle papers" that survive from the early modern period. They write that "everything that has been said about 'foul papers' has been conjectural. . . . [T]here has been no known example of foul papers" (3). Yet few of the alleged properties of "fowle papers" as Greg listed them are to be found in the Melbourne fragment in view of its tidiness and the regularity of its designation of the play's characters; its discovery leaves Greg's "fowle papers" the purely ideal formulation it has always been. Instead of "fowle papers," the Melbourne fragment may well be "a rejected early version" of a scene, to quote the remarks of I. A. Shapiro, whose view is no more speculative than Hammond and Delvecchio's (736).

In spite of this ongoing quest for "fowle papers," there are also indications that the influence of Greg's general theory is beginning to wane. Scott McMillin's study of the *Moore* manuscript challenges Greg's long-standing norms of immediate legibility and tidiness for theatrical manuscripts. And Harold Love can now write,

> Shakespeare may well have put work into circulation through the agency of scribes. . . . The sale or presentation to a wealthy patron of a manuscript of a favourite play would have offered an opportunity for additional income, and is intrinsically no less improbable than other explanations which have been brought forward for the genesis of the manuscripts which served as copy for the better quarto editions. (67–68)

In suggesting that early printed texts of Shakespeare's plays may be based on scribal transcripts that found their way to stationers through other agents besides the companies that performed the plays, Love is merely speculating. Yet in the course of his speculation, he correctly implies that what generations of scholars have accepted from Greg as a general theory is also only speculation.

Once Greg's theory is widely recognized as speculation, perhaps the study of manuscript drama can free itself from the restriction of his narrowly conceived and irrelevant categories. Each dramatic manuscript can then be appreciated in its uniqueness as the matrix of a variety of possible scholarly narratives about the inscription of early English drama. This present essay, written on the basis of investigation of a great number of the extant manuscripts, offers not a new taxonomy of them but an a posteriori conclusion that respects their variety and disuniformity and offers this conclusion in place of Greg's a priori theory of the categories "fowle papers" and "promptbooks," into which the manuscripts, he thought, *should* fit.

## NOTES

1. General editors of the Malone Society who have succeeded Greg include F. P. Wilson, Arthur Brown, G. R. Proudfoot, John Pitcher, and N. W. Bawcutt.
2. Greg actually included texts of only three actors' parts in *Dramatic Documents*, two medieval examples from the fourteenth and fifteenth centuries and Edward Alleyn's part of Orlando in *Orlando Furioso*; he did make reference to a fourth, the then newly discovered part from *Processus Satanae* (c. 1570–1580), which he arranged to have appear in the Malone Society's *Collections* II, part 3 (237–50). Since Greg's time a small book in which four other players' parts are preserved has been donated to Harvard (MS Thr 10.1). "The parts included . . . are Polypragmaticus in Burton's *Philosophaster*, Antonius in an unidentified Latin play, and Poore in an unidentified English play," as well as "the part of Amurath" from Thomas Goffe's *The Courageous Turk* (O'Malley, 56). A transcription of the part of "Poore" is in the Malone Society's *Collections* XV (111–69). It is fully described in two articles by Carnegie.
3. For more recent discussion of these plots, see Bradley and King.
4. For discussion of the form of dramatic manuscripts that antedate Greg's cutoff point, see Howard-Hill, "Evolution."

    The academic plays (and, with them, all Latin and Greek plays) excluded by Greg constitute a wide range of texts: those whose performance can be tied not only to Oxford and Cambridge but also to the Inns of Court, the London boys' schools (like Westminster), and English schools abroad, like St. Omers and Douay. For texts of much of the Latin drama, see the series Renaissance Latin Drama in England. For editions of the other kinds, see Harbage's *Annals* and its revisions.

    Although Greg excluded masques and entertainments from his 1931 work, he had already published *A List of Masques, Pageants, &c.* for the Bibliographical Society as its 1901 number in 1902. An important accidental consequence of Greg's exclusion of closet drama was the exclusion of the few women dramatists, for whom there was no place on the public stage, but who were nonetheless writing drama to be read. Witness the extant manuscripts of Lady Jane Lumley's *Iphigenia in Aulis*, a translation of Euripides, a transcription of which had been published by the Malone Society in 1910, or the manuscript of Queen Elizabeth's translation of *Hercules Oetaneus*, or Lady Mary Wroth's manuscripts of *Love's Victory*.

    Greg also paid no attention to manuscripts of such extra-literary phenomena as jigs and tilts, and he listed almost none of the many extant fragmentary manuscripts, none of the printed quartos containing manuscript theatrical annotation, none of the play manuscripts based on printed texts. (An exception to Greg's exclusion of fragments is his listing of Robert Wild's *The Benefice*.) There are recorded three quartos with manuscript theatrical annotation: the British Library copy of Edward Sharpham's *The Fleire*

(1607), discussed by Leech and Peter; the Folger copy of *The Two Merry Milke-Maids or, The Best Words Wear the Garland* (1620), discussed by Leslie Thomson; and the University of Chicago's copy of Lodge and Greene's *Looking Glasse for london and England* (lacking the title page), discussed by Baskervill. (My thanks to Leslie Thomson for her contributions to this note.) Perhaps the most famous dramatic manuscript based on printed copy is the Dering manuscript of the two parts of Shakespeare's *Henry IV*, but there are many others, contrary to the widespread impression that manuscript necessarily precedes print. (For extensive discussion of this issue, see Barbara Mowat's essay in this volume.)

5. Bald's study of the manuscripts has been superseded by Zimmerman's, his edition by Howard-Hill's.

6. Harbage's *Annals* have been twice revised, once by S. Schoenbaum in 1964 and again by Sylvia Stoler Wagonheim in 1989. The second revision needs to be used with great care; see Anne Lancashire's review of it in *Shakespeare Quarterly*.

7. Greg also rather contradictorily excludes from any of his classes the manuscript of Wilde's *The Converted Robber*, which was performed under the same auspices as *The Lovers' Hospital*. Other contradictions also obtrude in Class C, like the appearance in it of *The Royal Slave*, another academic play. It seems that Class C is scarcely a "class" at all, but merely a supplement to Classes A and B.

8. It is usually assumed that the essential and distinctive mark of the "Book" or, for Greg and his followers, the "prompt book" is that it contains the censor's license, which alone (it is said), under the law, could authorize performance. The assumption that this licensed copy was customarily the one that was marked up to regulate performance has enabled scholars to limit the number of possible manuscripts of a play in a way that flies in the face of evidence from the extant dramatic manuscripts. In this regard, as in many others, the extant manuscripts indicate that theatrical practice in its variability and disuniformity can be reduced to no rational norm. Sometimes the licensed manuscript was marked up for performance; sometimes another manuscript was—as is witnessed by the manuscripts in Greg's Class A; only five of the fifteen Class A manuscripts contain licenses on their final pages. (While in some cases the ends of manuscripts may be defective, such is not *always* the case. The final pages of both *Edmond Ironside* and *The Two Noble Ladies*—to cite just two random examples of plays in the British Library's MS Egerton 1994 marked up for the theater—are intact but lack licenses.)

9. As Greg could not have known, two of the manuscripts of *Hengist* (one in the Lambarde Collection at the Folger) do contain such typical theatrical annotations as the addition of what are apparently actors' names squeezed into the right margin in the same hand and ink as the playtext. In other respects, however, there are too many errors in both of these manuscripts for them to qualify as normative "prompt books" for Greg, or for R. C. Bald, who denies them any such status (Middleton, *Hengist*, ed. Bald, xxix). To explain the variation between the manuscript and printed texts of *Hengist*, Bald must nevertheless postulate the existence of two "prompt books" of the play, in each of which the play must have been cut down in a different way for production (xxxiv), a duplication not allowed in Greg's normative account of the production of "prompt books."

10. In his preface, Pollard thanked Greg for "ungrudging permission to use his work as my own" (*Shakespeare*, vi).

11. The foregoing two paragraphs appear with slight differences in wording in my "Shakespeare" chapter in *Scholarly Editing* (201–2).

12. The other document upon which Greg depended in trying to establish his general theory that playwrights deposited their own copies of their plays in the acting company's archives is a note from Robert Daborne to Henslowe (Greg, *Henslowe Papers*, 78). As Bowers wrote of this note, "There is no evidence whatever here or elsewhere in Henslowe that an author ever submitted for payment anything but a fair copy, or that the company required a dramatist to turn over his original foul sheets along with the fair copy" (*On Editing*, 15).

13. On August 19, 1623, Sir Henry Herbert, then Master of the Revels, recorded in his *Office Book*, according to Malone's transcription of it: "For the king's players. An olde playe called Winter's Tale, formerly allowed of by Sir George Bucke, and likewyse by mee on Mr Hemmings his worde that there was nothing profane added or reformed, thogh the allowed booke was missinge" (Chambers, *William Shakespeare*, 2:347). On the last leaf of the *Honest Man's Fortune* manuscript appear these words in the hand of Herbert: "This play. being an olde One and the Originall Lost was reallowd by mee."

14. For a critique of Greg's view that there are features distinctive to "fowle papers," see Long, "Stage-Directions," and Werstine, "McKerrow's 'Suggestion.'" As Long points out, theatrical annotators left intact in manuscripts those features that, according to Greg, are distinctive to "fowle papers"; thus those features simply cannot be regarded as unique to "fowle papers." In "McKerrow's 'Suggestion,'" I call attention to the single feature most often cited as a characteristic mark of "fowle papers"—namely, inconsistency in the naming of roles in stage directions and speech prefixes—and show how in an actual extant dramatic manuscript such inconsistency was demonstrably produced through the combined efforts of a censor and a theatrical scribe, with no evident contribution from an "author."

15. In *The Editorial Problem in Shakespeare* (1942), Greg also included as "fowle papers" "carelessly written additions . . . in . . . *The Faithful Friends*, and Shirley's *Court Secret*" (28), but he dropped these examples without comment in *The Shakespeare First Folio* (1955).

16. Greg also assumed that since the play is recorded in Herbert's *Office Book* as having been licensed, and since there is no license at the (undamaged) end of the extant manuscript, there must have been another manuscript that contained both the license and the final theatrical annotations—Greg's ideal norm, the "Book" or "prompt book." As already discussed in note 10 above, there is no reason to presume that license and theatrical annotations need always or even normally have been found in the same manuscript.

17. So anxious are scholars to find examples of Greg's ideal "fowle papers," however, that the Malone Society editor of *Escapes* terms the manuscript "technically . . . author's 'foul papers' " (ix).

18. In their reply to Werstine's " 'Foul Papers' or 'Prompt books' " in their *Textual Companion*, Wells and Taylor misreport the article's thesis. They say that the article sets out to prove that the copy for Folio *Errors* can be determined, and that it can be determined to be "author's papers . . . used as a playbook" or a theatrical manuscript (266).

# Bibliography

Achtert, Walter S., and Joseph Gibaldi. *The MLA Style Manual*. New York: Modern Language Association, 1985.

Adams, Barry B., ed. *John Bale's King Johan*. San Marino, Calif.: Huntington Library, 1969.

Adams, Henry Hitch. *English Domestic or Homiletic Tragedy, 1575 to 1642*. New York: Columbia University Press, 1943.

Adams, Joseph Quincy. "The *Massacre at Paris* Leaf." *The Library*, 4th ser., 14 (1934): 447–69.

——, ed. *The Dramatic Records of Sir Henry Herbert, Master of the Revels, 1623–1673*. New Haven: Yale University Press, 1917.

Adams, Robert P. "Critical Myths and Chapman's Original *Bussy D'Ambois*." *Renaissance Drama* 9 (1966): 141–62.

Adelman, Janet. *Suffocating Mothers: Fantasies of Maternal Origin in Shakespeare's Plays, "Hamlet" to "The Tempest."* New York: Routledge, 1992.

Adorno, Theodor. *The Culture Industry: Selected Essays on Mass Culture*. Edited by J. M. Bernstein. London: Routledge, 1991.

Aers, David, ed. *Culture and History: 1350–1600: Essays on English Communities, Identities, and Writing*. Detroit: Wayne State University Press, 1992.

Agnew, Jean Christophe. *Worlds Apart: The Market and the Theatre in Anglo-American Thought*. Cambridge: Cambridge University Press, 1986.

Albright, Evelyn May. *Dramatic Publication in England, 1580–1640*. New York: Modern Language Society of America, 1927.

Alexander, Robert, ed. "Records of Early English Drama: Bath." Unpublished transcriptions.

Allen, Michael J. B., and Kenneth Muir, eds. *Shakespeare's Plays in Quarto: A Facsimile Edition of Copies Primarily from the Henry E. Huntington Library*. Berkeley: University of California Press, 1981.

Althusser, Louis, and Etienne Balibar. *Reading Capital*. Translated by Ben Brewster. London: Verso, 1979.

Alton, R. E. "Marlowe Authenticated." *Times Literary Supplement*, April 26, 1974, pp. 446–47.

Amt, Emilie, ed. *Women's Lives in Medieval Europe: A Sourcebook*. New York: Routledge, 1993.

Amussen, Susan. *An Ordered Society: Gender and Class in Early Modern England*. Oxford: Blackwell, 1988.

Anderson, J. J., ed. *Records of Early English Drama: Newcastle Upon Tyne*. Toronto: University of Toronto Press, 1982.

Anglo, Sydney. "The Court Festivals of Henry VII." *Bulletin of the John Rylands Library* 40 (1960–1961): 12–45.

———. "The Evolution of the Tudor Disguising, Pageant and Masque." *Renaissance Drama*, n.s., 1 (1968): 3–44.

———. *Spectacle, Pageantry, and Early Tudor Policy*. Oxford: Oxford University Press, 1969.

———. "William Cornish in a Play, Pageants, Prison, and Politics." *Review of English Studies*, n.s., 10 (1959): 347–60.

Appleby, Joyce Oldham. *Economic Thought and Ideology in Seventeenth-Century England*. Princeton: Princeton University Press, 1978.

Arber, Edward, ed. *A Transcript of the Registers of the Company of Stationers of London; 1554–1640 A.D.* 5 vols. London: n.p., 1875–79; Birmingham: n.p., 1894.

Archer, Ian W. *The Pursuit of Stability: Social Relations in Elizabethan London*. Cambridge: Cambridge University Press, 1991.

Arnold, Janet. *"Lost from her Maiesties back": Items of Clothing and Jewels Lost or Given Away by Queen Elizabeth I Between 1561 and 1585*. London: Costume Society, 1980.

Aubrey, John. *"Brief Lives," Chiefly of Contemporaries, set down by John Aubrey, between the years 1669 and 1696*. Edited by Andrew Clark. 2 vols. Oxford: Clarendon Press, 1898.

Augustine. *Concerning the City of God Against the Pagans*. Translated by Henry Bettenson. London: Penguin, 1984.

Axton, Marie. *The Queen's Two Bodies: Drama and the Elizabethan Succession*. London: Royal Historical Society, 1977.

Axton, Richard. *Three Rastell Plays*. Cambridge: D. S. Brewer, 1979.

Bacon, Francis. *The Essayes or Covnsels, Civill and Morall, of Francis Lo. Vervlam, Viscovnt St. Alban*. London, 1625. Reprint, London: Oxford University Press, 1966.

Baines, Barbara J., ed. *Three Pamphlets on the Jacobean Antifeminist Controversy*. Delmar: Scholars' Facsimiles and Reprints, 1978.

Bakhtin, Mikhail. *Rabelais and His World*. Translated by Helene Iswolsky. Cambridge: MIT Press, 1968.

Bald, R. C. "Arthur Wilson's *The Inconstant Lady*." *The Library*, 4th ser., 18 (1938): 287–313.

———. *Bibliographical Studies in the Beaumont and Fletcher Folio of 1647*. London: Bibliographical Society, 1938 (for 1937).

———. "Sir William Berkeley's *The Lost Lady*." *The Library*, 4th ser., 17 (1937): 395–426.

Baldwin, Thomas Whitfield. *The Organization and Personnel of the Shakespearean Company*. Princeton: Princeton University Press, 1927.

———. *Shakspere's Five-Act Structure: Shakspere's Early Plays on the Background of Renaissance Theories of Five-Act Structure from 1470*. Urbana: University of Illinois Press, 1947.

Baldwyn-Childe, Mrs. "The Building of the Manor-House of Kyre Park, Worcestershire (1588–1618)." *The Antiquary* 21 (1890): 202–5, 261–64; and 22 (1890): 24–26, 50–52.

Bale, John. *The Complete Plays of John Bale*. Edited by Peter Happé. 2 vols. Cambridge: D. S. Brewer, 1986.

Barbaro, Daniele. *M. Vitruvii Pollionis de architectura libri decem*. Venice, 1567. Inigo Jones's annotated copy in the Devonshire Collection at Chatsworth.

Barish, Jonas. *The Antitheatrical Prejudice*. Berkeley: University of California Press, 1981.

Barnes, Barnabe. *The Devil's Charter*. Edited by R. B. McKerrow. Louvain: A. Uystpruyst, 1904.

Barnes, Warner, and O. M. Brack. "Remarks on Eclectic Texts." *Proof* 4 (1974): 31–76.

Barroll, J. Leeds. "Locating the Censor in Stuart England." Paper presented at the annual meeting of the Shakespeare Association of America, 1995.

———. "A New History for Shakespeare and His Time." *Shakespeare Quarterly* 39 (1988): 441–64.

———. *Politics, Plague, and Shakespeare's Theater*. Ithaca: Cornell University Press, 1991.

———. "The Social and Literary Context." In Clifford Leech and T. W. Craik, gen. eds., *The Revels History of Drama in English*, 3:1–94. London: Methuen, 1975.

Bartlett, Henrietta C., and Alfred W. Pollard. *A Census of Shakespeare's Plays in Quarto, 1594–1709*. 2d ed., rev. New Haven: Yale University Press, 1939.

Barton, Anne. *Ben Jonson, Dramatist*. Cambridge: Cambridge University Press, 1984.

———. Introduction to *A Midsummer Night's Dream*. In G. Blakemore Evans, ed., *The Riverside Shakespeare*, 217–21. Boston: Houghton Mifflin, 1974.

Baskerville, Charles Read. "A Prompt Copy of *A Looking Glass for London and England*." *Modern Philology* 30 (1932/33): 29–51.

Battenhouse, Roy. *Marlowe's Tamburlaine*. Nashville: Vanderbilt University Press, 1941.

Bawcutt, N. W. "Craven Ord Transcripts of Sir Henry Herbert's Office-Book in the Folger Shakespeare Library." *English Literary Renaissance* 14 (1984): 83–94.

———. "Evidence and Conjecture in Literary Scholarship: The Case of Sir John Astley Reconsidered." *English Literary Renaissance* 22 (1992): 333–46.

———. "New Revels Documents of Sir George Buc and Sir Henry Herbert, 1619–1662." *Review of English Studies*, n.s., 35 (1984): 316–31.

Beadle, Richard. "The York Cycle." In Richard Beadle, ed., *The Cambridge Companion to Medieval English Theatre*, 85–108. Cambridge: Cambridge University Press, 1994.

———. *The York Plays*. London: Edward Arnold, 1982.

Beaumont, Francis. *The Knight of the Burning Pestle*. In Fredson Bowers, ed., *The Dramatic Works in the Beaumont and Fletcher Canon*. Cambridge: Cambridge University Press, 1968.

———. *The Knight of the Burning Pestle*. Edited by Sheldon P. Zitner. Manchester: Manchester University Press, 1984.

Beaumont, Francis, and John Fletcher. *The Works of Francis Beaumont and John Fletcher*. Edited by Arnold Glover and A. R. Waller. 10 vols. Cambridge: Cambridge University Press, 1905–12.

Beckerman, Bernard. "Philip Henslowe." In Joseph W. Donohue, Jr., ed., *The Theatrical Manager in England and America*, 19–62. Princeton: Princeton University Press, 1971.

———. *Shakespeare at the Globe*. New York: Macmillan, 1962.

Bednarz, James P. "Representing Jonson: *Histriomastix* and the Origin of the Poets' War." *Huntington Library Quarterly* 54 (1991): 1–30.

Beier, A. L. *Masterless Men: The Vagrancy Problem in England, 1560–1640*. London: Methuen, 1985.

——. *The Problem of the Poor in Tudor and Early Stuart England*. London: Methuen, 1983.

Bell, Maureen. "Entrance in the Stationers' Register." *The Library*, 6th ser., 16 (1994): 50–54.

Belsey, Catherine. "Alice Arden's Crime." *Renaissance Drama* 13 (1982): 83–102.

——. *The Subject of Tragedy: Identity and Difference in Renaissance Drama*. London: Methuen, 1985.

Bennett, H. S. *English Books and Readers, 1558 to 1603: Being a Study in the History of the Book Trade in the Reign of Elizabeth I*. Cambridge: Cambridge University Press, 1965.

——. *English Books and Readers, 1603 to 1640: Being a Study in the History of the Book Trade in the Reigns of James I and Charles I*. Cambridge: Cambridge University Press, 1970.

Bentley, Gerald Eades. *The Jacobean and Caroline Stage*. 7 vols. Oxford: Clarendon Press, 1941–68.

——. *The Profession of Dramatist in Shakespeare's Time, 1590–1642*. Princeton: Princeton University Press, 1971.

——. *The Profession of Player in Shakespeare's Time, 1590–1642*. Princeton: Princeton University Press, 1984.

——. *The Seventeenth-Century Stage*. Chicago and London: University of Chicago Press, 1968.

Bergeron, David M. *English Civic Pageantry, 1558–1642*. Columbia: University of South Carolina Press, 1971.

——. "The Patronage of Dramatists: The Case of Thomas Heywood." *English Literary Renaissance* 18 (1988): 294–305.

Berry, Herbert. "Aspects of the Design and Use of the First Public Playhouse." In Herbert Berry, ed., *The First Public Playhouse: The Theater in Shoreditch 1576–1598*, 29–45. Montreal: McGill-Queen's University Press, 1979.

——. *The Boar's Head Playhouse*. Washington, D.C.: Folger Shakespeare Library, 1986.

——. "The Globe Bewitched and *El Hombre Fiel*." *Medieval and Renaissance Drama in England* 1 (1984): 211–30.

——. *Shakespeare's Playhouses*. New York: AMS Press, 1987.

——. "Shylock, Robert Miles, and Events at the Theatre." *Shakespeare Quarterly* 44 (1992): 183–201.

——. "The Stage and Boxes at Blackfriars." *Studies in Philology* 63 (1966): 163–86.

Berry, Herbert, and James Stokes. "Actors and Town Hall in the Sixteenth Century." *Medieval and Renaissance Drama in England* 6 (1993): 37–56.

Bevington, David. "Determining the Indeterminate: The Oxford Shakespeare." *Shakespeare Quarterly* 38 (1987): 501–19.

——. *From "Mankind" to Marlowe: Growth of Structure in the Popular Drama of Tudor England*. Cambridge: Harvard University Press, 1962.

——. "Literary Management in the Lord Admiral's Company, 1596–1603." *Theatre Research International* 2 (1977): 186–97.

——. *Tudor Drama and Politics: A Critical Approach to Topical Meaning*. Cambridge: Harvard University Press, 1968.

——, ed. Introduction to *The Complete Works of Shakespeare*. 4th ed. New York: Harper Collins, 1992.

———, ed. *Medieval Drama*. Boston: Houghton Mifflin, 1975.

Bevington, David, and Eric Rasmussen, eds. *Doctor Faustus: A- and B-Texts (1604, 1616)*. Manchester: Manchester University Press, 1993.

Bills, Bing D. "The 'Suppression Theory' and the English Corpus Christi Play: A Re-Examination." *Theatre Journal* 32 (1980): 157–68.

Birrell, T. A. "Reading as Pastime: The Place of Light Literature in Some Gentlemen's Libraries of the Seventeenth Century." In Robin Myers and Michael Harris, eds., *Property of a Gentleman: The Formation, Organisation and Dispersal of the Private Library, 1620–1920*, 113–31. Winchester: St. Paul's Bibliographies, 1991.

Black, Antony. *Guilds and Civil Society in European Political Thought from the Twelfth Century to the Present*. Ithaca: Cornell University Press, 1984.

Blackstone, Mary A. "Circles Within Circles: Touring Patterns and the Patron's Sphere of Influence." Paper presented in the seminar "Entertainers on the Road in Early Modern England" at the annual meeting of the Shakespeare Association of America, 1991.

———. "Patrons and Elizabethan Dramatic Companies." In C. E. McGee, ed., *Elizabethan Theatre X*, 112–32. Port Credit, Ontario: P. D. Meany, 1988.

Blayney, Peter W. M. "*The Booke of Sir Thomas Moore* Re-examined." *Studies in Philology* 69 (1972): 167–91.

———. *The Bookshops in Paul's Cross Churchyard*. London: Bibliographical Society, 1990.

———. *The First Folio of Shakespeare*. Washington, D.C.: Folger Library Publications, 1991.

———. *The Texts of "King Lear" and Their Origins*. Vol. 1, *Nicholas Okes and the First Quarto*. Cambridge: Cambridge University Press, 1982.

Blumenberg, Hans. *The Legitimacy of the Modern Age*. Translated by Robert M. Wallace. Cambridge: MIT Press, 1985.

Boas, F. S. "James I at Oxford in 1605." In *Collections*, vol. 1, pt. 3, pp. 247–59. London: Malone Society, 1909.

———. "A Lost and Found Volume of Manuscript Plays." *Times Literary Supplement*, July 4, 1935, p. 432.

———. *University Drama in the Tudor Age*. Oxford: Clarendon Press, 1914.

———, ed. *The Christmas Prince*. London: Malone Society, 1922.

Bodley, Sir Thomas. *The Life of Sir Thomas Bodley: The Honourable Founder of the Publique Library in the University of Oxford*. Oxford, 1647.

Boose, Lynda E. "Scolding Bridles and Bridling Scolds: Taming the Woman's Unruly Member." *Shakespeare Quarterly* 42 (1991): 179–213.

———. "*The Taming of the Shrew*, Good Husbandry, and Enclosure." In Russ McDonald, ed., *Shakespeare Reread: The Texts in New Contexts*, 197–225. Ithaca: Cornell University Press, 1994.

Bowers, Fredson. "Current Theories of Copy-Text." In O. M. Brack, Jr., and Warner Barnes, eds., *Bibliography and Textual Criticism*, 59–72. Chicago: University of Chicago Press, 1969.

———. *On Editing Shakespeare and the Elizabethan Dramatists*. Philadelphia: University of Pennsylvania Library, 1955. Reprint, Charlottesville: University Press of Virginia, 1966.

———. "Remarks on Eclectic Texts." *Proof* 4 (1974): 31–76.

Bowers, Rick. *John Lowin and Conclusions Upon Dances*. New York: Garland, 1988.

Bowsher, Julian M. C., and Simon Blatherwick. "The Structure of the Rose." In Franklin J. Hildy, ed., *New Issues in the Reconstruction of Shakespeare's Theater: Proceedings of the Conference Held at the University of Georgia February 16–18, 1990,* 55–78. New York: Peter Lang, 1990.

Bradbrook, Muriel C. *The Rise of the Common Player.* Cambridge: Harvard University Press, 1962.

——. *Shakespeare the Craftsman.* London: Chatto and Windus, 1969.

Bradley, David. *From Text to Performance in the Elizabethan Theatre.* Cambridge: Cambridge University Press, 1992.

——. *The Ignorant Elizabethan Author and Massinger's "Believe as you List."* Sydney: University of Sydney Press, 1977.

Brady, Jennifer, and W. H. Herendeen, eds. *Ben Jonson's 1616 Folio.* Newark: University of Delaware Press, 1991.

Brathwait, Richard. *The English Gentleman.* London, 1630.

Braunmuller, A. R., and Michael Hattaway. *The Cambridge Companion to English Renaissance Drama.* Cambridge: Cambridge University Press, 1990.

Bray, Alan. "Homosexuality and the Signs of Male Friendship in Elizabethan England." In Jonathan Goldberg, ed., *Queering the Renaissance,* 40–61. Durham: Duke University Press, 1994.

——. *Homosexuality in Renaissance England.* London: Gay Men's Press, 1982.

Braybrooke, Richard Griffin, ed. *The Private Correspondence of Lady Jane Cornwallis, 1613–1644.* London: Bentley, Wilson, and Fley, 1842.

Brayman, Heidi. "Impressions from a 'Scribbling Age': Recovering the Reading Practices of Renaissance England." Ph.D. diss., Columbia University, 1995.

Bredbeck, Gregory W. *Sodomy and Interpretation: Marlowe to Milton.* Ithaca: Cornell University Press, 1991.

*A Breefe Discourse, declaring and approuing the necessarie and inviolable maintenance of certain laudable customes of London.* London, 1584.

Brenan, Gerald. *A History of the House of Percy from the Earliest Times down to the Present Century.* 2 vols. London: Freemantle, 1902.

Brennan, Michael. *Literary Patronage in the English Renaissance: The Pembroke Family.* London: Routledge, 1988.

Brewer, John, James Gardner, and R. H. Brodie, eds. *Letters and Papers, Foreign and Domestic, of the Reign of Henry VIII.* 21 vols. London: HMSO, 1862–1918. *Addenda.* 2 vols. London: HMSO, 1929–32.

Brigden, Susan. "Youth and the English Reformation." *Past and Present* 95 (1982): 37–67.

Bristol, Michael D. *Carnival and Theater: Plebeian Culture and the Structure of Authority in Renaissance England.* New York: Methuen, 1985.

Brome, Richard. *The Antipodes.* Edited by Ann Haaker. Lincoln: University of Nebraska Press, 1966.

Brooke, C. F. Tucker, ed. *The Life of Marlowe and The Tragedy of Dido Queen of Carthage.* London: Methuen, 1930.

Brown, Arthur, ed. *The Lady Mother.* London: Malone Society, 1959.

Brown, Frank E. "Continuity and Change in the Urban House: Development in Domestic

Space Organisation in Seventeenth-Century London." *Comparative Studies in Society and History* 28 (1986): 558–90.

Bruster, Douglas. *Drama and the Market in the Age of Shakespeare.* Cambridge: Cambridge University Press, 1992.

Bullock-Davis, Constance, ed. *Menestrellorum Multitudo: Minstrels at a Royal Feast.* Cardiff: University of Wales Press, 1978.

———, ed. *Register of Royal and Baronial Domestic Minstrels 1272–1327.* Woodbridge, Suffolk: Boydell, 1986.

Bullokar, John. *An English expositor: teaching the interpretation of the hardest words used in our Language.* London, 1616.

Bulwer, John. *Chironomia: or, the art of manuall rhetorique.* London, 1644.

Burckhardt, Jacob. *The Civilization of the Renaissance in Italy.* Translated by S. G. C. Middlemore. Introduction by Benjamin Nelson and Charles Trinkaus. 2 vols. New York: Harper, 1959.

Burke, Peter. *Popular Culture in Early Modern Europe.* London: Temple Smith, 1978.

Burnett, Mark Thornton. *Authority and Obedience: Masters and Servants in English Literature and Society.* Cambridge: Cambridge University Press, 1996.

Burt, Richard. *"Licensed by Authority": Ben Jonson and the Discourses of Censorship.* Ithaca: Cornell University Press, 1993.

———. " 'Licensed by Authority': Ben Jonson and the Politics of Early Stuart Theater." *ELH* 54 (1987): 529–60.

Burt, Richard, and John Michael Archer, eds. *Enclosure Acts: Sexuality, Property, and Culture in Early Modern England.* Ithaca: Cornell University Press, 1994.

Butler, Judith. *Gender Trouble: Feminism and the Subversion of Identity.* New York: Routledge, 1990.

Butler, Martin. "Ecclesiastical Censorship of Early Stuart Drama: The Case of Jonson's *The Magnetic Lady*." *Modern Philology* 89 (1992): 469–81.

———. "Massinger's *The City Madam* and the Caroline Audience." *Renaissance Drama,* n.s., 13 (1982): 157–87.

———. *Theatre and Crisis, 1632–1642.* Cambridge: Cambridge University Press, 1984.

———. "Two Playgoers and the Closing of the London Theatres, 1642." *Theatre Research International* 9 (1984): 93–99.

Buttes, Henry. *Dyets Dry Dinner.* London, 1599.

Byrne, M. St. Clare. "Anthony Munday and His Books." *The Library,* 4th ser., 1 (1921): 225–56.

*Calendar of State Papers, Domestic Series of the Reign of Charles I.* Nendeln, Liechtenstein: Kraus, 1967.

Calvin, John. *The Institution of Christian Religion.* Translated by T[homas] Norton. 1561. 5th ed. London: 1582.

———. *The Sermons of M. John Calvin vpon the Fifth Booke of Moses Called Deuteronomie.* Translated by Arthur Golding. London: George Bishop, 1583.

*Cancer.* Edited by Thomas W. Best. Hildesheim: Georg Olms, 1987.

Capp, Bernard. "English Youth Groups and the Pinder of Wakefield." *Past and Present* 76 (1977): 127–33.

Carnegie, David. "Actors' Parts and the 'Play of Poore.'" *Harvard Library Bulletin* 30 (1982): 5–24.

——. "The Identification of the Hand of Thomas Goffe, Academic Dramatist and Actor." *The Library*, 5th ser., 26 (1971): 161–65.

Carpenter, Nan Cooke. *John Skelton*. New York: Twayne Publishers, 1968.

Carson, Neil. *A Companion to Henslowe's Diary*. Cambridge: Cambridge University Press, 1988.

——. "Literary Management in the Lord Admiral's Company, 1596–1603." *Theatre Research International* 2 (1977): 186–97.

Cartwright, William. *The Plays and Poems of William Cartwright*. Edited by Gwynne B. Evans. Madison: University of Wisconsin Press, 1951.

Cawley, A. C. "The Staging of Medieval Drama." In Lois Potter, gen. ed., *The Revels History of Drama in English*, 1:1–66. London: Methuen, 1983.

Ceresano, S. P. "The 'Business' of Shareholding, The Fortune Playhouses, and Francis Grace's Will." *Medieval and Renaissance Drama in England* 2 (1985): 131–51.

Chamberlain, John. *Letters*. Edited by Norman E. McClure. 2 vols. Philadelphia: American Philosophical Society, 1939.

Chambers, E. K. *The Elizabethan Stage*. 4 vols. Oxford: Clarendon Press, 1923.

——. *The Medieval Stage*. 2 vols. Oxford: Clarendon Press, 1903.

——. *William Shakespeare: A Study of Facts and Problems*. 2 vols. Oxford: Clarendon Press, 1930.

Chapman, George. *Bussy D'Ambois*. Edited by Nicholas Brooke. London: Methuen, 1964.

Chartier, Roger. *The Order of Books: Readers, Authors, and Libraries in Europe Between the Fourteenth and Eighteenth Centuries*. Translated by Lydia G. Cochrane. Stanford: Stanford University Press, 1994.

——, ed. *A History of Private Life: Passions of the Renaissance*. Vol. 3, Philippe Aries and Georges Duby, gen. eds. Translated by Arthur Goldhammer. Cambridge: Harvard University Press, 1989.

Chartres, John, ed. *Agricultural Markets and Trade, 1500–1750*. Cambridge: Cambridge University Press, 1990.

Chartrou, Josèphe. *Les Entrées Solennelles et Triomphales à la Renaissance, 1484–1551*. Paris: Les Presses Universitaires de France, 1928.

Cheal, David J. *The Gift Economy*. London: Routledge, 1989.

Cheney, Christopher Robert. *A Handbook of Dates for Students of English History*. London: Offices of the Royal Historical Society, 1978.

Clare, Janet. *"Art Made Tongue-Tied by Authority": Elizabethan and Jacobean Dramatic Censorship*. Manchester: Manchester University Press, 1990.

——. "'Greater Themes for Insurrection's Arguing': Political Censorship of the Elizabethan and Jacobean Stage." *Review of English Studies*, n.s., 38 (1987): 169–83.

Clark, Peter. "The Ownership of Books in England, 1560–1640: The Example of Some Kentish Townsfolk." In Lawrence Stone, ed., *Schooling and Society: Studies in the History of Education*. Baltimore: Johns Hopkins University Press, 1976.

——. "'The Ramoth-Gilead of the Good': Urban Change and Political Radicalism at Gloucester, 1540–1640." In Peter Clark, Alan G. R. Smith, and Nicholas Tyacke, eds.,

*The English Commonwealth, 1547–1640: Essays in Politics and Society Presented to Joel Hurstfield.* Leicester: Leicester University Press, 1969.

——, ed. *Country Towns in Pre-Industrial England.* Leicester: Leicester University Press, 1981.

Clark, Peter, and Paul Slack, eds. *Crisis and Order in English Towns, 1500–1700: Essays in Urban History.* London: Routledge and Kegan Paul, 1972.

Clement, Richard W. "Librarianship and Polemics: The Career of Thomas James (1572–1629)." *Libraries and Culture* 26 (1991): 269–82.

Clifford, Lady Anne. *The Diary of the Lady Anne Clifford.* Edited by V[ita] Sackville-West. London: Heinemann, 1924.

Clopper, Lawrence M. "Lay and Clerical Impact on Civic Religious Drama and Ceremony." In Marianne G. Briscoe and John C. Coldewey, eds., *Contexts for Early English Drama,* 103–34. Bloomington: Indiana University Press, 1989.

——, ed. *Records of Early English Drama: Chester.* Toronto: University of Toronto Press, 1979.

Coghill, Nevill. *Shakespeare's Professional Skills.* Cambridge: Cambridge University Press, 1964.

Cohen, Walter. *Drama of a Nation: Public Theater in Renaissance England and Spain.* Ithaca: Cornell University Press, 1985.

Cokain, Sir Aston. "An Epitaph on Mr. John Fletcher, *and Mr.* Philip Massinger, *who lie buried both in one Grave in St.* Mary Overie's Church *in* Southwark." Epigram 100. *Small POEMS of Divers sorts.* 186. London, 1658.

Coldewey, John C. "That Enterprising Property Player: Semi-professional Drama in Sixteenth-Century England." *Theatre Notebook* 31 (1977): 5–12.

——, ed. *Early English Drama.* New York: Garland, 1993.

——, ed. "Records of Early English Drama: Nottinghamshire." Unpublished transcriptions.

Collinson, Patrick. *The Birthpangs of Protestant England.* London: Macmillan, 1988.

Colvin, H. M., and John Summerson. "The King's Houses, 1485–1660." In H. M. Colvin, ed., *The History of the King's Works.* Vol. 4, 1485–1660, part 2, pp. 1–364. London: HMSO, 1982.

Connerton, Paul. *How Societies Remember.* Cambridge: Cambridge University Press, 1989.

Cook, Ann Jennalie. "The Audience of Shakespeare's Plays: A Reconsideration." *Shakespeare Studies* 7 (1974): 283–305.

——. "'Bargaines of Incontinencie'": Bawdy Behavior at the Playhouses." *Shakespeare Studies* 10 (1977): 271–90.

——. "The London Theater Audience, 1576–1642." Ph.D. diss., Vanderbilt University, 1972.

——. *The Privileged Playgoers of Shakespeare's London: 1576–1642.* Princeton: Princeton University Press, 1981.

——. "Shakespeare and His Audiences." In John F. Andrews, ed., *William Shakespeare: His World, His Work, His Influence,* 2:549–55. New York: Scribner's, 1985.

Cotgrave, Randle. *A Dictionarie of the French and English Tongves.* London, 1611.

Cowling, Jane, ed. "Records of Early English Drama: Winchester." Unpublished transcriptions.

Craik, T. W. "The Political Interpretation of Two Tudor Interludes: *Temperance and Humility* and *Wealth and Health.*" *Review of English Studies,* n.s., 4 (1953): 98–108.

———. *The Tudor Interlude.* Leicester: Leicester University Press, 1958.

Craster, Sir Edmund. *History of the Bodleian Library, 1845–1945.* Oxford: Clarendon Press, 1952.

Crouch, David J. F. "Paying to See the Play: The Stationholders on the Route of the York Corpus Christi Play in the Fifteenth Century." *Medieval English Theatre* 13 (1991): 64–111.

Davenant, William. *The Wits.* London, 1634.

———. *The Works of Sir William Davenant.* London, 1673.

Davis, Natalie Zemon. "The Reasons of Misrule: Youth Groups and Charivaris in Sixteenth-Century France." *Past and Present* 50 (1971): 41–75.

———. "The Sacred and the Body Social in Sixteenth-Century Lyon." *Past and Present* 90 (1981): 40–70.

Dawson, Giles. "An Early List of Elizabethan Plays." *The Library,* 4th ser., 15 (1935): 445–56.

———. *Records of Plays and Players in Kent. Collections,* vol. 7. London: Malone Society, 1965.

Dawson, Giles, ed. *July and Julian.* Reprint, London: Malone Society, 1955.

de Grazia, Margreta. "Fin-de-Siècle Renaissance England." In Elaine Scarry, ed., *Fins de Siècle: English Poetry in 1590, 1690, 1790, 1890, 1990,* pp. 37–63. Baltimore and London: Johns Hopkins University Press, 1995.

———. *Shakespeare Verbatim: The Reproduction of Authenticity and the 1790 Apparatus.* Oxford: Oxford University Press, 1991.

de la Marck, Robert, seigneur de Fleurange. "Mémoires." In Joseph François Michaud and Jean Joseph François Poujoulet, eds., *Nouvelle Collection des Mémoires relatif a l'histoire de France,* 5:1–79. Nouvelle édition. 34 vols. Paris: Didier, 1854.

Dekker, Thomas. *The Dramatic Works.* Edited by Fredson Bowers. 4 vols. Cambridge: Cambridge University Press, 1953–61.

———. *The Gull's Hornbook: or Fashions to Please All Sorts of Gulls.* In E. D. Pendry, ed., *Thomas Dekker: Selected Writings,* 63–109. London: Macmillan, 1967.

———. *A KNIGHTS Coniuring. Done in earnest: Discouered in Iest.* London, 1607.

———. *The Non-Dramatic Works.* Edited by Alexander B. Grosart. 5 vols. 1884. Reprint, New York: Russell and Russell, 1963.

Delpit, J. *Collection Générale des Documents Français qui se Trouvent en Angleterre.* Paris, 1847.

Derrida, Jacques. *Dissemination.* Translated by Barbara Johnson. Chicago: University of Chicago Press, 1981.

———. *Specters of Marx: The State of the Debt, the Work of Mourning, and the New International.* Translated by Peggy Kamuf. New York and London: Routledge, 1994.

Dessen, Alan. *Elizabethan Stage Conventions and Modern Interpreters.* Cambridge: Cambridge University Press, 1984.

Dickens, A. G. *The English Reformation.* 2d ed. University Park: Pennsylvania State University Press, 1989.

*The Digby Plays.* Edited and modernized by Alice J. Brock and David G. Byrd. Dallas: Paon, 1973.

Dillon, Janette. "Is There a Performance in This Text?" *Shakespeare Quarterly* 45 (1994): 74–86.

Dilthey, Wilhelm. "The Types of World-View and Their Development in the Metaphysical

Systems." In H. P. Rickman, ed., *W. Dilthey: Selected Writings*, 133–54. Cambridge: Cambridge University Press, 1976.

Dinsmoor, W. B. "The Literary Remains of Sebastiano Serlio." *Art Bulletin* 24 (1942): 55–91, 115–54.

Dobell, Bertram, ed. *"The partiall law; a tragi-comedy," by an unknown author, circa 1615–30*. London, the editor, 1908.

Dobson, R. B. "Admissions to the Freedom of the City of York in the Later Middle Ages." *Economic History Review* 26 (1973): 1–21.

Dolan, Frances E. *Dangerous Familiars: Representations of Domestic Crime in England, 1550–1700*. Ithaca: Cornell University Press, 1994.

Dollimore, Jonathan. *Radical Tragedy: Religion, Ideology, and Power in the Drama of Shakespeare and His Contemporaries*. Brighton: Harvester, 1984. 2d ed., Durham: Duke University Press, 1989.

Dollimore, Jonathan, and Alan Sinfield, eds. *Political Shakespeare: New Essays in Cultural Materialism*. Ithaca: Cornell University Press, 1985.

*The Domestick Intelligence, Or, News both from City & Country*. October 10, 1679. Number 28. Huntington RB 72730.

Douglas, Audrey, and Peter H. Greenfield, eds. *Records of Early English Drama: Cumberland, Westmorland, Gloucestershire*. Toronto: University of Toronto Press, 1986.

Dowling, Margaret. "The Printing of John Dowland's *Second Booke of Songs or Ayres*." *The Library*, 4th ser., 12 (1931–1932): 365–80.

Duffy, Eamon. *The Stripping of the Altars: Traditional Religion in England c. 1400–c. 1580*. New Haven: Yale University Press, 1992.

Dunbar, William. *Poems*. Edited by James Kinsey. Oxford: Clarendon Press, 1958.

Dutton, Richard. "Ben Jonson and the Master of the Revels." In J. R. Mulryne and Margaret Shewring, eds., *Theatre and Government Under the Early Stuarts*, 57–86. Cambridge: Cambridge University Press, 1993.

——. *Mastering the Revels: The Regulation and Censorship of English Renaissance Drama*. London: Macmillan, 1991.

——. "Patronage, Politics, and the Master of the Revels, 1622–40: The Case of Sir John Astley." *English Literary Renaissance* 20 (1990): 287–31.

——, ed. *Jacobean Civic Pageants*. Keele: Keele University Press, 1995.

Eagleton, Terry. *Ideology*. New York: Longman, 1994.

Earle, John. *Microcosmography*. Edited by Philip Bliss. London: John Harding, 1811.

E/BER: Records of the Trustees of the Bedford Settled Estates. Cited in F. H. W. Sheppard, ed., *The Theater Royal Drury Lane and The Royal Opera House Covent Garden, Survey of London* 35. London: Athlone Press for the Greater London Council, 1970.

Eccles, Mark. "Sir George Buc, Master of the Revels." In C. J. Sisson, ed., *Sir Thomas Lodge and Other Elizabethans*, 409–506. Cambridge: Harvard University Press, 1938.

Edelman, Lee. *Homographesis: Essays in Gay Literary and Cultural Theory*. New York: Routledge, 1994.

Edmond, Mary. "Pembroke's Men." *Review of English Studies*, n.s., 25 (1974): 129–36.

——. *Rare Sir William Davenant*. Manchester: Manchester University Press, 1987.

Edwards, Philip. "Society and the Theatre." In Lois Potter, gen. ed., *The Revels History of Drama in English*, 4:3–67. London: Methuen, 1981.

Eisenstein, Elizabeth L. *The Printing Revolution in Early Modern Europe*. Cambridge: Cambridge University Press, 1983.

Elliott, John R., Jr. "College and University Drama." In Nicholas Tyacke, ed., *The History of the University of Oxford*. Vol. 4. Oxford: Oxford University Press, forthcoming.

——. "Degree Plays." *Oxoniensia* 53 (1988): 341–42.

——. "Queen Elizabeth at Oxford: New Light on the Royal Plays in 1566." *English Literary Renaissance* 18 (1988): 218–29.

——, ed. "Records of Early English Drama: Oxford." Unpublished transcriptions.

Elliott, John R., Jr., and John Buttrey. "The Royal Plays at Christ Church in 1636: A New Document." *Theatre Research International* 10 (1985): 93–109.

Elton, G. R. *Policy and Police*. Cambridge: Cambridge University Press, 1971.

Erickson, Amy. *Women and Property in Early Modern England*. New York: Routledge, 1993.

Erickson, Peter. *Patriarchal Structures in Shakespeare's Drama*. Berkeley: University of California Press, 1985.

Esdaile, Katharine. *English Monumental Sculpture Since the Renaissance*. London: Society for Promoting Christian Knowledge, 1927.

Evans, G. Blakemore. "The Douai Manuscript—Six Shakespearean Transcripts (1694–95)." *Philological Quarterly* 41 (1962): 158–72.

——. "Records, Documents, and Allusions." In G. Blakemore Evans, ed., *The Riverside Shakespeare*, 1827–52. Boston: Houghton Mifflin, 1974.

——. "Shakespeare's *Julius Caesar*: A Seventeenth-Century Manuscript." *Journal of English and Germanic Philology* 41 (1942): 401–17.

——, ed. *The Plays and Poems of William Cartwright*. Madison: University of Wisconsin Press, 1951.

——, ed. *The Riverside Shakespeare*. Boston: Houghton Mifflin, 1974.

Everitt, Alan. "The Marketing of Agricultual Produce 1500–1640." In John Chartres, ed., *Agricultural Markets and Trade, 1500–1750*, 114–35. Cambridge: Cambridge University Press, 1990.

*"The fary knight; or, Oberon the Second," a manuscript play attributed to Thomas Randolph*. Edited by Fredson Bowers. Chapel Hill: University of North Carolina Press, 1942.

Fehrenbach, R. J. "Sir Roger Townshend's Books." In Fehrenbach and Leedham-Green, eds., *Private*, 1:79–135.

Fehrenbach, R. J., and E. S. Leedham-Green, eds. *Private Libraries in Renaissance England: A Collection and Catalogue of Tudor and Early Stuart Book-Lists*. 4 vols. to date. Binghamton, N.Y.: Medieval and Renaissance Texts and Studies, 1992–95.

Fennor, William. *Fennors Descriptions*. London, 1616.

Ferguson, Margaret W. "Running On with Almost Public Voice: The Case of E.C." In Florence Howe, ed., *Tradition and the Talents of Women*, 37–67. Urbana: University of Illinois Press, 1991.

Ferguson, Margaret W., Maureen Quilligan, and Nancy J. Vickers, eds. *Rewriting the Renaissance: The Discourses of Sexual Difference in Early Modern Europe*. Chicago: University of Chicago Press, 1986.

Ferguson, Wallace K. *The Renaissance in Historical Thought: Five Centuries of Interpretation*. Boston: Houghton Mifflin, 1948.

Ferris, Lesley, ed. *Crossing the Stage: Controversies on Cross-Dressing*. London: Routledge, 1993.

Feuillerat, Albert, ed. *Documents Relating to the Office of the Revels in the Time of Queen Elizabeth*. Louvain: A. Uystpruyst, 1908. Reprint, Vaduz: Kraus, 1963.

——. *Documents Relating to the Revels at Court in the Times of King Edward VI and Queen Mary*. Louvain: A. Uystpruyst, 1914. Reprint, Nendeln, Liechtenstein: Kraus, 1968.

Fineman, Joel. "Fratricide and Cuckoldry: Shakespeare's Doubles." In Murray M. Schwartz and Coppélia Kahn, eds., *Representing Shakespeare: New Psychoanalytic Essays*, 70–109. Baltimore: Johns Hopkins University Press, 1980.

Finkelpearl, Philip J. " 'The Comedians' Liberty': Censorship of the Jacobean Stage Reconsidered." *English Literary Renaissance* 16 (1986): 123–38.

Fisher, William. "Queer Money." Unpublished essay circulated in the seminar "The Politics of Pleasure" at the meeting of the Shakespeare Association of America, 1994.

Fitzgeffrey, Henry. *Satyres and Satyricall Epigrams: with Certaine Obseruations at Blacke-Fryars*. London, 1617.

Fleay, Frederick Gard. *A Chronicle History of the London Stage, 1559–1642*. London, 1890.

Fleming, Juliet. "The Ladies' Man and the Age of Elizabeth." In James Grantham Turner, ed., *Sexuality and Gender in Early Modern Europe: Institutions, Texts, Images*, 158–81. Cambridge: Cambridge University Press, 1993.

Florio, Iohn. *A WORLDE of Wordes, Or Most copious, and exact Dictionarie in Italian and English*. London, 1598.

Florio, John. *First Fruites*. London, 1578.

Foakes, R. A. *Illustrations of the English Stage, 1580–1642*. Stanford: Stanford University Press, 1985.

Forse, James H. *Art Imitates Business: Commercial and Political Influences in Elizabethan Theatre*. Bowling Green: Bowling Green State University Press, 1993.

Foucault, Michel. *The Archaeology of Knowledge*. Translated by A. M. Sheridan Smith. New York: Pantheon Books, 1972.

——. *Language, Counter-Memory, Practice*. Edited by Donald F. Bouchard. Ithaca and New York: Cornell University Press, 1977.

——. "What Is an Author?" In Paul Rabinow, ed., *The Foucault Reader*, 101–20. New York: Pantheon, 1984.

Fraser, Russell, and Norman Rabkin, eds. *Drama of the English Renaissance*. New York: Macmillan, 1976.

Freeman, Arthur. *Thomas Kyd: Facts and Problems*. Oxford: Clarendon Press, 1967.

Friedman, Alice T. *House and Household in Elizabethan England: Wollaton Hall and the Willoughby Family*. Chicago: University of Chicago Press, 1995.

Frye, Susan. *Elizabeth I: The Competition for Representation*. New York and Oxford: Oxford University Press, 1993.

——. "Ocular Textiles in *Othello*." Paper presented in the seminar "Visual Regimes" at the meeting of the Shakespeare Association of America, 1995.

Fulwell, Ulpian. *Like Will to Like*. In J. A. B. Somerset, ed., *Four Tudor Interludes*. London: Athlone, 1974.

Fumerton, Patricia. *Cultural Aesthetics: Renaissance Literature and the Practice of Social Ornament*. Chicago: University of Chicago Press, 1991.

Furness, Horace Howard, ed. *A New Variorum Edition of "King Lear."* Philadelphia: Lippincott, 1880.

Furnivall, F. J. "Sir John Harington's Shakspeare Quartos." *Notes and Queries* 9 (1890): 382–83.

Gaignebet, Claude, and Marie-Claude Florentin. *Le Carnaval: Essais de mythologie populaire.* Paris: Payot, 1979.

———. "Le Combat de Carnaval et de Carême de P. Breughel (1559)." *Annales: Economies, Sociétés, Civilisations* 27 (1972): 313–43.

Gair, Reavley. *The Children of Paul's: The Story of a Theatre Company, 1553–1608.* Cambridge: Cambridge University Press, 1982.

Galloway, David, ed. *Records of Early English Drama: Norwich 1540–1642.* Toronto: University of Toronto Press, 1984.

Galsworthy, John. "Some Platitudes Concerning Drama." In Toby Cole, ed., *Playwrights on Playwriting,* 45–52. New York: Hill and Wang, 1961.

Garber, Marjorie. " 'Infinite Riches in a Little Room': Closure and Enclosure in Marlowe." In Alvin Kernan, ed., *Two Renaissance Mythmakers: Christopher Marlowe and Ben Jonson,* pp. 3–21. Selected Papers from the English Institute, n.s., 1. Baltimore: Johns Hopkins University Press, 1977.

Gardiner, Harold C. *Mysteries' End: An Investigation of the Last Days of the Medieval Religious State.* New Haven: Yale University Press, 1946.

Garner, Shirley Nelson. " 'Let Her Paint an Inch Thick' ": Painted Ladies in Renaissance Drama and Society." *Renaissance Drama* 20 (1989): 123–39.

Gaskell, Philip. *A New Introduction to Bibliography.* Oxford: Clarendon Press, 1972.

Gatch, Milton. "Mysticism and Satire in the Morality of *Wisdom.*" *Philological Quarterly* 53 (1974): 342–62.

Gayton, Edmund. *Pleasant Notes upon Don Quixote.* London, 1656.

Geertz, Clifford. *Local Knowledge: Further Essays in Interpretive Anthropology.* New York: Basic Books, 1983.

George, David, ed. *Records of Early English Drama: Lancashire.* Toronto: University of Toronto Press, 1991.

Gibson, James, ed. "Records of Early English Drama: Kent." Unpublished transcriptions.

Gierke, Otto. *Political Theories of the Middle Age.* Edited and translated by F. W. Maitland. Cambridge: Cambridge University Press, 1987.

Gilbert, Felix. *History: Politics or Culture? Reflections on Ranke and Burckhardt.* Princeton: Princeton University Press, 1990.

Gilbert, Sandra, and Susan Gubar. *The Madwoman in the Attic: The Woman Writer and the Nineteenth-Century Literary Imagination.* New Haven: Yale University Press, 1984.

Gildersleeve, Virginia Crocheron. *Government Regulation of the Elizabethan Drama.* New York: Columbia University Press, 1908.

Gillam, Stanley. *The Divinity School and Duke Humfrey's Library at Oxford.* Oxford: Clarendon Press, 1988.

Girouard, Mark. *Life in the English Country House.* New Haven: Yale University Press, 1978.

Giustinian, Sebastian. *Four Years at the Court of Henry VIII.* Translated by Rawdon Brown. 2 vols. London: Smith, Elder, and Co., 1854.

Glapthorne, Henry. *Wit in a Constable.* London, 1640.

Goldberg, Jonathan. *Sodometries: Renaissance Texts, Modern Sexualities*. Stanford: Stanford University Press, 1992.

———. "Sodomy and Society: The Case of Christopher Marlowe." In David Scott Kastan and Peter Stallybrass, eds., *Staging the Renaissance: Reinterpretations of Elizabethan and Jacobean Drama*, 75–82. New York: Routledge, 1991.

———. "Speculations: Macbeth and Source." In Jean E. Howard and Marion F. O'Connor, eds., *Shakespeare Reproduced: The Text in History and Ideology*, 242–64. New York and London: Methuen, 1987.

———. *Writing Matter: From the Hands of the English Renaissance*. Stanford: Stanford University Press, 1989.

———, ed. *Queering the Renaissance*. Durham: Duke University Press, 1994.

Gordon, D. J. *The Renaissance Imagination*. Edited by Stephen Orgel. Berkeley: University of California Press, 1975.

Gosson, Stephen. *Playes Confuted in Five Actions*. London, 1582. Reprint, New York: Johnson, 1972.

Gouge, William. *Of Domesticall Duties*. London, 1622.

Gould, Cecil. "Drawing Into Painting: Raphael's Use of His Studies." *Apollo* 119 (1984): 8–15.

Grafton, Anthony, and Lisa Jardine. *From Humanism to the Humanities: Education and the Liberal Arts in Fifteenth and Sixteenth Century Europe*. Cambridge: Harvard University Press, 1986.

Greenblatt, Stephen, ed. *The Forms of Power and the Power of Forms in the Renaissance*. Norman: University of Oklahoma Press, 1984.

———. "Invisible Bullets: Renaissance Authority and its Subversion, *Henry IV* and *Henry V*." In Jonathan Dollimore and Alan Sinfield, eds., *Political Shakespeare: New Essays in Cultural Materialism*, 18–47. Ithaca: Cornell University Press, 1985.

———. *Renaissance Self-Fashioning from More to Shakespeare*. Chicago: University of Chicago Press, 1980.

———. *Shakespearean Negotiations: The Circulation of Social Energy in Renaissance England*. Berkeley: University of California Press, 1988; Oxford: Clarendon Press, 1988.

Greene, Thomas. *The Light in Troy: Imitation and Discovery in Renaissance Poetry*. New Haven: Yale University Press, 1982.

Greenfield, Peter H. "Entertainments of Henry, Lord Berkeley, 1593–4 and 1600–05." *Records of Early English Drama Newsletter* 8 (1983): 12–24.

———. "Professional Players at Gloucester: Conditions of Provincial Performing." In C. E. McGee, ed., *Elizabethan Theatre X*, 73–92. Port Credit, Ontario: P. D. Meany, 1988.

———, ed. "Records of Early English Drama: Hampshire, Hertfordshire, Bedfordshire." Unpublished transcriptions.

Greg, W. W. "Authorship Attribution in the Early Play-lists 1656–1671." *Edinburgh Bibliographical Society Transactions* 2 (1946): 305–29.

———. "Autograph Plays by Anthony Munday." *Modern Language Review* 8 (1913): 89–90.

———. "The Bibliographical History of the First Folio." *The Library*, 2d ser., 4 (1903): 258–83.

———. *A Bibliography of the English Printed Drama to the Restoration*. 4 vols. London: Bibliographical Society, 1939–59. Reprint, 1962.

———. *Dramatic Documents from the Elizabethan Playhouses: Stage Plots, Actors' Parts, Prompt Books*. 2 vols. Oxford: Clarendon Press, 1931.

——. *The Editorial Problem in Shakespeare*. Oxford: Oxford University Press, 1931.

——. "Entrance and Copyright." *The Library*, 4th ser., 26 (1945–1946): 308–10.

——. "Entrance, Licence, and Publication." *The Library*, 4th ser., 25 (1944–1945): 1–22.

——. "The First Folio and Its Publishers." In The Shakespeare Association, *Studies in the First Folio*, 129–56. London: Oxford University Press, 1924.

——, ed. *Gesta Grayorum*. London: Malone Society, 1914.

——. Introduction to *Pericles 1609* (Shakespeare Quartos in Collotype Facsimile, no. 5), 4 pp. unnumbered. London: Shakespeare Association, 1940.

——. *A List of Masques, Pageants, &c*. London: Bibliographical Society, 1902 [for 1901].

——, ed. *Marlowe's "Doctor Faustus" 1604–1616: Parallel Texts*. Oxford: Clarendon Press, 1950.

——. "Prompt Copies, Private Transcripts, and the 'Playhouse Scrivener.' " *The Library*, 4th ser., 6 (1926): 148–56.

——. "The Rationale of Copy-Text." In O. M. Brack and Warner Barnes, eds., *Bibliography and Textual Criticism*, 41–58. Chicago: University of Chicago Press, 1969.

——. Review of Fredson Bowers, *On Editing Shakespeare*. *Shakespeare Quarterly* 7 (1956): 101–4.

——. "Reviews and Notices." *The Library*, 4th ser., 9 (1928): 202–11.

——. *The Shakespeare First Folio: Its Bibliographical and Textual History*. Oxford: Clarendon Press, 1955.

——. *Some Aspects and Problems of London Publishing Between 1550 and 1650*. Oxford: Clarendon Press, 1956.

——. "Some Notes on the Stationers' Registers." *The Library*, 4th ser., 7 (1926–1927): 376–86.

——. *Two Elizabethan Stage Abridgements*. London: Malone Society, 1922.

——, ed. *"Bonduca" by John Fletcher*. Reprint, London: Malone Society, 1951.

——, ed. *The Book of Sir Thomas More*. 1911. Reprint, London: Malone Society, 1961.

——, ed. *A Companion to Arber*. Oxford: Clarendon Press, 1967.

——, ed. *Henslowe Papers: Being Documents Supplementary to Henslowe's Diary*. 2 vols. London: A. H. Bullen, 1907. Reprint, London: Scolar Press, 1977.

——, ed. *"Processus Satanae."* In *Collections*, vol. 2, pt. 3, pp. 239–50. London: Malone Society, 1931.

Greg, W. W., and E. Boswell, eds. *Records of the Court of the Stationers' Company, 1576 to 1602, from Register B*. London: Bibliographical Society, 1930.

Grose, Francis, comp. "The Earl of Northumberland's Household Book." In *The Antiquarian Repertory*, 4:25–302. London: E. Jeffery, 1809.

Grose, Francis, and Thomas Astle, eds. *The Antiquarian Repertory*. 4 vols. New ed. London, 1807–9.

Grossman, Marshall. *"Authors to Themselves": Milton and the Revelation of History*. Cambridge: Cambridge University Press, 1987.

Guizot, François Pierre Guillaume. *Shakespeare and His Times*. New York: Harper and Brothers, 1852.

Gurr, Andrew. "The General and the Caviar: Learned Audiences in the Early Theatre." *Studies in the Literary Imagination* 26 (1993): 7–20.

——. "The Loss of Records for the Travelling Companies in Stuart Times." *Records of Early English Drama Newsletter* 19 (1994): 2–19.

——. "Money or Audiences: The Impact of Shakespeare's Globe." *Theatre Notebook* 42 (1988): 3–14.

——. *Playgoing in Shakespeare's London.* Cambridge: Cambridge University Press, 1987.

——. "The Shakespearian Stages, Forty Years On." *Shakespeare Survey* 41 (1989): 1–12.

——. *The Shakespearean Stage, 1574–1642.* Cambridge: Cambridge University Press, 1980. 3d ed., Cambridge: Cambridge University Press, 1992.

——. "The 'State' of Shakespeare's Audiences." In Marvin and Ruth Thompson, eds., *Shakespeare and the Sense of Performance,* 162–79. Newark: University of Delaware Press, 1989.

——. "*The Tempest*'s Tempest at Blackfriars." *Shakespeare Survey* 41 (1988): 91–102.

——. "Three Reluctant Patrons and Early Shakespeare." *Shakespeare Quarterly* 44 (1993): 159–74.

——. With John Orrell. *Rebuilding Shakespeare's Globe.* London: Weidenfeld and Nicolson, 1989.

Haaker, Ann. "The Plague, the Theater, and the Poet." *Renaissance Drama* 1 (1968): 283–305.

Haigh, Christopher. *English Reformations.* Oxford: Oxford University Press, 1993.

Hale, John. *The Civilization of Europe in the Renaissance.* London: Fontana Press, 1993.

Hall, Edward. *Hall's Chronicle: The Vnion of the Two Noble and Illustre Famelies of York and Lancaster.* Edited by Henry Ellis. London: J. Johnson, 1809.

Hall, Hubert. *Society in the Elizabethan Age.* London: Swann, Sonnenschein, Lowrey, 1886.

Hall, Joseph. *Heaven Upon Earth and Characters of Vertues and Vices.* Edited by Rudolf Kirk. Manchester: Manchester University Press, 1948.

Hall, Kim F. *Things of Darkness: Economics of Race and Gender in Early Modern England.* Ithaca: Cornell University Press, 1995.

Hall, Peter. *Peter Hall's Diaries.* Edited by John Goodwin. London: Hamlish Hamilton, 1984.

Halliwell-Phillipps, James Orchard. *An Account of the Only Known Manuscript of Shakespeare's Plays, comprising some important variations and corrections in the Merry Wives of Windsor obtained from a playhouse copy of that play recently discovered.* London: J. R. Smith, 1843.

Hamilton, Alice, ed. "Records of Early English Drama: Leicester." Unpublished transcriptions.

Hamilton, Donna. *Shakespeare and the Politics of Protestant England.* Lexington: University of Kentucky Press, 1992.

Hammond, Antony, and Doreen Delvecchio. "The Melbourne Manuscript and John Webster; A Reproduction and Transcript." *Studies in Bibliography* 41 (1988): 1–32.

Hanawalt, Barbara A., ed. *Women and Work in Preindustrial Europe.* Bloomington: Indiana University Press, 1986.

Harbage, Alfred. *Annals of English Drama, 975–1700: An Analytical Record of All Plays, Extant or Lost, Chronologically Arranged and Indexed by Authors, Titles, Dramatic Companies &c.* Philadelphia: University of Pennsylvania Press, 1940. 2d ed., rev. by S. Schoenbaum. London: Methuen, 1964. 3d ed., rev. by Sylvia Stoler Wagonheim. London and New York: Routledge, 1989.

——. *As They Liked It*. New York: Macmillan, 1947.

——. *Shakespeare and the Rival Traditions*. New York: Macmillan, 1952.

——. *Shakespeare's Audience*. New York: Columbia University Press, 1941.

Harbage, Alfred, and Mary D. Harris, eds. *The Coventry Leet Book*. 4 vols. Early English Text Society, o.s., 134, 135, 138, 146. London: Oxford University Press, 1907–13.

Hardin, Richard F. "Marlowe and the Fruits of Scholarism." *Philological Quarterly* 63, no. 3 (1984): 387–400.

Hardison, O. B., Jr. *Christian Rite and Christian Drama in the Middle Ages*. Baltimore: Johns Hopkins University Press, 1965.

Harris, John, and Gordon Higgott. *Inigo Jones: Complete Architectural Drawings*. London: Royal Academy of Art, 1989.

Harrison, J. F. C. *The Common People: A History from the Norman Conquest to the Present*. London: Fontana, 1984.

Harrod, Henry. "Queen Elizabeth Woodville's Visit to Norwich in 1469." *Norfolk Archaeology* 5 (1859): 32–33.

Harvey, Gabriel. *Letter Book*. Edited by E. J. L. Scott. Camden Society Publications, n.s., 33 (1884).

Hattaway, Michael. *Elizabethan Popular Theatre: Plays in Performance*. London: Routledge and Kegan Paul, 1982.

Hawkesworth, Walter. *Leander/Labyrinthus*. Edited by Susan Brock. Hildesheim: Georg Olms, 1987.

Hay, D. *Europe: The Emergence of an Idea*. Edinburgh, 1957.

Hayes, Rosalind, and C. E. McGee, eds. "Records of Early English Drama: Dorset." Unpublished transcriptions.

Hazlitt, W. Carew, ed. *A Selection of Old Plays*. London: Reeves and Turner, 1875.

Hedback, Ann-Mari. "The Douai Manuscript Reexamined." *Papers of the Bibliographical Society of America* 73 (1979): 1–18.

Hegel, Georg Wilhelm Friedrich. *Lectures on the History of Philosophy: Medieval and Modern Philosophy*. Translated by E. S. Haldane and Frances H. Simpson. Lincoln: University of Nebraska Press, 1995.

——. *The Philosophy of History*. Translated by J. Sibree. New York: Dover, 1956.

——. *Reason in History*. Translated by Robert S. Hartman. New York: Macmillan, and London: Collier Macmillan, 1953.

Heidegger, Martin. "The Age of the World Picture." In *The Question Concerning Technology and Other Essays*, 115–54. Translated by William Lovitt. New York: Harper and Row, 1977.

Heinemann, Margot. "Drama and Opinion in the 1620s: Middleton and Massinger." In J. R. Mulryne and Margaret Shewring, eds., *Theatre and Government Under the Early Stuarts*, 237–65. Cambridge: Cambridge University Press, 1993.

——. "Political Drama." In A. R. Braunmuller and Michael Hattaway, eds., *The Cambridge Companion to English Renaissance Drama*, 161–205. Cambridge: Cambridge University Press, 1990.

——. *Puritanism and Theatre: Thomas Middleton and Opposition Drama Under the Early Stuarts*. Cambridge: Cambridge University Press, 1980.

——. "Rebel Lords, Popular Playwrights, and Political Culture: Notes on the Jacobean Patronage of the Earl of Southampton." *Yearbook of English Studies* 21 (1991): 63–86.

Helgerson, Richard. *Self-Crowned Laureates: Spenser, Jonson, Milton, and the Literary System*. Berkeley: University of California Press, 1983.

Henderson, Diana E. "Many Mansions: Reconstructing *A Woman Killed with Kindness*." *Studies in English Literature, 1500–1900* 26 (1986): 277–94.

Henderson, Katherine Usher, and Barbara F. McManus. *Half Humankind: Contexts and Texts of the Controversy About Women in England, 1540–1640*. Urbana: University of Illinois Press, 1985.

Hendricks, Margo, and Patricia Parker, eds. *Women, "Race," and Writing in the Early Modern Period*. New York: Routledge, 1994.

Henslowe, Philip. *The Diary of Philip Henslowe*. Edited by John Payne Collier. London, 1845.

——. *Henslowe's Diary*. Edited by R. A. Foakes and R. T. Rickert. Cambridge: Cambridge University Press, 1961.

——. *Henslowe's Diary*. Edited by W. W. Greg. 2 vols. London: A. H. Bullen, 1904, 1908.

Herbert, Henry. *The Dramatic Records of Sir Henry Herbert*. Edited by Joseph Quincy Adams. New Haven: Yale University Press, 1917.

Herbert, William. *The History of the Twelve Great Livery Companies of London*. 2 vols. London, 1837.

Hermann, Thomas Arthur, and Isobel Dorothy Thornley, eds. *The Great Chronicle of London*. London: G. W. Jones, 1938.

Hersey, George. *The Lost Meaning of Classical Architecture*. Cambridge: MIT Press, 1988.

Hexter, J. H. "Property, Monopoly, and Shakespeare's *Richard II*." In Perez Zagorin, ed., *Culture and Politics from Puritanism to the Enlightenment*, 1–24. Berkeley: University of California Press, 1980.

Heylyn, Peter. *Memorial of Bishop Waynflete*. Edited by J. R. Bloxam. London: Caxton Society, 1851.

Heywood, Thomas. *"An Apology for Actors" (1612) with "A Refutation of the Apology for Actors" (1615)*. Edited by Richard H. Perkinson. New York: Scholars' Facsimiles and Reprints, 1941.

——. *An Apology for Actors*. London, 1612.

——. *The Escapes of Jupiter*. Edited by Henry D. Janzen. London: Malone Society, 1978.

——. *If You Know Not Me, You Know Nobody*. Edited by Madeleine Doran. 2 vols. London: Malone Society, 1935.

——. *A Woman Killed with Kindness*. Edited by Brian Scobie. New York: Norton, 1985.

——. *A Woman Killed with Kindness*. Edited by R. W. Van Fossen. London: Methuen, 1961.

Higgins, Anne. "Medieval Notions of the Structure of Time." *Journal of Medieval and Renaissance Studies* 19 (1989): 227–50.

——. "Work and Plays: Guild Casting in the Corpus Christi Drama." *Medieval and Renaissance Drama in England* 7 (1995 [for 1992]): 76–97.

Hill, W. Speed, ed. *New Ways of Looking at Old Texts: Papers of the Renaissance English Text Society, 1985–1991*. Binghamton: Renaissance English Text Soceity, 1993.

Hillebrand, H. N. *The Child Actors: A Chapter in Elizabethan Stage History*. Urbana: University of Illinois Press, 1926. Reprint, New York: Russell and Russell, 1964.

Hinman, Charlton, ed. *The Norton Facsimile: The First Folio of Shakespeare*. New York: Norton, 1968.

Historical Manuscripts Commission. *Report on the Manuscripts of the Late Reginald Rawdon Hastings, Esq. olf the Manor House, Ashby de la Zouche*. Vol. 1. London, 1928.

Hjort, Mette. *Strategy of Letters*. Cambridge: Harvard University Press, 1993.

Holden, William. *Anti-Puritan Satire: 1572–1642*. New Haven: Yale University Press, 1954.

Holderness, B. A. *Pre-Industrial England: Economy and Society from 1500–1700*. London: J. M. Dent, 1976.

Holdsworth, R. V., ed. *A Fair Quarrel*. New York: Hill and Wang, 1974.

*The Holy Bible*. London, 1611. As reproduced in *The Holy Bible: A Facsimile in a reduced size of the Authorized Version published in the year 1611*. Introduction by A. W. Pollard. Oxford: Oxford University Press, 1911.

Honigmann, E. A. J. "The Date and Revision of *Troilus and Cressida*." In Jerome J. McGann, ed., *Textual Criticism and Literary Interpretation*, 38–54. Chicago: University of Chicago Press, 1985.

——. *Shakespeare: The "Lost Years."* Totawa, N.J.: Barnes and Noble, 1985.

——. "Shakespeare's Revised Plays: *King Lear* and *Othello*." *The Library*, 6th ser., 4 (1982): 142–73.

——. *The Stability of Shakespeare's Text*. London: Arnold, 1965.

Honigmann, E. A. J., and Susan Brock, eds. *Playhouse Wills, 1558–1642: An Edition of Wills by Shakespeare and His Contemporaries in the London Theater*. Manchester: Manchester University Press, 1993.

Hooker, Richard. *Works*. Edited by Isaac Walton. 2 vols. Oxford: Oxford University Press, 1841.

Hope, Jonathan. *The Authorship of Shakespeare's Plays: A Socio-linguistic Study*. Cambridge: Cambridge University Press, 1994.

Hopkins, Lisa. "The False Domesticity of *A Woman Killed with Kindness*." *Connotations* 4 (1994/95): 1–7.

Hosley, Richard. "The Playhouses." In Clifford Leech and T. W. Craik, gen. eds., *The Revels History of Drama in English*, 3:119–235. London: Methuen, 1975.

Hotson, Leslie. *The Commonwealth and Restoration Stage*. Cambridge: Harvard University Press, 1928.

——. *Shakespeare's Wooden O*. London: Hart-Davis, 1959.

Houlbrooke, Ralph A. *The English Family, 1450–1700*. London: Longman, 1984.

Howard, Jean E. *The Stage and Social Struggle in Early Modern England*. London: Routledge, 1994.

Howard-Hill, T. H. "Another Warwickshire Playwright: John Newdigate of Arbury." *Renaissance Papers 1988*, pp. 51–52.

——. "Boccaccio, *Ghismonda*, and Its Foul Papers, *Glausamond*." *Renaissance Papers 1980*, pp. 19–28.

——. "Buc and the Censorship of *Sir John Van Olden Barnavelt* in 1619." *Review of English Studies*, n.s., 39 (1988): 39–63.

——. "The Evolution of the Form of Plays in English During the Renaissance." *Renaissance Quarterly* 43 (1990): 112–45.

———. "Marginal Markings: The Censor and the Editing of Four English Promptbooks." *Studies in Bibliography* 36 (1983): 168–77.

———. *Ralph Crane and Some Shakespeare First Folio Comedies.* Charlottesville: University of Virginia Press, 1972.

———, ed. *Thomas Middleton: "A Game at Chess."* Manchester: Manchester University Press, 1993.

Hoy, Cyrus. "Critical and Aesthetic Problems of Collaboration in Renaissance Drama." *Research Opportunities in Renaissance Drama* 19 (1976): 3–6.

———. *Introductions, Notes, and Commentaries to Texts in "The Dramatic Works of Thomas Dekker."* Cambridge: Cambridge University Press, 1980.

———. "The Shares of Fletcher and His Collaborators in the Beaumont and Fletcher Canon (I)." *Studies in Bibliography* 8 (1956): 129–46.

———. "The Shares of Fletcher and His Collaborators in the Beaumont and Fletcher Canon (III)." *Studies in Bibliography* 11 (1958): 85–106.

Hoy, James F. "On the Relationship of the Corpus Christi Plays to the Corpus Christi Procession at York." *Modern Philology* 71 (1973): 166–68.

Hughes, Charles, ed. *Shakespeare's Europe: A Survey of the Conditions of Europe at the End of the Sixteenth Century, Being Unpublished Chapters of Fynes Moryson's Itinerary.* 2d ed. New York: Benjamin Bloom, 1967.

Hughes, Paul, and James Larkin, eds. *Tudor Royal Proclamations.* 3 vols. New Haven: Yale University Press, 1964.

Huizinga, Johann. *Men and Ideas: History, the Middle Ages, and the Renaissance.* New York: Harper Torchbooks, 1959.

Hunter, G. K. *John Lyly: The Humanist as Courtier.* London: Routledge, 1962.

Hunter, Robert. *Shakespeare and the Mystery of God's Judgments.* Athens: University of Georgia Press, 1976.

Hutson, Lorna. *The Usurer's Daughter: Male Friendship and Fictions of Women in Sixteenth-Century England.* New York: Routledge, 1994.

Hutton, Ronald. *The Rise and Fall of Merry England: The Ritual Year 1440–1700.* Oxford: Oxford University Press, 1994.

Hyland, Peter. "'A Kind of Woman': The Elizabethan Boy-Actor and the Kabuki Onnagata." *Theatre Research International* 12, no. 1 (1987): 1–8.

Ingram, Martin. *Church Courts, Sex and Marriage, 1570–1640.* Cambridge: Cambridge University Press, 1990.

Ingram, R. W., ed. *Records of Early English Drama: Coventry.* Toronto: University of Toronto Press, 1981.

Ingram, William. *The Business of Playing: The Beginnings of the Adult Professional Theater in Elizabethan London.* Ithaca: Cornell University Press, 1992.

———. "The Cost of Touring." *Medieval and Renaissance Drama in England* 6 (1993): 57–62.

———. *A London Life in the Brazen Age.* Cambridge: Harvard University Press, 1978.

———. "The Playhouse as Investment, 1607–14: Thomas Woodford and Whitefriars." *Medieval and Renaissance Drama in England* 2 (1985): 9–30.

Ioppolo, Grace. *Revising Shakespeare.* Cambridge: Harvard University Press, 1991.

Jackson, MacD. P. *Studies in Attribution: Middleton and Shakespeare.* Salzburg: University of Salzburg, 1979.

Jackson, William A. "Variant Entry Fees of the Stationers' Company." *Papers of the Bibliographical Society of America* 51 (1957): 103–10.

——, ed. *Records of the Court of the Stationers' Company, 1602 to 1640*. London: Bibliographical Society, 1957.

James I, King. *The Works of the Most High and Mighty Prince James*. London, 1616.

James, Mervyn. "Ritual, Drama, and Social Body in the Late Medieval English Town." *Past and Present* 98 (1983): 3–29.

James, Thomas. *Catalogus Universalis Librorum in Bibliotheca Bodleiana*. Oxford, 1620.

Jameson, Fredric. *Postmodernism, or, the Cultural Logic of Late Capitalism*. London and New York: Verso, 1991.

Jayne, Sears. *Library Catalogues of the English Renaissance*. Berkeley: University of California Press, 1956.

Jeayes, Isaac H., ed. *Letters of Philip Gawdy*. London: Nichols, 1906.

Jencks, Charles. *Towards a Symbolic Architecture: The Thematic House*. New York: Rizzoli, 1985.

Jenkins, Harold. "Supplement to the Introduction." In W. W. Greg, ed., *The Book of Sir Thomas More*, xxxiii–xlvi. 1911. Reprint, London: Malone Society, 1961.

Johnson, Francis R. "Notes on English Retail Book-prices, 1550–1640." *The Library*, 5th ser., 5 (1950–1951): 83–112.

Johnson, Samuel. *Johnson on Shakespeare*. Edited by Arthur Sherbo. Vols. 7–8 of *The Yale Edition of the Works of Samuel Johnson*. New Haven: Yale University Press, 1968.

——. *Selected Poetry and Prose*. Edited by Frank Brady and W. K. Wimsatt. Berkeley: University of California Press, 1977.

Johnston, Alexandra F. "The Procession and the Play of Corpus Christi in York After 1426." *Leeds Studies in English*, n.s., 7 (1973): 55–62.

——. "The York Corpus Christi Play: A Dramatic Structure Based on Performance Practice." In Herman Braet, Johan Nowe, and Gilbert Tournoy, eds., *The Theatre in the Middle Ages,* 362–73. Leuven: Leuven University Press, 1985.

——, ed. "Records of Early English Drama: Berkshire." Unpublished transcriptions.

Johnston, Alexandra F., and Margaret Rogerson, eds. *Records of Early English Drama: York*. 2 vols. Toronto: University of Toronto Press, 1979.

Jonson, Ben. *Ben Jonson*. Edited by C. H. Herford, Percy Simpson, and Evelyn Simpson. 11 vols. Oxford: Clarendon Press, 1925–52.

——. *The Complete Poems*. Edited by George Parfitt. Harmondsworth: Penguin, 1975.

——. *Epicoene or The Silent Woman*. Edited by L. A. Beaurline. Lincoln: University of Nebraska Press, 1966.

——. *Every Man in His Humour*. A Parallel-Text Edition of the 1601 Quarto and the 1616 Folio. Edited by J. W. Lever. Lincoln: University of Nebraska Press, 1971.

——. *The Magnetick Lady: Or, Humors Reconcil'd*. London, 1640.

——. "To the memory of my beloued, The AVTHOR Mr. William Shakespeare: And what he hath left vs." In Hinman, *The Norton Facsimile*, pp. 9–10.

Jonson, Ben, George Chapman, and John Marston. *Eastward Ho!* Edited by C. G. Petter. London: Ernest Benn, 1973.

Kahn, Coppélia. *Man's Estate: Masculine Identity in Shakespeare*. Berkeley: University of California Press, 1981.

Kahrl, Stanley J. "Medieval Staging and Performance." In Marianne G. Briscoe and John C. Coldewey, eds., *Contexts for Early English Drama*, 219–37. Bloomington: Indiana University Press, 1989.

——, ed. *Records of Plays and Players in Lincolnshire, 1300–1585. Collections*, vol. 8. London: Malone Society, 1974.

Kantorowicz, Ernst H. "The 'King's Advent' and the Enigmatic Panels in the Doors of Santa Sabina." *Art Bulletin* 26 (1944): 207–31.

——. *Laudes Regiae: A Study in Liturgical Acclamations and Mediaeval Ruler Worship.* Berkeley: University of California Press, 1946.

Kastan, David Scott. " 'Holy Wurdes' and 'Slypper Wit': John Bale's *King Johan* and the Poetics of Propaganda." In Peter C. Herman, ed., *Rethinking the Henrician Era*, 267–82. Urbana: University of Illinois Press, 1994.

——. "Proud Majesty Made a Subject: Shakespeare and the Spectacle of Rule." *Shakespeare Quarterly* 37 (1986): 458–75.

Kelly, Joan. *Women, History, and Theory: The Essays of Joan Kelly.* Chicago: University of Chicago Press, 1984.

Kelly, Thomas. *Early Public Libraries: A History of Public Libraries in Great Britain Before 1850.* London: Library Association, 1966.

Kendall, Ritchie. *The Drama of Dissent.* Chapel Hill: University of North Carolina Press, 1986.

Kermode, Jenny, and Garthine Walker, eds. *Women, Crime, and the Courts in Early Modern England.* London: UCLP, 1994.

Kernan, Alvin B. "Courtly Servants and Public Players: Shakespeare's Image of Theater in the Court of Elsinore and Whitehall." In Maynard Mack and George deForest Lord, eds., *Poetic Traditions of the English Renaissance*, 103–21. New Haven: Yale University Press, 1982.

Kerridge, Eric. "Early Modern English Markets." In L. Anderson and A. J. H. Latham, eds., *The Market in History*, 120–47. London: Croom Helm, 1986.

Kerrigan, John. "Revision, Adaptation, and the Fool in *King Lear.*" In Gary Taylor and Michael Warren, eds., *The Division of the Kingdoms: Shakespeare's Two Versions of "King Lear,"* 195–246. Oxford: Clarendon Press, 1983.

Kerrigan, William, and Gordon Braden. *The Idea of the Renaissance.* Baltimore and London: Johns Hopkins University Press, 1989.

Kiessling, Nicolas K. *The Library of Robert Burton.* Oxford: Oxford Bibliographical Society, 1988.

King, John N. *English Reformation Literature.* Princeton: Princeton University Press, 1982.

King, T. J. *Casting Shakespeare's Plays.* Cambridge: Cambridge University Press, 1992.

——. *Shakespearean Staging, 1599–1642.* Cambridge, Mass.: Harvard University Press, 1971.

——. "Staging of Plays at the Phoenix in Drury Lane, 1617–52." *Theatre Notebook* 19 (1964/65): 146–66.

Kipling, Gordon. " 'Grace in This Lyf and Aftirwarde Glorie': Margaret of Anjou's Royal Entry Into London." *Research Opportunities in Renaissance Drama* 29 (1986/87): 77–84.

——. "The London Pageants for Margaret of Anjou: A Medieval Script Restored." *Medieval English Theatre* 4 (1982): 5–27.

——. "Richard II's 'Sumptuous Pageants' and the Idea of the Civic Triumph." In David M.

Bergeron, ed., *Pageantry in the Shakespearean Theater*, 83–103. Athens: University of Georgia Press, 1985.

——, ed. *The Receyt of the Ladie Kateryne*. Early English Text Society, o.s., 296. London: Oxford University Press, 1990.

Kirschbaum, Leo. *Shakespeare and the Stationers*. Columbus: Ohio State University Press, 1955.

Klausner, David N., ed. *Records of Early English Drama: Herefordshire, Worcestershire*. Toronto: University of Toronto Press, 1990.

Klein, Joan Larsen, ed. *Daughters, Wives, and Widows: Writings by Men About Women and Marriage in England, 1500–1640*. Urbana: University of Illinois Press, 1992.

Klink, Dennis R. "Calvinism and Jacobean Tragedy." *Genre* 11 (1978): 333–58.

Knowles, Richard. "The Case for Two *Lears*." *Shakespeare Quarterly* 36 (1985): 115–20.

Knutson, Roslyn L. "The Commercial Significance of Payments for Playtexts in *Henslowe's Diary*, 1597–1603." *Medieval and Renaissance Drama in England* 6 (1991): 117–63.

——. "Elizabethan Documents, Captivity Narratives, and the Market for Foreign History Plays." *English Literary Renaissance* 26 (1996): 75–110.

——. "*Henslowe's Diary* and the Economics of Play Revision for Revival, 1592–1603." *Theatre Research International* 10 (1985): 1–18.

——. "Influence of the Repertory System on the Revival and Revision of *The Spanish Tragedy* and *Doctor Faustus*." *English Literary Renaissance* 18, no. 2 (1988): 257–74.

——. "The Puzzle of Short Runs in *Henslowe's Diary*." *Publications of the Arkansas Philological Association* 13 (1987): 54–67.

——. *The Repertory of Shakespeare's Company, 1594–1613*. Fayetteville: University of Arkansas Press, 1991.

Koselleck, Reinhart. *Futures Past: On the Semantics of Historical Time*. Translated by Keith Tribe. Cambridge: MIT Press, 1985.

Krivatsy, Nati H., and Laetitia Yeandle. "Sir Edward Dering." In Fehrenbach and Leedham-Green, eds., *Private*, 1:137–269.

[Kyd, Thomas]. *The First Part of Ieronimo*. London, 1605.

Kyd, Thomas. *The Spanish Tragedie . . . Newly corrected and amended of such grosse faults as passed in the first impression*. London, [1592?].

——. *The Spanish Tragedie: Or Hieronimo is mad againe*. London, 1615.

——. *The Spanish Tragedy*. Edited by Philip Edwards. Cambridge: Harvard University Press, 1959.

Lachmann, Richard. *From Manor to Market: Structural Change in England, 1536–1640*. Madison: University of Wisconsin Press, 1987.

Lake, David J. *The Canon of Thomas Middleton's Plays: Internal Evidence for the Major Problems of Authorship*. Cambridge: Cambridge University Press, 1975.

——. "Webster's Additions to *The Malcontent*: Linguistic Evidence." *Notes and Queries* 226 (1981): 153–57.

Lancashire, Anne. Review of Sylvia Stoler Wagonheim, ed., *Annals of English Drama 975–1700*. 3d ed. *Shakespeare Quarterly* 42 (1991): 225–30.

——, ed. *The Second Maiden's Tragedy*. Manchester: Manchester University Press, 1978.

Lancashire, Ian. "The Auspices of *The World and the Child*." *Renaissance and Reformation* 12 (1976): 96–105.

——. *Dramatic Texts and Records of Britain: A Chronological Topography to 1558*. Toronto: University of Toronto Press, 1984.

——. "Orders for Twelfth Day and Night *circa* 1515 in the Second Northumberland Household Book." *English Literary Renaissance* 10 (Winter 1980): 7–45.

——. *Two Tudor Interludes: Youth and Hickscorner*. Manchester: Manchester University Press, 1980.

Laroque, François. *Shakespeare's Festive World: Elizabethan Seasonal Entertainment and the Professional Stage*. Translated by Janet Lloyd. Cambridge: Cambridge University Press, 1991.

Lee, Jr., Maurice, ed. *Dudley Carleton to John Chamberlain, 1603–1624*. New Brunswick, N.J.: Rutgers University Press, 1972.

Leech, Clifford. "The Plays of Edward Sharpham: Alterations Accomplished and Projected." *Review of English Studies* 11 (1935): 69–74.

Leedham-Green, E. S. *Books in Cambridge Inventories: Book-Lists from Vice-Chancellor's Court Probate Inventories in the Tudor and Stuart Periods*. 2 vols. Cambridge: Cambridge University Press, 1986.

Lefebvre, Lucien. *The Production of Space*. Translated by Donald Nicholson-Smith. Oxford: Blackwell, 1991.

Leggatt, Alexander. *Citizen Comedy in the Age of Shakespeare*. Toronto: University of Toronto Press, 1973.

——. *Jacobean Public Theatre*. London: Routledge, 1992.

Legge, Cantrell. "A direction to value most Bookes by the charge of the Printer & Stationer as paper was sould Anno Dñi: 1622." Manuscript. Cambridge University Archives, 33. 2. 95: 25–27.

LeGoff, Jacques. *Time, Work, and Culture in the Middle Ages*. Translated by Arthur Goldhammer. Chicago: University of Chicago Press, 1980.

Leinwand, Theodore B. "Shakespeare and the Middling Sort." *Shakespeare Quarterly* 44 (1993): 284–303.

Leishman, J. B., ed. *The Three Parnassus Plays, 1598–1601*. London: Nicholson and Watson, 1949.

Leland, John, and Nicholas Udall. "Leland's and Udall's Verses Before the Coronation of Anne Boleyn." In F. J. Furnivall, ed., *Ballads from Manuscripts*, 1:364–401. London, 1868–73.

Leland, John, ed. *De Rebus Britannicis Collectanea*. 6 vols. London, 1770.

Lever, J. W., ed. *The Wasp*. Reprint, London: Malone Society, 1976.

Levin, Richard. "The Contemporary Perception of Marlowe's *Tamburlaine*." *Medieval and Renaissance Drama in England* 1 (1984): 51–70.

Levine, Laura. *Men in Women's Clothing*. Cambridge: Cambridge University Press, 1994.

Lewalski, Barbara Kiefer. *Writing Women in Jacobean England*. Cambridge: Harvard University Press, 1993.

——, ed. *Renaissance Genres: Essays on Theory, History, and Interpretation*. Cambridge: Harvard University Press, 1986.

Lewis, C. S. *English Literature in the Sixteenth Century Excluding Drama*. Oxford: Clarendon Press, 1954.

Lindley, David, ed. *The Court Masque*. Manchester: Manchester University Press, 1984.

Lindley, E. S. "The Manor of Yate." *Transactions of the Bristol and Gloucestershire Archae-ological Society* 85 (1967): 156–63.

Llewellyn, Martin. *Men-Miracles, With Other Poems*. London, 1646.

Loengard, Janet. "An Elizabethan Lawsuit: John Brayne, His Carpenter, and the Building of the Red Lion Theater." *Shakespeare Quarterly* 34 (1982): 298–310.

Loewenstein, Joseph. "The Script in the Marketplace." *Representations* 12 (1985): 101–14.

Long, William B. " 'A Bed / for woodstock': A Warning for the Unwary." *Medieval and Renaissance Drama in England* 2 (1985): 91–118.

———. "Bookkeepers and Playhouse Manuscripts: A Peek at the Evidence." *Shakespeare Newsletter* 44 (1994): 3.

———. "Bookkeepers in Action: *The Two Merry Milkmaids* and the Manuscript Playbooks." Paper presented at the annual meeting of the Shakespeare Association of America, 1994.

———. "The Occasion of *Sir Thomas More*." In T. H. Howard-Hill, ed., *Shakespeare and "Sir Thomas More": Essays on the Play and Its Shakespearian Interest*, 45–56. Cambridge: Cambridge University Press, 1989.

———. "Stage-Directions: A Misinterpreted Factor in Determining Textual Provenance." *TEXT* 2 (1985): 121–38.

Louis, Cameron, ed. "Records of Early English Drama: Sussex." Unpublished transcriptions.

Love, Harold. *Scribal Publications in Seventeenth-Century England*. Oxford: Clarendon Press, 1993.

Lowenthal, Leo. *Literature, Popular Culture, and Society*. Palo Alto: Pacific Books, 1961.

Lumiansky, R. M., and David Mills, eds. *The Chester Mystery Cycle*. 2 vols. Early English Text Society, s.s., 3, 9. London: Oxford University Press, 1974, 1986.

Lydgate, John. *The Minor Poems*. Part 2. Edited by Henry N. MacCracken. London: Oxford University Press, 1961.

Lyly, John. *The Complete Works of John Lyly*. Edited by R. Warwick Bond. 3 vols. Oxford: Clarendon Press, 1902.

MacDonald, A. A. "Mary Stewart's Entry Into Edinburgh: An Ambiguous Triumph." *Innes Review* 42 (1991): 101–10.

MacIntyre, Jean. *Costumes and Scripts in the Elizabethan Theatres*. Edmonton: University of Alberta Press, 1992.

MacLean, Sally-Beth. "Players on Tour: New Evidence from Records of Early English Drama." In C. E. McGee, ed., *Elizabethan Theatre X*, 55–72. Port Credit, Ontario: P. D. Meany, 1988.

———. "The Politics of Patronage: Dramatic Records in Robert Dudley's Household Books." *Shakespeare Quarterly* 44 (1993): 175–82.

———. "Tour Routes: 'Provincial Wanderings' or Traditional Circuits?" *Medieval and Renaissance Drama in England* 6 (1993): 1–14.

———. "Tracking Leicester's Men: Patterns and Incentives." Paper presented in the seminar "Entertainers on the Road in Early Modern England" at the annual meeting of the Shakespeare Association of America, 1991.

Madan, F., G. M. R. Turbutt, and S. Gibson. *The Original Bodleian Copy of the First Folio of Shakespeare*. Oxford: Clarendon Press, 1905.

Mann, David. *The Elizabethan Player: Contemporary Stage Representation*. London: Routledge, 1991.

Manning, Roger B. *Village Revolts: Social Protest and Popular Disturbances in England,* *1509–1640.* Oxford: Clarendon Press, 1988.

*Manuscripts of the Duke of Rutland.* Historical Manuscripts Commission, 4th Report. London: HMSO, 1874.

Marcus, Leah. "Pastimes and the Purging of Theater: *Bartholomew Fair.*" In David Scott Kastan and Peter Stallybrass, eds., *Staging the Renaissance,* 196–209. New York: Routledge, 1991.

———. *The Politics of Mirth: Jonson, Herrick, Milton, Marvell, and the Defense of Old Holiday Pastimes.* Chicago: University of Chicago Press, 1986.

———. *Puzzling Shakespeare: Local Reading and Its Discontents.* Berkeley: University of California Press, 1988.

———. "The Shakespearean Editor as Shrew-Tamer." *English Literary Renaissance* 22 (1992): 177–200.

Marlowe, Christopher. *The Complete Works of Christopher Marlowe.* Edited by Fredson Bowers. 2 vols. Cambridge: Cambridge University Press, 1973. 2d ed., Cambridge: Cambridge University Press, 1981.

———. *The Complete Works of Christopher Marlowe.* Edited by Roma Gill. Vol. 2, *Doctor Faustus.* Oxford: Clarendon Press, 1990.

———. *Doctor Faustus.* Ed. John Jump. London: Methuen, 1962.

———. *Tamburlaine the Great, Parts I and II.* Edited by W. Harper. New York: Hill and Wang, 1971.

———. *The troublesome raigne and lamentable death of Edward the second, King of England . . .* Written by Chri. Marlow Gent. London, 1594.

———. *The Works of Christopher Marlowe.* Edited by C. F. Tucker Brooke. Oxford: Clarendon Press, 1910.

Marotti, Arthur F. *Manuscript, Print, and the English Renaissance Lyric.* Ithaca: Cornell University Press, 1995.

Marsh, Bower, transcriber and editor. *Records of the Worshipful Company of Carpenters.* Vol. 3. Oxford: Oxford University Press, 1915.

Marston, John. *Iacke Drum's Entertainment.* London, 1601.

———. *The Malcontent.* Edited by Bernard Harris. London: Ernest Benn, 1967.

———. *The Malcontent.* Edited by G. K. Hunter. London: Methuen, 1975.

———. *Plays.* Edited by H. Harvey Wood. 3 vols. London: Oliver and Boyd, 1934.

Marx, Karl. *The Marx-Engels Reader.* 2d ed. Edited by Robert C. Tucker. New York: Norton, 1978.

Massinger, Philip. *Believe as You List.* Edited by C. J. Sisson. London: Malone Society, 1927.

———. *The Excellent Comedy, called The Old Law: Or A new way to please you.* [By Phil. Massinger. Tho. Middleton. William Rowley.] London, 1656.

Masten, Jeffrey. "Beaumont and/or Fletcher: Collaboration and the Interpretation of Renaissance Drama." *ELH* 59 (1992): 337–56.

———. "My Two Dads: Collaboration and the Reproduction of Beaumont and Fletcher." In Jonathan Goldberg, ed., *Queering the Renaissance,* 280–309. Durham: Duke University Press, 1993.

———. "Pressing Subjects; Or the Secret Lives of Shakespeare's Compositors." In Jeffrey Masten, Peter Stallybrass, and Nancy Vickers, eds., *Language Machines: Technologies of*

*Cultural Production*. Papers from the 1995 English Institute. New York: Routledge, forthcoming 1997.

———. *Textual Intercourse: Collaboration, Authorship, and Sexualities in Renaissance
Drama*. Cambridge: Cambridge University Press, 1996.

Maydiston, Richard. "The Reconciliation of Richard II. with the City of London." In
Thomas Wright, ed., *Political Poems and Songs Relating to English History Composed
During the Period from the Accession of Edw. III. to That of Ric. III*, 1:282–300. 2 vols. Lon-
don, 1859–61.

McConica, James, ed. *The History of the University of Oxford*. Vol. 3, *The Collegiate University*. Oxford: Oxford University Press, 1986.

McDonald, Russ, ed. *Shakespeare Reread: The Texts in New Contexts*. Ithaca: Cornell University Press, 1994.

McFarlane, Kenneth. *The Nobility of Later Medieval England*. Oxford: Clarendon Press, 1957.

McGann, Jerome J. *Critique of Modern Textual Criticism*. Chicago: University of Chicago
Press, 1983.

McGee, C. E. "Travelling Players: The Case of Dorset." Paper presented in the seminar
"Entertainers on the Road in Early Modern England" at the meeting of the Shakespeare
Association of America, 1991.

McKenzie, D. F. *The Cambridge University Press, 1696–1712: A Bibliographical Study*. 2 vols.
Cambridge: Cambridge University Press, 1966.

———. "Notes on Printing at Cambridge c. 1590." *Transactions of the Cambridge Bibliographical Society* 3 (1959–1963): 96–103.

———. "Printers of the Mind: Some Notes on Bibliographical Theories and Printing-House
Practices." *Studies in Bibliography* 22 (1969): 1–75.

McKerrow, Ronald B. *An Introduction to Bibliography for Literary Students*. Oxford: Clarendon Press, 1927.

———. *Prolegomena for the Oxford Shakespeare: A Study in Editorial Method*. Oxford:
Oxford University Press, 1939.

———. "A Suggestion Regarding Shakespeare's Manuscripts." *Review of English Studies* 11
(1935): 459–65.

McLaverty, James. "The Concept of Authorial Intention in Textual Criticism." *The Library*,
6th ser., 6 (1984): 121–38.

McLuskie, Kathleen E. "The Poets' Royal Exchange: Patronage and Commerce in Early
Modern Drama." *Yearbook of English Studies* 21 (1991): 53–62.

———. *Renaissance Dramatists*. Atlantic Highlands, N.J.: Humanities International, 1989.

McMillin, Scott. *The Elizabethan Theatre and "The Book of Sir Thomas More."* Ithaca: Cornell University Press, 1987.

———. "The Ownership of *The Jew of Malta*, *Friar Bacon*, and *The Ranger's Comedy*." *English Language Notes* 9 (1972): 249–52.

———. "The Plots of *The Dead Man's Fortune* and *2 Seven Deadly Sins*." *Studies in Bibliography* 26 (1973): 235–44.

———. "The Queen's Men and the London Theatre of 1583." In C. E. McGee, ed., *Elizabethan Theatre X*, 1–17. Port Credit, Ontario: P. D. Meany, 1988.

McMullan, Gordon. *The Politics of Unease in the Plays of John Fletcher*. Amherst: University
of Massachusetts Press, 1994.

McPherson, David. "Ben Jonson's Library and Marginalia: An Annotated Catalogue." *Studies in Philology* 71 (1974): 1–106.

Meadowcroft, J. W. R. "Playing King Lear: Donald Sinden Talks to J. W. R. Meadowcroft." *Shakespeare Survey* 32 (1980): 81–87.

Medwall, Henry. *The Plays of Henry Medwall.* Edited by Alan H. Nelson. Cambridge: D. S. Brewer, 1980.

Mercer, Eric. "The Decoration of the Royal Palaces from 1553–1625." *Archaeological Journal* 110 (1953): 150–63.

*Middlesex County Records.* Edited by John Cordy Jeaffreson. 4 vols. London: Middlesex County Records Society, 1886–92.

Middleton, Thomas. *The Collected Works of Thomas Middleton.* Edited by Gary Taylor. Oxford: Oxford University Press, forthcoming.

——. *"A Game at Chesse" by Thomas Middleton.* Edited by R. C. Bald. Cambridge: Cambridge University Press, 1929.

——. *"Hengist, King of Kent; or The Mayor of Queenborough" by Thomas Middleton.* Edited by R. C. Bald. New York: Scribner's, 1938.

——. *The Roaring Girle.* London, 1611.

——. *The Works.* Edited by A. H. Bullen. 8 vols. 1885–86. Reprint, New York: AMS Press, 1964.

Mill, Anna Jean. *Mediaeval Plays in Scotland.* Edinburgh and London: William Blackwood, 1927.

Milo, Daniel S. *Trahir le Temps (Histoire).* Paris: Les Belles Lettres, 1991.

Minsheu, Iohn. *Ductor in Linguas The Guide into the tongues.* London, 1617.

Moeslein, M., ed. *The Plays of Henry Medwall: A Critical Edition.* New York: Garland, 1981.

Mommsen, T. E. "Petrarch's Conception of the 'Dark Ages.' " *Speculum* 17 (1942): 226–42.

Montagu, Elizabeth. *An Essay on the Writings and Genius of Shakspeare, Compared with the Greek and French Dramatic Poets with Some Remarks upon the Misrepresentations of Mons. de Voltaire.* 6th ed. London: R. Priestley, 1810.

Montaigne, Michel de. *The Essayes Or Morall, Politike and Millitairie Discourses of Lo: Michaell de Montaigne . . . now done into English.* Translated by John Florio. London, 1603.

Montrose, Louis Adrian. "The Place of a Brother in *As You Like It*: Social Process and Comic Form." *Shakespeare Quarterly* 32 (1981): 28–54.

More, Thomas. *The Booke of Sir Thomas More.* Edited by W. W. Greg. 1911. Reprint, London: Malone Society, 1961.

——. *The History of Richard III.* Vol. 2 of *The Complete Works of Sir Thomas More.* Edited by Richard Sylvester. New Haven: Yale University Press, 1963.

Morgan, Paul. "Frances Wolfreston and 'Hor Bouks': A Seventeenth-Century Woman Book-Collector." *The Library,* 6th ser., 11 (1989): 197–219.

Mowat, Barbara A. "Lavinia's Message: Shakespeare and Myth." *Renaissance Papers 1981:* 55–69.

——. "Rogues, Shepherds, and the Counterfeit Distressed: Texts and Infracontexts of *The Winter's Tale* 4.3." *Shakespeare Studies* 23 (1994): 58–76.

——. "Shakespeare's Text as Construct." *Style* 23 (1989): 335–51.

———. *"The Tempest*: A Modern Perspective." In Barbara A. Mowat and Paul Werstine, eds., *The Tempest*, 185–99. Washington, D.C.: Folger Library, 1994.

Mowl, Timothy. *Elizabethan and Jacobean Style*. London: Phaidon, 1993.

Moxon, Joseph. *Mechanick Exercises on the Whole Art of Printing (1683–4)*. Edited by Herbert Davis and Harry Carter. 2d ed. London: Oxford University Press, 1962.

Muir, Kenneth. Introduction to *The Painfull Adventures of Pericles Prince of Tyre*. Liverpool: University of Liverpool, 1953.

Mulcaster, Richard. *Positions wherein those primitive circumstances be examined, necessary for the bringing up of children*. London, 1581.

[Mulcaster, Richard]. *The Quenes Maiesties Passage Through the Citie of London to Westminster the Day Before Her Coronacion*. Introduction by Sir John Neale. Edited by James M. Osborn. New Haven: Yale University Press, 1960.

Mullaney, Steven. *The Place of the Stage: License, Play, and Power in Renaissance England*. Chicago: University of Chicago Press, 1988.

Munro, John, ed. *The Shakspere Allusion-Book: A Collection of Allusions to Shakspere from 1591 to 1700*. 2 vols. New York: Duffield, 1909.

Murray, John Tucker. *The English Dramatic Companies, 1558–1642*. 2 vols. London: Constable, 1910. Reprint, New York: Russell and Russell, 1963.

Murray, Timothy. *Theatrical Legitimation: Allegories of Genius in Seventeenth-Century England and France*. New York and Oxford: Oxford University Press, 1987.

Myers, Alec Reginald. *The Household Book of Edward IV: The Black Book and the Ordinance of 1478*. Manchester: Manchester University Press, 1959.

Myers, Robin. *The Stationers' Company Archive: An Account of the Records, 1554–1984*. Winchester: St Paul's Bibliographies, 1990.

———, ed. *Records of the Worshipful Company of Stationers, 1554–1920*. Microfilm, 112 reels. Cambridge: Chadwyck-Healey, 1985.

Myers, Robin, and Michael Harris, eds. *Property of a Gentleman: The Formation, Organisation, and Dispersal of the Private Library, 1620–1920*. Winchester: St. Paul's Bibliographies, 1991.

Nabbes, Thomas. *Tottenham Court*. London, 1638.

Nashe, Thomas. *The Works of Thomas Nashe*. Edited by R. B. McKerrow. 5 vols. London: Sidgwick and Jackson, 1910. Reprint, Oxford: Blackwell, 1958.

Naudé, Gabriel. *Instructions Concerning Erecting of a Library*. Translated by John Evelyn. London, 1661.

Neill, Michael. " 'Wit's most accomplished Senate': The Audience of the Caroline Private Theaters." *Studies in English Literature* 18 (1976): 341–60.

Nelson, Alan H. *Early Cambridge Theatres: College, University, and Town Stages, 1464–1720*. Cambridge: Cambridge University Press, 1994.

———. *The Medieval English Stage: Corpus Christi Pageants and Plays*. Chicago: University of Chicago Press, 1974.

———, ed. *Records of Early English Drama: Cambridge*. 2 vols. Toronto: University of Toronto Press, 1989.

Newman, Karen. *Fashioning Femininity and English Renaissance Drama*. Chicago: University of Chicago Press, 1991.

Newton, Stella Mary. *Renaissance Theatre Costume and the Sense of the Historical Past.* London: Rapp and Whiting, 1975.

Newton, Thomas, trans. *Fovvre Severall Treatises of M. Tvllivs Cicero: Conteyninge his most learned and Eloquente Discourses of Frendshippe: Oldage: Paradoxes: and Scipio his Dreame. All turned out of Latine into English, by Thomas Newton.* London, 1577.

Nicholl, Charles. *The Reckoning: The Murder of Christopher Marlowe.* London: Picador, 1992.

Nichols, John Gough, ed. *The Chronicle of Queen Jane and of Two Years of Queen Mary and Especially of the Rebellion of Sir Thomas Wyatt. Written by a Resident in the Tower of London.* London: Camden Society, 1850.

Nixon, Antony. *Oxfords Triumph.* London, 1605.

Nochimson, Richard L. "Robert Burton's Authorship of *Alba.*" *Review of English Studies,* n.s., 21 (1970): 325–31.

Norbrook, David. "The Masque of Truth." *The Seventeenth Century* 1 (1986): 81–109.

Norden, John. *Civitas Londini.* London, 1600.

Nosworthy, J. M. "Hand B in *Sir Thomas More.*" *The Library,* 5th ser., 11 (1956): 47–50.

———. "The Marlowe Manuscript." *The Library,* 4th ser., 26 (1946): 158–71.

Nungezer, Edwin. *A Dictionary of Actors and of Other Persons Associated with the Public Representation of Plays in England Before 1642.* New Haven: Yale University Press, 1929. Reprint, New York: Greenwood Press, 1968.

Oates, Mary I., and William J. Baumol. "On the Economics of Theatre in Renaissance London." *Swedish Journal of Economics* 74 (1972): 136–60.

*The Oldcastle Controversy: "Sir John Oldcastle, Part 1" and "The Famous Victories of Henry V."* Edited by Peter Corbin and Douglas Sedge. Manchester: Manchester University Press, 1991.

Oliver, H. J., ed. *Dido Queen of Carthage; The Massacre at Paris.* London: Methuen, 1968.

O'Malley, Susan Gushee, ed. *A Critical Old-Spelling Edition of Thomas Goffe's "The Courageous Turk."* New York: Garland, 1979.

Ong, Walter J. "Latin Language Study as a Renaissance Puberty Rite." *Studies in Philology* 56 (1959): 103–24.

Orgel, Stephen. *The Illusion of Power: Political Theater in the English Renaissance.* Berkeley and Los Angeles: University of California Press, 1975.

———. *The Jonsonian Masque.* Cambridge: Harvard University Press, 1967.

———. "Making Greatness Familiar." In David Bergeron, ed., *Pageantry in the Shakespearean Theater,* 19–25. Athens: University of Georgia Press, 1985.

———. "Nobody's Perfect: Or, Why Did the English Stage Take Boys for Women?" *South Atlantic Quarterly* 88 (1989): 7–29.

———. "What Is a Text?" In David Scott Kastan and Peter Stallybrass, eds., *Staging the Renaissance: Reinterpretations of Elizabethan and Jacobean Drama,* 83–87. New York: Routledge, 1991.

Orgel, Stephen, and Roy Strong. *Inigo Jones: The Theatre of the Stuart Court.* 2 vols. Berkeley: University of California Press, 1973.

Orlin, Lena Cowen. *Elizabethan Households: An Anthology.* Washington, D.C.: Folger Shakespeare Library, 1995.

——. *Private Matters and Public Culture in Post-Reformation England.* Ithaca: Cornell University Press, 1994.

Orrell, John. "The Architecture of the Fortune Playhouse." *Shakespeare Survey* 47 (1994): 15–27.

——. "Beyond the Rose: Design Problems for the Globe Reconstruction." In Franklin J. Hildy, ed., *New Issues in the Reconstruction of Shakespeare's Theater: Proceedings of the Conference Held at the University of Georgia, February 16–18, 1990,* 95–118. New York: Peter Lang, 1990.

——. "Building the Fortune." *Shakespeare Quarterly* 44 (1993): 127–44.

——. *The Human Stage: English Theatre Design, 1567–1640.* Cambridge: Cambridge University Press, 1988.

——. "Inigo Jones at the Cockpit." *Shakespeare Survey* 30 (1977): 157–68.

——. "The London Stage in Florentine Correspondence, 1604–1618." *Theatre Research International* 3 (1978): 157–76.

——. "The Private Theatre Auditorium." *Theatre Research International,* n.s., 9 (1984): 79–93.

——. *The Quest for Shakespeare's Globe.* Cambridge: Cambridge University Press, 1983.

——. "Scenes and Machines at the Cockpit, Drury Lane." *Theater Survey* 26 (1985): 103–19.

——. "The Theatre at Christ Church, Oxford, in 1605." *Shakespeare Survey* 35 (1982): 129–40.

——. *The Theatres of Inigo Jones and John Webb.* Cambridge: Cambridge University Press, 1985.

Osberg, Richard H. "The Jesse Tree in the 1432 London Entry of Henry VI: Messianic Kingship and the Rule of Justice." *Journal of Medieval and Renaissance Studies* 16 (1986): 213–32.

Palliser, D. M. "Civic Mentality and the Environment in Tudor York." *Northern History* 18 (1982): 78–115.

Panofsky, Erwin. *Renaissance and Renascences in Western Art.* London: Paladin, 1970.

Parker, Mark. "*Measure and Counter-measure: the Loving joy—Wellek Debate and Romantic Periodization.*" In David Perkins, ed. *Theoretical Issues in Literary History.* Cambridge: Harvard University Press, 1981.

*Inescapable Romance: Studies in the Poetics of a Mode.* Princeton: Princeton University Press, 1979.

Parker, Patricia. *Literary Fat Ladies: Rhetoric, Gender, Property.* London and New York: Methuen, 1987.

Parry, Graham. *The Golden Age Restor'd: The Culture of the Stuart Court.* Manchester: Manchester University Press, 1981.

——. "The Politics of the Jacobean Masque." In J. R. Mulryne and Margaret Shewring, eds., *Theatre and Government Under the Early Stuarts,* 87–118. Cambridge: Cambridge University Press, 1993.

Paster, Gail Kern. *The Body Embarrassed: Drama and the Disciplines of Shame in Early Modern England.* Ithaca: Cornell University Press, 1993.

Patterson, Annabel. *Censorship and Interpretation: The Conditions of Reading and Writing in Early Modern England.* Madison: University of Wisconsin Press, 1984.

——. *Reading Holinshed's Chronicles.* Chicago: University of Chicago Press, 1994.

——. *Shakespeare and The Popular Voice.* Oxford: Blackwell, 1989.

Peacham, Henry. *The Compleat Gentleman.* London, 1622.

——. *Thalia's Banquet*. London, 1620.

Peacock, John. *The Stage Designs of Inigo Jones: The European Context*. Cambridge: Cambridge University Press, 1995.

Peat, Derek. "Looking Back to Front: The View from the Lords' Room." In Marvin Thompson and Ruth Thompson, eds., *Shakespeare and the Sense of Performance*, 180–94. Newark: University of Delaware Press, 1989.

——. "Looking Up and Looking Down: Shakespeare's Vertical Audience." *Shakespeare Quarterly* 35 (1984): 563–70.

Peck, Linda Levy. "Court Corruption and Patronage in Early Stuart England." In Guy Fitch Little and Stephen Orgel, eds. *Patronage in Early Modern England*, 27–46. Princeton: Princeton University Press, 1981.

Pepys, Samuel. *The Diary of Samuel Pepys*. Edited by Robert Latham and William Matthews. 9 vols. Berkeley: University of California Press, 1970.

Peter, C. G., ed. *A Critical Old-Spelling Edition of the Works of Edward Sharpham*. New York: Garland, 1986.

Philip, Ian. *The Bodleian Library in the Seventeenth and Eighteenth Centuries*. Lyell Lectures, Oxford, 1980–81. Oxford: Clarendon Press, 1983.

——. Introduction to Gwen Hampshire, ed., *The Bodleian Library Account Book, 1613–1646*. Oxford: Oxford Bibliographical Society, 1983.

Phythian-Adams, Charles. "Ceremony and the Citizen: The Communal Year at Coventry, 1450–1550." In Peter Clark and Paul Slack, eds., *Crisis and Order in English Towns, 1500–1700: Essays in Urban History*, 57–85. London: Routledge and Kegan Paul.

——. "Ceremony and the Citizen: The Communal Year at Coventry, 1450–1550." In Richard Holt and Gervase Rosser, eds., *The English Medieval Town: A Reader in English Urban History, 1250–1540*, 238–64. London: Longman, 1990.

Pilkinton, Mark. "The Playhouse in Wine Street, Bristol." *Theatre Notebook* 37 (1983): 14–21.

——, ed. "Records of Early English Drama: Bristol." Unpublished transcriptions.

*Pimlyco, or Runne Red-Cap*. London, 1609.

Pinciss, F. M. "Thomas Creede and the Repertory of the Queen's Men, 1583–1592." *Modern Philology* 67 (1970): 321–30.

Pitcher, John. "Editing Daniel." In W. Speed Hill, ed., *New Ways of Looking at Old Texts*, 57–74. Binghamton, N.Y.: Renaissance English Text Society, 1993.

Pittenger, Elizabeth. "Dispatch Quickly: The Mechanical Reproduction of Pages." *Shakespeare Quarterly* 42 (1991): 389–408.

Platter, Thomas. *Thomas Platter's Travels in England, 1599*. Translated by Clare Williams. London: J. Cape, 1937.

Plomer, Henry R. *A Dictionary of the Booksellers and Printers Who Were at Work in England, Scotland, and Ireland from 1641–1667*. London: Blades, East, and Blades, 1907. Reprint, London: Bibliographical Society, 1968.

Pollard, Alfred W. *Shakespeare Folios and Quartos: A Study in the Bibliography of Shakespeare's Plays, 1594–1685*. London: Methuen, 1909.

——. *Shakespeare's Fight with the Pirates and the Problems of the Transmission of His Text*. London: Moring, 1917. 2d ed., rev., Cambridge: Cambridge University Press, 1920.

——, ed. *Shakespeare's Hand in "Sir Thomas More."* Cambridge: Cambridge University Press, 1923.

Pollard, Alfred W., and G. R. Redgrave, comps. *A Short-Title Catalogue of Books Printed in England, Scotland, and Ireland, and of English Books Printed Abroad, 1475–1640*. 2d ed., rev. and enlarged by W. A. Jackson, F. S. Ferguson, and Katharine F. Pantzer. 3 vols. London: Bibliographical Society, 1976–91.

Pollard, Graham. "The Early Constitution of the Stationers' Company." *The Library*, 4th ser., 18 (1937–1938): 235–60.

———. "The Sandars Lectures, 1959." *Publishing History* 4 (1978): 7–48.

Pollet, Maurice. *John Skelton*. Translated by John Warrington. London: Dent and Sons, 1971.

Poole, Kristen. "Saints Alive! Falstaff, Martin Marprelate, and the Staging of Puritanism." *Shakespeare Quarterly* 46 (1995): 47–75.

Poole, Reginald. *Medieval Reckonings of Time*. New York: Macmillan, 1921.

Prest, Wilfrid R. *The Inns of Court Under Elizabeth I and the Early Stuarts, 1590–1640*. Towtowa, N.J.: Rowman and Littlefield, 1972.

Price, David. *Patrons and Musicians of the English Renaissance*. Cambridge: Cambridge University Press, 1981.

Price, George R., ed. *A Fair Quarrel*. Lincoln: University of Nebraska Press, 1976.

Prior, Mary, ed. *Women in English Society, 1500–1800*. New York: Methuen, 1985.

Prynne, William. *Histrio-Mastix. The Players Scourge, or, Actors Tragaedie*. London, 1633.

Quint, David. *Origin and Originality in Renaissance Literature: Versions of the Source*. New Haven: Yale University Press, 1983.

Raine, Angelo. *Mediaeval York*. London: John Murray, 1955.

Rainolds, John. *Th'Overthrow of Stage-Playes*. Middelburgh, 1599.

[Ralegh, Walter]. *The History of the World*. London, 1614.

Rambuss, Richard. *Spenser's Secret Career*. Cambridge: Cambridge University Press, 1993.

Randolph, Thomas. *The Muses Looking-Glasse*. London, 1638.

Rappaport, Steve. *Worlds Within Worlds: Structures of Life in Sixteenth-Century London*. Cambridge: Cambridge University Press, 1989.

Rasmussen, Eric. "Setting Down What the Clown Spoke: Improvisation, Hand B, and *The Book of Sir Thomas More*." *The Library*, 6th ser., 13 (1991): 126–36.

———. "Shakespeare's Hand in *The Second Maiden's Tragedy*." *Shakespeare Quarterly* 40 (1989): 1–26.

———. *A Textual Companion to "Doctor Faustus"*. The Revels Plays Companion Library. Manchester: Manchester University Press, 1994.

Rastell, William. *The Pardoner and the Friar and the Four Ps*. Edited by G. R. Proudfoot. Oxford: Oxford University Press, 1984.

Rawcliffe, Carole. *The Staffords, Earls of Stafford and Dukes of Buckingam*. Cambridge: Cambridge University Press, 1978.

Reynolds, George F. *The Staging of Elizabethan Plays at the Red Bull Theater*. New York: Modern Language Association, 1940.

Richards, E. J., ed. *The Christmas Prince. Renaissance Latin Drama in England*. First Series 11. Hildesheim and New York: Georg Olms, 1982.

Richardson, H. *The Medieval Fairs and Markets of York*. York: St. Anthony's Press, 1961.

Riggio, Milla, ed. *The Wisdom Symposium: Papers from the Trinity College Medieval Festival*. New York: AMS Press, 1986.

Roberts, Jeanne Addison. "Ralph Crane and the Text of *The Tempest.*" *Shakespeare Studies* 13 (1980): 213–33.

Roberts, Julian, and Andrew G. Watson, eds. *John Dee's Library Catalogue*. London: Bibliographical Society, 1990.

Robertson, William. *History of the Reign of Charles V*. Edinburgh, 1769.

Rowley, William. *The Witch of Edmonton: A known true Story*. Composed into A Tragi-Comedy By divers well-esteemed Poets; William Rowley, Thomas Dekker, John Ford, &c. London, 1658.

Rozett, Martha Tuck. *The Doctrine of Election and the Emergence of Elizabethan Tragedy*. Princeton: Princeton University Press, 1984.

Rubin, Gayle. "The Traffic in Women: Notes on the 'Political Economy' of Sex." In Rayna Reiter, ed., *Toward an Anthropology of Women*, 157–210. New York: Monthly Review Press, 1975.

Rubin, Miri. *Corpus Christi: The Eucharist in Late Medieval Culture*. Cambridge: Cambridge University Press, 1991.

Russell, Joycelyne G. *The Field of Cloth of Gold: Men and Manners in 1520*. London: Routledge and Kegan Paul, 1969.

Rutter, Carol Chilington, ed. *Documents of the Rose Playhouse*. Manchester: Manchester University Press, 1984.

Said, Edward. *Beginnings: Intention and Method*. New York: Basic Books, 1975.

Salter, H. E., ed. *Registrum Annalium Collegii Mertonensis 1483–1521*. Oxford: Oxford Historical Society, 1923.

Scarisbrick, J. J. *The Reformation and the English People*. Oxford: Blackwell, 1984.

Scattergood, V. J. "Literary Culture at the Court of Richard II." In V. J. Scattergood and J. W. Sherborne, eds., *English Court Culture in the Later Middle Ages*, 29–44. New York: St. Martin's, 1983.

Schalkwyk, David. " 'She never told her love': Embodiment, Textuality, and Silence in Shakespeare's Sonnets and Plays." *Shakespeare Quarterly* 45 (1994): 381–407.

Schanzer, Ernest. Introduction to *Pericles, Prince of Tyre*. New York: Signet, 1977.

Sheingorn, Pamela. "Illustrations in the Manuscript of the Lille Plays." *Research Opportunities in Renaissance Drama* 30 (1988): 173–76.

Schwartz, Hillel. *Century's End: A Cultural History of the Fin-de-Siècle from the 990s through the 1990s*. New York: Doubleday, 1990.

Schwartz, Murray M., and Coppélia Kahn. *Representing Shakespeare: New Psychoanalytic Essays*. Baltimore: Johns Hopkins University Press, 1980.

Schwarz, Marc L. "Sir Edward Coke and 'This Scept'red Isle': A Case of Borrowing." *Notes and Queries*, n.s., 35 (1988): 54–56.

Scott, Michael. *John Marston's Plays: Theme, Structure, and Performance*. London: Macmillan, 1978.

Seaver, Paul S. *The Puritan Lectureships*. Stanford: Stanford University Press, 1970.

*The Second Maiden's Tragedy*. Edited by Anne Lancashire. Manchester: Manchester University Press, 1978.

"Second Northumberland Household Book." Unpublished Bodleian Library Manuscript. English History b.208.

Sedgwick, Eve Kosofsky. *Between Men: English Literature and Male Homosocial Desire.* New York: Columbia University Press, 1985.

Serlio, Sebastiano. *Architettura.* In Bernard Hewitt, ed., *The Renaissance Stage: Documents of Serlio, Sabbattini, and Furenbach.* Coral Gables: University of Miami Press, 1958.

——. *The First [-fift] Booke of Architecture, Made by Sebastian Serly . . . Translated out of Italian into Dutch, and of Dutch into English.* London, 1611.

Shaaber, M. A. "The Meaning of the Imprint in Early Printed Books." *The Library,* 4th ser., 24 (1943–1944): 120–41.

Shakespeare, William. *The Complete Works.* Edited by Peter Alexander. London: Collins, 1951.

——. *The Complete Works of Shakespeare.* Edited by David Bevington. 4th ed. New York: Harper Collins, 1992.

——. *Hamlet.* Edited by G. R. Hibbard. Oxford: Oxford University Press, 1987.

——. *Hamlet.* Edited by Harold Jenkins. London: Methuen, 1982.

——. *I Henry IV.* Edited by David Bevington. Oxford: Clarendon Press, 1987.

——. *King Henry IV, Part 1.* Edited by A. R. Humphreys. London: Methuen, 1960.

——. *King Lear.* Edited by Kenneth Muir. London: Methuen, 1952.

——. *The Late, And much admired Play, Called Pericles, Prince of Tyre.* London, 1609.

——. *A Midsummer Night's Dream.* Edited by Harold F. Brooks. London: Methuen, 1979.

——. *The most excellent Historie of the Merchant of Venice.* London, 1600.

——. *A Most pleasaunt and excellent conceited Comedie, of Syr Iohn Falstaffe, and the merrie Wiues of Windsor.* London, 1602.

——. *The New Cambridge Shakespeare.* Edited by John Dover Wilson and Arthur Quiller-Couch. 42 vols. Cambridge: Cambridge University Press, 1921–66.

——. *The Norton Facsimile: The First Folio of Shakespeare.* Edited by Charlton Hinman. New York: Norton, 1968.

——. *Othello.* Edited by M. R. Ridley. London: Methuen, 1958.

——. *Pericles.* Edited by F. D. Hoeniger. London: Methuen, 1963.

——. *A Pleasant Conceited Comedie Called, Loues labors lost. Newly corrected and augmented By W. Shakespere.* London, 1598.

——. *The Riverside Shakespeare.* Edited by G. Blakemore Evans. Boston: Houghton Mifflin, 1974.

——. *Shakespeare's Sonnets.* Edited by Stephen Booth. New Haven: Yale University Press, 1977.

——. *The Taming of the Shrew.* Edited by H. J. Oliver. Oxford: Oxford University Press, 1982.

——. *The Taming of the Shrew.* Edited by Ann Thompson. Cambridge: Cambridge University Press, 1982.

——. *The Tempest.* Edited by Stephen Orgel. Oxford: Oxford University Press, 1987.

——. *The Tragœdy of Othello, The Moore of Venice.* London, 1622.

——. *The Tragicall Historie of Hamlet Prince of Denmarke.* London, 1603.

——. *The Two Gentlemen of Verona. Mr. William Shakespeares Comedies, Histories & Tragedies.* London, 1623. In Hinman, *The Norton Facsimile.*

———. *The Two Noble Kinsmen: Mr. John Fletcher, and Mr. William Shakspeare*. London, 1634.

———. *William Shakespeare: The Complete Works*. Edited by Gary Taylor and Stanley Wells. Oxford: Clarendon Press, 1986.

Shann, Richard. "The Commonplace Book of Richard Shann." Unpublished manuscript held by the British Library. Add. MS 38,599.

Shapiro, I. A. "The Melbourne Manuscript." *Times Literary Supplement*, July 4, 1986, pp. 735–36.

Shapiro, Michael. *Children of the Revels: The Boy Companies of Shakespeare's Time and Their Plays*. New York: Columbia University Press, 1977.

Sharpe, Kevin. *Criticism and Compliment: The Politics of Literature in the England of Charles I*. Cambridge: Cambridge University Press, 1987.

Sharpe, Robert Bois. *The Real War of the Theaters: Shakespeare's Fellows in Rivalry with the Admiral's Men, 1594–1603*. Boston: D. C. Heath, 1935.

Sherman, William H. *John Dee: The Politics of Reading and Writing in the English Renaissance*. Amherst: University of Massachusetts Press, 1995.

Shillingsburg, Peter L. *Scholarly Editing in the Computer Age*. Athens: University of Georgia Press, 1986.

Shuger, Deborah. *Habits of Thought in the English Renaissance: Religion, Politics, and the Dominant Culture*. Berkeley: University of California Press, 1990.

Siemon, James R. *Shakespearean Iconoclasm*. Berkeley: University of California Press, 1985.

———. "Sporting Kyd." *English Literary Renaissance* 24 (1994): 553–82.

Sinfield, Alan. *Faultlines: Cultural Materialism and the Politics of Dissident Reading*. Berkeley: University of California Press, 1992.

Sisson, C. J. "The Laws of Elizabethan Copyright: The Stationers' View." *The Library*, 5th ser., 15 (1960): 8–20.

———. "Shakespeare's Quartos as Prompt-copies." *Review of English Studies* 18 (1942): 129–43.

Slack, Paul. *The Impact of Plague in Tudor and Stuart England*. Cambridge: Cambridge University Press, 1985.

Smith, Bruce. *Homosexual Desire in Shakespeare's England: A Cultural Poetics*. Chicago: University of Chicago Press, 1991.

Smith, Charles R., ed. and trans. "Richard Moydiston's 'Concordia: Foeta Inter Regem Riccardum II et Civitatem Londonie." Ph.D. diss., Princeton University, 1972.

Smith, George Charles Moore. *College Plays Performed in the University of Cambridge*. Cambridge: Cambridge University Press, 1923.

Smith, Irwin. *Shakespeare's Blackfriars Theater: Its History and Its Design*. New York: New York University Press, 1964.

———. *Shakespeare's Globe Playhouse*. New York: Scribner's, 1956.

Smyth, John. *The Berkeley Manuscripts*. Edited by Sir John Maclean. Gloucester, 1883–85.

Smythson, Robert. "The Banketinge House at the White Hall in London." Drawing. Smythson Collection I/10. Royal Institute of British Architects, London.

Somerset, J. A. B. " 'How chances it they travel?': Provincial Touring, Playing Places, and the King's Men." *Shakespeare Survey* 47 (1994): 45–60.

——. "Local Drama and Playing Places at Shrewsbury: New Findings from the Borough Records." *Medieval and Renaissance Drama in England* 2 (1985): 1–32.

——. "The Lords President, Their Activities and Companies: Evidence from Shropshire." In C. E. McGee, ed., *Elizabethan Theatre X*, 93–111. Port Credit, Ontario: P. D. Meany, 1988.

——. "New Historicism: Old History Writ Large? Carnival, Festivity and Popular Culture in the West Midlands." *Medieval and Renaissance Drama in England* 5 (1991): 245–56.

——. "Unremarked, But Not Unremarkable: The Lady Elizabeth's Men." Paper delivered at the annual meeting of the Shakespeare Association of America, 1995.

——, ed. *Records of Early English Drama: Shropshire*. Toronto: University of Toronto Press, 1994.

Soule, Lesley. "Character, Actor, and Anti-Character." Ph.D. diss., University of Exeter, 1994.

——. "Subverting Rosalind: Cocky Ros in the Forest of Arden." *New Theatre Quarterly* 26 (1991): 126–36.

Southern, Richard. *The Seven Ages of the Theatre*. New York: Hill and Wang, 1961.

——. *The Staging of Plays Before Shakespeare*. London: Faber and Faber, 1973.

Spalding, Jack J. "The Sequence of Cigoli's Studies in the Uffizi for the *Martyrdom of St. Stephen*." *Master Drawings* 19 (1981): 293–99.

Spector, Stephen, ed. *The N-Town Play*. 2 vols. Early English Text Society, s.s. 11, 12. Oxford: Oxford University Press, 1991.

Spenser, Edmund. *The Faerie Qveene*. London, 1596.

Spevack, Marvin, J. W. Binns, and Hans-Jurgen Weckermann. *Renaissance Latin Drama in England*. Hildesheim: G. Olms, 1981–91.

Spikes, Judith Doolin. "The Jacobean History Play and the Myth of the Elect Nation." *Renaissance Drama* 8 (1977): 117–48.

Spufford, Margaret. "Puritanism and Social Control?" In A. J. Fletcher and J. Stevenson, eds., *Order and Disorder in Early Modern England*, 41–57. Cambridge: Cambridge University Press, 1985.

——. *Small Books and Pleasant Histories: Popular Fiction and Its Readership in Seventeenth-Century England*. Cambridge: Cambridge University Press, 1981.

Stallybrass, Peter. "Patriarchal Territories: The Body Enclosed." In Margaret W. Ferguson, Maureen Quilligan, and Nancy J. Vickers, eds., *Rewriting the Renaissance: The Discourses of Sexual Difference in Early Modern Europe*, 123–42. Chicago: University of Chicago Press, 1986.

——. "Shakespeare, the Individual, and the Text." In Lawrence Grossberg, Cary Nelson, and Paula Treichler, eds., *Cultural Studies*, 593–610. New York: Routledge, 1992.

Stallybrass, Peter, and Allon White. *The Politics and Poetics of Transgression*. Ithaca: Cornell University Press, 1986.

*The Statutes of the Realm*. 11 vols. Great Britain Records Commission. London: Dawson of Pall Mall, 1963.

Stevens, David. "The Staging of Plays at the Salisbury Court Theater, 1630–1642." *Theater Journal* 31 (1979): 511–25.

Stevens, John. *Music and Poetry in the Early Tudor Court*. London: Methuen, 1961.

Stevens, Martin. *Four Middle English Mystery Cycles*. Princeton: Princeton University Press, 1987.

Stevenson, W. H., and H. E. Salter. *The Early History of St. John's College Oxford*. Oxford: Oxford Historical Society, 1939.

Stockwood, John. *A Sermon Preached at Paules Crosse*. London, 1578.

Stokes, James, ed. "Records of Early English Drama: Somerset." Unpublished transcriptions.

Stone, Lawrence. *The Crisis of the Aristocracy, 1558–1641*. Oxford: Clarendon Press, 1965.

———. *The Family, Sex and Marriage in England, 1500–1800*. New York: Harper and Row, 1977.

———. "Office Under Queen Elizabeth: The Case of Lord Hunsdon and the Lord Chamberlainship in 1585." *The Historical Journal* 10 (1967): 279–85.

Stone, P. W. K. *The Textual History of "King Lear."* London: Scolar Press, 1980.

Stowe, John. *Annales or a Generall Chronicle of England . . . continued . . . [b]y Edmond Howes*. London, 1631.

Streitberger, W. R. *Court Revels, 1485–1559*. Toronto: University of Toronto Press, 1994.

———. *Edmond Tyllney, Master of the Revels and Censor of Plays: A Descriptive Index to His Diplomatic Manual on Europe*. New York: AMS Press, 1986.

———. "On Edmond Tyllney's Biography." *Review of English Studies*, n.s., 29 (1978): 11–35.

———, ed. *Jacobean and Caroline Revels Accounts, 1603–1642*. Collections, vol. 13. London: Malone Society, 1986.

Stringer, Philip. "A Brief of the Entertainment Given to Queen Elizabeth at Oxford." Cambridge University Library, MS. 34, fols. 3–9.

Strong, Roy. *Art and Power: Renaissance Festivals, 1450–1650*. Berkeley and Los Angeles: University of California Press, 1984.

———. *Splendour at Court: Renaissance Spectacle and Illusion*. London: Weidenfeld and Nicolson, 1973.

Stubbs, William, ed. *Chronicles of Edward I and II*. Vol. 1. London, 1882.

Sturdy, David. "Bodley's Bookcases: 'This Goodly Magazine of Witte.' " *John Donne Journal* 5 (1986): 267–89.

Sturman, Berta. "The 1641 Edition of Chapman's *Bussy D'Ambois*." *Huntington Library Quarterly* 14 (1950/51): 171–201.

Summerson, John. *Inigo Jones*. Harmondsworth: Penguin, 1966.

Swanson, Heather. "Artisans in the Urban Economy: The Documentary Evidence from York." In Penelope J. Corfield and Derek Keene, eds., *Work in Towns 850–1850*, 42–56. Leicester: Leicester University Press, 1990.

———. *Medieval Artisans: An Urban Class in Late Medieval England*. Oxford: Blackwell, 1989.

T.K. [Thomas Kyd?] *The housholders philosophie. Wherein is perfectly described, the true oeconomia of housekeeping*. London, 1588. Reprinted in Frederick S. Boas, ed., *The Works of Thomas Kyd*, 231–84. Oxford: Clarendon Press, 1901.

Tannenbaum, Samuel A. *The Booke of Sir Thomas More: A Bibliotic Study*. New York: Tenny Press, 1927.

Tanselle, G. Thomas. "The Editorial Problem of Final Authorial Intention." *Studies in Bibliography* 29 (1976): 167–211.

———. "Historicism and Critical Editing." *Studies in Bibliography* 39 (1986): 1–46.

Taylor, Frank, and John S. Roskell, ed. and trans. *Gesta Henrici Quinti.* Oxford: Clarendon Press, 1975.

Taylor, Gary. "The Fortunes of Oldcastle." *Shakespeare Survey* 38 (1985): 85–100.

———. *"King Lear*: Date and Authorship of the Folio Version." In Gary Taylor and Michael Warren, eds., *The Division of the Kingdoms: Shakespeare's Two Versions of "King Lear,"* pp. 351–468. Oxford: Clarendon Press, 1983.

———. "*Pericles.*" In Stanley Wells and Gary Taylor, eds., *William Shakespeare: A Textual Companion,* 556–92. Oxford: Clarendon Press, 1987.

———. *Three Studies in the Text of "Henry V."* Oxford: Oxford University Press, 1979.

Taylor, Gary, and Michael Warren, eds. *The Division of the Kingdoms: Shakespeare's Two Versions of "King Lear."* Oxford: Clarendon Press, 1983.

Taylor, John. "The Trve Cavse of the Watermens Suit Concerning Players." In *Workes,* 171–76. London, 1630.

Teague, Frances. *Shakespeare's Speaking Properties.* Lewisburg: Bucknell University Press, 1991.

Tennenhouse, Leonard. *Power on Display.* London: Methuen, 1986.

*A Third Blast of Retrait.* In *A Second and Third Blast of Retrait from Plaies and Theaters.* London, 1580.

Thomas, David, and Arnold Hare. *Restoration and Georgian England, 1660–1788.* Theatre in Europe: A Documentary History. Cambridge: Cambridge University Press, 1989.

Thompson, Craig R. *Schools in Tudor England.* Washington, D.C.: Folger Shakespeare Library, 1958.

Thompson, E. P. "Patrician Society, Plebeian Culture." *Journal of Social History* 7 (1974): 382–405.

———. "Rough Music: Le Charivari anglais." *Annales: Economies, Sociétés, Civilisations* 27 (1972): 285–312.

Thomson, Leslie. "A Quarto 'Marked for Performance': Evidence of What?" *Medieval and Renaissance Drama in England* 8 (1996): 176–210.

Thomson, Peter. *Shakespeare's Professional Career.* Cambridge: Cambridge University Press, 1992.

Thomson, Peter, and Gamini Salgado. *The Everyman Companion to the Theatre.* London: J. M. Dent, 1985.

Thomson, R. S., ed. "*Boote and Spurre*: A Jacobean Quete from Folger MS. J.a.I." *English Literary Renaissance* 18 (1988): 275–93.

Tillot, P. M., ed. *A History of Yorkshire: The City of York.* The Victoria History of the Counties of England. Oxford: Oxford University Press, 1961.

Tillyard, E. M. W. *The Elizabethan World Picture.* New York: Macmillan, 1944.

———. *The English Renaissance: Fact or Fiction?* Baltimore: Johns Hopkins University Press, 1952.

Tilney, Edmund. *The Flower of Friendship: A Renaissance Dialogue Contesting Marriage.* [1568]. Edited by Valerie Wayne. Ithaca: Cornell University Press, 1992.

Tittler, Robert. *Architecture and Power: The Town Hall and the English Urban Community c. 1500–1640.* Oxford: Clarendon Press, 1991.

*Tom a Lincoln.* Edited by G. R. Proudfoot. London: Malone Society, 1992.

Traister, Barbara. " 'Who's in, who's out': John Dee, The London College of Physicians, and

Simon Forman." Unpublished seminar paper circulated at the meeting of the Shakespeare Association of America, 1991.

Traub, Valerie. *Desire and Anxiety: Circulations of Sexuality in Shakespearean Drama.* New York: Routledge, 1992.

Traver, Hope. *The Four Daughters of God.* Bryn Mawr: Bryn Mawr College, 1907.

Tricomi, Albert H. "Philip, Earl of Pembroke, and the Analogical Way of Reading Political Tragedy." *Journal of English and Germanic Philology* 85 (1986): 332–45.

———. "The Revised *Bussy D'Ambois* and *The Revenge of Bussy D'Ambois*: Joint Performance in Thematic Counterpoint." *English Language Notes* 9 (1972): 253–62.

———, ed. "*A Dialogue betweene Pollicy and Piety* by Robert Davenport." *English Literary Renaissance* 21 (1991): 190–216.

Trompf, G. W. *The Idea of Historical Recurrence in Western Thought from Antiquity to the Reformation.* Berkeley: University of California Press, 1979.

Trousdale, Marion. "A Second Look at Critical Bibliography and the Acting of Plays." *Shakespeare Quarterly* 41 (1990): 87–96.

———. *Shakespeare and the Rhetoricians.* Chapel Hill: University of North Carolina Press, 1982.

Turpyn, Richard. "The Chronicle of Calais." In John Gough Nichols, *The Chronicle of Calais in the Reigns of Henry VII and Henry VIII.* London: Camden Society, 1846.

Twycross, Meg. " 'Places to Hear the Play': Pageant Stations at York, 1398–1572." *Records of Early English Drama Newsletter* 3 (1978): 10–33.

———. "The Theatricality of Medieval English Plays." In Richard Beadle, ed., *The Cambridge Companion to Medieval English Theatre*, 37–84. Cambridge: Cambridge University Press, 1994.

Twycross, Meg, and Sarah Carpenter. "Masks in Medieval English Theatre: The Mystery Plays." *Medieval English Theatre* 3 (1981): 7–44, 69–113.

Ullman, B. L. "Renaissance—The Word and the Concept." *Studies in Philology* 49 (1952): 105–18.

Underdown, David. "The Taming of the Scold: the Enforcement of Patriarchal Authority in Early Modern England." In Anthony Fletcher and John Stevenson, eds., *Order and Disorder in Early Modern England*, 116–36. Cambridge: Cambridge University Press, 1985.

Ure, Peter. "Chapman's *The Tragedy of Bussy D'Ambois*: Problems of the Revised Quarto." *Modern Language Review* 48 (1953): 257–69.

Urkowitz, Steven. *Shakespeare's Revision of "King Lear."* Princeton: Princeton University Press, 1980.

———. " 'Well-sayd olde Mole': Burying Three *Hamlets* in Modern Editions." In Georgianna Ziegler, ed., *Shakespeare Study Today*, 37–70. New York: AMS Press, 1986.

Van Brun Jones, Paul. *The Household of a Tudor Nobleman.* Urbana: University of Illinois Press, 1918.

Veevers, Erica. *Images of Love and Religion: Queen Henrietta Maria and Court Entertainments.* Cambridge: Cambridge University Press, 1989.

Visser, Colin. "*The Descent of Orpheus* at the Cockpit, Drury Lane." *Theatre Survey* 24 (1983): 35–53.

Vives, J. L. "The Instruction of a Christian Woman." In Foster Watson, ed., *Vives and the Renascence Education of Women.* London: Edward Arnold, 1912.

Vogt, George McGill. "Richard Robinson's *Eupolemia* (1603)." *Studies in Philology* 21 (1924): 629–48.

Voltaire. "Dissertation sur La Tragédie Ancienne et Moderne (1749)." *Oeuvres Complète Voltaire*, 4:487–503. 52 vols. Paris: Garnier Frères, 1877–85.

Wager, Lewis. *Life and Repentance of Mary Magdalene*. Edited by Frederic Ives Carpenter. Chicago: University of Chicago Press, 1904.

Wake, Isaac. *Rex Platonicus*. Oxford, 1607.

Wall, Alison. "Elizabethan Precept and Feminine Practice: The Thynne Family of Longleat." *History* 75 (1990): 23–38.

Wall, Wendy. *The Imprint of Gender: Authorship and Publication in the English Renaissance*. Ithaca: Cornell University Press, 1993.

Wallace, Charles W. "Three London Theatres of Shakespeare's Time." *Nebraska University Studies* 9 (1909): 287–342.

Walsingham, Thomas. *Historia Anglicana*. Edited by H. T. Riley. 2 vols. London, 1875.

Walter, John Henry, ed. *Charlemagne*. London: Malone Society, 1938.

Wapull, George. *The Tide Tarrieth No Man*. In Edgar T. Schell and J. D. Schuchter, eds., *English Morality Plays and Moral Interludes*, 309–66. New York: Holt, Rinehart, Winston, 1969.

*A Warning for Fair Women: A Critical Edition*. Edited by Charles Dale Cannon. The Hague: Mouton, 1975.

Warren, Michael. "Quarto and Folio *King Lear* and the Interpretation of Albany and Edgar." In David Bevington and Jay L. Halio, eds., *Shakespeare: Patterns of Excelling Nature*, 95–107. Newark: University of Delaware Press, 1978.

Wasson, John M. "Elizabethan and Jacobean Touring Companies." *Theatre Notebook* 42 (1988): 51–57.

——, ed. "Records of Early English Drama: Derbyshire." Unpublished transcriptions.

——, ed. *Records of Early English Drama: Devon*. Toronto: University of Toronto Press, 1986.

Wasson, John M., and David Galloway, eds. *Records of Plays and Players in Norfolk and Suffolk, 1330–1642. Collections XI*. London: Malone Society, 1980.

Watt, Tessa. *Cheap Print and Popular Piety, 1550–1640*. Cambridge: Cambridge University Press, 1991.

Weber, Max. *The Protestant Ethic and the Spirit of Capitalism*. Translated by Talcott Parsons, with a foreword by R. H. Tawney. New York: Scribner, 1930.

Webster, John. *The Complete Works*. Edited by F. L. Lucas. 4 vols. London: Chatto and Windus, 1927.

——. *The Duchess of Malfi*. Edited by John Russell Brown. London: Methuen, 1964.

Weimann, Robert. *Shakespeare and the Popular Tradition in the Theater: Studies in the Social Dimension of Dramatic Form and Function*. Translated and edited by Robert Schwartz. Baltimore: Johns Hopkins University Press, 1978.

Wells, Stanley. "The Once and Future *King Lear*." In Gary Taylor and Michael Warren, eds., *The Division of the Kingdoms: Shakespeare's Two Versions of "King Lear,"* 1–22. Oxford: Clarendon Press, 1983.

Wells, Stanley, and Gary Taylor, with John Jowett and William Montgomery. *William Shakespeare: A Textual Companion*. Oxford: Clarendon Press, 1988.

Welsford, Enid. *The Court Masque*. New York: Russell and Russell, 1962.

Wentersdorf, Karl P. "*Arden of Faversham* and the Repertory of Pembroke's Men." *Theater Annual* 31 (1975): 57–71.

——. "The Repertory and Size of Pembroke's Company." *Theater Annual* 33 (1977): 71–85.

Werstine, Paul. "Close Contrivers: Nameless Collaborators in Early Modern Plays." In A. L. Magnusson and C. E. McGee, eds., *Elizabethan Theatre XV*. Forthcoming.

——. " 'Foul Papers' and 'Prompt-books': Printer's Copy for Shakespeare's *Comedy of Errors*." *Studies in Bibliography* 41 (1988): 232–46.

——. "McKerrow's 'Suggestion' and Twentieth-Century Shakespeare Textual Criticism." *Renaissance Drama* 19 (1988): 149–73.

——. "Narratives About Printed Shakespeare Texts: 'Foul Papers' and 'Bad' Quartos." *Shakespeare Quarterly* 41 (1990): 65–86.

——. "Shakespeare." In *Scholarly Editing: A Guide to Research*, 190–218. New York: Modern Language Association, 1995.

——. "The Textual Mystery of *Hamlet*." *Shakespeare Quarterly* 39 (1988): 1–26.

Westfall, Suzanne R. *Patrons and Performance: Early Tudor Household Revels*. Oxford: Clarendon Press, 1990.

Wheeler, G. W., ed. *Letters of Sir Thomas Bodley to Thomas James, First Keeper of the Bodleian Library*. Oxford: Clarendon Press, 1926.

——, ed. *Letters of Sir Thomas Bodley to the University of Oxford, 1598–1611*. Oxford: Printed for Private Circulation at Oxford University Press, 1927.

Whigham, Frank. *Ambition and Privilege: The Social Tropes of Elizabethan Courtesy Theory*. Berkeley: University of California Press, 1984.

White, Eileen. "Places for Hearing the Corpus Christi Play in York." *Medieval English Theatre* 9 (1987): 23–63.

White, Paul Whitfield. *Theatre and Reformation: Protestantism, Patronage, and Playing in Tudor England*. Cambridge: Cambridge University Press, 1992.

Whiting, Robert. *The Blind Devotion of the People: Popular Religion and the English Reformation*. Cambridge: Cambridge University Press, 1989.

Wickham, Glynne. *Early English Stages, 1300–1660*. 3 vols. in 4. London: Routledge and Kegan Paul, 1959–81.

——. "Heavens, Machinery, and Pillars in the Theater and Other Early Playhouses." In Herbert Berry, ed., *The First Public Playhouse: The Theatre in Shoreditch 1576–1598*, 1–15. Montreal: McGill-Queen's University Press, 1979.

——. "The Privy Council Order of 1597 for the Destruction of All London's Theaters." In David Galloway, ed., *The Elizabethan Theater*, 21–44. Toronto: Macmillan, 1969.

Wilcox, Donald J. *The Measure of Times Past: Pre-Newtonian Chronologies and the Rhetoric of Relative Time*. Chicago and London: University of Chicago Press, 1987.

Wilks, John S. *The Idea of Conscience in Renaissance Tragedy*. London: Routledge, 1990.

Williams, George Walton, and Gwynne Blakemore Evans, eds. *The History of King Henry the Fourth, as revised by Sir Edward Dering, Bart*. Charlottesville: University of Virginia, for the Folger Library, 1974.

Williams, Neville. *Thomas Howard, Fourth Duke of Norfolk*. London: Barrie and Rockliff, 1964.

Williams, Raymond. *Keywords: A Vocabulary of Culture and Society.* New York: Oxford University Press, 1976.

——. *Writing in Society.* London: Verso, 1983.

Williams, William P. "The Castle Ashby Manuscripts: A Description of the Volumes in Bishop Percy's List." *The Library,* 6th ser., 2 (1980): 391–412.

Willis, Deborah. *Malevolent Nurture: Witch-hunting and Maternal Power in Early Modern England.* Ithaca: Cornell University Press, 1995.

Wilson, F. P. *Shakespeare and the New Bibliography.* 1945. Revised and edited by Helen Gardner. Oxford: Clarendon Press, 1970.

——. "Shakespeare's Reading." *Shakespeare Survey* 3 (1950): 14–21.

——, ed. *The Plague Pamphlets of Thomas Dekker.* Oxford: Clarendon Press, 1925.

Wilson, John Dover, ed. *The Manuscript of Shakespeare's "Hamlet" and the Problems of Its Transmission.* Cambridge: Cambridge University Press, 1934.

Wilson, Richard. " 'A Mingled Yarn': Shakespeare and the Cloth Workers." *Literature and History* 12 (1986): 164–80.

——. "Observations on English Bodies: Licensing Maternity in Shakespeare's Late Plays." In Richard Burt and John Michael Archer, eds., *Enclosure Acts: Sexuality, Property, and Culture in Early Modern England,* 121–50. Ithaca: Cornell University Press, 1994.

——. *Will Power: Essays on Shakespearean Authority.* London: Harvester Wheatsheaf, 1993.

Withington, Robert. *English Pageantry: An Historical Outline.* 2 vols. Cambridge: Harvard University Press, 1918–26.

Womack, Peter. "Imagining Communities: Theatres and the English Nation in the Sixteenth Century." In David Aers, ed., *Culture and History 1350–1600: Essays on English Communities, Identities, and Writing,* 91–146. Detroit: Wayne State University Press, 1992.

Wood, Anthony à. *The History of the University of Oxford.* Edited by John Gutch. 4 vols. Oxford, 1786–1996.

Woodbridge, Linda. *Women and the English Renaissance.* Urbana: University of Illinois Press, 1984.

Woodmansee, Martha. "The Genius and the Copyright: Economic and Legal Conditions of the Emergence of the 'Author.' " *Eighteenth-Century Studies* 17 (1984): 425–48.

Woodworth, Allegra. *Purveyance for the Royal Household in the Reign of Queen Elizabeth.* Philadelphia: American Philosophical Society, 1945.

Wright, H. G., ed. *Ghismonda, A Seventeenth Century Tragedy.* Manchester: Manchester University Press, 1944.

Wright, James. *Historia Histrionica: An Historical Account of the English Stage.* London, 1699.

Wrightson, Keith. *English Society, 1580–1680.* London: Hutchinson, 1982.

Würzbach, Natascha. *The Rise of the English Street Ballad, 1550–1650.* Translated by Gayna Walls. Cambridge: Cambridge University Press, 1990.

Yachnin, Paul. "The Powerless Theatre." *English Literary Renaissance* 21 (1991): 49–74.

Yeandle, Laetitia. "The Dating of Sir Edward Dering's Copy of 'The History of King Henry the Fourth.' " *Shakespeare Quarterly* 37 (1986): 224–26.

Young, William. *The History of Dulwich College*. 2 vols. Edinburgh: Printed for the author by Morrison and Gibb, 1889.

Zeller, Hans. "A New Approach to the Critical Constitution of Literary Texts." *Studies in Bibliography* 28 (1975): 231–64.

Zika, Charles. "Hosts, Processions, and Pilgrimages: Controlling the Sacred in Fifteenth-Century Germany." *Past and Present* 118 (1988): 25–64.

Zimmerman, Susan. "The Folger Manuscripts of Thomas Middleton's *A Game at Chesse*." *Papers of the Bibliographical Society of America* 76 (1982): 159–95.

Žižek, Slavoj. *The Sublime Object of Ideology*. London and New York: Verso, 1989.

Zwicker, Steven. "Reading the Margins." Lecture delivered at "The Early Modern Book," November 19, 1994, College Park, Maryland.

# Contributors

Peter W. M. Blayney is a Distinguished Research Fellow at the Folger Shakespeare Library and is the author of several studies of the London printing trade, including *The Texts of King Lear and Their Origins*.

Michael D. Bristol, Professor of English at McGill University, is the author of *Carnival and Theatre*, *Shakespeare's America*, *America's Shakespeare*, and, most recently, *Big-Time Shakespeare*.

Ann Jennalie Cook, Professor of English at Vanderbilt University, is the author of *The Privileged Playgoers of Shakespeare's London* and *Making a Match: Courtship in Shakespeare and His Society*. Executive Director of the Shakespeare Association of America for twelve years, she has served most recently as Chairman of the International Shakespeare Association and is now its Vice President.

John D. Cox teaches English at Hope College. He is the author of *Shakespeare and the Dramaturgy of Power* and of many articles on early drama.

Margreta de Grazia, Professor of English at the University of Pennsylvania, is the author of *Shakespeare Verbatim* and a coeditor, with Maureen Quilligan and Peter Stallybrass, of *Subject and Object in Renaissance Culture*. She is completing a book on the periodizing of the early modern.

Felicity Dunsworth teaches at the University of Kent at Canterbury and is writing a dissertation on motherhood in early modern drama.

Richard Dutton, Professor of English at Lancaster University, has published *Ben Jonson: To the First Folio*, *Mastering the Revels*, and *Ben Jonson: Authority: Criticism*. He is general editor of the Macmillan Literary Lives.

John R. Elliott, Jr. is Professor of English at Syracuse University, and a former Senior

Research Fellow at New College, Oxford. Among his publications on early English drama is *Playing God: Medieval Mysteries on the Modern Stage.*

Garrett P. J. Epp, Associate Professor of English at the University of Alberta, has published numerous articles on producing early drama and regularly directs productions of early drama, both educationally and professionally.

Peter H. Greenfield, University of Puget Sound, has coedited the Records of Early English Drama for Cumberland/Westmorland/Gloucestershire and authored articles on early dramatic activity in the provinces. He is currently completing an edition of the Hertfordshire and Hampshire records for REED.

Heidi Brayman Hackel, Assistant Professor of English at Randolph-Macon College, is completing a book to be titled *Impressions from a "Scribbling Age,"* on reading practices in sixteenth-century England.

Diana E. Henderson is Associate Professor of Literature at the Massachusetts Institute of Tecnnology and the author of *Passion Made Public: Elizabethan Lyric, Gender, and Performance,* as well as numerous articles on early modern authors.

Anne Higgins, Associate Professor of English at Dalhousie University, has published essays about Chaucer, Shakespeare, medieval notions of time, and the civic drama.

David Scott Kastan is Professor of English and Comparative Literature at Columbia University. He is the author of *Shakespeare and the Shapes of Time,* coeditor with Peter Stallybrass of *Staging the Renaissance,* and one of the general editors of the Arden Shakespeare.

Gordon Kipling, Professor of English at UCLA, has published a number of articles on civic triumphs and other aspects of medieval theater. He recently edited *The Receyt of the Ladie Kateryne* (EETS, 1990) and is writing a book on theater, liturgy, and ritual in the medieval civic triumph.

Roslyn L. Knutson, Professor of English at the University of Arkansas at Little Rock and author of *The Repertory of Shakespeare's Company, 1594–1613,* is currently working on the nature of commerce among the Elizabethan playing companies.

Jean MacIntyre, Professor of English at the University of Alberta, is the author of *Costumes and Scripts in the Elizabethan Theatres,* as well as articles on costume symbolism. She is currently working on politics in the drama of John Fletcher and the masque.

Kathleen E. McLuskie is Professor of English at the University of Southampton and the author of, most recently, *Dekker and Heywood: Professional Dramatists.*

Jeffrey Masten teaches in the Department of English at Harvard University. He is the author of *Textual Intercourse: Collaboration, Authorship, and Sexualities in Renaissance Drama,* and, along with Peter Stallybrass and Nancy Vickers, editor of a collection of essays from the English Institute, titled *Language Machines: Technologies of Cultural Production.*

Barbara A. Mowat, Director of Academic Programs at the Folger Shakespeare Library, is the editor of *Shakespeare Quarterly,* and coeditor with Paul Werstine of the New Folger Library Shakespeare edition. She has written widely on Shakespeare and editing.

Alan H. Nelson, Professor of English at the University of California, Berkeley, edited the

Cambridge volumes of the Records of Early English Drama and recently published *Early Cambridge Theatres*.

John Orrell, University Professor in English at the University of Alberta and principal historical adviser to the Bankside Globe reconstruction project, is the author of *Rebuilding Shakespeare's Globe* and other books and articles on early stages.

Graham Parry teaches English at the University of York, England. His most recent book is *The Trophies of Time*, on the antiquarian movement in the seventeenth century.

Eric Rasmussen, Associate Professor of English at the University of Nevada, Reno, and coeditor with David Bevington of *Dr. Faustus* in the Revels Plays Series, is the author of *A Textual Companion to Doctor Faustus* and coeditor of the forthcoming New Variorium *Hamlet*.

W. R. Streitberger, Professor of English at the University of Washington, is the author, most recently, of *Court Revels, 1485–1559*.

Peter Thomson, Professor of Drama at Exeter University, is the author of *Shakespeare's Theatre* and *Shakespeare's Professional Career*.

John M. Wasson, Emeritus Professor of English at Washington State University, is editor of the Records of Early English Drama for Devon and the Malone Society's Suffolk and Norfolk records, as well as the author of numerous articles on early drama.

Paul Werstine teaches English at King's College and the Graduate School at the University of Western Ontario. He has written widely about the manuscript inscriptions, printing, and editing of early modern English drama and is editing the New Folger Library Shakespeare with Barbara A. Mowat.

Suzanne Westfall, Associate Professor and theater director in the Department of English/Theater at Lafayette College, is the author of *Patrons and Performance* and is presently, with Paul Whitfield White, editing a collection to be titled *Theatrical Patronage and the Royal Court*.

Paul Whitfield White, Associate Professor of English at Purdue University, has published *Theatre and Reformation* and *Reformation Biblical Drama*. He edits *MSA Book Reviews* for the Marlowe Society of America and is currently editing a collection of essays on Christopher Marlowe.

# Index

# Index of Plays